The Politics of Deference

The Politics of Deference

a study of the mid-nineteenth century English Political System

David Cresap Moore

*Professor of History,
University of California,
Los Angeles.*

THE HARVESTER PRESS, HASSOCKS

BARNES & NOBLE, NEW YORK

First published in 1976 by
THE HARVESTER PRESS LIMITED
Publisher: John Spiers
2 Stanford Terrace, Hassocks, Sussex
and in the USA by
Harper and Row Publishers Inc.
Barnes & Noble Import Division
10 East 53rd Street, New York 10022

Copyright © 1976 D C Moore

Harvester Press
ISBN 0 901759 0 74

Barnes and Noble
ISBN 0-06-494932-X
Library of Congress Catalog Card Number 74-26187

Typeset by
Input Typesetting Ltd. London
Printed in Great Britain by
Redwood Burn Ltd, Trowbridge, Wiltshire

To Sally

Contents

Maps

Acknowledgements

In the course of writing this book I have incurred many obligations. For permission to cite manuscript material I am grateful to the Marquess of Salisbury, the Earl Fortescue, the Earl of Halifax (Hinckleton Papers), the Earl St Aldwyn, Lord St Oswald (Nostell Papers), and Colonel Sir Robert Adeane. For assistance in using papers deposited in their care, I am grateful to Mr P. I. King, M.A., archivist at the Northamptonshire Record Office (Daventry Papers, Fitzwilliam Papers and Gotch Papers), and to Mr P. A. Kennedy, M.A., archivist at the Devonshire Record Office (Burrows Papers) and to Mr P. L. Hull, M.A., archivist at the Cornwall Record Office (Vyvyan Papers).

Various of the arguments here presented have already appeared in articles published in *Victorian Studies* ['The other face of reform', V (1961), 'Political morality in Mid-Victorian England: concepts, norms, violations', XIII (1969), and 'Reply to E. P. Hennock, "The sociological premises of the first Reform Act: a critical note"', XIV (1971)], in the *Economic History Review* ['The corn laws and high farming', 2nd Ser., XVIII (1965)], in *The Historical Journal* ['Concession or cure: the sociological premises of the first Reform Act', IX (1966)], in R. Robson, (ed.), *Ideas and Institutions of Victorian Britain: Essays in Honour of George Kitson Clark* (London, 1967), and in *Albion* ['The matter of the missing contests: towards a theory of the mid-century British political system', VI (1974)]. I am grateful to the several editors for permission to repeat myself.

My research was begun during my tenure of a Fulbright Fellowship. It was continued with grants from the John Simon Guggenheim Memorial Foundation and the University of California.

Dr George Kitson Clark has generously encouraged me over the many years since I began my research under his supervision.

Mr John Spiers, of the Harvester Press, has been very patient and helpful.

D. C. M.
February 1976

Prologue: The evidential problem

I

In their studies of nineteenth century English politics historians have generally ignored an important body of evidence which symbolizes an important social fact. Until the adoption of the secret ballot, in 1872, voters voted in public. When they went to the polls they declared their choices before all to see and hear. In consequence, many of their voices can still be heard: in many constituencies after many contested elections, lists were published showing how each voter voted. In some cases these lists — or poll books, as they were called — were copies of the poll book which the returning officer in each constituency was legally obliged to keep. In others they were copies of the poll book which someone else compiled and which, in a few details, might differ from the returning officer's poll book. But, whichever the case, many poll books exist. In particular, their existence raises two questions: how, for so many years, could men endure the revelations they contain and why, ultimately, did these revelations become unendurable? Presumably — at least in part, the answers to these questions are implicit in the answers to certain others: for whom were poll books published, and how were they used? The apparent answer to these various questions suggest the need to revise certain of the generally accepted propositions concerning the nature of the nineteenth century English political system and the ways in which and the reasons why changes occurred within this system.

Mainly, poll books were published for the use of local politicians and others who hoped to understand each voter's behaviour in the light of their knowledge of the communities and networks within the constituency. This is suggested in part by the phenomenon of bloc voting which can be seen in certain poll books — the blocs in these cases reflecting obvious groups – and, in part, by the efforts of various election managers to learn the composition of the effective communities and networks within the constituencies with which they were concerned. As these efforts reveal, the procedures recommended by the authors of various electoral handbooks were frequently applied. According to Edward W. Cox and Standish Grove Grady, whose handbook reached its eleventh edition in 1872, the principal responsibility of the election manager was to learn exactly what influence or influences might be brought to bear upon each prospective voter. Or – to put it differently – it was the manager's responsibility to identify each voter in terms of his membership of the communities or networks in which such influences obtained. As they described it, local political organization existed within the context of this function: it existed to supervise the canvassers, the men used to discover, as appropriate, the identity of each voter's 'employer, sect, landlord, customer or creditor'.[1] And, they went on, only when the election manager possessed such information could he perform his 'real business', that of bringing favourable influences to bear and using them to counteract the unfavourable.[2] In the light of their implication, that contests occurred as confrontations between the various groups within each constituency which these different influences helped to define, the answer to the question how men endured the publication of poll books would obviously lie in the fact, which the publication of poll books itself tends to suggest, that many men regarded these communities and networks as natural attributes of the world in which they lived. Clearly, poll books could not have been published if, in significant fashion, the information they contain as to how the voters *did* vote offended against the predominant contemporary assumptions as to how the voters *should* vote. By the same token, poll books would become unpublishable when, either because the assumptions changed, the behaviour changed, or both, the necessary correspondence between the voters' behaviour and the relevant assumptions waned.

II

Poll books were muster lists of the effective groups within the different constituencies to which the members of the *pays legal* belonged. As such, if we could see them as contemporary election managers tried to see them they would obviously reveal the effective agencies of electoral recruitment. Further, they would allow various questions to be asked which have not usually been asked and which could otherwise scarcely be asked – or only in the hope of somewhat speculative answers: on what varieties of relationship did these different agencies of electoral recruitment depend; by which factors were they strengthened or weakened; why did particular contests turn out as they did; and, more generally, what was the nature of the political system within which such agencies and factors operated; and why, in the context of these agencies and factors, did changes in the system occur?

Unfortunately, however we cannot see the poll books as election managers tried to see them. The keys they used have in most cases been lost. Few of the canvassers' books have survived – or, at least, few have been found – and few items of the election managers' correspondence. These latter were evidently working papers which were rarely kept beyond the time of their immediate usefulness. Where they have been found they confirm the general picture of the mid-century political scene which is implicit in Cox and Grady's recommendations.[3] But in certain cases substitute keys can be fashioned. Ideally, these substitutes would be of the same kind as the originals: they would allow each voter's behaviour to be understood in terms of the effective nexus which conditioned his behaviour. With the evidence presently available substitutes of this nature cannot be had. But in certain cases substitutes of a somewhat inferior nature can be had. These derive not from individual identifications external to the poll booth evidence which might explain why each voter voted as he did but rather from those corporate identifications which the poll books themselves implicitly provide when they reveal that certain voters voted in agreement with one another. In the context of the fairly large number of alternative modes of behaviour available to most voters throughout most of the poll book periods such electoral agreement sometimes provides a useful test of the existence of a group.

During the period for which poll books are available most English constituencies were represented by two or three Members. Thus, because until 1868 the voters in any constituency could cast as many votes as there were seats to be filled at the contest, most voters during this period could cast two or three votes. Not that each voter was obliged to use all his votes. He could vote for a single candidate, or 'plump', as it was called, withholding his other vote or votes. Or, if he were voting in a three or four member constituency, he could vote for only two or three candidates. In 1868, in consequence of the minority vote clause of the second Reform Act, the number of alternative modes of behaviour available to the voters in three and four member constituencies was somewhat limited. Thereafter, a voter in a three member constituency could only cast two votes, a voter in a four member constituency only three. This reduced but slightly the number of alternative modes of behaviour available to these men. In effect, throughout the poll book period the number of modes of behaviour available to most voters was considerable. Or – to put it differently – most voters could identify themselves by means of their votes rather more precisely than they could had all constituencies been single member constituencies. These identifications are crude. But in many cases they are useful. At any given contest in any given constituency many men voted for the same candidates. But fewer men plumped for the same candidates or voted for the same combinations of candidates. And fewer, again, who plumped for the same candidates or who voted for the same combinations of candidates continued to vote in agreement with one another at successive contests. Where this did happen among men who had certain common attributes the explanation suggests itself that their behaviour reveals the existence of the group which their attributes define. In effect, where voters who had certain common attributes voted in agreement with one another, it is possible to fashion substitute keys. Unfortunately, however, in the light of the information concerning these attributes which is available in fairly large quantity – essentially that which the poll books themselves contain – these conditions are only met in certain circumstances.

In most of the borough poll books each voter was identified by his place of residence. In most of the county poll books, especially after 1832, he was identified by the location of the property in respect of which he was qualified to vote. Occasionally, in county as well as borough poll books, each voter was further identified by his occupation and by the nature of his electoral qualification. As a rule, however, only the geographical identifications are relevant to the problems raised by the voters' behaviour. Further, these identifications are only relevant to their behaviour in the rural parishes of the county constituencies.

By and large, there was no correlation between the voters' behaviour and their electoral qualifications. Borough freemen rarely voted as freemen. Nor did £10-householders in the boroughs vote as £10-householders. Furthermore, while 40s-freeholders in the counties were often more numerous on one side of the political divide, £50-tenants-at-will on the other, it is usually clear that such differences were not functions of these qualifications themselves but of the orientations of the groups to which freeholders on the one hand and tenants-at-will on the other tended to belong. Proportionately, 40s-freeholders were far more numerous in and around the towns than they were in the countryside, £50-tenants-at-will far more numerous in the countryside than they were in and around the towns.[4] In effect, in many counties the 40s-freehold franchise was essentially an urban franchise. Thus, where politics was polarized between town and countryside – and such was very often the case – those who qualified to vote as 40s-freeholders tended to vote as members of what might be called the urban interest group. In certain cases, again, members of certain occupational categories showed considerable homogeneity. Most butchers were Tory or Conservative; most grocers Whig or Liberal.[5] In many constituencies most retail tradesmen were Liberal or Radical.[6] Such correlations are extremely important. But the nature of their importance is not on the face of it clear. What does this behaviour reveal? Did butchers, grocers and tradesmen really constitute groups, or did the members of certain groups tend to be butchers, grocers or tradesmen? And, in any event, these men were somewhat exceptional. As a rule, voters did not vote as members of occupational categories. Indeed, the principal significance of the occupational identifications of the voters which many poll books provide lies in what they reveal of the usual *lack* of correlation between electoral behaviour and occupation or, more generally, between electoral behaviour and class membership. As Professor Vincent recently noted, generalizing from a large quantity of raw poll book data, during the period for which poll books are available, 'Class as stratum, . . . class in the colloquial sense, cannot really be used to describe voting patterns or to explain them.'[7] But in many cases in the counties voters voted in agreement with their immediate neighbours.

As a rule, where local electoral agreement is apparent it suggests its own dynamic. Generally, the groups which these blocs reflect were the obvious functions of landed estates: not only did such voters vote in agreement with one another, they generally voted in agreement with the principal local landowner. As such, their behaviour testifies to the electoral importance of the relationships which obtained on the particular estates which these men owned. However – and the point illustrates the limitations of the evidence which the poll books themselves contain – such blocs can only be seen where the boundaries of the group which the bloc reflected were coterminous with the boundaries of the parish in which the group existed. Obviously, if some voters in a parish were members of one group which one bloc reflected, others of another, and others, possibly, unattached to any group, the existence of the different groups would be obscured by one another, by the unattached voters, or by both. Thus, in practice, poll books rarely reveal the effective agencies and mechanisms of electoral recruitment except in the countryside and except where these agencies were landed estates with ramifications which affected the entire body of the voters – or at least a very large proportion of them – in the parish in which the estate was located. These conditions were frequently met. In some constituencies large proportions of the voters – perhaps majorities – behaved as members of such blocs. But frequently, too, the conditions were not met. Of course, the appearance of these blocs cannot be used to demonstrate the existence of other blocs which are not apparent. But, in view of the widespread efforts of election managers to gather information in the light of which the general existence of blocs might be understood, and in view of the factors to which the appearance of these blocs should be attributed, these blocs acquire an importance which far exceeds the specific incidence of their appearance. Furthermore, various groups obviously existed which, with the available evidence, cannot be seen.

In all probability, if the poll books for Cornwall could be found – none, apparently, exist for the county – they would fail to reveal the nexus which made it possible for the Reverend Thomas Gurney to offer Sir Richard Vyvyan eight votes in 1825. Nor do the Northamptonshire poll books reveal the identities of the men who were the tenants of the Reverend William Deane Ryland and whose prospective behaviour gave Ryland so much to worry about in 1837, Obviously, numerous electorally important groups existed in South Nottinghamshire in 1846. However, while more than half of the voters, at the South Nottinghamshire by-election of 1846 voted in overwhelming agreement with their immediate parish neighbours the remainder voted from parishes in which such local electoral agreement did not obtain. By and large, these voters voted from urban parishes where, if blocs existed, their existence is obscured by the existence of other blocs or by the existence of voters who were not members of blocs. And, again, certain blocs obviously existed in Carlisle in 1868. However, while their existence is apparent their full composition and possible importance are not.

Gurney's situation is understandable. He was an aging vicar in a far from wealthy living. Furthermore, he had offended certain of the powerful men in the county by his political activities in his youth. Thus he had no patron. He therefore tried to buy Vyvyan's patronage. He suggested that if Vyvyan agreed to help him obtain a cathedral stall or a more wealthy living he would help him with eight votes at the coming election, his own and the seven others he claimed were in his gift. While his offer was a bit crude – indeed, it may suggest why he was without a patron – it was not without a certain logic. Vyvyan had just been returned at an uncontested by-election. But a contest at the next general election was widely anticipated. Gurney preferred to use his influence in Vyvyan's favour. But he made no bones about it: if Vyvyan refused to help him – and he did refuse – he would then offer his eight votes to Vyvyan's prospective opponent.[8] Even if the relevant poll book existed, it would presumably be impossible to identify the seven men whose votes he claimed were really his to cast. Thus, it would be impossible to define the nature of the relationship which underlay his offer.

Ryland's situation was different. He had a patron. By the mid-thirties, however, if not before, he and his patron had become politically opposed. He was dependent upon the Whig Spencer family for preferment. By 1837 he was a Tory. Hence his dilemma when rumours began to spread, in 1837, that Captain Spencer, the brother of the former Lord Althorp, was going to stand for South Northamptonshire. He would have been professionally lost, he claimed, had he voted against a member of the Spencer family. At the same time, he was reluctant to use his 'influence' except in support of his own political principles. His proposed solution was simple. If faced with a choice between his own political principles and his future in the Church he would absolve himself of all responsibility for his tenants' behaviour. As he explained to William Cartwright, one of the Tory members for the division, if Spencer were the candidate he would have to vote for him but he would publicly announce that he had 'set his tenants free to decide . . . for themselves' how they would vote. On the other hand, if any other Whig candidate were chosen he would use both his 'votes and influence' against him.[9] Fortunately for Ryland, perhaps, no contest occurred in South Northamptonshire in 1837. But the available poll books which might have revealed his 'influence' at other contests do not do so.

The evidential problem can be seen even more clearly in South Nottinghamshire at the by-election of February, 1846. This *election* was occasioned by the appointment of the Earl of Lincoln, one of the Members for the division, to a new office in the Cabinet Peel formed after the announcement of his decision to repeal the corn laws. But in the constituency in which no *contest* had ever occurred the *contest* was in the nature of a referendum on the decision itself. Lincoln was beaten by the protectionist candidate, T. B. T. Hildyard, by 1,736 votes to 1,049. Of his total of votes Hildyard received 492 from parishes from which no voter voted for Lincoln. He received an additional 564 from parishes from which Lincoln only received 79. In turn, Lincoln received 195 votes from parishes from which no voter voted for Hildyard. He received an additional 184 from parishes from which Hildyard only received 37. In effect, over 24 per cent of the voters at this contest voted from parishes in which absolute unanimity prevailed. An additional 31 per cent voted from parishes in which less than absolute unanimity prevailed but in which more than 86 per cent of the voters voted in agreement with their immediate parish neighbours. Altogether, some 56 per cent of the voters voted from parishes in which, in the aggregate, some 92 per cent of the voters voted in agreement with their immediate parish neighbours. But some 44 per cent of the voters voted from parishes from which, in the aggregate, approximately 52 per cent of the voters voted for one candidate and 48 per cent for the other. The unanimous and quasi-unanimous parishes contained 1,551 voters who gave Hildyard 1,093 votes and Lincoln 458.

The other parishes contained 1,234 voters who gave Hildyard 643 votes and Lincoln 591. Among these latter parishes were those in the sizeable towns of Nottingham, Newark and Southwell. [10]

With the evidence presently available it is impossible to decide whether any significant proportions of the voters from these latter parishes voted as members of blocs. Thus we cannot ask what groups these blocs reflected, why they existed and, to what extent their existence was contingent upon the terms in which the corn law question was formulated. The evidence available provides no means of sorting out the voters into the blocs they *may have* formed. But the available evidence does provide a means of sorting out the other voters. Thus, while little or nothing can be said about the essential nature of the behaviour of the urban voters much can be said about the essential nature of the behaviour of many of the others. The corn law issue presumably, provided the terms in which their behaviour was rationalized. But the extent of their local electoral agreement strongly suggests that many of them voted as they did because of influences brought to bear upon them. These influences could obviously not have been exercised had the voters not been members of groups in which such influence obtained and, presumably, which they helped to strengthen.

The available evidence is equally reticent on the nature of the electorally important relationships in Carlisle. After the passing of the second Reform Bill the electorate in the borough included sizeable numbers of men employed by two railway companies, the London and North Western, and the Maryport and Carlisle. William Hodgson, a Conservative, was a director of the former Sir William Lawson, a Liberal, was a director of the latter. Both Hodgson and Lawson were candidates at the contest of 1868. The majority of the voters in the borough who were employed by the London and North Western voted for Hodgson. The majority of the voters who were employed by the Maryport and Carlisle voted for Lawson and his Liberal colleague. But no poll book reveals this. It can only be known today because certain men in the borough who knew where the different voters were employed were deeply disturbed by the fact that many employees of the London and North Western had voted for Hodgson. Believing that such men were Liberals by definition they also believed that such votes were *prima facie* evidence of coercion. Thus the behaviour of *both* groups of employees was ultimately brought to the attention of the Select Committee on Parliamentary and Municipal Elections. There, the vehemence with which the assumption, that railway workers were Liberals by definition, was stated prompted the statement of the other assumption, that votes for Hodgson by employees of the London and North Western, and votes for Lawson and his Liberal colleague by

employees of the Maryport and Carlisle, were both evidence of an
'*esprit de corps* in the different establishments to go the same way as the
leading members.' [11] The conflict of assumptions concerning the
relative legitimacy of the rival varieties of nexus suggests an important
reason why publication of the poll books would soon be impossible.
But the available evidence does little more than reveal the existence of
the conflict. Beyond the few men whose names were mentioned in
evidence before the Committee the documentation does not tell us
whose behaviour was involved. Thus it says nothing about the degree
to which the outcome of this contest was a function of the numbers of
voters in the borough who were associated with these or other
'establishments'. Nor does it tell us to what extent the outcome of the
contrast was a function of the means by which the loyalties of men to
these various 'establishments', or their loyalties to other possible
sodalities, were strengthened or weakened.

In effect, because many voters in the rural areas of the counties did
vote as members of geographically definable blocs, county poll books
often reveal the groups which these blocs reflected and, by extension,
the electoral importance of the means by which the cohesion of these
groups was strengthened or weakened. They do so because the
evidence they contain is directly relevant to the structure of the
predominant variety of endogenous group. But this is not the case for
the boroughs and for the urban areas of the counties. To discover why
urban voters voted as they did each of them would have to be
identified individually in terms of the nexus which conditioned his
behaviour. Or – to put it differently – evidence would be required
analogous to that which election managers tried to gather.

The relationships of rural society undoubtedly provided a stronger
basis for influence than those of urban society. In the countryside such
relationships tended to reinforce each another more frequently and,
perhaps, more intensively than was the case in the towns. But the
differences would appear to have been more of degree than of kind.
For example, it was stated in 1852 that not a single Dissenter resided in
the Cambridgeshire parish of West Wratting. [12] This probably reflected
one of the consequences of the widespread practice of giving
prospective tenants an informal religious test. [13] The sociological – and,
thus, the political consequences – of landlords only admitting on to
their estates tenants of the same religion as themselves are obvious. The
community which the estate often represented would be strengthened
at a time when, for purposes of administration, many estates were
becoming far more tightly organized than ever before. [14] But for
many towns it was widely assumed that men would sort themselves out
in analogous ways. Indeed, in 1843 the Radical William Ewart was
able to establish – presumably, at least, to his own satisfaction – exactly

how many Anglicans and Dissenters were employed in the Lancashire cotton mills by simply specifying the number of men employed in mills owned by Anglicans and the number employed in mills owned by Dissenters.[15] He left it to his audience to complete his syllogism by supplying his major premise, that no Anglican would employ a Dissenter, no Dissenter an Anglican. His point was not overtly political. But its political implications are clear. Only when different aspects of individual identity reinforced one another – when religion, for example, was not only a matter of individual confession but an explanation of a man's place of employment – could poll books have been published, because only then was the information which poll books contain sufficiently *un*important, sufficiently a matter of public knowledge or, at least, sufficiently a matter of public assumption. And, of course, it was only when this was the case that it was worth the while to gather the information in organized form which, according to Cox and Grady, was 'among the most valuable' which the election manager could possess, that concerning each voter's 'employer, sect landlord, customer or creditor.'[16]

III

Bloc voting was extremely widespread: this is an important point which ever county poll book reveals. The corollary, which successive poll books for the same county constituency reveal, is even more important: the changes in the overall polls from one contest to another which account for the returns of different candidates at different contests were largely the products of changes of orientation and changes in the relative size and cohesion of specific blocs.[17] These points suggest that those historians who in dealing with nineteenth century English elections, have focused *on what* the different voters voted for instead of *with whom* they voted have been asking the wrong question.[18] The question which they have asked is one which the political culture dictates and the usual parliamentary perspective prescribes. But, their approach has deflected our attention from two questions which hold important keys to the basic political problems of the nineteenth century: first, how were the groups and nexus which poll books reveal perpetuated and, second, how and why were these groups and nexus supplanted by other groups and nexus – supplanted, at least, as the characteristic groups and nexus on which the character of the system was based.

As a rule, politics, considered from a parliamentary perspective, have been interpreted not only as a goal-oriented activity but as one in which the goals are functions of the needs of men who belong to certain assumedly *a priori* groups. Hence, from this perspective voters' behaviour in elections has been explained in terms of the subsequent behaviour of the Members they chose, the behaviour of these Members in terms of the 'wishes' or 'opinions' expressed by the voters when they chose them. Furthermore — and thus is the circle closed — these 'wishes' or 'opinions' are generally regarded as either the spontaneous expressions of the voters' *a priori* social identities, or the equally spontaneous expressions of their moral or intellectual positions.

Within the system as a whole in which, at any given time, the voters and their representatives are both involved, the importance of these several propositions is undeniable. They help to strengthen the confidence without which no system of representative government could long endure. The evidence of the county poll books, however, and the procedures recommended by Cox and Grady, suggest that a distinction must be made between the functional value of these propositions and their descriptive value. Descriptively they imply that the systems which, functionally, they help to perpetuate, do not exist. Considered from a parliamentary perspective politics is the mechanism of legislation; legislation is the product of class, ideology, or some other of what are usually treated as unmoved movers. Considered from a poll book perspective politics is less the mechanism of legislation and more the means by which the relevant action groups are perpetuated — and sometimes jeopardized — in consequence of their rivalries with one another;[19] political class and ideology are less unmoved movers and more the products of the exigencies of cohesion of particular varieties of group in particular varieties of circumstance and the exigencies of stability of the leaders of the group. Indeed, to consider politics from a poll book perspective is to enter the world which the parliamentary perspective has tended to obscure, the world in which neither individual nor social identity is always quite as unambiguous as it is usually made out to be, the world in which, because such ambiguities exist, the fact that a group is a group for which a goal is a goal is important.

When men associated with a given estate or factory voted as a bloc, and when they voted for the same candidate or candidates as the owner of the estate or factory — or, in the case of a peer, as he would have voted — their behaviour can scarcely be explained except in terms of the cohesion of the group to which they belonged and the orientation of the influence to which, in many cases, the very existence of the group itself should be attributed. But such behaviour does more than illustrate the structure of the society it reflects. It also helps to explain the perpetuation of this structure, the perpetuation of the related political system, and the peculiar selection and formulation of political issues within the system. The voters who voted with their landlords or employers not only gave weight to the political decisions which these

men made. They also validated their claims to make these decisions.
Thus, they not only helped to perpetuate the conditions in which, as a
rule, political leadership roles were functions of certain quite specific
non-political leadership roles. They also helped to perpetuate the
conditions in which the selection and formulation of political issues
were principally conditioned by the exigencies of cohesion of the
particular varieties of group they formed and the exigencies of status of
the leaders of these groups.

The statement is tautological but useful: the political system which
poll books help to illustrate endured as long as sufficient proportions of
the voters could be recruited through the particular varieties of agency
of electoral recruitment which poll books reflect. As a rule, these
agencies were not class agencies: they did not recruit men for their class
identities. Rather, they were the means by which men of different
classes were organized, men who generally lived in fairly close
proximity to one another, who were connected by the same economic
'interest' – land, cotton, shipping, etc . . . – who were often of the
same religion, all of which would seem to have prompted them – and
this was the most important aspect of the matter – to acknowledge the
same individual as their ideological or 'opinion' leader. As a rule, these
latter were men of high socio-economic status. But whatever their
status their leadership roles did not derive from their status alone.
Rather, they derived from their status in their own communities.
Indeed, Bagehot and others notwithstanding, status alone on a
generalized scale does not explain their influence. Nor was the
mechanism of their influence that which Bagehot in particular
described.

According to Bagehot, influence obtained because a sufficient
proportion of the electorate was composed of men of at least middling
status, who were thus sufficiently *intelligent* to recognize the greater
intelligence of their social superiors; the viability of the mid-nineteenth
century English political system was the consequence of generalized
relationships among the members of different classes, classes which
differential *intelligence* served to define, and relationships which the
objective recognition of this differential *intelligence* served to explain.[20]
This is patent nonsense. Influence and deference were crucial factors in
mid-nineteenth century English politics. But influence and deference
only occurred in what might be called 'deference communities' or
'deference networks'. In effect, the behaviour which poll books reveal
cannot be understood in terms of the explanations provided by
Bagehot and various of his contemporaries. It was not *intelligence* which
was demonstrated by those men whose behaviour can be seen in the
county poll books. Rather, it was their membership of one or another
of those hierarchically structured communities or networks which

were the essential action groups of mid-nineteenth century English politics and which the issues of this politics served both to legitimize and challenge. However, while the assumptions implicit in Bagehot's and others' arguments are both foolish and demonstrably wrong they are no less important for being foolish and wrong. They cannot be used to describe the realities of the mid-nineteenth century English political system. But they can be used to describe how those realities appeared to many men at the time. And this is not only a reality in its own right. It also defines a problem and suggests a cause. The problem is why Bagehot and various others substituted an intellectual for a social dynamic when they tried to explain mid-century electoral behaviour. The cause is the probable role of their explanation in perpetuating the system they were thereby distorting. Indeed, to the extent that the explanations they provided were convincing, these undoubtedly helped to reinforce the traditional deference communities and deference networks – and this at a time when these traditional communities and networks were being weakened by their continued rivalries with one another and by the growing importance of quite other nexus.

When Cox and Grady observed in 1872 that canvassers rarely had any difficulty in eliciting the information they sought, they were referring to the residual strength of the traditional communities and networks.[21] But it was because these groups were becoming weaker that well *before* 1872 various election managers were ceasing to be able to predict the outcome of a prospective contest with their accustomed accuracy in the light of the information which canvassers were used to gathering.[22] To some extent, the growing bureaucratization of local politics in the latter sixties and seventies was obviously prompted by the hope of restoring, and even enhancing, the earlier accuracy. But the problem which the election managers faced was not the consequence of inefficient organization. Rather, it was the consequence of changes in the organizational importance of different nexus in English society. The traditional groups were losing their cohesion; men who had previously been able to exercise leadership roles in the context of these groups were ceasing to be able to do so. It was this phenomenon to which the leader writer in *The Times* implicitly referred, in 1872, when he noted that 'Large numbers of voters . . . are now fixed in the belief that they will be exposed to unknown evils if they have not the power of screening their votes in darkness.'[23]

The adoption of the secret ballot was symptomatic. So, too, were the development of the mass-membership political party, the assumption of extra-parliamentary leadership roles by parliamentary leaders, the growing power of the State, and the emergence of class issues upon the

surface of electoral and parliamentary politics. The structural
conditions which poll books reflect and which made their publication
possible were ceasing to exist. New agencies and mechanisms of
electoral recruitment which characterized the new political system
were coming into being.

, IV

As a rule, those who have considered politics from a parliamentary
perspective have tended to assume that the mid-nineteenth century
English political system and the changes which occurred within it were
both principally – if not solely – the products of legislation which
reformers demanded in the context of the general processes of
population growth, urbanization and industrialization. In effect, they
have tended to assume that changes in the distribution of political
power in the nineteenth century not only ran parallel to demographic
and economic changes but did so in consequence of the legislative
victories of reformers over anti-reformers. The importance of
legislation is not to be denied, nor the importance of reformers'
activities, nor, again, the political importance of the general processes
of population growth, urbanization and industrialization. But the
changes in the distribution of political power in the nineteenth century
were far more complex than this formulation allows. Not only were
certain pieces of nineteenth century legislation far less effective in
producing change than some reformers wished; not only were certain
changes less the products of legislation than they were the products of
antecedent political activities; even more important, certain pieces
of legislation were obviously designed to control or counteract some of
the changes which these activities and processes were effecting.

By and large, when dealing with the problems of political change in
England in the mid-nineteenth century, historians have tended to focus
their attention upon the first two Reform Acts and upon certain of the
provisions of these Acts contained – those which enlarged the
electorate, abolished certain categories of constituency reduced the
electoral weights of certain other categories of constituency, and
created new constituencies. Had these Acts contained only these
provisions and had the social identities of the voters been more fixed
than they were conditional, then there would perhaps be little reason
to criticise this general procedure. But these Acts contained other
provisions. Furthermore, the social identities of few men are so firmly
fixed as to be unaffected by the immediate institutional surroundings in
which they find themselves. Hence it is important to note that those
provisions normally neglected by historians in fact had considerable
impact upon these surroundings. They were the means by which, at

two important points in the general processes of population growth, urbanization and industrialization, those men who had been jumbled together by urbanization and industrialization were sorted out into different constituencies. In the context of the evidence provided by the poll books the implications of these provisions are clear. At two important points in time, when the continued existence of the traditionally structured deference communities and deference networks was being threatened, steps were taken to perpetuate them and thus to perpetuate the roles and status of the traditional elites.

Note: As this book goes to press Patrick Joyce has shown that poll books *can* be used to reveal the existence of electoral bloc in certain industrial towns ('The factory politics of Lancashire in the later nineteenth century', *The Historical Journal,* XVIII (1975), pp. 525-553). His work illustrates the error of my insistence that poll books are only really valuable in dealing with the rural areas of the countries. Obviously, the conditions which make them valuable in these areas are also obtained in certain towns.

Part I

Politics from a poll book perspective

Introduction

The evidence contained in isolated poll books is valuable but that in poll books for successive contests in the same constituency is far more so. Not only does the latter give a truly meaningful answer to the question who voted with whom; it also makes it possible to identify those men responsible for whatever differences of outcome may have occurred at these contests. Thus, one may ask and, to some extent, answer the question 'why did these differences of outcome occur?'

Among the most important elections in the nineteenth century were those which took place in the English county constituencies between 1830 and 1841. The reasons for this are simple. A majority of the English county Members who were returned at the elections of July and August 1830, voted against the Government on the civil list division the following November.[1] It was this vote which caused Wellington's resignation and the subsequent appointment of the Grey Ministry. Even more important, perhaps, were the consequences of the English county elections of May 1831. All but six of the 82 Members returned at these elections voted with the Grey Ministry on the crucial second reading of their second Reform Bill in July.[2] Their votes provided the necessary margin. But scarcely less important were the cummulative results of the English county elections in 1832, 1835, 1837 and 1841. In 1841, all but 24 of the English county Members, since 1832 enlarged to a total of 144, voted to restore Peel to office.[3] Again their votes provided the necessary margin.

As a rule, the changes of orientation of the majority of the English county Members between 1830 or 1831 and 1841 have been explained either in terms of ostensible differences between the relative coercibility of the 40s. freeholders who comprised the county electorates before 1832 and that of the new categories of voter enfranchised in 1832,[4] or in terms of an ostensible movement of public opinion[5] – that is to say, either in terms of the arguments which certain Whigs and many Radicals used at the time, or in terms of the arguments which various Tories or Conservatives used in replying to their arguments. Undoubtedly, neither of these explanations is 'wrong': evidence could be found for both. As the poll book evidence suggests, however, neither is adequate. Nor are they adequate when taken together. Primarily, each reflects a way of looking at the problem consistent with the interests of the viewer. The Radicals' argument reflects their effort to assuage their own disappointments with the Reform Act: the Tories' their effort to legitimize their own restored ascendancy in Parliament in terms which the Radicals defined while articulating their disappointments. But neither reflects the essential structure of county politics before the Bill was passed. And neither reflects the changes in this structure which occurred at the time the Bill was passed and which, in large measure, are attributable to it.

When the Radicals saw the results of the post-reform county elections their own logic and self-esteem required them to cry 'Coercion'! Such a cry was consistent with the notion that anti-liberalism, or anti-radicalism, could only subsist on the basis of the rotten boroughs or their moral equivalent. Its cogency was strengthened by the prominent roles which many of the former borough mongers played in the new coalitions which were forming around Wellington and Peel, by the terms of discussion of the reform crisis in general and the Chandos amendment[6] in particular, and by the arguments that were used to explain why, in 1831, most county Members were reformers.

In the pre-reform period the counties were often described as the means whereby the so-called 'popular' voice in politics was expressed. The reasons for this are not far to seek. They reflect an amalgam between the meaning, or meanings, of 'popularity', and the sizes of the various county electorates. When so many other English constituencies were controlled by individuals who used them at the beck and call of the Tory Ministers of the 1820s the fact – which the poll books reveal – that in most counties electoral influence was hardly weaker, merely more diffuse and partly urban, was largely ignored. When so many English county Members voted for the Bill the fact was completely ignored, which the poll books also reveal, that many of these men owed their seats to local coalitions which, especially in 1830, contained strong coteries of rural peers and squires who conceived of reform either as a means of punishing Wellington for his apostasy on the Catholic question or, more generally, as a means of destroying the Ministers' powers to enact liberal measures.

Apart from the fact that parliamentary reform had been a radical demand for many years there are two principal reasons why, in 1831

and 1832, urban and radical leaders became the major symbolic
spokesmen of reform. The one concerns the process by which a new
Tory or Conservative Party was created. The other concerns an
important aspect of the pre-reform constituency structure. During the
reform crisis many Ultra-Tories who had gone into opposition over
the Catholic Relief Bill in 1829 and who had played such important
roles in the anti-Wellingtonian coalitions of 1830 either withdrew
from politics, at least temporarily, or returned to the Tory fold. While
their behaviour obscured their own former roles in these coalitions
their arguments swelled the chorus that the Bill was indeed a radical
measure not only constitutionally but socially. In the context of these
arguments, which a number of former Whig peers and squires
evidently found convincing, a new set of coalitions came into being
which provided the basis of the new Conservative Party. Then, too, at
the county elections in 1826, 1830 and 1831 many urban Radicals
exploited a power which, presumably, had existed for many years but
which, previously, they had not exploited. In large measure, the
answer to the question why the overwhelming majority of English
county Members voted for the Bill in 1831 lies in the breadth of the
anti-Wellingtonian coalitions of 1830 and the relative slowness of the
process by which a new Conservative Party came into being. But in
large measure, too, it lies in the power which urban leaders were able
to exercise in many counties in the pre-reform period. In part, the
contingent nature of the anti-Wellingtonian coalitions of 1830 can be
seen in the relative rapidity with which the new Conservative Party
emerged. In part, it can be seen in those provisions of the first Reform
Act which either destroyed or seriously weakened the powers of urban
leaders to interfere in county elections.[7]

These two sets of factors – the disintegration and restoration of Tory
unity on the one hand and the electoral power which many urban
leaders could exercise in many counties if they chose to do so, on the
other, were extremely important. The results of the partnerships
between rural Whigs, dissident Tories and urban Radicals are apparent
in various county elections in 1830. The effects of the power which
many urban leaders continued to exercise in various counties after these
partnerships were dissolved but before the Bill was passed are apparent
in certain counties in 1831. Most county Members in 1831 were
members of the gentry. But many of these men owed their seats less to
their neighbours in the countryside than to the support of urban leaders
and the proportions of the total county electorates on whom these men
could bring effective influence to bear. In some counties in which
contests occurred in 1831 urban and quasi-urban freeholders exercised
even greater relative strength than they had in 1830. Presumably, in
many counties in which contests did not occur in 1831 it was the

prospective electoral weight of these freeholders together with the lack
of unity among the opponents of the Bill, which prevented their
occurrence. Thus, in the post-reform period the stage was set for a
fundamental redefinition of the counties as 'rural' constituencies: many
former Tories had returned to the fray; they had been joined in their
coalitions by many former Whigs; new categories of rural voter had
been enfranchised, many freeholders with freeholds in the boroughs
had been deprived of their county votes; many new boroughs had been
created; borough boundaries had been redrawn, and many urban
leaders restricted their own electoral energies to the new or newly
defined boroughs. In effect, the relationship between county Members
and their constituents was essentially the same in 1841 as in 1831 but the
constituents were different.

As a rule, these structural factors were not at the time publicly
acknowledged. Understandably – and especially in the post-reform
period – most politicians preferred to attribute their own powers to
their 'popularity' – and their opponents' to coercion – rather than
acknowledge that both frequently had a structural foundation. And
generally the discussion has been continued in the same vein. This has
served to obscure certain provisions of the first Reform Act which,
once noted, suggest that the Act should be considered not as the means
by which changes were effected in the locus of political power within
the State but rather as the means by which such changes stemming
from non-legislative sources, were controlled or counteracted.

II

Fortunately, the principal changes of orientation among Members of
Parliament between 1831 and 1841 occurred among the county
Members. Had it been otherwise these changes could scarcely be
explained – at least, with the procedures presently available. Yet the
necessary evidence is available for only a few, even of the county
constituencies. In the pre-reform period, particularly, most county
elections were uncontested. Contests occurred in only 10 of the 40
English counties in 1826, in 10 again in 1830, and in 1831, including
two by-elections, in 12.[8] Nor do poll books exist for all of the contests
which did occur. Hence the importance of the evidence for those
counties in which contests took place with some frequency in both the
immediate pre-reform and immediate post-reform periods, for which
poll books are available.

The evidence for Cambridgeshire is uniquely valuable. Contests
occurred in Cambridgeshire in 1826, 1830, 1831 – a by-election – 1832
and 1835. Furthermore, a poll book exists for each of these contests.
The evidence for Huntingdonshire and Northamptonshire is only

slightly less valuable. Contests took place in Huntingdonshire in 1826, 1831 and 1837 and poll books are available. In Northamptonshire a contest occurred in 1831 and a poll book exists for it. Contests for which poll books are available occurred in North Northamptonshire in 1832 and 1835 — a by-election. Furthermore, all three counties returned, in 1830 or 1831, reformers who subsequently retired or were defeated.

These three counties are next to each other. In consequence, the evidence which their poll books contain cannot reflect possible differences in electoral behaviour in different parts of the kingdom. Furthermore, the sheer number of contests within these counties raises the question whether these counties were not grossly a-typical and, assuming such to have been the case, raises the additional question of the nature of their a-typicality. The frequency of contested elections perhaps served to strengthen electoral blocs. More probably, it served to weaken them. In any event, without a contest there can be no poll book, without a poll book there can be no evidence, and the questions upon which this evidence can be brought to bear are extremely important.

1

Huntingdonshire, 1826-37

I

Two Tories were returned for Huntingdonshire in 1826, William Henry Fellowes, of Ramsey Abbey, who had sat for the county for many years, and Viscount Mandeville, the son of the fifth Duke of Manchester.[1] Defeated was Lord John Russell, son of the sixth Duke of Bedford, who had been returned without a contest in 1820. In 1830 Fellowes retired. In his place and – so rumour had it – with his blessing, Viscount Strathaven was nominated.[2] The son of the fifth Earl of Aboyne, Strathaven was regarded as an Ultra-Tory candidate. But if the Church question was that with which he was principally identified it was not that which either he or his supporters principally emphasized. As a correspondent reported in *The Times* – and the report reflects the frequent tendency of Ultra-Tories in 1830 to substitute certain economic questions for Church questions – 'In the absence of even a pretence for raising the howl of "No Popery", Lord Strathaven's committee call for the suffrages of the farmers on the ground of his enmity to "free trade in corn" . . .'[3]

In 1830 Russell refused to stand. He was strongly urged to do so on the grounds that the 50-vote margin, by which Fellowes had beaten him in 1826, no longer existed. Fellowes, it was argued, had polled his full strength in 1826 while 'many, very many additional [pro-Russell] votes have been made since then.'[4] Furthermore, according to those who pressed him, no other 'independent' candidate would have a chance if Mandeville and Strathaven 'coalesced'.[5] Finally, when these inducements failed, John Bonfoy Rooper, of Abbotts Ripton, was nominated in his place. Whether or not it proves the accuracy of the contention that no other 'independent' candidate besides Russell could win, Rooper was beaten. In 1831 the same candidates stood as in 1830.

HUNTINGDONSHIRE

Huntingdonshire in the mid-nineteenth century

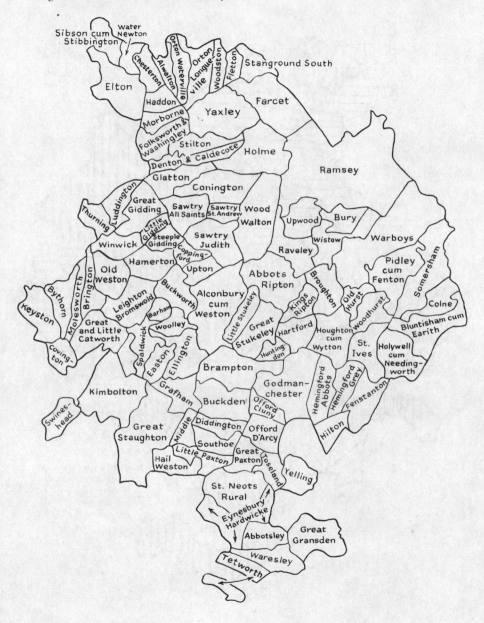

Sibson cum Stibbington

Water Newton

Orton Waterville

Chesterton

Alwalton

Orton Longueville

Woodston

Fletton

Stanground South

Elton

Haddon

Morborne

Yaxley

Farcet

Folksworth & Washingley

Stilton

Denton & Caldecote

Holme

Glatton

Ramsey

Luddington

Conington

Great Gidding

Sawtry All Saints

Sawtry St. Andrew

Wood Walton

Upwood

Bury

Thurning

Little Gidding

Steeple Gidding

Sawtry Judith

Wistow

Warboys

Winwick

Coppingford

Raveley

Pidley cum Fenton

Somersham

Hamerton

Upton

Abbots Ripton

Broughton

Old Hurst

Woodhurst

Colne

Old Weston

Buckworth

Alconbury cum Weston

Kings Ripton

Bluntisham cum Earith

Brington

Leighton Bromswold

Barham

Little Stukeley

Great Stukeley

Hartford

Houghton cum Wytton

St. Ives

Holywell cum Needingworth

Bythorn

Molesworth

Keyston

Woolley

Hunting don

Great and Little Catworth

Spaldwick

Easton

Ellington

Brampton

Godmanchester

Hemingford Abbots

Hemingford Grey

Fenstanton

Covington

Kimbolton

Grafham

Buckden

Offord Cluny

Hilton

Swineshead

Great Staughton

Middle

Diddington

Offord D'Arcy

Southoe

Hail Weston

Little Paxton

Great Paxton

Toseland

Yelling

St. Neots Rural

Eynesbury Hardwicke

Abbotsley

Great Gransden

Waresley

Tetworth

Location of the different voting patterns at the Huntingdonshire contests of 1826, 1831 and 1837

1826

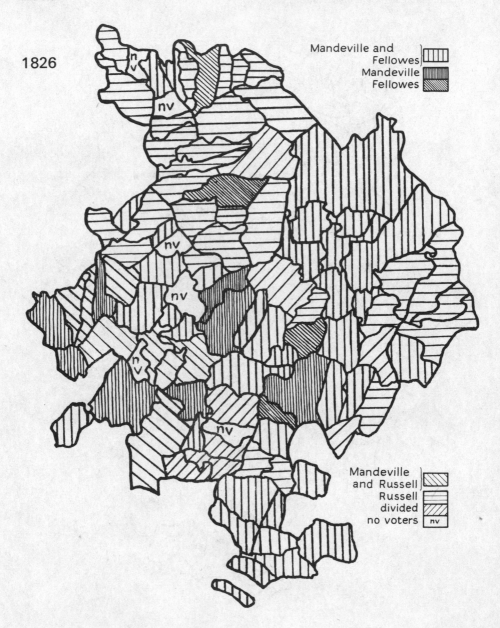

Mandeville and
Fellowes
Mandeville
Fellowes

Mandeville
and Russell
Russell
divided
no voters

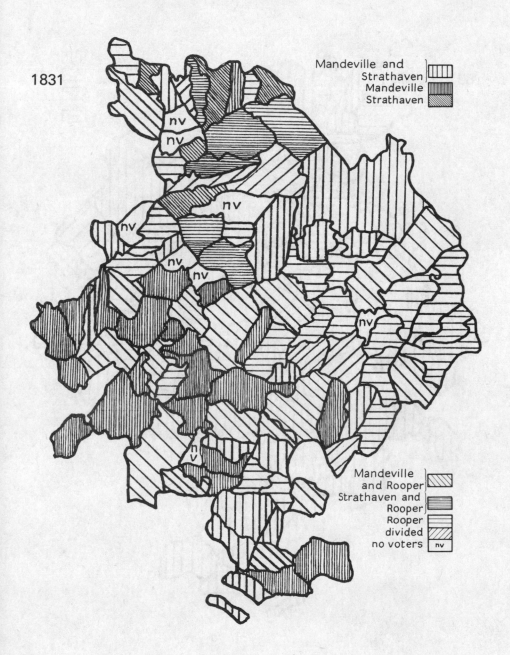

1831

Mandeville and
Strathaven
Mandeville
Strathaven

Mandeville
and Rooper
Strathaven and
Rooper
Rooper
divided
no voters   nv

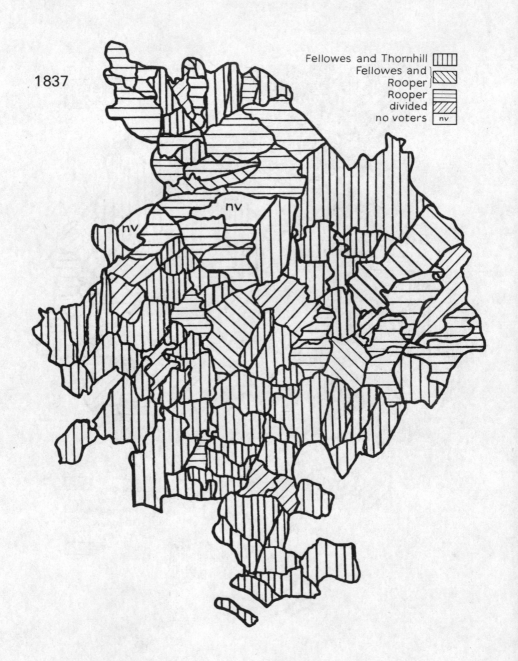

1837

Fellowes and Thornhill

Fellowes and
Rooper }

Rooper

divided

no voters   nv

But on this occasion Rooper was returned along with Mandeville. Mandeville and Rooper continued to sit for the county without opposition until 1837 when Mandeville retired and two Tory or Conservative candidates were nominated, Edward Fellowes, the son of the former Member, and George Thornhill, of Diddington. At the ensuing contest Rooper was beaten. Thereafter, no contest occurred in the county until 1857.

The total polls of the Huntingdonshire voters in 1826, 1830, 1831 and 1837 were as indicated in table 1. However, while these total polls tell us who would fill the county seats they do not tell us why.

Table 1[6]

Total polls of the Huntingdonshire voters at the contests of 1826, 1830, 1831 and 1837

1826		1830	
Voters who polled	1,281		
Mandeville (Tory)	968	Mandeville (Tory)	1,068
Fellowes (Tory)	911	Strathaven (Tory)	990
Russell (Whig)	858	Rooper (Whig)	840
1831		1837	
Voters who polled	1,214	Voters who polled	2,250
Rooper (Whig)	841	Fellowes (Tory)	1,393
Mandeville (Tory)	813	Thornhill (Tory)	1,332
Strathaven (Tory)	575	Rooper (Whig)	990

II

Replying to a complaint made in *The Times* during the elections of 1831 to the effect that only one reformer was being nominated in Huntingdonshire, a correspondent explained the situation in the county rather simply. Mandeville, he wrote, was being supported by the Duke of Manchester's interest, by the Earl of Sandwich's interest, by most of the squires, and he was one of the *two* candidates being supported by the Earl of Carysfort's interest.[7] Presumably, to those who understood the exigencies of multi-member constituency politics, and who knew something of the previous orientations of the major interests in the county, his statement constituted an adequate explanation.

To vote for a single candidate was to declare a strong individual preference. But in a two-member constituency in which each voter could cast two votes to vote for a single candidate was to leave very much to others the question of who would fill the second seat. To vote for two candidates was to play more part in answering this question. But in 1831, no candidate in the county was allied with any other candidate. Strathaven, the Ultra-Tory, had voted for the Reform Bill. By so doing, he had forfeited the support of two significant Tory interests in the county, those of the Duke of Manchester and the Earl of Sandwich.[8] As *The Times'* correspondent pointed out, these interests were now supporting Mandeville, by implication *not* supporting Mandeville *and* Strathaven. Presumably, those who knew that previously the Manchester and Sandwich interests had supported the *two* Tory candidates not only understood what the correspondent was saying, but also understood the electoral ramifications of the withdrawal of support from Strathaven. Those who knew that in 1826 the Carysfort interest had supported Russell alone also presumably understood the electoral ramifications of the statement that the Carysfort interest was now supporting two candidates, of whom Mandeville was one.[9] Clearly, the correspondent was saying that the reformers could not hope for more than Rooper's return. Perhaps he was also saying that they could only hope for Rooper's return because many of their opponents were no longer willing to support Strathaven.

For Rooper's friends Strathaven's behaviour in 1831 created both an opportunity and a problem. Some reformers, with their attention focussed upon reform, argued that Strathaven should be supported as the lesser of two evils. But Rooper himself was, as he put it, 'uncharitable enough to think, we must attribute his vote on reform, rather to an habitual subservience to Courts and Ministers, than to any regard for, or conviction of, the necessity of the measure.'[10] Thus, in his eyes, Strathaven may even have become the greater evil. Nor should certain quite practical considerations which may have made Strathaven seem, if not the greater evil, at least the greater threat be ignored. While certain Tory interests were focussing their support upon Mandeville alone, others were continuing to support Strathaven as well as Mandeville. Thus, since Rooper could only be returned if either Mandeville or Strathaven could be beaten, and since Mandeville was the stronger of the two, those men were jeopardizing Rooper's return who supported Strathaven against Mandeville.

After the contest was over the Earl of Sandwich's agent complained, 'Never were the Tories so unnecessarily beaten.'[11] In the light of his own earlier opposition to support being withdrawn from Strathaven[12] his meaning is clear. Tory dissension was responsible for Tory defeat. The poll books show that this was largely true.

In effect, Rooper's return in 1831 can principally be attributed to a split in the local Tory elite. His defeat, in 1837, can principally be attributed to the healing of this split. When the poll book of 1831 is compared with those of 1826 and 1837 what is apparent is not so much the weakening of local electoral agreement – signifying the weakening of the relevant influences and groups – as changes of orientation of different influences. True, in certain parishes local electoral agreement was weaker in 1831 than it was in 1826 and 1837, in particular in those parishes where at other times, Tory influences were strong. But the electoral consequences of the weakening of Tory influences were far less important than the electoral consequences of the changes of orientation of these influences. Furthermore, in most cases these changes of orientation can themselves be explained without necessarily assuming that changes of basic priority had taken place. The point is important. Like the vote which Strathaven cast for the Bill itself it suggests that the reform crisis was really the consequence of the loss of correspondence between political 'parties' and certain coherent sets of priorities.

III

In somewhat gross terms the importance of the breakdown and restoration of Tory unity can be seen from the behaviour of the outvoters.[13] In 1826 the Huntingdonshire outvoters cast rather more votes for Russell than for Mandeville or Fellowes. But the differences were not as great as they were in 1831.[14] In 1831 the outvoters cast somewhat fewer votes for Rooper than, previously, they had cast for Russell. But the numbers of votes they cast for Mandeville and Strathaven dropped sharply. In consequence of this drop Rooper had a plurality among the outvoters in 1831 which more than made up for Mandeville's plurality among the resident voters. In 1837, the outvoters cast roughly the same numbers of votes for each of the three candidates. Such can be seen from table 2.

The reasons for the drop in the numbers of votes which the outvoters cast for Mandeville and Strathaven in 1831 compared with the numbers they cast for Mandeville and Fellowes in 1826, are presumably not far to seek. Since voting had to be done in person, and since many voters – especially outvoters – would only vote if their travelling expenses were covered (or more than covered) – the behaviour of the outvoters was often a measure of the needs and organization of the candidate or candidates for whom they voted and of the amounts of money these candidates and their supporters were willing to spend. Whether or not the outvoters who polled for Rooper in 1831 did so because of his popularity, and the popularity of the cause he symbolized, it seems obvious that the outvoters who failed to poll for Mandeville and Strathaven failed to poll for them because Mandeville and Strathaven

Table 2

Polls of the resident voters and of the outvoters at the Huntingdonshire contests of
1826, 1831 and 1837

1826		Votes for		
		Mandeville (Tory)	Fellowes (Tory)	Russell (Whig)
Resident Voters		760	685	608
Outvoters		208	226	250
	totals	968	911	858

1831		Votes for		
		Mandeville (Tory)	Strathaven (Tory)	Rooper (Whig)
Resident Voters		716	496	619
Outvoters		97	79	222
	totals	815	575	841

1837		Votes for		
		Fellowes (Tory)	Thornhill (Tory)	Rooper (Whig)
Resident Voters		1,113	1,006	728
Outvoters		279	266	262
	totals	1,392	1,332	990

were no longer allied with one another. Presumably, with
Mandeville's own election effectively assured by the resident voters,
neither he nor his own supporters were willing to go to the trouble and
expense of bringing to the polls those outvoters who might have voted
for him alone. And, they were probably even less willing to bring to
the polls those outvoters who might have voted for the *two* 'Tory'
candidates. Nor, in the circumstances of 1831, did Strathaven possess
many ardent individual supporters. By 1837, Tory unity had been
restored.

IV

With the evidence presently available, the outvoters can only be dealt
with as members of that category. The resident voters, on the other

hand, can often be dealt with as members of specific groups the existence of which is revealed by their behaviour. Thus, their behaviour opens rather more interesting vistas and raises rather more interesting questions than that of the outvoters. In particular, these vistas and questions have to do with the existence of a socio-political system in which large numbers of voters consistently voted in agreement with the majority of their immediate neighbours, and in which the results of successive contests were products of changes in the cohesion of these local blocs, of changes in their individual orientations, and of changes in the relative numbers of voters which the differently oriented aggregates or groups of blocs contained.

No county poll book can reveal every electoral bloc which might have existed in the county. Thus, with the evidence presently available, a full measure of the political importance of these blocs cannot be had. But some indication of their importance can be gained from the simple existence of those which can be identified and from the degree to which support for the different candidates at the different contests in Huntingdonshire, Cambridgeshire and Northamptonshire between 1826 and 1857 was concentrated in particular parishes. For various reasons, particular aspects of the mid-century political system are more apparent from the poll books of one county in one year or succession of years than from those of another – e.g., in Northamptonshire the general political consequences of the relative changes in the numbers of voters who polled from the different types of parish between 1831 and 1832; in Cambridgeshire, in 1835, the relationship between private influence' and 'party' behaviour. But the importance of bloc behaviour and the varieties of factors to which the outcome of the different contests should be attributed are as apparent from the Huntingdonshire poll books as from those of these or other counties.

All, or significant majorities of the resident voters of certain parishes in Huntingdonshire split their votes between the two Tory candidates in 1826, 1831 and 1837 (group 1 of table 3). [15] In 1826, the voters who resided in these parishes constituted 32 per cent of the resident electorate. They contributed 40 per cent of the votes which Mandeville received from this electorate, 48 per cent of the votes which Fellowes received from them, but only 15 per cent of the votes which Russell received from them. In 1831, the voters who resided in these parishes comprised 33 per cent of the resident electorate. They contributed 40 per cent of the votes which Mandeville received from this electorate, 55 per cent of the votes which Strathaven received from them, but only 20 per cent of the votes which Rooper received from them. In 1837, the voters from these parishes only comprised 26 per cent of the total electorate. On balance, the proportional increase in the numbers of voters in other parish groups was greater – this, largely, because of the impact of the borough freeholder clause of the first Reform Act in the borough of Huntingdon.[16] They contributed 33 per cent of the votes which Fellowes and Thornhill received, but only 16 per cent of the votes which Rooper received.

All or significant majorities of the voters of certain other parishes in the county split their votes between the two Tory candidates in 1826 and 1837 and plumped for Mandeville in 1831 (group 2). In 1826, when the voters who resided in these parishes comprised 11 per cent of the resident voters, they contributed 17 per cent of the votes which Mandeville received from these voters, 16 per cent of the votes which Fellowes received from them, but only 3 per cent of the votes which Russell received from them. In 1831, when the voters who resided in

Table 3

An analysis of the local bases of power of the different candidates at the Huntingdonshire contests of 1826, 1831 and 1837

Parishes and Parish Groups	1826				1831				1837			
	Numbers of voters	*Votes for*			Numbers of voters	*Votes for*			Numbers of voters	*Votes for*		
		Mandeville	*Fellowes*	*Russell*		*Mandeville*	*Strathaven*	*Rooper*		*Fellowes*	*Thornhill*	*Rooper*
Group 1												
Bury	8	8	8	–	10	8	8	1	23	21	19	2
Chesterton	1	1	1	–	1	1	1	–	5	4	4	1
Diddington	–	–	–	–	1	1	1	–	6	6	6	–
Everton cum Tetworth	1	1	1	–	1	1	1	–	10	8	9	2
Eynesbury	16	14	12	3	17	13	13	4	28	21	21	7
Haddon	–	–	–	–	–	–	–	–	3	3	3	–
Hemingford Grey	16	12	10	4	21	19	16	3	66	34	37	31
Huntingdon	135	103	98	42	123	72	69	59	97	74	72	31
Little Gidding	1	1	1	–	1	1	1	–	3	3	3	–
Luddington	1	1	1	–	–	–	–	–	–	–	–	–
Offord Darcy	5	5	4	1	8	8	8	–	24	17	17	7
Old Hurst	1	1	1	–	–	–	–	–	4	3	2	2
Ramsey	142	100	133	17	133	112	110	22	209	189	169	34
St. Neots	68	54	48	20	72	45	40	32	102	71	68	34
Southoe	6	3	3	3	7	5	3	3	5	4	4	1
Steeple Gidding	–	–	–	–	–	–	–	–	3	3	3	–
Upwood	7	7	7	–	4	4	4	–	9	8	6	3
totals	408	311	328	90	399	290	275	124	597	466	443	155

Table 3 *(continued)*

Parishes and Parish Groups	1826 Numbers of voters	Votes for Mandeville	Fellowes	Russell	1831 Numbers of voters	Votes for Mandeville	Strathaven	Rooper	1837 Numbers of voters	Votes for Fellowes	Thornhill	Rooper
Group 2												
Barham	3	3	2	1	3	3	–	1	5	4	4	1
Brampton	25	24	24	1	23	22	11	5	47	43	40	6
Brington	4	4	1	2	3	3	–	1	9	6	6	3
Covington	2	2	–	–	3	3	–	–	7	4	4	3
Grafham	5	5	3	–	4	4	1	1	11	7	8	4
Gransden	22	18	18	4	17	15	2	7	20	19	19	1
Hamerton	1	1	1	–	2	2	1	–	8	7	7	1
Hemingford Abbots	9	5	6	4	6	6	1	1	34	22	21	13
Keyston	2	2	1	1	3	3	1	–	16	13	13	3
Kimbolton	44	44	33	6	51	49	3	7	68	58	59	10
Leighton	6	6	6	–	7	7	–	–	10	10	10	–
Stow	–	–	–	–	1	1	–	–	6	5	4	2
Stukely Little	6	5	6	–	8	8	4	2	7	6	6	1
Swineshead	5	5	4	–	5	5	–	1	20	20	20	–
Upton	3	2	2	1	1	1	–	–	4	4	4	–
Waresley	2	2	2	–	3	3	1	–	5	5	5	–
Wooley	2	2	2	–	1	1	–	–	3	3	3	–
totals	141	130	111	20	141	136	25	26	280	236	233	48

Table 3 continued on next page

Table 3 (continued)

	1826				1831				1837			
		Votes for				Votes for				Votes for		
Parishes and Parish Groups	Numbers of voters	*Manderville*	*Fellowes*	*Russell*	Numbers of voters	*Manderville*	*Strathaven*	*Rooper*	Numbers of voters	*Fellowes*	*Thornhill*	*Rooper*
Group 3												
Bluntisham	17	1	1	16	14	1	–	13	54	17	15	40
Colne	13	2	2	11	9	–	–	9	46	9	7	38
Denton	1	–	–	1	–	–	–	–	3	1	1	2
Earith	18	4	5	13	17	–	–	17	38	10	7	31
Fletton	4	–	–	4	1	–	–	1	18	4	4	14
Great Gidding	9	–	–	9	6	–	–	6	17	2	2	15
King's Ripton	1	–	–	1	1	–	–	1	7	3	2	5
Lutton cum Washingley	1	–	–	1	1	–	–	1	10	1	1	9
Pidley cum Fenton	10	2	6	8	10	2	–	9	22	10	9	13
Morborn	2	–	–	2	–	–	–	–	3	–	–	3
Sawtry St. Andrew	9	–	–	9	9	–	1	8	19	1	2	17
St. Ives	50	26	23	27	76	31	22	53	74	36	34	42
Sibson cum Stibbington	5	–	–	5	4	–	1	4	7	1	1	6
Woodhurst	5	1	2	4	5	1	–	5	10	3	2	9
totals	145	36	39	111	153	35	24	127	328	98	87	244
Group 4												
Farcet	9	–	–	9	9	–	9	7	33	15	13	21
Orton Waterville	3	1	–	3	2	–	2	1	12	3	6	9
Sawtry All Saints	5	–	–	5	8	–	4	6	9	1	2	9
Sawtry St. Judith	6	–	–	6	4	–	3	3	7	–	–	7
Stilton	29	11	8	22	29	3	20	18	46	22	18	37
Yaxley	31	3	1	29	23	8	17	14	48	17	14	36
totals	83	15	9	74	75	11	55	49	155	58	53	119
Totals, groups 3 & 4	228	51	48	185	228	46	79	176	483	156	140	363
Group 5												
Buckworth	–	–	–	–	1	1	–	1	8	–	–	8
Elton	30	1	–	30	26	21	4	19	45	9	10	36
totals	30	1	–	30	27	22	4	20	53	9	10	44

Table 3 (continued)

Parishes and Parish Groups	1826 Numbers of voters	Votes for Mandeville	Fellowes	Russell	1831 Numbers of voters	Votes for Mandeville	Strathaven	Rooper	1837 Numbers of voters	Votes for Fellowes	Thornhill	Rooper
Group 6												
Abbotsley	6	4	4	2	4	2	1	3	10	7	7	3
Offord Cluny	5	3	5	2	5	3	2	3	9	6	6	3
Yelling	1	1	1	–	5	4	1	4	8	7	7	1
totals	12	8	10	4	14	9	4	10	27	20	20	7
Group 7												
Abbots Ripton	12	7	8	5	5	3	–	5	16	8	8	8
Warboys	32	20	24	10	36	21	5	26	63	32	27	37
totals	44	27	32	15	41	24	5	31	79	40	35	45
Group 8												
Alconbury cum Weston	12	9	5	6	11	9	3	6	34	21	16	18
Buckden	25	17	13	14	19	14	5	9	34	24	29	8
Godmanchester	87	52	44	43	78	46	14	57	83	50	53	37
Hail Weston	8	4	4	4	9	5	1	7	14	9	11	6
totals	132	82	66	67	117	74	23	79	165	104	109	69
Group 9												
Catworth	24	21	4	18	17	14	1	11	32	22	24	8
totals	24	21	4	18	17	14	1	11	32	22	24	8
Group 10												
Great Staughton	29	18	3	24	26	13	2	19	58	35	34	28
Old Weston	5	5	1	4	7	5	2	5	19	12	12	10
Spaldwick	11	10	2	9	10	6	–	9	11	6	6	6
totals	45	33	6	37	43	24	4	33	88	53	52	44
Totals, Groups 5–10	287	172	118	171	259	167	41	184	424	248	250	197

Table 3 continued on next page

Table 3 (continued)

Parishes and Parish Groups	1826 Numbers of voters	Mandeville	Fellowes	Russell	1831 Numbers of voters	Mandeville	Strathaven	Rooper	1837 Numbers of voters	Fellowes	Thornhill	Rooper
Group 11												
Folkesworth	6	2	–	6	4	1	3	1	8	7	7	1
Glatton	5	–	1	5	3	–	3	–	10	3	3	7
Orton Longueville	4	2	4	2	4	1	4	–	8	7	7	1
Stanground	10	3	2	9	11	4	11	1	34	21	20	15
Water Newton	–	–	–	–	1	–	1	–	5	1	1	4
totals	25	7	7	22	23	6	22	2	70	39	39	34
Group 12												
Holywell cum Needingworth	15	11	8	6	11	5	4	7	34	16	13	21
Houghton cum Wytton	5	4	3	2	5	2	2	3	13	8	5	9
totals	20	15	11	8	16	7	6	10	47	24	18	30
Group 13												
Fenstanton	24	9	14	12	21	6	8	16	44	27	27	18
Great Paxton	6	1	1	5	4	–	–	4	15	7	9	8
Somersham	51	10	13	41	46	11	7	42	73	39	39	39
Toseland	1	–	–	1	2	–	–	2	6	3	3	3
Winwick	5	2	–	4	8	3	4	7	15	11	9	7
totals	87	22	28	63	81	20	19	71	153	87	87	75
Group 14												
Broughton	6	5	5	1	3	1	–	3	10	9	5	4
Easton	1	1	–	1	1	–	–	1	14	10	10	4
Great Ravely	1	1	1	–	1	–	–	1	8	7	6	2
Great Stukely	5	3	3	2	3	1	1	2	15	10	10	5
Hilton	8	5	4	4	6	3	3	3	8	6	6	2
Wistow	6	4	5	2	7	1	1	6	23	14	14	11
totals	27	19	18	10	21	6	5	16	78	56	48	28

Table 3 (continued)

Parishes and Parish Groups	1826 Numbers of voters	Mandeville	Fellowes	Russell	1831 Numbers of voters	Mandeville	Strathaven	Rooper	1837 Numbers of voters	Fellowes	Thornhill	Rooper
Group 15												
Bythorn	9	6	2	7	9	8	4	2	15	15	14	1
Copingford	1	–	–	1	–	–	–	–	1	1	1	–
Ellington	8	7	3	5	8	8	4	1	23	19	14	9
Molesworth	11	7	2	9	5	5	5	–	15	12	11	4
Papworth	3	2	1	2	2	2	1	1	2	2	2	–
Little Paxton	4	2	2	2	5	5	1	–	5	3	4	2
Thurning	2	1	–	2	1	1	1	–	4	3	3	1
Woodstone	1	–	–	1	2	2	–	–	10	8	8	2
Woodwalton	4	1	1	3	3	2	2	1	5	4	4	1
totals	43	26	11	32	35	33	18	5	75	67	61	20
Group 16												
Hartford	2	1	2	–	2	1	1	1	21	7	7	14
Midloe	1	1	1	–	–	–	–	–	3	1	1	2
totals	3	2	3	–	2	1	1	1	24	8	8	16
Group 17												
Holme	5	2	2	3	5	3	3	2	10	1	1	10
totals	5	2	2	3	5	3	3	2	10	1	1	10
Group 18												
Allwalton	1	1	1	–	2	1	1	1	6	3	3	3
Caldecote	2	1	–	2	2	1	1	1	3	2	1	2
Connington	4	–	3	1	–	–	–	–	–	–	–	–
totals	7	2	4	3	4	2	2	2	9	5	4	5
Totals, Groups 11–18	217	95	84	141	187	78	75	109	466	287	266	218

Table 3 (continued)

Analysis, showing the locus of support of the different candidates

	1826						1831						1837					
	numbers of voters	these as %s of total poll	Mandeville	Fellowes	Russell		numbers of voters	these as %s of total poll	Mandeville	Strathaven	Rooper		numbers of voters	these as %s of total poll	Fellowes	Thornhill	Rooper	
			votes for						votes for						votes for			
Group 1	408	32	311	328	90		399	33	290	275	124		597	26	466	443	155	
votes received from group as %s of total votes received			40	48	15				40	55	20				33	33	16	
%s of voters in the group who voted for			76	80	22				73	70	31				78	74	26	
Group 2	141	11	130	111	20		141	12	136	25	26		280	12	236	233	48	
votes received from group as %s of total votes received			17	16	3				19	5	4				17	17	5	
%s of voters in the group who voted for			92	79	14				96	18	18				84	83	17	
Groups 3-4	228	18	51	48	185		228	19	46	79	176		483	22	156	140	363	
votes received from group as %s of total votes received			7	7	30				6	16	28				11	10	37	
%s of voters in the group who voted for			22	21	81				20	35	77				32	29	75	
Groups 5-10	287	22	172	118	171		259	21	167	41	184		424	20	248	250	197	
votes received from group as %s of total votes received			23	17	28				23	8	30				18	19	20	
%s of voters in the group who voted for			60	41	60				64	16	71				58	59	46	
Groups 11-18	217	17	95	84	141		187	15	78	75	109		466	20	287	266	218	
votes received from group as %s of total votes received			13	12	23				11	15	18				20	20	22	
%s of voters in the group who voted for			44	39	65				42	40	58				62	57	47	

these parishes comprised 12 per cent of the resident electorate, they contributed 19 per cent of the votes which Mandeville received from this electorate, but only five per cent of the votes which Strathaven received from them – clearly, these men did much to defeat Strathaven – and four per cent of the votes which Rooper received from them. In 1837, when the voters from these parishes comprised 12 per cent of the total electorate, they contributed 17 per cent of the votes which Fellowes and Thornhill received but only five per cent of the votes which Rooper received.

Large majorities of the voters from other parishes plumped for Russell in 1826, for Rooper in 1831, and for Rooper again in 1837 (group 3). Significant majorities of the voters from others plumped for Russell in 1826, split their votes between Rooper and Strathaven in 1831, and plumped for Rooper again in 1837 (group 4). Presumably, in these parishes votes for Strathaven were either votes for the man who had voted for the Bill or votes against Mandeville, the man who had voted against it. In either case, there is no need to assume any change of priorities or of basic political orientation to explain the votes cast for Strathaven.

The parishes in groups 3 and 4 contained fewer voters than those in groups 1 and 2. This political fact helps to explain the general lack of success of Whig candidates. But while the voters from what might be called the Whig parishes were fewer than those from what might be called the Tory parishes, their behaviour was similar to that of the others. They tended to act as members of geographically definable blocs – indeed, it is only because they did so that they are visible. Also, they cast a disproportionate share of the votes received by the candidates for whom they voted. In 1826, when they comprised 18 per cent of the resident electorate they contributed 30 per cent of the votes which Russell received from this electorate but only seven per cent of the votes which Mandeville and Fellowes received from them. In 1831, when they comprised 19 per cent of the resident electorate, they contributed 28 per cent of the votes which Rooper received from this electorate, 16 per cent of the votes which Strathaven received from them, but only six per cent of the votes which Mandeville received from them. In 1837, when they comprised 22 per cent of the total electorate, they contributed 37 per cent of the votes which Rooper received but only 11 per cent of the votes which Fellowes received and only 10 per cent of the votes which Thornhill received.

The orientations of the majorities of the voters in the parishes in groups 1 through 4 can be described in 'party' terms and understand in terms of parliamentary perspectives. Certain of these orientations might be called Tory, others Whig, but obviously the mechanisms which conditioned the behaviour of these voters were not 'party' mechanisms.

Nor did they derive from Parliament. They were intensely local. As such, they were obviously functions of the communities in which they existed. In certain other parishes the behaviour of the majorities of the voters cannot be described in 'party' terms or understood in terms of simple parliamentary perspectives. In other parishes, again, the political importance of cohesive social groups is less clear. However, in only a very few parishes did changes of orientation occur which parallel the changes in the aggregate county polls. In effect, there were very few men whose behaviour confirms the validity of the assumptions which have generally been used to explain the changes of orientation of the majority of English county Members between 1830 or 1831 and 1841.

Paradoxical as it may seem, there were certain parishes, together containing over 20 per cent of the resident voters in 1831, from which majorities of the voters split their votes in 1831 between Rooper the reformer and Mandeville the anti-reformer (groups 5 – 10). Except in these parishes such splits were extremely rare. In effect, as with other patterns of behaviour, where the pattern occurred it tended to occur as the dominant pattern. However, there was no general rule governing how voters who split their votes in 1831 between Rooper and Mandeville would vote at other contests.

Rooper-Mandeville splits occurred in 1831 in some parishes where, at other contests, majorities of the voters plumped for the Whig candidates (group 5). Presumably, in these parishes, votes for Mandeville in 1831 were votes against Strathaven the Ultra-Tory. They occurred in some parishes where, at other contests, majorities of the voters split their votes between the two Tory candidates (group 6). Possibly, in these parishes, votes for Rooper in 1831 were votes against Strathaven the renegade Tory. They also occurred in some parishes where, either in 1837 or 1826, there was no strong 'party' consensus (groups 7 and 8). And, again, they occurred in some parishes where, in 1826, majorities of the voters split their votes between Fellowes and Russell. The majority of the voters from one of these parishes split their votes between the two Tory candidates in 1837 (group 9). From the others the three candidates received fairly equal support in 1837 (group 10).

Voters in the parishes in clusters 5 through 10 obviously helped to return Rooper and Mandeville in 1831 and thus to defeat Strathaven. Altogether, in 1831, they comprised 21 per cent of the resident electorate. They provided Rooper with 30 per cent of the votes he received from this electorate, Mandeville with 23 per cent of the votes he received from them, and Strathaven with a mere eight per cent of the votes he received from them. In 1826, the voters from these parishes did little to reinforce the aggregate polls. They comprised 22 per cent of the resident electorate. The votes they cast made the largest proportional contribution to the votes received by Russell, the loser. They provided him with 28 per cent of the votes he received from this electorate, Mandeville with 23 per cent of the votes he received from them, and Fellowes with 17 per cent of the votes he received from them. In 1837, their proportional contributions to the totals of votes which the three candidates received were approximately the same for each. They comprised 20 per cent of the total electorate. They provided Rooper with 20 per cent of the votes he received, Thornhill with 19 per cent of the votes he received, and Fellowes with 18 per cent of the votes he received. Whatever the reason, the voters from these parishes no longer provided the same strong support for Rooper as in 1831. Their behaviour helps to illustrate the point that the aggregate polls were the consequence of the convergence of very different factors.

The voters who plumped for Strathaven in 1831 help to illustrate the same point (group 11). But the parishes were few in which such behaviour occurred. Nor did these parishes contain many voters.

There were, of course, some parishes from which majorities of the voters changed their orientation in ways which, in general, paralleled the changes in the aggregate county polls between 1826 and 1831 (group 12), between 1831 and 1837 (group 13), and even between 1826 and 1831 and, again, between 1831 and 1837 (group 14). The voters from these parishes obviously helped to return Rooper in 1831 and to defeat him in 1837. But the question arises whether the parliamentary significance of the behaviour of these men is that to which their behaviour itself should be attributed. Furthermore, there were other parishes from which majorities of the voters changed their orientation in ways which ran counter to the changes in the aggregate county polls between 1826 and 1831 (group 15), between 1831 and 1837 (group 16), and even between 1826 and 1831 and, again, between 1831 and 1837 (group 17). Together with a few politically nondescript parishes (group 18) these parishes contained the total county electorate. Except in 1826, the contributions which the voters from the parishes in groups 11 through 18 made to the totals of votes which the different candidates received did not differ by more than three per cent from the percentages of the total electorates in the county which these parishes contained. In the aggregate, the voters from these parishes affected the outcome of the contests of 1826, 1831 and 1837 rather less than the voters from certain other parishes.

V

The patterns of bloc voting define the question, why did these patterns exist? To some extent the localism of these patterns provides a means of answering the question – or, at least, a means of defining the terms in which, in all probability, satisfactory answers might be found. Clearly, these electoral blocs reveal the effects of discrete local influences. Presumably, the influences which conditioned the behaviour of the members of these blocs also had something to do with the existence of these blocs themselves.

In certain cases we can begin to see why these blocs existed and why members of them voted in ways which not only reveal the existence of the blocs but their own identities as members of them. For example, one of the parishes from which majorities of the voters consistently voted for the two Tory or Conservative candidates – even in 1831, when the two candidates were at odds with one another – was Ramsey (group 1). Ramsey Abbey was the seat of the Fellowes family[17] which provided the county with several Tory members. The behaviour of the Ramsey voters was presumably a measure of the family's local influence, an influence which – it seems obvious – was exerted in favour of Strathaven not only in 1830[18] but in 1831 too. The family's influence presumably also explains similar electoral patterns in the adjacent parishes of Bury and Upwood. For Bury, this assumption is to some extent confirmed by the marginal notation of a prominent Whig who wrote beside the parish entries in his own copy of the poll book of 1837: 'all Fellowes.'[19] In Warboys, however, which is also adjacent to Ramsey, a different electoral pattern is apparent both in 1831 and in the years following. A majority of the Warboys voters voted for the two Tory candidates in 1826. But, in 1831, a significant number of them split their votes between Rooper the reformer and Mandeville the anti-reformer (group 7).

The Rooper-Mandeville splits in 1831 are doubly significant: not only do they suggest the possible electoral importance of certain considerations which the usual parliamentary perspective has tended to obscure; they also suggest where and, possibly, through what channels, these considerations made themselves felt. One of the parishes from which majorities of the voters split their votes between Rooper and Mandeville in 1831 was Elton (group 8). It was there the Carysfort seat was located. As *The Times*' correspondent explained in 1831, Mandeville was one of the *two* candidates the Carysfort interest was supporting.

Unfortunately, only four of the parishes from which majorities of the voters split their votes between Rooper and Mandeville in 1831 are included in the available portion of the poll book for 1830. These are Alconbury-cum-Weston, Catworth, Elton and Warboys – and Elton only in part. In all four parishes significant numbers of voters split their votes across 'party' lines in 1830. With available evidence, it is impossible to discover whether a cross 'party' split was always the reflection of the orientation of a single influence or whether it was sometimes the consequence of the convergence of two opposing influences. Even so, the evidence is clear in certain cases and suggests the importance of those coalitions between Whigs and ministerial Tories which emerged in the immediate pre-reform period and which the reform crisis helped to destroy. After the Whig Duke of Bedford had voted with Wellington on the regency question in July 1830, James Duberly, a local Whig, complained, '. . . no one can understand the Duke of Bedford's vote.'[20] But whatever it was that prompted Bedford to vote as he did,[21] and whatever it was that prompted him to return to his former Whig affiliation by the summer of 1831, his flirtation with the Tories had an obvious electoral impact in Cambridgeshire, where it can be seen reflected in the poll book for 1830,[22] and presumably had some effect in Huntingdonshire. As Bedford's agent reported to Milton in 1830, Bedford was supporting Mandeville.[23] Unfortunately, he neglected to say whether Bedford was supporting Mandeville alone. Obviously, in Cambridgeshire in 1830, Bedford supported Osborne, the Whig and Manners, the Tory against Adeane, the Independent. This is clear from the voting in the parish of Thorney, where Bedford's Cambridgeshire estates were located. However, the available portion of the Huntingdonshire poll book for 1830 does not include any of the parishes in which Bedford's Huntingdonshire estates were to be found. At other times the voters from Sibson cum Stibbington, for example (group 3), behaved as they might be expected to behave: almost all of them plumped for the Whig or Liberal candidates. However, the available evidence is silent upon their behaviour in 1830. On the other hand, the available portion of the Huntingdonshire poll book for 1830 includes certain of the Elton voters and thereby suggests that the Carysfort influence, as exercised by the dowager Countess and the Carysfort trustees, was being exercised in favour of both Rooper and Mandeville.[24] But why did such coalitions endure rather longer in Huntingdonshire than in most other counties?[25] With the evidence available the existence of these coalitions is rather clearer than the specific reasons for their existence.

For Kimbolton, on the other hand, the available evidence clearly explains why most of the voters polled for the two Tory candidates in 1826 and 1837, but plumped for Mandeville in 1831 (group 2). Kimbolton Castle was the seat of the Dukes of Manchester. Similar patterns of behaviour are apparent in various other parishes in the county in which the Manchester estates were spread, some adjacent to Kimbolton, others lying at a distance, among them Brington, Stow and Swineshead. In Catworth, Great Staughton and Spaldwick on the other hand, which lie directly adjacent to Kimbolton, different patterns are apparent (groups 9 and 10). In 1826, large numbers of voters from these parishes split their votes between Mandeville and Russell, in 1831 between Mandeville and Rooper. While the proximity to Kimbolton might explain the votes for Mandeville, it scarcely explains the votes for Russell and Rooper. With the evidence presently available they cannot be explained.

The available evidence does, nevertheless, provide a means of explaining the behaviour of the voters from Orton Longueville (group 11). Orton Longueville was the seat of the Earls of Aboyne. The majority of the voters from Yaxley who voted for Strathaven in 1831 possibly did so because Strathaven had voted for the Bill (group 4). On the other hand, Strathaven had little appeal in 1831 in various other parishes in the county in which, as in Yaxley, majorities of the voters polled for the Whig or Liberal candidates at other contests. Whatever the reasons for the majorities of the Yaxley voters voting for the Whig or Liberal candidates at other contests, it seems very possible that the strength of Strathaven's appeal in Yaxley in 1831 had some connection with the fact that Yaxley lies next to Orton Longueville.

Then there were the parishes in which estates belonging to prominent Whigs who did not enter into coalition with Tories in the immediate pre-reform period were located. Thus Great Gidding, where the Whig Earl Fitzwilliam was a significant landowner (group 3). Great Gidding is included in the available portion of the Huntingdonshire poll book for 1830. Of the six voters who polled from the parish in that year, all but one plumped for Rooper; this one split his votes as was done in Elton between Rooper and Mandeville.

VI

Clearly defined blocs cannot be seen in every parish. With the evidence presently available the groups which these blocs undoubtedly reflected cannot be identified, except circumstantially and in many cases, cannot be identified at all. But if the behaviour of the majorities of the voters in the different parishes is considered in the light of their behaviour at earlier and later contests, it becomes clear that Rooper's return in 1831 was very largely due to the breakdown of those alliances among individual leaders to which the return of the two Tory candidates in 1826 should be attributed. By the same token, his defeat in 1837 was very largely due to the restoration of those alliances. The Earl of Sandwich's agent was presumably implicitly noting the importance of these alliances when he complained, after the contest of 1831, 'Never were the Tories so unnecessarily beaten.'

Rooper received fewer votes when he was returned in 1831 than Russell received in defeat in 1826. Indeed, Rooper received only one more vote in 1831 than in 1830 when he was himself beaten. Thus –

and, presumably, it was this which elicited the complaint of the Earl of Sandwich's agent – since Mandeville trailed Rooper by fewer than thirty votes in 1831, he might possibly have headed the poll with the help of the outvoters. By the same token, since the margin between Mandeville and Strathaven was in part a function of the votes of those Tories who voted against Strathaven either directly or indirectly, Strathaven might possibly have been returned instead of Rooper had not those men who were able to bring effective influence to bear upon

Table 4

Polls of the resident voters in 1826, 1831 and 1837; polls of the voters in the parishes in which majorities of the voters generally voted for the two Tory candidates but in which, in 1831, they either plumped for Mandeville or split their votes between Mandeville and Rooper; and polls of the voters in the parishes in which majorities of the voters polled for Rooper in 1831 and against him in 1837 where votes for Rooper in 1831 were not really votes against Strathaven

| | 1826 | | | 1831 | | | 1837 | | |
| | *Votes for* | | | *Votes for* | | | *Votes for* | | |
	Mandeville	*Fellowes*	*Russell*	*Mandeville*	*Strathaven*	*Rooper*	*Fellowes*	*Thornhill*	*Rooper*
Resident voters	760	685	608	716	496	619	1,113	1,006	728
Group 2	130	111	20	136	25	26	236	233	48
6	8	10	4	9	4	10	20	20	7
7	27	32	15	24	5	31	40	35	45
8	82	66	67	74	23	79	104	109	69
9	21	4	18	14	1	11	22	24	8
10	33	6	37	24	4	33	55	52	44
totals	301	229	161	281	62	190	475	473	221
resident voters less those in Groups 2 and 6–10	459	456	447	435	434	429	638	533	507
Group 13	22	28	63	20	19	71	87	87	75
14	19	18	10	6	5	16	56	48	28
totals	41	46	73	26	24	87	143	135	103

these voters decided to oppose him. Obviously, the only 'necessity' in Strathaven's defeat was the reason why it happened. The same is true of Rooper's defeat in 1837. Hence the importance of the behaviour of the voters from the generally Tory parishes from which majorities of the voters either plumped for Mandeville in 1831 or split their votes between Mandeville and Rooper. The results of the poll of the resident voters in the county as a whole would not have been significantly different in 1826 and 1837 had the voters from these parishes not voted. Had the voters from these parishes not voted, however, in 1831 the results of the poll of the resident voters would have been different in a way which confirms the thrust of the argument of Sandwich's agent (see table 4).

After the 1837 contest, Rooper complained that 'the screw' had been used against him.[26] In effect, he implied that the factors determining the behaviour of significant numbers of voters in 1837 were different from those determining their behaviour in 1831. Ostensibly, in 1831, they voted for him because they *wished* to do so. Ostensibly, in 1837, they voted against him because they were *forced* to do so. Of course, the poll books have nothing to say about who was coerced and who was not. Thus, they have nothing to say about the accuracy of Rooper's implicit contention. But these points should be noted: the only parishes from which majorities of the voters polled for Rooper in 1831 and against him in 1837, and where votes *for* Rooper in 1831 were not really votes *against* Strathaven, were those in groups 13 and 14. The voters from these parishes did much to return Rooper in 1831. But they were too few in number to have had the impact he attributed to them later whatever their reasons for changing sides (see table 4).

Nor should it be forgotten that these men changed sides at a time when the Tories were trying to create an image for themselves as the 'party' of the landed interest. As General Denzil Onslow put it while nominating Thornhill in 1837, Rooper himself might be a friend of the farmer. But his party was not.[27] Perhaps, such an argument helps to explain Henry Sweeting's political switch. In 1830 Sweeting had been reported as using his influence exclusively for Rooper.[28] In 1837, he seconded Thornhill's nomination. Clearly, there were several ways of looking at all this. One of them was that reflected in the speaker's statement at the consolation dinner given for Rooper in 1838: 'The Tory landlords, and the priestly tyranny combine against us. And then there are "the little Squires" – the *novi homines* – who set up for squires, and think that, when a man becomes a Tory it makes him a gentleman.'[29]

CAMBRIDGESHIRE

Cambridgeshire in the mid-nineteenth century

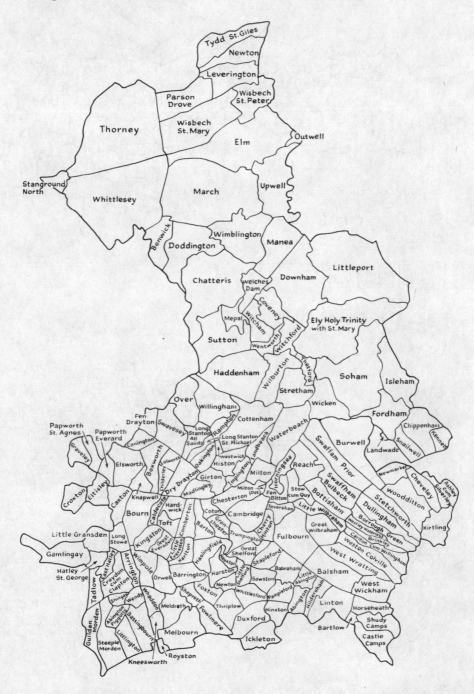

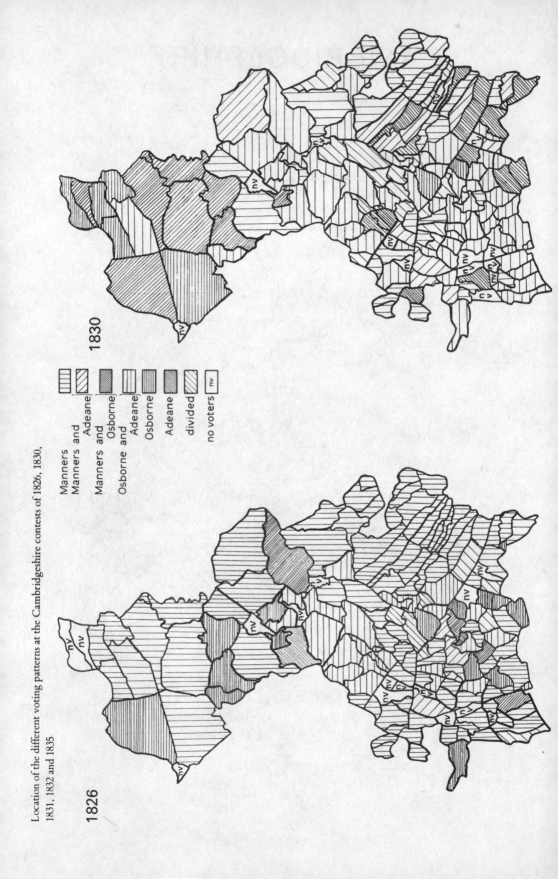

Location of the different voting patterns at the Cambridgeshire contests of 1826, 1830, 1831, 1832 and 1835.

Manners

Manners and Adeane

Manners and Osborne

Osborne and Adeane

Adeane

Osborne

Adeane

divided

no voters

1830

1826

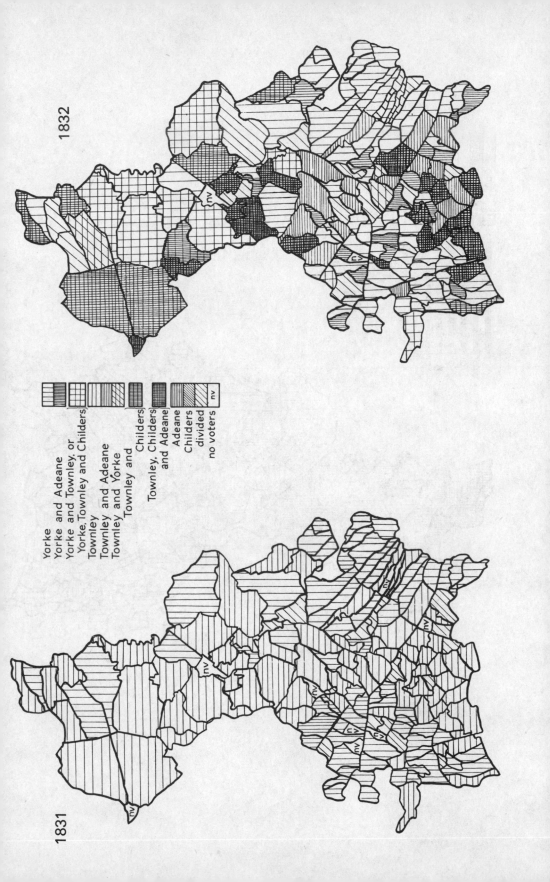

1832

Yorke
Yorke and Adeane
Yorke and Townley, or
Yorke, Townley and Childers
Townley
Townley and Adeane
Townley and Yorke
Townley and Childers
Townley, Childers
    and Adeane
Adeane
Childers
divided
no voters   nv

1831

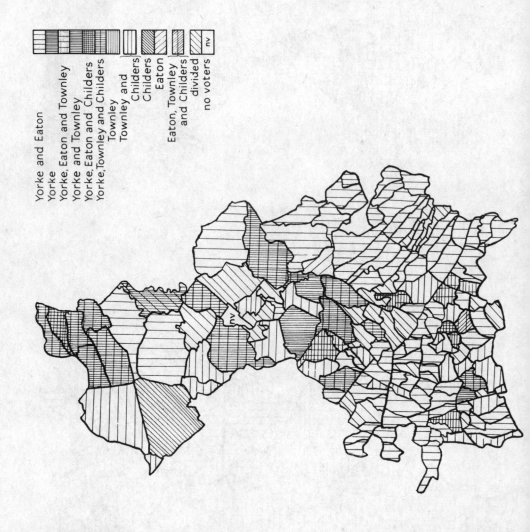

Yorke and Eaton

Yorke

Yorke, Eaton and Townley

Yorke and Townley

Yorke, Eaton and Childers

Yorke, Townley and Childers

Townley

Townley and Childers

Childers

Eaton

Eaton, Townley and Childers

divided

nv   no voters

1835

2

Cambridgeshire: 1826-1835

I

In the early nineteenth century Cambridgeshire was the close preserve of the principal local aristocratic families. These were the Manners, Dukes of Rutland, who owned large estates centring on their seat at Cheveley, near Newmarket, and the Yorkes, Earls of Hardwicke, whose estates were even larger, some centring on their seat at Wimpole, near Cambridge, others scattered.[1] Indeed, writing in 1816 Thomas Oldfield declared that the Rutland and Hardwicke influence in the county was so strong 'that it intimidates every person who might be otherwise disposed to offer himself as a candidate.' He added, however, that the Duke of Bedford, 'having great property in this county, has a considerable interest.'[2]

During the late eighteenth century the Rutland and Hardwicke families dominated the representation of the county and occasionally fought with each other for exclusive control. In the early years of the nineteenth century however the politics of the county were complicated by the formation of a so-called 'Independent' party, based largely in the borough of Cambridge, and generally supported by Bedford.[3] At the time it was formed this party was primarily aimed against Hardwicke.

It achieved its first lasting victory in 1810, six years before Oldfield wrote. At a county by-election, caused by the appointment of Charles Yorke as teller of the exchequer, the 'Independent' party, assisted by the Bedford interest, secured the return of Lord Francis Godolphin Osborne, son of the fifth Duke of Leeds. Although the election evidently reflected a decrease of Hardwicke influence the ways in which this was manifest are obscure: no contest took place. Yorke retired before the poll. But this much is certain: the Hardwicke family was effectively humbled. Thereafter, they never fought alone. Rather, they sought alliances first with one, then with another electoral group until finally, in 1831, they joined Rutland and those other peers and squires who joined him to oppose the Bill.

During the next 20 years county representation remained in the hands of Osborne and Lord Charles Somerset Manners, son of the Duke of Rutland, who had first been returned in 1802. Both men were evidently regarded with at least some charity and until 1826 their membership was never seriously challenged. In that year a group of persons from Cambridge promoted a contest in the county with the evident intention of exerting their influence in the only place it could be effective.

In the borough of Cambridge the franchise was restricted to the members of a small self-selected corporation. There, Rutland had built an impregnable basis for his power. Efforts to breach it failed in 1818.[4] Efforts failed again in 1826 when George Pryme, the political economist, tried. He stood as an anti-Rutland candidate and received four votes before he retired. The close constituency gave the Rutland candidates 24 and 23 votes, respectively.[5] Immediately after the borough contest Pryme and his various urban supporters announced their intention of precipitating a contest in the county.[6] They chose as their champion Henry John Adeane of Babraham, chairman of quarter sessions, who had fought against the Rutland interest in the borough in 1818.[7] In the county Rutland was vulnerable in a way in which he was not in the borough. While his own estates were large other estates were larger. Furthermore – and especially in the pre-reform period – many county voters were members of communities in which the effective influences were opposed to those of the world of landed estates.

II

While population was, of course, important it was sociological and geographical factors which primarily determined the number of voters which the different communities – and the different varieties of community – contained, especially in the pre-reform period. In Cambridgeshire the principal geographical factor had to do with the Fens. The line of the Fens separated two fairly distinct and fairly homogeneous regions. In neither were freeholders very numerous. In proportion to the population as a whole, however, freeholders were somewhat more numerous in the northern Fens than they were in the southern uplands. Except for certain Fen parishes such as Thorney, in which the Duke of Bedford was the sole landowner, the Fens were a region in which landownership was fairly widely distributed. It was a region of small farms where much land remained unenclosed until well into the nineteenth and even the twentieth century. By the mid-nineteenth century, however, the southern uplands contained few if any unenclosed parishes. The uplands were a region of sizeable estates.

The adjacent hundreds of Staine and Radfield illustrate the effects of such factors upon the size of the electorate. Much of Staine is Fenland. Radfield contains no Fen areas. Although the population of Staine was smaller than that of Radfield far more voters polled from Staine in the pre-reform period than polled from Radfield. After 1832 the relative electoral weights of the two hundreds came to be somewhat closer to their relative populations. Both the differences in the proportions of voters to population, and the changes in them, may be seen in table 5.

Table 5[8]

Showing the populations of Radfield and Staine in 1801 and 1841, and the numbers of voters who polled from the two hundreds at the several contested elections in Cambridgeshire between 1722 and 1835

	Population in		Numbers of voters in							
	1801	1841	1722	1780	1802	1826	1830	1831	1832	1835
Radfield	3,117	5,580	69	85	98	60	61	57	159	154
Staine	2,967	4,883	160	106	140	89	138	90	177	177

The same story is told elsewhere. From the Fen parish of Wittingham, for example, which had a population of 1,403 in 1831, 88 persons polled in that year, roughly five per cent of the population. From the Fen parish of Cottenham, with a population of 1,635, 94 persons polled, almost six per cent of the population. But from the upland and enclosed parish of Little Abington, with a population of 253, a maximum of two persons polled before 1832; from Whaddon, with a population of 339, a maximum of four persons polled before 1832; from Babraham, with a population of 473, a maximum of three persons polled before 1832. These parishes were the centres of large estates.

In the larger towns the proportions of freehold voters to population were sometimes scarcely greater than they were in the enclosed agricultural parishes. In Wisbech, the second largest town in the county, only some three per cent of the local population polled before 1832. But three per cent of Wisbech's population could swamp a hundred Little Abington's. From Wisbech in 1830, 248 voters polled. An even larger electoral weight was concentrated in the borough of Cambridge. Although the maximum number of voters who polled from the borough before 1832 was only slightly more than two per cent of its population this amounted to 471. Indeed, if the numbers of men who voted be a measure of the numbers qualified to vote then, before 1832, almost 14 per cent of the Cambridgeshire electorate was concentrated in the borough of Cambridge: almost 20 per cent was concentrated in Cambridge and Wisbech.

The factors which affected the relative sizes of the electorates in the different towns and parishes in the county frequently also affected the political orientations of the majorities of the local voters. In the enclosed agricultural parishes electoral leadership was generally exercised from the local manor house or parsonage. Squires and parsons did, of course, disagree on political matters. As a rule, however, the points at issue between them did not include the question whether or not they should jointly continue to exercise that degree of influence within the Kingdom which made their disagreements so important; in many towns and unenclosed villages comparable leadership was often exercised by men for whom this question was important. The religious division between Church and Chapel frequently reinforced this other division. In consequence, the occasional efforts of Anglican squires to exclude nonconformists from their own estates undoubtedly helped to concentrate nonconformist leaders in those communities where, in the pre-reform period, the largest numbers of voters proportionate to population were also concentrated. The Duke of Rutland was not referring to the electoral aspect of this phenomenon when he later claimed that most agricultural labourers preferred to live in their own communities, especially their own religious communities, and walk to work, rather than live in 'close' parishes, those in which landownership was concentrated, and where they might not feel at home.[9] But it was the phenomenon itself which provided the logic of his statement. What with the close correlation between religion and politics it is scarcely surprising that in many market towns and unenclosed parishes majorities of the voters were Radical.

Before the latter twenties and early thirties, however, there was little direct political significance in this concentration of electoral weight. The nonconformist and urban leaders seldom challenged the political control of the local aristocracy and gentry. In practical affairs each county was guided by small groups of men recruited exclusively — or almost exclusively — from among the larger landowners. Within the upper hierarchies of county society the patterns of allegiance which bound most of the gentry to one or another magnate's interest were clear. Possibly, as Professor Asa Briggs suggests, the urban leaders considered the county members chosen from the aristocracy and gentry, or the members for neighbouring boroughs, to be adequate representatives of their interests.[10] In any event, the continuity of membership for the various counties until the eve of the reform crisis is a clear reflection of the stability of these various political groupings and of the fact that until then their powers were seldom contested by groups which represented an alternative social focus. In Cambridgeshire the contest of 1826 constituted such a challenge.

III

In 1826 Adeane did not want to stand. He was no friend of the Rutland interest. But neither was he a friend of certain of his backers. In particular, he strongly disliked the politics of the man who nominated him, William Wells, of Huntingdon.[11] Furthermore, he was personally pledged to Osborne. In these circumstances, and believing that he could only be returned if Osborne were defeated, he declared that he would apply for the Chiltern Hundreds if he were elected.[12] His supporters, however, were not deterred. They kept the polls open for seven days. But to no avail. Manners and Osborne were returned, Manners at the head of the poll.

In 1830 Adeane was back in the field, this time of his own volition. And this time, the same men standing, Manners was defeated.

When the poll book for 1830 is compared with that for 1826 two principal reasons emerge for Manners' defeat in 1830. Firstly he was deserted by a number of men whose influence was clearly responsible for the sizeable Tory majorities in certain parishes at other contests. *The Times* obviously exaggerated in reporting that only one local squire, St.Vincent Cotton, of Madingley, remained with Manners to the end[13] but the story the poll book tells is not so very different. Secondly, – and even more important electorally – many more voters were brought to the polls in 1830 than in 1826. While the polls were kept open a full week in 1826, many men from certain parishes simply did not vote although they were obviously qualified to do so. In 1830 they voted. In 1830, over 70 per cent more voters polled. In some cases the absentees of 1826 resided in parishes far distant from the polling place in Cambridge, but in other cases they lived fairly close by. In 1826 the networks had obviously not been brought into operation which were in 1830 and which resulted in a far larger poll, especially from parishes where, when the voters voted, they generally supported the anti-Tory candidates.

No contest occurred in the county in May 1831 – Manners began to canvass but gave it up[14]. A contest did occur at a by-election the following October occasioned by Osborne's resignation. At this contest Richard Greaves Townley, of Fulbourn, a reformer, defeated Charles Yorke, an anti-reformer, who was heir presumptive to the Earl of Hardwicke. By then, however, certain alliances had come into being on which the politics of the county were to be based until 1885.

IV

Ostensibly, Hardwicke had been allied with Bedford in 1826. Both men gave their exclusive support to Osborne. In 1830 Hardwicke and Bedford parted company. Hardwicke supported Osborne and Adeane jointly. In effect, he opposed Manners, the ministerial candidate. Bedford, on the other hand, supported Manners as well as Osborne. However, after Grey had formed a Government in which one of Bedford's sons held office, Bedford rejoined the main body of the Whigs. Meanwhile, various other Whigs formed enduring alliances with their former opponents and various anti-Ministerial Tories returned to the Tory fold. After the failure of Manners' canvassing in 1831 – or perhaps before – Hardwicke and Rutland placed a permanent moratorium on their unpaid grudges. They joined together in opposing the Bill. In this endeavour they gained support from Osborne's father, the Duke of Leeds, among others, and from most of the local squires, both those who had remained faithful to Manners in 1830 and those who deserted him.

In some cases the changes of orientation which produced this new coalition were reported in the press. In others they can be seen in the division lists in *Hansard* or in the poll books. In yet others, they can only be inferred. Such are the cases where the evidence lies in the behaviour of the voters from parishes where certain estates were located. Such evidence is only circumstantial. No specific explanations should be based upon it. In some cases, however – and these are perhaps the most interesting – the different sources tell confirming stories. Hardwicke's orientations – or ostensible orientations – at the contests of 1826, 1830 and 1831 were reported in *The Times.*[15] There is no question of the accuracy of this report for 1831. Hardwicke voted against the Bill.[16] From various parishes in which the Hardwicke estates were located, Charles Yorke received an essentially personal vote in 1831. However, questions do arise concerning the accuracy of the report for the earlier years. There was no consensus among the voters from these parishes in 1826 and 1830.[17] The Earl de la Warr voted against the Bill. His behaviour was directly mirrored in that of the voters from Bourn, where his estates in the county were situated.[18] The Duke of Leeds voted against the Bill. His behaviour was mirrored – although somewhat more slowly – in that of the voters from Stapleford, where his estates in the county were located.[19]

The list might be enlarged. However, while such a list would go one step towards explaining the behaviour of the majority of the voters from certain parishes in 1831 and the years following it would only be one step: the questions why Hardwicke, de la Warr and Leeds behaved

as they did would remain. In effect, it is impossible to explain fully the
coalition which supported Yorke in 1831. But this can be said about it:
it reflected the emergence of a new agricultural-aristocratic 'party' in
the county. Furthermore, the emergence of this 'party' helps to clarify
the roles of the various candidates.

In 1826 Adeane had simply been used by the Radicals. In 1830 when
he stood of his own volition he spoke in terms of premises which
provided a bridge between his own essentially Conservative position
and the Radical position of the men who had promoted his candidacy
in 1826. However, while this bridge served to join these positions, the
positions themselves remained distinct. The bridge had to do with
opposition to Wellington, the positions with the grounds of
opposition.

By 1830 Wellington had succeeded in offending significant members
of just about every important political group in the kingdom, currency
reformers and sound money men, protectionists and free traders,
'Protestants' and 'Catholics,' in effect, just about everyone who lacked
a strong personal reason for supporting him. Since this amounted to
just about everyone who lacked a 'job' the ostensible basis of his power
helped to define the grounds on which his various opponents tended to
meet, his alleged use of public money to keep himself in office.

Reflecting, perhaps, the way in which traditional political labels,
were losing their meaning, Adeane refused to call himself either a
Whig or Tory in 1830.[20] He stood as an 'Independent.' When his own
return together with Osborne began to seem assured, he explained the
defeats of various ministerial candidates in other counties by declaring
that they, like Manners, 'had not supported retrenchment'.[21] On the
hustings Pryme, and others, urged the voters to vote for him as well as
for Osborne because of the number of offices in Church and State
which were filled by members of the Rutland family, and because
Manners was part of the ministerial tail in Parliament.[22] Their
comments suggest that perhaps as far as they were concerned Adeane
was merely the lesser of two evils. And such he proved to be. While he
spoke of the need for reform in 1830, the essentially anti-Radical nature
of his concern for reform became clear when he not only voted but
spoke for Chandos' motion to extend the county franchise to
tenants-at-will of agricultural land who paid rents of at least £50 a
year.[23] Subsequently, this vote cost him the support of his former urban
backers. In effect, by 1831, those men who had been drawn together by
events of the pre-reform period had begun to part company. In 1831
some of Adeane's supporters of 1830 voted for Yorke. Others voted for
Townley.

The essential nature of this split is apparent from another source.
While Townley was the squire of Fulbourne, a significant proportion

of the committee which chose him in 1831 was composed of men who were not part of the rural world.[24] The chairman was the Reverend Algernon Peyton, of Doddington, later described as 'the great dry nurse of Whig candidates [in the county].'[25] Obviously, Peyton operated in close conjunction with Bedford.[26] In addition, the committee included the Reverend John Hailsham, of Bottisham, and William Nash, squire of Hinxton. But the other members of this committee were urban, Radical and significantly non-Anglican. They included George Pryme, Ebenezer Foster, a nonconformist banker whose bank was affiliated with that of George Grote, in London, Henry Hatfield, editor of the Radical *Independent Press,* and three Cambridge merchants, at least one of whom was probably a nonconformist.[27] These men had no effective influence in the borough as it was then constituted. But they had considerable influence in the county and it was based in those communities where, in the pre-reform period, the largest numbers of voters were concentrated.

V

The first Reform Act assigned a third seat to Cambridgeshire. The leaders of the urban-nonconformist coalition chose John Walbank Childers as their candidate for the seat. Their choice presumably reflects a complete split between them and the local men whose social positions were analogous to Childers'. While Childers was a member of the gentry, he was not a member of the local gentry. He was a Yorkshireman who allowed that he had no personal connection with the county. Clearly he regarded this as something of a drawback. On the hustings he promised that if he were elected he would buy land in the county.[28] The members of this urban-nonconformist coalition were obviously happy with Childers – Pryme seconded his nomination.[29] But they were not entirely happy with the prospect of merely adding Childers. They would have liked to drop Adeane.[30] It is a measure of the relations between them and Adeane that Adeane had one election committee, Townley and Childers another.

Throughout the early summer the members of the new anti-Radical coalition were quiet. Possibly, in these circumstances, their opponents assumed that Adeane, Townley and Childers would not be opposed. In any event, when Yorke announced that he would stand again, the Townley and Childers committee attempted to join forces with Adeane.[31] Adeane refused. He presumably hoped to be returned in 1832 as he had been returned in 1830, supported by men who were themselves opposed to one another. He came close to succeeding. Many voters in 1832 split their votes between him and Yorke. Others split their votes between him, Yorke and Townley. Others, again, split their votes between him, Townley and Childers. But those who did so were not sufficiently numerous to save him from those others who plumped for Yorke, who split their votes between Townley and Childers, or who, with possibly greater vindictiveness, split their votes between Townley, Childers and Yorke. Yorke, Townley and Childers were returned, Yorke at the head of the poll.

The leader writer for the Radical *Cambridge Independent Press* was rather concerned that Yorke headed the poll. He sought to explain his position in terms of 'the divisions which unfortunately existed among his opponents.' [32] In part, of course, he was right. But his ingenuity was far greater than his logic when he tried to show that in spite of Yorke's position on the poll 'the friends of Liberal opinions were numerically stronger than the Tories.' Arguing that votes for Adeane were really votes for a Liberal – in effect, that the 'divisions' to which he referred did not exist – he argued further that those men who had cast one vote for Yorke and one for either Adeane, Townley or Childers, could be divided into half-Tories and half-Liberals, and that those others who had cast one vote for Yorke and two for any combination of Adeane, Townley or Childers could be divided into one-third Tories and two-thirds Liberals. Upon this basis he used the poll book totals to show that of the 5,923 voters who polled 3,323 were Liberals and only 2,602 were Tories. [33]

Of course, from the nature of the case Yorke's position was favourable. He was the only Tory candidate in a field of four. And the other candidates were not united. In these circumstances, with each voter able to cast one, two or three votes, he benefited from the votes both of his own exclusive supporters and of those others who split their votes across 'party' lines. But the conclusion that Yorke's position on the poll was primarily a function of such splits was scarcely justified. Indeed, to make this suggestion was to obscure the basis of former anti-Tory power in the county and the ways in which the political complexion of the county was being changed.

VI

Once the Act was passed, and once the £10-householders in the borough of Cambridge had destroyed the corporation's power, those urban leaders who had precipitated the contest in the county in 1826 and had been so heavily represented on the committee which chose Townley in 1831 rapidly retired from county politics. They returned Pryme and Thomas Spring Rice for the borough in 1832. Thereafter, relatively little was done to recruit and organize the potential anti-Tory strength in the county. The statement that after 1832 the anti-Tory leaders paid absolutely no attention to the electoral register in the county was presumably something of an exaggeration.[34] But these men scarcely strained themselves in trying to perpetuate their powers. From this an important question arises. Could their power, in fact, have been perpetuated? This question is posed partly by the ways in which the decline of their own strength in the county was manifest. But partly too by the steps which urban leaders took to restore their strengths in certain other counties later in the century, and from the success of those steps.[35] However, in Cambridgeshire, in 1834, Eliot Thomas Yorke was allowed to succeed quietly to the seat vacated by his brother, Charles, when Charles succeeded as Earl of Hardwicke. The following year, Childers was defeated at the polls by a second Tory candidate, Richard Jefferson Eaton, of Stetchworth. After Childers' defeat different anti-Tories recriminated among themselves, each claiming someone else was to blame.[36] What they did not do was what the Tories did. Effectively, they relinquished all initiative to their opponents. Both organizationally and ideologically this initiative was symbolized by the Cambridge and Isle of Ely Farmers' Association.

The Farmers' Association provided an ideological frame of reference. Furthermore, its members gathered signatures on petitions to Parliament on all manner of agricultural questions. These were questions with which both Charles and Eliot Thomas Yorke were identified, with which Eaton was identified, and with which John Peter Allix, of Swaffham Prior, was identified – Allix was returned as third Tory member in 1841. They included such things as malt tax repeal, currency reform, whether the agricultural interest was really depressed, whether foreign grain should be imported in bond to be ground for export, and the question of the corn laws themselves.[37]

In all probability, when the members of the Farmers' Association took up positions on these various questions, and when they gathered signatures on petitions to Parliament, they were performing important political functions. However, when considering these functions certain points should be noted: for analytical purposes the distinction between influence and ideology is clear; but for practical purposes it breaks down. Not only were many men of influence active disseminators of ideology. In many cases the ideologies they disseminated served to legitimize and thus strengthen their influence. However, some men were apparently concerned to make an institutional distinction between influence and ideology which would parallel the analytical distinction. This is suggested by the way in which the Farmers' Association was initially organized and structured. And, possibly, the logic of this organization and structure is revealed by the terms of Childers' attack on Yorke in 1832, to the effect that Yorke's candidacy reflected the attempt of the various local aristocratic families to 'dominate' the county.[38] Possibly, to be effective their 'domination' had to be covert. Or, to put it somewhat differently, they had to create an ideological context in which their 'domination' would be understood as 'leadership.'

The Farmers' Association was organized a month before the elections of 1832. It was organized by one of Yorke's elections agents, George J. Twiss.[39] Twiss was a solicitor. For some reason, however – perhaps to obscure the political nature of the Association – Twiss was not given a fee for his political services even though, as a solicitor, such services did not lie outside his normal field of work. Not that his services were unrewarded. Indeed his ultimate rewards were perhaps greater than any fee he might have been paid. His services provided him with a claim upon the gratitude of the local Tory squires. Some months after the contest many of these men joined in giving him a testimonial dinner at which John Bendyshe, the chairman of Yorke's election committee, spoke in glowing terms of the importance of his work and presented him with a piece of plate worth 180 guineas. In replying, Twiss not only expressed his gratitude but spoke of his eagerness to serve again.[40]

It was also perhaps to obscure the political nature of the Association that its initial rules excluded country gentlemen as members. But if the gentry were not there in person they were clearly there by proxy. The great majority of the men who attended the meetings of the Association voted exclusively for Manners or Yorke in 1826, 1830, 1831 and 1832. By and large, they resided in parishes in which Tories were the predominant landowners. And, without exception, those men who attended these meetings and who had not voted for Tory candidates before 1832 did so thereafter. Furthermore – and almost without exception – where this occurred the men concerned resided in parishes where their own change in political allegiance ran parallel to that of the majority of their neighbours.[41]

Of course, there may have been no connection at all between the activities of these men in the Farmers' Association and the political orientation of the predominant landowners in the parishes where most of them lived. On the other hand, such connections were often assumed to exist. When the question arose, in 1852, for example, whether Rutland was supporting the candidacy of the nonconformist tenant farmer, Edward Ball, of Burwell, the question was answered – whether accurately or not is another question – by the observation that none of Rutland's tenants had attended a meeting in favour of Ball which they might have attended without inconvenience as it was held near the Rutland estates.[42] And 30 years later, in West Cornwall, similar assumptions produced consternation among the local Liberal wire-pullers when they learned that one of Lord Falmouth's tenants had resigned from his local Liberal association. Coming on top of the

rumours that Falmouth was deeply disturbed by the presence of Bright
and Chamberlain in Gladstone's second Cabinet these men assumed
that the tenant's resignation meant that Falmouth had changed his
political affiliations from Liberal to Conservative. They were only
satisfied that the tenant spoke for himself alone, and that his behaviour
might be a measure of his health, not his politics, when one of the two
Liberal members for the division had an interview with Falmouth.[43]

In all probability, what with the overwhelmingly Tory membership
of the Farmers' Association, and what with the rather contrived way in
which Twiss managed to retain his amateur status in politics – he was
secretary of the Association at least until 1841 – the Farmers'
Association was simply a 'party' association operating under another
name.[44] Clearly, several such bodies existed. Indeed, after the elections
of 1835 the general point was made that Tories had gained considerable
numbers of seats in those counties where 'CONSERVATIVE, or, still
better, AGRICULTURAL ASSOCIATIONS were early organized,
and have been conducted with dilligence and spirit.'[45]

As the author of this statement went on to say, he preferred the
name, 'agricultural association,' because such a name rendered possible
common action which a party name might preclude: while agricultural
associations 'afford the opportunity of carrying into effect any desirable
object, they are not characterized by any title which can by the
perversity of faction be construed into a party or offensive
signification.'[46]

From the beginning relations between the Farmers' Association and
the Tory gentry were close. But they were rather one-sided. Indeed, it
is scarcely an exaggeration to say that the Farmers' Association served
to articulate demands which gave a representative character to the
decisions of the Tory gentry. When a 'Conservative Meeting' was held
in the county in the late autumn of 1834 to discuss whether a second
Tory or Conservative candidate should be nominated at the
forthcoming elections the most vociferous proponents of such a course
were the members of the Farmers' Association. They took no part in
the choice of the candidate. As Edward Ball explained – he had voted
for the Tory candidates exclusively in 1826, 1830, 1831 and 1832 – the
farmers were 'willing to submit . . . to the gentlemen who usually took
the lead in politics.'[47] And, subsequently, it was Ball who seconded the
nomination of Eaton, the candidate the 'gentlemen' chose.[48]

By the time Eaton was elected the conditions which had prompted
the adoption of the rule excluding gentlemen from membership in the
Farmers' Association had perhaps ceased to apply. By this time the
ideological currents which the Farmers' Association may possibly have
helped to produce had become so strong that the relationship between
influence and ideology need no longer be obscured. In any event, after

Eaton's election in 1835, and Childers' defeat, the rule was rescinded. [49]

If that rule had reflected a concern to legitimize the influences of the local aristocratic families by obscuring the close relationship between influence and ideology its removal made the Farmers' Association a semi-formal adjunct of the new agricultural-aristocratic coalition. But it did not affect the Association's role. Members of the Association had no more control over the behaviour of the members for the county once they had been elected than they had in the choice of the candidates. The question of the malt tax is an example of this. At the first reported meeting of the Association this tax was described as an 'onerous burden' which gave farmers 'peculiar claims to legislation.' [50] In 1835, however, after Peel had been appointed to office, and after he had refused to agree to the Marquis of Chandos' demand that he commit himself to the repeal of the malt tax, the Association framed two petitions on agricultural questions and neglected to mention the tax. As the Radical *Independent Press* put it, this was 'political complacency with a witness.' [51] Nor did Eliot Thomas Yorke vote with Chandos when the malt tax question was raised in Parliament. As he explained from the hustings in 1837 — and his explanation reflects the relative strengths of his commitments to his agricultural supporters in the county and to his party leaders in Parliament — the Government could not have done without the money which the tax produced. [52]

VII

Before the elections of 1835 a member of the Farmers' Association urged the Tory leaders to nominate not two but three candidates. In defending their refusal to do so Allix declared that while the Whigs were not entitled to more than one of the three county seats, they were entitled to that one. [53] In effect, he implied that the Tories could have taken the third seat had they wished to do so, that they were simply exercising self-restraint in the interest of fairness. The elections of 1837 passed quietly in the county. Yorke, Eaton and Townley were returned without a contest. But two years later the Tory leaders changed their minds about the third seat. [54] Once they had decided to try to evict Townley the Association became an informal committee for the return of Allix, the candidate chosen to replace him. [55] And, presumably, it was at least in part to assist Allix' return that the members of the Association spent the remainder of the year raising petitions on the corn laws 'from every town and village in the county and isle.' [56] Not that Townley was a free trader. But Townley was a Whig. As such, and even though he had voted *against* various free trade proposals, he was condemned for the deeds and activities of his party associates much as Rooper had been condemned in Huntingdonshire in 1837. Shortly before the elections of 1841, when Earl Fitzwilliam introduced a petition in favour of corn law repeal, the Conservative *Chronicle* told its readers, 'Mr. Townley's friends – remember that – Mr. Townley's friends have brought things to this pass. It is the mean Whigs who have unsettled and imperilled the farmer's interests, and Mr. Townley has done all that in him lies to keep the mean Whigs in office.'[57] Such arguments were perhaps essential as a means of defeating Townley. Perhaps they prompted the efforts to do so. But whichever the case – and whether these and other arguments were more effective in determining the behaviour of the voters at the polls or in providing some of them with the necessary rationalization for their behaviour – Townley retired on the eve of the elections.

In 1847, when Townley stood again, his retirement was attributed, not to any loss of support for him in the county, but to his own loss of confidence in the different parliamentary leaders. As Peyton put it when nominating him, Townley had been unhappy with Lord John Russell's proposal to substitute a fixed duty for the sliding scale corn law then in effect, and he had not trusted Peel.[58] Clearly, in 1847, this argument was tactically relevant. Both earlier and later, however, Townley's retirement was explained in terms which made him somewhat less the master of his fate. In 1865 Thomas St. Quintin contended that Townley had retired after discovering that Allix' committee, of which St. Quintin was chairman, had a subscription fund of £5,000.[59] The story was told for the moral it contained. St. Quintin wished to show his brother Conservatives what the consequences might be of having such a fund available at all times. According to him, had such a fund been available the Conservatives would have regained the third county seat in 1865. And, according to him, such a fund would have been available had there been a permanent Conservative organization in the county. The ostensible circumstances of 1841 provided the moral for 1865. But in spite of its clear ulterior purpose the story may well have been not only accurate but relevant. Townley was not a rich man. His election expenses in 1831 had been paid, at least in part, by public subscription: he was reportedly returned 'free of expense.'[60] Furthermore, if, as seems likely, Bedford paid the lion's share of this public subscription then Townley may have cut himself off from the source of financial support without which he could not afford to stand when he voted against Lord John Russell's corn law proposals. Nor are these various explanations mutually incompatible. As Townley put it in his own retirement address in 1841, he had found 'that the same feverish alarm which in other agricultural counties had deprived many Whig candidates of their supporters, had equally operated against . . . [himself], and largely reduced the numbers . . . [he] had hoped to rely on.'[61]

Unfortunately, since Townley retired in 1841, no poll book exists which, together with the poll book of 1835, might otherwise have been used to identify those former supporters on whom he could no longer rely. By the same token, the fact that only two Tories were nominated in 1835 makes it impossible to identify those men who might have voted for a third, and the fact that only one Tory was nominated in 1832 makes it impossible to identify those men who might have voted for a second or a third. However, while the poll books do not allow such men to be identified, they do provide fairly clear indications as to why the successful candidates were returned in 1832 and 1835, just as the earlier poll books provide fairly clear indications as to why other candidates were returned in 1826, 1830 and 1831. In addition, these poll books have a good deal to say about the nature of electoral behaviour in the county and the relations between electoral behaviour and the conduct of elections. In the county as a whole the polls for the contests of 1826, 1830, 1831, 1832 and 1835 were as indicated in table 6.[62]

Table 6

Total polls at the Cambridgeshire contests of 1826, 1830, 1831, 1832 and 1835

1826

| | as reported in the poll book | | | as revealed in the poll book evidence |
	residents	*outvoters*	*totals*	*resident voters*
voters	2020	116	2136	2025
votes for				
Manners (Tory)	1324	70	1394	1323
Osborne (Whig)	841	56	897	835
Adeane (Ind.)	605	23	628	611

1830

| | as reported in the poll book | as revealed in the poll book evidence |
	totals	*totals*
voters	3717	3722
votes for		
Osborne (Whig)	2339	2347
Adeane (Ind.)	2086	2083
Manners (Tory)	1757	1754

Table 6 continued on next page

1831

	as reported in the poll book			*as revealed in the poll book evidence*
	residents	*outvoters*	*totals*	*resident voters*
voters	3107	319	3426	3105
votes for				
Townley (Whig)	1829	152	1981	1827
Yorke (Tory)	1278	167	1445	1278

1832

	as reported in the poll book	*as revealed in the poll book evidence*
	totals	*totals*
voters	5923	5923
votes for		
Yorke (Tory)	3693	3692
Townley (Whig)	3261	3261
Childers (Whig)	2862	2861
Adeane (Ind.)	2850	2849

1835

	as reported in the poll book	*as revealed in the poll book evidence*
	totals	*totals*
voters	5895	5891
votes for		
Yorke (Tory)	3870	3872
Eaton (Tory)	3261	3261
Townley (Whig)	3070	3071
Childers (Whig)	2979	2978

But these total polls obscure the factors which produced them.

In Cambridgeshire, as in Huntingdonshire, the basic political fact was the existence of certain definable groups. Thus in Cambridgeshire, as in Huntingdonshire, the outcome of a contest was largely the function of the size, cohesion, and orientation of these groups. In some years it was obviously easier to perpetuate the cohesion of those groups which were oriented in one direction, in other years of those which were oriented in another. With respect to some of them, however — irrespective of their orientation — it made very little difference: their cohesiveness was little influenced by what might be called outside circumstances. Furthermore, whether issues and arguments were themselves conditioned by the problems of cohesion in the different varieties of group, it was apparently in the context of such groups that issues and arguments had their impact. And again, the exercise of political power in the county was the effective prerogative of those men who were themselves the leaders of cohesive groups.

In part, Adeane's contention that Manners was defeated in 1830 because he failed to support retrenchment, may have been accurate. But this failure scarcely provides a full explanation of his defeat. While his failure to support retrenchment may have affected the behaviour of many voters, no attempt to explain his defeat would be at all satisfactory which did not at least ask why this failure only affected the behaviour of certain voters in certain parishes. Similarly, on the other side of the general problem, no effort to explain, for example, Townley's election in 1831, would be at all satisfactory if it merely cited his support of the Bill without asking why his support of the Bill only prompted certain voters in certain parishes to vote for him.

It is, of course, impossible to say why blocs existed and why the members of the different blocs behaved as they did. But to recognize the existence of blocs is to recognize the essential nature of the problem which requires explanation. Blocs *did* exist; many were intensely hierarchical in structure; in many cases attitudes towards issues obviously served to enhance the cohesion of the social groups which these blocs reflected and to legitimize the roles of the leaders of these groups. Furthermore, many group leaders were directly involved in the articulation and dissemination of these rallying cries. In Cambridgeshire, as in Huntingdonshire, contests were won and lost because certain blocs changed their orientations, because certain blocs lost their cohesion — or gained it, and because certain blocs were larger than others. In effect, the principal reasons for Manners' defeat in 1830 were, first, that majorities of voters from certain parishes deserted him and, second, that larger numbers of voters who had not voted in 1826 came to the polls from certain other parishes and voted against him.

It was the same socio-political world as that in which Yorke was defeated in 1831 and returned in 1832. In many parishes where Tory desertions occurred in 1830 majorities of the voters had returned to their former allegiance by October 1831. However, while Yorke was thus supported by majorities of the voters from the majority of the parishes in the county, these parishes only contained a minority of the effective electorate. If the poll book for 1831 is compared with the poll books for the immediately preceding and immediately succeeding contests, it becomes apparent that Yorke's defeat was due in part to the relative concentration of freeholders in those parishes in which the influences associated with extensive landownership were weak.

In 1832 Yorke was returned at the head of the poll. After the contest various Liberals pointed to the numbers of voters who had split their votes between Yorke and one or two of the other candidates while trying both to explain Yorke's position at the head of the poll and to reassure themselves that 'the friends of Liberal opinions were numerically stronger than the Tories'. In part, of course, they were right: Yorke would not have headed the poll without the support which these others provided. But when these Liberals went on to argue that Yorke's position at the head of the poll – indeed, possibly, his return itself – should be attributed to 'the divisions which unfortunately existed among his opponents' they were saying more about their own problems of electoral discipline than about the reasons for Yorke's victory. Five hundred and fifty-three voters split their votes in 1832 among Yorke, Townley and Childers. But 859 voters either split their votes among Yorke, Adeane and Townley or between Yorke and Adeane. Those who split their votes among Yorke, Townley and Childers were those who defeated Adeane, who replaced him with Childers. Most of these votes were cast from otherwise Whig or Radical parishes. Those who split their votes among Yorke, Adeane and Townley – in all, 443 voters – were voting against Childers. Like the Yorke-Adeane splits, of which there were 416, most of these votes were cast from otherwise Tory parishes. In effect, while Yorke benefited from numerous split votes, many of these were not the consequence of 'the divisons which unfortunately existed among his opponents'. Rather, they were the result of the efforts of certain basically Tory voters to choose which of the non-Tory candidates would fill the other two seats.

Then, too, in various parishes between 1831 and 1832 changes occurred in the orientations of the majorities of the voters – in all but three cases in favour of Yorke. Also, changes occurred in the relative electoral weights of different parishes. Between 1831 and 1832 the average increment of voters in the parishes from which Yorke received majorities both in 1831 and 1832 was roughly 123 per cent. The average increment of voters in the parishes from which Townley received majorities both in 1831 and 1832 was roughly only 65 per cent. Not that political orientation was the crucial factor in determining the relative increments of voters between 1831 and 1832. But it was often related to the crucial factor, or factors. Certain of these had to do with the effective limitation which the 40s-freehold franchise placed upon the numbers of voters from certain categories of parish in the pre-reform period. Others had to do with the ways in which the Act itself and the tendencies of urban leaders to withdraw from county politics once they had been provided with constituencies of their own, affected the balance of power in the county. In the parishes which were parts of large estates, those in which Yorke's principal supporters were located, the very existence of the estate tended to limit the numbers of pre-reform voters. In the parishes which were not parts of estates, those in which the proportions of freeholders to population were relatively large, the effective influences were often opposed to Yorke. In many of these parishes, however, in the post-reform period, the voters were less efficiently recruited for political action than they were in the others. The point is important for what it tells us of the effective agencies and mechanisms of electoral recruitment in the county in the mid-century and for what it tells us of the political concerns of the urban leaders. In part, the changes which occurred in most counties between the pre-reform and post-reform periods in the relative numbers of voters who responded to different orientations of influence were obviously due to the enfranchisement of copyholders, leaseholders and occupiers, to the disfranchisement of many borough freeholders, to the redrawing of borough boundaries, and, in the counties where it occurred, to the creation of new boroughs. But in part, too, these changes occurred because urban leaders tended to withdraw from county politics once they had been provided with appropriate constituencies of their own.

Had the Cambridgeshire Tories tried, they might perhaps have taken more county seats than they took in either 1832 or 1835. But their decision to try for all three in 1841 was obviously related to their belief that Townley was vulnerable. Clearly, Townley agreed. As he said in his retirement address, he refused to contest without a clear certainty of victory.[63] While he was referring to a specific set of circumstances, his explanation is useful for what it reveals of mid-century electoral practices in general and of the relationship between social structure and politics.

VIII

As in Huntingdonshire, so in Cambridgeshire, there were certain parishes where the orientation of the majorities of the voters were both constant and clearly understandable from a parliamentary perspective. But the usual intensity of local electoral agreement among the voters in these parishes suggests that the context in which their behaviour might be said to 'make sense' was not the context in which their behaviour occurred. In other parishes majorities of the voters changed their orientation between 1826 and 1835, sometimes once, sometimes twice.

In some of these parishes the orientation of the majorities of the voters is, on each occasion, understandable from a parliamentary perspective. In other cases it is not. But whichever the case, these voters behaved as members of blocs. In other parishes whether blocs existed whose existence might be taken to indicate the existence of definable collectivities is less clear. But the existence of such parishes scarcely affects the importance of the other parishes in conditioning generalizations about mid-century county politics.

Among the parishes from which majorities of the voters behaved in terms of parliamentary considerations were those where the Rutland estates were to be found (see group 1.1 of table 7). Their behaviour, however, was very little different from that of the majorities of the voters from certain other parishes where there were estates belonging to men who were not only politically but also actively allied with Rutland, who attended meetings, nominated candidates, or were candidates themselves (group 1.2). In Boxworth, for example, the predominant landowner was George Thornhill, of Diddington, Hunts, who was returned as Tory member for Huntingdonshire in 1837. In Croxton, land was predominantly in the hands of the Newton family, a member of which attended the meeting in 1841 at which a requisition was presented to John Peter Allix, inviting him to stand.[64] In Dullingham and Stetchworth, most of the land was in the hands of the Eaton family, a member of which sat as Tory member for Cambridgeshire from 1835 until 1847. In Hatley, Thomas St. Quintin was the predominant landowner. Besides urging the formation of a permanent Conservative organization in Cambridgeshire in 1865 he nominated Eliot Thomas Yorke in 1837 and 1841.[65] In Madingley, St. Vincent Cotton was the predominant landowner, ostensibly the only squire who remained with Manners to the end in 1830.[66] And in Westley Waterless and Weston Colville the Hall family was the main landowner and one of its members was initially invited to stand as the second Tory candidate at the elections of 1835.[67] Obviously, the priorities of the men who exercised effective influence within these parishes were somewhat different from those of the men who exercised effective influence in, e.g., Knapwell and Newton (group 1.3 of table 7). In 1826, 1830 and 1831 majorities of the voters from these parishes voted exclusively for the Tory candidates. Yet in 1832 they split their votes between Yorke and Adeane. In Newton, in 1835, they split their votes between Yorke, Eaton and Townley. But however their priorities differed their socio-political roles were similar. In Newton, most of the land was in the hands of the Pemberton family. Colonel Christopher Pemberton nominated Yorke in 1835.[68] But he himself split his votes between Yorke, Eaton and Townley in 1835 much as he had split his votes between Yorke, Adeane and Townley in 1832.

Table 7

An analysis of the local bases of power of the different candidates at the Cambridgeshire contests of 1826, 1830, 1831, 1832 and 1835.

parishes and parish groups	1826				1830				1831			1832					1835					
	numbers of voters	Manners	Osborne	Adeane	numbers of voters	Manners	Osborne	Adeane	numbers of voters	Yorke	Townley	numbers of voters	Yorke	Adeane	Townley	Childers	numbers of voters	Yorke	Eaton	Townley	Childers	votes cast per voter
Group 1.1																						
Ashley	10	10	–	–	12	12	1	–	9	9	–	24	22	3	2	2	20	19	19	1	1	
Cheveley	15	15	1	–	17	17	1	2	13	13	–	19	18	1	–	1	22	22	21	–	1	
Newmarket	27	26	3	1	17	17	2	2	25	21	4	24	19	2	6	6	23	20	21	5	2	
Wood Ditton	15	15	–	–	12	12	–	–	10	10	–	29	29	–	–	–	24	24	24	–	–	
1.1 total	67	66	3	1	58	58	4	2	57	53	4	96	88	6	9	9	89	85	85	6	4	2.02
Group 1.2																						
Arrington	–	–	–	–	–	–	–	–	1	1	–	5	5	–	–	–	4	4	4	–	–	
Barton	3	2	1	–	3	2	–	1	3	3	–	7	7	1	3	1	7	5	6	1	1	
Boxworth	2	2	–	–	1	1	–	–	1	1	–	8	8	–	–	2	6	6	6	–	–	
Chippenham	6	6	–	–	7	7	–	1	6	6	–	17	17	4	–	–	15	15	15	–	–	
Croxton	1	1	–	–	2	2	–	–	2	2	–	8	8	–	–	2	5	5	3	–	–	
Dullingham	12	12	–	–	7	7	2	1	7	7	–	27	25	1	3	2	24	19	23	2	1	
Hardwicke	1	1	–	–	9	1	2	2	4	2	2	9	9	2	1	2	8	6	6	3	2	
Hatley	1	1	–	–	1	1	–	–	3	3	–	6	6	–	1	–	7	6	5	2	3	
Horseheath	16	16	1	–	16	10	5	–	12	12	–	19	18	–	1	–	23	23	22	3	1	
Kennett	2	2	–	–	3	3	–	–	2	2	–	10	10	2	–	–	11	11	11	–	–	

parishes and parish groups	1826				1830				1831			1832					1835					
	numbers of voters	Manners	Osborne	Adeane	numbers of voters	Manners	Osborne	Adeane	numbers of voters	Yorke	Tounley	numbers of voters	Yorke	Adeane	Tounley	Childers	numbers of voters	Yorke	Eaton	Tounley	Childers	votes cast per voter
Madingley	2	2	–	–	2	2	–	–	2	2	–	6	6	1	–	–	5	5	5	1	–	
Papworth	4	4	–	–	4	4	–	–	6	6	–	10	10	1	–	–	11	11	11	–	–	
Snailwell	1	1	–	–	1	1	–	–	2	2	–	3	3	1	–	–	3	2	3	–	–	
Stetchworth	3	3	–	–	2	2	–	–	4	4	–	13	13	–	–	–	20	20	20	–	–	
Westley Waterless	1	1	–	–	–	–	–	–	–	–	–	4	4	–	–	–	4	10	4	2	2	
Weston Colville	8	8	1	–	8	7	1	–	9	9	–	15	14	–	2	1	14	10	12	4	1	
Whaddon	5	5	–	–	–	–	–	–	4	4	–	3	3	–	1	–	5	5	2	–	–	
Great Wilbraham	6	6	–	–	11	9	3	4	13	8	5	17	14	2	7	4	18	14	13	6	5	
Little Wilbraham	11	11	2	–	12	10	4	3	6	3	3	13	10	3	4	2	11	10	10	2	1	
Wimpole	2	2	2	–	–	–	–	–	3	3	–	8	8	–	–	–	8	8	8	–	–	
1.2 total	85	84	7	1	89	75	15	17	90	80	10	208	198	19	22	13	209	189	189	26	17	2.01
Group 1.3																						
Abington Piggotts	1	1	–	–	1	1	–	–	2	2	–	1	1	1	–	–	3	3	3	–	–	
Graveley	1	1	–	–	1	1	–	–	1	1	–	5	4	3	1	1	5	3	3	1	2	
Knapwell	1	1	–	–	–	–	–	–	–	–	–	4	3	3	1	–	3	3	3	–	–	
Lolworth	–	–	–	–	1	1	–	–	1	1	–	2	2	2	–	–	3	3	3	–	1	
Newton	2	2	–	–	1	1	–	–	2	2	–	3	3	3	1	–	3	3	3	2	–	
Wentworth	–	–	–	–	7	6	1	2	1	1	–	10	7	6	4	4	7	6	5	1	2	
1.3 total	5	5	–	–	10	9	1	2	7	6	1	25	20	18	7	6	24	21	20	4	4	2.04

parishes and parish groups	1826 numbers of voters	Manners	Osborne	Adeane	1830 numbers of voters	Manners	Osborne	Adeane	1831 numbers of voters	Yorke	Townley	1832 numbers of voters	Yorke	Adeane	Townley	Childers	1835 numbers of voters	Yorke	Eaton	Townley	Childers	votes cast per voter
Group 1.4																						
Burwell	61	61	–	–	75	61	16	23	56	45	11	83	72	21	21	21	83	70	79	21	5	
Soham	109	109	2	–	155	129	25	34	130	123	7	222	199	27	30	32	202	176	181	34	34	
1.4 total	170	170	2	–	230	180	41	57	186	168	18	305	271	48	51	53	285	246	260	55	39	2.10
Group 1 total	327	325	12	2	387	322	61	78	340	307	33	634	578	91	89	81	603	541	554	91	63	2.07
Group 2																						
Bottisham & Reach	38	37	3	4	53	38	14	35	33	25	8	53	42	26	18	12	52	41	40	18	12	
Bourn	1	1	–	1	7	4	3	4	3	3	–	12	12	–	–	–	18	17	17	1	1	
Caxton	1	1	–	1	7	6	1	3	6	5	1	20	18	8	2	2	21	19	18	3	4	
Coton	2	1	–	1	4	2	2	2	3	3	–	7	7	–	–	–	6	6	6	–	–	
Fen Drayton	4	4	–	–	8	5	5	4	8	8	–	17	16	5	1	1	19	16	15	1	3	
Girton	6	5	1	–	2	1	1	1	5	3	2	7	5	4	2	3	7	4	4	3	3	
Gransden	7	7	–	–	13	10	2	6	10	10	–	26	22	4	4	4	25	23	23	1	2	
Kirtling	13	13	–	–	14	9	2	6	13	13	–	24	23	4	–	–	28	27	27	1	1	
Shudy Camps	3	3	1	–	3	3	–	2	3	3	–	13	11	7	2	1	12	9	9	3	3	
Swaffham Prior	20	20	2	–	36	29	5	19	23	22	1	56	54	22	7	6	57	56	54	7	4	
Group 2 total	96	92	7	6	147	107	35	82	107	95	12	235	210	80	36	29	245	218	213	38	33	2.05

parishes and parish groups	1826				1830				1831			1832					1835					votes cast per voter
	numbers of voters	Manners	Osborne	Adeane	numbers of voters	Manners	Osborne	Adeane	numbers of voters	Yorke	Townley	numbers of voters	Yorke	Adeane	Townley	Childers	numbers of voters	Yorke	Eaton	Townley	Childers	
Group 3.1																						
Littleport	25	24	1	–	90	54	32	54	63	43	20	133	108	42	62	43	134	110	100	33	47	
Manea	18	18	–	–	23	16	8	7	13	8	5	36	28	20	20	19	40	29	14	27	28	
West Wratting	14	13	1	1	14	9	1	8	13	8	5	22	18	10	6	4	22	19	17	11	4	
3.1 total	57	55	2	1	127	79	41	69	89	59	30	191	154	72	88	66	196	158	131	71	79	2.24
Group 3.2																						
Elm	13	12	1	1	39	28	18	3	24	21	3	104	88	18	46	42	104	96	83	30	32	
Newton-in-the-Isle	–	–	–	–	19	12	12	4	11	8	3	24	19	6	9	8	26	25	19	8	15	
3.2 total	13	12	1	1	58	40	30	7	35	29	6	128	107	24	55	50	130	121	102	38	47	2.37
Group 3 total	70	67	3	2	185	119	71	76	124	88	36	319	261	96	143	116	326	279	233	109	126	2.29
Group 4.1																						
Croydon	2	2	–	–	1	–	–	1	2	2	–	6	5	2	–	–	6	6	3	4	1	
Dry Drayton	3	3	–	–	6	3	2	4	4	3	1	17	13	5	4	5	15	14	14	2	1	
Eltisley	7	7	–	–	6	3	3	6	4	4	1	17	16	1	1	–	17	16	16	–	1	
Great Eversden	3	2	1	1	1	–	2	6	3	2	2	8	6	2	2	2	10	8	8	2	2	
Little Eversden	2	1	–	1	3	–	2	3	3	3	2	7	5	2	2	2	8	7	7	1	1	
Grantchester	4	3	1	1	6	2	4	4	6	4	2	14	10	7	4	3	15	13	13	3	3	

parishes and parish groups	1826				1830				1831			1832					1835					
	numbers of voters	Manners	Osborne	Adeane	numbers of voters	Manners	Osborne	Adeane	numbers of voters	Yorke	Townley	numbers of voters	Yorke	Adeane	Townley	Childers	numbers of voters	Yorke	Eaton	Townley	Childers	votes cast per voter
Harlton	2	2	–	1	4	2	3	3	4	3	1	10	10	6	5	–	10	9	9	1	1	
Kingston	1	1	–	–	3	1	2	2	2	3	1	9	8	–	1	1	8	8	8	–	–	
Litlington	9	6	3	4	21	10	16	13	12	9	3	24	22	10	5	6	20	20	16	3	1	
Steeple Morden	5	5	–	–	13	4	10	9	10	9	1	20	17	5	3	4	23	19	14	9	8	
West Wickham	3	3	–	–	6	1	1	6	6	5	1	11	9	2	1	1	9	7	7	2	1	
4.1 total	41	35	5	8	70	26	44	52	56	45	11	143	121	42	28	24	141	127	115	27	20	2.05
Group 4.2																						
Great Abington	2	1	1	1	5	3	–	4	4	2	2	7	5	5	1	1	3	3	2	2	–	
Little Abington	1	1	–	–	2	–	1	2	–	–	–	4	3	4	1	–	6	5	5	3	–	
Castle Camps	6	6	2	–	6	3	3	6	4	4	–	21	18	16	1	–	16	16	16	1	–	
4.2 total	9	8	3	1	13	6	4	12	8	6	2	32	26	25	3	1	25	24	23	6	–	2.12
Group 4 total	50	43	8	9	83	32	48	64	64	51	13	175	147	67	31	25	166	151	138	33	20	2.06
Group 5.1																						
Elsworth	14	14	1	–	22	7	17	15	11	6	5	35	22	19	22	17	36	21	21	19	18	
Landbeach	3	2	1	1	4	2	2	3	3	3	–	16	11	8	5	8	17	11	9	10	9	
5.1 total	17	16	2	1	26	9	19	18	14	9	5	51	33	27	27	25	53	32	30	29	27	2.23

parishes and parish groups	1826				1830				1831			1832					1835					votes cast per voter
	numbers of voters	Manners	Osborne	Adeane	numbers of voters	Manners	Osborne	Adeane	numbers of voters	Yorke	Tounley	numbers of voters	Yorke	Adeane	Tounley	Childers	numbers of voters	Yorke	Eaton	Tounley	Childers	
Group 5.2 Stretham	26	22	10	3	43	22	25	28	20	11	9	49	40	12	26	24	51	43	23	28	33	2.49
Group 5 total	43	38	12	4	69	31	44	46	34	20	14	100	73	39	53	49	104	75	53	57	60	2.35
Group 6 Stow-cum-Quy	6	6	-	-	6	2	2	5	6	3	3	12	10	9	3	3	10	4	5	6	6	
Tadlow	2	2	-	-	-	-	-	-	1	1	-	4	3	1	2	2	3	1	1	2	2	
Group 6 total	8	8	-	-	6	2	2	5	7	4	3	16	13	10	5	5	13	5	6	8	8	2.08
Group 7 Wisbech St. Mary	5	5	-	-	4	1	3	3	10	6	6	112	73	60	83	65	132	87	59	91	91	
Group 7 total	5	5	-	-	4	1	3	3	10	6	6	112	73	60	83	65	132	87	59	91	91	2.48
Group 8 Fordham	31	26	3	5	54	14	37	44	30	8	22	58	51	45	27	6	55	45	50	6	15	
Haslingfield	8	5	2	4	9	2	8	8	10	4	6	19	13	9	7	6	21	17	17	5	6	
Wendy	2	2	-	-	-	-	-	-	2	-	2	4	4	1	-	-	4	4	3	-	-	
Group 8 total	41	33	5	9	63	16	45	52	42	12	30	81	68	55	34	12	80	66	70	11	21	2.10

parishes and parish groups	1826 numbers of voters	Manners	Osborne	Adeane	1830 numbers of voters	Manners	Osborne	Adeane	1831 numbers of voters	Yorke	Townley	1832 numbers of voters	Yorke	Adeane	Townley	Childers	1835 numbers of voters	Yorke	Eaton	Townley	Childers	votes cast per voter
Group 9																						
Balsham	8	4	4	3	9	4	4	7	8	2	6	27	11	20	17	14	23	17	18	9	5	
Duxford	12	10	2	1	22	5	11	19	15	6	9	29	15	22	9	6	31	27	22	11	9	
Linton	29	26	7	1	38	11	11	37	33	16	17	56	31	47	23	19	54	42	38	25	19	
Swaffham Bulbeck	8	6	2	2	20	9	7	13	9	3	6	26	17	21	6	5	29	22	26	16	5	
Group 9 total	57	46	15	7	89	29	33	76	65	27	38	138	74	110	55	44	137	108	104	61	38	2.27
Group 10																						
Borough Green	5	5	1	–	10	5	5	6	8	3	5	25	13	13	13	11	25	14	15	15	12	
Brinkley	4	4	–	1	7	5	1	5	6	–	6	13	4	7	8	5	7	4	4	3	–	
Carlton	5	3	2	1	4	1	1	3	2	–	2	13	5	7	8	6	15	7	8	7	6	
Foxton	3	3	2	–	6	1	6	4	6	2	4	8	5	6	5	3	12	6	6	6	6	
Kneesworth	1	1	–	–	4	1	2	4	1	–	1	8	5	2	3	3	7	4	3	4	4	
Milton	2	1	1	–	12	6	7	8	2	–	2	22	16	17	14	7	24	15	14	11	10	
Little Shelford	15	10	5	3	13	5	8	8	14	6	8	24	17	11	13	10	20	14	15	7	11	
Teversham	2	1	1	1	5	1	4	4	4	–	4	9	5	4	7	3	8	5	5	5	3	
Group 10 total	37	28	12	6	61	25	34	42	43	11	32	122	70	67	71	48	118	69	70	58	52	2.11
Group 11																						
Chatteris	50	50	2	–	68	50	26	18	78	35	43	162	103	47	93	92	166	92	72	97	103	

parishes and parish groups	1826 numbers of voters	1826 Manners	1826 Osborne	1826 Adeane	1830 numbers of voters	1830 Manners	1830 Osborne	1830 Adeane	1831 numbers of voters	1831 Yorke	1831 Townley	1832 numbers of voters	1832 Yorke	1832 Adeane	1832 Townley	1832 Childers	1835 numbers of voters	1835 Yorke	1835 Eaton	1835 Townley	1835 Childers	votes cast per voter
Upwell	11	11	–	–	70	52	41	6	59	22	37	104	83	31	77	43	98	76	58	79	40	
Group 11 total	61	61	2	–	138	102	67	24	137	57	80	266	186	78	170	135	264	168	130	176	143	2.34
Group 12 Impington	2	2	–	–	7	5	3	3	1	–	1	11	5	7	6	6	11	5	5	6	6	
Waterbeach	21	18	4	5	28	18	11	14	36	10	26	71	41	52	46	35	64	39	35	43	40	
Group 12 total	23	20	4	5	35	23	14	17	37	10	27	82	46	59	52	41	75	44	40	49	46	2.39
Group 13 Foulmire	4	4	–	1	2	–	2	2	3	1	2	14	2	9	11	11	17	3	3	15	14	
Shepreth	4	3	1	1	9	2	6	9	5	1	4	8	–	8	8	8	9	–	–	9	9	
Group 13 total	8	7	1	2	11	2	8	11	8	2	6	22	2	17	19	19	26	3	3	24	23	2.04
Group 14.1 Whittlesea	85	71	25	5	138	86	112	49	92	29	63	317	165	114	229	255	322	192	116	209	268	2.44
Group 14.2 Outwell	3	3	1	–	24	13	17	1	22	4	18	23	16	10	20	15	23	19	11	19	11	2.61

parishes and parish groups	1826				1830				1831			1832					1835					votes cast per voter
	numbers of voters	Manners	Osborne	Adeane	numbers of voters	Manners	Osborne	Adeane	numbers of voters	Yorke	Townley	numbers of voters	Yorke	Adeane	Townley	Childers	numbers of voters	Yorke	Eaton	Townley	Childers	
Group 14 total	88	74	26	5	162	99	129	50	114	33	81	340	181	124	249	270	345	211	127	228	279	2.45
Group 15.1																						
Leverington and Parson Drove	16	16	1	–	68	32	54	33	36	12	24	119	83	75	75	70	125	92	49	85	98	
Tydd St. Giles	–	–	–	–	55	20	47	24	31	1	30	68	33	37	64	57	71	43	27	56	61	
Wisbech St. Peter	77	74	20	2	248	112	208	129	193	51	142	365	180	209	269	227	352	211	130	248	246	
15.1 total	93	90	21	2	371	164	309	186	260	64	196	552	296	321	408	354	548	346	206	389	405	2.46
Group 15.2																						
Downham	6	5	1	–	38	5	33	32	32	5	27	66	34	37	52	44	63	39	35	36	38	
Histon	10	6	3	4	26	7	19	21	16	4	12	38	20	21	24	21	39	21	18	22	23	
15.2 total	16	11	4	4	64	12	52	53	48	9	39	104	54	58	76	65	102	60	53	58	61	2.27
Group 15.3																						
Ely	54	43	27	3	130	60	95	68	117	45	72	214	119	122	152	128	201	139	88	112	122	2.29
Group 15.4																						
Isleham	41	34	5	7	68	33	33	38	59	15	44	97	37	43	67	71	99	57	70	50	46	2.25

parishes and parish groups	1826				1830				1831			1832					1835					
	numbers of voters	Manners	Osborne	Adeane	numbers of voters	Manners	Osborne	Adeane	numbers of voters	Yorke	Townley	numbers of voters	Yorke	Adeane	Townley	Childers	numbers of voters	Yorke	Eaton	Townley	Childers	votes cast per voter
Group 15 total	204	178	57	16	633	269	489	345	484	133	351	967	506	544	703	618	950	602	417	609	634	2.38
Group 16																						
Bassingbourn	11	9	7	1	35	10	30	28	22	6	16	49	17	38	37	38	49	21	13	38	37	
Melbourn	12	9	3	–	39	7	34	31	26	2	24	79	25	51	64	64	74	34	26	47	50	
Whittlesford	6	3	3	2	14	3	12	11	11	2	9	15	3	12	11	10	17	6	9	12	8	
Group 16 total	29	21	13	3	88	20	76	70	59	10	49	143	45	101	112	112	140	61	48	97	95	2.15
Group 17 March	26	26	–	–	100	67	74	31	97	42	55	250	159	98	144	133	239	152	137	118	124	
Group 17 total	26	26	–	–	100	67	74	31	97	42	55	250	159	98	144	133	239	152	137	118	124	2.22
Group 18																						
Bartlow	5	1	3	1	4	2	1	3	3	3	–	7	7	4	–	–	5	5	5	2	–	
Fen Ditton	7	1	7	6	7	5	4	5	5	3	2	19	17	9	8	4	19	13	10	11	8	
Longstanton	10	–	9	9	16	7	8	15	11	9	2	19	15	8	5	7	18	13	13	5	5	
Orwell	1	1	1	1	5	4	4	5	4	4	1	9	9	2	1	3	8	8	6	1	1	
Rampton	3	–	3	3	2	1	1	2	–	–	–	9	8	6	5	1	8	7	7	5	1	
Toft	2	–	1	2	16	7	9	8	9	5	4	21	17	14	5	7	17	13	11	7	6	

parishes and parish groups	1826				1830				1831			1832					1835					
	numbers of voters	Manners	Osborne	Adeane	numbers of voters	Manners	Osborne	Adeane	numbers of voters	Yorke	Townley	numbers of voters	Yorke	Adeane	Townley	Childers	numbers of voters	Yorke	Eaton	Townley	Childers	votes cast per voter
Group 18 total	28	2	24	22	50	23	27	38	32	23	9	84	73	43	19	22	75	61	52	31	21	2.20
Group 19																						
Swavesey	13	4	8	8	41	5	35	38	25	15	10	51	30	47	32	25	51	35	25	35	36	
Group 19 total	13	4	8	8	41	5	35	38	25	15	10	51	30	47	32	25	51	35	25	35	36	2.57
Group 20																						
Babraham	–	–	–	–	3	1	1	3	2	–	2	6	3	6	3	–	6	4	4	5	–	
Cherry Hinton	11	1	10	6	11	2	8	8	10	2	8	28	16	22	18	9	33	21	21	14	10	
Comberton	5	2	3	3	11	5	5	6	5	1	4	19	16	10	5	4	18	10	8	9	9	
Gamlingay	4	2	3	1	36	10	28	26	28	12	16	62	35	27	33	32	55	36	31	23	27	
Hildersham	–	–	–	–	1	–	1	1	3	1	2	5	5	3	3	–	7	5	6	3	1	
Longstow	–	–	–	–	3	–	2	3	2	–	2	5	3	4	3	3	8	6	6	2	1	
Pampisford	3	–	3	1	6	1	4	5	7	–	7	7	2	6	2	3	6	6	6	2	–	
Great Shelford	10	7	10	3	16	5	13	13	14	4	10	21	14	11	11	8	21	16	15	10	7	
Stapleford	11	3	10	2	14	4	11	13	13	5	8	13	8	8	6	5	14	9	9	6	6	
Triplow	6	1	5	3	6	1	6	5	4	–	4	14	9	11	5	6	12	10	8	3	4	
Trumpington	6	3	1	6	8	5	4	5	13	6	7	25	18	13	11	6	27	19	20	13	8	
Group 20 total	56	19	45	25	115	34	83	78	101	31	70	206	129	121	100	75	207	142	134	90	73	2.12

parishes and parish groups	1826 numbers of voters	Manners	Osborne	Adeane	1830 numbers of voters	Manners	Osborne	Adeane	1831 numbers of voters	Yorke	Tounley	1832 numbers of voters	Yorke	Adeane	Tounley	Childers	1835 numbers of voters	Yorke	Eaton	Tounley	Childers	votes cast per voter
Group 21 Cambridge	378	171	260	195	456	217	325	245	471	168	303	376	225	185	231	184	394	216	196	238	199	
Group 21 total	378	171	260	195	456	217	325	245	471	168	303	376	225	185	231	184	394	216	196	238	199	2.15
Group 22.1 Doddington	8	3	7	–	29	19	26	8	21	2	19	58	15	13	52	50	57	14	8	49	50	
Thorney	5	–	5	–	12	11	12	–	19	–	19	57	3	8	57	57	53	–	–	53	53	
22.1 total	13	3	12	–	41	30	38	8	40	2	38	115	18	21	109	107	110	14	8	102	103	2.02
Group 22.2 Mepal	1	–	1	–	10	6	7	4	15	3	12	14	4	9	13	9	14	7	6	8	10	2.29
Group 22 total	14	3	13	–	51	36	45	12	55	5	50	129	22	30	122	116	124	21	14	110	113	2.08
Group 23 Wimblington	1	–	1	–	24	21	20	4	19	3	16	47	39	12	26	26	46	25	21	22	22	
Group 23 total	1	–	1	–	24	21	20	4	19	3	16	47	39	12	26	26	46	25	21	22	22	2.13

parishes and parish groups	1826 numbers of voters	1826 Manners	1826 Osborne	1826 Adeane	1830 numbers of voters	1830 Manners	1830 Osborne	1830 Adeane	1831 numbers of voters	1831 Yorke	1831 Townley	1832 numbers of voters	1832 Yorke	1832 Adeane	1832 Townley	1832 Childers	1835 numbers of voters	1835 Yorke	1835 Eaton	1835 Townley	1835 Childers	votes cast per voter
Group 24 Welney	4	2	2	1	12	7	9	1	12	7	5	12	7	8	11	6	16	12	8	13	8	
Group 24 total	4	2	2	1	12	7	9	1	12	7	5	12	7	8	11	6	16	12	8	13	8	2.56
Group 25.1																						
Barrington	2	–	2	1	6	1	4	5	5	1	4	8	1	6	7	7	9	2	2	8	7
Benwick	2	–	2	1	6	1	5	5	5	1	4	17	4	13	15	14	17	8	3	13	14
Caldecot	–	–	–	–	1	–	1	1	–	–	–	6	2	4	4	4	5	2	2	4	4
Childerly	1	–	–	–	1	–	1	1	–	–	–	–	–	–	–	–	1	–	–	1	1
Coveney	2	1	2	1	32	8	25	27	24	6	18	37	12	26	27	26	40	17	13	28	28
Fulbourn	21	2	20	14	37	11	32	27	30	3	27	50	22	38	44	27	51	17	15	45	29
Harston	8	2	5	6	15	2	15	13	14	1	13	31	8	28	23	22	29	12	11	22	19
Hauxton	1	–	–	1	3	–	3	3	2	–	2	7	–	5	7	7	5	–	–	5	5
Over	33	2	31	31	64	5	58	59	38	4	34	84	17	64	67	66	82	21	16	69	67
Royston	21	6	16	12	19	3	16	15	34	3	31	25	7	16	20	20	22	6	4	18	19
Sawston	8	1	7	4	22	2	16	20	16	4	12	30	11	24	19	14	30	9	11	27	19
Stanground	–	–	–	–	–	–	–	–	–	–	–	7	–	3	7	7	7	2	1	6	7
Sutton	7	2	–	5	63	18	51	44	50	7	43	73	33	52	53	46	70	30	26	46	57
Wilburton	5	1	5	4	14	–	14	14	13	1	12	18	5	14	14	12	24	9	5	19	19
25.1 total	110	16	90	80	283	51	241	234	231	31	200	393	122	293	307	272	392	135	109	311	295	2.17

parishes and parish groups	1826 numbers of voters	1826 Manners	1826 Osborne	1826 Adeane	1830 numbers of voters	1830 Manners	1830 Osborne	1830 Adeane	1831 numbers of voters	1831 Yorke	1831 Townley	1832 numbers of voters	1832 Yorke	1832 Adeane	1832 Townley	1832 Childers	1835 numbers of voters	1835 Yorke	1835 Eaton	1835 Townley	1835 Childers	1835 votes cast per voter
Group 25.2																						
Cottenham	75	10	65	66	84	14	70	75	94	7	87	124	70	114	79	67	121	68	58	73	80	
Oakington	9	2	6	8	13	3	7	12	10	4	6	13	7	12	6	7	18	7	6	12	11	
25.2 total	84	12	71	74	97	17	77	87	104	11	93	137	77	126	85	74	139	75	64	85	91	2.26
Group 25.3																						
Guilden Morden	2	1	1	1	26	10	20	14	18	7	11	33	14	12	23	22	30	12	8	23	21	2.13
Group 25 total	196	29	162	155	406	78	338	335	353	49	304	563	213	431	415	368	561	222	181	419	407	2.19
Group 26																						
Haddenham	40	1	39	37	70	6	65	65	47	20	27	103	71	58	59	43	101	79	46	51	59	
Witchford	4	1	3	3	11	5	8	6	8	2	6	14	12	7	3	4	12	11	6	7	6	
Group 26 total	44	2	42	40	81	11	73	71	55	22	33	117	83	65	62	47	113	90	52	58	65	2.34
Group 27																						
Ickleton	3	1	3	1	14	4	5	11	8	1	7	23	7	21	15	16	22	15	12	13	10	
Westwick	2	–	2	2	2	1	1	2	2	1	1	2	1	2	1	1	3	2	2	2	1	
Wicken	3	1	2	2	24	10	16	15	24	11	13	48	22	27	29	29	44	27	33	23	18	
Willingham	67	3	63	64	84	16	61	79	88	11	77	111	63	80	64	57	121	73	64	64	58	

parishes and parish groups	1826 numbers of voters	Manners	Osborne	Adeane	1830 numbers of voters	Manners	Osborne	Adeane	1831 numbers of voters	Yorke	Townley	1832 numbers of voters	Yorke	Adeane	Townley	Childers	1835 numbers of voters	Yorke	Eaton	Townley	Childers	votes cast per voter
Group 27 total	75	5	70	69	124	31	83	107	122	24	98	184	93	130	109	103	190	117	111	102	87	2.19
Group 28																						
Chesterton	14	6	9	8	16	5	12	10	23	1	22	42	22	20	24	21	41	23	19	26	23	
Hinxton	6	–	6	–	12	5	8	10	7	3	4	11	5	6	4	6	9	5	6	5	5	
Horningsea	5	2	3	3	10	2	8	8	8	1	7	10	5	6	6	5	11	6	6	7	5	
Meldreth	13	5	10	5	27	1	23	26	20	4	16	36	22	22	20	28	34	21	13	21	23	
Witcham	4	–	3	4	35	11	25	28	18	8	10	31	17	20	19	16	31	16	14	18	18	
Group 28 total	42	13	31	20	100	24	76	82	76	17	59	130	71	74	73	76	126	71	56	77	74	2.21
Group 29																						
Conington	1	1	–	–	1	1	–	–	2	1	1	5	3	1	2	3	4	2	2	2	2	
Shingay	–	–	–	–	–	–	–	–	2	1	1	2	1	–	1	1	2	2	1	1	1	
Group 29 total	1	1	–	–	1	1	–	–	4	2	2	7	4	1	3	4	6	4	3	3	3	2.17
Group 30																						
Thetford	–	–	–	–	–	–	–	–	8	4	4	15	11	6	9	7	19	16	6	15	14	
Group 30 total	–	–	–	–	–	–	–	–	8	4	4	15	11	6	9	7	19	16	6	15	14	2.68

The behaviour of the voters from Hardwicke, Whaddon and Wimpole (group 1.2) cannot be explained so simply – at least until 1831. The Earl of Hardwicke was the predominant landowner in these parishes. According to the published report, he had supported Osborne individually in 1826 and Osborne and Adeane jointly in 1830. But most of the voters from the parish of Hardwicke plumped for Manners both in 1826 and 1830. From Whaddon, where no one voted in 1830, most of those who had voted in 1826 plumped for Manners. And from Wimpole, where Hardwicke's seat was located, and where no one voted in 1830, those who voted in 1826 split their votes between Manners and Osborne. Perhaps, *The Times'* report was wrong. Perhaps, Hardwicke made no serious effort to exercise his influence among these voters in 1826 and 1830. If so, we can understand why in 1831, when Hardwicke's nephew was the candidate, a personal consensus came into being in certain of the parishes on the Hardwicke estates. The polls for these parishes can be seen in table 8.

If so, we can also understand why, in Haddenham, one of the other parishes in which Hardwicke was a significant landowner, there is a significant change in the orientation of large numbers of voters in 1831 (see Haddenham in group 26 of table 7). Both in 1826 and 1830 the vast majority of the Haddenham voters split their votes between Osborne and Adeane. Their behaviour in 1830 accords with Hardwicke's current, reported orientation. But their behaviour in 1826 does not. Furthermore, in 1831, more than half of them voted for Townley. But almost half of them – and therein lay the change – voted for Yorke. In 1832 and 1835 majorities of the Haddenham voters polled for members of the Yorke family. But they did not vote for them as members of a 'party'. In 1835, when 101 voters polled from Haddenham, 79 of them voted for Eliot Thomas Yorke. But only 35 of these voters cast 'party' votes for Yorke and Eaton. The remainder either plumped for Yorke or split their votes across 'party' lines between Yorke and Townley, Yorke and Childers, or Yorke, Townley and Childers. Presumably, in Haddenham, Hardwicke could affect the behaviour of certain voters, both those who were qualified to vote before 1832, and those who were not qualified to vote until 1832. Presumably, he could affect their behaviour through the nexus his properties provided. But whatever that particular nexus these men were also involved in others.

The voters from the parishes in group 1 of table 7 were well organized for political action. And, as a rule, the political action for which they were organized was 'party' action – 'party' defined in a parliamentary sense. At none of the general elections before 1841 did the Cambridgeshire Tories nominate as many candidates as there were seats to be filled, or – to put it differently – as many candidates as the voters had votes. In these parishes, however, (Haddenham, and the

Table 8

Polls for the parishes in which Hardwicke estates were located and in which appropriate consensus came into being in 1830 or 1831 [69]

1826		1830	
Voters	25	Voters	23
Votes for		*Votes for*	
Manners (Tory)	18	Manners (Tory)	5
Osborne (Whig)	4	Osborne (Whig)	14
Adeane (Ind.)	2	Adeane (Ind.)	19

1831		1832	
Voters	30	Voters	62
Votes for		*Votes for*	
Yorke (Tory)	27	Yorke (Tory)	53
Townley (Whig)	3	Adeane (Ind.)	11
		Townley (Whig)	8
		Childers (Whig)	9

1835	
Voters	67
Votes for	
Yorke (Tory)	58
Eaton (Tory)	50
Townley (Whig)	14
Childers (Whig)	13

parishes in group 1.3 of table 7 are, of course, exceptions) majorities of the voters not only voted for the Tory candidates, they voted for them exclusively. In effect, they generally abstained on the question of who should fill the seats for which Tory candidates had not been nominated. This tendency suggests a useful measure of the relative 'party' commitments of the voters in the different parishes and thus a useful clue to one of the essential aspects of 'party' in the county – the numbers of votes cast per voter in the different parishes in 1835, when two Tory and two Whig candidates were nominated.

Altogether, in 1835, the 5,891 voters in the county cast 13,182 votes, an average of 2.24 votes per voter. At this election 1,551 voters polled for three candidates. An additional 96 voters polled for two candidates of different 'parties'. And 161 votes cast plumped votes, non-'party' votes of a somewhat different nature. In effect, over 30 per cent of the voters in the county cast non-'party' votes of one form or another. But the 603 voters who polled from the parishes in group 1 only cast 1,249 votes, an average of only 2.07 votes per voter. Furthermore, only 83 of these voters cast non-'party' votes of whatever nature, less than 14 per cent.

The loci of these different modes of behaviour are important: they suggest that many voters who behaved in 'party' terms were doing so for non-'party' reasons. Possibly, the voters from the parishes in group 1 of table 7 regarded themselves as Tories. Possibly, when they discussed their own behaviour at the polls, they did so in terms of the prospective parliamentary behaviour of the men for whom they voted. But the intensity of electoral agreement within each of these parishes, and the frequently demonstrable correspondence between the political orientations of the voters in these parishes and the political orientations of the predominant local landowners, suggest that these voters did not vote as members of a 'party', nor as men determined to return candidates to Parliament who would behave in certain ways. However they may have rationalized it their behaviour suggests that when they went to the polls they simply declared themselves to be members of particular groups. If, indeed, they described their behaviour in other terms this would only suggest that these were more satisfying, not more realistic.

Most of the parishes in which such discipline is apparent were parts of significant agricultural estates. Thus, presumably, when the relative electoral weights of such parishes were increased – and this would appear to have been the principal consequence of the Act in the counties – the importance of 'party' was increased. But in many cases the men who voted as members of such 'parties' only did so because they were members of quite specific groups of an essentially non-political nature. Obviously, within these groups, men behaved in 'party' terms because the effective influences were exerted in 'party' terms. From this the conclusion follows: 'parties' were not themselves agencies of electoral recruitment. Rather, they were products of the coalitions of the men who were themselves the recruiters – who were able to perform political recruitment roles in respect of their other roles. Hence the paradox: the definition of 'party' behaviour as ideological behaviour was largely a nineteenth century phenomenon; furthermore, this definition was used to distinguish 'party' behaviour from deferential behaviour; but in many cases 'party' behaviour was strongest where it was the obvious expression of deference – in the counties, where it was the obvious measure of the ramifications of an estate. By and large, 'party' voting was weakest in the parishes where no significant estate was located – those parishes in which, especially in the pre-reform period, the largest proportions of voters had been concentrated, those parishes in which effective influence was often exercised by radicals.

But in certain parishes where landownership was divided strong mechanisms of electoral recruitment did exist and were in the hands of Tories. Clearly, they existed in Burwell and Soham (group 1.4 of table 7). And, presumably, the general similarity between the electoral patterns in these parishes and the patterns in the Rutland parishes was the consequence of roughly equivalent causes, the influence of men who were themselves organizationally involved in the local Tory 'party'. In both Burwell and Soham, however, these influences seem to have radiated from neighbouring parishes. According to a later reporter, five-sixths of the Soham voters were 'afraid to vote against [John] Dobede.'[70] The Dobede family did not own any land in Soham but they were large landowners in the adjacent parish of Exning, Suffolk. Possibly, since many Soham freeholders owned plots of land which, while large enough to provide them with electoral qualifications, were too small to provide them with any economic independence, the Dobede family possessed an influence in Soham which was a measure of the size of their own neighbouring estates, of the lack of alternative local sources of political leadership – there were no significant Whig estates in the area – and of the extreme division of local landownership.[71] In any event – and whether their influence in Soham was 'legitimate' or 'illegitimate' – the family was intimately involved with the Cambridgeshire Tories. It was at their home, in 1839, that Allix was introduced as the prospective third Tory candidate for Cambridgeshire.[72] And, in 1847, when the Rutland connection with the county was restored after a lapse of 17 years, it was John Dobede who nominated Lord George Manners.[73] For Burwell the effective influence or influences are not so easily defined, but perhaps the consistent Toryism of the majority of the Burwell voters was a measure of how near the parish was to the Rutland estates.

The parishes in group 1 of table 7 were the only parishes from which majorities of voters retained an exclusively Tory allegiance in all five contests between 1826 and 1835. From certain other parishes majorities of voters plumped for Manners in 1826. But most of the parishes where this occurred fall into either of two general categories. In the one, majorities of voters subsequently defected from their Tory allegiance. In the other, the potential anti-Tory voters simply did not poll in 1826.

As a rule, anti-Tory defections were a phenomenon of 1830. In some parishes these defections were both slight and of short duration (group 2 and 3 of table 7). In these parishes Manners retained his edge in 1830 or received as many votes as Adeane or Osborne. Furthermore, while the numbers of voters from these parishes tended to drop off rather more sharply between 1830, and 1831 than was the case, for example, among the voters from the parishes in Clusters 1.1, 1.2 and 1.3 of table 7, in 1831 majorities of voters from these parishes polled for Yorke. In some of these parishes Tory candidates received strong 'party' support in 1832 and 1835 (group 2). In others the subsequent 'party' orientation was less intense (group 3). In two of these latter parishes significant numbers of voters split their votes in 1830 between Manners and Osborn (group 3.2). These parishes were in the vicinity of Thorney, the base of Bedford's influence in the county. In the others, significant numbers of voters split their votes between Manners and Adeane (group 3.1).

The decline of exclusive support from the voters in the parishes in groups 2 and 3 made things more difficult for Manners: when other voters were splitting their votes between Osborne and Adeane split votes between Manners and Osborne and Manners and Adeane raised the hurdle which Manners had to overcome. But in other parishes the defections were even more serious. In some of these they were also more enduring.

In some parishes there were clear changes of orientation between 1826 and 1830, and again between 1830 and 1831: majorities of the voters plumped for Manners in 1826, put either Osborne or Adeane at the head of the poll in 1830, and voted for Yorke in 1831 (group 4). In certain of these parishes majorities of voters plumped for Yorke in 1832 (group 4.1). In others, they split their votes between Yorke and Adeane (group 4.2). By 1835, however, majorities of the voters from both subgroups were polling for the Tory candidates and for them alone. Strong 'party' patterns had become established. The average number of votes cast per voter from these parishes in 1835 was 2.06.

There were other parishes from which majorities of the voters plumped for Manners in 1826, defected in 1830, and from which at least half of the voters voted for Yorke in 1831. In some of these the Tory candidates received slight majorities both in 1832 and 1835 (groups 5.1 and 5.2). In others Yorke received a majority in 1832 but not in 1835 (group 6). In another, Townley received slight majorities both in 1832 and 1835 (group 7). In some of the parishes in groups 5, 6 and 7 'party' discipline was average. In Elsworth and Landbeach (group 5.1) in 1835 the average number of votes cast per voter in 1835 was 2.23. In others, 'party' discipline was stronger. In Stow-cum-Quy and Tadlow (group 6) the average number of votes cast per voter was 2.08. In others it was weaker. In Streatham (group 5.2) the average number of votes cast per voter was 2.49. In Wishbech St. Mary (group 7) the average number of votes cast per voter was 2.48.

The evidence does not allow any hard and fast rule. But more often than not the lack of local 'party' pattern was associated with the lack of 'party' discipline, not with the coexistence of rival disciplines within the same parish – evidentially, with large porportions of triple votes in 1835 or, in view of the relatively small number of plumped votes in 1835, what usually comes to the same thing, large numbers of votes cast per voter.

In other parishes the defections were more enduring: majorities of voters plumped for Manners in 1826, split their votes between Adeane and Osborne in 1830, and polled for Townley in 1831. In these parishes significant numbers of voters split their votes between Yorke and Adeane in 1832, sometimes preferring Yorke (group 8 of table 7), sometimes Adeane (group 9), before returning to the Tory fold and adopting those 'party' patterns which their behaviour reveals in 1835. In group 8 the average number of votes cast per voter in 1835 was 2.10. In group 9 it was 2.27. In other parishes where serious defections occurred in 1830, and where majorities of the voters polled for Townley in 1831, no clear 'party' patterns are subsequently apparent (group 10). In these parishes, however, the lack of 'party' pattern reflects not so much a lack of 'party' discipline as the existence of more than one fairly well disciplined bloc in each parish. From these parishes only 19 of the 118 voters who polled in 1835 cast three votes. The average number of votes cast per voter was only 2.11.

In other parishes the Tory majorities of 1826 persisted in 1830 but disappeared in 1831. In some of these, significant numbers of voters split their votes in 1830 between Manners and Osborne (group 11). These parishes were in the general vicinity of Thorney. In others, which lay elsewhere in the county, such splits did not occur (group 12). Subsequently, in both groups, 'party' discipline was relatively weak. In group 11 in 1835, the average number of votes cast per voter was 2.34. In group 12 it was 2.39. In two parishes on the other hand where majorities of the voters plumped for Manners in 1826 the defections of 1830 were both sharp and permanent. In these parishes in both 1832 and 1835 majorities of voters polled for the non-Tory candidates and polled for them as members of a 'party' (group 13).

The parishes in groups 1 to 13 should be clearly distinguished from certain other parishes. Apparently the changes of orientation which the poll books reveal for certain of these parishes resulted from changes in the orientation of effective local influences. While more voters may have polled from these parishes in 1830 than in 1826 these additional voters were not responsible for whatever changes of orientation may have occurred within them. In West Wickam, for example (group 4.1), twice as many voters polled in 1830 as in 1826. Almost twice as many polled in 1832 as in 1830 or 1831. But the two changes of orientation which occurred among these voters – the first between 1826 and 1830, the second between 1830 and 1831 – cannot be attributed to any change in the nature of the electorate, merely to changes in the ways they voted. Since the voters retained their essential cohesion their altered behaviour was presumably a result of changes in the influences which were effective among them. When additional voters polled, they merely increased the electoral weight of the predominant influence in the parish. In certain other parishes, however, changes of orientation occurred between 1826 and 1830 which are principally attributable to the participation of men at the second contest who had not participated at the first. In many cases, the 'party' orientations of these men were relatively weak.

Whittlesey was such a parish (group 14.1 of table 7). There, in 1826, the majority of the voters plumped for Manners. In 1830, more than half as many voters again polled from Whittlesey as polled in 1826. Many of those who had plumped for Manners in 1826 now split their votes between Manners and Osborne. But most of those who had not polled in 1826 split their votes between Osborne and Adeane. There is still the question of the significance of the Manners-Osborne split in Whittlesey — in particular, whether it was a measure of Bedford influence newly emanating from the adjacent parish of Thorney. But be this as it may, 'party' discipline in Whittlesey was weak. In 1835 almost half the 322 voters who polled from Whittlesey split their votes across normal 'party' lines. The average number of votes cast per voter was 2.44. Outwell was another such parish (group 14.2). With marginal differences in 1832 and 1835 the patterns of behaviour of the Outwell voters were the same as those of the Whittlesey voters. Nor did the similarity stop there. In 1835, 15 of the 23 Outwell voters cast three votes. The average number of votes cast per voter was 2.61.

There were other parishes from which the majorities of the voters who polled in 1826 plumped for Manners, and where changes of orientation occurred between 1826 and 1830 which are principally attributable to the participation of voters in 1830 who had not participated in 1826. In some of these, as in Whittlesey and Outwell, 'party' discipline was weak. In others it was fairly strong. By and large, 'party' discipline was weaker where subsequent changes of orientation occurred (groups 15.1-15.4). In 1835 roughly 40 per cent of the voters from these parishes cast three votes. The average number of votes cast per voter was 2.38. It was stronger where subsequent changes of orientation did not occur (group 16). In these parishes in 1835, only some 20 per cent of the voters cast three votes. The average number of votes cast per voter was only 2.15. Significantly, perhaps, one of the 'parties' for which this discipline was exercised included Adeane as well as Townley and Childers. In this respect, these parishes differed sharply from March (group17). There, in the shadow of Thorney — and, thus, presumably, in the area of Bedford influence — Adeane had rather less support. Most of the voters who polled from March in 1830, and who had not polled in 1826, split their votes between Osborne and Manners. Presumably, Bedford influence was also responsible for the relatively small number of March voters who polled for Adeane in 1832. But in March 'party' discipline was somewhat stronger than it was in many of the other parishes in which the effective influence in 1830 would seem to have come from beyond that parish boundaries. While Tory candidates had a slight edge in 1832 and 1835, the average number of votes cast per voter in 1835 was only, 2.22, considerably below the numbers in Outwell and Whittlesey

The behaviour of the voters in the parishes in groups 14 and 15 has much to suggest about the exercise of effective political power in the county. Both in the pre- and post-reform periods these parishes contained significant proportions of the total county electorate – or, at least, of the *potential* county electorate. When they voted, the voters from these parishes comprised some 20 per cent of the county electorate. But especially in the pre-reform period, when there was but one polling place in the county – and that located at the far end of the county, in the borough of Cambridge – fluctuations of electoral participation among the voters from these parishes were rather larger than the county average. In the post-reform period, when additional polling places were provided – one in the northern town of Wisbech – the electoral participation of the voters from these parishes was more constant. However, the proportions of votes split across normal 'party' lines cast by these voters was rather larger than the county average. In effect, majorities of the voters from these parishes could be brought to the polls to vote for Osborne in 1830, and for Townley in 1831, but they did not provide a base for stable political power in the county. Clearly, in these parishes, significant numbers of voters were not members of communities or networks which were politically enmeshed. Either the ties which bound them to one another were weak, or the ties by which the groups they may have formed were bound to other groups in other parishes in the county were weak. Whichever the case, the reason was presumably the same: none of these parishes was part of any significant estate.

Nor did any significant estate exist in the parishes in group 16 of table 7. But these parishes were centres of old nonconformity and hence, 'party' discipline within them was fairly strong. However, if such discipline existed as a more permanent attribute it was not always applied in the county arena. In 1826, many qualified men in these parishes did not vote. If they had done so, they would presumably have voted for Osborne and Adeane. Nor did they have the same excuse for not voting as the others: these parishes were on the outskirts of Cambridge.

In most of the parishes from which majorities of the voters plumped for Manners in 1826 Tory orientations were restored by 1832, but the new anti-radical coalition which came into being during and after the reform crisis drew its strength from others besides the faithful Tories and the returning defectors of 1830. In some parishes where majorities of the voters polled for Osborne and Adeane in 1826 significant increments in Tory strength are apparent in 1830. In these parishes majorities of voters polled for Yorke in 1831 and went on to poll for the Tory candidates both in 1832 and 1835 (group 18). In one parish where majorities of voters polled for Osborne and Adeane both in 1826 and 1830 and for Yorke in 1831 they tended to split their votes in 1832 in such ways as to put Adeane at the head of the poll (group 19). Nor did they accommodate themselves to the new 'party' alliances by 1835. Whether they hung onto the old alliances or were merely not engaged in the new 28 of the 51 voters who polled from this parish in 1835 voted for three candidates. The average number of votes cast per voter was 2.57.

In other parishes where majorities of the voters polled for Osborne, Adeane or both in 1826 and 1830 and for Townley in 1831 a number of them split their votes in 1832 between Yorke, Adeane and Townley, and in 1835 between Yorke, Eaton and Townley – in effect, voting *against* Childers (group 20). Significantly, such patterns are apparent both in Babraham and Stapleford, the former the centre of Adeane's estates, where all the voters polled for Adeane in 1830 and 1832, the latter the centre of the Duke of Leeds estates, where sizeable numbers of voters plumped for Osborne both in 1826 and 1830. Presumably, the non-'party' behaviour of the Babraham voters was not unrelated to the fact that after 1832 the Adeane family withdrew from any active political involvement for a generation.

In the borough of Cambridge, too, a change occurred in the orientation of the aggregate poll between 1831 and 1832 (group 21). In 1826 and 1830 the voters from Cambridge gave Osborne significant pluralities over both Adeane and Manners; in 1831 almost twice as many of them polled for Townley as for Yorke. Yet in 1832, when their number was sharply reduced – obviously, as a result of the borough freeholder clause – Townley had but a slight margin over Yorke, and Adeane and Childers were effectively even. The same pattern obtained in 1835.

Thorney was the centre from which Bedford's influence in the county emanated (group 22.1). In 1826, the Thorney voters all plumped for Osborne. In 1830, all but one of them split his votes between Manners and Osborne. In 1831 they all voted for Townley. In 1832, they all voted for Townley and Childers. A few voted for Adeane, and fewer still for Yorke. In 1835, when only two Whig candidates were nominated all 53 Thorney voters polled for them and for them alone.

In only a few other parishes did significant proportions of the voters split their votes between Manners and Osborne in 1830. Most of the parishes in which such splits occurred were in the immediate vicinity of Thorney. In a few cases, however, it would appear that split votes between Manners and Osborne were not so much evidence of direct Bedford influence as of indirect influence – his ability to condition the ways in which other people's influences were exercised. In the county as a whole, in 1830, roughly eight per cent of the voters split their votes between Manners and Osborne. In the North Witchford hundred, where Thorney is located, and in the neighbouring hundred of Wisbech, 33 per cent of the voters split their votes between Manners and Osborne. In most parishes the means by which these results were achieved are obscure. But in one they are fairly clear.

In Doddington (group 22.1 of table 7), which lies close to Thorney, majorities of the voters not only split their votes between Manners and Osborne in 1830; they polled *á la* Thorney at each of the five contests between 1826 and 1835. In all probability, the cohesion of the Doddington voters was a measure not of Bedford's direct influence but of the influence of the Peyton estate. The Peyton family were the predominant landowners in the parish. Bedford's influence upon the Doddington voters was probably only felt indirectly, through his influence upon members of the Peyton family. The relations between the two families were close. Not only did the Reverend Algernon Peyton perform various political roles in the county which Bedford could not perform because of being a peer, but by the forties the two families were linked by marriage.[74] Similar factors may have been responsible for behavioural patterns in Mepal (group 22.2). But with the evidence presently available the reason for these patterns remains obscure.

Similar factors may also have been responsible for behavioural patterns in Wimblington (group 23), but in 1832 the correspondence between the behaviour of the Thorney and the Wimblington voters ceased: almost all of the Wimblington voters polled for Yorke. Had only some of the enlarged complement of Wimblington voters in 1832 polled for Yorke, and had those who voted for him in 1832 not voted before, it might be argued that the Reform Act had enfranchised men in the parish who were members of a group which was politically opposed to the group from which the pre-reform voters had been drawn. However, the behaviour of the Wimblington voters in 1832 tends to undermine that hypothesis without supplying another. Welney (group 24) raises separate problems.

In Barrington, Benwick *et al* (groups 25.1-25.3) majorities of the voters consistently polled for the anti-Tory candidates. In some of these parishes the probable source of effective influence can be specified: the Townley family in Fulbourn, the Pell family in Wilburton, the Huddleston family in Sawston, the Lilley family in Hauxton. In the fen parish of Over and the market town of Royston it was probably not a family's influence transmitted through the agency of an estate which conditioned the voters' behaviour but religious nonconformity. From certain of these parishes majorities of the voters split their votes among Adeane, Townley and Childers in 1832 (group 25.1). From others, including Oakington, where the Adeane family was one of the principal landowners, majorities of the voters gave Adeane a strong individual support at each of the contests at which he stood (group 25.2). From another of these parishes relatively few voters polled for Adeane (group 25.3). But there the lack of split votes between Manners and Osborne in 1830 suggests that lack of support for Adeane was not the result of Bedford influence. In these several parishes 'party' discipline was fairly strong. The average number of votes cast per voter in 1835 was 2.17.

In Haddenham and Witchford members of the Yorke family received an essentially personal support in 1832 and 1835 (group 26) – in Haddenham, presumably, for reasons suggested above. In other parishes majorities of the voters followed other progressions which reflect the growth of Tory influences or the weakening of Whig influences (groups 27 and 28). Conington and Shingay are somewhat difficult to characterize: they contained too few voters (group 29). By and large, however, their voters behaved as members of 'parties': the average number of votes cast per voter in 1835 was 2.17. In Thetford, on the other hand, the effective influence or influences were so strongly oriented in non-'party' terms that 13 of the 19 Thetford voters in 1835 voted for three candidates (group 30). On average, each Thetford voter cast 2.68 votes.

IX

If the Cambridgeshire voters be considered as individual actors then we will never know why the Cambridgeshire contests between 1826 and 1835 turned out as they did: their outcomes would reflect multiplicities of factors the sheer number of which would defy efforts at description. To some extent, the same is true if the Cambridgeshire electorate at each contest be considered as the sum of its geographically definable components. But the number of variables is sharply reduced if the results of these contests are considered less in terms of what conditioned each voter's behaviour, and more in terms of how the behaviour of the different aggregates of voters affected the final poll. In effect, if each of the Cambridgeshire poll books is compared with the preceding poll book the changes in size, orientation and cohesion of the different blocs or aggregates can be seen and it is to these that at one level of explanation, the results of the different contests should be attributed. This level is not the final one: these changes do not fully 'explain' the results of these contests. But they illustrate the varieties of factor on which such explanations would focus.

In 1826, the parishes from which majorities of the voters polled for Manners contained well over half of the resident voters. Ninety-one per cent of these men voted for Manners (See Table 9 and Figure 1). To explain the cohesions and orientation of these men and the failures of certain other men to vote in 1826 would explain why Manners was returned. In addition, it would illustrate the vulnerability of his position. In some of the parishes from which majorities of the voters polled for Manners in 1826 they polled for him again in 1830 – although rather less exclusively (group 1 of table 9). In others, majorities of the voters deserted him in 1830 but later returned to a Tory allegiance (group 2). In others, again, they deserted him and never returned to a Tory allegiance (group 3). Principally, it was the voters from these parishes who both revealed and symbolized the vulnerability of Manners' position.

The decline in the exclusiveness of support for Manners in what might be called the consistently Tory parishes was extremely important in 1830. It deprived him of the means of overcoming the consequences of two other but obviously related phenomena. In certain parishes the decline of exclusive support went so far as to place Manners at the bottom of the local poll. In other parishes many men who had not voted in 1826 voted solidly against Manners in 1830. Because these voters took part in the election what were then the Whig parishes contained two-thirds of the voters in the county. Until the passing of the Reform Bill, which enabled the leaders of the local landed party to restore their position – but probably only because their opponents were willing to allow the restoration to occur – the voters whom the leaders of the landed party could organize were an impotent minority

However many men were qualified to vote in Cambridgeshire in the pre-reform period,[75] roughly 75 per cent more voters polled in 1830 than in 1826. But the increments were by no means uniform. In what might be called the consistently Whig parishes, those in groups 4 and 5 of table 9, the average increments were not very different from those in what might be called the consistently Tory parishes. In the consistently Whig parishes the average increments were roughly 71 per cent. In the consistently Tory parishes they were roughly 68 per cent. But in the parishes in group 3 they were more than 200 per cent. To explain why voters from these parishes polled in 1830 but had not in 1826 would go a long way towards explaining why, as a consequence of the new

Table 9
Why Manners lost in 1830

Parishes from which majorities of voters polled for :	1826								1830							
	numbers of voters	these as % of total voters	votes for Manners (Tory)	these as % of total votes he received	votes for Osborne (Whig)	these as % of total votes he received	votes for Adeane (Ind.)	these as % of total votes he received	numbers of voters	these as % of total voters	votes for Manners (Tory)	these as % of total votes he received	votes for Osborne (Whig)	these as % of total votes he received	votes for Adeane (Ind.)	these as % of total votes he received
1) Manners in both 1826 and 1830 (groups 1-3, 11-12, 14, 17, 24 and 29 of Table 7)	696	34	668	51	56	7	21	3	1167	31	847	48	460	20	359	17
%s of voters in the group who voted for			96		8		3				73		39		30	
2) Manners in 1826 but not in 1830, but who later returned to a Tory allegiance (groups 4-10 and 13 of Table 7)	249	12	208	16	53	6	37	6	386	10	138	8	217	9	299	14
%s of voters in the group who voted for			84		21		15				36		56		78	
3) Manners in 1826 but not in 1830, who never returned to a Tory allegiance (groups 15-16 of Table 7)	233	12	199	15	70	8	19	3	721	19	289	17	565	24	415	20
%s of voters in the group who voted for			85		30		8				40		78		58	
4) Osborne and Adeane in 1826 and 1830 (groups 18-21, 25-28 of Table 7)	832	41	245	19	642	77	534	87	1373	40	423	24	1040	44	994	48
%s of voters in the group who voted for			29		77		64				31		76		72	

Table 9 (continued)
Why Manners lost in 1830

Parishes from which majorities of voters polled for :	1826								1830							
	numbers of voters	these as %s of total voters	votes for Manners (Tory)	these as %s of total votes he received	votes for Osborne (Whig)	these as %s of total votes he received	votes for Adeane (Ind.)	these as %s of total votes he received	numbers of voters	these as %s of total voters	votes for Manners (Tory)	these as %s of total votes he received	votes for Osborne (Whig)	these as %s of total votes he received	votes for Adeane (Ind.)	these as %s of total votes he received
5) Osborne in 1826 and Osborne and Manners in 1830 (groups 22-23 of Table 7)	15	1	3	0	14	2	0	0	75	2	57	3	65	3	16	1
%s of voters in the group who voted for			20		93		0				76		87		21	
Totals from 'Tory' parishes (groups 1–3 above in 1826 and 1 in 1830)	1178	58	1075	81	179	21	77	12	1167	31	847	48	460	20	359	17
%s of voters in the group who voted for			91		15		7				73		39		31	
Totals from 'Whig' parishes (groups 4–5 above in 1826 and 2-5 in 1830)	847	42	248	19	656	79	534	87	2555	69	907	35	1887	80	1724	83
%s of voters in the group who voted for			29		77		63				35		74		67	

balance of power in the county which the participation of these men created, Manners was defeated in 1830. The parishes in which Manners was at the bottom of the local poll in 1830 contained more than two-thirds of the voters in the country.

In most cases the orientations of 1830 were those of 1831: almost 80 per cent of the voters of 1831 voted from parishes in which majorities of the voters had had the same basic orientation in 1830 (see table 10). And again, as in 1830, the principal changes of orientation were against the Tory candidate. As a result, the parishes in which Townley headed the poll contained more than three-quarters of the voters who polled. Furthermore the average degree of local electoral agreement was perhaps greater in the Tory parishes of 1831 than it had been in those of 1830. In 1830, only 73 per cent of the voters from the Tory parishes polled for Manners (See table 9: 'Totals from "Tory" parishes'). In 1831, 81 per cent of them polled for Yorke (See table 10: 'Totals from "Tory" parishes'). In the Whig parishes consensus was somewhat less (See Table 10: 'Totals from "Whig" parishes'). Indeed, even in 1826, when the consensus of the voters from such parishes was greatest, only 78 per cent of them polled for Osborne (See table 9: 'Totals from "Whig" parishes'). But as long as the Whig parishes contained such large proportions of the voters the differences in the levels of organization or discipline among them were not politically significant. They became significant in 1832.

Between 1831 and 1832 a fundamental change occurred in the balance of political power in the county which was principally the result of a change in the relative electoral strengths of different categories of parish. In the county as a whole roughly 90 per cent more voters polled in 1832 than in 1831 (see table 11). However, in the parishes from which majorities of the voters polled for Yorke both in 1831 and 1832, those in group 1 of table 11, 120 per cent more voters polled in 1832 than in 1831. In the parishes from which majorities of the voters polled for Townley in 1831, and for Townley, Adeane or Childers in 1832, those in group 4 of table 11, only 69 per cent more voters polled in 1832 than in 1831. The Whig parishes still contained a majority of the electorate in the county. But the agencies of electoral recruitment in these parishes were far less capable of delivering votes to the Whig candidates than those in the Tory parishes of delivering votes to the Tory candidates. There was less consensus in the Whig parishes in 1832 than there had been in 1831 – markedly less than in the Tory parishes in 1832. Furthermore, the principal changes of local political orientation were now occurring in favour of Yorke (see figure 1). And, again – which table 11 clearly reveals – there was a far greater disparity between the numbers of votes which Yorke received from the voters, in the Tory parishes and the numbers of votes which Adeane,

Table 10

Why Townley was returned in 1831

Parishes from which majorities of voters polled for:	1830								1831					
	numbers of voters	these as % of total voters	votes for Manners (Tory)	these as % of total votes he received	votes for Osborne (Whig)	these as % of total votes he received	votes for Adeane (Ind.)	these as % of total votes he received	number of voters	these as % of total voters	votes for Yorke (Tory)	these as % of total votes he received	votes for Townley (Whig)	these as % of total votes he received
1) Manners in 1830 and Yorke in 1831 (groups 1-3, 24 and 29-30 of Table 7)	732	20	556	32	176	7	237	11	595	19	503	39	92	5
%s of voters in the group who voted for			76		24		32				85		15	
2) Manners in 1830 and Townley in 1831 (groups 11-12, 14 and 17 of Table 7)	435	12	291	17	284	12	122	6	385	12	142	11	243	13
%s of voters in the group who voted for			67		65		28				37		63	
3) Osborne and Adeane or Osborne and Manners in 1830 and Townley in 1831 (groups 8-10, 13, 15-16, 20-23 and 25-28 of Table 7)	2302	62	813	46	1728	74	1530	73	1953	63	514	40	1439	79
%s of voters in the group who voted for			35		75		66				26		74	
4) Osborne and Adeane in 1830 and Yorke in 1831 (groups 4-7, 18-19 of Table 7)	253	7	94	5	159	7	194	9	172	6	119	9	53	3
%s of voters in the group who voted for			37		63		77				69		31	

Table 10 (continued)
Why Townley was returned in 1831

Parishes from which majorities of voters polled for :	1830								1831					
	number of voters	these as % of total voters	votes for Manners (Tory)	these as % of total votes he received	votes for Osborne (Whig)	these as % of total votes he received	votes for Adeane (Ind.)	these as % of total votes he received	number of voters	these as % of total voters	votes for Yorke (Tory)	these as % of total votes he received	votes for Townley (Whig)	these as % of total votes he received
Totals for 'Tory' parishes (groups 1-2 above in 1830 and 1 and 4 in 1831)	1167	31	847	48	460	20	359	17	767	25	662	49	145	8
%s of voters in the group who voted for			73		39		31				81		19	
Totals for 'Whig' parishes (groups 3-4 above in 1830 and 2 and 3 in 1831)	2555	69	907	52	1887	80	1724	83	2338	75	656	51	1682	92
%s of voters in the group who voted for			35		74		67				28		72	

Table 11

Why Yorke was returned at the head of the poll in 1832

Parishes from which majorities of voters polled for:	1831						1832									
	number of voters	these as % of total voters	votes for Yorke (Tory)	these as % of total	votes for Townley (Whig)	these as % of total he received	number of voters	these as % of total voters	votes for Yorke (Tory)	these as % of total he received	votes for Adeane (Ind.)	these as % of total he received	votes for Townley (Whig)	these as % of total he received	votes for Childers (Whig)	these as % of total he received
1) Yorke in both 1831 and 1832 (groups 1-6, 18, 29 and 30 of Table 7)	720	23	594	46	126	7	1585	28	1370	37	433	15	388	12	338	12
%s of voters in the group who voted for			83		17				86		27		24		21	
2) York in 1831 but not in 1832 (groups 7, 19 and 24 of Table 7)	47	2	28	2	19	1	175	3	110	3	115	3	126	4	96	3
%s of voters in the group who voted for			60		40				63		66		72		55	
3) Townley in 1831 and Adeane, Townley or Childers in 1832 (groups 9-10, 12-16, 21-22, 25 and 27-28 of Table 7)	1887	61	489	38	1398	77	3196	54	1548	42	1872	66	2211	68	1999	70
%s of voters in the group who voted for			26		74				48		59		69		63	
4) Townley in 1831 and Yorke in 1832 (groups 8, 11, 17, 20, 23 and 26 of Table 7)	451	15	167	13	284	16	967	16	664	18	429	15	536	16	428	15
%s of voters in the group who voted for			37		63				69		44		55		44	

Table 11 (continued)

Why Yorke was returned at the head of the poll in 1832

Parishes from which majorities of voters polled for :	1831						1832									
	numbers of voters	these as % of total voters	votes for Yorke (Tory)	these as % of total votes he received	votes for Townley (Whig)	these as % of total votes he received	numbers of voters	these as % of total voters	Votes for Yorke (Tory)	these as % of total votes he received	votes for Adeane (Ind.)	these as % of total votes he received	votes for Townley (Whig)	these as % of total votes he received	votes for Childers (Whig)	these as % of total votes he received
Totals for 'Tory' parishes (groups 1-2 above in 1831 and 1 and 4 in 1832)	767	25	622	49	145	8	2552	43	2034	55	862	30	924	28	766	27
%s of voters in the group who voted for			81		19				80		34		36		30	
Totals for 'Whig' parishes (groups 3-4 above in 1831 and 2-3 in 1832)	2338	75	656	51	1682	92	3371	57	1658	45	1987	59	2337	69	2095	73
%s of voters in the group who voted for			28		72				49		59		69		62	

Table 12

Why Childers was defeated in 1835

Parishes from which majority of voters polled for:	1832										1835										
	numbers of voters	these as % of total voters	votes for Yorke (Tory)	these as % of total votes he received	votes for Adeane (Ind.)	these as % of total votes he received	votes for Townley (Whig)	these as % of total votes he received	votes for Childers (Whig)	these as % of total votes he received	numbers of voters	these as % of total voters	votes for Yorke (Tory)	these as % of total votes he received	votes for Eaton (Tory)	these as % of total votes he received	votes for Townley (Whig)	these as % of total votes he received	votes for Childers (Whig)	these as % of total votes he received	votes cast per voter
1) 'Tory' candidates in both 1832 and 1835 (groups 1-5, 8, 17-18, 20, 23, 26 and 29-30 of Table 7)	2270	38	1835	50	774	27	749	23	626	22	2229	38	1820	47	1666	51	676	22	645	22	2.16
%s of voters in the group who voted for			81		34		33		28				82		75		30		29		
2) York in 1832 and either Townley or Childers in 1835 (groups 6 and 11 of Table 7)	282	5	199	5	88	3	175	5	140	5	277	5	173	4	136	4	184	6	151	5	2.32
%s of voters in the group who voted for			71		31		62		50				62		49		66		55		
3) 'Whig' candidates in both 1832 and 1835 (groups 7, 12-16, 19, 21-22, 24-25 and 28 of Table 7)	2927	50	1421	38	1680	59	2102	64	1900	66	2940	50	1585	41	1174	36	1990	65	2005	67	2.30
%s of voters in the group who voted for			49		57		72		65				54		40		68		68		

Table 12 (continued)

Why Childers was defeated in 1835

Parishes from which majority of voters polled for :	1832 numbers of voters	these as % of total voters	votes for Yorke (Tory)	these as % of total votes he received	votes for Adeane (Ind.)	these as % of total votes he received	votes for Townley (Whig)	these as % of total votes he received	votes for Childers (Whig)	these as % of total votes he received	1835 numbers of voters	these as % of total voters	votes for Yorke (Tory)	these as % of total votes he received	votes for Eaton (Tory)	these as % of total votes he received	votes for Townley (Whig)	these as % of total votes he received	votes for Childers (Whig)	these as % of total votes he received	votes cast per voter
4) Adeane, Townley or Childers in 1832 and for York or Eaton in 1835 (groups 9-10 and 27 of Table 7)	444	7	237	6	307	11	235	7	195	7	445	8	294	8	285	9	221	7	177	6	2.20
%s of voters in the group who polled for			53		69		53		44				66		64		50		40		
Totals for 'Tory' parishes (groups 1-2 above for 1832 and 1 and 4 for 1835)	2552	43	2034	55	862	30	924	28	766	27	2674	45	2114	55	1951	60	897	29	822	28	2.16
%s of voters in the group who polled for			80		34		36		30				79		73		34		31		
Totals for 'Whig' parishes (groups 3-4 above for 1832 and 2 and 3 for 1835)	3371	57	1658	45	1987	70	2337	72	2095	73	3217	55	1758	45	1310	40	2174	71	2156	72	2.30
%s of voters in the group who polled for			49		59		69		62				55		41		67		67		

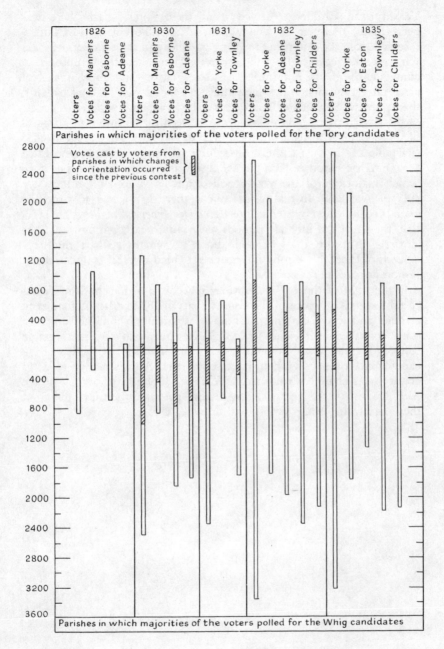

Fig 1
Sources of support for the different candidates in Cambridgeshire, 1826-35.

Townly and Childers received from these voters, than there was between the numbers of votes which Adeane, Townley and Childers received from the voters in the Whig parishes and the numbers of votes which Yorke received from these voters. These were the symptoms: in consequence of the inferiority of the agencies and mechanisms of electoral recruitment on which they depended, the Whigs had lost their previous advantage. In large part, the advantage which the leaders of the landed party now enjoyed can be seen in the different numbers of votes cast per voter from the different categories of parish in 1835 (see table 12). In the parishes from which majorities of the voters polled for Yorke or Eaton in 1835 the average was 2.16. In the parishes from which majorities of the voters polled for Townley or Childers the average was 2.30. In reality, of course, there is no way to assess the claim of the leader writer in the *Cambridge Independent Press,* in 1833, that 'the friends of Liberal opinions were numerically stronger than the Tories.'[76] But this may be said about it: whatever their numbers, 'friends of Liberal opinions' no longer provided a viable foundation for political power in the county.

In the light of these considerations it seems possible that the Tories could have taken more of the county seats in 1832 and 1835 than they claimed and took. But their diffidence was scarcely unique. In many other county constituencies in 1832 Tories only laid claim to a single seat. Nor was Cambridgeshire the only county in which Tory candidates won seats without contests in 1841. Altogether, in 1841, 13 county seats changed hands from Whigs to Tories without the active participation of the voters. Recognizing, perhaps, the inevitability of their defeat, the Whigs simply withdrew.

North Northamptonshire in the mid-nineteenth century

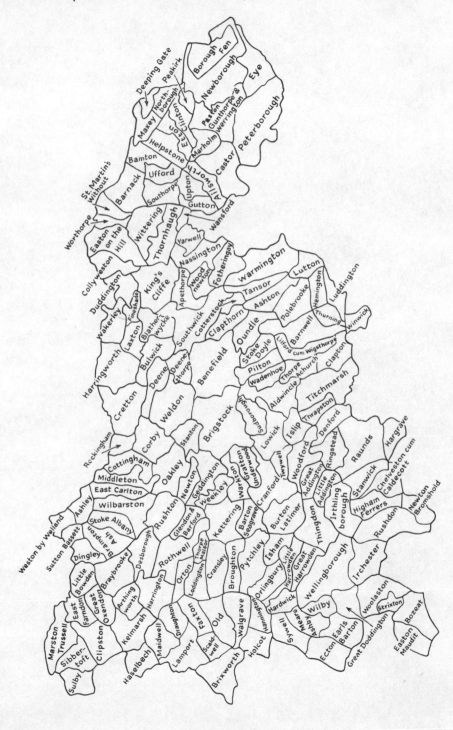

3

Northamptonshire and North Northamptonshire, 1831-57

I

Before 1831 there had not been a contest in Northamptonshire for many years. When Parliament was dissolved the sitting members were Viscount Althorp, Chancellor of the Exchequer in the Grey Ministry, and William Cartwright of Aynhoe, a Tory who had voted against the Bill. But Cartwright's vote notwithstanding, many reformers were reluctant to try to oust him. Their ostensible reasons reflect their belief in the importance of influence, and the importance of the communities and networks in which different influences obtained. But they also suggest inadequate consideration of the intensity of feeling on the substantive questions at issue which, in some cases, obviously affected the ways in which influence was exercised and in others may well have weakened the effectiveness of influence when it was not exercised on behalf of reform candidates. Many men, they claimed, who deplored Cartwright's vote, would not use their influences against him because they liked him personally.[1] Presumably, it was they, speaking largely for themselves, who delayed the formal announcement of a contest. There was talk of opposition from the time Parliament was dissolved. Notices were even put in some local newspapers to the effect that the freeholders of certain parishes were committed to vote for Althorp and for any other candidate of the same persuasion, and to vote for them 'free of expense'.[2] But Cartwright and Althorp were the only candidates announced until Viscount Milton, the son of the fourth Earl Fitzwilliam, was nominated from the hustings. The Tories responded by nominating a second candidate, the Ultra-Tory, Sir Charles Knightley.

The choice of Knightley probably reveals the Tories' concern both to restore their own cohesion in the county and to weaken the residual coalition among certain Whigs, Radicals and Ultra-Tories. Deeply offended by Catholic Emancipation, Knightley had welcomed the defeat of the Wellington Government in November, 1830.[3] Whether accurately or not, it was men such as he to whom the ostensible change of orientation in the county in 1830 was sometimes attributed. As a friend of Cartwright's put it in 1830, Althorp had in years past had more reason to fear a contest than Cartwright. But, because Cartwright had supported Wellington on the Catholic question, the situation had changed. And, he added – thereby laying claim to Cartwright's gratitude for helping to avoid a contest in 1830 – whenever he had met anyone who spoke of Cartwright's new vulnerability he declared that Cartwright would go to the polls and had £20,000 he was prepared to spend.[4] But 1831 was not 1830. By February, Knightley had become suspicious of the Grey Ministry.[5]

Whether he was chosen because it was hoped he would show others the way back into the Tory fold his own return was earlier than some. The Earl of Winchilsea, for example, who had significant properties in the county, did not formally desert the Grey Ministry until June. He signed a requisition in April convening a reform meeting in the county.[6] If his own political orientation can be deduced from the votes cast from those parishes in the northern area of the county in which his own estates were located he remained a reformer – although not an enthusiastic one – until after the May elections.[7]

In any event, whatever the reasons for Knightley's candidacy, it was clearly the reformers' concern to prevent the erosion of their strength among the Ultra-Tories which conditioned their treatment of Cartwright. To perpetuate the local anti-Wellingtonian coalition the Ultra-Tories could not be allowed to forget why many of them had gone into opposition between 1829 and 1830. Not that the substantive issue of Catholic emancipation was emphasized. Indeed, to have done so would scarcely have been politic. It would have emphasized one of the principal causes for division between different groups of reformers. Rather, Wellington's apostasy was emphasized and, by implication, the powers by which he had apparently influenced others to become apostates too. In effect, as the reformers put it, Cartwright was part of Wellington's tail. Their treatment of Cartwright is an example of the ways in which, after the Catholic Relief Act was passed, the substantive question of Catholic emancipation often became merged into the political or constitutional question of how the Relief Act was passed – in substance, into the question of why the tail existed. As one of their broadsheets put it:–

Who voted against the extension of Civil and Religious Liberty
when brought forward by the men composing the present Ministry?
  Cartwright!
Who became an apostate, when the same measure was brought
forward by the Duke of Wellington?
  Cartwright![8]

Both Whig candidates were returned from the county in 1831. At
the elections which followed the passage of the Bill, however, one
Whig and one Tory were returned from each of the two divisions into
which the county had been divided. Althorp and Cartwright were
returned without a contest from the new southern division. In the new
northern division, where various Whig peers had large estates, a total
of four candidates was nominated, two Whigs, Milton and William
Hanbury, of Kelmarsh, and two Tories, Viscount Brudenell, son of the
seventh Earl of Cardigan, and Thomas Tryon of Bulwick. Milton and
Burdenell were returned.

The following year the fourth Earl Fitzwilliam died. Fortunately for
the family's interests in Northamptonshire his grandson had already
come of age. Thus, when Charles William Wentworth succeeded his
father as fifth Earl Fitzwilliam, his eldest son, William Charles
Wentworth, was ready to fill the vacancy in the county. This new
Viscount Milton was twice returned without a contest, first at the
by-election of 1833 and, subsequently, along with Brudenell, at the
general election of 1835. But the following November this new Lord
Milton himself died. This time there was no immediate member of the
family available to replace him. As heir apparent to his father William
Charles Wentworth was succeeded by his brother, William Thomas
Wentworth. But as member for North Northamptonshire William
Thomas Wentworth could not succeed. At the time his brother died he
had only just turned 20. In these circumstances another candidate was
chosen, the formerly-defeated William Hanbury and Philip Maunsell,
of Thorpe Malsor, went through with his previously announced plan
of contesting the seat at the first opportunity. The Whigs made much
of the question whether Maunsell's candidacy was not somehow
disrespectful to Milton's memory.[9] But their apparent effort to salvage
their poltical fortunes by an essentially non-ideological appeal was a
failure. Hanbury was beaten badly. Another contest occurred in 1837
when Brudenell retired. On this occasion the Fitzwilliam family
produced a candidate from their own ranks for William Thomas
Wentworth was now old enough to sit in Parliament. He was beaten
by two Tory or protectionist candidates, Maunsell and Viscount
Maidstone, the son of the ninth Earl of Winchilsea. Thereafter, no
contest occurred in the division for 20 years. Then, at a by-election, the

Liberal candidate, Fitzpatrick Vernon, was defeated by the Conservative candidate, George Ward Hunt.

The northern division included those parishes where the total polls in 1831, 1832, 1835, 1837 and 1857 were as indicated in table 13.[10]

Table 13

Total polls for North Northamptonshire, at the contests of 1832, 1835, 1837 and 1857, and for the parishes subsequently included in North Northamptonshire at the contest of 1831

1831		1832	
Voters	1754	voters	3063
Votes for		*Votes for*	
Althorp (Whig)	1073	Brudenell (Tory)	1541
Milton (Whig)	1030	Milton (Whig)	1562
Cartwright (Tory)	720	Hanbury (Whig)	1455
Knightley (Tory)	492	Tryon (Tory)	1269

1835		1837	
Voters	2866	Voters	3149
Votes for		*Votes for*	
Maunsell (Tory)	1737	Maunsell (Tory)	1842
Hanbury (Whig)	1129	Maidstone (Tory)	1801
		Milton (Whig)	1404

1857	
Voters	2438
Votes for	
Hunt (Conservative)	1419
Vernon (Liberal)	1019

As in Huntingdonshire and Cambridgeshire, however, these total polls obscure their own essential components. By doing so they obscure the factors which produced them.

II

Since the contest of 1831 was the first in this series of contests there is no way to measure the possible impact of the circumstances in which it occurred upon the sizes, orientations and cohesions of the various electoral blocs which the county contained. But three important factors are apparent.

First, there was the assessor's decision in the case of some 500

Northampton freemen who tried to vote in the county in respect of their rights to the use of certain common lands. The questions were legal: whether their rights to the use of these lands made them freeholders by inheritance, and whether the lands to which each had a right was of sufficient value. Had the assessor decided in their favour – or, more precisely, had he decided in Cartwright's favour, for it was Cartwright who brought them to the polls – Cartwright would have been returned in place of Milton.[11]

Second, within the body of the electorate as the assessor defined it there was the relative Liberalism or Radicalism of the voters who resided in the parishes from which the largest numbers of voters polled. If the voters who resided in the towns and villages from which 30 or more voters polled had not voted, Cartwright would have been returned in place of Milton. Furthermore, it was to a considerable degree the ratio of voters to population within these towns and villages in the pre-reform period which enabled these voters to return Milton. There is no way of determining whether, if the ratio of voters to population had been equal in all parishes in the county in 1831, Milton would have been returned. There would still be the question whether the effective local influences would have been the same in both cases. But the question illustrates certain of the political consequences of the 40s freehold franchise: voters were principally concentrated in

Table 14

An analysis of the Northamptonshire poll book of 1831

	Voters	Votes for:				Popu-lation (1831)	Ratio, voters to popu-lation
		Cartwright (Tory)	Knightley (Tory)	Althorp (Whig)	Milton (Whig)		
Totals	4,182	1,995	1,401	2,462	2,113	179,300	1:43

Poll of the voters from the parishes from which 30 or more voters polled

	1,569	642	438	1,043	901	54,989	1:35
Contributions (%)							
	37.5	32.2	31.2	42.4	42.6	30.6	

Poll of the voters from the parishes from which 29 or fewer voters polled

	2,613	1,353	963	1,419	1,212	124,311	1:48
Contributions (%)							
	62.5	67.8	68.8	57.6	57.4	69.4	

parishes in which landownership was divided; thus, the effective influences in these parishes were the effective influences in the county as a whole. This is apparent from table 14.

It was principally in the south of the county, among the parishes which were later included in South Northamptonshire, that there was a correlation between division of landownership and political orientation. Nor was the correlation inconsiderable. Indeed, if only those voters had polled in 1831 who resided in the parishes which were later included in the southern division of the county and from which 24 or fewer voters polled – these including roughly half of the voters who polled from this area of the county – Cartwright would have headed the poll. followed by Althorp, Knightley and Milton. But the same conditions did not exist in the area later included in North Northamptonshire. If only those voters had polled in 1831 who resided in the parishes which were later included in the northern division of the county and from which 20 or fewer voters polled – these including roughly half of the voters who polled from this area of the county – the results would have been the same as those provided by the actual poll in the county as a whole. This is apparent from table 15.

In effect, in the north of the county there was little difference between the aggregate behaviour of the voters from the parishes from which small numbers of voters polled in 1831, and the aggregate behaviour of the voters from the parishes from which large numbers of voters polled. True, the voters who polled from the parishes in the former category contributed a slightly larger proportion of the votes which Cartwright and Knightley received, the voters in the latter category contributed a slightly larger proportion of the votes which Althorp and Milton received. But the differences were marginal. In the south of the county, however, the differences were sizeable. The explanation for this presumably lies in large part in the relative numbers, and sizes of Whig estates in the north. In the south of the county – and the same is true for most other counties – there were relatively few estates which provided the means of channelling Whig influences to an estate electorate. Thus, political orientation could often be predicted according to the concentration or division of local landownership. But in the north there were sizeable estates belonging to Earl Fitzwilliam, the Duke of Bedford, Earl Spencer – although his principal estates were in the south, Lord Lilford, Lord Sondes, the Earl of Carysfort, and Lord Bateman – as William Hanbury was known after his elevation to the peerage in 1837.[12] The existence of these estates and the influences which radiated from them, obviously help to explain why, in the north, the differential increments of electoral weight in the different categories of parish between 1831 and 1832 had, in themselves, so little impact upon the effective balance of local power.

In 1831, from the parishes which were later included in the northern division of the county, 1,754 voters polled. From these parishes, in 1832, 3,063 voters polled, an increase of roughly 75 per cent. But in 1832 only 28 per cent more voters polled from the parishes from which 21 or more voters polled in 1831 than had polled from these parishes in 1831. From the other parishes in the area 122 per cent more voters

Table 15

An analysis of the Northamptonshire poll book of 1831

	Voters	Votes for:				Popu-lation (1831)	ratio, voters to popu-lation
		Cartwright (Tory)	Knightley (Tory)	Althorp (Whig)	Milton (Whig)		
Totals	4,182	1,995	1,401	2,462	2,113	179,300	1:43
Area of the Northern division							
	1,754	720	492	1,073	1,030	73,766	1:42
Contribution (%)							
	42.0	36.1	35.2	43.6	48.7	41.2	
21 or more voters							
	883	349	241	556	531	26,020	1:29
Contribution (%)							
	50.3	48.5	49.0	51.8	51.5	35.6	
20 or fewer voters							
	871	371	251	517	499	47,746	1:55
Contribution (%)							
	49.7	51.5	51.0	48.2	48.5	64.6	
Area of the Southern division							
	2,428	1,275	909	1,389	1,083	105,534	1:43
Contribution (%)							
	58.0	63.9	64.8	56.4	51.3	58.8	
25 or more voters							
	1,201	561	373	772	614	41,945	1:35
Contribution (%)							
	49.4	44.0	41.1	55.6	56.7	39.6	
24 or fewer voters							
	1,227	714	536	617	469	63,589	1:52
Contribution (%)							
	50.6	56.0	58.9	44.4	43.3	60.4	

polled in 1832 than had polled in 1831. In consequence of these relative increments there was a greater equality in 1832 than in 1831 between the ratios of voters to population in the different categories of parish. In 1831, in the parishes from which 21 or more voters polled and which were later included in the northern division, the ratio of voters to population was 1:29. In the other parishes in the area the ratio was 1:55. In 1832, in the parishes from which 21 or more voters polled in 1831 the ratio of voters to population was 1:23. But in the other parishes in the area the ratio had dropped far more sharply: it was now 1:25. In the south of the county where Tory influences obviously operated over a far larger proportion of the land surface, such differential increments – if, indeed, they occurred – would presumably have altered the balance of power themselves.[13] By and large, in the counties, the new voters voted as their neighbours voted: the same influences affected them both. Hence, had the number of voters from the two categories of parishes increased in the south of the county in the same way as in the north this would itself help to explain why when Althorp succeeded as third Earl Spencer in 1934, Sir Charles Knightley was returned without opposition to his former seat in the House of Commons. But in the north of the county the proportional contributions which the votes in these different categories of parish made to the totals of votes which the different candidates received in 1832 and 1835 were roughly equal – as they had been in 1831 – to the proportions of the total electorate in the area which they comprised. This is apparent from table 16.

Presumably the circumstances which the evidence suggests help to account for the existence of the evidence: had the proportional contributions of the voters from the different categories of parish in the north been what they were in the south there might have been no contests in the north. This is not to say that many voters in the north did not vote as members of cohesive blocs. Rather, that the orientations of the various electoral blocs in the north were not as predictable in terms of the concentration or division of local landownership as they were in the south.

III

Among the Cartwright Papers in the Northamptonshire Record Office is a list of contributors to the election expenses of the two Tory candidates in 1831.[14] Cartwright and Knightley were themselves down for £1,000 each. Of the remaining £11,110, £5,825 were assigned to men who, or whose heirs, were later identified as significant landowners in parishes in the northern division. In their own ways, most of the voters from these parishes made important contributions to the Tory cause.

The largest contributor was the Duke of Buccleugh. He was down for £2,500. He had property in a number of northern division parishes. In some of these he was the only landowner listed. In others, he was listed as one of several principal landowners. From the parishes for which he was the only landowner listed only one vote was cast for other than Tory or Conservative candidates at any of the contests for

Table 16

An analysis of the North Northamptonshire poll books of 1832 and 1835

1832

	voters	votes for			
		Brudenell (Tory)	Tryon (Tory)	Milton (Whig)	Hanbury (Whig)
total poll	3,063	1,541	1,269	1,562	1,455
Voters from the parishes from which 21 or more voters polled in 1831					
	1,068	524	444	562	536
% contribution	34.8	34.0	35.0	36.0	36.8
Voters from the parishes from which 20 or fewer voters polled in 1831					
	1,995	1,017	825	1,000	919
% contribution	65.2	66.0	65.0	64.0	63.2

1835

	voters	votes for	
		Maunsell (Tory)	Hanbury (Whig)
total poll	3,088	1,841	1,247
Voters from the parishes from which 21 or more voters polled in 1831			
	1,115	661	454
% contribution	36.2	35.9	36.4
Voters from the parishes from which 20 or fewer voters polled in 1831			
	1,973	1,180	793
% contribution	63.8	64.1	63.6

which a pool book is available (group 1 of table 17). If the behaviour of the voters from these parishes is any indication, Buccleugh was opposed to Tryon's candidacy in 1832: large majorities of the voters from these parishes plumped for Brudenell. Such behaviour presumably reflected Buccleugh's reluctance to oppose Fitzwilliam. Votes for Tryon as well as for Brudenell were votes *against* Milton, and thus against the family to which he belonged. But plumped votes for Brudenell were not. In some of the parishes for which Buccleugh was listed as only *one* of the principal landowners the voters' behaviour was similar (group 2). But in others there was no real consensus until 1835 – and in one of them that consensus was lost in 1857 (group 3).

Other peers who owned estates in parishes later included in the northern division contributed to this fund. Down for £500 each were the Marquis of Exeter, the Earl of Cardigan, Lord Brudenell, Cardigan's son and heir, and Lord Carbery. The majorities of the voters in the parishes in which their estates were located made their contributions at the polls (group 4).

Various commoners contributed to this fund too. Among those who did so and who were significant landowners in parishes later included in the northern division were J. W. Russell – down for £500, Sir Justinian Isham and A. E. Young – £200 each, H. H. Hungerford, A. Isted, W. R. Rose and J. Tryon – £100 each, J. D. Smith – £20, and F. G. P. Stopford – £5. In certain of the parishes for which they were listed as principal landowners appropriately oriented consensus generally obtained – appropriate to the assumption of their influence (group 5). In others appropriately oriented consensus did not obtain until 1832 or 1835 (group 6).

There were other parishes where land was owned by other prominent Tories who either did not contribute to this fund or whose contributions were channelled through a local committee – the 'London committee' was down for a total of £2,000. There were the Earls of Dysart, Sandwich and Westmoreland and Lord Willoughby de Brooke, each of whom voted against the Bill. There were Maunsell himself, George Payne, who nominated him, William Whitworth, who seconded Brudenell's nomination in 1832, and who was chairman of the annual dinner of the North Northamptonshire Conservative Association in December, 1835, and Sir John Trollope, who seconded Tryon's nomination in 1832 and who was later returned as Tory Member for South Lincolnshire.[15] Apparently, none of these men contributed to the Cartwright-Knightley fund. But in most of the parishes in the area in which their estates were located majorities of the voters polled for the Tory or Conservative candidates at every contest for which a poll book is available (group 7).

There were other parishes, where the probable sources of influence

1831, 1832, 1835 and 1857

Legend (1832):
- Brudenell and Tryon
- Brudenell
- Brudenell and Milton
- Milton and Hanbury
- divided
- em evidence misplaced
- nv no voters

1832

Legend (1831):
- Cartwright and Knightley
- Cartwright
- Cartwright and Althorp
- Althorp and Milton
- divided
- nv no voters

1831

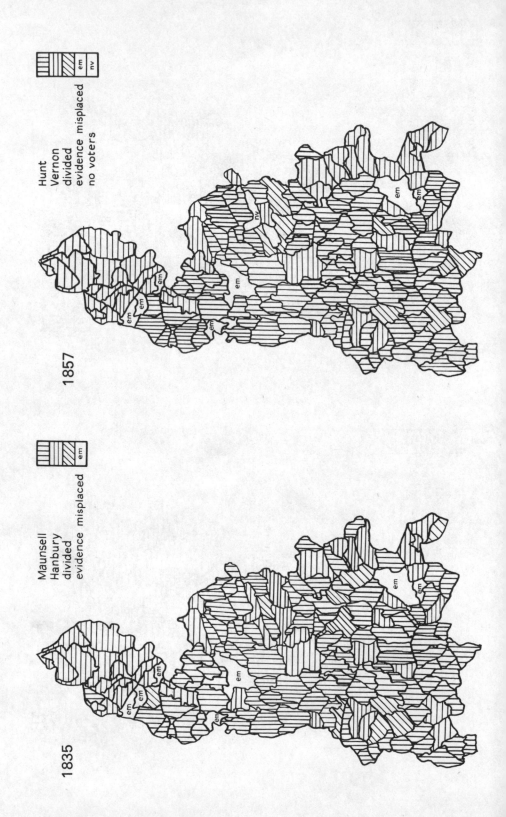

1835

Maunsell
Hanbury
divided
evidence misplaced
em

1857

Hunt
Vernon
divided
evidence misplaced
no voters
em
nv

remain obscure, from which majorities of the voters consistently polled for the Tory or Conservative candidates (group 8), or polled for the Tory or Conservative candidates except in 1831, when they split their votes between Cartwright and Althorp (group 9), or polled for the Tory or Conservative candidates until 1857 (group 10). It is presumably only the lack of relevant evidence that distinguishes these parishes from those in which probable sources of influence can be specified.

Comparable cohesion and continuity of orientation are apparent among majorities of the voters from the parishes in which prominent Whigs were listed among the principal landowners. Few voters from the parishes for which the Duke of Bedford, Earl Fitzwilliam, Earl Spencer. Lord Lilford,[16] Lord Sondes, Lord Carysfort or Lord Bateman were listed as principal landowners voted against their interests (group 11). Somewhat larger proportions of the voters from the parishes for which Sir James Langham,[17] Sir Culling Eardley Smith, and Vernon Smith were subsequently listed as principal landowners voted against theirs (group 12). But the differences were not very great. There were other parishes from which majorities of the voters consistently polled for the Whig or Liberal candidates but in which the probable mechanisms of influence cannot be specified (group 13).

The case of parishes for which the Earl of Winchilsea is listed as a principal landowner is different. In 1832, 1835 and 1857, overwhelming majorities of the voters from these parishes polled for the Tory or Conservative candidates. But in 1831 a smaller majority of them polled for Althorp and Milton (group 14). Their behaviour suggests that Winchilsea did not, in fact, 'lose confidence in the Grey Ministry,' as he put it, until shortly before he made the relevant announcement.[18] On the other hand, their behaviour also suggests that Winchilsea's signature on the petition convening a reform meeting in the county in April notwithstanding, he scarcely exerted himself on behalf of the reform candidates the following month.

There were other parishes from which majorities of the voters polled for Althorp and Milton in 1831 and for the Tory candidates in 1832 and 1835. From some of these they also polled for Hunt, the Conservative, in 1857 (group 15.1). From others they polled for Vernon the Liberal (group 15.2). Unfortunately, with the evidence available it is impossible to discover why the voters from these parishes voted together, and why they changed their orientations when they did.

In certain parishes parallel changes of orientation occurred, but not until 1835. In some of these parishes the new orientations held in 1857 (group 16.1). In others, the earlier orientation was then restored (group 16.2). In one of the former parishes, Cranford St. Andrew, it is

Table 17

Sources of support for the different candidates at the Northamptonshire and North Northamptonshire contests of 1831, 1832, 1835 and 1857

	1831					1832					1835			1857		
landowners and parishes	numbers of voters	Cartwright	Knightley	Althorp	Milton	numbers of voters	Brudenell	Tryon	Milton	Hanbury	numbers of voters	Maunsell	Hanbury	numbers of voters	Hunt	Vernon
1 Duke of Buccleugh: principal landowner																
Barnwell All Saints	—	—	—	—	—	3	3	—	—	—	3	3	—	3	3	—
Barnwell St. Andrew	1	1	1	—	—	4	4	2	—	—	5	5	—	3	3	—
Hemington	—	—	—	—	—	3	3	1	—	—	3	3	—	4	4	—
Luddington	1	1	1	—	—	3	3	3	—	—	1	1	—	1	1	—
Newton	—	—	—	—	—	6	6	1	—	—	5	5	—	4	4	—
Little Oakley	—	—	—	—	—	3	3	—	—	—	3	3	—	2	2	—
Warkton	1	1	1	—	—	4	4	1	—	1	3	3	—	4	4	—
Weekley	1	1	—	—	—	4	4	1	—	—	11	11	—	5	5	—
Group 1	4	4	3	—	—	30	30	8	—	1	34	34	—	26	26	—
2 Duke of Buccleugh: one of several landowners																
Broughton	14	12	5	5	4	22	14	16	6	7	20	16	4	35	27	8
Grafton Underwood	—	—	—	—	—	3	3	—	—	—	3	3	—	4	3	1

Polebrook cum Armston	17	10	3	5	7	19	14	9	6	5	18	14	4	16	16	—
Group 2	31	22	8	10	11	44	31	25	12	12	41	33	8	55	46	9
3 Duke of Buccleugh: one of several landowners																
Stanion	5	4	2	2	1	9	7	4	2	3	8	7	1	7	5	2
Twywell	6	4	4	2	2	9	5	5	4	4	8	8	—	6	6	—
Winwick	9	6	5	2	4	17	8	9	9	6	19	15	4	10	4	6
Group 3	20	14	11	6	7	35	20	18	15	13	35	30	5	23	15	8
4 Marquis of Exeter: principal landowner and one of several																
Barnack	9	5	5	4	4	19	18	18	1	1	17	17	—	15	15	—
Collyweston	4	4	4	—	1	9	8	7	1	1	13	12	1	17	16	1
Easton-on-the-Hill	25	24	22	1	1	48	48	48	—	—	45	44	1	47	41	6
King's Cliffe	15	12	7	3	4	70	57	53	13	12	64	56	8	35	32	3
Stamford St. Martin	24	15	15	8	9	25	15	16	10	8	24	18	6	16	14	2
Wakerley	1	1	1	—	—	5	3	4	4	1	4	3	1	5	5	—
Whittering	1	1	1	—	—	8	8	8	—	—	8	8	—	8	8	—
Woothorpe	3	2	2	1	1	7	4	5	2	2	9	7	2	4	4	—
	80	64	57	17	19	191	161	159	28	25	184	165	19	159	147	12

Table 17 continued on next page

Table 17 (continued)

landowners and parishes	1831					1832					1835			1857		
	numbers of voters	Cartwright	Knightley	Althorp	Milton	numbers of voters	Brudenell	Tryon	Milton	Hanbury	numbers of voters	Maunsell	Hanbury	numbers of voters	Hunt	Vernon
4 (continued) Earl of Cardigan: principal landowner and one of several																
Deene	1	1	1	—	—	4	4	2	—	—	4	4	—	5	5	—
Deenethorpe	—	—	—	—	—	6	5	1	—	—	7	7	—	5	5	—
Glapthorne	3	3	3	—	—	9	7	3	2	1	5	5	—	8	7	1
Corby	—	—	—	—	—	16	14	11	3	3	17	15	2	19	16	3
	4	4	4	—	—	35	30	17	5	4	33	31	2	37	33	4
Lord Carberry Laxton	1	1	1	—	—	1	1	1	—	—	3	3	—	2	2	—
Group 4	36	69	62	17	18	227	192	177	34	30	220	199	21	198	182	16

5 J. W. Russell																
Benefield	2	1	1	1	1	17	16	–	1	1	20	18	2	20	19	1
Sir Justinian Isham																
Lamport	3	3	3	–	–	8	8	7	1	–	12	12	–	5	5	–
A. E. Young																
Orlingbury	4	2	2	2	2	8	7	7	1	1	11	10	1	6	5	1
H. H. Hungerford																
Dingley	3	3	0	1	–	10	10	9	1	1	10	9	1	7	6	1
Draughton	–	–	–	–	–	6	6	6	–	–	5	5	–	4	4	–
East Farndon	23	18	13	7	5	26	20	16	7	7	24	18	6	23	19	4
Maydwell	1	1	1	–	–	8	8	7	–	–	10	10	–	8	7	1
Orton	–	–	–	–	–	5	5	2	–	–	5	5	–	3	3	–
A. Isted																
Ecton	2	2	1	1	–	18	17	15	1	2	17	16	1	18	15	3
W. R. Rose																
Cranley	5	5	4	–	–	11	10	10	–	–	12	12	–	6	6	–
J. Tryon																
Bulwick	6	6	4	–	–	9	8	9	1	–	11	11	–	9	9	–
Harringworth	2	1	1	1	1	11	9	10	1	1	16	15	1	15	15	–
F. G. P. Stopford																
Lowick	4	4	4	–	–	12	12	12	–	–	11	11	–	9	9	–
Slipton	1	1	1	–	–	3	3	3	–	–	4	4	–	3	3	–
Group 5	56	47	37	12	9	152	139	113	14	12	168	156	12	136	125	11

Table 17 continued on next page

Table 17 (continued)

landowners and parishes	1831 numbers of voters	Cartwright	Knightley	Allhorp	Milton	1832 numbers of voters	Brudenell	Tryon	Milton	Hanbury	1835 numbers of voters	Maunsell	Hanbury	1857 numbers of voters	Hunt	Vernon
6 J. W. Russell																
Oundle	59	21	12	38	37	87	50	39	40	36	79	44	35	52	35	17
A. E. Young																
Little Harroden	15	6	5	7	9	21	12	8	13	8	19	11	8	11	7	4
Sir Justinian Isham																
Haslebeech	2	1	–	2	1	10	7	8	1	3	11	9	2	7	6	1
Old	23	15	9	13	9	31	19	18	11	13	31	19	12	17	10	7
F. G. P. Stopford																
Islip	10	4	2	5	6	16	9	10	7	6	15	10	5	9	9	–
Woodford	23	12	11	9	10	35	22	16	13	14	30	21	9	26	19	7
Group 6	134	59	39	74	72	200	119	99	85	80	185	114	71	122	86	36
7 Earl of Dysart																
Harrington	–	–	–	–	–	7	7	7	–	–	7	7	–	6	5	1
Earl of Sandwich																
Thurning	–	–	–	–	–	1	1	–	–	–	3	3	–	4	4	–

Earl of Westmoreland																
Apethorpe	1	1	1	–	–	5	5	1	–	–	5	5	–	7	7	–
Cotterstock	4	4	4	–	–	8	8	5	–	–	9	9	–	7	7	–
Nassington	6	5	5	1	1	24	22	20	2	2	21	20	1	17	17	1
Tansor	7	4	1	3	3	8	7	6	–	1	12	11	1	11	10	1
Woodnewton	5	5	4	–	–	18	16	12	2	1	16	16	–	12	12	1
Yarwell	–	–	–	–	–	8	7	7	1	1	10	9	1	9	8	1
Lord Willoughby de Brooke																
Sulby	3	3	2	1	–	15	12	13	3	2	15	10	5	7	7	–
T. P. Maunsell																
Thorpe Malsor	7	4	4	3	3	11	10	10	–	1	8	7	1	11	11	–
Rothwell	102	60	43	51	40	99	56	39	44	45	100	69	31	60	42	18
G. Payne																
Sibbertoft	19	11	6	10	8	28	18	16	9	11	28	17	11	23	16	7
W. Whitworth																
Earl's Barton	22	13	10	9	10	40	32	32	8	8	41	35	6	49	26	23
Group 7	176	110	80	78	65	272	201	168	69	72	275	218	57	223	172	51
8																
Great Addington	6	5	3	1	1	12	8	8	3	4	16	8	8	9	9	2
Little Addington	3	2	2	–	1	8	6	6	2	2	9	6	3	9	7	2
Arthlingworth	5	5	2	2	–	9	7	3	1	5	8	7	1	9	8	1
Ashley	14	14	9	3	–	23	20	11	2	3	24	21	3	15	13	2
Carlton	–	–	–	–	–	4	4	2	–	–	7	7	–	2	2	–
Catworth	6	6	4	–	–	–	–	–	–	–	9	9	–	2	2	–
Cottingham	2	2	2	–	–	16	14	3	6	2	16	14	2	14	8	6
Cransley	5	5	4	–	–	11	10	10	–	–	12	12	–	9	9	–
Finshade	–	–	–	–	–	1	1	1	–	–	1	1	–	–	–	–

Table 17 continued on next page

Table 17 (continued)

landowners and parishes	1831 numbers of voters	Cartwright	Knightley	Alborp	Milton	1832 numbers of voters	Brudenell	Tryon	Milton	Hanbury	1835 numbers of voters	Maunsell	Hanbury	1857 numbers of voters	Hunt	Vernon
8 (continued)																
Glendon and Barford	3	3	3	–	–	4	3	1	1	1	3	3	–	3	3	–
Hardwick	–	–	3	–	–	1	1	1	–	–	2	2	–	2	2	–
Hannington	10	7	4	4	3	14	8	5	6	6	16	10	6	12	9	3
Great Oatley	–	–	1	–	–	5	4	2	1	1	3	3	–	7	5	2
Rushton	1	–	–	–	–	14	14	13	–	1	13	13	–	10	9	1
Stoke Doyle	4	4	3	1	–	6	6	5	–	–	7	7	–	6	6	6
Wadenhoe	2	–	1	1	1	4	2	1	1	1	7	3	–	3	3	3
Ashton	–	–	–	1	–	11	8	10	3	1	13	13	–	11	10	1
Barton Seagrave	2	2	2	–	–	5	4	2	–	1	7	6	1	7	5	2
Group 8	63	57	40	11	6	148	120	84	26	28	169	145	24	130	108	22
9																
Little Bowden	25	17	7	16	7	28	21	15	10	10	25	18	7	24	14	10
Geddington	16	9	4	9	7	18	14	8	4	5	22	20	2	17	14	3
Marston Thrussell	10	5	3	7	5	18	14	14	4	4	17	16	1	12	12	1
Great Oxenden	20	10	8	12	9	18	14	13	3	6	21	17	4	8	6	2
Sutton Bassett	5	4	2	3	–	5	4	1	3	1	5	4	1	3	3	–
Walgrave	14	10	5	8	4	31	22	13	10	11	36	25	11	25	19	6
Group 9	90	55	29	55	32	118	89	64	34	37	126	100	26	89	68	21

Brixworth	23	21	44	12	42	54	17	21	22	29	45	8	11	10	18	26
Faxton	2	–	2	–	4	4	1	1	1	3	3	–	–	–	–	–
Fotheringay	4	2	6	–	9	9	–	–	7	7	7	–	–	–	–	–
Group 10	29	23	52	12	55	67	18	22	30	39	55	8	11	10	18	26
11 Earl Fitzwilliam																
Ailsworth	12	–	12	7	1	8	9	10	–	–	10	3	3	–	–	3
Castor cum Milton	30	–	30	17	4	21	17	22	1	1	22	10	10	2	3	13
Chelveston cum Caldecote	7	4	11	6	2	8	6	10	1	2	10	5	5	–	–	5
Deeping Gate	16	3	19	16	5	21	19	21	4	2	23	16	13	3	3	19
Etton and Woodcroft	5	–	5	8	1	9	4	4	1	1	5	5	3	–	–	5
Great Harroden	6	–	6	5	–	5	6	6	–	–	6	1	1	–	–	1
Helpstone	25	4	29	16	3	19	16	19	6	3	23	21	20	2	2	23
Higham Ferrers	16	–	16	8	–	8	9	10	–	1	10	5	3	1	1	6
Lutton	11	–	11	8	1	9	6	6	–	1	7	4	4	–	–	4
Marholm	4	–	4	4	–	4	5	5	–	–	5	1	1	–	–	1
Maxey	5	–	5	15	5	20	14	17	6	1	20	11	11	–	–	11
Upton	4	1	5	3	–	3	3	3	–	–	3	–	–	–	–	–
Earl Fitzwilliam	141	12	153	113	22	135	114	133	19	11	144	82	74	8	9	91
Duke of Bedford																
Eye	11	13	24	30	14	44	28	33	6	6	37	6	6	2	2	8
Stibbington & Wansford	3	1	4	11	3	14	11	11	2	2	13	1	1	–	–	1
Thornyhaugh	4	–	4	3	–	3	4	5	1	–	5	6	6	–	1	7
Duke of Bedford	18	14	32	44	17	61	43	49	9	8	55	13	13	2	3	16

Table 17 continued on next page

Table 17 (continued)

landowners and parishes	1831 numbers of voters	Cartwright	Knightley	Althorp	Milton	1832 numbers of voters	Brudenell	Tryon	Milton	Hanbury	1835 numbers of voters	Maunsell	Hanbury	1857 numbers of voters	Hunt	Vernon
11 (continued)																
Lord Lilford																
Aldwinkle	17	–	–	14	15	29	4	5	25	24	30	8	22	26	13	13
Tichmarsh	30	4	3	26	26	39	8	7	32	28	35	13	22	27	12	15
Lord Lilford	47	4	3	40	41	68	12	12	57	52	65	21	44	53	25	28
Lord Bateman																
Kelmarsh	2	1	1	1	1	9	2	1	5	7	11	1	10	5	3	2
Earl Spencer																
Strixton	–	–	–	–	–	5	–	–	5	5	4	–	4	2	–	2
Lord Carysford																
Warmington	31	7	4	23	25	43	6	9	37	34	36	11	25	32	6	26
Lord Sondes																
Kettering	2	–	1	1	2	102	27	10	85	83	118	41	77	79	34	45
Rockingham	–	–	–	–	–	3	–	–	3	3	3	–	3	2	–	2
Stoke Albany	17	7	6	10	10	17	5	3	13	12	21	5	16	12	9	3
Wilbarston	17	4	3	14	13	38	10	8	30	27	37	18	19	25	11	14
Lord Sondes	36	11	10	25	25	160	42	21	131	125	179	64	115	118	54	64

12																
Sir James Langham Raunds	56	6	2	41	50	65	10	8	55	55	67	31	36	60	16	44
Sir Culling Eardley Smith Newborough with Borough Fen	2	1	1	1	1	50	13	14	37	32	63	20	43	69	29	40
Vernon Smith																
Brigstock	14	2	–	11	12	38	10	7	27	28	36	8	28	23	9	14
Pilton	1	–	–	1	1	3	–	1	3	2	4	–	4	4	2	2
Group 12	73	9	3	54	64	156	33	30	122	117	170	59	111	156	56	100
13																
Bozeat	14	4	3	9	10	35	9	13	26	21	32	15	17	30	10	20
Great Doddington	8	1	–	8	7	19	8	4	14	11	15	6	9	13	–	13
Glinton	14	1	–	13	13	15	–	1	15	14	22	3	19	20	5	15
Paston	9	–	–	7	9	17	2	2	15	15	10	4	6	5	–	5
Peakirk	1	–	–	1	1	12	–	–	12	12	11	1	10	14	2	12
Peterborough	51	9	8	43	43	65	10	7	58	51	65	29	36	102	18	84
Rushden	13	4	3	8	9	40	16	14	28	21	38	13	25	39	15	24
Sywell	3	1	1	2	2	8	3	3	4	5	6	3	3	5	–	5
Werrington	4	–	–	3	4	16	3	2	14	13	13	–	13	14	1	13
Wollaston	44	13	6	35	31	60	15	14	45	44	48	14	34	42	12	30
Gunthorpe	1	–	–	1	1	3	–	–	3	3	3	–	3	5	–	5
Hoothorpe	1	–	–	1	1	3	–	–	3	3	3	–	3	1	–	1
Group 13	163	33	21	136	131	293	66	60	237	213	266	88	178	290	63	227

Table 17 continued on next page

Table 17 (continued)

landowners and parishes	1831					1832					1835			1857		
	numbers of voters	Cartwright	Knightley	Althorp	Milton	numbers of voters	Brudenell	Tryon	Milton	Hanbury	numbers of voters	Maunsell	Hanbury	numbers of voters	Hunt	Vernon
14 Earl of Winchilsea																
Gretton	21	9	6	13	12	34	25	27	9	7	29	28	1	40	34	6
Weldon	14	7	4	8	7	22	20	19	3	2	23	21	2	22	19	3
Group 14	35	16	10	21	19	56	45	46	12	9	52	49	3	62	53	9
15.1																
Ashton (Polebrook Hundred)	3	1	1	2	2	6	6	1	–	–	8	8		4	4	–
Denford	10	4	1	7	7	10	8	7	3	2	9	8	1	8	7	1
Hargreave	20	7	6	11	13	21	13	13	8	7	21	16	5	10	7	3
Scaldwell	13	5	1	10	7	22	11	11	10	11	18	12	6	15	8	7
Thrapston	44	19	12	28	25	63	37	26	25	24	50	33	17	43	28	15
Weston cum Welland	9	5	3	6	4	13	7	8	6	5	10	8	2	6	6	–
15.1	99	41	24	64	58	135	82	66	52	49	116	85	31	86	60	26

15.2																
Newton Bromshold	3	–	–	3	3	11	10	7	2	1	9	8	1	8	2	6
Pytchley	6	2	2	4	4	13	9	11	3	2	13	12	1	10	4	6
15.2	9	2	2	7	7	24	19	18	5	3	22	20	2	18	6	12
Group 15	108	43	26	71	65	159	101	84	57	52	138	105	33	104	66	38
16.1																
Burton Latimer	27	6	4	21	22	35	16	16	17	18	45	26	19	26	15	11
Clapton	1	–	–	1	1	4	2	1	2	2	6	5	1	4	4	–
Cranford St. Andrew	4	1	–	3	3	4	1	–	3	2	5	4	1	5	5	–
Desborough	40	13	7	31	24	40	18	10	20	26	45	24	21	32	17	15
Thingdon	36	15	12	21	21	43	20	19	23	23	51	31	20	48	28	20
16.1	108	35	23	77	71	126	57	46	65	71	152	90	62	115	69	46
16.2																
Holcot	16	4	1	14	12	18	10	7	9	10	20	12	8	17	7	10
Irchester	12	3	1	9	9	18	8	4	14	10	20	13	7	15	2	13
Northborough	8	1	1	5	7	9	2	2	8	6	9	6	3	13	5	8
Ringstead	21	7	5	15	14	20	10	5	11	10	29	17	12	25	11	14
Stanwick	27	3	2	19	24	20	8	4	15	11	23	16	7	16	5	11
16.2	84	18	10	62	66	85	38	22	57	47	101	64	37	86	30	56
Group 16	182	53	33	139	137	211	95	68	122	118	253	154	99	201	99	102

Table 17 continued on next page

Table 17 (continued)

landowners and parishes	1831					1832					1835			1857		
	numbers of voters	Cartwright	Knigbtley	Altborp	Milton	numbers of voters	Brudenell	Tryon	Milton	Hanbury	numbers of voters	Mansell	Hanbury	numbers of voters	Hunt	Vernon
17																
Blatherwycke	2	–	–	2	2	5	–	–	5	5	4	–	4	2	2	–
Clipston	28	5	2	24	24	44	10	10	34	34	49	22	27	37	21	16
Cranford St. John	4	1	1	3	3	6	–	–	6	6	7	2	5	5	5	–
Irthlingborough	29	7	5	18	22	48	12	9	38	31	42	20	22	38	24	14
Loddington	5	1	1	4	4	10	5	5	5	5	9	3	6	8	5	3
Middleton	5	3	–	5	2	12	7	1	7	5	9	4	5	6	5	1
Southorpe	–	–	–	–	–	7	2	4	5	3	2	1	1	9	9	–
Group 17	73	17	9	56	57	132	36	29	100	89	122	52	70	105	71	34
18.1																
Lilford cum Wigsthorpe	1	1	–	–	–	–	–	–	–	–	1	–	1	–	–	–
Sudborough	2	2	2	–	–	9	5	1	7	4	7	2	5	3	2	1
18.1	3	3	2	–	–	9	5	1	7	4	8	2	6	3	2	1

18.2																
Braybrook	22	11	7	15	11	28	14	14	15	12	29	15	14	16	12	4
Mear's Ashby	15	11	5	7	4	20	8	7	13	11	19	11	8	22	19	3
18.2	37	22	12	22	15	48	22	21	28	23	48	26	22	38	31	7
18.3																
Brampton Ash	3	2	2	1	–	10	5	5	5	5	10	5	5	4	–	4
Eaton Maudit	–	1	–	–	–	3	2	2	1	1	2	1	1	1	–	1
Thorpe Achurch	1	1	–	–	–	4	2	1	2	2	4	2	2	4	–	4
18.3	4	3	2	1	–	17	9	8	8	8	16	8	8	9	–	9
18.4																
Isham	4	–	–	3	4	13	6	6	7	6	13	5	8	7	4	3
18.4	4	–	–	3	4	13	6	6	7	6	13	5	8	7	4	3
Group 18	48	28	16	26	19	87	42	36	50	41	85	41	44	57	37	20

reasonably clear what conditioned local electoral agreement, the orientation in 1831 and 1832, and the change of allegiance between 1832 and 1835. It was there that the Robinson estates were located. Sir George Robinson, sixth baronet, sat as Whig Member for Northampton borough from 1826 to 1832. His nephew and heir presumptive, the Reverend George Robinson, nominated Milton in 1832. Three years later, after succeeding his uncle as seventh baronet, the Reverend Sir George Robinson declared from the hustings that he was 'satisfied' with Milton, the son of his previous nominee.[19] But the following December he supported Maunsell.[20] He probably deserted Whigs because while he was an ardent protectionist the Fitzwilliam clan were ardent freetraders.[21] In effect, the question raised by Robinson's behaviour in 1835 is not so much why he supported Maunsell in December as why he declared he was 'satisfied' with Milton in January. The answer to this question, taken together with our knowledge of the Robinson influence in Cranford St. Andrew, would tell us why majorities of the voters from Cranford St. Andrew polled for Milton and Althorp in 1831, for Milton in 1832, and for Maunsell in 1835. Unfortunately, however, the available evidence it is impossible to explain the behaviour of the voters from those other parishes where the majorities did change their orientations at this time – or even why they tended to vote in agreement with one another.

There were other parishes, again, from which majorities of the voters polled for the Whig candidates in 1831, 1832 and 1835 and for Hunt the Conservative in 1857 (group 17). In one of these, Blatherwycke, it is fairly clear what conditioned local electoral agreement, the orientation of 1831, 1832 and 1835, and the change of allegience between 1835 and 1857. It was there the O'Brien estates were located. Both in 1832 and 1835 Stafford O'Brien nominated Hanbury. In 1841, however, after Maidstone resigned, O'Brien was returned without a contest as Protectionist Member for the division. Unfortunately, with the evidence now available, it is impossible to explain the behaviour of the voters from these other parishes where the majorities changed their allegiance between 1835 and 1857 – or even why they tended to vote in agreement with one another.

In a few other parishes majorities of the voters took other paths (group 18). But the voters from these parishes only represented small proportions of the total electorate in the division.

IV

By 1835 the basis of Whig power in North Northamptonshire had been destroyed. This is evident from the returns of Althorp and Milton in 1831. Some of the mechanisms responsible for this are clear, and are distinguishable from one another.

In the first place, in certain parishes changes of orientation in favour of the Tory candidates occurred between 1831 and 1832 (see group 1 of table 18). In certain other similar parishes changes occurred between 1832 and 1835 (group 2). But no comparable changes occurred in favour of the Whig candidates. In the second place, in the consistently Tory parishes of the early thirties – those from which majorities of the voters polled for Cartwright and Knightley, or Cartwright alone, in 1831, for Brudenell and Tryon, or Brudenell alone, in 1832, and for Maunsell in 1835 – significant gains occurred in the cohesion of the voters (group 3). But in the consistently Whig parishes of the early 'thirties no comparable changes (group 4). Indeed, in some of these parishes the voters showed less consensus in 1835 than in 1831 or 1832.

Table 18

An analysis of the changing bases of power in North Northamptonshire, 1831–1835

	1831					1832					1835		
	numbers of voters	*Cartwright*	*Knightley*	*Althorp*	*Milton*	*numbers of voters*	*Brudenell*	*Tryon*	*Milton*	*Hanbury*	*numbers of voters*	*Maunsell*	*Hanbury*
Group 1 (including the parishes in groups 6, 14 and 15 of table 16)													
	277	118	75	166	156	415	265	229	154	141	375	268	107
%s	17.4	42.6	27.1	59.9	56.2	14.7	63.8	55.4	37.1	34.0	13.1	71.4	28.6
Group 2 (including the parishes in group 16 of table 16)													
	182	53	33	139	137	211	95	68	122	118	253	154	99
%s	11.4	29.1	18.1	76.3	75.2	7.4	45.0	32.2	57.8	55.9	8.8	60.8	39.2
Group 3 (including the parishes in groups 1–5 and.7–10 of table 16)													
	552	396	280	200	156	1,054	834	679	226	222	1,104	939	165
%s	34.7	71.7	50.7	36.2	28.2	37.2	79.1	64.4	21.4	21.0	38.5	85.0	15.0
Group 4 (including the parishes in groups 11, 12, 13 and 17 of table 16)													
	532	94	61	416	439	1,065	216	190	876	799	1,049	335	714
%s	33.4	17.6	11.4	78.2	82.5	37.6	20.3	17.8	82.1	75.0	36.6	32.0	68.0
Group 5 (including the parishes in group 18 of table 16)													
	48	28	16	26	19	87	42	36	50	41	85	41	44
%s	3.0	58.3	33.3	54.2	39.5	3.0	48.2	41.3	57.4	47.1	3.0	48.2	51.8
totals	1,591	689	465	947	907	2,832	1,452	1,202	1,428	1,321	2,866	1,737	1,129
%s	99.9	43.3	29.2	59.5	57.0	99.9	51.2	42.4	50.4	46.6	99.9	60.6	39.4

Then, too, changes occurred in the relative electoral importance of the different parish groups. But these latter changes contributed far less than the others to the overall change in the balance of political power in the area. Indeed, initially their impetus ran counter to that of the others. This was probably the result of the number and size of Whig estates in the area.

In most counties Whig strength was principally a function of the orientation of influence in those parishes in which landownership was most widely divided — these the parishes in which, as a rule, the smallest increments of electoral strength occurred between 1831 and 1832. But in North Northamptonshire the number and size of Whig estates provided the means by which Whig influences could be brought to bear upon the voters in many of the parishes in which the largest increases in electoral strength occurred. In most counties between 1831 and 1832 radical changes took place in the ratio of voters to population in the different categories of parish and this greatly weakened the relative electoral weights of the parishes from which the largest numbers of voters polled in the pre-reform period. As a rule, because of the influences in these different categories of parish, these changes of relative electoral weight had considerable impact upon the effective balance of political power. But this was not the case in North Northamptonshire. Indeed, between 1831 and 1832 the increases in electoral weight in North Northamptonshire were slightly larger in the consistently Whig parishes than they were in the consistently Tory parishes. Exactly twice as many voters polled from the former in 1832 as in 1831. From the latter the average increment of electoral strength was only some 91 per cent. From the consistently Whig parishes, however — and this obviously reflects the impact of the same varieties of factor to which the declining consensus of the voters from these parishes between 1832 and 1835 should be attributed — slightly fewer voters polled in 1835 than polled in 1832. From the consistently Tory parishes, on the other hand, not only was consensus greater in 1835; slightly more voters polled. Voluntary political activities must have been to some extent responsible for these phenomena — the varieties of activity to which Maunsell referred, in 1835, when he noted the importance of 'registration' in securing his own return. [22]

The number and size of Whig estates probably affected the situation in other ways too. Certain Tories were obviously reluctant to use their own influences for 'party' purposes in 1831 and 1832. They were presumably reluctant to oppose Althorp or Milton or the families to which they belonged. Almost 72 per cent of the voters from the consistently Tory parishes voted for Cartwright in 1831, only some 50 per cent for Knightley. Approximately 80 per cent of the voters from these parishes voted for Brudenell in 1832, only some 64 per cent for

Tryon (group 3 of table 18). Nor should it be said that Knightley and Tryon were simply 'bad' candidates. The split votes across 'party' lines and the plumped votes for Cartwright and Brudenell were far too geographically discrete, far too much the attributes of specific parishes. But similar restraint did not obtain in the consistently Whig parishes. In 1831, some 82 per cent of the voters from these parishes voted for Milton, some 78 per cent for Althorp. In 1832, again, some 82 per cent of the voters from these parishes voted for Milton, 75 per cent for Hanbury (group 4). It is tempting to assume that the slightly increased margin which Milton enjoyed over Hanbury in these parishes in 1832 compared with that which he enjoyed over Althorp in 1831 is attributable to Althorp's status as a member of the Spencer family. But this much is clear. In 1831, the parishes from which majorities of the voters polled for Milton and Althorp contained well over 60 per cent of the voters in the area. As a result, the overall pluralities which Milton and Althorp received from the voters in the area were independent of the votes they received from other parishes. But in 1832 Milton's return was largely attributable to the refusal of certain Tories to use their influences against him. Hence the importance of the series of deaths in the Fitzwilliam family which left them without a champion of their own in December 1835. Hence, too, the importance of the efforts of the more 'party' oriented Tories to induce their neighbours to use their influences for 'party' purposes.

In October, 1831, while the tempo of radical agitation was rising, Cartwright and Knightley began the campaign. Together with Sir Henry Gunning and William Willes, Cartwright's son-in-law, they agreed to extend an interest-free loan to Willoughby Marshall Smithson to enable him to start a newspaper in the county in the interests of the 'High Tory Party.[23] Thus was the *Northampton Herald* begun. Later, the operating deficit of the paper was referred to as part of the cost of trying to defeat Milton in 1832.[24] The men who launched the paper were later joined by others to form the Conservative Club which defrayed the expenses of electoral registration in the northern division.[25] It was the same men, again, who formed the Northamptonshire Association for the Protection of Agriculture. The Northamptonshire Association was one of those 'CONSERVATIVE, or better still, AGRICULTURAL ASSOCIATIONS', which, ostensibly, helped the Tories increase their share of the county representation in 1835.[26] It was presumably organized as a means of challenging the Fitzwilliam influence in the county. However – and it helps to reveal the nature of this influence, initially the challenge was somewhat turned against the challengers.

At the best of times the free-trade enthusiasms of the Fitzwilliam clan severely strained their relations with some of their friends and neighbours. In 1830 Rooper told Milton that his anti-corn law position was distinctly unpopular in Huntingdonshire.[27] The following year, when Hanbury was being considered as a possible co-candidate with Althorp in Northamptonshire, Sir John Trollope explained to Milton that he would be happy to join in trying to replace Cartwright with Hanbury 'provided Hanbury supports the present corn law'.[28] Trollope's proviso obviously indicates the fissure into which various Tories tried to drive a wedge – men like Cartwright, permanent chairman of the Northamptonshire Association for the Protection of Agriculture, the Earl of Westmoreland, the president of the Association, and Gunning, the chairman of the first annual meeting.[29] Hence their dilemma when, after they had followed normal practice and invited all noblemen and large landowners in the county to join the organization they were founding, they received Milton's note accepting their invitation.

As a member of the Association later explained, had the provisional committee *not* issued the original invitation they would have been charged with 'political bias'. Invitations were sent out, 'presuming that no gentleman would accept . . . who was not prepared at the same time, to adopt the declarations of the society'.[30] But when Milton accepted while indicating his opposition to the corn laws, and when those who had invited him to join refused to allow him to join, the charge of political bias was made from the other side. In the light of Milton's importance the question soon became a matter of public discussion. Some argued that Milton should have been allowed to join so that he would learn the errors of his ways.[31] Others, realizing, perhaps, the improbability of such an outcome, tried to resolve the conflicts between their relations with the Fitzwilliam family and their positions on the corn laws by resigning from the Association. One who did so was the Reverend Sir George Robinson.

In 1832 Robinson nominated Charles William Wentworth. In January 1835, the month in which he resigned from the Northamptonshire Association for the Protection of Agriculture, he announced that he was 'satisfied' with William Charles Wentworth, the son of his former nominee.[32] Such 'satisfaction' was presumably a measure of friendship. It could obviously not have been a measure of agreement on those questions of public policy which were becoming increasingly important and which had induced him to join the Northamptonshire Association. Thus, at the by-election the following autumn which followed the death of William Charles Wentworth, there was more to Robinson's support for Maunsell than the fact that Hanbury's name was not Fitzwilliam. While Milton's death may have released Robinson from a personal or family loyalty the loyalty itself had clearly been under strain for quite some time. The decline in the numbers of men from the consistently Whig parishes who voted between 1832 and 1835 and in the proportions of these who voted for Hanbury are indications that others besides Robinson had been released from such loyalties. Without the support which these loyalties provided the Whigs no longer had a chance. A contest occurred in the division in 1837 which obviously served to confirm this. Thereafter, no serious contest took place in the county for twenty years.

Part II

Towards the social definition of constituencies

4

The first Reform Act

I

It is, of course, impossible to say whether Wellington really believed every one of the public statements he made during the reform crisis. But whether he believed them or not – whether all were sincerely made or whether some were made with a consciously instrumental intent – they should be read in the context of the problems he faced when he made them.

There were two principal problems. The first was parliamentary: how to defeat the Bill. The second was both parliamentary and extra-parliamentary: how to restore the Tory coalition of the twenties. However, the evidence which various county poll books contain suggests that these problems were closely related. In large measure, the return of anti-Wellingtonian candidates in 1830 and 1831 and the ultimate introduction of the Bill resulted from numerous urban leaders deciding to exploit their potential powers within the pre-reform constituency structure. They were also the result of the breakdown of the Tory coalition. Essentially the coalition collapsed because spokesmen for the landed interest lost confidence in the policies of Wellington's Government, and because of the growing belief that the powers of government, alias crown, had been used tyrannically, for the private benefit of the members of the Government, and to implement policies which were injurious to the landed interest. In these circumstances, Wellington's only hope of restoring the coalition lay in convincing the various defectors of either of two propositions– ideally, that his own Government had been not tyrannical but strong, and had used its strength to implement policies which were both politically necessary and really favourable to the landed interest, or, at the very least, that the Grey Ministry was a far greater danger to the landed interest than his own Government had ever been. This is why the interpretation of the Bill which the Grey Ministry had introduced was of such importance.

The interpretation on which Wellington and most of his former colleagues insisted is that contained in his speech of 4 October 1831. Here, he emphasized those provisions of the Bill by which the close boroughs would be disfranchised, various towns enfranchised, and the electorate (especially, the borough electorate) enlarged. He argued that such provisions would inevitably destroy the only supports on which the landed interest could depend. Inevitably, he claimed, the Members for the new boroughs and for many of the old boroughs would be Radical because the proposed £10-household voters would be Radical. Thus, since the close boroughs would be gone, the only possible anti-Radical constituencies to remain would be the counties. And, he went on, in a statement, which has often been quoted in part but seldom in its entirety,

> I doubt the county representation, as it stands at present, being capable of protecting the landed interest of the country without the assistance of the Members of the close boroughs. These are the true protectors of the landed interest of the country. The increase of manufactures and commerce, has given great influence to the inhabitants of towns in all county elections.[1]

Furthermore, according to Wellington, the changes in the county constituencies which the Bill proposed would inevitably *increase* the strength of urban influences in the counties. From this he concluded,

> The Members for counties will, therefore, be nearly as much under the control of constituencies residing in towns, as the Members for the towns themselves will.[2]

In effect, then, the proportional increase in the number of county Members which the Bill proposed would merely aggravate the problems of the landed interest. Having reached this conclusion there was a further one: such a radical reform must be the prelude to further Radical legislation.[3]

Obviously, if Wellington was right in saying that the social role of the close boroughs was largely a function of the growing 'influence . . . [of] the inhabitants of towns in all county elections', then, if nothing were done to limit the influence of the urban voters in the counties, the abolition of the close boroughs would seriously alter the balance of power in the State between the landed and urban interests. But the Grey Ministry *did* propose to limit the influence of urban voters in the counties. In effect, by emphasizing certain provisions and by ignoring certain others, Wellington was distorting the essential nature of the Bill. It presumably testifies to the general respect in which Wellington has been held by subsequent historians that they, too, have tended to emphasize the provisions he emphasized and ignore those he ignored. However, as Lord John Russell explained while introducing the Bill in March, 1831, 'At the same time that the towns will have themselves a proper share in the representation, we do not intend that they shall interfere with the representation of the counties.'[4]

In general, the Tories refused to acknowledge those provisions of the Bill to which Russell implicitly referred. Their reasons for this are not far to seek. The landed interest as they defined it was that which a strong government was required to protect; a strong government was that which, all else failing, could depend for support upon the Members for the close boroughs. Thus, while Tories might recognize that townsmen should be stopped from 'interfering with the representation of the counties', and might even try to make the exclusion of townsmen from the county constituencies even more complete than the Ministers proposed, they could scarcely recognize the simple exclusion of townsmen from the counties as a solution, or even a partial solution, to the essential political or constitutional problem as they understood it – how a strong Government could be kept in being. Then, too – and on a somewhat different level – they could scarcely allow that the curtailment of urban influences in the counties was one of the principal objectives of the Grey Ministry when the very men to whom they themselves were appealing for support were those most concerned to curtail such influences.

As various poll books reveal, the alliances of 1830 between anti-Wellingtonian Tories and rural Whigs on the one hand and urban Radicals on the other were crucial factors in bringing down Wellington's Government. But, as the poll books and other evidence reveals – for example, Knightley's change of heart in Northamptonshire by February 1831[5] and the composition of the committee which asked Townley to stand as a reform candidate in Cambridgeshire the following October[6] – these were limited alliances which, in some cases, scarcely endured beyond Wellington's resignation.

Obviously, with Arbuthnot reporting on changes of heart about reform in Northamptonshire, and others reporting from other counties, Wellington and his friends were not unaware that it might be possible to restore something approximating to the Tory coalition of the twenties.[7] Of course, they could scarcely hope to restore this coalition or to defeat the Bill unless they could convince their would-be allies that the constitutional argument against the Bill which reflected its essential nature – that it would reduce the powers of the crown – was really a social argument. Presumably, they themselves believed that only a strong Government could defend the landed interest and thus that since the Bill would weaken the Government by abolishing the close boroughs on which the strength of the Government so largely depended, it would weaken the landed interest. The arguments of many Radicals undoubtedly helped their cause. But, these arguments notwithstanding, there were many difficulties in their way, not the least being the strength of the residual belief among their would-be allies that the close boroughs had served not as 'protectors of the landed interest' but as sources of strength which the Wellington Government had used to implement policies which were injurious to the landed interest. In effect, whether Wellington's statements and the statements of his various colleagues be explained in tactical terms, or in terms of that on-going controversy over the policies of the Wellington Government which came to a head in the immediate pre-reform period, they must be read in the context of these controversies. [8] One of the questions at issue had to do with the role of the close boroughs in the pre-reform period. Another had to do with the question whether the Bill which the Grey Ministry had introduced would effectively restore the political hegemonies of the leaders of the landed interest in their own neighbourhoods, thus destroying the circumstances in which the uneasy alliances of 1830 had come into being.

The Bill as the thing men·argued about must be distinguished from the Bill as a piece of prospective legislation. But neither as the one nor as the other should it be considered in abstraction from the political problems of the pre-reform period, the political structure of this period which poll books help to reveal, or the modes of behaviour which this structure encouraged. In particular, the structural problem was a problem of the counties. Wellington put it quite succinctly when he observed, 'the increase of manufactures and commerce, has given great influence to the inhabitants of towns in all county elections'.

II

The English counties were, traditionally, the political preserves of the local aristocracy and gentry. However, the evidence of the various county poll books suggests that before 1832 the powers of these men were somewhat precarious. The legal situation no longer provided them with an effective defence for their powers should they be challenged by those who might seek to exploit the consequences of economic growth and population movement.

The reasons for this are extremely simple. Before 1832, when the minimum voting qualification in a county election was simply the

ownership of real property in the county worth not less than 40s. a year
and either assessed to the land tax or redeemed, no distinction was
made between the rural and urban areas of the counties. True,
freeholders whose properties were located in certain of the so-called
'county boroughs' could not vote in the county in which the 'borough'
was located. But such inhibitions were few. They only obtained in 15
of these 'boroughs'.[9] Except in these 'boroughs' a freeholder with
property within a borough had just as much right to vote in the county
in which the borough was located as a freeholder whose property lay
in the smallest rural hamlet. And, of course, for electoral purposes
towns which lacked borough status were merely parts of the counties
in which they were located. Hence the importance of the growth of
urban population, the growth of urban wealth which found investment
in urban real property, and the growing concentration of rural
landownership.

In symbolic terms the plaints of the men of Manchester, Leeds and
Birmingham that they had no separate representation of their own, are
understandable, But these men were not always the impotent
bystanders at the game of politics they have often been described as
being. In many cases the plaints should have come – as they sometimes
did – from those who generally considered themselves their principal
opponents.[10] Where sizable towns existed and, in particular, perhaps,
where such towns either lacked borough status or electoral power was
out of reach of the local town magnates – it lay in the hands of
borough patrons or borough corporations – these magnates tended to
focus their political energies upon the counties. In 1830, the *Manchester
Mercury* carried a notice requesting 'the freeholders of the county
resident in Manchester, in Preston, in Warrington, and other great
towns in Lancashire . . . to withold the promise of their votes for a few
days, when a [commercial] candidate [would] be announced to
them.'[11] No 'commercial' candidate materialized in Lancashire in
1830. But in 1826 John Marshall, a flax-spinner from Leeds, had been
returned for Yorkshire without a contest. While discussing Marshall's
election Turberville and Beckwith noted one of its principal aspects,
that 'Leeds having no parliamentary representative of its own, the
ardent politicans of the town devoted their thoughts and energies to the
county elections.'[12] But more was involved in Marshall's election, and
the subsequent election of Henry Brougham, than the fact that Leeds
itself was unenfranchised. There was also the question of the number of
county voters over whom the town magnates could exercise significant
influence. Leeds contained 1,700 freeholders.[13] Of course, these alone
could not have swamped the rural areas of the county. In 1807, the last
time a real contest occurred in the county before 1832, 23,007 voters
polled.[14] But the Leeds freeholders were not alone. Yorkshire

contained other towns, some enfranchised, some not, for which Marshall 'could fairly claim to be a spokesman'. [15]

During the reform debates the role of these towns was clearly recognized. As Brougham noted with respect to his own election for Yorkshire in 1830, ' . . .he had never thought of canvassing the squires though he had taken great care to canvass the towns.' He acknowledged the fact that 'the squires were at first violently opposed to him, . . . [They had] actually held a meeting for the purpose of preventing his standing.' But this had not deterred him. Nor should it have done so. As he explained, ' . . . he had not placed any dependence upon the squires: all his reliance was upon the towns, for they were sure to carry the election.' [16] And later he added that considering the numbers of urban freeholders in Yorkshire, 'if you could make sure of two or three large towns, you had an exceedingly good chance of being returned for the county.' [17]

Yorkshire was not the only county in which the supposedly unrepresented towns had sufficient electoral power either to swamp the rural areas or at least to innundate them severely. To say that the unrepresented town of Birmingham contained 2,000 Warwickshire freeholders was probably an exaggeration. [18] But exaggerated or not, the leaders of the Birmingham Political Union were, apparently, in full control of the county by the time the elections of 1831 were held. [19] And, if contemporary allegations are accurate, their control was a function of the number of freeholders the town contained. [20]

Nor were the manufacturing counties the only ones in which such general conditions obtained. Because of the relative numbers of freeholders in the different communities which made up each county and, as the evidence for Northamptonshire suggests, the relative proportions of freeholders to population in these different communities, many counties were becoming quasi-urban or, at least, politically urban constituencies. [21] In Cambridgeshire, in 1830, over half of the freeholders who polled were concentrated in some 10 per cent of the towns and villages. From the borough of Cambridge alone some 456 freeholders polled, over 12 per cent of the 3,717 men who polled at this contest. [22] In Oxfordshire, in 1831, over half the voters were concentrated in fewer than seven per cent of the towns and villages. At this contest 2,934 voters polled. Of these 333, or more than 11 per cent, polled from the borough of Oxford. [23] As the poll books for Cambridgeshire and Northamptonshire reveal, the return of reform candidates in 1830 and 1831 was partly caused by the defection of many Tories. But it was also caused by various urban leaders deciding to exploit the power that was potentially theirs because of the concentration of freeholders in those communities in which their own influences were dominant. In effect, from the point of view of many leaders of the landed interest, a major political problem had come into being in many counties. The nature of this problem is revealed by the question Brougham asked when, after describing how the distribution of political power in Yorkshire between town and countryside had been responsible for his own return in 1830, he asked the House of Lords 'whether that was a state of representation which ought to be satisfactory to the country'.[24] A possible explanation for his question is his customary flippancy. But this does not explain those provisions of the first Reform Bill which historians have tended to ignore.

III

As John Cannon has noted – and quite rightly – the Ministers' 'top priority was the abolition of the nomination boroughs'.[25] There were two principal reasons for this. In the first place, the abolition of these boroughs was the means of rooting out one variety of 'corruption' in the State. In the second, the abolition of these boroughs cleared the way for the reconstruction of the representative system along the lines on which the Ministers hoped to reconstruct it. Their thinking can to some extent be seen from the gross redistribution scheme they initially proposed. Had the first Bill[26] been passed in the form in which it was introduced 62 seats belonging to the nomination boroughs would have been abolished outright, 106 would have been assigned to other constituencies, some with new names, others with old, but all fundamentally changed. Nine of these seats would have gone to Scotland, Wales and Ireland, 42 to new English boroughs, and 55 to the English counties.[27] If Wellington's principal contention of 4 October be allowed – that the close boroughs were the 'true protectors of the landed interest' – then, notwithstanding the fact that 13 more seats were being offered to the English counties than to the English boroughs the Bill would scarcely have gladdened the hearts of the leaders of the landed interest. But if Wellington's contention be disallowed, and if those provisions which he ignored be noted – provisions which further reveal the lines along which the Ministers hoped to reconstruct the representative system – then the leaders of the landed interest would have had good reason to be pleased. Indeed, within limits, they would have had reason to be pleased by the enfranchisement of each additional town. For according to the first Bill – and the same was true of the second Bill until it was amended in August – when a town became a borough most of the freeholders in the town automatically lost their county votes.

To emphasize this point is not to suggest that the exclusion of townsmen from the counties was the Ministers' 'over-riding consideration'.[28] Rather, it is to focus upon an obvious, important and hitherto neglected symbol of the sort of political world they hoped to create after the close boroughs had been abolished. As such, it provides an essential basis from which the values and assumptions which informed their handiwork might be considered. Furthermore, because they themselves amended the relevant provisions, greatly reducing the degree of exclusion they initially proposed, it poses the question why these provisions were amended.

The relevant provisions of the first published version of the first Bill, of the second published version of this Bill – the greatly lengthened version with which the House went into Committee in April – and of the first published version of the second Bill, introduced in June, were essentially the same: as stated in the first published version of the second Bill, clause 18, no man was to vote – or, to be precise, no man was to be registered as a prospective voter[29] – in any future county election 'in respect of any house, warehouse, or countinghouse, or of any land occupied together with a house, warehouse or countinghouse, by reason of the occupation of which respectively he or any other person shall be entitled to vote . . . for any city or town, being a county of itself, or for any other city or borough.'[30] As a result of other clauses of these Bills every major town was to be a borough and every man was to be entitled to vote in a borough who had resided there for at least six months and who occupied premises in the borough which were valued at £10 a year or more. In effect, most of the townsmen who, previously, had been able to 'interfere with the representation of the counties' would no longer have been able to do so.

The intent of clause 18 is clear – to isolate the counties from urban influences. But to recognize this intent is to raise various questions: to what extent was the Bill as a whole designed to separate different categories of voter into different constituencies? What experiences and assumptions would account for such a Bill? And to what extent could such a separation be achieved by means of legislation – and, of course, be achieved by such means in a complex world of different rights and competing values? This clause would have deprived of his county vote any borough freeholder whose property was worth more than £10 a year : in effect, whose property provided him 'or any other person' with a borough vote. If he were able to satisfy the proposed residence requirement for the borough franchise he would not lose his right to vote in respect of that property. The right would merely be transferred from the county to the borough. But if he failed to satisfy this residence requirement he would lose his right to vote altogether – at least in respect of that property. But the clause would not have deprived all borough freeholders of their county votes. It would not have affected the right to vote of the man who owned property in a borough which was worth the 40s. necessary for him to qualify as a county voter but less than the £10 necessary for him 'or any other person' to qualify as a borough voter. And, in conjunction with another clause, in some towns it would have enfranchised borough freeholders in the counties. The reasons for this are somewhat complex.

In the pre-reform period electoral rights in the boroughs proper differed greatly. Before 1832, however, the boroughs proper had this in common: every 40s.-freeholder whose property was located in the borough was qualified to vote in the surrounding county – assuming, of course, that his property was assessed to the land tax or redeemed. But no such rule applied to the freeholders of property in the 19 towns which had county status, what were often called the 'county boroughs'. In six of these the freeholders voted in the 'borough'. In four they voted in the surrounding county. But in nine a freeholder, *per se,* could not vote in either the 'borough' or the surrounding county.[31] If these 'boroughs' were only a minor problem as they were so few in number, they were a problem, nevertheless, which the Ministers tried to solve in their efforts to simplify the overall constituency system. As Althorp explained on one occasion, 'He saw no reason why persons residing in counties of cities should be placed in a situation different from those who resided in boroughs.'[32] The same £10 occupation qualification was proposed for both, and the same limits upon the rights of freeholders within them to vote in the counties proper. However, since the freeholders in 15 of the 'county boroughs' had not had the right to vote in the surrounding counties in the pre-reform period, when the Ministers proposed that each 'county borough' become, for purposes of parliamentary election, part of the county in which it was located, a proposal contained in clause 15 of the second Bill, they were in fact proposing that various townsmen be allowed to 'interfere with the representation of the counties' in the future when they had not been able to do so in the past.

The numbers of men who might have retained their county votes in spite of clause 18 of the second Bill could not have been very large. Nor could many men have acquired county votes in consequence of clause 15. Only fifteen 'boroughs' were really affected. And, of course, the impact of clause 15 would have been tempered by clause 18.[33] But the numbers of these men had no bearing upon the polemical uses to which they were put. Some Members argued that these various provisions were both inconsistent and unfair. Furthermore – and what was even more important within the context of the problems the Ministers faced in trying to get their overall scheme through a Parliament in which their own support came largely from the county Members – some of those who criticised these provisions managed to build a case around clause 15 saying that it revealed the Ministers' true intent of 'overwhelming' the landed interest.[34] To achieve consistency and, presumably, fairness, and to defend the landed interest, they tried to make the exclusion of the borough freeholders from the counties complete. Their arguments concerning the Ministers' true intent are dubious to say the least. But their arguments had considerable impact at the time. And, in the context of their contemporary impact, their arguments have helped to obscure the essential nature of the initial ministerial scheme.

Then, too – further obscuring the nature of this scheme – in August 1831, during the Committee stage of the second Bill, the Ministers amended clause 18. As the clause was then amended – and the sense of the amended clause was that which the Act contained – each borough freeholder who was not *himself* able to qualify for the borough franchise in respect of the particular property which allowed him to claim a county vote, was allowed to retain his county vote.[35] This amendment did not allow any man to vote in a county in respect of a freehold in a borough proper who would not have been able to do so in the pre-reform period. But, in consequence of this amendment, many men retained their electoral rights in the counties who would otherwise have lost these rights. The man who owned property in a borough where he himself resided and which provided *him* with a borough franchise was still disfranchised in the county. But the non-resident freeholder in a borough whose property was worth more than £10 a year, thus whose property provided 'any other person' with a borough franchise, was allowed to retain his county vote. So, too, the resident freeholder who owned property in a borough which was occupied by someone else and which provided this 'other person' with a borough vote.

Clause 15 was also amended later. But the importance of this amendment was quite different. If the amendment to clause 18 might be used to cast doubt on the sincerity of the Ministers' concern to prevent townsmen from 'interfer[ing] with the representation of the counties', then the amendment to clause 15 might be used to confirm their sincerity. In their third Bill, introduced in December, the Ministers deleted from the schedule to which the 'county borough' clause referred the six 'county boroughs' in which freeholders voted in the 'borough' in the pre-reform period. As a result of this deletion, a freeholder whose property was located in one of these 'boroughs' continued to vote in the 'borough' – if, of course, he was able to satisfy the new residence requirements for the borough franchise.[36] There was now no single and uniform category of borough, as would have been the case had the deletion not been made. On the other hand, a freeholder in a 'county borough' could now only vote in the surrounding county if he had been able to do so in the pre-reform period or if, in the pre-reform period, his freehold had not provided him with an electoral qualification in either the 'borough' or the surrounding county. While 'precedent' would help to explain the Ministers' decision in the former case, their decision in the latter presumably reflects their general concern lest the borough electorates be swamped by faggot voters.[37]

We should not forget that these amendments were *admendments to the Bill*. The effect of amending clause 18 was merely to *reduce* the numbers of borough freeholders who were *deprived* of their county votes. The only 'borough' freeholders who acquired the right to vote in a county in consequence of the Act were those whose freeholds were located in the nine 'county boroughs' where, previously, the freeholders *per se* had not voted in either the 'borough' or the surrounding county.

IV

Because of the amendment to clause 18 the Act failed to achieve that degree of separation of interests between town and countryside which the initial Bills would have achieved. Until recently, however, it had not been realised that the initial Bills would have achieved such a separation. The reasons for this obviously partly result from the prevalence of certain assumptions about the Bill, and about the reform process in general, in the context of which the initial borough freeholder provisions are somewhat anomalous. According to most historians, the Bill was a means of placating various urban middle class critics of the existing representative system by increasing their powers within the State at a time when their criticisms, augmented by those of the working class were acquiring a proto-revolutionary edge because of economic depression. Those who have studied the Bill, and the reform crisis in general, have also tended to focus their attention more upon the things which some men said about the Bill than upon the provisions of the Bill itself. The Bill is there to be read in its several versions. As a rule, however, it has not been read. Instead, statements about it have been read, statements which obviously reveal far less about the Bill itself than about attitudes towards the Bill, and about the tactical considerations of politicians during one of the severest political crises in Britain in the nineteenth century.

Because the borough freeholders were an important symbol – more important as a symbol, perhaps, at the time the Bill was passed than as a real political force: that came later – it was important where they would vote. The Ministers themselves proposed that those who could qualify to vote in the boroughs in which their properties were located should vote in these boroughs, that many – or, possibly, most – of those who could not thus qualify should be disfranchised in respect of that property. But many reformers were not satisfied by such an arrangement. Some were concerned to perpetuate the rights of all borough freeholders to vote – and to vote in the counties. Others, whether concerned or not that some borough freeholders might be disfranchised, wanted to exclude the whole lot of them from voting in the counties. And, on this point, the majority of the anti-reformers were with them.

The incipient coalition between the anti-reformers and what might be called the rural reformers was extremely important both for what it augured for the future and for what it reveals of the logic of the anti-reformers' procedures once they realized that the close boroughs could not be saved. They sought the total exclusion of the borough freeholders from the counties as a means of strengthening the landed interest in the conditions which the Bill would create. In arguing that such an exclusion was desirable they were not only abandoning but also implicitly contradicting the two principal constitutional or theoretical arguments they used in opposing the Bill as a whole: first that only those men who were not constrained by interests could have an objective understanding of the national legislative needs and, second, that politics would become dangerously polarized if all constituencies were defined in terms of interests. But simple opposition to the Bill would scarcely have allowed the anti-reformers, while continuing to oppose the Bill, to try to make those changes to the Bill which, from their point of view, would improve it. Nor would simple opposition to the Bill have allowed them to attract the support of the various rural reformers without whose help they could scarcely hope to amend the Bill to suit their needs or, in the longer term, to be restored to office. One lesson became clear as the debates wore on: if the nomination boroughs which according to Wellington had been 'the true protectors of the landed interest', were doomed then, possibly, the counties might be conditioned to perform their ostensible role. Towards this end – or these ends – it was essential that all borough freeholders be excluded from the counties, or that the effort be made to exclude them.

In both the pre-amendment and post-amendment periods the Ministers resisted the various efforts to exclude all borough freeholders from the counties. By and large, in the post-amendment period they did so in terms of the argument that interests should not be separated into different constituencies. Speaking in January 1832, Russell declared: 'The great objection to ... [the proposal to make the exclusion of townsmen from the counties complete] was ... that it would produce a division of interests between the inhabitants of towns and counties.'[38] But nine months earlier, while introducing the first Bill, he had implicitly proclaimed the merits of just such a division. And two or three months earlier Palmerston had thought of him as a prospective supporter of certain changes in the Bill which, in fact, were never discussed in the Cabinet, but which he hoped would be proposed as a means of making the Bill more acceptable to the Lords. Among these changes was one which would have removed the towns completely from the counties.[39] Indeed, as Grey noted in November 1831, it had been the ministers' 'original intention' to do just that – to provide that '*no* right of voting for counties should be derived from any property within the towns to be represented.'[40] If only the Ministers' statements in the post-amendment period are read, and if these statements are read without reading the provisions of the various Bills themselves – or otherwise noting the fact that, initially, the Ministers had proposed to deprive most borough freeholders of their county votes – one might conclude that the Ministers and the anti-reformers were at odds on the important question whether interests should or should not be separated into different constituencies. Unfortunately, this is what has happened. Russell's statement in January 1832, has received considerable attention, being not long ago described as containing one of 'the clearest ministerial statements' on the general question.[41] Until fairly recently, however, his statement of March 1831, and – what is even more significant – the provisions of the Bill to which this statement obviously referred, have been effectively ignored. It is difficult to say why these provisions and this statement have been ignored. Presumably because these various assumptions concerning the political reform process in general are far more compatible with Russell's statement of January 1832, than with his statement of March 1831. And, presumably, the strength of these assumptions is responsible for the fact that the one fairly recent historian of the nineteenth century parliamentary process who recognized the importance of the borough freeholder question, an historian on whom others have depended, got the story wrong.

Professor Charles Seymour obviously did not realise that the borough freeholder clause which the Act contained was not the same as the one in the first two Bills. Thus, because he noticed the efforts of the anti-reformers to amend the clause, and because he noticed the arguments of the Ministers while resisting these efforts, he approached the problem from the wrong end. According to Seymour, it was only those who opposed reform who tried to separate the counties from the towns. Their efforts were a measure of their opposition to reform. The Ministers' resistance to their efforts was a measure of the Ministers' commitment to reform. As a means of illustrating this commitment Seymour quoted from Russell's statement of January 1832. And there he left it. He failed to quote from Russell's statement of January 1831, or from the provisions of the first and second Bills to which this statement obviously referred. And, of course, he failed to note the particular context in which the final borough freeholder arrangement, that which he described as a measure of the *Ministers'* commitment to reform, was adopted.[42]

Recently, two historians in particular who make very similar assumptions to Seymour's about the reform process as a whole have tried to accommodate the fact that, initially, the Ministers themselves proposed to exclude most townsmen from the counties. Their concern reveals the importance of the problem. But their efforts suggest that the problem cannot be easily solved without changing their basic assumptions. There is too much that has to be argued away.

John Cannon, for example, is willing to grant that 'a clause prohibiting urban freeholders from voting in the counties was included in the first Bill, and defended by Russell on the grounds that the towns should not "interfere" with the rural areas, but [he goes on] it was modified in the second bill.' This statement, suggesting as it does that the clause was modified *before* the second Bill was introduced, not after, and, possibly, that it was modified in the light of a belated recognition of what it would achieve – in effect, that it was modified in the light of some recourse to 'principle', rather than in the context of political pressures and bargains – is grossly misleading. But Cannon's subsequent argument builds upon these suggestions: 'Had the main consideration been to preserve the sanctity of the counties at all costs, ministers would neither have modified the clause, nor offered any opposition to the Chandos amendment.' Whatever the significance of the phrase, 'at all costs', this argument not only obscures the context in which the clause was modified, and distorts the grounds for the Ministers' opposition to the Chandos amendment, it seeks to convey the rather dubious message that a provision which, in fact, appeared in each of the first three published versions of the Bill, a provision in which two changes of wording were made without any change of thrust, a provision which was ultimately modified but not deleted, had nothing to do with the "main considerations of the Government: [it] was included in the first bill, . . . but . . . modified in the second"; it was an error which was rapidly corrected.[43]

Mr Brock also tries to save the reputation of the Ministers as good democrats – or, at least, as good proto-democrats. He makes two principal suggestions concerning the initial clause, first, that it might have been a simple 'inadvertence' – the word which John Cannon forbore to use except by implication, and, second, that it might have been a measure of the importance of Ultra-Tory support at the time the Bill was drafted.[44] An 'inadvertence' it certainly was not. Nor should it be dismissed as the product of temporary Ultra-Tory influence. The amendment to the clause was obviously in part a consequence of waning Ultra-Tory support, a consequence of the Ministers' need to find compensating support in another quarter. But the clause reflects certain fundamental assumptions concerning English, or British, society in the early nineteenth century which were prevalent far beyond the areas of Ultra-Tory discourse. What has presumably served to obscure this fact is the need to endow the various reformers with liberal or democratic values as a means of explaining how, ultimately, a liberal or democratic society came into being. But the apparent effort to apply a combination of biological and mechanical analogies – liberals and democrats much have been responsible for the creation of a liberal and democratic society; legislation must have been the instrument of change – distorts the nature of the Bill, the nature of the change, and the values and assumptions of the men who not only drafted the Bill but lived in the world which poll books reflect.

According to Seymour, who obviously did not know that the borough freeholder clause was amended, the final borough freeholder arrangement was that which the Ministers initially intended. In trying to preserve the validity of Seymour's general interpretation, Cannon and Brock have tried to argue that the final arrangement was the one the Ministers *really* intended all along. But can an interpretation which, in large part, depends on a fundamental error, remain valid once the error is discovered?

Seymour apparently had some trouble in coping with the fact that the final borough freeholder arrangement *did* limit the rights of borough freeholders to vote in the counties. But when this arrangement was compared with that which the anti-reformers tried to impose – the complete exclusion of the borough freeholders from the counties – it was clearly possible to describe the arrangement itself and the men who produced it in at least proto-democratic terms, and to apply such terms to the overall scheme. Such terms, however, are scarcely appropriate in describing the scheme which the Ministers, in fact, had drafted.

V

Reporting in his diary for 14 August, the day the Cabinet decided to amend their initial borough freeholder provisions, Lord Holland noted, 'The reason for altering our former determination [to exclude most borough freeholders from the counties] was a persuasion that we should hardly be able to carry a provision so injurious to the rights of persons connected with town population.' [45] As reported in *Hansard* for 26 August, a few days after the amended clause had been adopted, Althorp explained that the clause had been amended 'in consequence of the amendment of the noble Marquis (the Marquis of Chandos) having been carried'. [46] Assuming that neither man's explanation was wrong, their statements are extremely useful for what they suggest of the social and political values which, in the aggregate, the members of the Grey Ministry possessed; for what they suggest of the difficulties which these men faced when, in the context of the many existing rights, they tried to draft an internally consistent Bill by which these values would be implemented; and for what they suggest of the further difficulties they faced when, unable to exercise any effective discipline over their motley crowd of supporters in the House, they were faced with the possibility that even if they were successful in rooting out one variety of "corruption" in the State it would only be replaced by others.[47]

Obviously, there were several factors limiting the Ministers' efforts to exclude townsmen from the counties even before 14 August. Indeed, these contributed to their difficulties. They had chosen not to disfranchise the smaller freeholders. They had also chosen not to assign the smaller borough freeholders to vote in the boroughs in which their freeholds were located. Whatever their principal reason for not disfranchising the smaller freeholders – whether it was their historical importance as had been revealed by all the fuss that was made about the disfranchisement of the 40s-freeholders in Ireland at the time of Catholic emancipation, or, as Grey reported to the King, the belief that the retention of the 40s-freehold franchise would be more favourable than otherwise to the landed interest – Althorp went to some length to explain why the Ministers decided to assign the smaller borough freeholders to vote in the counties.[48] As he puts it, had the Ministers decided to assign them to vote in the boroughs two problems would have arisen: the one had to do with the new residence requirements for the borough franchise, the other with the dangers of encouraging the creation of faggot votes. In the light of the fact that the non-resident voters in the boroughs were pre-eminent symbols of venality the Ministers felt very strongly that the new borough electorates should be resident electorates. And there was no residence requirement attached to the 40s-freehold franchise. Furthermore, when annuities and various other incorporeal rights were regarded as freeholds, when these could be easily created, and when the householder electorates projected for some of the post-reform boroughs were very small, the Ministers were deeply concerned lest, in allowing freeholders to vote in boroughs, they might encourage the wholesale creation of what were often called 'fictitious freeholds'. As Althorp put it, the Ministers 'were . . . anxious to distinguish *bona fide* freeholders from those who were created for the purpose of assisting elections.'[49] Their goal was not that which, on the basis of *some* of their public and private statements, has been attributed to them – the simple enlargement of the electorate. Rather, it was the enfranchisement of men in each constituency who were members of the community which the constituency as they hoped to define it, would symbolize. Indeed – and it helps to illustrate the community principle on which their Bill was based - they regarded the '*fictitious* freeholders', or 'freeholders . . . who were created for the purpose of assisting elections', as but another form of 'corruption'. In effect, while the exclusion of the borough freeholders from the counties which the Ministers proposed in their first two Bills would not have been complete, the Ministers had good reasons – or, at least, reasons which in their eyes were good, and reasons which help to illustrate the kind of political system they were trying to create – for handling the borough freeholder problem as they handled it. Their refusal to exclude *all* borough freeholders from the counties illustrates, on the one hand, their reluctance to disfranchise men against whom no general charges of 'corruption' could be brought and, on the other, their reluctance to encourage the creation of faggot voters. Within the limits which these concerns defined, however, they had proposed to exclude from the counties almost all borough freeholders who did not have separate qualifications beyond the borough boundaries. Indeed – and and it helps to illustrate the grounds on which one of the so-called Waverers wavered in his support of the Bill – when Lord Wharncliffe launched his first public attack on the Bill it was the failure of the Bill to exclude *these* men which he principally criticised.

Speaking in March, 1831, before the Bill had been formally introduced in the House of Lords – a procedure which some regarded as somewhat unconstitutional – Wharncliffe acknowledged the fact that the borough freeholder clause had prompted many members of the landed interest to support the Bill 'under the notion that it would be a benefit to them'.[50] But, he went on, the Bill which contained this and other provisions – in particular, those by which additional county Members would be created, and those by which constituency boundaries would be redrawn – would not really benefit the landed interest *because it did not go far enough*. Coming from Yorkshire, and understanding the conditions to which Brougham referred, he wanted a far more radical measure. As he put it, even if *most* townsmen were deprived of their rights to vote in the counties in respect of properties located in towns, many of these men would still be able to vote in the counties in respect of properties located beyond the borough boundaries.[52] The following year, when he repeated this complaint, Brougham observed that he seemed to be saying that the Bill was creating the evil, not reducing it.[54]

By and large, however, both in their public and certain of their private statements the anti-reformers and the rural critics of the Bill were even less generous than Wharncliffe in recognizing the very considerable benefit which the landed interest would have enjoyed in consequence of these provisions. Instead, they fastened upon the treatment of the smaller borough freeholders and, in particular, the treatment of those whose freeholds were located in the 'county boroughs', as confirmation of their contention that the Bill as a whole was designed to destroy the political powers of the landed interest. Replying privately to the question why the freeholders of Bristol should vote in the county instead of in the 'borough' where they had voted in the past – Bristol was one of the six 'county boroughs' in which, before 1832, freeholders had voted in the 'borough'; ultimately, in consequence of the alteration of the 'county borough' schedule they continued to vote in the 'borough' – Peel explained that the Ministers were involved in a simple attempt to delude the country gentlemen by professing to give them a power which, in fact, they were taking from them.[55] In Parliament, Wellington's Solicitor General, Sir Edward Sugden, argued from the same text. Speaking on 4 August, he declared that the Ministers' handling of the smaller borough freeholder question revealed their wish to destroy the landed interest by allowing these men *to retain* their power to 'overwhelm the influence of the agricultural portion of the county'.[56] Obviously, it was in the hope of strengthening his case that on 12 August he added a new dimension to his argument: 'The principle never could be right which allowed the smaller freeholder to retain his rights and took them from the larger freeholder.[57]

In illustrating this latter point Sugden cited two hypothetical situations. Each concerned an absentee freeholder in Brighton, the one who owned 20 houses, each worth well over £10 a year, the other a single property worth barely 40s. At present, he noted, each had a vote in Sussex. But if the Bill were passed as it stood the larger freeholder would lose his vote in Sussex while each of his tenants would gain a vote in Brighton. The other, whose tenant would not be able to qualify to vote in the borough, would retain his county vote. However, while thus criticising the 'inequities' of the borough freeholder provisions, Sugden was not suggesting that the larger freeholders be given the same rights as the smaller. He was suggesting that all borough freeholders be excluded from voting in the counties. Sugden did not propose – any more than did the Ministers – to disfranchise these men. Instead, he and most of the Bill's opponents urged that all borough freeholders be assigned to vote in the boroughs in which their properties were located.

On the 17th August Althorp announced the Ministers' decision to amend the borough freeholder clause. As reported in *Hansard* he then explained that the Ministers had been convinced by Sugden's equity argument. It certainly was an 'anomaly', he declared,

> that a person should have a vote for the county merely by retaining
> a forty-shilling freehold in a town, which he did not himself

occupy; whereas, if it was an occupancy of a larger amount, he would lose that right. This objection was of considerable weight, and had occupied much attention. One great object which . . . [the Ministers] had originally in view, in arranging the Bill was, to diminish the influence of towns in county elections. With such views, the eighteenth clause was framed as it now stood. The hon. and learned Gentlemen, however, had so fully satisfied them of its defects, that he meant to propose an alternation, the effect of which would be, that no person should be deprived of his vote for a county which he derived from property held in a town, unless he should acquire a vote for such town.[58]

E. P. Hennock has recently suggested that Althorp's statement on *this* occasion should be taken at face value both for what he said and for what he did not say. On *this* occasion he said nothing about the Chandos motion, which was down for the following evening. Thus, presumably, there was no connection between the amendment of the borough freeholder clause and the Chandos motion. According to Hennock, the Ministers 'amended the borough freeholder clause for reasons of equity, not wishing to deprive a freeholder of his vote in the county unless he was entitled on the strength of that property to a borough vote instead.' But, he allowed, a connection did develop later within the context of the continuing debate on the amended borough freeholder clause. 'From now on', he explained, 'whenever fears were expressed that the agricultural interest would suffer from the admission [sic!] of borough freeholders to the county register [sic!] the government had the perfect answer to hand. They could point out that the landed interest had gained considerably more by the Chandos clause then they would lose by means of the borough freeholders. In retrospect the two amendments came to be linked for debating purposes, but such debating points, intended to calm the fears of the landed interest, do not provide an explanation of the amendment itself.' As confirmation of his argument, Dr Hennock notes that Althorp's statement of 26 August was not a 'premeditated statement'. It was, he declares, 'a retrospective explanation . . . clearly at variance with what had been said eleven days [sic!] previously.' Furthermore, it contained 'errors of fact and *non sequiturs* which . . . are indications of the stress of the debate.'[59]

Dr Hennock's reference to what had been said 'eleven days previously' is presumably a typographical error. The relevant discussions were not on the 15th but on the 17th. But the principal grounds on which he discounts Althorp's statement of the 26th raise an important methodological question. Would Althorp's statement have been more cogent had it been 'premeditated'?

Althorp's statement of the 26th was made in response to certain wide-ranging criticisms of the Bill by Stuart Wortley, Wharncliffe's son. Wortley was willing, he said, to admit the need 'in the formation of the new system, to enfranchise large towns, but the noble Lords had gone beyond that necessity, and proceeded, on the most vague foundation, to change our whole political system.'[60] In replying to these criticisms Althorp mentioned, among other things, the county franchise provisions. While doing so, he made an important distinction between changes in the political system which the Ministers had themselves proposed and changes which they had felt constrained to make because of pressure from others.

> ... no change whatever had been made in the rights of freeholders, [he declared] except by adding copyholders and certain classes of leaseholders, which, he thought, was a judicious measure. The Ministers intended, that in the newly-created boroughs all those classes of persons resident within them should have votes for such places, but in consequence of the amendment of the noble Marquis (the Marquis of Chandos) having been carried, they proposed that certain classes of such persons, viz: those who possessed freeholds under [sic!] a given value, should continue still to vote for the respective counties, as a balance to prevent the agricultural interest in the county having the whole influence in returning of county Members.[61]

Dr Hennock refers to 'errors of fact and *non sequiturs*' in this statement. But the only clear error concerns the identities of those whose rights to vote were affected by the amendment of the borough freeholder clause. The amendment of this clause did not affect those who possessed freeholds *under* a given value, only those who possessed freeholds *over* a given value. Possibly, the reporter was at fault, possibly, Althorp. But if Althorp was at fault we should ask what conclusion should be drawn from the fault.

Dr Hennock is, of course, quite right in saying that Althorp was not delivering a prepared speech. Rather, he was making an impromptu reply to Stuart Wortley's criticisms. In such circumstances, errors of detail are not surprising: the Bill was extremely complex. But the description of relationships and causes in such circumstances is another matter: it does not require the same technical memory, the same verbal precision. Indeed, unless either Althorp or the reporter was making up the whole story which Althorp's statement of the 26th reflects – and the latter is improbable in the light of the fact that *The Mirror of Parliament* contains essentially the same report, but without the error – the very existence of the error in Althorp's statement as reported in *Hansard* would almost strengthen the presumption of accuracy in his description of relationships and causes.[62]

On a less methodological level, Dr Hennock's explanation is

vulnerable at several points. Not the least important of these is the suggestion that 'equity' means something quite apart from the values to which it implicitly refers. The Ministers did, of course, amend the clause in the way Dr Hennock describes. Indeed, Althorp's description of the change in the clause – at least, his description on the 17th – is the obvious source of Dr Hennock's description of the Ministers' motives. But the suggestion that they 'wished' to effect this end, and the further and more basic suggestion that their 'wishes' were conditioned by a concern for 'equity', are scarcely compatible with Holland's reference to the Ministers' 'earlier determination', or with the differences between the arrangement Sugden urged in the interests of 'equity' and the arrangement Althorp described on the ostensible grounds of 'equity'. Then, too, there is the implication that the Ministers had not, in fact, understood the full ramifications of their own initial borough freeholder provisions until Sugden pointed these out to them. This is scarcely possible – if only because the wording of the clause had been changed twice in the first three published versions of the Bill without any change in its thrust. The Ministers were obviously well aware of the 'anomalies' of their own initial borough freeholder provisions. They were presumably willing to pay this price to achieve the 'One great object which', as Althorp explained on the 17th, 'they had originally in view, ... to diminish the influence of towns in county elections.' Indeed, had they abandoned an object thus described simply 'for reasons of equity' it would suggest that their own Bill had been drafted in something resembling absent mindedness. Nor did Holland mention 'equity' or any related *principle* in his diary. As he put it, the decision to amend the clause was made on the grounds of pure expedience. Nor did Althorp mention equity in his explanation of the 26th.

Of course, since the decision to amend the clause was made on 14 August, the Chandos amendment not carried until 18 August, it might be complained that Althorp's explanation of 26 August violates the simplest rules of chronology. But if the Ministers had become convinced by the 14th that they could not defeat the Chandos amendment or, alternatively, if they had good reasons to fear this would be so, then the chronological problem would be solved and a connection would appear between Holland's explanation and Althorp's *two* explanations. It would lie in the Ministers' response to the developing coalition between the Wellingtonian Tories and the rural reformers to which the Ministers' defeat on 18 August should principally be attributed.

Certain points are clear. The Ministers tried to prevent this coalition from developing or succeeding. Failing in these efforts, they made several changes in their Bill. In particular, they abandoned that important expression of the community principle on which their Bill was based, that which the initial borough freeholder provisions represent. Their willingness to do so was a measure of the damage to their overall scheme which, in their eyes, the coalition had effected. As revealed in part by Althorp's arguments against letting the smaller borough freeholders vote in the boroughs, in part by the terms of the Minister's general opposition to the Chandos amendment itself, the Ministers were deeply concerned lest they allow new varieties of 'corruption' to grow while trying to extirpate the old varieties. In the context of their initial borough freeholder provisions their opposition to the Chandos amendment illustrates the crucial distinction they made between 'legitimate' and 'illegitimate' influence, the one a function of the community in which it obtained, the other a simple function of property. They opposed the Chandos amendment because of their belief that the £50-tenants-at-will of agricultural land whom Chandos sought to enfranchise would behave not as members of an agricultural community but as the simple creatures of their landlords.

The Ministers sought to protect the landed interest both by excluding from the countries as many townsmen as their other considerations allowed and by enlarging the agricultural components of the county electorates. In the eyes of many of their rural supporters, however, these means were inadequate. They sought a more effective way of protecting the landed interest which led them to subvert the Ministers' distinction between 'legitimate' and 'illegitimate' influence and – equally important – which led them into coalition with the anti-reformers. Presumably, it was in these circumstances that the anti-urban aspect of the initial borough freeholder provisions acquired that importance to which Holland referred. The Ministers perhaps hoped to bring the Radicals onto their side over the Chandos amendment by proposing to alter those provisions which, as Holland noted, were 'so injurious to the rights of persons connected with town population'. If this were so then their tactics obviously failed: many Radicals voted for the Chandos amendment. They may also have hoped to keep their rural supporters in line by indicating the consequence – or *possible* consequence – of their defection. In effect, their decision of the 14th may have been a *contingent* decision. The manner and timing of Althorp's announcement suggests this.

VI

It was on the 17th that the first formal expression of the developing coalition between the Wellingtonian Tories and the rural reformers occurred. The symbol of this coalition was the motion brought by Colonel Thomas Davies, a usual ministerialist, that the 'county borough' clause, clause 15, be rejected on the grounds 'that freeholders of cities and boroughs should vote for the towns within which their freeholds were situated, and not for the counties in which such towns were placed.'[63]

Davies was, as he put it, happy to cast silent votes for most of the Bill's provisions.[64] But he strongly disliked two sets of them, those which assigned the smaller borough freeholders to vote in the counties, and those which directed the boundary commissioners to enlarge the areas of those boroughs which contained fewer than 300 £10 houses. In the Ministers' eyes these provisions were important both for their substantive content and, perhaps even more, for their relationships to other provisions. In the anti-reformers' eyes these provisions were important because they provided the grounds for an alliance between themselves and various rural reformers.

Within the logic of the Ministers' overall scheme there was good reason to enlarge the boundaries of the smaller boroughs. If this were not done many boroughs would continue to exist whose electorates – so it was argued – would be too small to prevent bribery and other forms of 'illegitimate' influence from having a significant impact upon the State. By the same token, when 'fictitious freeholds' were so easily created, and when the prospective electorates in many boroughs were so small, there was good reason *not* to allow freeholders to vote in the boroughs. The essential thrust of their measure was reflected in Davies' observation, that "the Bill provided constituencies for the places to which it allotted Members."[65] But Davies' further observation was sheer caricature, that

> The Bill as it stood said, that if there were not ten pound householders enough in the towns, they must be taken from the counties, and the deficiency in the counties so created must be made up from the freeholders in the towns. Thus, on the one hand, they would take the farmer to choose Representatives for a commercial or manufacturing population, and, on the other, they would send the weaver, or the gun-maker, or the sailor from Liverpool, who believed their interests to depend upon a repeal of the Corn-laws, to elect a Member for those who thought they could only be protected from ruin by further restrictions.[66]

In general, while dealing with the borough freeholder problem the anti-reformers focused their attention less on clause 18, the borough freeholder clause, than on clause 15, the 'county borough' clause. Obviously, in view of the number of men whom clause 15 would affect, the essential importance of this clause derived less from its own prospective impact than from its usefulness in describing – or distorting – the prospective impact of clause 18. The same relationship obtained for Davies. His motion was directed against clause 15. But he objected to this clause not because of what *it* would do – assimilate the 'county boroughs' into the simple category of borough – but because of what clause 18 would *not* do: clause 18 would *not* deprive all borough freeholders of their county votes. As he explained – thus indicating what dangers he really did see and, suggesting who had taught him to see them – he wished to prevent townsmen from 'overwhelm[ing] the counties, and return[ing] both their own Members and those for the county'.[67] As the Bill then stood all borough freeholders whose freeholds were worth more than £10 a year would have been deprived of their county votes. True, the Bill would have given county votes to the smaller freeholders whose freeholds were located in certain of the 'county boroughs'. But before the debate on Davies' motion occurred Althorp had tried to explain the logic of the Ministers' procedure. The Ministers 'had felt considerable difficulty', he declared,

> with respect to the vote which should be given to freeholders whose freeholds were situated within the limits of cities or borough towns . . . It was reasonable and necessary that they should have votes somewhere, and the question was, whether they should be allowed to vote for the city or the county . . . The principle which had all along been maintained, and which Ministers wished to carry into effect, was, to grant the right of voting in boroughs to inhabitant householders paying a certain amount of rent; and they were also anxious to distinguish *bona fide* freeholders from those who were created for the purpose of assisting elections. Balancing the evils which appeared on both sides, and looking particularly to that which was connected with non-residentship, Ministers conceived that, on the whole, it would be better to give to freeholders possessing freeholds within the limits of boroughs or cities, the right of voting for counties, instead of running the risk of allowing non-residents to vote for boroughs.[68]

And then he announced the Ministers' intention of making certain amendments to certain future clauses – in particular, of amending the Bill so as to make the creation of 'fictitious freeholds' rather more difficult. Because of this prospective amendment no future annuitant would receive a county vote for an annuity of less than £10 a year.[69] In effect, it would be impossible to use 'fictitious freeholds' in the towns to swamp the rural vote.

Althorp's statements on this occasion are important not only for what he said but for what he did not say. The decision – or, possibly, the *contingent* decision – to amend clause 18 had been made three days earlier. While Davies' motion was a motion to reject clause 15 its logic derived from clause 18. Before sitting down and allowing the debate on Davies' motion to proceed Althorp described certain amendments the Ministers intended to make to clauses yet to come, amendments obviously designed to assuage the concern of Davies and his prospective supporters. But on this occasion Althorp failed to mention what would have been, from Davies' point of view the far more important amendment of clause 18. He indicated the reasons why the Ministers' wished the borough freeholders to vote in the counties. But he did not say whether the freeholders he had in mind were those specified in the Bill as it stood, those whose freeholds were worth *less* than £10 a year, or those others whose freeholds were worth *more* than £10 a year. Until clause 18 was amended there was no question of men continuing to vote in the counties in respect of freeholds located in boroughs which were worth *more* than £10.

It was later that evening, just before the division on Davies' motion, that Althorp announced the Ministers' decision to amend clause 18. He interrupted Sugden, who had just begun to warm to his theme of the inequity of allowing the smaller borough freeholders to retain rights of which the larger were to be deprived. Such an interruption was itself somewhat unusual. To have withheld such an important item of information until that point in the debate was, perhaps, even more so, As he put it, indicating the Ministers' basic agreement with Davies, 'One great object which . . . [the Ministers] had originally in view, in arranging the Bill was, to diminish the influence of towns in county elections. With such views, the eighteenth clause was framed as it now stood.' Then, he went on, presumably turning to Sugden. 'Then hon. and learned Gentleman, . . . had so fully satisfied . . . [the Ministers] of . . . [the] defects [of the clause] that he meant to propose an alteration, the effect of which would be, that no person should be deprived of his vote for a county which he derived from property held in a town, unless he should thereby acquire a vote for such town.'

Sugden was dismayed. He certainly did not appreciate, perhaps he did not even comprehend, what Althorp was about: to grant his premises and then use his premises to defeat his object. As he put it, he feared the Ministers had not understood the reasons why he objected to the borough freeholder provisions. He then explained them all over again, why it would be inequitable to deprive the larger borough freeholders of rights which the smaller freeholders were allowed to retain, why, in solving this problem of *equity,* all borough freeholders should be assigned to vote in the boroughs in which their properties were located and not in the counties lest the landed interest 'be deprived of the share of the Representation it ought to possess'.[70]

As the terms of Sugden's statement suggest – in particular, his criticisms of the Bill for not giving the landed interest 'the share of the Representation it ought to possess – he was not only talking about the Bill. He was also trying to restore his own and his former colleagues' political fortunes by casting them in the roles of defenders of the landed

interest, thus implying that the Ministers were attacking the landed
interest. Whatever the reason for his failure to understand the thrust of
the initial borough freeholder clause – or refusal to acknowledge this
thrust – it is obvious that his political object was far more easily
attained when this clause was seen in conjunction with the 'county
borough' clause. Clearly, Sugden was stretching things a bit when he
suggested that 'if 300 or 400 smaller freeholders were thrown in upon
the county constituencies ... the due influence of the aristocracy
[would be destroyed].' Yet much was at stake in this suggestion and in
the further suggestion that the Ministers' wish to destroy the influence
of the aristocracy was revealed in their refusal to exclude the smaller
borough freeholders from the counties.[71] Althorp was obviously trying
to restore a certain measure of sanity to the general discussion when he
explained that even if the changes which he described were adopted
they would not give the borough freeholders any *new* rights 'because
they had already votes for the county'.[72] But the Bill was not being
debated in a theoretical vacuum. It was being debated by men whose
political fortunes would in part depend on what provisions the Bill
contained, and even more on what interpretation was placed upon
these provisions. In such circumstances hyperbole are not surprising –
including those which men believed. Nor, in such circumstances, is the
attempt to control the flow of information surprising. Althorp
presumably had good reason both to withhold the crucial piece of
information and to produce it when he did.

The question whether, by 17 August, the Ministers had definitely
decided to amend the borough freeholder clause no matter what the
division on Davies' motion and what the division on Chandos' motion
will, it is hoped, soon be answered. The decision of the 14th had
perhaps been irrevocably made. But perhaps, when Althorp staggered
his announcements, reserving the crucial one until just before the
division on Davies' motion, he was hoping he would not have to make
it. Perhaps, had the debate on Davies' motion progressed differently
the crucial announcement would never have been made.

Davies' motion was defeated. Only 12 other usual ministerialists
voted with him. But the following evening Chandos' motion was
carried decisively, 232 to 148. The majority contained 85 usual
ministerialists.[73]

VII

In part the importance of the vote on the Chandos amendment lies in
the fact, noted by Mr. Brock, that it was the Ministers' 'one committee
defeat'.[74] Principally, however, it lies in the fact that for various
reasons a large majority of the House had repudiated the fundamental

distinction on which the Bill was based, that between 'legitimate' influence on the one hand and 'illegitimate' influence and 'corruption' on the other. Once this had happened the Ministers made several related changes in their Bill. In particular, they amended the borough freeholder clause, thus allowing certain men back into the county electorates who were foreign to that ideal of the counties which their initial borough freeholder provisions help to illustrate. As Althorp explained on 26 August, these men 'should continue . . . to vote for the respective counties, as a balance to prevent the agricultural interest . . . having the whole influence in returning of county Members.'[75] The essential clue to the Ministers' behaviour lies in the relationship between the nature of the county constituencies as these were initially projected and the grounds for their opposition to the Chandos amendment.

Notwithstanding Althorp's statement of the 26th, that the Ministers wished 'to prevent the agricultural interest . . . having the whole influence in returning of county Members', the Ministers had sought to exclude as many townsmen as possible from the county electorates. However, as Althorp explained on 17 August, *before* the debate of Davies' motion, they had sought to do so without disfranchising any large number of existing voters and without encouraging the growth of 'corruption' in other constituencies. In addition, the Ministers proposed to enfranchise various categories of copyholder and leaseholder in the counties. As Palmerston explained soon after the first Bill was introduced, the enfranchisement of these men was conceived as a means of increasing the relative size of the agricultural elements in the county electorates.[76] But it was not simply agriculturists that the Ministers sought to enfranchise in the counties. Had this been the case they would scarcely have opposed the Chandos amendment. Rather, it was a certain category of agriculturist. One might ask whether the category was legally definable. But the effort itself is clear. The men they sought to enfranchise in the counties were those who, while recognizing themselves as members of an agricultural community – thus, while being potentially responsive to the 'legitimate' influences which obtained within this community – would also be proof against 'illegitimate' influence. Essentially, the changes that were made in the Bill on 19 and 20 August were a measure of the fact that while a large number of rural reformers were happy to join in abolishing the nomination boroughs they wanted to guarantee the absolute nature of rural power in the counties in a way that violated the distinction between 'legitimate' and 'illegitimate' influence. The Ministers were successful in deterring many of these men from voting for Davies' motion – or, as the Ministers saw it, voting to increase the number of 'fictitious freeholders' in the boroughs. But the Ministers failed to deter them from voting for Chandos' motion – or, as the Ministers saw it, voting to enfranchise men who could not be described as members of an agricultural community but only as their landlords' dependants.

From the present perspective the distinction they made might appear somewhat fine. From any perspective it must be recognized as somewhat metaphysical. But the metaphysics was not theirs alone. Indeed, in one way or another many of their contemporaries – even including James Mill – made the same or analogous distinctions.[77] But it was *their* distinction which the Bill as it was initially drafted reflects. And it was *their* response to the practical repudiation of this distinction by numerous of their rural supporters which explains the changes they made in their Bill. Failing to prevent the enfranchisement of the £50-tenants-at-will in the counties they allowed back into the county electorates various men who, while foreign to their ideal of the counties, were, as Althorp explained, expected to provide a political 'balance' against the anticipated impact of the tenants-at-will. And, presumably, it is the difficulty of recognizing this distinction in the vastly different social context of the present day which accounts both for the tendency to ignore the role of this distinction in the arguments of such men as James Mill and for the recent suggestion that since the Ministers were opposed to the Chandos amendment they could not really have wanted 'to preserve the sanctity of the counties'.[78]

As a rule, reformers assumed that the ability to resist 'illegitimate' influence was a function of the possession of property, the legal guarantee that such possession would be undisturbed, and, finally, membership in a stable, hierarchical community. The model to which they looked – but on which they wished to improve – was the 40s-freeholder. In part, at least, the security of a freehold was supposed to compensate for its occasional deficiency in value. Making allowance for 400 years of intermittent inflation, the Ministers pegged their new copyhold franchise at a £10 level and saw it approved without much demur. All who spoke were agreed on the prospective 'independence' of the £10 copyholder.[79] However, because the rights which leaseholders enjoyed, unlike those which copyholders enjoyed, were matters of temporary contract and thus periodically dependent upon some other person, there was no similar agreement about the 'independence' of the leaseholders especially if their leases were of short duration and its value small. When, in the second Bill, the Ministers reduced the necessary rent as well as the necessary length of time the lease had to run for its holder to qualify as a county voter, the difference of degree which originally separated the proposed leasehold voters from the existing freeholders became a difference of kind. In their first Bill the Ministers specified £50 leaseholders whose leases ran for not less than 21 years. In their second Bill they proposed to enfranchise £10 leaseholders whose leases ran for not less than seven years. Because of these changes in the Bill many men feared that the leasehold franchise might become a major vehicle for the creation of faggot votes.[80] But before they could mount a concerted attack upon the clause, either to remove it, or to reinstate it in its original form, the leasehold question became submerged beneath the issues raised by Colonel Sibthorp and Lord Chandos.

Colonel Sibthorp and Lord Chandos proposed that men be enfranchised in the counties who were tenants-at-will of agricultural land for which they paid rents of not less than £50 a year. These amendments were far more radical in their departure from the existing freehold franchise than the leaseholder provisions.[81] Undoubtedly, the £50-tenants-at-will had far more property than many 40s-freeholders. Undoubtedly, many of them had far more property than many £10 borough occupiers. But they had minimal security. Holding their land at the will of their landlords they could be evicted, legally, at six months' notice.

At the time when many leases negotiated during the Napoleonic period were falling due, and when the unsettled state of agriculture made many farmers and landlords reluctant to bind themselves for long periods, Sibthorp and Chandos sought – or so they said – to make the Bill accord with economic reality. As Chandos noted – and rightly – very few Buckinghamshire farmers had leases.[82] But from the Ministers' point of view this was not altogether relevant. They were concerned to enfranchise agriculturists in the counties, to define the counties as agricultural constituencies. But they were not concerned to enfranchise *any* agriculturalist. Their worldly wisdom made them realize that any tenant in county or borough might be evicted for political reasons. With this possibility in mind – and while trying to increase the correspondence between constituencies and communities – they had drafted their Bill so as to prevent those men being enfranchised whose properties, or lack of property, might make them peculiarly vulnerable to 'illegitimate' influence. The initial borough freeholder clause, and the residence requirements for the borough franchise, are evidence of their concern to define constituencies in terms of communities. But within the limits of the constituencies thus defined they sought to exclude those men from the franchise whom it might be possible to bribe because of their *lack* of property, or possible to coerce because of the kind of property they possessed.

In its economic and legal aspects the question raised by the Chandos amendment was later known as tenant right. For most of the century, with certain local exceptions, no agricultural tenant had any right of ownership over the capital he might invest in the exploitation of his farm. If he were turned out unexpectedly he stood to lose his total investment except for that which his stock and growing crops might represent. In these circumstances, as Althorp explained, the leaseholder tended to conduct his farming operations so as to 'get out of the land the value of the capital he had embarked in it, within the time for which his lease was given . . .'[83] Thus, according to Althorp, since a leaseholder would be ready to quit his farm at the expiration of his lease, he might vote against his landlord with relative impunity. But only those leaseholders could do so, Althorp insisted, who had a minimum tenure of seven years. According to Althorp the backers of the Chandos amendment had failed to consider the social consdquences of these economic and legal realities. As he put it, citing the case which various proponents of the Chandos amendment made,

> The argument was, that you gave the ten pound householder in the borough a right to vote, and you ought, on the same principle, to give farmers paying a certain rent a right to vote for the county; but . . . there was . . . this distinction, that it was in the power of the landlord of the farmer to do his tenant a greater injury than the landlord of the [borough] householder could do his . . . Look . . . to the householder who carried on a business in a shop in a town. It would, no doubt be an inconvenience to such a man to be removed from a place where he had carried on his business; but in removing, he could carry all, or nearly all, his business with him, and could remove the whole of his stock, and in this respect he was much more independent of his landlord than the farmer.[84]

This was an essential part of the logic on which the Bill was based. By and large, those who supported the Chandos amendment did so on the grounds that it would strengthen the landed interest. For some – for Chandos himself – this was necessary to balance the potential strength of the Radical voters in the unenfranchised towns.[85] For others – and their arguments illustrated their failure to understand the logic of the initial borough freeholder provisions – it was necessary because new towns were being enfranchised. This, for example, was the principal argument of St. John Mildmay, a usual ministerialist.[86] In effect, Chandos and most of his supporters ignored the logic of Althorp's argument, or, at most, tried to answer him in the terms which 'Squire' Western suggested: that farmers were respectable men, and that eviction for political reasons was improbable as long as the agricultural depression endured. As Western put it – M.P. for Essex, he, like Mildmay, was usually found in the ministerial lobby – 'In the present state of the country, a good tenant was as necessary to the landlord as the landlord was to . . . [the tenant].'[87]

A number of Radicals also supported the amendment. According to their lights their doing so was not anomalous. Some argued that the ballot would soon provide the tenant with a prospective anonymity behind which he could safely express his own interests – interests which, they assumed, would be opposed to his landlords' and thus allied with theirs.[88] Others evidently believed that once the corn laws had been repealed – and many looked for repeal as soon as the Bill was passed – a change would occur in the relative powers of landlord and tenant. With the further reduction of agricultural prices which, they assumed, would inevitably follow repeal, 'the landlord would become more anxious to let his land than the tenant to hire it.'[89]

In the short term, and for the reasons given, the Radicals' assumptions demonstrate nothing so much as their sociological naiveté and their ignorance of rural society. 'Squire' Western's assumptions are somewhat more valid – although he was greatly in error in ignoring the power differential between landlord and tenant. As might be expected, Peel made no such error. But within the context of this differential when he looked at the countryside he saw a somewhat different danger from that which Althorp saw. According to Peel, if a farmer were tempted to invest in his farm on the security of a short lease he would be even more vulnerable to the pressures of his landlord than the tenant-at-will who was not thus tempted.[90] The same essential logic, but focused upon the prospective relationship between landlord and leaseholder, not landlord and tenant-at-will, can be seen in the statement of the rather radical Hughes Hughes: 'He would not consent to give the power of withholding or conferring the franchise to the landlord, which would be the case if the right of voting depended upon his granting or refusing a seven years' lease, and therefore he would vote for the amendment of the noble Marquis.'[91]

Clearly, it was not to Hughes Hughes that Althorp had been appealing on 11 August when he explained that the Ministers

> ... felt the necessity, while they were adding to the democratic share of the Representation, by extending the franchise generally, and adding to the Members for the large towns, of preserving the balance of the aristocratic share, by increasing the influence of the great landed proprietors in the counties.[92]

Nor, again, was it Hughes Hughes to whom Althorp had appealed on 12 August when he explained that it was the Ministers' intention

> ... that the voters in towns and boroughs should be excluded from voting for the counties, and by this means the town and county Representation would be kept distinct, and the landed interest would claim an advantage which at present it did not possess.[93]

Rather, it was those others, the Adeanes, the Davies, and the Mildmays, who, by voting with Chandos and Sugden, either prompted the Ministers' decision to amend the borough freeholder clause or induced them to make good their threat to do so.

VIII

After their defeat on the 18 August the Ministers made several related changes in the Bill. First, having induced Chandos to withdraw his amendment 'in order that . . . [it] might be embodied in technical form', they proceeded to rewrite it in such a way as to somewhat defeat Chandos' purpose.[94] Speaking on the 19th, Althorp noted that Chandos' own version applied to farmers and to farmers only. Then, in bland contradiction of everything Chandos himself and most of his supporters had argued the evening before, Althorp went on to say that it could not have been Chandos' intent to enfranchise farmers alone.[95] The draft amendment he then read provided for the enfranchisement of the men Chandos proposed to enfranchise – the £50-tenants-at-will of agricultural land. But it also provided for the enfranchisement of £50 tenants-at-will of gardens and – a more significant addition – of houses. Whether or not the instrument of tenancy-at-will was ever used for suburban residences, these suburbanites, like the larger borough freeholders, were presumably given county votes so that they too might provide a political 'balance' against the agricultural tenants-at-will.

The following evening Althorp introduced the amended borough freeholder clause to which a new section had been added referring to borough copyholders and borough leaseholders. The clause with respect to freeholders had been amended by deleting the words, 'or any other person'. But these words appeared in the new section. As Althorp explained, this section had been added to guarantee that the rights now being retained by those borough freeholders who were not themselves able to qualify for the borough franchise in respect of their own properties, were not extended to borough copyholders and borough leaseholders. No copyholder or leaseholder, he declared, was to vote in a county in respect of any property by reason of the occupation whereof 'he or any other person might acquire a vote . . . [in a] city or borough'.[96]

From the Ministers' point of view, they should have left well enough alone. Althorp's statement is clear; the new section was part of the final Bill; but the legislative draftsman erred: according to the final version of the Bill the copyholders and leaseholders who were excluded from the county franchise were those who 'occupied' property, not those who 'held' it. Evidently, borough copyholders were relatively few. But there were many borough leaseholders who 'held' property which they did not 'occupy' – who 'held' several premises by lease and sub-let one or more of them. Subsequently, in the light of the legal maxim that a specific exclusion implies the inclusion of the others, and in the context of the general argument that the Reform Act had been designed primarily to enlarge the electorate – thus, that further enlargements were consistent with its principles, many borough leaseholders who 'held' property which they did not 'occupy' managed to qualify as county voters. Some men objected. But until 1867, when the second Reform Act effectively disfranchised these borough leaseholders in the counties, their votes were considered good.[97]

In the years immediately before the passing of the second Reform Act there was a sharp increase in certain counties in the numbers of men who were qualified to vote in respect of property located in boroughs. With the evidence presently available it is impossible to discover whether these men were qualified in respect of leasehold, copyhold or freehold properties. But, in the context of the Ministers' response to Sibthorp's and Chandos' efforts to guarantee the absolute power of the landed interest in the counties, the phenomenon not only illustrates the irony of these efforts it also explains an important dynamic of the second Reform Act which has so far not been noted. As Disraeli observed in 1859, while the majority of the tenants-at-will were more affected by rural than by urban influences, in many counties they were far outnumbered by men who qualified in respect of property in boroughs, and most of these were more affected by urban than by rural influences.[98] The Reform Bill he was then introducing was essentially designed to deal with this phenomenon. Of course, the Bill of 1859 was defeated. But it and the Act of 1867 had much in common between them.[99]

These developments lay in the future. Thus, while they illustrate certain aspects of the working of the system which the Act of 1832 defined, and certain responses to these workings, they scarcely illustrate the motives of the men who drafted or passed the Bill. These motives are to some extent revealed by Althorp's statement, in 1831, that the object of the amended borough freeholder clause was the original one, 'that the county constituency should not be overpowered by the inhabitants of towns, which they would have been if all those who had the right of voting for property in towns were admitted indiscriminately to vote for the counties' – in effect, if the conditions which obtained in the pre-reform period had been allowed to remain unchanged.[100]

Althorp's statement presumably failed to placate the Adeanes, the Davies, and the Mildmays. Nor did it placate the Ministers' more urban-oriented supporters. Indeed, according to Lord Milton the borough freeholder clause in both its original and amended form was an unwonted innovation. He was no doubt referring to the abolition of the close boroughs when he declared his admiration for 'the principle and general character of this measure of Reform. I admire its boldness, too', he said. 'But', he went on,

I must say, at the same time, that many of the principles of the details of it have not been based, as they ought to have been, upon the ancient institutions of the country. It should have been so founded, instead of trying to make a balance between the trading and commercial interests on the one side, and the landed interest on the other – instead of trying an experiment, the success of which is obviously impossible, for no ingenuity will be sufficient to render that balance so nice as not to excite dissatisfaction on the one side or the other.[101]

Yet it was precisely this ingenuity which the Ministers tried to demonstrate. Nor did they lack an historical rationale. Indeed, such a rationale informed Althorp's reply to Milton: 'If all interests were the same, why should there be separate rights of voting for towns and counties?'[102] But Althorp neglected to answer the substantive point of Milton's criticism. Had he done so he might have provided that coherent statement of the social and political assumptions which informed the Ministers' efforts to reconstruct the representative system. As he did not, such a 'statement' can only be put together from the evidence of what they did, – although such evidence must obviously be handled with far greater care – from the evidence of what they and others said about it, and from the more general evidence contained in the arguments of various contemporary political theorists.

IX

The intent of the initial borough freeholder provisions should have been clear to everyone who read the Bills : except, of course, those whose understandings were affected by a *deformation politique*. But, from the Bills themselves, there was no way of knowing how the boundaries question was to be handled. Clues might have been found in the instructions which the boundary commissioners received from the Home Office between August and November, 1831, but the complete picture did not become clear until the Government's boundary proposals were published as a whole in the spring of 1832.

The boundary sections of the various nineteenth century Reform Acts have never been accorded the attention they deserve. Redistribution has not suffered the same neglect. However, redistribution has suffered equivalent distortion since it has been considered almost solely in urban terms, as a means of creating new boroughs – in effect, since the question of what happened to the counties when certain urban areas were abstracted from them has generally been ignored. As the populations of various of the boroughs had considerably overspilled the existing borough boundaries the initial borough freeholder provisions would scarcely have allowed the

Ministers to achieve the goal which Russell defined – that townsmen should no longer 'interfere with the representation of the counties' – unless the boundaries of these boroughs were significantly redrawn. Hence the importance of the task which was assigned to the boundary commissioners. But the commissioners exceeded their initial charge. Their work had an important bearing upon the logic of redistribution itself.

Initially, the Cabinet committee made a clear procedural distinction between the two principal aspects of their measure, that of abolishing nomination, and that of creating the desired conditions of representation. In drafting their Bill they implied that nomination was a simple problem which they themselves were capable of handling without any special information. On the other hand, they implied that representation involved complex questions, some of which could not be handled without detailed study of the demographic circumstances in and around each prospective constituency. To perform these local studies the initial Bills provided for the appointment of two committees of the Privy Council, the one to be charged with the final determination of the boundaries between borough and county, the other with the final division of the counties. But these committees were not to concern themselves with the *schedule A* boroughs, those which the Ministers proposed to disfranchise.

The initial plan to exclude the *schedule A* boroughs from the purview of these committees was perhaps intended to save time: inquiries for which there would be no use would not be made. Perhaps it was intended to allow the members of the borough committee to go about their business of adjusting boundaries without becoming embroiled in the more hotly controversial question of the schedules themselves. But whatever the Ministers' motives it is obvious that they wished to keep the schedules they had drawn up entirely separate from the work of the boundaries men. They might perhaps have succeeded in this had they not used population figures as a means of rationalizing the lines between the different categories of borough: those in *schedule A*, which were to be totally disfranchised; those in *schedule B*, which were to lose one seat; and those which were unscheduled and which were to retain their existing representative strengths. Not only were these figures 10 years old they were simply not appropriate to the use that was made of them.

The Ministers used the census figures of 1821. They had good reason for using these rather than those then to be assembled during the decennial census of 1831. Had they made such political importance of the figures of 1831 these might have been grossly distorted. But they had no excuse for the ways in which they used the 1821 figures. They made the logically unwarranted assumption that the population of each borough as a legal entity was an accurate measure of the borough's relative importance as a social entity — as a town. Initially, they obviously failed to consider the possible existence of population concentrations in the areas immediately beyond the borough boundaries, concentrations which would not have shown up in the population figures for the boroughs themselves no matter which figures they used, those for 1821 or those for 1831. They proposed to disfranchise completely those boroughs which had fewer than 2,000 inhabitants within their existing boundaries. Those boroughs which had 2-4,000 inhabitants within their existing boundaries were placed in *schedule B*.

As a result of this procedure, the Ministers faced two very important problems. They had to justify the 2,000 dividing line between *schedules A* and *B*. And they had to explain their decision to take one seat from each of the *schedule B* boroughs. In dealing with the first, one of their supporters used a moral argument which was consistent with the Ministers' decision to keep the boundaries men away from the *schedule A* boroughs. He praised the Ministers for their ability 'in selecting as a line that amount of population which coincided with the boroughs which *ought to be disfranchised*.'' [103] But this moral argument was of no use when the question why the *schedule B* boroughs were to be deprived of one member was asked. Since one of the main declared purposes of the Bill was to abolish nomination, the Ministers were precluded by their own logic from claiming that the *schedule B* boroughs should be deprived of one of their seats for reasons analogous to those for which the *schedule A* boroughs were being disfranchised entirely. They could only point to the 'insignificance' of these boroughs as the reason why each should lose one member. [104] Yet to an audience for which the mere size of a community was not an adequate reason to recognize it as a constituency — or to disfranchise it — the inherent weakness of such an argument was aggravated by the explicit admission in the Bill that some of the boroughs which found their way into *schedule B* by passing the population test might still lack the 300 £10 houses — implying 300 potential voters — believed to be essential as a further guarantee against 'illegitimate' influence. The logic of the Ministers' position was gravely undermined by their suggestion that such 'deficient' boroughs might be given adequate constituencies if their boundaries were adequately enlarged. It required little skill to make the point that if such a technique had been applied to the boroughs in *schedule A* most of them might have been redeemed. [105] In effect, the powers which the Ministers proposed to grant to the boundaries men in dealing with the *schedule B* boroughs were completely inconsistent with their initial refusal to allow the boundaries men to deal with the *schedule A* boroughs too.

Ultimately, because of widespread criticism, the redistribution and boundary procedures were both altered. When protests developed that the Privy Council committees would not have been responsible to Parliament – according to the first two Bills they would have reported to the King, who would then have issued proclamations enforcing their recommendations – the relevant provisions were modified.[106] By an amendment to the second Bill specific commissioners were named whose reports would have been submitted not to the King but to Parliament. By then, however, the commissioners had already been appointed and begun their work. Although the Bill which named them was defeated in the Lords in October the commissioners continued their investigations throughout the autumn. In all probability, it was the evidence they gathered which finally undermined the initial procedural distinction between *schedules A* and *B*. Considered in the abstract, the legal boundaries of a borough might have no relation to the boundaries of the 'town' of which the borough might be only a small part. Thus, the population of a borough was not necessarily a fair measure of its relative significance. The implications of this were obviously realized when, late in October, the borough boundary commissioners were given new instructions by which their frames of reference were enlarged to include the boroughs in *schedule A*.[107]

As a result of the commissioners' investigations, new criteria were developed for *schedules A* and *B*. In their third Bill the Ministers abandoned the simple population tests based on the geographical limits of the boroughs as legal entities. Instead, they developed composite criteria based upon the number of houses in the 'town', and the amount of the assessed taxes paid by the 'town'.[108] As Russell acknowledged when introducing the third Bill, the new line between *schedules A* and *B* had been drawn in purely arbitrary fashion and not to distinguish the redeemable from the unredeemable boroughs – such a distinction, with its moral implications, had been totally abandoned – but merely to provide the vacant seats which the other schedules required if the size of the House were not to be enlarged.[109]

The new schedules were in effect drawn up by Lieutenant Drummond of the Royal Engineers. Drummond had supervised the boundary commissioners' activities. Later, he sat on the small committee appointed by the Government to study the commissioners' recommendations before they were embodied in the Boundaries Bill to which the Reform Act referred, and which was an integral part of it. When Drummond had used the new composite criteria to identify the 100 least significant boroughs, and had arranged these boroughs in their relative order, the Ministers had merely drawn a line between *schedules A* and *B* so as to lop off an arbitrary 56 boroughs. It indicates the degree to which the different criteria overlapped – in effect, the degree to which the power to nominate was a function of certain socio-economic conditions – that the new *schedule A* differed only slightly from the old. But once the Ministers had turned the commissioners loose on *schedule A* boroughs there were no longer any major sections of the Bill which could be rationalized in purely moral terms. Sociological categories had replaced the moral. The question was no longer, which boroughs should be abolished because they are the places where nomination occurred? The question had become, what are the circumstances in which nomination may be expected to obtain? Russell's defence of this procedure was entirely pragmatic and sociological, not moral,

> . . . that it was necessary to take a certain number of small boroughs, where freedom of election could not be hoped for, or obtained, and to draw a line between them and the boroughs of somewhat more consideration, and into which we could introduce a greater number of electors, so as to establish more fully the principle of this Bill, . . . that elections ought of right to be free.[110]

X

The reports of the boundary commissioners and the various instructions issued to them between August and November reflect the increasing importance of their work as well as the reasons why certain aspects of it were so complex. However, while the new rationalizations for *schedules A* and *B* derived from their work on the smaller boroughs it was not on these but on the larger boroughs that their most important work was done.

As long as it was a matter of the smaller boroughs the commissioners' instructions defined a simple mechanical procedure. Where a borough contained fewer than 300 £10 houses its 'deficiency' was to be made good by including a neighbouring district within its boundaries. It reveals the spuriousness of Davies' criticism of the enlargement of the boroughs that where such enlargement was necessary it would scarcely involve a merging of essentially distinct communities and possibly conflicting interests. Almost by definition, such 'deficient' boroughs were part of the same rural-agricultural-aristocratic complex as the adjoining county areas from which their necessary supplementary electors would be drawn. A square mile more or less of farmland might have important consequences in terms of *party* politics. The question whether the member or members for a borough would be Whig or Tory might well depend on whether a given estate was or was not included within its boundaries. But the socio-political consequences of such a question were slight. For these boroughs the Ministers could therefore ignore all but legal questions and simply require that their new boundaries coincide with those of 'parishes, townships, chapelries, or other divisions of known legal denomination'.[111] Ultimately, parish boundaries took precedence. In November the commissioners were told that if a borough were 'deficient', but the parish in which it was situated contained the requisite number of householders, then the boundaries of the borough were to be defined as those of the parish. If such boundaries were still inadequate one or more adjacent parishes were to be added.[112] The requirement that each borough contain at least 300 householders had already been dropped.[113] Nevertheless, in only two cases did the commissioners have to go beyond the stipulated seven mile limit to obtain a constituency which they hoped would contain such a number.[114]

But when the commissioners were concerned with those boroughs which already possessed adequate constituencies they were given other instructions which reflected both the greater social complexity of the consequent boundary problems and the greater importance of their task. Again, as with the smaller boroughs, the Ministers preferred that the new boundaries coincide with those of recognized local government units, but insisted that the boundaries of the larger boroughs be determined on the basis of social and economic criteria. The party political consequences of allowing a local Whig dynasty to compete with a local Tory dynasty in the same constituency were obviously considered far less important than the consequences of allowing the leaders of different varieties of social group to compete in the same constituency. The point is important for the same reason that the initial borough freeholder clause is important: it suggests the Ministers' concern to perpetuate the traditional agencies of electoral recruitment by separating the principal varieties of such agency into different constituencies. Whatever conflicts occurred between the leaders of the groups which these agencies reflected — and thus, by assimilation, between the members of these groups themselves — would only occur in the parliamentary arena, not in those other arenas in which the groups themselves existed and, thus in which their own existence might be jeopardized. For those boroughs which possessed adequate constituencies but which were not growing rapidly — that is, were not the major urban centres — the Ministers instructed the commissioners to use the boundaries of the present 'town' even when these boundaries conflicted with those of recognized local government units.[115] On the other hand, for those towns which were growing rapidly they instructed the commissioners to project the borough boundaries beyond the limits of the present 'town'. The commissioners, they wrote, should pay close attention

. . .to the direction in which . . . [the] Town . . . [was] increasing, to the principal lines of communication that now exist, or such as

are likely, from the nature of the surrounding country, or other circumstances, to be opened; and [to make] a liberal allowance . . . for the extension of the Town in such direction; so that the boundary determined today may not require alteration tomorrow.[116]
The commissioners' instructions differed according to the problems they were called upon to deal with. The constituency boundaries, when finally drawn up, helped to isolate the two most important types of community, the urban and the rural, for many years to come. And because of the borough freeholder clause – even in its amended form – redistribution served much the same purpose.

To isolate such gross types of community from one another was the most important function of the borough boundary commissioners. As a general rule, and particularly when it concerned new boroughs, such isolation was certainly considered more important than the isolation of neighbouring urban communities from one another if the latter implied the neglect of the former. Although the formal grouping of boroughs was never adopted in England as it was in Scotland and Wales, a number of urban districts were created in England in which a principal town was forced to share its right of separate representation with one or more adjacent towns. In dealing with the new borough of Wolverhampton, for example, the commissioners declared that 'the Towns of Wolverhampton, and Bilston, and the population immediately connected with their trade and manufactures, should form the principal object of [their] attention.'[117] In effect, they defined their problem as that of isolating these towns from the non-manufacturing parts of North Staffordshire. As they observed,

> These towns are intimately connected in interest. They are separated by an interval not exceeding a mile; and their increasing wealth and population renders it probable that this separation will in process of time become imperceptible.[118]

Acting on this basis, they recommended boundaries which defined the borough so as to include the parishes of Wolverhampton and Smedley. The former contained five townships, those of Wolverhampton, Bilston, Willenhall, Wednesfield, and Pelsall. While Smedley was partly agricultural its inclusion was rationalized on the grounds that it contained a number of manufacturing villages which would otherwise have diluted the county division.[119] In effect, because the boundaries of Wolverhampton defined the borough in terms of the hardware manufacturing area which Wolverhampton symbolized, and because the boundaries of other Black Country boroughs were similarly defined, the relevant county divisions of Staffordshire, Worcestershire and Warwickshire were largely insulated from most of the men 'immediately connected with their trade and manufacture'.

The same results were obtained in other parts of the kingdom where other industrial pockets had come into being. In North Lancashire, for example, the borough of Clitheroe was defined as the textile district between the River Ribble and the Pendle Hills. As such, the borough extended far beyond the immediate township of Clitheroe to include the chapelries of Clitheroe and Downham, and all parts of the chapelry of Whalley with the exception of the agricultural township of Read. [120] And its boundaries therefore helped to insulate the county division from the impact of those men who might look to the 'Clitheroe' mill-owners for their political guidance. Had no changes been made in the initial borough freeholder provisions these boundaries would have created a rural sea dotted with urban islands. As Disraeli noted later, the amendment of the borough freeholder clause provided the means by which urban leaders largely redrew the map. But from the evidence of Althorp's statement while introducing the amended borough freeholder clause, the Ministers did not intend to do more than slightly blur the outlines.

Social criteria were crucial. But they were applied within a framework of existing relationships and rights. Thus, as was explained by the subsequent committee which studied the commissioners' recommendations, the commissioners had been reluctant to provide the same 'board margin' for the old boroughs as they had provided for the new. The ambiguity which informed the Ministers' handling of the old franchise qualifications also informed their handling of the boundaries question. The Ministers perpetuated the freeman and other old franchises where these existed – provided, of course, that the would-be voters were resident. So the boundary commissioners keep an eye open for local feelings. For the new boroughs they drew their boundaries so that men

> ... connected with the same interest, and deriving employment from the same source, [might] participate with the Town itself in the exercise of a political privilege now conferred for the first time. [121]

But they also considered the 'jealousy and dislike which an old borough might feel to the extension of such a privilege to its surrounding neighbours'. [122]

XI

To isolate whatever urban areas might remain in the counties was one of the aims behind the Ministers' decision to divide all but one of the larger counties into two divisions, each of which would return two members, and to divide Yorkshire into three divisions, each to return two members. The Ministers hoped that these divisions would be equal in population, and that their boundaries would follow those of existing local government units. As with the boundaries of the boroughs, however, such hopes were often incompatible with the more important social and economic considerations which underlay their total scheme. They did not want to separate 'Districts and Places which, from their community of interest and feeling, manifestly ought to be placed in the same Division of their County.'[123] Ultimately, as between population and 'community of interest and feeling', community of interest generally won out. Lancashire, for example, was so divided that the population of the Northern Division, not including the population of the North Lancashire boroughs, was 258,190, while that of the Southern Division on the same basis was 392,431.[124] The rationale of such a division lay in the claim that the boundary separated 'almost all the agricultural portion of the county' – North Lancashire – from the commercial and manufacturing portion to the south.[125] As the commissioners themselves observed with regard to Leicestershire, the boundaries they proposed would best realize the 'object of separating the manufacturing from the agricultural population.'[126]

Perhaps because the proposal to divide the counties was made in public – it was contained in the Bill itself – it raised significant protest from those men who, had they known of the boundary commissioners' instructions, would undoubtedly have protested even more vehemently. Since electoral influence in most counties was associated with extensive landownership, and since many of the larger landowners were active political partisans, many urban reformers were concerned lest the division of the counties take place in such a way as to create new constituencies which, in their eyes, would be functionally similar to the nomination boroughs. No doubt facetiously, *The Times* even suggested that, instead of dividing the counties, an equal number of 'rotten boroughs' be restored. 'There was something in the unblushing effrontery of the rotten boroughs', they declared,

> that put people fairly on their guard, and gave them the consolation of feeling that if they were plundered, it was openly – *they were not ensnared and cheated*. But in a half-county election there is some semblance of popularity, on which if the freeholders, etc . . . place reliance, *it will be to have the mortification of finding themselves miserably duped and betrayed.*[127]

But the Ministers were not thinking in terms of *The Times'* implicit distinction between a 'free' and an 'unfree' electorate. They were thinking in terms of 'legitimate' and 'illegitimate' influence, the one a matter of face-to-face communities and groups of men who were joined together in the same 'interest', the other a mere matter of property and power. They saw little danger that the 'illegitimate' influence they associated with the nomination boroughs would ever find a home in the counties. As Althorp explained,

The patron of a borough could elect at his bidding whomsoever he pleased. But however influential a person might be in a county, he could not have that power. Without doubt, there would always be an influence exercised by a person possessed of property, and this was neither to be wondered at, nor objected to, but that influence would depend upon his popularity in some degree. [128]

Althorp's explanation is consistent with his arguments on the Chandos amendment. Indeed, before this amendment was forced upon the Ministers the only danger he saw in the counties was their growing tendency to return well-known Radicals, or the scions of noble families, on the basis of their 'mere popularity'. [129] He attributed this tendency to the extreme size of the electorate in many counties, and the consequent difficulty of a candidate's being returned unless his 'chief merit is, that his name is best known to all.' [130] Thus, for Althorp, the division of the counties served two related purposes, to increase the number of county members, and to increase the localism of political action in the counties. What with the greater intimacy and social homogeneity implied by a smaller geographical area he hoped that the division of the counties would encourage 'gentlemen of retiring habits [to stand, who] holding large property in the county . . . [would be] well qualified to represent its interests.' [131]

XII

The same concerns were reflected in the reconstruction of the borough electorates.

It has often been said that the post-reform borough electorates not only comprised a single electorate but a single electorate definable in class terms and that the Ministers sought to define it in these terms. But such a description of the Ministers' intentions makes no allowance for their adamant refusal to allow any man to vote in a borough who failed to satisfy the new residence requirements for the borough franchise. A great deal of time was, of course, spent discussing the prospective class composition of the £10-householders and these discussions reveal the depth of concern about the class question. But they scarcely resolve that other question, namely, whether the Ministers did in fact seek to create a *class* electorate in the boroughs – with all the social implications such a question came to have in subsequent political and historical discussion – or whether they sought to resolve the mounting problems of class relationship by emphasizing those other varieties of nexus which might possibly dull the importance of class differentiation. Indeed, since no man was to vote in a borough who did not reside in that borough, or within a seven-mile radius of it, it might be more appropriate to say that the Ministers' intended to create, not a single class electorate in the boroughs but a congeries of local or corporate electorates, each composed of men who were clearly associated with the borough where they each had the right to vote. But, however, the borough electorates be described, the Ministers' provisions for distribution reveal that they were trying to establish an overall balance within the State between or among the different interests which the different constituencies symbolized.

XIII

The redistribution schedules which the final Bill contained differed from those which the first Bill contained. But the differences were more of size than of balance. While the first Bill would have reduced the size of the house by 62 Members the final Bill left the size of the House as it was. This it did by reprieving a number of the smaller boroughs, by creating more new boroughs and by giving more seats to the English counties.

By the terms of the final Bill only 142 seats were redistributed. Thus, since the first Bill would have affected 168 seats – 62 abolished outright, 106 redistributed to other constituencies, some new, some old – for purposes of comparison, it might be said that the final Bill 'assigned' 26 more seats to the smaller English boroughs than the first Bill would have 'assigned' to them. In addition, it assigned seven more seats to the English counties. As against these 33 seats, which might reasonably be credited to the landed-*cum*-aristocratic interests, it only assigned 22 more seats to the English boroughs. The majority of these boroughs were located in the midlands and north where the social world was changing rapidly. But in several instances the interests subsequently represented from these boroughs were only indirectly those of a manufacturing and commercial community. Like Whitehaven, in Cumberland, where the Lonsdale interests were admittedly dominant, certain of these new boroughs provided seats for lordlings, or dependents of peers, who only differed from their more rural cousins in their perhaps greater ability, or eagerness, to profit from their landed wealth in an increasingly commercial world.[132]

Of course urban magnates retained their influence in the majority of the 60-odd seats for English open boroughs which had existed in the pre-reform period. They gained control of the majority of the 64-new English borough seats. However – and whatever the degree to which the one phenomenon was the cause of the other – after the Bill was passed and things had settled down a bit the leaders of the landed interest found that their own powers had been *restored* in most of the 82 pre-reform seats for the English counties. And, by the same token, they found that they were able to gain control of most of the 62 new

English county seats. In most of the smaller boroughs the powers of individual members of the aristocracy and gentry had never been questioned. All that had been questioned were the uses to which these powers were put. It was this question that Wellington sought to answer in such a way as might be expected to restore the political coalition which had finally broken up between 1829 and 1830.

XIV

It was a different sort of problem that the Ministers tried to deal with by creating electoral registers, increasing the number of polling booths, and reducing the time polling booths would be open. These provisions were principally designed to reduce the expense of contested elections. However, while the problems were different, the means by which the Ministers hoped to solve these problems reflect corporate assumptions similar to those which informed the other parts of their Bill.

On occasion, before 1832, contested elections – especially contested elections in the counties – were almost incredibly expensive, and for three main reasons: the existence of only one polling place in each constituency, the lack of direct political involvement on the part of many voters and – and especially in the counties – the legal problems of validating each would-be voter's right to vote.[133] Numerous freeholders refused to make the sometimes long and arduous journey to the single polling place in each county unless their expenses were fully covered and they were well entertained *en route*. Furthermore, it was standard practice for the partisans of one candidate to challenge the electoral qualifications of those who were the known partisans of a rival candidate. And it was also standard practice to use every available means not only to identify these partisans before the polling occurred – indeed, to identify partisans on *all* sides – but to discover the specific grounds on which any of those who might possibly be open to challenge, could be challenged.[134] Thus, the length of time which a voter might have to spend in the county town – and the size of the bill his candidates, of his candidates' friends, might have to pay – was, in part, a measure of the sometimes complex legal problems which were raised by the questioning of his right to vote. The right to vote in the counties was enjoyed by freeholders whose properties were assessed to the land tax or redeemed. Since much property had been redeemed from this tax without prejudice to the electoral rights belonging to it, the land tax assessment lists were grossly inaccurate as electoral registers.[135] Furthermore, many county elections were decided less at the polls than in the offices of the assessors who decided whether each would-be voter whose right to vote had been challenged was really qualified.[136] It was presumably not irrelevant to these general problems that voters might be more willing to vote, and at a lower price, if they were more closely identified with the interests the different constituencies symbolized. More specifically, however, the Ministers proposed to establish numerous polling places in each county and to provide, at public expense, a register of the men who were qualified to vote at each polling place. Under these circumstances they also proposed that no poll would remain open for more than two days.

Few M.P.s can have enjoyed what were probably the increasing costs of politics in the pre-reform period.[137] They gladly agreed to the increased numbers of polling places and the shortened duration of the poll. But there were many who looked askance at the suggested procedures for drawing up the electoral registers, particularly in the counties. A number of men objected to the initial proposal that the cost of drawing up the electoral registers be placed on the county rates or, in the boroughs, upon the rates of the respective parishes. They also objected to making the parish overseers responsible for drawing up the county registers. They granted that the overseers might successfully draw up lists of the voters who were also occupiers of property in their respective parishes, but they doubted that these men would include the names of the non-resident freeholders.[138] Since rates were paid by the occupiers of property, and since the rate books were kept by the overseers, even the simplest overseer might be competent to list the occupiers in either county or borough whose assessments were of the requisite value. However, since there were no readily available records of landownership which might secure the inclusion of the non-resident freeholders it was feared that many of these would be omitted.

In answer to these criticisms the Ministers cited the inherent self-knowledge which they attributed to the members of local communities. Indeed, in their various drafts of the Bill they provided means by which this self-knowledge might be used to compensate for the overseers' possible deficiencies. Once drawn up, the registration lists were to be posted on the doors of all churches and chapels within the parish for two successive Sundays. Qualified voters who were not included might then discover their plight. The inclusion of unqualified persons might similarly be noticed. Claims and objections were to be heard later by specially appointed barristers. When the Bill's opponents asked how the non-resident freeholders might learn that they had been omitted from the lists Althorp had an answer at hand which confirms the premises of many of his other statements: 'Their tenantry . . . would . . . apprize them.'[139]

But the Bill's opponents were not convinced. As one of them argued, this system would require the appointment of attorneys either by each non-resident freeholder, to make sure his name was included, or by each Member, 'to make sure that his friends were put upon the list, and to prevent improper persons from being inserted on it. And', he added, 'as the list was to be made out annually, these agents must be retained annually.'[140] To Althorp, on the other hand, such fears were groundless. 'Every candidate', he said, 'would have plenty of intelligent friends who would look at the lists for him, and give him the necessary information.'[141]

Yet by the time the final Bill was passed the Ministers had acknowledged the sense of some of these criticisms. For the boroughs, the registration procedure remained the same as that defined in the early drafts of the Bill. But in their third Bill they placed the full burden of claiming the right to vote upon the would-be county voter himself. Furthermore, while the registration lists in both county and borough were to be revised annually, the county lists would be quasi-permanent: any man, once registered in a county, would remain registered unless, for whatever reason, his right to vote were challenged and he failed to respond adequately to the challenge.[142] During the committee stage of this Bill they also accepted Joseph Hume's suggestion that the county voter pay the expense of registering his claim.[143] The clause was amended to provide that each person who claimed a county vote should accompany his claim with a shilling.

Placing these registration procedures within the context of the overall scheme Althorp happily prophesied that 'gentlemen of small forture [would be able] to stand for Representation of their respective counties, without incurring ruinous expense.'[144] Russell was more specific. He ventured that a seat for a divided county would now cost no more than £500 and for an undivided county no more than £1,000.[145]

XV

The Bill was a complex measure and particularly so in that some of its provisions were conditioned or triggered by others. As a rule, however, those who have studied the Bill have not only ignored these conditioning or triggering *relationships*, they have also ignored the principal provisions which either influenced, or were influenced by, the provisions on which they have concentrated. Or, as recently, while acknowledging the existence of one of these provisions, the borough freeholder clause, they have sought to discount its importance, first, by noting that it was, after all, amended – which is an important point but its bearing, as the reasons for amendment suggest, upon the Ministers' intentions should not be overestimated – and, second, by suggesting that the initial formulation of this clause was either an 'inadvertence' or, at most, the product of a passing and essentially superficial political alliance. These observations and suggestions both reflect and confirm certain assumptions, namely that the effective demands for reform were *urban* demands, that the Ministers hoped to afford sure ground of resistance to further innovation' by 'conceding' additional political power to the new interests which urbanization and industrialization were creating. But, is the interpretation of the Bill which fitted Professor Seymour's evidence still appropriate when the errors in his evidence have been revealed?

Certainly, in the late twenties and early thirties there were many urban critics of the existing socio-political system. The exigencies of their positions *vis-à-vis* their followers perhaps led them not only to claim but to believe that they were, in fact, controlling the course of events during the reform crisis – that the Ministers had drafted the Bill because of *their* demands and agitations and that *they,* by their continued agitations, were keeping the Ministers up to the mark.[146] This argument is implicit in John Cannon's conclusion to his recent work where he quotes Lady Belgrave's statement that the Bill 'will clip the aristocracy', and her observation, that 'a great deal must be sacrificed to save the rest.'[147] But if the Bill be considered *as a whole,* and if its various provisions be considered both in relation to one another and in relation to the contemporary political scene – a part of which was, of course, those agitations, we find ourselves asking whether the Ministers, as full or partial members of the aristocracy, were really trying to buy their own survival and, if so, to whom the ransom was being paid. We are concerned with much more basic problems than whether the Ministers were 'attend[ing] to grievances . . . [or] yield[ing] to the demands to which these grievances had given rise'.[148] We are concerned with the identities of those whose grievances were the effective ones; the role of legislation in effecting those changes in the locus of political power which are often subsumed under the general heading, the growth of political democracy; the nature of the nineteenth century political system; the role of Parliament within this system; and the reasons why it is so often assumed that Parliament was – and is – composed of essentially disinterested agents of 'the peoples' ' will.

If the new residence requirements for the borough franchise and the borough freeholder clause are both ignored, and if the boundaries question is dismissed as unimportant, then nothing stands in the way of two related conclusions: first, that the new household franchise in the boroughs was a 'class' franchise, and, second, that this franchise, taken together with the creation of new boroughs was 'the technical means of infusing fresh life into the narrow and unpopular governing system.'[149] These conclusions are sound within the context of the remaining provisions of the Bill, but their fundamental cogency must depend upon the validity of the logically antecedent but totally implicit premise that the Bill may be described without distortion in terms of its remaining provisions. With these other provisions in mind it might be more appropriate to say that the new household franchise in the boroughs was the means of creating a set of electoral communities, that this franchise, together with the creation of new boroughs, were 'the technical means' of channelling and counter-acting those infusions of 'fresh life' which were already occurring. Indeed, if the Bill be considered as a whole, and if its various provisions be considered both in relation to one another and in relation to the contemporary political scene, we find ourselves asking if the various Radical demands and agitations were really steps on the way to the solution of the problem as the Ministers saw it or part of the problem. Or – to put it differently – in Norman Gash's words, were the Ministers trying 'to restore to the government that broad basis of national confidence which it had previously lacked and without which it could not effectively exist', primarily by sociological and psychological means or primarily by means of that real transference of political power which the concession theory tries to explain.[150]

This is not to suggest that the Bill was a Machiavellian device designed to provide the semblance of power without the reality. Rather, that the social interpretation of the Bill usually adopted by historians was primarily a function of the political needs and related political perspectives of the Radicals and the anti-reformers. The Radicals and the anti-reformers both proclaimed that the Bill would basically alter the balance of political power between the landed and urban interests. But the Ministers themselves made no such claim. Instead, they spoke of the need to abolish nomination and to establish the requisite conditions for representation. And, to remind their various opponents and supporters what the Bill was all about, they frequently referred to those provisions of the Bill which the others tended to ignore. As Palmerston put it on the third night of debate, one of the major defects of the existing constituency structure was the lack of separate representation for the larger manufacturing towns. To correct this defect, he observed, the Government proposed to enfranchise these towns. 'And,' he went on,

> because this was done a cry had been raised that the balance between the agricultural and manufacturing interests was destroyed. But the plan went to *restore* to the landed interest that influence which he thought indispensable to the safety and prosperity of the country, by giving fifty-five Members to the counties, and still further, by conferring votes on copyholders, and not permitting those who had votes for towns to enjoy the same privilege in counties.[151]

The Bill cannot be divorced from the general context of accelerating industrialization and population movement, and growing intellectual ferment. However – and perhaps because of the tendency to look at the Bill through the eyes of the various polemicists – these symptoms of the problem which the Ministers tried to deal with have become confused with the cure they prescribed. ' . . . in the long run', Professor Gash declares,

> the politician is the servant of the forces he directs. The deliberations of the cabinet committee on reform, and the Reform Act itself, were only symptoms of a much wider movement in the country. To ascribe solely to the decisions of a handful of ministers or to a single statute the immense political developments after 1832 is scarcely a tenable proposition. The Whigs must bear responsibility for the Reform Act of 1832, but as instruments rather than as creators. [152]

The questions raised here are extremely important but the crucial ones are begged – and begged, it would seem, because certain of the Bill's provisions were considered in isolation from others with which they had a causal link.

All reformers agreed in criticising the pre-reform structure: this is a simple tautology. But they did not agree on why the structure should be changed. Nor did they agree on the form or forms of the changes. Without detailing the reasons, or combinations of reasons, why different men were reformers, it should nevertheless be noted that some were reformers because they believed reform would be a step towards the abolition of the monarchy, the House of Lords and the Established Church; others because they believed it would strengthen these institutions; some because they believed it would accelerate the progress towards free trade; others because they believed it would reverse this progress; some because they believed it would guarantee the currency settlement of 1819; others because they believed it would be the prelude to the undoing of this settlement. Nor can we say who was right and who was wrong, because the effects of the Act cannot be distinguished from the effects of the efforts of the men who worked within the structure defined by the Act. [153]

The multiplicities of reasons why men were reformers helps to explain why the Bill was passed. But they also reveal the importance of a problem which, as a rule, historians have ignored. The nature of this problem can be seen from the Tory journalist's statement; in 1830, that certain changes should be made in the ways MPs were chosen. Of course, he never ceased to oppose 'reform' when the term was used to describe what the Radicals had in mind. He merely sought to reduce the excessive 'dependence' of many MPs. [154] Yet, by proposing reforms while opposing 'reform', he illustrates the problem whose very existence has been obscured by the obvious choices which the Ministers made. Reform had perhaps become essential by the time the Grey

Ministry took office. But to say there were no alternatives to their proposals is to obscure the many alternatives which, in fact, did exist until their own proposals displaced them.[155] The Bill obviously reflected dissatisfaction with the existing political structure. But *whose* dissatisfaction did it reflect? This question will remain unanswered unless we understand that different men had different grounds for dissatisfaction. But to note the point does not solve the problem. We have to identify all those men whose dissatisfaction taken together explains the Bill in its entirety. And, for some historians, the problem thus formulated apparently raises serious methodological difficulties.

Once the Bill was introduced it became such an important factor in the efforts of rival politicians to secure or gather strength that many of *their* statements about it must be read more for what they reveal of these efforts and the reasons for them than what they reveal of the Bill itself. But the Bill exists, and exists in its several versions. Thus, it is evidence of the textual changes that were made between the first and last drafts. More important, it is a potential frame of reference against which the statements of the various polemicists might be tested for their particular relevance. And its value for this purpose is particularly enhanced when its own provisions are seen in the context of the behaviour of various men in various constituencies in the immediate pre-reform period. Problems are obviously raised by each of the several varieties of evidence available to historians – especially when the evidence is used to describe motives and related values. Recently, Dr. Milton-Smith warned of the dangers of trying to infer motives and values from actions. 'It is precarious', he observed, 'to draw general conclusions about the motives of a whole Cabinet by concentrating upon its enactments'.[156] He is, of course, quite right. But it is even more precarious to search for motives in 'the private and public statements of actors and observers – his preferred locus – while failing to note exactly what these men were doing and seeing.[157] John Cannon's observation is similar: since 'sociological analysis has yet to provide a wholly satisfactory explanation of the motivation of the bill . . . [historians] must fall back on the more conventional evidence provided by private letters and public statements.'[158] But, if the test of the value of evidence be the usefulness of the conclusions to which it ostensibly leads, the temptations to 'fall back on the more conventional evidence' will not be very great. According to Dr. Cannon,

> The impression which these sources leave is that the ministers introduced reform primarily because they believed that the old system had lost the confidence of the country and could not go on. Grey was a reluctant reformer, moved mainly by the desire to restore public tranquillity, while Durham, Althorp and the more radical members of his cabinet welcomed the need for change. The

solution, acceptable to both groups, was to strengthen the institutions of the country by bringing into the representation the prosperous middle class and to eliminate those features of the old system that had, over the years, brought it into disrepute. [159]

Whatever the differences between Grey on the one hand and 'the more radical members of his cabinet' on the other, such a conclusion is open to several criticisms. In the first place, it obscures the elements of balance within the Bill. If, in fact, the Bill really served to bring 'the prosperous middle class' in the representation – and such a proposition might be challenged in each of its particulars – was no compensation offered to the others? If compensation was offered how does this affect the proposition itself? In the second place, it obscures the nature of the process by which 'the old system . . . [was] brought . . . into disrepute.'

After 1 March 1831 the question whether the members of the Grey Ministry believed 'that the old system . . . could not go on' was presumably irrelevant. But, the question whether, in trying to create a new system, they were trying to provide a means by which, in Cannon's words, 'the prosperous middle class' might be brought 'into the representation', or by which, in Gash's words, the 'forces' generated by industrialization could be transmitted into the political world does require an answer. If the Bill be considered *as a whole,* and if its various provisions be considered both in relation to one another and in relation to the contemporary political scene, it seems clear that the Ministers were, in fact, trying to control the effects of the antecendent impact of 'the prosperous middle class' upon 'the representation', trying to prevent the 'forces' which neither they nor anyone else could control from destroying the existing balance of political power and the traditional forms of social power.

What with the functional definition of the nomination boroughs which the anti-reformers provided, and about which many Radicals agreed, it is understandable that these Radicals were subsequently very disappointed that the Act was not the prelude to such things as the repeal of the corn laws and of the law of primogeniture. In 1837, as a means of attaining *these* ends – 'the advantages', as Thomas Wakley put it, 'that were intended to be conferred on . . . ["the people"] by the Reform Bill' – Wakley proposed a further extension of the franchise, the adoption of the secret ballot, and the repeal of the Septennial Act. [160] To which Russell made the following reply:

> . . . at the time the Reform Act was passed, I stated my belief that it must necessarily give a preponderance to the landed interest; and, although it may be deemed that such a preponderance has been somewhat unduly given, I still think that a preponderance in favour of that interest tends to the stability of the general institutions of the country. It is my opinion that to frame a plan of reform which

should give weight only to the large towns, to the exclusion of the greay body of the landed interest, meaning by the term not merely the landlords, but the farmers and the tenants of the country, would be to introduce elements of general disorder; and I cannot suppose that those who would be thus unjustly deprived of their franchise would never rest quite under that plan of government until they had, by every means, endeavoured to reinstate themselves in their due position in the country.[161]

Of course, this says nothing about the mechanisms which the Ministers hoped to strengthen in their obvious effort 'to afford sure ground of resistance to further innovation'. But one point at a time.

XVI

As a rule, the first Reform Act has been considered in the context of that historical model often associated with James Harrington's *Oceana,* according to which changes in the balance of economic power inevitably produce concomitant changes in the balance of political power. In much the same way that Harrington atrributed the defeat of Charles I to the growing wealth of the gentry, most historians have attributed the first Reform Act to the growing wealth of the new middle class or classes. In their attempts to define the dynamics of the Act they have focused their attentions upon industrialization, Radical agitation, and the ostensible Whig belief that 'concession to a sustained popular demand ... [is] the wisest policy for a governing aristocracy.'[162] And then they have gone on to discuss the sort of measure Wakley thought had been passed, the sort of measure Wellington described, the sort of measure which might be explained as the product of such phenomena. But that measure was never drafted. To account for the measure which was drafted another model is required as a means of organizing a somewhat different set of causal phenomena.

5

The background and social logic of the Act

I

Speaking in October, 1831, Wellington claimed that the 'spirit of Reform' which the Bill reflected 'was a consequence of the French Revolution [1830].' [1] Speaking in March, two days after the Bill was introduced, Peel pointed to a different source. Without naming Sir James Graham directly he charged that Graham was responsible 'who [the previous spring] called for the Pension List of the Privy Council, for the express purpose of holding up the members of that Council to public indignation.' [2]

Wellington's claim makes no sense at all. By obscuring those demands for reform which preceded the Paris Revolution, and to which the Bill is related, he not only distorted the nature of the reform crisis, he distorted the nature of the Bill. As for Peel's charge, it makes no sense as it stands. Its weakness lies in its personal nature. The effective demands for reform which the Bill reflects cannot be attributed to Graham's request for a return of all salaries, pensions and emoluments received by Privy Councillors. [3] But the importance of this information to Graham, to Peel, and to many others, both in Parliament and out, points to certain problems to which the effective demands for reform can be attributed and to which the Bill itself was directly related. At the core of these problems was the existence of a governmental system in which many important elements within the kingdom has lost confidence. In part, their loss of confidence was a function of structure: the governmental system failed to provide adequate nexus between Ministers, Members of Parliament, and the leaders of the significant groups or communities throughout the kingdom. But the structural problem only came to a head because the question arose whether certain policies to which there was widespread opposition were not themselves functions of this structure.

II

The members of the Liverpool and Wellington Governments were not party leaders in the modern sense. Parties did not exist as they do today as agencies of parliamentary discipline because they did not exist either as agencies of ideological consensus or as agencies of electoral recruitment. Nor were these men party leaders in the eighteenth century sense. By the early nineteenth century the numbers of placemen had been greatly reduced: numerous sinecures had been abolished; numerous jobs within the Government had been removed from Treasury control. Nor did many members of these Cabinets have significant influence of their own to compensate for the declining influence of the crown. By and large, their qualifications for office were training, ability, or capacity for work, not social position, ownership of wide estates, or possession of borough influence.[4] Hence, in large part, their problems. Many of these men participated actively in the intellectual life of their time. But the governmental machinery through which they tried to adapt the kingdom to the circumstances of a new era – or, at least, to the circumstances as they understood them – was, if anything, even less efficient than that which others before them had used to deal with rather less exacting problems. In alliance with many individual backbenchers some of them worked to establish the stable currency and the reduced tariffs which, they hoped, would allow British manufacturers and merchants to gain an increasing share of the world's markets. Others, with similar help, sought to increase the efficiency of the legal and administrative systems. From their offices in Whitehall or Dublin Castle they prepared their measures in theoretical or pragmatic terms. Then, to obtain the necessary parliamentary sanction, they depended primarily upon the same cosmopolitan opinion of these matters which informed their own positions and upon the traditional confidence in the wisdom of the king's advisors. The effective influence they were able to exercise was minimal. The main functions of Parliament in this scheme of things were to approve their proposals and, on occasion, to criticise their conduct. This was natural. As the governmental system was then constituted M.P.s could not have done more. Certainly, they could not have served as the channels of an effective extra-parliamentary dynamic. Nor could they have provided the means of securing essential support for ministerial policies throughout the kingdom. The Ministers' mode of procedure was a function of the absence of formal nexus between themselves and the various M.P.s and, again, between these M.P.s and the increasingly articulate groups in the kingdom. But the reactions both to their policies and to their modes of procedure were also functions of the absence of these nexus.

Before 1832 the formal constituency structure of the kingdom was not very different from what it had been a century or two earlier. But the roles of these constituencies had changed in ways suggested by the theory of virtual representation. Originally constituencies had tended in many cases to coincide with the significant communities of the kingdom. They had provided means of representation for important local interests. As such, they had also provided means by which the support of some at least of these interests might be secured for government policies. But in many cases in the early nineteenth century they no longer performed either role. Many boroughs had decayed into sheep-run or pasture. Many new towns had grown up to confuse the political world of the counties. And, in the meantime, the intensity of politics was rising: phenomena were becoming problems.

According to the theory of virtual representation the merchants of Manchester were represented by the Members for Liverpool, London or Preston, the Yorkshire squires who had been unable to prevent the return of John Marshall and Henry Brougham by the Members for a more rural county. Such a theory, and the political structure it served to rationalize, were all very well for those who considered themselves adequately represented. But as British society became more complex, and as pressures on Parliament to enact legislation for this, that or another group increased the confidence and patience which this theory presupposed were increasingly dissipated. In these circumstances it was almost inevitable that more and more people should have come to feel they were virtually unrepresented.

Furthermore – and in spite of the degree to which the Government had been weakened by the abolition of sinecures and the prohibitions against certain categories of placemen and Government contractors sitting in the House of Commons – those beliefs in the context of which these sinecures were abolished and these prohibitions adopted had hardly been weakened. It was still thought that where money or money's worth passed between the members of a political group the cohesion of that group was simply a function of such ostensible 'corruption.' Indeed, while the various administrative reforms and declarations of ineligibility to sit in the House of Commons were designed primarily to reduce the influence of the crown – in effect, to reduce the influence of the Government – they may have served more to intensify than to ease the suspicions from which they derived. Writing in 1820, Russell claimed, 'there still remain[ed] enough [jobs] to support an independent, unpopular, incapable administration' And, he went on, revealing the degree to which the structural problem was not to be solved by the means thus far adopted, while it had been said

. . . that the reduction of establishment and offices diminishes the influence of the crown, yet an establishment once reduced, is on the contrary a source of increased influence; for persons who have served will be much more anxious to be appointed to a vacancy, than those who have not already devoted themselves to a profession.[6]

Juxtaposed on certain other assumptions, this assumption led him to conclude that the influence of the crown had 'not only been augmented, but organized and directed in a manner never before known'.[7]

This statement has been described as a gross exaggeration.[8] Clearly, it was. But whatever the degree of exaggeration it contained, it was still important. What with the growing problems of policy in the immediate pre-reform period, the assumptions it reflects help to explain why Graham requested a return of all salaries, pensions and emoluments received by Privy Councillors. They also help to explain why this information was so important.

III

Considered in terms of abstract power and abstract relationships the case which Graham and various others put together in the immediate pre-reform period was scarcely new. Its principal elements can be found in the arguments of many eighteenth century reformers. They can also be found in the arguments of Sir James Mackintosh, in 1809, about the large numbers of men who were seeking jobs in the military, religious, legal, civil and colonial 'establishments', the amounts of money these 'establishments' required, and the consequent power of the men who controlled appointments within them.

As Mackintosh put it, 'almost every man above the rank of labouring mechanic, has pretensions, more or less direct or immediate, to some . . . appointment [within one of these establishments].' And, he went on, since England had become 'a nation of public functionaries, . . . a prodigious proportion of the whole national income [had been placed] in the gift of those who have the nomination of these functionaries.'[9] Russell perhaps saw the problem of Government influence in more extreme terms than Mackintosh. With respect to Graham, however, there is no question. By then the structural aspects of these problems had been magnified by their policy aspects.

Mackintosh was concerned about the problem of taxes. As he noted, the burden of taxes was one of the principal evils from which the demand for parliamentary reform had arisen.[10] But these taxes scarcely played the same role in his analysis as they did in Graham's, or even in Russell's. According to Mackintosh, taxes were not the symbol of corruption they became in Graham's eyes when their burden had been aggravated by deflation. Nor did Mackintosh place quite the same emphasis as Russell did later on the ways in which these taxes served to consolidate the interests of the holders of the national debt with the interests of the Government. Mackintosh observed, as Russell observed after him, that the burden of taxes helped to increase the demand for parliamentary reform. But, he noted, these taxes were required to pay for wars which had been and still were popular.[11] Thus, not much could really be said against them. Nor did he protest against the high level of salaries. As he explained, unless salaries were high good men could not be attracted into government service.[12] Nor, again, did he protest against the number of offices in the State. Rather, he focussed upon the patronage system by which these offices were filled. According to Mackintosh, M.P.s were 'debased' by the patronage system. Not that they were the direct beneficiaries of the system. The benefits accrued to others. But the system encouraged them to support the Government of the day in the hope of influencing the distribution of patronage much as 'the people' supported the Government in the hope of receiving this patronage.[13]

In effect, issues *qua* issues had little to do with Mackintosh's analysis. He was far less concerned about the uses to which the powers of government were put than with the monopoly of power in certain hands 'to the discomfiture of others'.[14] As such, his argument reveals that jealousy of the 'outs' for the 'ins' which was such an important factor in early nineteenth century politics. In addition, it reveals that basic distrust of the central government which, by definition, the 'ins' controlled. Yet on this point Mackintosh found himself in something of a dilemma. According to him, the plethora of offices which were an adjunct of the central government could not simply be abolished. And if the patronage were taken away from the M.P.s whom it 'debased' – obviously, he conceived no other way of filling these offices except by patronage – then he who fell heir to it would be supreme in the State.[15] The only 'remedy' he could see was one he rejected: to destroy much of the power of the central government by letting counties and parishes choose their own tax gatherers, clergy and magistrates.[16] As he noted, this would strengthen 'local partialities'.[17] And, from his point of view, this was not desirable. The only 'palliative' he could see was the 'increased intelligence and spirit of the people'.

Mackintosh was clearly being pulled two ways, one way by his strong nostalgia for an idealized pre-urban or pre-industrial society, another by his even stronger belief that a Government based on such a society would not be adequate to the needs of the day. His dilemma itself, and his choice between the alternatives he defined, are important, and not only because the problems of patronage were important. They are important because they reveal the differences between his own choice and the choice which the members of the Grey Ministry made some 20 years later. The grounds on which he rejected his 'remedy' for the problems of patronage were closely related to those on which he argued the need for parliamentary reform. However, as various provisions of the Bill reveal, the members of the Grey Ministry were less reluctant than he to strengthen 'local partialities'.

As with the problems of patronage, so with the other problems with which he dealt, the grievances which defined these problems as 'problems' were fairly abstract. He argued the need for parliamentary reform not in the context of any substantive issues but in the context of a general process which gave weight to two related distinctions. The one had to do with forms of government, the other with varieties of influence. The process was that by which these varieties of influence had become distinct.

According to Mackintosh, there were two forms of government, the old and the new. The old were more stable, the new more vigorous and able. The stability of the old was a measure of 'the natural tendency of influence derived from wealth, to settle and consolidate into a sort of patriarchal chieftainship, which gains strength by descent and duration.' As he put it,

> An old government is a mass made up of a congeries of little circles, each of which has its own fixed centre and point of radiation. Every county, and district, and parish, and village, has its settled heads and leaders, through whom, as their natural organ, their sentiments and wishes are made known, and by whose influences they may be greatly impressed with the wishes and sentiments of others. [18]

Clearly, his 'remedy' for the problems of patronage was to enlarge the roles of these 'congeries of little circles'. However – this obviously explains his rejection of the 'remedy' – while an 'old government' might be more stable than a 'new', it would inevitably be less enlightened. As he described it, the reasons for this lay in the varieties of influence associated with each sort of government.

According to Mackintosh, since property could be accumulated over time and transmitted from one generation to another, its concentrations were constantly growing. Thus, the influences which derived from property were constantly growing. But such was not the case with respect to the influences which derived from 'personal gifts and accomplishments'. Because such 'gifts and accomplishments' could not be passed on from one generation to another the influences which derived from them were 'stationary'. [19] In effect, as a general rule, parliamentary reform was needed to countervail the relative incremental tendencies of these two varieties of influence. And, he argued, it was particularly needed because those who comprised the '[aristocracy] of rank or hereditary wealth' were no longer those who comprised the 'aristocracy of personal merit'.

'In order to make any government secure and peaceful', he explained, 'these two aristocracies must be *united*.[20] And in former times, he argued, they had been united. When the duties of rulers were easy, and when luxuries did not exist, rulers were generally suited to their tasks. They monopolized education and had no other ambition than that of performing their duties. But this was before the 'privileged orders' had been seduced by luxuries and before the 'common people' acquired education. In effect, in feudal times the necessary virtues were all to be found in the same men. But in the early nineteenth century they were not. Hence the need for parliamentary reform: since the requisite unity between the two aristocracies could no longer be found in the 'superior skill, valour and accomplishments of hereditary chieftains', it was necessary that these relinquish 'a large share of political power to those who have become their equals in all kinds of personal endowments.'[21]

Russell's observation of 1826 incorporated both these and certain other assumptions. While Huskisson, in Liverpool, was promising his constituents the rapid and total repeal of the corn laws, Russell teased the Ministers with the notion that unless Parliament were reformed their own 'liberal' policies might come a 'cropper': those M.P.s, he explained,

> who were returned ... not by the people, but by those who regularly opposed themselves on all occasions to the people, would protest in very strong terms against the liberal system of policy which ministers had lately pursued.[22]

He was right about the general course of ministerial policy. He was also right about the general source of prospective opposition. But in his short and teasing observation he ignored the question whether, as Ministers continued to pursue liberal policies certain of those who opposed these policies might not themselves become reformers. In effect, two points were ignored: first, that reform meant change, and that change could occur in any direction; and, second, that the borough patrons were less the members of a social class than they were the members of an administrative clique. It was this latter point which Graham recognized. And, recognizing this point his argument was very different.

Of course, all three men had certain common concerns. All three were deeply disturbed by the increase in taxes, the increase in the national debt, the increase in the numbers of fundholders, and the growing size of the various 'establishments'. But Mackintosh and Russell saw these problems more as problems of power than as conditioners of policy. Writing in 1820, Russell expressed the belief that .when fundholders, office holders and M.P.s supported the Government their support was essentially a measure of the benefits they derived from the Government or hoped to derive from it. Writing in the latter twenties, Graham expressed the same belief. But in the latter twenties, when the burden of taxes and the problems faced by producers for the domestic market were being aggravated by deflation, the belief led Graham to distinguish, as Mackintosh had not, between the 'settled heads and leaders' of the 'congeries of little circles' on the one hand, and the borough patrons on the other. It was this distinction which the Bill reflected.

IV

The currency question and the related question of the malt tax played important roles in the growth of an effective demand for reform because they provided the means by which the structural arguments of such men as Mackintosh and Russell were transformed into social arguments or, to put it somewhat differently, they played important roles because they provided the means of identifying ostensible villains.[23] Nor was the political importance of these questions lessened by the fact that the economic roles of the malt tax and of 'Peel's Act', as it was often called – the measure of 1819 by which the convertibility of paper money into gold was restored – were matters of such intense controversy. On the currency question there was agreement on the substantive points alone: many prices had risen during the wars when nonconvertible paper money was issued in fairly large quantities; and many prices had fallen after peace was restored and the convertibility of paper money into gold at the pre-war rate of exchange was also restored. But there was no agreement on why prices rose or why they fell. In part, the reasons for this had to do with the novelty of such price movements and the total lack of relevant information except that of the prices themselves. But obviously – what with the political use that was made of these price phenomena – this lack of agreement also had to do with the differential advantages of inflation and deflation to different groups in British society. It was upon these differential advantages that Graham and others focussed.

During the wars, Graham argued, when the principal need had been to increase domestic food production, many landowners had mortgaged their properties to raise money both for land improvement and for land purchase preliminary to land improvement. They had done this in the light of the parliamentary declaration that the pound notes they used were equivalent in value to the legal coin of the realm.[24] Then, when the wars ended, in 1815, they had sought – and, according to him, somewhat foolishly sought – to keep domestic agricultural prices at levels above those which would fairly compensate them for their immediate fiscal burdens. According to Graham, landowners had a legitimate claim to protection equivalent to their fiscal burdens.[25] But they had sought and obtained a larger amount of protection, one principally designed, as he put it, to perpetuate high rents and thus the cultivation of inferior soils.[26] Since the prices required to support such rents put pressure on urban wages and urban profits, the corn law had intensified urban hostility towards them. Nor had the corn law been successful in the countryside. According to Graham, the ostensible effort to perpetuate high prices as a means of perpetuating high rents had made farming hazardous and rents unpredictable. '. . . Whether the price of wheat will rise to 78s. per quarter,' he explained, 'when the profit of the farmer would be enormous, or touch the maximum of 80, when, by the opening of the ports and of the granaries of corn in bond, wheat would instantly fall at least 50 per cent to his utter ruin, is a matter almost of accident, frequently influenced by fraud.'[27] In effect, according to Graham, the corn law of 1815 had failed to provide landowners with the positive benefits they hoped for. But even more important in his eyes, by isolating them politically the corn law had raised a barrier against the development of an effective alliance between themselves and others who were the common victims of deflation. Such an alliance had become essential lest English society be convulsed by the consequences of deflation.

As Graham described it, the measure of 1819 was not the consequence of any villainy. It had been adopted out of ignorance. No one had understood how the sudden restoration of convertibility would affect prices, the value of money and the burden of taxes after 20-odd years during which the Bank of England had issued paper money without the limitation implied by the legal requirement that they redeem their paper in gold. Furthermore, at the time 'Peel's Act' was passed special circumstances affecting the price of gold had confirmed the notion that paper money might again be tied to gold at the pre-war rate of exchange without any significant effect upon the general level of prices. In consequence, the need to cushion the impact of the restoration of convertibility had not been recognized. Parliament had, as Graham put it, '. . . carried the restoration of the ancient standard of value without any adjustment of contracts made in a debased currency or provision for the increased incumbrances of all debts, taxes, and annuities [which such an action inevitably entailed].'[28] The Act they passed did little more than set the date at which all contracts negotiated in paper would become payable in gold.

During the subsequent contraction of the currency many prices, especially agricultural prices, fell sharply. About this there was no disagreement. The price of wheat, for example, fell by half between 1819 and 1822. It never regained its former levels and scarcely ever reached such levels as would have allowed it to be imported under the provisions of the corn law of 1815. But there the agreement stopped. There was no agreement about why so many prices had fallen nor about what should be done. According to Ricardo, the return to cash payments had affected wheat prices at most by 10 per cent. The remainder of the roughly 50 per cent change he attributed to other factors, primarily to increases in supply.[29] Thus, according to his lights, there was nothing to be done about these prices except what was being done by allowing those lands to go out of cultivation which could not be cultivated at such prices. According to Graham and many others, however, increases in supply had far less to do with the existing levels of price than those reductions in the amount of money in circulation which had been the consequence of restoring convertibility. In effect, according to their lights, these prices were themselves the consequence of legislation. Thus, a solution might be found in legislation.

As a rule, the different explanations for these price movements, and the different proposals as to how these movements should be dealt with were directly related to the ways in which the explainers or proposers were themselves affected. In general, the men who suffered most were those who had either borrowed money when prices were high, or who had goods to sell at home. They saw the real value of their debts increase and the prices fall with which these debts could be paid. On the other hand, the men who thrived were those who had loaned money when prices were high, who had fixed money incomes, or who had goods to sell abroad. In occupational categories, those who suffered most included farmers, landowners, and manufacturers for the domestic market. Those who thrived most included fundholders, government officials, pensioners, annuitants, mortgagees, and the foreign merchants and manufacturers for the foreign market who found the rates of exchange turning in their favour. In many cases, however, the same man found himself in both camps. This was particularly true among landowners. As receivers of rent which, at any given level of productivity, was largely a function of price, many landowners were eager to restore war-time prices by reinflating the currency. But as creditors of the State, as receivers of official salaries and pensions, and·as annuitants, others were concerned to prevent that inflation which would erode their other forms of capital and income. And, quite apart from the question of crude economic interest, since landowners provided the major group from which ministerial offices were filled, a number of the most prominent among them were drawn into the ideological orbits which the political economists were able to influence through their influence both in the City and the Treasury.

Undoubtedly, the non-agricultural roles of many landowners – or the ambiguities of their roles – somewhat limited the extent of the rural demand for currency reform. Furthermore, the non-agricultural roles of these men undoubtedly facilitated their use of the Ricardian argument, that post-war prices were less a function of the currency than of increases in supply. However – and the point is crucial – these increases in supply were generally conceived more in terms of the greater areas of land which had been brought under cultivation during the wars, and improved means of transportation, than in terms of increasing efficiency and increasing yields. Such a conception reflected traditional agricultural practice. On certain estates, however, agricultural practices were changing rapidly. Indeed, much the same thing was happening in the countryside as in the towns. But it was happening in the countryside without that theoretical appreciation of the possibility of its happening there which informed the classical economic attitude towards the growth of productivity in the towns.

The classical economists were well aware that the efficiency of manufacture might be increased immeasurably as a consequence of investment. But they denied that this could occur in agriculture, except to a negligible degree.[30] And, as yet, no statistics were available which could help to establish whether the existing levels of price in both town and countryside were attributable more to the currency than to increases in supply, and, in turn, whether these increases were themselves attributable more to efficiencies of production than to larger market areas. In these circumstances the various men who disagreed about these price phenomena tended to focus upon their opponents' arguments or behaviour and to analyse their arguments or behaviour in terms of the logic of advantage. Hence the political potential of the issue.

Whatever the validity of Graham's economic argument, his social argument was clearly valid: deflation was tending to divide English society along new lines. The melodramatic elements of his case were those which the activist cause required. He hoped to encourage that alliance to which, as he put it, the corn law of 1815 had been the principal barrier.

> ... amidst the ruin of the farmer and the manufacturer, [he explained] the distress of the landlords, and the insurrection of a populace without bread and without employment, one class flourished and was triumphant; the annuitant and the taxeater rejoiced in the increased value of money; in the sacrifice of productive industry to unproductive wealth.[31]

Nor did it weaken his case to argue that the problem was self-reinforcing. As he put it, with their own salaries and pensions and claims upon the State fixed in amounts which others had to pay through taxes the Ministers and their various allies would have injured themselves had they abandoned the policy upon which their new wealth was founded. Furthermore, according to Graham, as the belief that wealth was not to be had from productive activities spread, increasing numbers of ambitious men looked to the State 'in the hope of sharing its patronage, and of making that provision out of the public purse which the hereditary family estates ... [would] no longer bear.'[32]

Mackintosh and Russell before him had referred to the positive attractions of official jobs. But they had emphasized the security such jobs offered, not the wealth. As Russell put it, more money could be made in other professions. But the 'prudent man' would try to get for his son a Government job in which he could ultimately hope for £2,000 a year.[33] As most Government salaries had not been reduced in any way commensurate with the increased value of money after 1819 – and many of the higher among them had not been reduced at all – the distinction between the security factor which Russell emphasized and the wealth factor which Graham emphasized became somewhat blurred. It was not this point exactly which Graham was trying to make when he charged that 113 privy councillors received salaries or pensions which averaged more than £7,000 a year.[34] However, as the Ultra-Tory *Morning Herald* observed, while commenting on Graham's statement, this was 'certainly to be "Right Honourable" to some purpose.'[35] Mackintosh and Russell before him had criticised government influence. But for Graham, and for many others who, like him, attributed their economic problems to deflation, this influence ceased to be simply an abstract structural problem. It acquired an immediate importance which was entirely a measure of the uses to which, ostensibly, it was put. And with a somewhat different initial concern the same was true of men like the Marquis of Blandford. Infuriated by the Catholic Relief Act, by which the Protestant monopoly of political office had been destroyed, Blandford denounced 'the system' to which he attributed its passage. What he meant by the term was the same government influence which Mackintosh and Russell had criticized. But his argument, like Graham's, was scarcely abstract. According to him, it was only by means of 'the system' that the liberal policies which he deplored had been implemented. It was the Catholic Relief Act to which he referred when he argued that 'the system' was responsible for 'the largeness of that majority which lately overthrew the constitution, and proved to the people how very little their prayers were heard or heeded.'[36] Illustrating that conjunction of issues which came to dominate the political scene in the immediate pre-reform period, he also held 'the system' responsible for

 ... the success of the odious principle of free trade; a principle which, if persisted in, will spread the desolation still further, which so fearfully prevails, and is now pressing so severely on our commerce.[37]

And, again, he held it responsible for the laws by which the value of money had been increased.[38] Indeed, while he disagreed with Graham on the Catholic question he recognized the same essential divisions in English society which Graham recognized. 'The system,' he declared,

> ... work[s] well for the jobbers in the borough-market; it ... work[s] very well for all who go to power, and profit, and distinction, by ... [it]; and I dare say ministers will be the last to say it works ill. But ... it works destructively for the empire at large – ... against every one of the great interests of this country – against the well-being of its trade, its manufactures, its agriculture.[39]

For these reasons he proposed a reform of Parliament. For these reasons he joined the Birmingham Political Union soon after it was organized, in January 1830.[40] Under the leadership of Thomas Attwood the Union became one of the principal means of organizing pressure for parliamentary reform. Like Blandford, Attwood was a Tory. Like Blandford, he believed reform would weaken 'liberal' influences within the State, in particular the influences of the political economists.

V

As Peel noted in his reply to Blandford's motion in 1829, since Blandford argued the need for reform on the ground that neither the policy of free trade nor Catholic Emancipation would have been adopted if the close boroughs had not existed, he doubted that many of the habitual supporters of reform would vote with him.[41] In fact, several of them did so. As John Cam Hobhouse was careful to explain, however, he voted with Blandford not because he agreed with him about the effects reform would have upon government policy. Rather, he voted with him because he disagreed with him about these effects. He believed a reformed Parliament would be even more strongly committed than an unreformed Parliament to 'the great principles of civil and religious liberty and free trade.'[42]

The beliefs which Hobhouse expressed are intimately related to those pressures for reform on which the concession theory has focussed. But the effective pressures for reform in the immediate pre-reform period had less to do with such beliefs than with those others which Attwood, Blandford, and Graham expressed. Indeed, between the Catholic Relief Act and the dissolution of Parliament in July 1830, many of those men who agreed with Hobhouse, that all forms of liberalism were merely forms of the same thing, found themselves defending the Wellington Government against the mounting attacks of such men as Attwood,

Blandford, and Graham, who, opposing the liberal policies of the Government, became the most vociferous spokesmen of parliamentary reform. In some cases, what triggered their behaviour were those liberal economic policies which Graham emphasized. In others it was the Catholic Relief Act. But for these latter the Relief Act was important not only because it violated the constitutional principle, that political power in the State should be a Protestant monopoly. It was also important because, for them, it revealed the essential accuracy of Graham's political analysis. According to their lights, Governments were holding office not to further specific policies, but simply to enjoy the fruits of office.

The existence of these anti-liberal reformers has not been adequately noted. As a rule, both the Act itself and the reform crisis from which the Act emerged have been described as if the only men who had reason to be dissatisfied with the existing political system were those who might be described as 'liberal' – in particular, Dissenters, free traders and theoretical Radicals. As a rule it has been forgotten that others had reasons to be dissatisfied too, among them Ultra-Tories, currency reformers and protectionists. In consequence, those pressures for reform which stemmed from their dissatisfaction have received rather a bad press. Most historians have ignored them completely. Others, like Elie Halevy, have deprecated their importance on two grounds, that they 'lacked popular support' and that they 'lacked the support of the Whig or Liberal party leaders.' [43] The former argument is tied to the notion that the course of history in both the long and short term is defined by ostensibly popular desires. The latter is tied to the notion that the Reform Ministry was a Whig Ministry. But this notion is scarcely compatible with the presence of such men as Godrich, Melbourne, and Richmond, in the Grey Cabinet. As Professor Aspinall has pointed out, 'The Reform Ministry . . . was not so much a Whig Ministry as a non-Party Government representing, with the exception of the Radicals, all the groups which had combined to defeat the Duke.' [44] As for the former notion, while it must be allowed that it has some pertinence today, when means for discovering popular desires and for transforming them into law have been highly developed, when social communities are extremely fluid, and when political leaders are more often made than born, to apply it to the early nineteenth century without significant reservation is a simple anachronism. Indeed, while the question whether reform can be isolated as the principal cause of the growth of political democracy is debatable the question whether 'democracy' was the cause of reform is not.

We must not forget that the House of Commons in which the first Reform Bill was passed was chosen by the unreformed constituencies – in effect, that the men who sat in this Parliament did so in consequence of the various influences which obtained within these constituencies. In certain cases traditionally based influences were clearly weaker during the reform crisis than they were at other times. But in other cases they were scarcely affected at all. At least in certain counties – and the counties are particularly important in this respect both because they were the pre-eminent 'open' constituencies and because so many county members voted for the Bill – the behaviour of many voters was obviously affected by the same factors in 1830 and 1831 as on other occasions. In both years large numbers of county voters voted in overwhelming agreement with their immediate neighbours and – for the two criteria were generally the same – in agreement with the predominant landowner in the parish in which they resided. Of course, many county voters who had not voted before were brought to the polls in these years. Most of these men voted for reform candidates. Many of them were urban or quasi-urban, thus confirming the argument in *Blackwood's Edinburgh Magazine,* that the outcome of the county elections in these years had been the consequence of the balance of power between the urban and rural areas of the counties. [45] As the Cambridgeshire poll books in particular reveal, however, especially in 1830 certain local influences were exerted on behalf of reform candidates which, on other occasions, were exerted on behalf of Tory candidates. In some cases the relevant influences can be identified. But even where they cannot it is clear that the temporary changes in the political orientation of the voters reflected temporary changes in orientation of the men who exercised effective influence among them: by and large, the different local blocs retained their cohesion.

To emphasize the electoral importance of these changes in orientation is not to deny the existence of that Foxite tradition of reform which many historians have emphasized and which provides the obvious reason for their tendency to stress Grey's role. Grey, a friend of Fox, a Friend of the People, a man who had introduced a motion for parliamentary reform in 1793, was an obvious carrier of this tradition. Nor is it to deny the existence of that far more Radical tradition, going back to Thomas Paine and beyond, from which Grey and his various allies of the nineties had somewhat vainly tried to dissociate themselves. Nor, again, is it to deny the existence of 'Captain Swing'. Rather, it is to focus upon the essential arena and to ask the questions which the factors of power in these arena tend to suggest. In metaphysical terms, perhaps, Professor Oakeshott is right that, in John Cannon's paraphrase, 'the only proper historical explanation is a complete account of the antecedent events.' [46] But the metaphysical elements in politics are few. Where the problems are problems of power operating within a structure of a certain nature historians can make certain choices. Obviously, in trying to explain events in the prereform world too much time should not be spent discussing the attitudes of those who lacked power in this world. Rather, emphasis should be placed upon those who possessed power in this world. Many of these – on this point Russell was right in 1826 – were violently opposed to all policies which they believed to be 'liberal'. Yet on this occasion, Russell ignored the point whose importance he should have recognized, what with his own earlier criticisms of the influence of the crown: because the borough patrons were less the members of a social class than they were the members of an administrative clique the existence of nomination boroughs did not threaten 'the liberal system of policy which ministers had lately pursued'. Indeed, it was the existence oof these boroughs that allowed the policy to be pursued.

Whatever the principal reason why historians have tended to discount the importance of 'opportunism' in politics – and, obviously, a possible reason would lie in the intensification of the problems which behaviour of any sort would represent if it were first assumed that men are by nature opportunistic: it would no longer be possible to try to explain their behaviour as the working-out of clearly defined ideological positions – the importance of opportunism is not to be denied. By the same token, while certain ideologues tried to make Liberalism an exclusive creed their efforts were constantly being undermined by politicians who, forced to deal with real-life situations, found that eclecticism and pragmatism were necessary virtues.

To emphasize the role of the anti-liberal reformers is not to suggest that it was *they* who drafted the Bill. Nor is it to suggest that either in whole or in part the Bill was drafted specifically *for them*. Indeed, to suggest that those provisions of the Bill which offend against the urban and individualistic model in terms of which historians have generally conceived the Bill were the price the Ministers were willing to pay for Ultra-Tory support is to obscure the very prevalence of the sociological assumptions which these provisions reflect.[47] Implicitly and, in some cases, explicitly, these assumptions can be found in the works of men as different from one another politically as James Mill and Robert Southey.[48] Rather, to emphasize the role of the anti-liberal reformers is to provide a means of approaching the question which, considering the limitations upon liberal power in the various constituencies in the pre-reform period, could otherwise scarcely be approached: why and how were those men who were responsible for Wellington's defeat returned to Parliament in 1830. As such, it is to provide a means of approaching the further question: why, as a means of defining the political character of the Grey administration, was the myth of the Bill being a Radical measure produced?

VI

With tempers high – raised by the Catholic Relief Act – and with nothing being done by the Government to relieve the mounting depression which many men in both town and countryside attributed to deflation, Graham's political analysis acquired increasing pertinence. In the context of this depression many men came to contend that the Ministers were happily conspiring with the fundholders to feather their own nests. Pointing to the fact that Wellington had refused to surrender office even though he surrendered his opposition to Catholic Emancipation which had largely prompted him to accept office in the first place, the Ultra-Tory *Morning Journal* proclaimed, '. . . the Most Noble Arthur Duke of Wellington is proud, overbearing, grasping, dishonest, and unprincipled, and capable of a design to overturn the crown, and prostrate the laws and liberties of this kingdom'. [49] Nor did the response to this accusation calm the tempers which produced it. The owners of the *Morning Journal* were charged with libel and found guilty.

The journalistic response to the suit reflects that alliance between certain of the Ultra-Tories and Radicals on the one hand and the ministerial Tories and certain Whigs and Liberals on the other which attended the development of the reform crisis but which the crisis largely dissolved. Notwithstanding their earlier criticism of Catholic Emancipation, the Ultra-Tory *Morning Herald* dated their opposition to Wellington from the time the suit was brought. According to them, the suit was the 'first great blow which the Duke's Administration received.'[50] In the context of the suit, the Ultra-Tory *Standard* lost almost all restraint. And, noting the slowness with which the 'liberal' papers responded – *The Times, Star, Globe,* and *Sun* – they warned them of the principle involved: '. . . their turn is only postponed until the Tories are disposed of; the power which hates us hates them'. [51] Their tone was echoed in various provincial Tory papers, among them the *Sheffield Courant, Durham County Advertiser,* and *Birmingham Journal.* Their concern, if not their tone, was also echoed in the Radical *Examiner.* Indeed, when the jury's verdict was returned, the *Examiner* compared the jury's behaviour with that of a panel of judges in France who had recently acquitted the editors of *Journal des Debats* of similar charges. And, they concluded, since the judge in the English case – Lord Tenterden, an Ultra-Tory – would presumably have found the owners of the *Morning Journal* innocent, the jury's behaviour raised the question of whether trial by jury was really such a good thing. [52] But *The Times* was not only slow in responding. Its response was somewhat equivocal. While regretting the libel suit it attacked the owners of the *Morning Journal* for having made it necessary, for *their* 'blow . . . on the liberty of the press,' for *their* effrontery in attacking 'a powerful and respected Government.' [53] And while the Whig *Morning Chronicle* disapproved of the prosecutions it explained their occurrence in terms which effectively condoned them. [54]

Writing in the Ultra-Tory *Blackwood's Edinburgh Magazine* the following spring David Robinson made an even more violent accusation than the *Morning Journal's* and escaped, perhaps because of the outcry which the libel suit had produced. He declared, 'The plea of the Minister – I did this because I could not carry on the government without – is precisely in effect the plea of the pickpocket or murderer – I robbed or murdered because I had no other means of obtaining wealth.' [55]

Perhaps, it was the role of deflation in the logic of this case which brought the editors of the *Morning Herald* over to the side of the currency reformers. As late as 9 June 1829 they were still criticising the currency reformers' position, arguing that the cause of distress was not the currency but overproduction. However, by mid-July they were speaking of the need for a 'Radical Reform' of Parliament in terms which reflected their acceptance of the logic of Graham's case, that the political alliance which deflation encouraged was self-reinforcing.

The greater part of the Members [of Parliament, they declared], get in by bribery of some description; and when in, the greater part are under the influence of the Ministry – because the greater part are gaping for pension, place, and power, both for themselves as well as for their relations and friends. [56]

And, by October, they were complaining that while Wellington had sacked Huskisson he had failed to abandon his policy; that while Wellington had forced Peel to give up his opposition to Catholic Emancipation he had failed to make him change his currency ideas. [57]

In effect, from the summer and autumn of 1829, while various Whigs and Liberals were helping to keep Wellington's Government in office as a means of perpetuating the liberal policies which the Government was pursuing, the principal attacks on the Government came from those Members of Parliament who accepted the accuracy of Graham's political analysis. Ostensibly, some of these men merely sought to reverse the policy of deflation. While moving for the appointment of a committee to consider the distressed state of the country Edward Davenport asserted that he did not wish to turn the Ministers out. [58] But this brought a laugh. Others sought to destroy the Ministers' powers or to weaken them.

Speaking in 1830, Blandford declared that the problems of distress would never be solved until all sinecures and pensions and useless places had been abolished. [59] Clearly, what concerned him was not only the expense of these sinecures, *et cetera,* and the burden of the taxes that were required to support them. Clearly, what principally concerned him was the political function these sinecures ostensibly performed. In his renewed motion for parliamentary reform he included demands that all placemen and pensioners be dismissed from the House of Commons, and that all nomination boroughs be abolished.[60] According to the *Standard,* his speech on reform was a 'noble speech'.[61] Noting, however, that few 'Protestant tories' had supported him – in fact, as it also noted, few of these men had voted on either side – the paper complained that Blandford had gone too far: his motion was 'made to be defeated'.[62]

David Robinson's proposals, published in the pages of *Blackwood's Edinburgh Magazine,* were more judicious. Implicitly, he assumed the correctness of Blandford's and Graham's analysis. But he merely sought to control the system they described, not to destroy it. He recognized that the nomination boroughs were a major source of ministerial power. But he also recognized that they were havens of administrative talent. In consequence, he proposed to leave these boroughs intact to provide seats for ministers and potential ministers. To the other constituencies he assigned the task of controlling and directing these men, of strengthening an

> Independent Party . . . whose leaders would be wholly free from the wish for office, . . . who must originate no measures; . . . [a party which] must act the part of a disinterested and impartial judge [between the Ministerial and Opposition parties, and thus which] must be, as far as possible, purified from everything which can make it interested and partial – which can render it partisan.[63]

Primarily, as Robinson conceived it, 'partisanship' was a function of office, and of the policies which officeholders favoured. And these policies were symbolized by the 'new commercial system' according to which, he declared,

> . . . each interest is taught to regard protection against the foreigner as an evil, and to believe that its profit lies in the injury and ruin of . . . [other domestic interests] . . . Those who are engaged in foreign and retail trade [he went on], need no direct protection; they are clamourous for abolishing it to all others, and especially to the agriculturists, and they now elect or control the part of Parliament which holds the scale between parties. The growth of manufactures and trade has enabled them to take precedence of agriculture in dictating to the county members, as well as to fill many seats with men engaged in them, which were previously to a recent period occupied by independent gentlemen.[64]

His proposals for reform were directly related to the means by which he believed those men who depended on 'the new commercial system' had intruded themselves into parliamentary constituencies where ostensibly, they did not belong. According to him, such intrusions were the simple consequence of wealth. His various proposals were obviously conceived as means of enabling the return to Parliament of those men who were identified with the interests their constituencies traditionally symbolized, and of restoring to the different types of constituency the balance of interests which had been destroyed by the intrusion of the wealthy. His proposals were far more limited than those which the Bill later contained. But among other things, he proposed that outvoters be disfranchised in the counties, that borough freemen vote where they resided, and that various steps be taken to reduce the expense of elections so that local men might stand a better chance of being returned.[65]

Of course, it was not only those who opposed the Catholic Relief Act who were deeply disturbed by the powers the Ministers had shown in passing it. Shortly after its passage a correspondent of the Radical *Examiner* observed,

> Although no one more heartily than myself rejoices at the passing of the Catholic Relief Act, yet we may certainly look at the means by which it was passed and ask whether the power of the Ministry has not arrived at a pitch perfectly alarming to the liberty of the subject. It is not because on one or two instances the power is exerted beneficially, that we are to admire the principle.[66]

On the other hand, as the *Examiner* had already noted – and perhaps together with the subsequent requests for office on the part of the Whigs the phenomenon bears upon the question whether much should really be made of the theoretical concern of the Whigs with the problem of consent – *Edinburgh Review* was turning cold on parliamentary reform.[67]

VII

After the Catholic Relief Act was passed few men, even the most ardent Ultra-Tories, seriously hoped to undo it. At a testimonial dinner for Sir Edward Knatchbull in Kent even the Earl of Winchilsea remarked that the Act was law, whatever they might think of it – Winchilsea who had fought a duel with Wellington after Wellington's apostasy had been announced.[68] Indeed, with the Act on the books, what principally remained in Winchilsea's mind were the memory of the apostasy itself and a bitter distaste for the political system through which the apostasy had been legislatively reinforced. Anticipating his subsequent – if temporary – coalition with Grey and advocacy of the Bill, he went on to distinguish between those men who had 'conscientiously advocated' Catholic Emancipation all along, and 'that Government or Administration which had ousted the others, and made the profession of Protestantism their stepping-stones to office'.[69]

Perhaps Knatchbull never became a reformer. Yet for him the problem of government influence which the passage of the Catholic Relief Act revealed was clearly an on-going problem. And the seriousness of the problem in his eyes was a measure of his belief that this influence provided the mechanism through which liberal policies were being implemented.

> ... when the Ministers of the day had canvassed his sentiments, [he declared] and sought his support for a change in the constitution, he had refused obedience – he had dissented from the dictation of the Ministers ... [And, he went on] had he submitted to dictation on so important a measure, upon the mere volition of the Government, how would he have been afterwards placed? The Government might equally say, 'We approve and confirm those principles of free trade (as they were called), and we require you to submit to the opinions which we entertain, although we know you were always opposed to them.'[70]

But on the question of free trade, and the liberal economic policies which free trade symbolized, the dangers of 'submission' both for Knatchbull and for many other M.P.s were purely rhetorical. When Parliament reassembled in February, Knatchbull and Blandford moved an amendment to the Address which would have brought down Wellington's Government had not certain Whigs and Liberals voted in Wellington's favour.[71] The question at issue was whether that 'distress' which Attwood in Birmingham and many agriculturists attributed to the policies of the liberal economists was 'universal' or merely prevailed 'in some parts of the kingdom'. As proclaimed in the Speech from the Throne, distress only prevailed 'in some parts of the kingdom'. According to Knatchbull and Blandford, however, distress was 'universal.' The importance of the question derived from the logic of the currency reformers' case: if distress was universal then, clearly, 'Peel's Act' was to blame.

The debate was abstract, or – more to the point – polemical. Without any significant statistical evidence to speak of, those who took part did little more than flex their premises. Seconding the Address in the Lords, Saltoun declared that a change had occurred 'from obtaining large profit on small ventures to getting only small profits on large transactions'.[72] During the wars, he went on, when world trade had been relatively small, Britain had enjoyed a monopoly of it. But now, when the trade was larger, and when others besides British manufacturers and merchants were engaged in it, the unit prices were smaller. Later, in the Commons John Herries added another dimension when, in replying implicitly to the arguments of Thomas Attwood, he claimed that the economic and social problems in the towns derived not from the currency but from the introduction of new productive techniques. According to him, when these techniques had been fully assimilated the intensity of the problems which their introduction was causing would decrease. Indeed, according to him, the *former* depression in Birmingham, where Attwood's following was concentrated, and in the neighbouring towns of Walsall and Wolverhampton, was already lifting.[73] The previous month Wellington had granted that distress was widespread. But, he had added – and his argument had much in common with Herries' 'there are symptoms which show that the country is advancing.' Exports were increasing, traffic on canals and railroads was increasing.[74] And, while Knatchbull in the Commons was describing the increase of exports as 'overtrading,' Wellington went on to assert that the retail traders were certainly not distressed.[75] And, he added, if distress was universal, how could one account for the volume of new construction in the cities?[76]

Significantly missing from the ministerial arguments, however, was anything about agriculture. Indeed, with respect to agriculture the Ministers and their deflationist allies held out little hope. Peel put it simply: during the wars poor lands had been brought into cultivation in England which, now that improved transportation was available, found themselves competing with the good soils of Scotland and Ireland.[77] He recognized the importance of differential efficiencies. But, according to him, they could not be changed. They were inherent in different qualities of land. Thus, any effort to raise prices would merely lower the general level of agricultural efficiency. Logically, if prices were raised to such levels as to remove the pressures from the owners and tenants of the poorer lands, then rents on the better lands would be commensurately increased. In effect, such prices would simply increase the proportion of the national income which rent represented while reducing the proportion of the national income which profit and wage represented. Peel complained that the plight of the agriculturists pained him. He had no wish, he declared, to 'depress the landed interest'. But he saw nothing Parliament could do about the problems they faced.[78] Indeed, according to the logic of his argument there were only two possible solutions to their problems, currency reform – which he rejected out of hand – and allowing the poorer lands to revert to waste. In effect, there was not any solution. Nor, indeed, did any solution emerge until it began to be recognized that in certain cases and to some extent the differential efficiencies of different agriculturists were functions of their relative technological sophistication – this, reflected in their relative productivities and costs of production. Then there was some basis for action: Parliament could take steps to encourage the less efficient producers to emulate their more efficient neighbours. Whatever the degree to which the rural protests of 1829 and 1830 were the consequence of such technologically based differential efficiencies, it was not until some years later that the general problems of rural prosperity were reformulated in terms which not only recognized the existence of such differential efficiencies, but which also recognized the factors responsible for their existence.[79] In the meantime, rejecting the alternative of currency reform, Peel was understandably pained.

The Times was less pained. Not because it saw any other alternatives. Rather, because it welcomed those reductions in the price of agricultural commodities about which the agriculturists were complaining. *The Times* even announced that it would no longer publish letters from farmers complaining of distress.[80] If manufacturers were prosperous, it explained, they would be able to pay more for food and food prices would rise. But if efforts were made to increase food prices artificially then the manufacturers would become bankrupt. And, the paper added, if the manufacturers were bankrupt then the producers of food would have no one to whom they could sell.[81] According to *The Times,* 'Rents must come down to the state at which they were before the great war began.'[82]

On the other hand, to the general body of landowners, whose incomes derived from rents, this was scarcely an attractive prospect. Focussing upon the fiscal burdens which aggravated the problem of agricultural prices, but which were necessary to pay the interest on the national debt, the *Morning Herald* replied that 'the sacredness of one contract is as good as the sacredness of another contract' – in effect, that the farmer's obligation to pay rent at the rate initially agreed upon with his landlord was equally as 'sacred' as the Treasury's obligation to pay a stipulated interest on the national debt.[84] Ignoring the possibility that such rents might be paid if production were increased – or if farmers focussed their energies upon more remunerative products – the *Morning Herald* directed attention to those other variables, prices, and particularly, taxes. It was this argument of equivalent sanctity which allowed the *Morning Herald* to add what it claimed *The Times* had '[forgotten] to add, that *taxes* should also come down to the same level.'[85] A month later, in the *Morning Herald* – but not in *The Times* – ministerial salaries and pensions were added to the list of items which would have to come down to pre-war levels.[86]

But the real issue was not prices, or rents, or taxes, or ministerial salaries and pensions. These were symbols. The real issue was the status of the landed classes under prevailing conditions of production, and the structure of the society in which this status was recognized. As the *Standard* explained, landowners could scarcely expect to maintain their rank in society if, with rents at the levels of 1792, they had to pay taxes at the levels of 1829.[87] Indeed, the *Standard* welcomed *The Times'* attack because of the consequences they anticipated from it. It would, the *Standard* hoped, put landowners 'on their guard'. And, it went on, 'if [landowners] be not content to sink in the scale of society, they must make up their minds for a most serious investigation into the fiscal, financial, and commercial state of the country ...' [88] Obviously, what the paper had in mind were the policies associated with the liberal economists. And, at this time, these policies were being discussed at a series of county meetings which were focussed on the question of malt tax.

VIII

The malt tax question was not a simple one. It was the point at which several problems converged. Because of the size of the tax – it produced between four and five million pounds a year in the early thirties, roughly a tenth of the annual revenue – the Treasury could scarcely do without it unless an alternative source of revenue were found, or unless the expenses of the government were radically reduced. Thus, because the generally assumed alternative to the malt tax was a property tax, which would fall upon the fundholders, and because the interest on the national debt which went to pay the fundholders was the largest item in the budget, the malt tax question was directly related to the fundholder question. As such, it was also related both to the question of deflation and to the further question of why the policy of deflation was being pursued.

But there were other aspects of the question as well. These had nothing to do with the political structure of the kingdom, or with the relations between the landed interest and other groups. Rather, they had to do with the effects of the increase in the tax since the early eighteenth century upon patterns of consumption, and upon the differential prosperity of different agriculturists. According to most of the critics of the tax who convened the county meetings in the winter of 1829-30, the increased rate of the tax had, by raising the price of beer, reduced its per capita consumption. As such, according to them, the increased rate of the tax was responsible for increasing the rate of crime in England because many of those men who formerly drank beer were turning to strong drink.[89] More important, however, if the increase in the malt tax could be held responsible for reducing the per capita consumption of beer then it could also be held responsible for reducing the general demand for barley, the principal ingredient of beer. Furthermore, since the malt tax was paid on barley destined for the maltster, not on malt – it was not really a malt tax but a barley tax – and since it was paid at a flat rate per bushel, its increased rate tended to enhance the maltsters' preferences for those barleys which would give them the largest yields of malt. Thus, since the light lands and drained clays produced a thin-skinned barley which yielded more malt per bushel than the thick-skinned barley produced on the undrained clays, the increased rate of the tax effectively limited both the market and price of the clay land barley.[90]

In 1829 and 1830, however, this latter aspect of the malt tax question was rarely, if ever, mentioned. The question of how far the malt tax *raised* the price of the so-called best barley, the only barley on which the tax was paid was effectively ignored. As such, the tax was not then used to explain why those agriculturists who produced this barley might be more prosperous than the others. By 1835 this had become the principle argument against the tax. By then most repealers were claiming that the tax was a piece of discriminatory legislation *in favour* of the owners and farmers of the light lands and drained clays.[91] It was this argument which Peel tried to answer when, in replying to Chandos' motion for repeal of the tax, he contended that repeal would not help the landed interest because the real depression in agriculture was on the clay lands, the wheat lands, not on the light lands, the barley lands. Thus, arguing that it was not the malt tax which had limited the consumption of beer, but the preference for other drinks, Peel went on to claim that repeal of the tax would scarcely benefit the landed interest if it encouraged clay land farmers to sow barley instead of wheat when no increase in the demand for barley could be anticipated.[92]

But in 1829 and 1830 few men argued for repeal in terms of the differential prosperity of different agriculturists. Instead – and implicitly denying the existence of such a differential – they argued that the malt tax was a means of both reducing the price of barley and of transferring roughly five million pounds a year from the pockets of the agriculturists into those of the fundholders.[93] Whether the two points could each be valid scarcely bothered them. They were right that the tax was worth between four and five million pounds a year to the Treasury. But not all farmers paid it: only those whose barley was bought by a maltster. Furthermore, as was later recognized, those who paid it not only received the highest price for their barley; by and large, they were the most prosperous.

In effect, in 1829 and 1830 the tax was used to explain why rural depression was ostensibly universal. As such, in almost every speech, the tax was treated as an appropriate point from which to discuss the relations between the landed interest and the fundholders.[94] In certain speeches it was also treated as an appropriate point from which to discuss the factors which affected ministerial policy and the structural changes which might be necessary before this policy could be changed.

According to most of the men who spoke at these meetings it was the depth and universality of rural depression which demonstrated the errors inherent in the theories of the political economists. They demanded malt tax repeal not only as a means of easing the pressures upon farmers and landowners. They also demanded it as a token that the economic policies to which they attributed these pressures would not be pursued further. According to Lord Teynham, relief of the landed interest was available within the existing political structure. As he explained to the initial public meeting in London, from which the call was issued to convene the subsequent county meetings, while Wellington wanted to repeal the malt tax he did not know how he could do so without simply shifting the burden to other groups.[95] Cripps made substantially the same point when he explained that Wellington had only agreed to continue the system of free trade with which the policy of deflation was associated because the Cabinet could not agree on abandoning the system.[96] But Teynham and Cripps and many others believed that Wellington could be pressured. Indeed, it was to do so — and, occasionally to rehearse the reasons why the effort to do so would inevitably fail — that the meetings were held. Hence the importance of the Government's assertion, contained in the Speech from the Throne in February, that depression only prevailed 'in some parts of the kingdom'. And hence the importance of Knatchbull's and Blandford's amendment to the Address in which they claimed that depression was 'universal'. As Attwood explained in Birmingham,

> It is well known that Consols have advanced from 60 to 93, whilst land has fallen from 60 to 30. During the war these two great interests were upon an equality, or nearly so — whilst now the one is three times as great as the other.[97]

IX

The Government survived the vote on Knatchbull's and Blandford's amendment. But they only did so because various Whigs and Liberals came to their rescue. And soon thereafter Arbuthnot was telling Peel that if taxes such as the malt tax which pressed on 'industry' were not removed, and a modified property tax substituted for them, the Government would definitely be beaten.[98] In effect, Arbuthnot neglected the possibility that the Government's tenure of office might be continued by perpetuating the coalition upon which, increasingly, the Government depended. During the winter of 1830, however, this was clearly the consummation which *The Times* and *Morning Chronicle* sought. Following the vote on Knatchbull's and Blandford's amendment both journals claimed that those Whigs who had kept the Government in being should be rewarded with office. *The Times* did so directly.[99] But while the *Morning Chronicle* was not so brazen the implications of its argument can scarcely have been missed – that since the Catholic Relief Act Wellington had ceased to be a party leader and had become a national one.[100] Nor was it only the resolution of the Catholic issue which prompted the paper to emphasize Wellington's 'national' stature. It stated that there were positive reasons for coalition as well. Although the Whig leaders were scarcely of one mind on the currency question – indeed, in April 1830, Grey declared he had a somewhat open mind on the question[101] – this pre-eminent Whig journal joined with *The Times* in ridiculing the currency reformers' contention that distress was universal.[102] In effect, its argument as to why those Whigs who had kept the Government in being should be rewarded with office was based upon the premise that those men who wished to defend the currency settlement of 1819 should stand together.

But from a different perspective the *Morning Herald* saw the behaviour of these men as evidence of avarice pure and simple. Commenting in January on those journalistic arguments which were subsequently repeated in Parliament it claimed that those Whigs who belittled the extent of distress merely wished to share the salaries which, depending on taxes, and enhanced in value by deflation, could not reasonably be perpetuated at the existing levels unless the contention that distress was universal were denied. And, they went on,

> . . . the landed proprietors of England will have to thank themselves for their own ruin if they allow the Ministers to go on as they have been for a long time doing without determined constitutional resistance and energetic remonstrance.[103]

To a large extent, the response of the *Morning Herald's* constituency explains the defeat of many ministerial candidates during the elections of August 1830. After these elections, when the Wellington Government was in even greater trouble, the *Morning Chronicle* renewed their request that 'places' be found for the Whigs. Likening the effects of the elections to the effects of a tropical fever, they observed in September that the Wellington Government 'is at present like a Regiment returned from the West Indies, with the colours, drums, and one or two officers – a very good Regiment, only requiring to be renewed.' [104] And the same tone of coy expectation was reflected in their subsequent observation that what Parliament did when it convened would depend upon who the Ministers were and what measures they proposed. Wellington, they claimed, was not vindictive. '. . . if the Duke grant advantages to the country, it would be foolish in the country to refuse them.' [105]

X

As a rule, Wellington's speech of 2 November 1830, in which he denied the need for reform, has been read as a statement of principle. It has not been read in the context of the problems his Administration faced from the autumn of 1829 through to the dissolution in July 1830. Nor has it been read in the context of the results of the August elections. Nor has it been read in the light of the domestic reactions both to the July Revolution in France and the mounting tempo of Radical agitation at home. Nor has it been read to the end. Wellington did not limit himself to a simple eulogy of the existing representative system. He explained why the system deserved this eulogy: '. . . the representation of the people at present,' he declared, 'contained a large body of the property of the county, and in which the landed interest have a prepondering influence.' [106]

In the winter and spring of 1830 Wellington's principal parliamentary opponents would scarcely have agreed with this contention. However, by the following autumn many of them had begun to doubt the validity of their earlier assumptions. The impact of revolution in France and growing unrest at home gave an immediacy to their demands for currency reform. As William Johnstone declared in *Blackwood's Edinburgh Magazine,*

> The best way to prevent revolution, is to show the people that they have nothing to gain by it; and that those whom they permit to govern them, take as good care of them as any others they might choose: [And, he went on], . . . while property continues in the hands of the few, and the mass of the people have nothing but their labour to exchange for so much of it as their daily wants require, it is easy to see how the depression of the value of labour may be carried so far as to compel them to resort to the law of nature. [107]

In effect, revolution was natural what with Parliament's failure to deal with the problem of distress.

Earlier, many Ultra-Tories had criticised the Government severely for refusing to allow that distress might be universal. But now the ostensible consequences of this earlier refusal made them fear the lack of strong executive leadership. '. . . no William Pitt is at hand to guide us,' De Quincey complained. And the parties which, together, 'express[ed] the truth of . . . [the] constitution,' the one representing 'the conservative charge of the popular powers, . . . the other the powers of the crown' had been shattered. [108] Previously, when times were quieter, the 'congeries of little circles' represented points from which that ministerial power to which Robinson had attributed the passage of liberal legislation might be controlled. But, with unrest and agitation increasing, and Captain Swing on his nocturnal escapades in

Kent, the failure of these 'congeries' to defend law and order was patent. Clearly, these phenomena were responsible for that gradual reconstruction of the Tory or Conservative party which began in the autumn of 1830. And, in the context of these phenomena, the close boroughs began to acquire a function in the eyes of many of Wellington's former opponents analogous to that which, presumably, they had in his. The previous spring the close boroughs had loomed as agencies by which the power and wealth of the rural aristocracy and gentry were being destroyed. But in October, as De Quincey put it, these boroughs had to be preserved as means of preserving the powers of the aristocracy itself.[109] Clearly, it was this general change of attitude which the author of *Tory Union, our only Safeguard against Revolution* hoped to invoke.[110] What with the dangers of democratic revolution which threatened from Paris, Brussels and Blackfriars Rotunda, those factors which had driven many Ultra-Tories into opposition waned in importance.

Furthermore, during the late summer and autumn two other things occurred which promised to make Ultra-Tory coalition with Wellington easier: Huskisson died, and Wellington failed to arrange a juncture with the Canningites and Whigs. Huskisson's death in early September removed a man who was *personna non grata* to many Ultra-Tories. In large measure, he symbolized those liberal economic policies to which they attributed their economic ills. Indeed, on 17 September Arbuthnot reported to Peel what he had heard from two of the principal Ultra-Tories, Lord Salisbury and William Bankes – many of their friends who would have gone into total opposition immediately had Huskisson rejoined the Government were now favourably disposed towards Wellington.[111] Then, on the heels of Huskisson's death, while anti-Tory polemic mounted in the Whig press, Wellington's negotiations with the Canningites and Whigs failed.[112]

These various phenomena were, presumably, not unrelated. During the winter and spring of 1830 the Government had been kept in office by the Whigs. During the elections of August 1830, many ministerial candidates were beaten who symbolized the general complex of policies which this coalition reflected. In these circumstances, with the Whig leaders placing a price on their continued support of the Government which Wellington was reluctant to pay, and with various Ultra-Tories beginning to reconsider the advantages of a strong executive Government, Wellington and his colleagues apparently decided to turn from dependence upon the Whigs and Liberals to dependence upon the Ultra-Tories. The symptom of this decision was presumably the implication – or, possibly, the promise – that the self-designated spokesmen of the landed interest would have a greater influence in their councils. Such is the story which the circumstances strongly suggest. Such is also the story contained in Mrs. Arbuthnot's *Journal.* As she noted at the time, following Palmerston's interview with Wellington, when Palmerston demanded so many places for Whigs 'that . . . [the Government] would be a Whig Government, the Duke and Peel allowed to stay,' Wellington and Peel had decided 'that we must make up our minds to fight the battle as we are . . . We shall have a desperate fight,' she went on, 'but, if our people are bold, as we have numbers I have no notion we shall be beat.' [113] Her reference to 'numbers' is significant. What with the results of the August elections the only 'numbers' she could have meant were those which Ultra-Tory coalition would bring. In this respect it is important to note that she not only considered the failure of these negotiations as they might affect the behaviour of the Canningites and Whigs. She also considered their failure as they might affect the Ultra-Tories. 'I think the not making this junction,' she went on, 'and the hostility that will necessarily ensue, will bring back our Tory party.' [114] Wellington perhaps believed all along that his Government had acted for the positive benefit of the landed interest, that the self-designated spokesmen of the landed interest were simply deluded. But whether he believed this or not — and his arguments about distress during the winter of 1830 might be mustered on the other side — his comments about the 'preponderating influence' of the landed interest in the existing representative system were probably made with a tactical intent which was only obscured by the slowness of reaction of those men to whom they were addressed. The memory of those measures which had prompted Ultra-Tory opposition was not easily erased. As Lord Hertford observed to Croker the following spring, 'I regretted the Duke's sweeping denial of all change, not as bad in itself, but as unwise and unnecessary, as it did not even secure the rejunction of the Tories'. [115] But Wellington had other difficulties to contend with besides the difference between the reactions of bodies of troops and of M.P.s. He also had to contend with the consequences of Earl Grey's prior declaration, that he had a somewhat open mind on the currency question. [116]

XI

From the meeting of Parliament in February, 1830 until some time after Wellington's defeat the following November, the crucial political fact was the refusal of Wellington's Government to acknowledge the validity of the argument that depression had reached such a point as to call the theories of the political economists into question. According to *The Times,* this was the main issue during the elections in the summer of 1830.[117] In November, when the Wellington Government was finally defeated, the defeat occurred on the question of economy in government. Furthermore, the man most widely touted as Wellington's probable successor was the man who, not seven months earlier, had advertised his differences with Wellington on the currency question. In announcing the policies of his new Government, Grey promised they would deal with reform. But he also promised that the relief of 'distress' – the existence of which the Wellington Government had previously denied – would be their 'first and most anxious object'.[118] With this combination the *Standard* declared themselves satisfied. The 'great distinction,' they observed, 'that formerly existed between ... Whigs and Tories, who were not mere political adventurers, exists no longer.' While Catholic Emancipation had been passed by 'apostates' it had destroyed this point of division. Reform had become the point of meeting.[119]

At the same time, however, the *Standard* recognized the existence of grounds for concern. The Grey Ministry was a coalition of Whigs, Canningites, and Ultra-Tories whose only point of positive agreement was the need for parliamentary reform. Lord Goderich was a known free trader; Sir Henry Parnell was a known opponent of currency reform. In the *Standard* these points were mentioned to show that those men of whose opinions they disapproved would be held in check: Grey was particularly known for his protectionist sentiments, Graham for his sentiments on the currency.[120] But in citing these differences of opinion within the Cabinet the *Standard* implicitly acknowledged the possibility that Grey and Graham would be held in check, not Goderich and Parnell. By January, various Ultra-Tories were giving thought to the problem of what they should do if they 'turn[ed] from supporting Grey's views by his being overruled by the Radical particles of his Cabinet.'[121]

Whether Grey was thus overruled, the belief that he was had a crucial impact upon subsequent British politics. Grey's failure to live up to his promise, that the relief of distress would be his 'first and most anxious object', was a severe blow to many of those men who, believing that no solution to their economic and social problems was possible without a change in the structure of government, had contributed to Wellington's defeat. It implied that Grey's scheme of reform might be designed not to restore their prosperity and status but to undermine them further.

The development of such a fear can be seen in successive issues of the *Standard*. On the basis of Grey's initial policy statement the *Standard* expected the relief of distress to precede reform. Towards the end of January, when its editors heard rumours that reform would precede the relief of distress, they began to be concerned. Reform, it observed, might remove the causes of distress. But it would not end distress itself. It approved the Government's handling of the disorders which distress had produced. However, it believed that more had to be done: credit had to be revived; capital had to be diffused. Thus, initially, the *Standard* refused to believe the rumours that a full plan of reform was to be submitted to Parliament early in March. Instead – and citing Grey's initial pledge it argued that a parliamentary committee would be appointed to consider the question of reform. According to the *Standard,* Wellington, Grove Price, Peel and Holmes 'stand alone in maintaining that the present constitution of the House of Commons is perfection.'[122] But a day or so later, realizing the accuracy of the rumours, it were urging the members of the 'country party' to force the Government to redeem its pledge.[123] Its attitude reflected its evident fear that under pressure of the political economists the relief of distress might be forgotten. As it went on to explain, 'The repeal of the currency bill of 1819 would be a far more remedial measure for instant purposes'.[124] Concern increased when Althorp announced that the pensions which had legally expired with the death of George IV would be continued at the previous rates.[125] It increased further when Althorp acceded to the protests of Peel, Goulburn and the fundholders, and dropped the proposed transfer taxes on funded and landed property from the budget.[126] But when the paper discovered that Poulett Thompson, the 'chief representative of the political economists', had a hand in drawing up the budget its concern became dismay.[127] For reform ought to be a means of destroying the influence of these men. And, reflecting the mounting pressures of Ultra-Tory coalition with Peel and Wellington, the *Standard* went on to declare that if Grey did not throw Thompson overboard and turn to Graham he would soon be replaced by Peel.[128] Ten days later it had come to believe that the men in the Government of whose opinions they disapproved would also have a hand in drafting the scheme of reform.[129] And when the Bill was finally introduced the paper totally ignored the many points of similarity between it and the earlier schemes proposed by Blandford and Robinson. They declared it was 'not reform but *revolution* . . .'[130]

XII

There are several reasons why such a designation might have seemed appropriate. Not least among them was the sheer bulk of *schedule A,* the list of the boroughs which the Ministers proposed to disfranchise. In 1829 and 1830 so long a list might have been attractive to many Ultra-Tories. But with the progress – albeit the slow progress – of Tory regrouping, the earlier questions as to the political functions which many of these boroughs performed within the State tended to lose their significance. The majority of the men who controlled the representation of these boroughs were ministerial Tories. Thus, among the Ultra-Tories, the meaning of *schedule A* changed as Tory regrouping progressed. The *schedule* became a threat, not to enemies but to allies. Furthermore, what with the mounting intensity of those proletarian and Radical agitations which helped to encourage Tory regrouping, confidence in the social cohesion of the local communities on which the ministerial scheme was based was eroded.[131]

Then, too, and complementing Wellington's efforts to define his Government in terms which would appeal to the spokesmen of the landed interest – or his party in such terms once his Government had been defeated – there were the efforts from the other side of the social or economic spectrum to make the Whigs into spokesmen of the middle class. In each case the efforts are understandable – in the one case to keep a Government in office, or to provide the basis on which the members of this Government might return to office, in the other case to gain an ideological control over what initially promised to be a hostile Government. What with the importance of the currency question in the winter and spring of 1830, and the relevance of the problem of distress to the currency reformer's arguments, *The Times'* constituency can scarcely have been pleased when Grey declared that the 'first and most anxious object' of his Government would be the relief of distress. Remembering Grey's earlier statement, that he had 'an open mind' on the currency question, this declaration buoyed the hopes of the *Standard*. What buoyed their hopes, however, can only have brought despair to *The Times*. Indeed it was presumably Grey's openness of mind on the currency question which prompted *The Times* to assert in August 1830, 'As to the Whigs, we plainly . . . deny that the country looks to them as its saviours in any great emergency.'[132]

But with Wellington's defeat the problems with which *The Times* was faced changed. The question no longer was how to keep a Government in office, which, by and large, was favourably disposed towards them and their constituency. Rather, the question was how it could increase its influence upon a Government which not only included Grey and Graham but which also included those other men whom the *Standard* hoped Grey and Graham would keep in check.

The rivalry between *The Times* and the *Standard* in adulation of Grey during his early months in office is not only farcical; it is extremely revealing.[133] No one knew where the balance of power in the Ministry would lie. And except for those ministerial Tories who were now committed to opposition because of having held office under Wellington, or because of having supported him to the end, no one was willing to give up hope that the balance of power would lie in the hands of those with whom he was politically allied. If the Ministry fulfilled the promise which Grey had made when he described his Government's policies, some sort of reform would be proposed. But, in the context of the political situation which existed from the summer of 1830 into the spring of 1831, to say this was not to say anything meaningful. The question remained — what sort of reform? One which would weaken the influence of the political economists? One of which Graham might approve? Or one which would strengthen their influence? One of which Poulett Thompson might approve? In this respect, the Government's initial fiscal measures would seem to have been important not only for their fiscal content but for what they promised for the future. When Althorp suggested the imposition of transfer taxes on funded and landed property the men on *The Times* were appalled. Their observation harked back to Grey's 'open mind' on the currency question, that 'the views of a Whig Administration are held in the city to be necessarily unfavourable to public credit.' As they added, however, '[this was] an opinion which practical proof to the contrary can drive out'.[134] And, presumably, much as the men who provided the *Standard*'s constituency were dismayed when these taxes were dropped from the budget, so were those others reassured who provided *The Times*'s constituency.

These various reactions scarcely bear upon the nature of the Bill. But they bear directly upon the ways in which the Bill was perceived and thus upon the nature of the political alliances which came into being during the reform crisis. As a result of these alliances political groups became polarized in terms less artificial than new. On the one side an urban middle class complex was developing, on the other a rural aristocratic complex. Essentially, it was the development of these new alliances which conditioned the way the story of reform was subsequently told.

XIII

Before 1831 the rivalries of town and countryside were growing rapidly. But there was little correspondence between the different social groups outside Parliament and the major political groups within. Insofar as the major groups in Parliament represented ideological positions they were far less sharply defined by the rivalries of economic interest as by those other rivalries between the advocates of strong government and the opponents of ministerial absolutism. Wellington's appeal helped to change this. So too did the efforts of the Liberals and Radicals to convince themselves that the balance of power in the Cabinet lay in the hands of its liberal economic wing. And, what with these polarities, the Act itself helped to change this: in most cases the constituencies it defined were appropriate to this new polarization. Yet while many men found the Act surprisingly extensive, and while the Act helped to polarize political groups, it scarcely affected that change in the locus of political power for which many of its supporters hoped and many of its opponents feared. Indeed, it was scarcely a Radical measure unless the essence of Radicalism be defined as the curtailment of government influence. For their own obvious reasons this was the definition the Bill's opponents tried to make. However, it was only somewhat gradually that they came to criticize the Bill in these terms.

In moving the introduction of the first Bill, Russell tried to justify it within the wide sweep of English history. He left it to others to place the measure in its immediate context or − to put it somewhat differently − to define the context in which it should be placed. In particular, this was done not by the Bill's supporters but by its opponents.

The initial opposition speakers had, of course, no knowledge of what Russell would say, or of what the Bill would contain. Thus − and whatever allowance be made for their abilities as debaters − their statements should obviously be considered more as replies to what they *assumed* Russell would say than as replies to his specific statements, more as comments upon what they *assumed* the Bill would contain than as comments upon its actual provisions as Russell described them. In these circumstances it is significant that the initial opposition speakers hardly touched upon the Radical case for reform, the argument to which Wellington later contributed, that the Bill would be a means of shifting political power from one social group to another. In effect, they had been prepared to continue the arguments of the immediate pre-reform period, those which Graham and others had been putting together. Yet for the anti-reformers to continue to argue in these terms was to place themselves at a considerable tactical disadvantage. On this ground alone were all groups of reformers substantially agreed. Thus, to argue in these terms was to help perpetuate that anomalous coalition of Radicals, Liberals, Ultra-Tories, and Whigs which, in many constituencies, had affected the outcome of the elections of August 1830.

The choice of Sir Robert Inglis as the initial anti-reform speaker suggests that the anti-reformers appreciated something of the nature of their dilemma. In 1829, when Peel resigned his seat for the University of Oxford over the Catholic question and then stood for re-election, it was Inglis who emerged as the Ultra-Tory champion and beat him. Yet while the actor may have been chosen with the Ultra-Tories in mind, his script was probably not very effective among them. He made the point that the king's writ summoned members to Parliament to treat about national affairs, not about those of the various communities

of which the kingdom was composed.[135] The point was a valid one.
Yet its validity was far more constitutional than social. According to
constitutional logic the establishment of a closer nexus between
members of Parliament and the significant communities of the realm
would weaken the relative powers of the crown and the House of
Lords. Yet for many of the men who had opposed the liberal
legislation of the twenties such constitutional logic was hardly relevant.
In all probability most men were willing to grant that the whole was
more than the sum of its parts. But Inglis' line of argument begged the
important question of how the whole might be defined. Many of the
petitions against the Catholic Relief Bill had originated at county and
borough meetings. Considering how these petitions were ignored, and
how important the Catholic question was among the Tories, Baring
Wall's contention during the second night of debate that a reformed
Parliament might not have passed the Relief Bill can scarcely have
helped his cause.[136] Nor can Inglis' warning have been very effective,
that the essential character of the House would be destroyed if
members of Parliament acceded to external pressures.[137] A number of
others joined Inglis in asserting, 'every year we have been becoming
more independent of the Crown.'[138] Yet with only two years
separating these assertions from the apostacies of 1829 it seems probable
their impact upon the readers of such Ultra-Tory organs as *Blackwood's
Edinburgh Magazine,* the *Morning Herald,* and the *Standard,* was not very
great. In effect, the tactical political problems the anti-reformers faced
required that they change their script. Their case was far more strongly
put by those who argued, that the total impact of the ministerial plan
would weaken the landed interests and, by extension, the stable society
it symbolized. Wellington's needs and Radical orthodoxy were both
served by this social argument. Its ultimate logic implied that Grey's
cohorts were no different from Robespierre's.

This was, of course, absurd. Yet in the circumstances of 1831 it
gained cogency from the fears of many Ultra-Tories who, like the
Marquis of Londonderry, Sir Charles Knightley, and the editors of the
Standard, became increasingly apprehensive about the growth of
Radicalism and suspicious of the influence of the political economists in
the Government. It also gained cogency from the hopes and activities
of the Radicals. In effect, throughout the reform crisis relatively few
men saw the Bill for what it really was, a measure designed to weaken
ministerial influence and to increase the powers of the 'settled heads
and leaders' of the established communities of the kingdom – a measure
that was not only socially conservative but socially conservative in the
old sense which Mackintosh's dilemma helps to illustrate. And, clearly,
those who failed to see it in this sense helped to destroy the reality –
helped to effect that substitution of a new criterion of conservatism for

the old which serves, in part, to mark the boundaries between the old *régime* and the new.

To a large extent the dynamics of this substitution was the search for power; to a large extent the mechanism was the merging of the constitutional argument against the Bill with the social argument. Wellington's constitutional argument was clear: 'The King could not perform the duties of his high station, nor the House of Lords, if the House of Commons were formed on the principle and plan proposed.'[139] But in isolation this constitutional argument could scarcely have been very compelling to those of his would-be supporters who had been embittered by the Catholic Relief Act and by the failure of his Government to do anything about the currency or the malt tax. It was basic to his argument that the property whose influence was predominant both in the elections to the House of Commons and in its proceedings was landed property. But according to them this was exactly what it was not.

Many of the men who reiterated Wellington's argument probably believed it. On the other hand, their insistence upon it may have been more a measure of their recognition of their need to alter their own public image for political purposes, their need to find an answer to the arguments of Graham and Blandford and Knatchbull. Indeed, in considering the question of how 'sincere' was their belief in the social argument against the Bill it is important to note that in the summer of 1832, when Croker tried to explain why the reformed Parliament would inevitably promote a revolution in British policy, he called it 'a miserable delusion to consider the agricultural interests as essentially Conservative.'[140]

This statement was made in private, to another member of the old Tory party. Thus, Croker could ignore the need to confirm the pedigree of the new Conservative party which may have affected the public statements of other old Tories. Instead, he could note how the tithe question and, presumably, the other fiscal questions with which the last Parliament of George IV had been primarily concerned during its final months, and which had also been extensively agitated out of doors, would unite the 'small farmers and great gentlemen, in a common assault upon the whole social system'.[141]

Nor in the early thirties did Peel believe that the agricultural interest was conservative. And, from his point of view he was quite right. Whatever the proportion of landlords who remained reformers throughout the reform crisis, once the Bill was passed and a new Parliament had been returned, most of the county Members voted for Thomas Attwood's motion, that a committee be appointed 'to inquire into the causes of the general distress existing among the industrious classes'.[142] Attwood's motion was defeated by a coalition of Whigs and ministerial Tories much as Knatchbull's amendment to the Address had been defeated in February 1830. But when Peel saw that Attwood's supporters included anti-reformers as well as reformers — both Knatchbull and the Marquis of Chandos voted with him — he concluded that the coalition between the Radicals and the Ultra-Tories which had come into being in 1830 and which had largely broken down during the reform crisis had been strengthened. As Croker explained to Lord Hertford, 'He seemed to think that there would be an entirely new [political] combination of which the Currency question would be the basis.'[143] It was to combat this 'new combination' that he decided to return to active political leadership. But this 'combination' was not stronger in 1833 than it had been in 1830. It was weaker. It was this 'combination' which had precipitated the reform crisis. But it was this 'combination' which the reform crisis served to dissolve.

Peel's criticism of Graham, in March 1831, for having 'called for the Pension List of the Privy Council, for the express purpose of holding up the members of that Council to public indignation' reveals his awareness of the importance of the attitudes which this 'combination' reflected. From a later perspective, however, the existence and importance of this 'combination' would seem to have been obscured both by the subsequent development of the Conservative party as the party of the landed interest and by the widespread tendency to subscribe to the assumptions implicit in Russell's observation of 1826, that men 'who opposed themselves on all occasions to the people' would also oppose 'the liberal system of policy which ministers had lately pursued'. Such assumptions were clearly useful in parliamentary *badinage*. But they scarcely provide a valid means of explaining the behaviour of M.P.s. As the behaviour of Peel, Huskisson and Canning reveals, those economic policies which have become identified with 'liberalism' were not incompatible with an intense suspicion of 'the people'. And, as is revealed by the behaviour of those various Ultra-Tories, currency reformers and protectionists, who were often called the Country Party, confidence in 'the people' — or, rather, confidence in the cohesion of those 'congeries of little circles' to which Mackintosh referred — was not incompatible with a violent antipathy towards the theories of the liberal economists and the policies to which these theories were related. In effect, political, religious and economic 'liberalism' were not merely different forms of the same thing.

In part, the behaviour of the men who coalesced with Wellington and Peel to oppose the Bill, and who were later joined by many other spokesmen of the landed interest, was a measure of the political skill of the Conservative leaders. But it was due even more to circumstances which the Conservative leaders could not control — the basic parliamentary weakness of the landed interest, and to circumstances for which they would hardly claim credit – the continuing threat of Radicalism. The leaders of the landed interest had no ministerial tradition of their own which might have defined them as a party. Nor did they have any parliamentary leaders of their own who might have formed a landed party Government. At best they were a marginal group which, while sizeable, and thus able to influence ministers could never control them. That they ultimately returned, by and large, to the Tory allegiance from which most of them had come, instead of continuing their flirtation with the Whigs and Radicals, was due far less to the positive attractions of the former than to the increasingly negative attractions of the latter. Many rural leaders never lost their suspicions of Wellington and Peel. The sentiment, expressed in 1836, that 'the landed interest of this country has not a more decided, determined and dangerous enemy than Sir Robert Peel' was far from rare.[144] Yet support them they did. By so doing they tended to confirm Wellington's definition of his party as the party of the landed interest. As later events reveal, however, the interests of 'the land' as they defined them were rather different from the interests of 'the land' as Wellington and Peel defined them.

The concerted reaction of the leaders of the landed interest to the policies which ultimately led to the repeal of the corn laws only lasted a short time. But it was long enough to have a considerable political impact. It conditioned the results of many of the elections at which were chosen men who not only joined in defeating Wellington but in passing the second reading of the first Bill by the small but adequate majority of one. The general process which ultimately led to the Conservative victory of 1841 began soon after these elections were over. In the light of the events of 1846 the process might seem somewhat anomalous. Considering the role of the Bill – meaning the interpretation of the Act – and the role of the Act – meaning the changes in the representative structure – in producing the majorities of 1841 the anti-reformers' arguments might also seem somewhat anomalous. But the *Act* itself simply provided the machinery. The arguments about the *Bill* helped to condition the ways the machinery would be used. And, of course, scholastic arguments which fail to recognize that identities are always conditional have no place in history except as historical phenomena.

XIV

Opportunism provides much of the answer to the question why certain men both in and out of Parliament found themselves working in alliance with certain other men before, during and after the reform crisis. But statements to the contrary notwithstanding, the Bill itself reveals a coherent set of social and political values and assumptions.[145] In the light of the evidence the Bill contains it is clear that the members of the Grey Ministry were principally concerned to change the modes of political action without greatly changing the relative powers of the different interests in the State — or, at least, without increasing the powers of the urban interest beyond the point to which the urban activists had already brought them. There is still the question of the extent to which the Bill was designed, as Palmerston put it, 'to *restore* to the landed interest that influence which he thought indispensable to the safety and prosperity of the country'.[146] But this much is clear: for all the hopes of the Radicals, and for all the fears of the more ardent anti-reformers, the members of this highly aristocratic Cabinet were not traitors to their estate or class. They intended not social revolution but the reconstruction of a governmental system in which many important elements within the Kingdom had lost confidence. Apparently, as they conceived it, this loss of confidence was largely due to the failure of numerous M.P.s to remain true to their declared principles in the face of cosmopolitan opinion, ministerial influence, and the influence of individual patrons. To restore confidence they proposed a plan which, while integrated in concept and legislation, involved two distinct procedural steps, first, the disfranchisement of those constituencies which were not communities and which were considered incapable of the necessary rehabilitation and, second, the creation of new constituencies, some with new names, others with old, which would be communities. In functional terms the first of these steps implied a significant weakening of ministerial and other non-constituency influences in the House of Commons. In functional terms the second implied a strengthening of the 'independence' of M.P.s by mustering communities in their support. The underlying assumptions of their plan were very simple. First, that M.P.s could not be expected to resist the various pressures they faced unless their ability to do so was strengthened by countervailing pressures focussed on them from the communities which chose them. Second, that the internal cohesion of such communities, enhanced by their relations with the M.P.s they chose, would provide a guarantee of social peace.

If democracy be defined in terms of the size of the electorate and the relative powers of the representative and other branches of government then it must be allowed that the Bill's opponents were right in portraying the measure as a step towards democracy. The Bill proposed to increase the numbers of potential voters. Furthermore, the Bill was passed against violent opposition from the majority of the members of the House of Lords and more temperate opposition from the King. Thus, to pass the Bill was to register the increasing relative strength of the so-called democratic element of the constitution. In these circumstances, what with the occasional violence of reform agitation and the fact that no clear answer has even yet been found to the question, at what point riot becomes revolution, historians have often implied that Grey's behaviour in appointing the Cabinet committee which drafted the Bill was somewhat analogous to Wellington's behaviour when, absenting himself from the House of Lords, he allowed the Bill to pass. The term, clearly appropriate to Wellington's behaviour, has been applied to Grey's as well: they were both 'conceding'. Furthermore, noting that the ostensible concessions which the Act contained were not, in fact, very large – that later measures contributed far more to the growth of democracy – twin conclusions have been drawn: the Act was conservative *because* its concessions were small; its provisions were less important than the fact of its existence.[147]

John Cannon is perhaps right, in saying that 'the true conservative is one who suspects those who declare that the supreme crisis is at hand, resists invitations to die in the last ditch, and comforts himself with the unheroic virtues of patience and resilience, conscious that reform, like income tax, death duties and capital gains tax, may not be as deadly as it seems.'[148] But before the Act be used to mark 'the beginning of the transformation from one political system to another', and before it be used to illustrate the 'foundation achievement of modern conservatism' which, in turn, would illustrate the role of the 'true conservative', two fundamental questions must be answered.[149] The first concerns the nature of these political systems. The second concerns the nature of the process by which the one system was transformed into the other.

Obviously, those who die in the last ditch are dead: survival is crucial. Since political and social identities are nothing if not changeable, however, the criteria of political and social survival are not always clear. Obviously, few men in politics or out achieve exactly what they set out to achieve. Compromise is often essential, sometimes concession. However, while compromise is one thing, concession another, the relevance of this distinction to the politics of the early thirties has been obscured – and this, it would seem, for two principal and related reasons. In the first place, not sufficient notice has been taken of the fact that reform meant change – nature and direction unspecified – and that while certain Radicals were at pains to claim the Bill as their own – others, of course, to deny all responsibility for it – the Ministers were at pains to clarify the differences between their Bill and the sort of Bill the Radicals might have produced. In the second place, when statements have been found referring to the Bill as a 'concession' these have been read more in the light of the assumption that reform must have meant the thing the Radicals had in mind than in the light of the rhetorical tradition according to which parliamentary actions of whatever nature were often described as 'concessions' to extra-parliamentary demands. The provisions of the Bill confirm the validity of the Ministers' description. As such, they provide an effective means of approaching the question of the context within which the Bill should be described as a 'conservative' measure.

In the years after 1832, the years in which the term, 'conservative', came into widespread use, many men sorted themselves out politically along the lines which the term itself suggests into a party nominally committed to the encouragement of change and a party nominally committed to the resistance to change. In the light of this polarity there were, perhaps, as John Cannon suggests, 'few fundamental differences' between Peel and Grey.[150] But the very fact that Grey was a reformer, Peel an anti-reformer, suggests that whatever the *number* of their differences the fundamental importance of these differences should not be ignored. And, to a significant extent, these differences were fundamental because they concerned the nature and mechanism of what might be called 'conservatism' itself. According to that orthodox Tory theory to which Peel subscribed, ministerial influence was a 'conservative' factor in the State because it allowed the King's government to be carried on above the rough and tumble of conflicting interests. While it was this influence – this 'conservatism' – which the Bill was designed to weaken the effort to do so can only be described as 'radical' by ignoring the nature of the constituency system which the Ministers tried to create. As Mackintosh had noted in 1809, the stability of 'old governments' was a function of the strength of the 'congeries of little circles' on which they were based; the fact, as he put it, that 'Every county, and district, and parish, and village, has its settled heads and leaders.' Clearly, the Ministers tried to strengthen these 'settled heads and leaders'. Clearly, their efforts were 'conservative' in the sense which Mackintosh helps to illustrate. To the extent that 'conservatism' in this sense should be distinguished from 'conservatism' in the sense which Dr. Cannon's 'true conservative' helps to illustrate so should the sort of 'concession' in which fundamental power is at stake be distinguished from the sort of 'concession' whose logic is found in parliamentary usage.

Obviously, John Cannon is right, that 'where Grey sowed, Peel reaped'.[151] But obviously, neither Peel nor Grey anticipated such a result. Possibly, as Cannon suggests, 'Grey deserves a place of honour in the pantheon of the Conservative party.'[152] But unless we realise that such a desert illustrates the irony in human affairs, and thus that such a statement is simply a question in disguise, the statement itself will simply breed confusion. Not only will the differences between the executive basis of Peel's 'conservatism' and the social or corporate basis of Grey's 'conservatism' be obscured, the differences between these two 'conservatisms' on the one hand and the new 'conservatism' on the other will also be obscured. And two further questions will be begged; how and why did old 'conservatisms' become merged in the new?

The constituency arrangement which the Ministers proposed presumably illustrates their sense of what a constituency should look like as a *political* entity – of what it should represent. Presumably it illustrates their sense of what a constituency should look like as a *social* entity – of what the agencies and mechanisms of electoral recruitment should be within it, of how it should fulfil its political role. Presumably their constituency arrangement reveals an aspect of the general problem with which they sought to deal which bears on the question of the degree to which the Act should be used to mark 'the beginning of the transformation from one political system to another', the degree to which it should be used to mark one of the first constitutional efforts to arrest this transformation.

If the principal measure of democracy be the size of the electorate then, clearly, the Act might be used to mark the crucial first step towards democracy. But if the principal measure of democracy be the relative fluidity of the groups within the society and the relative weakness of the hierarchies which these groups support, then, just as clearly, the Act itself should not be used to mark any first step towards democracy. Rather, the steps – first, second, or whatever – would consist in the weakening of the traditional nexus of English society. In this context three important points should be noted. First, as the poll books help to illustrate, that, other things being equal, the mere size of the electorate is rather less significant than the distribution of voters in relation to the various mechanisms within society through which these voters might be recruited and organized. Second, that the Act was the means by which – although less efficiently than the initial Bills: in this respect, in particular, the Act was a compromise – different categories of voters were assigned to different constituencies. And, third, as is assumed in several contemporary analyses, among them the analyses of several contemporary reformers, that the very dissatisfactions which the demands for reform reflected were functions of the weakening of the traditional nexus of English society which reform itself would correct. Together, these arguments and phenomena confirm the judgment that 'the men who drafted the Bill were primarily concerned to correct the conditions from which they believed the demands for reform had arisen – not to yield to these demands,' that the Bill was not a 'concession' whose essential 'conservatism' would lie in the paucity of the things 'conceded' but an effort to impose a 'conservative' 'cure'.[153]

XV

The importance of the traditional nexus of English society was basic to the arguments of many members of the Grey Ministry. It was that which informed the distinction Russell made between two sections of the aristocracy while introducing the first Bill. The one, he said, resided on their estates, 'receiving large incomes, performing important duties, relieving the poor by charity, and evincing private worth and public virtue'. The other did not 'live among the people, . . . [knew] nothing of the people, and . . . care[d] nothing for them'. As for the first, he declared, 'It is not in human nature that they should not possess a great influence upon public opinion.' [154] But for the second he had no sympathy: 'The sooner its influence is carried away with the corruption on which it has thriven, the better for the country, in which it has repressed so long every wholesome and invigorating influence.' [155]

It was the same distinction which Graham made when he explained that the main trouble with the existing constituency structure lay not in the influence it allowed but in its failure to distinguish between different types of influence. In the unreformed system, he declared, it made little difference whether property was held by good or bad landlords, whether influence was transmitted through a social community or exercised at a distance, ruthlessly and impersonally. But, in the reformed system, he went on, 'Character would begin to be necessary, residence to be necessary.' [156] Taking the bull by the horns, perhaps, he cited the borough of Tavistock to explain what he meant. In spite of the strength of the Duke of Bedford's influence in Tavistock the Ministers did not propose to disfranchise the borough. To various anti-reformers this only showed that the Ministers were able to recognize their friends. But Graham had another explanation which, however useful in explaining the Ministers' treatment of Tavistock, reveals an important aspect of their general logic. He allowed that even after the Bill had been passed Bedford would retain considerable influence in Tavistock. But, he insisted, his residual influence would not then exceed 'his legitimate influence'. [157]

In effect, Graham distinguished – as Thomas Oldfield had distinguished some forty years earlier – between two types of influence, the one 'legitimate', the other 'illegitimate'. Regarding that influence which 'prevails in counties and popular cities and towns', Oldfield declared, '[it] only derived from extensive property, eminent personal qualities, or from good neighbourhood and hospitality.' He reserved the term, 'corruption', for that other type of influence which, he explained, existed irrespective of social community, and which was to be found 'in limited corporations and burgage tenures, and [in] what are termed rotten boroughs, with only ten or twelve houses in each'. The deserted hill of Old Sarum symbolized this second type of influence. The borough contained no one through whom the influence of the Earl of Caledon might be channelled. In consequence, the Caledon influence in Old Sarum was not a matter of social relationship. It was simply a matter of property. It was a 'saleable commodity . . . carried to market . . . with as little secrecy and caution as an estate is carried to the hammer at a public auction'.[158] In a different way the Chandos amendment also symbolized this second type of influence. While tenants-at-will might be fairly numerous their dependence upon their landlords was such that, in the eyes of the Ministers, the influences which their landlords would obtain in consequence of their enfranchisement would not be matters of social relationship but simple matters of property.

The question of influence is crucial to the understanding of both the Bill itself and the mid-century political system. But nothing has done so much to confuse the true nature of the Bill and the true nature of this system as the problems relating to it. Most observant men from James Mill on the one hand to Robert Southey on the other understood the role of influence in English society and politics. They also appreciated the fact that influence obtained in the context of hierarchical relationships. Furthermore – and, presumably, because few men of status conceived of a society except as the framework for the peculiar varieties of heriarchical relationships with which they were familiar – they tended to recognize the differences between 'legitimate' and 'illegitimate' influences: the one was a function of such relationships and tended to perpetuate them; the other was not and did not. But these men did not always agree on which influences were 'legitimate' and which were 'illegitimate'. Nor are their disagreements on this point to be wondered at. Indeed, such is the nature of politics that in the heat of political battle the measure of the legitimacy of any influence tends to lie not in the sources from which it derives but in the uses to which it is put. And, presumably, it was largely as a result of such disagreements and of the question which such disagreements reflected – whether those groups and relationships were themselves legitimate which 'legitimate' influence reflected – that, as time went on, many men tended to substitute the distinction between a 'free' and an 'unfree' electorate for the earlier distinction between 'legitimate' and 'illegitimate' influence.[159] As a rule, both the Bill itself and the mid-century political system have been considered in the light of this substitute distinction.

But neither distinction helps to reveal the logic of the Bill's opponents. Indeed, from the orthodox Tory point of view the various Old Sarums were simply necessary because they facilitated the exercise of power. The question whether the type of influence which obtained within them was 'legitimate' or 'illegitimate', whether the voters within them were 'free' or 'unfree' was scarcely relevant. But those who opposed the policies, some liberal, some not, the implementation of which was facilitated by the existence of these boroughs did not, of course, agree. And, whether these boroughs were used more to implement liberal or anti-liberal policies, they ceased to be useful for either purpose as the opposition to these policies increased – as that confidence which the exercise of power requires was dissipated. It was this which made reform necessary, not any growing appreciation of the 'disreputable' nature of the pre-reform system – as if 'disreputability', like beauty, did not lie more in the eyes of the beholder than in the thing beheld, and not in any growth in 'the basic Whig disposition to welcome the "march of mind" and extend civil liberties.' [161] In effect, the Old Sarums were not abolished as a means of eradicating influence. They were abolished as a means of eradicating 'illegitimate' influence. Nor were they abolished by men who regarded all their fellow subjects as equal members of English society, or who regarded this society as an unstructured aggregate of essentially rational individuals. Much has been made of the fact that most of the adult population remained unenfranchised after 1832. Less has been made of the related fact that as far as possible the new constituencies were to be composed of men who were members of the communities which these constituencies symbolized, men who might thus be recruited and organized through the 'legitimate' agencies and mechanisms of electoral recruitment which these constituencies contained. In effect, while eradicating those 'illegitimate' influences which, they believed, were increasingly being used to jeopardize their powers and status – and this is a not inappropriate definition of 'illegitimate' influence – the men who passed the Bill sought to maximize those 'legitimate' influences which, they believed, both reflected and supported their powers and status.

XVI

Obviously, the Bill's opponents failed to appreciate the extent of their own prospective influence in the constituencies the Ministers were trying to create. Yet their opposition was, perhaps, as much principled as it was pragmatic. Even those anti-reformers who tried to increase their own prospective influences in the counties – the Chandoses, the Sibthorps, and the Sugdens – tended to accept the orthodox Tory argument, that no political system could really survive whose essential strength was a function of such influences exercised in such constituencies. In part, perhaps, this belief was a measure of their lack of practical experience. As a group the anti-reformers had not tried to organize their own bases of power throughout the Kingdom before

1832. Instead, they had depended upon the executive powers to protect them. Their consequent impotence before the reformers' onslaught at the elections of May 1831, both aggravated their problems and reveals something of their nature. As in previous years, most elections were not contested. The Bill's opponents lost by default. Nor is their quiescence entirely to be wondered at. Indeed, had the anti-reformers tried to organize opposition to the measure throughout the Kingdom they would have been contradicting the grounds of their opposition to the Bill itself. They would have been accepting its essential premise, that the choice between rival policies should depend more upon the social powers of the various protagonists than upon the wisdom of the King's Ministers and the executive powers of the State. As Wellington explained to a friend who was doing his utmost to assist the anti-reform cause in Kent, 'I quite concur in all that you suggest as steps to be taken, with the exception of the formation of societies.' He approved the circulation of petitions against the Bill which individuals might sign. But he refused to countenance that organization of individuals into societies without which they could scarcely have played effective political roles.[162] His reasons were presumably those which Croker specified when he explained why he opposed the formation of anti-Radical associations. These, he explained, would 'sanction the principle of association independent of the Crown, and would legitimatize the Radical National Guard. ... When it becomes a matter of association and counter-association', he went on, 'it is a mere affair of numbers, and eventually of physical force.' [163]

Except when they tried to exclude the borough freeholders from the counties and to enfranchise the tenants-at-will, the anti reformers evidenced a consistent position whose logic derived from the importance of that objectivity and power which they associated with the close boroughs. Except when they amended the initial borough freeholder clause and made those other adjustments to their Bill following the adoption of the Chandos amendment the Ministers evidenced a similarly consistent position whose logic derived from the importance of those agencies of social discipline which were implicit in the phrase, 'legitimate' influence. There was no question of intentionally enfranchising men who were not members of communities. Yet, from the anti-reformers' point of view – and this is what made their efforts to exclude all borough freeholders from the counties somewhat anomalous – influence was not to be confused with wisdom nor social cohesion with power. In effect, most of the Bill's opponents tended to doubt that the Kingdom could ever be secure if its main anchor were the ties which bound the members of local communities together. Few of them denied that constituencies could be fashioned in such a manner as to provide for the representation of interests. But most of them doubted that these interests could provide the dynamic of a coherent policy which would not end in the ultimate destruction of the landed interest, the aristocracy, and the crown. They believed that the various interests in the Kingdom would lock, not as gears mesh in an engine, their motions complementary, but as opposing forces converge, their final vector determined by the failure of the weakest. And, of course, those of them who had worked within the existing political system to implement the liberal reforms of the 'twenties saw how the Bill would destroy the machinery they had used. As Baring Wall observed, a reformed Parliament would probably not have passed the Catholic Relief Bill.[164] Peel's criticism was similar: no Government could operate efficiently unless it possessed more influence than the Bill would leave it.[165] When Charles Baring compared the relative assertiveness and organizational ability of the magnates of the new northern towns with that of the country gentlemen he was considering a different but related problem. The country gentlemen, he explained, could not withstand the pressures which the others would generate unless a strong executive were retained to help them.[166]

In fact, Baring's apprehensions were somewhat exaggerated. To some extent the country gentlemen did rise to the challenge but in doing so they not only confirmed the anti-reformers' general apprehensions, they even convinced Russell that these apprehensions were somewhat justified. As Russell explained while introducing his Reform Bill of 1854, there was a 'defect' in the first Reform Act which subsequent events had revealed.[167] The word he used was fairly mild. As he described it, however, the 'defect' was anything but superficial. Indeed, what was 'defective' were the very premises on which the reconstruction of constituencies had been based, those responsible for the fact, as he put it, that the Act had 'tended to divide the country in a way it was not divided before; in short, into opposite camps according as the districts might be connected with land or trade'. And, he went on, thus explaining why he came to believe that such a division had been a mistake, 'I think that since the passing of the Act we have seen – what had not occurred before – we have seen county Members too generally exclusive in respect of the interest they cared for, and Members for the great cities too exclusive also for theirs'.[168]

In consequence of the changes that were made to the Bill on 19 and 20 August 1831, the division of the country which the Act effected was far milder than that which the Ministers initially proposed. But even with these amendments a sharp break was made with the past. The close boroughs were gone. Also, while the Act did not erect impassable barriers at the boundaries of the boroughs it provided the means by which voluntary political activists might enhance the interest orientations of both the residual and the new constituencies by registering certain prospective voters in these constituencies and not registering others, and by disseminating appropriate ideologies among the men they registered. To some extent, of course, such means had existed in the pre-reform period. Indeed, it was largely by exploiting these means that urban activists had been able to enhance their powers in the counties at the elections of 1830 and 1831. But, in the circumstances created by the abolition of the close boroughs, the type of behaviour which these voluntary political activists help to illustrate acquired a new importance. To what extent was the 'defect' to which Russell referred a 'defect' in the Act? To what extent was it a product of the efforts of men to develop bases of power within 'their own' constituencies – those which they helped to make 'their own' when they developed bases of power within them?[169] But, whatever the answer to these questions, a new political system came into being which the various elites helped to create when, responding to the suggestions which the Act implicitly conveyed, they tried to identify themselves with the interests their constituencies symbolized and, of course, tried to define these interests according to their own roles within them. Such a system presumably helped to solve the related problems of confidence and social cohesion. But it only did so by intensifying the rivalries between, or among, the relevant interests. As John Cannon notes, there has been a tendency of late 'to downgrade the [first] Reform Act'.[170] Indeed, the tendency is one to which he contributes when he describes the Act as a 'conservative' measure because of the 'comparative modesty of the changes it wrought'.[171] But these changes were only 'modest' if measured against the wrong scale. They were 'modest' as steps along the path towards democracy for the very simple reason that they were steps in another direction entirely.

In part, the direction in which these changes tended can be seen from the anti-reformers' complaints that the Bill would intensify the rivalries between, or among, the various interests in the State while weakening the ability of any Government to govern. Of course, various anti-reformers tried to make the division of the country even sharper than the Ministers proposed in order to enhance the powers of the landed interest within the system which the Ministers were trying to create. But it was just such an intensification of interests against which they warned when opposing the Ministers' efforts to create this system. According to Peel, if the close boroughs were abolished no Government would have the powers it needed to operate efficiently. According to Inglis, if the close boroughs were abolished and constituencies refashioned in terms of interests the institutional basis of parliamentary objectivity would be destroyed: no M.P.s would be left who would be able to consider national affairs other than according to the narrow perspectives of the interests they represented. Whether Russell remembered that it was the anti-reformers, by and large, who had uttered these warnings, he had obviously come, by 1854, to believe that the dangers of which they warned were very real.

In part, too, the direction in which these changes tended can be seen from the fact that in the thirties few reformers recognized the validity of the anti-reformers' criticisms. True, in January 1832, Russell argued that a *complete* exclusion of the borough freeholders from the counties 'would produce a division of interests between the inhabitants of towns and counties'.[172] And that, he said, would be bad. But this was more a tactical than a principled argument. In the context of the continued efforts of various anti-reformers and certain reformers to exclude all borough freeholders from the counties it was a means of defending the amended borough freeholder clause. Furthermore, as Althorp explained in August 1831, while discussing the amended clause, even though the exclusion of townsmen from the counties was not to be as complete as that initially proposed the difference was only a difference of degree. The object of the amended clause was the same as that of the original clause: 'that the county constituency should not be overpowered by the inhabitants of towns, which they would have been if all those who had the right of voting for property in towns were admitted indiscriminately to vote for the counties'.[173] True, Milton criticised the amended clause on the ground that no effort 'to make a balance between the trading and commercial interests on the one side, and the landed interest on the other ... [could be successful because] no ingenuity ... [could] render that balance so nice as not to excite dissatisfaction on the one side or the other'.[174] But the amended clause was contained in the final Bill. Indeed, in the eyes of most of the men who were ultimately responsible for the Bill, who drafted it or helped to pass it, the point which Milton criticised was, presumably, a reason for satisfaction: what else was 'legitimate' influence but the political consequence of certain varieties of social relationship? As the provisions of the Bill themselves suggest, the dangers which these men saw were not those which Milton imagined or those to which Russell later referred. Rather, they were those which the mutual re-enforcement of political and social relationships might help to avoid, the dangers of the possible disintegration of the traditional groups in English society, the dangers of the possible loss of status of the leaders of these groups. These dangers were manifest in two forms: the close borough, and the jumbling of differently oriented groups within the same constituency. The substantive grievances which derived from these manifestations differed from one another. But the departures from the ideal, as illustrated in the provisions of the Act were similar: in the one case political power was abstracted from social power; in the other case social power was jeopardized by the locus of competition; in neither case was political power a function of social roles.

XVII

It has often been claimed that the first Reform Bill was passed because the reformers, by and large, believed in the individual intelligence or wisdom of the members of the 'middle classes' — by presumptive definition, members of the urban 'middle classes'. In describing the background of the Bill references have often been made both to the growth of towns and to the growth of 'public opinion' — what might ostensibly be measured by the increasing press runs of *The Times* and other newspapers.[175] Various reformers' statements, redolent of praise for townsmen and suggestive of the need to make certain adjustments to the representative system in consequence of the growth of towns have often been quoted. These statements were, of course, made. The Bill was, of course, passed. But various provisions of the Bill suggest that if, indeed, 'the cause of reform was the growing wealth and intelligence of the middle classes', the relations between reform on the one hand and 'middle class' wealth and intelligence on the other were rather more complex than has usually been allowed.[176] Possibly, the key to these relationships lies in the answer to this question: what did the reformers really mean when they referred — as many of them did — to 'public opinion'.

Various of the themes of the third chapter of Macaulay's *History of England* were anticipated by his observation, in 1831, that 'New forms of property . . . [had come] into existence, . . . [that] new portions of society [had risen] into importance',[177] and by his assertion that 'The great cause of revolution is this, that while nations move onwards, constitutions stand still.'[178] But the parallel progression model which informed his argument both in 1831 and in his subsequent *History* was not the model on which the Bill was based. Brougham's reference was the same when he spoke of

> Large towns, densely peopled, marts of commerce, emporia of manufactures, the abodes of honest and industrious men who, in time of peace contributed to advance the prosperity of their country by the sweat of their brows, and who, in war defended their country by the sinews of their arms, and by the blood of their veins; but who, because they had not been formerly congregated into masses in certain small districts, had not hitherto been thought worthy of being represented in the legislative council of the nation.[179]

However, while Brougham was clearly eager to provide these men with representatives *of their own* in Parliament these were precisely the men who, he said, should be deprived of their influences in county elections as a means of 'restor[ing] the state of Representation to what it ought to be'.[180] Presumably, his much advertised esteem for townsmen was no less real because of this. But whatever his own esteem for townsmen, in discussing the Bill he was obviously led to adopt a wider political perspective than that with which he is sometimes credited and a somewhat different social perspective. For the purposes of discussing the Billl he had to acknowledge the importance of that rural power in the counties which the growth of urban power was tending to undermine. Also — at least by implication — he had to acknowledge the differences among the nexus through which the different categories of voters were recruited.

Undoubtedly, many men — Macaulay, possibly, among them — conceived of 'public opinion' in somewhat unstructured terms as a simple product of the media. But when many men referred to 'public opinion' the thing to which they referred was not the product of the media but the product of definable relationships. A case in point is James Mill. Mill presumably never used the phrase, 'deference community'. But he described the essential attributes of such a community when he explained that men would inevitably adopt the 'opinions' of those of their superiors

> ... who come the most immediately in contact with them, to whom they fly for advice and assistance in all their numerous difficulties, upon whom they feel an immediate and daily dependence in health and in sickness, in infancy and in old age; to whom their children look up as models for their imitation, whose opinions they hear daily repeated and account it their honor to adopt.[181]

This is not to suggest that the reformers as a whole — and, in particular, the men who drafted the Bill — were crypto-Benthamites. Rather, it is to illustrate an aspect of the climate of assumptions in which the Bill was drafted which helps to explain the contents of the Bill. It is to illustrate a social component in the contemporary understanding of 'public opinion' — or, at least, in Mill's understanding — which those historians and political scientists have obviously ignored who try to explain the Bill in terms of such ostensible occurrences as the growth in 'the basic whig disposition to welcome the 'march of mind' and extend civil liberties'.[182] However the recent statement be explained, that '[James] Mill's consideration of the suffrage was shaped by his belief that men would choose their representatives according to their individual wishes and interests', many reformers in the thirties — or, at least, many who were in a position to impose the consequences of their beliefs upon the Kingdom — believed that certain specific extensions of the franchise were not only safe but desirable if they served to strengthen certain deference communities or deference networks.[183] Because they did so the Bill contained the provisions it contained. In substance, the very factors which made reform possible in 1832 were those which produced the 'defect' to which Russell referred in 1854.

Part III

The mid-century political system

6

The creation of the system: the Act and the activists

I

The political system which came into being after 1832 was in part the product of the first Reform Act. But it was also the product of the efforts of the men who grasped the potentialities of power which the Act provided, thus the product of the factors which conditioned their efforts. The distinction between the role of the Act and the role of voluntary political activity is somewhat analogous to that which Dicey and, to some extent, Freeman before him made between the laws and conventions of the constitution.[1] It is important because it provides a means of organizing the various questions which arise concerning the origin and nature of the mid-century political system and the reasons why changes occurred within it.

The Act determined the distribution and boundaries of the different constituencies and the conditions which the would-be voters in each constituency would have to satisfy. But the Act did not determine which of the qualified men would be registered to vote. Nor did it determine how those men who were registered would behave at the polls should their presence be required there to answer the questions which only they could answer and only there. In effect, the Act defined the tasks which those man who hoped to exercise power in the various constituencies would have to perform. But for no constituency did it really determine who these men would be or how they would behave. Historians have frequently told us who these men were and what tasks they performed. But the relationships between these men, the tasks they performed, and the structure of the society within which they operated have not been adequately considered. It has for example, often been noted that in many constituencies the various local elites tried to register their own potential supporters, to block the registration of their opponents' potential supporters and, failing this, to purge their opponents' supporters from the register. As a rule, however, no-one has fully considered how the information was gathered which enabled the various supporters to be identified, why the gathering of this information was tolerated, how gathering it might have affected the structure of the society to which it was pertinent, and hence how it might have affected the very pertinence of this information itself. In effect, the mid-century political system has not been considered *as a system* which those who worked it helped to create and change. Instead, it has been described somewhat abstractly as the simple product of the first Reform Act which was altered subsequently by the second Reform Act. The importance of the role which the first Reform Act ostensibly played in conditioning the nature of this system can be seen from the question which various historians have tried to answer: in exactly what ways did the first Reform Act affect the size and composition of the various electorates? Efforts to answer this question not only reveal a lack of understanding of the evidence. Even more importantly, perhaps, they reveal a lack of understanding of the mid-century political system itself.

The point is this: while certain provisions of the Act not only came into effect automatically, but came into effect in definable fashion, other provisions were entirely permissive. And, when the question has to do with the size and composition of the various electorates, these were the more important. The only truly automatic provisions were those which determined the distribution and boundaries of the various constituencies. These placed certain limits, fairly broad ones, upon the size and character of the different electorates. The franchise provisions also placed certain limits upon the size and character of the different electorates. However, since registration was not automatic – since the franchise provisions merely defined the qualifications necessary for registration – these limits were broader still. For the boroughs which the Act created, and for certain of the pre-reform boroughs in which, in the pre-reform period, electorates were effectively non-existent, the significance of these points is obscured by the sheer size of the post-reform electorates. But to ignore these points is to ignore the implications of the evidence which the poll books contain, that is, that the principal function which the mid-century voters performed was to support the political ambitions of their leaders. Politics had to do with the rivalries of these men with one another and, within the context of a changing environment, one which they themselves helped to change, the means by which the members of a given set of established leaders tried to retain the loyalties of their respective followers, the means by which they tried to pry their opponents' followers free from their loyalties, and the means by which other would-be leaders tried to displace them. The rest is administration.

II

The Act defined *potential* electorates. Thus, to measure the effects upon the size of the electorates of the Act itself it would be necessary to know the size of the potential electorates both in the pre-reform period and post-reform periods. But the very reasons for adopting a system of electoral registration in 1832 suggest why the size of the potential electorates in the pre-reform period must be forever unknown. And the very nature of the franchise provisions in the mid-century suggest why the size of the potential electorates which the Act defined must also remain unknown.[2]

Before 1832 the potential electorate in any English county included all men, not peers or otherwise disqualified, who possessed freehold or equivalent interests in any real property in the county which was worth at least forty shillings a year above all charges and which had either been assessed to the land tax for at least six months or redeemed. Land tax assessment lists might be used to measure the numbers of men who possessed landed property of the requisite value which had been assessed to the land tax. But much land had been redeemed from the tax without prejudice to the landowners' electoral rights.[3] Furthermore, many categories of property besides land and houses were often regarded as real property for the purposes of the franchise and for these no lists are available. But even if the size of the potential pre-reform electorates were known precisely such knowledge could not be used to measure the effects of the *Act*. While the Act defined a potential electorate there is no way to measure the size of the potential electorate which the Act defined. The closest approximation to such a potential electorate would be that other potential electorate composed of the men whose names were enrolled in the new electoral registers. But unless these registers were significantly corrected they would not even provide accurate measures of the numbers of men whose names they contained.

Electoral registers were not drawn up for a constituency as a whole. They were drawn up separately for each parish. They were simply lists – and by no means exhaustive lists – of the men in the various parishes who possessed the necessary qualifications. In effect, there was no such thing as a single electoral register for a constituency any more than there was a single polling booth within the constituency. When reference was made to a constituency register the thing referred to was the collection of registers for the various parishes, or for the various polling districts, into which the constituency was divided. In consequence, because some men were qualified in respect of more than one qualification and, in the counties, because some men possessed qualifications in different parishes of the same county or county division, the number of entries on the registers for a given constituency might well exceed the number of men who might vote at a contest within the constituency. The problem was that to which the clerk of the peace for Bedfordshire referred, in 1837, while reporting the number of entries on the electoral register for the county – ostensibly, the number of registered electors in the county: there were obviously more entries than potential voters because 'the names of several people are repeated, their property being situate in more parishes than one'. [4]

Obviously there could not have been very many cases of the same men registering twenty times within a given constituency, once for each of twenty different properties, [5] or even nine times, once for each of nine different properties. [6] But if such cases were few it was not because the registration procedures prevented their occurrence. Rather, it was because there were few men whose properties were appropriately located.

There was a logic to the situation which the various procedures reflected. In the boroughs the Reform Act came close to establishing a single set of franchise requirements which the would-be registree had to satisfy. Furthermore, in the boroughs these requirements were such that who qualified was often a matter of public knowledge. Except for the compound rate payer, the man whose rates were paid by his landlord, the borough rate books should have contained the information necessary to determine which men were qualified to be registered as £10-householders. The freemen lists contained the information necessary to determine which men were qualified to be registered as freemen. In consequence, the Act empowered those men who kept the rate books and the freemen lists to draw up preliminary lists of borough voters. When these preliminary registers had been corrected and approved by the revising barristers they became the official registers for the coming year.

But in the counties such a system was scarcely viable. In the counties the ways in which a man might qualify were legion. [7] Furthermore, many of these ways involved complex legal questions. And, again, in many cases, none of the relevant information was publicly available. In consequence, while in the boroughs the initiative in drawing up the lists from which the registers were made was put in the hands of the overseers, who kept the rate books, and the town clerks, who kept the freemen lists, in the counties the initiative was put in the hands of the would-be registrees themselves. Thus, in the counties, the overseers were primarily receivers of claims, the revising barristers primarily referees. [8] And the questions referred to them were among the most difficult which human ingenuity and a complex legal system could in combination devise. In consequence, as long as sixty or seventy men were employed as revising barristers, and as long as there was so superior authority to standardize their interpretations of the Act, the county registers not only reflected the different factors to which the various claims should be attributed, they also reflected the different factors to which the many conflicting decisions of the revising barristers should be attributed. Such inconsistencies were scarcely new. As Russell noted, however, the problems resulting from the fact that, for example, the revising barrister for Middlesex recognized the possession of shares in the New River Company as a valid qualification while the revising barrister for Hertfordshire did not, were far more acute when the revising barristers gave their judgments in public than they had been when the assessors had given their judgments in the privacy of the sheriffs' rooms.[9] Indeed, ultimately, the acuteness of the problem overrode the initial concern that if appeals from the revising barristers' decisions were heard in a court of law public confidence in the court's impartiality might be jeopardized.[10] To put an end to such inconsistencies the Court of Common Pleas was given appellate jurisdiction on points of law in registration cases. This was done by the Registration Act of 1843, 6 Victoria, c. 17. Subsequently, the Court used its powers to alter the franchise law in ways which obviously violated the intent of the reformers of 1832.[11] In part, their intentions were incorporated in a provision of the second Reform Act which historians have tended to ignore.[12] But the registration procedure remained a judicial procedure. In the counties this was particularly important. As the members of the Select Committee on Registration of Voters in Counties in 1870 noted, it was always possible that an objection against a valid qualification would be sustained. For this reason they defended the duplication of entries on the county registers. But they only defended them up to a point. To save the rate payers' money they argued that no man should be registered more than twice. The logic of their argument was simple: while the costs of initial registration were ostensibly borne by the would-be registree – each claim for registration in a county had to be accompanied with a shilling – the subsequent expenses of compiling and printing the registers were paid from the county rates. The Committee's further comment, that no one who was registered twice should be counted twice, had an obvious bearing upon the general ways in which the electoral registers would have to be corrected if they were to provide accurate measures of the numbers of men who might have voted at a given contested election.[13] But there is no way of knowing exactly what corrections should be made in any given case.[14]

However, the figures which the electoral registers contain are not without value. While they cannot be used to measure the effects of the Act they can be used to illustrate the importance of other factors. In 1833 the registers for the English counties contained 344,564 entries.[15]

By 1836 and 1837 the number had grown to approximately 440,000.[16] Thereafter, the increase was more gradual. By 1845 the number had only reached 476,232,[17] an increase of less than ten per cent for the decade.[17] Twenty years later it had only reached 499,617, an increase of less than five per cent for the two decades.[18]

In certain cases, this growth might perhaps be explained in terms of the general growth of population and prosperity in mid-century. Indeed, it was this assumption which informed Walter Bagehot's argument, in the fifties, that a reform of Parliament was desirable. If the number of entries on the register for a given constituency were growing then, according to Bagehot, the constituency itself was growing in 'prosperity, and therefore . . . presumable intelligence'. For these reasons, he went on, it should be accorded greater representative weight than those other constituencies on whose registers the numbers of entries were not growing.[19] In some cases, the dynamic to which he referred was perhaps the appropriate one. Usually, however, it probably was not. Indeed, in this instance as in various others Bagehot's formulation would appear to be more important for what it reveals of the logic of mid-century discourse than for what it reveals of mid-century realities.[20] In some boroughs the relationships between the numbers of entries on the registers and the numbers of qualified men were, perhaps, constant. But they were not constant in all. As the secretary of the City of London Liberal Registration Association observed, in 1860, the 'expansive and contractive nature of the franchise' was largely the consequence of changes in the levels of exertion of local registration societies.[21] Where such levels were constant, and constantly high, the great majority of qualified men may have been registered at any given time. But in many cases in the counties, where registration was often handled in highly informal fashion, the relationships between the numbers of entries and the numbers of qualified men were obviously not constant.[22] Whatever the merits of Bagehot's overall argument about changing the relative parliamentary weights of the different varieties of constituency, he vitiated the logic of his case by failing to allow for the obvious effects of high levels of political activity in the places where the relationships between the numbers of registered electors and the numbers of qualified men were such as to suggest that the one was a function of the other.

In very few county constituencies did the numbers of entries on the registers show those patterns of growth which might be expected if population, 'prosperity, and . . . presumable intelligence' were the principal dynamics of growth. Indeed, in sixteen county constituencies, in some of which significant increments of population occurred, there were fewer entries on the electoral registers in the mid-sixties –

suggesting fewer electors: than there had been in the mid-thirties (see table 19).[23] In thirty-three the numbers of such entries increased but did so by less than twenty per cent during this period. In nineteen the numbers of such entries increased by more than twenty per cent. Nor were the increases always constant where they did occur. Indeed, in a number of county constituencies in which the numbers of entries increased significantly between the years 1836 and 1864 there were fewer entries on the registers in 1857 than there had been in 1836. Such was the case in North Hampshire, South Shropshire, North Leicestershire, West Worcestershire and North Devonshire. In these constituencies the overall increments between 1836 and 1864 reflect reversals of earlier declines.

The correlations and lack of correlations between the changes in the numbers of entries on the registers for these constituencies and the changes in their populations are extremely revealing. As a rule, where correlations did obtain they did so somewhat more closely between the numbers of entries and the populations *exclusive* of the borough populations than they did between the numbers of entries and the populations *inclusive* of the borough populations. This suggests the essentially rural nature of the men who generally concerned themselves with county politics. But in most cases there was no correlation at all. In most county constituencies the proportional increases in population and entries between the thirties and sixties were quite unequal whether the borough populations be included or not.

The explanation is obvious: since registration was not automatic there was no way in which the numbers of qualified men, or changes in the numbers of qualified men, might have been directly reflected on the registers. This alone can be said: within the limits which population and prosperity helped to define the numbers of entries on each register were principally measures of the intensity of local political life.

By and large, the intensity of local political life was in turn a function of the degree to which different varieties of community or group were jumbled together in the same constituency. Presumably, in part at least, this is the significance of the fact that contested elections occurred somewhat more frequently in the more urbanized than in the less urbanized counties. Presumably this also helps to explain why the rates of population growth and the rates of growth of entries on the electoral registers tended to be somewhat closer where larger numbers of contests occurred.

The fact that some men exerted themselves to register their own supporters or prospective supporters – and that others did not – bears upon the argument that might be made, that the different categories of registered electors could be used to test the effects of the Act. In many of the returns of registered electors in the counties the different

Table 19

Numbers of entries on the electoral registers of the English county constituencies, 1832–68, together with their populations, inclusive and exclusive of boroughs, and the numbers of contested elections in each

constituency	entries on the registers				% change		population (000)						numbers of contests Dec. 1832–Oct. 1868
	1832	1836	1857	1864	'36–'57	'36–'64	inclusive of boro's 1831	1861	% change	exclusive of boro's 1831	1861	% change	
Constituencies in which the number of entries was smaller in 1864 than in 1836													
W. Sussex	2,365	3,122	2,914	2,607	−6	−20	100	109	+9	55	53	−4	1
N. Essex	5,163	5,833	5,553	4,904	+8	−16	167	191	+14	147	162	+10	5
W. Suffolk	3,326	4,952	4,084	4,269	−17	−14	137	147	+7	119	127	+7	4
Berkshire	5,582	5,843	4,884	5,066	−16	−13	147	176	+20	112	129	+15	5
S. Devonshire	7,453	10,946	9,625	9,592	−12	−12	323	412	+28	193	220	+14	3
S. Warwicks.	2,550	3,997	3,522	3,517	−12	−12	81	102	+25	72	91	+26	3
E. Riding, Yorks.	5,559	7,965	7,382	7,400	−7	−7	164	235	+43	107	127	+19	1
N. Derbys.	4,370	5,410	5,336	5,055	−1	−7	102	159	+56	102	159	+56	3
W. Norfolk	4,396	6,980	7,179	6,534	+3	−6	165	181	+10	148	161	+9	5
Cambs.	6,435	7,391	6,298	7,063	−15	−4	144	176	+22	123	150	+22	3
W. Somerset	7,884	8,854	7,323	8,632	−17	−3	165	186	+12	146	160	+11	4
E. Norfolk	7,041	8,098	7,755	7,939	−4	−2	229	258	+11	144	149	+3	6
Dorset	5,632	6,320	5,621	6,203	−11	−2	160	190	+19	115	136	+18	1
E. Gloucs.	6,437	7,584	7,891	7,515	+4	−1	175	208	+19	88	104	+18	3
S. Cheshire	5,130	6,852	7,068	6,826	+3	0	145	243	+68	119	160	+35	3
S. Notts.	3,170	3,432	3,654	3,427	+6	0	109	157	+44	59	71	+20	2
												average	3.2

Constituencies in which the number of entries was larger in 1864 than in 1836 by less than 20%.

Herefords.	5,013	7,175	7,330	7,179	+2	0	110	123	+12	94	102	+9	3
N. Wilts.	3,614	5,059	4,400	5,146	−13	+2	134	147	+10	80	80	0	3
Westmoreland	4,392	4,846	4,168	4,937	−14	+2	55	61	+11	43	49	+14	1
N. Cheshire	5,105	5,900	6,693	6,026	+13	+2	193	273	+41	124	182	+47	3
N. Warwicks.	3,730	6,505	6,832	6,710	+5	+3	252	455	+81	81	117	+44	6
S. Hampshire	3,143	5,475	5,525	5,677	+1	+4	163	269	+65	82	113	+38	3
W. Cumberland	3,848	4,406	4,389	4,602	0	+4	78	100	+28	56	74	+32	4
N. Shropshire	4,682	5,016	4,227	5,315	−16	+6	120	136	+13	98	114	+16	1
S. Northumber.	5,192	5,121	5,608	5,511	+10	+8	157	250	+59	80	107	+34	2
Bucks.	5,306	5,689	5,353	6,126	−6	+8	147	168	+14	104	119	+14	8
Hunts.	2,647	2,744	2,918	2,999	+6	+9	53	64	+21	48	58	+21	3
S. Wilts.	2,540	3,059	3,239	3,343	+6	+9	101	101	0	74	74	0	3
E. Suffolk	4,265	6,147	5,907	6,769	−4	+10	155	185	+19	135	147	+9	6
N. Staffs.	8,756	9,611	9,536	10,703	−1	+10	187	290	+55	120	163	+36	5
N. Northants.	3,363	3,627	3,800	4,016	+5	+10	81	103	+27	74	91	+23	6
N. Devons.	5,368	7,889	7,264	8,746	−8	+11	171	171	0	152	150	−1	2
W. Surrey	2,912	3,681	3,920	4,081	+7	+11	87	118	+36	81	110	+36	6
S. Lincs.	7,956	8,215	8,287	9,260	+1	+13	145	184	+27	118	147	+23	2
Monmouths.	3,738	4,360	5,099	4,909	+17	+13	98	175	+79	85	144	+69	1
W. Worcs.	3,122	4,615	4,015	5,221	−13	+13	107	121	+13	57	67	+18	2
E. Kent	7,026	7,228	8,000	8,250	+11	+14	183	247	+35	130	165	+27	8

Table continued on next page

Table 19 (continued)

constituency	entries on the registers				% change		population (000)						numbers of contests	
	1832	1836	1857	1864	'36–'57	'36–'64	inclusive of boro's		% change	exclusive of boro's		% change	Dec. 18	Oct. 18
							1831	1861		1831	1861			
N. Leicesters.	3,658	4,144	3,899	4,767	–6	+15	84	92	+10	84	92	+10	4	
N. Northumber.	2,322	2,703	3,296	3,109	+22	+15	80	93	+16	60	66	+10	3	
Oxfordshire	4,721	5,055	5,119	5,798	+1	+14	153	171	+12	119	125	+5	3	
N. Durham	4,267	5,208	5,847	6,042	+12	+16	153	388	+154	78	170	+118	3	
Beds.	3,966	4,152	4,231	4,845	+2	+17	96	135	+41	89	122	+37	4	
S. Shrops.	2,791	3,566	3,183	4,170	–11	+17	94	104	+11	64	69	+8	2	
E. Worcs.	5,161	5,867	6,065	6,875	+3	+17	116	186	+40	83	130	+57	5	
E. Cumberland	4,035	4,623	5,693	5,455	+23	+18	92	105	+14	73	76	+4	3	
W. Kent	6,678	8,322	8,949	9,811	+8	+18	297	492	+66	187	277	+48	9	
S. Northants.	4,425	4,478	4,675	5,253	+4	+18	97	123	+27	82	90	+10	6	
North Hants.	2,424	3,508	3,149	4,185	–10	+19	114	157	+38	96	132	+38	4	
Middlesex	6,939	12,431	14,977	14,847	+20	+19	1,359	2,206	+62	193	368	+91	7	

average 4.0

Constituencies in which the number of entries was larger in 1864* than in 1836 by more than 20%.

S. Derbys.	5,541	6,630	7,102	7,976	+7	+20	135	180	+33	111	137	+23	6
N. Notts.	2,889	3,379	4,028	4,065	+19	+20	105	136	+30	65	89	+37	3
S. Lancs.	10,039	17,800	20,460	21,555	+15	+21	986	1,771	+80	363	628	+42	7
N. Lincs.	9,134	10,165	12,435	12,372	+22	+22	173	230	+33	155	194	+25	4
Herts.	4,245	5,098	6,011	6,228	+19	+22	144	174	+21	137	167	+21	6
Rutland	1,296	1,391	1,822	1,774	+31	+28	19	22	+16	19	22	+16	1
E. Cornwall	4,462	4,446	6,261	5,781	+41	+30	130	155	+19	155	137	+19	3
N. Lancs.	6,593	9,943	12,352	13,006	+24	+31	344	547	+59	259	374	+44	0
N. Riding, Yorks	9,539	11,768	12,238	15,438	+4	+31	229	300	+31	161	201	+25	4
W. Cornwall	3,353	3,504	4,542	4,615	+30	+32	171	214	+25	137	170	+24	0
W. Gloucs.	6,521	6,859	9,250	9,368	+35	+37	224	297	+33	120	143	+19	4
S. Leicesters.	4,125	4,590	5,205	6,283	+13	+37	113	145	+28	72	77	+7	2
W. Riding, Yorks.	18,056	29,456	37,513	40,695	+27	+38	975	1,498	+54	639	881	+38	6
E. Sussex	3,437	4,824	6,114	6,670	+27	+38	172	254	+48	104	126	+21	7
S. Essex	4,488	5,286	6,169	7,338	+17	+39	150	213	+42	145	207	+43	10
E. Somerset	8,996	8,504	10,592	11,867	+25	+39	227	240	+6	161	173	+7	2
S. Staffs.	3,107	7,534	11,202	10,841	+49	+41	224	461	+106	129	260	+102	3
S. Durham	4,336	4,864	5,565	7,263	+14	+49	79	170	+115	79	170	+115	4
E. Surrey	3,150	5,308	7,197	9,913	+35	+86	398	707	+78	106	209	+97	7

average 4.1

categories of prospective voter were separately tabulated. In the English counties as a whole in the latter thirties approximately 66 per cent of the entries were for men registered as freeholders, approximately 22 per cent for men registered as occupiers, roughly 5 per cent each for men registered as copyholders and leaseholders, and somewhat less than 2 per cent for men registered as trustees, mortgagees, etc. ... [24] These total proportions notwithstanding, however, it might be grossly inaccurate to say that the total English county electorate was half as large again after the Bill was passed. Apart from the problems raised by duplicate entries and those raised by the fact that the proportions of freeholders in 1837 ranged from a low of 37 per cent in West Cornwall to a high of 82 per cent in East Kent, there are those others raised by the provision of the Act which removed the requirement that a freeholder of unredeemed land be assessed to the land tax. In consequence of this provision the freeholder category undoubtedly included some men who were enfranchised by the Act. But even if the figures were corrected in the several ways these problems might require, the assertion that the Act itself was responsible for the increase in the electorate thus revealed would reflect a distortion of the essential nature of the mid-century political system. It would fail to reflect the degree to which the post-reform electorates were created by the men who used them to support their own political ambitions. In many parts of the kingdom the freehold franchise was primarily in urban or quasi-urban franchise. [25] In effect, in many county constituencies the proportion of freeholders on the register was in part a measure of the continuing interest – or, later in the century, a measure of the *renewed* interest – of urban politicians in county politics.

III

There is no simple answer to the question why, once the Bill was passed by which many boroughs were constituted and others reconstituted, many urban leaders withdrew from the county arena, leaders whose exploitation of certain radical nexus in the counties had done so much to affect the outcome of the immediate pre-reform county elections. Nor is there any simple answer to the question why, in the years immediately *before* the second Reform Bill was passed, many urban leaders returned to the county arena. But whatever the reasons – or whatever the *principal* reasons – for the behaviour of these men it provides a crucial key to the nature of the mid-century political system, to the ways in which and the reasons why changes occurred within this system and, in certain respects, to the relationship between changes within this system and legislation.

Undoubtedly, the shifts in the balance of electoral weight among the different varieties of community which occurred in most counties at the time of the first Reform Act were factors in the tendency of urban leaders to retire from county politics.[26] These shifts obviously weakened, in some cases they may have destroyed, the rationale for their earlier activities in the counties. But to recognize these shifts and the role they played is to ask why they occurred.

In part, of course, these shifts were the consequence of certain provisions of the Act, those by which new boroughs were created, by which the boundaries of various old boroughs were enlarged, by which certain categories of copyholder, leaseholder and occupier were enfranchised in the counties, and by which many borough freeholders were disfranchised in the counties. But to some extent these shifts were also the consequence of the tendencies of urban leaders to concentrate their electoral energies upon the boroughs once the boroughs had been so constituted, or reconstituted, as to make them appropriate foci for their energies.

By the same token, the powers which urban leaders enjoyed once they returned to the county arena were undoubtedly enhanced by the continuing penetration of essentially urban populations beyond the limits which the redistribution and boundary provisions of the Act of 1832 had recognized. Undoubtedly, these powers were enhanced by the results of various of the decisions of the Court of Common Pleas once the Court was given appellate jurisdiction on points of law in registration cases. But their tendencies to return obviously reflect some other dynamic.

The crucial point is that when the members of the Grey Ministry amended the initial borough freeholder clause they provided the leaders in many boroughs with the means of perpetuating their powers in the counties. As a rule, however, the urban leaders did not avail themselves of these means until many years had passed. In consequence, in the mid-century, many men were not registered who were perfectly well qualified to be registered, and who, if they had been registered and brought to the polls, would have made significant differences to the local balances of power, thus, in the aggregate, significant differences to the balance of power in Parliament. One example, which does not however have to do with the withdrawal of urban leaders from the county arena, helps to illustrate the reasons why their tendency to withdraw was so important: In the Northleach polling district in East Gloucestershire, in 1863, there were at least 102 men who were not registered although they were perfectly well qualified. The Conservative registration agent who reported their existence had not submitted registrations claims on their behalf. Indeed, he lived in some trepidation that his Liberal opponents might one day do so. As he put it, the existence of these men showed 'what havoc

might be made if the other side knew the sources of their strength'. [27]
Had these men been registered the potential electorate in the district
would have been 15 or 20 per cent larger. Had they voted as he
assumed they would vote the Conservative majority in the district
might have been seriously jeopardized. Indeed, if comparable situations
existed in other polling districts in the constituency a more active
Liberal registration effort might well have destroyed the Conservative
hegemony in the constituency as a whole.

Possibly, the Conservative agent was right – that the Liberals in East
Gloucestershire did not know 'the sources of their strength'. But to
argue from analogy it seems more likely they were simply not
concerned to exploit these resources. Certainly, it was not from any
want of knowledge of the sources of their strength that the Liberals in
North Warwickshire had to wait until 1866 before they could boast
that they had a majority of 59 on the county register. Nor did those
Liberals in South Leicestershire lack the requisite knowledge of the
sources of their strength: after the first Reform Bill was passed, and
after the Members they returned in 1831 had both retired, they had to
wait until 1867 before being able to return another Liberal candidate. [28]
In some cases – in Cambridgeshire, perhaps – any radical urban leaders
who continued to devote a considerable effort to the county might
have been wasting their time. But in other cases – in South
Leicestershire and North Warwickshire, perhaps – the power of these
men would seem to have languished because it was simply not
exercised, or effectively exercised. This is suggested by the apparent
ease with which the urban leaders in Leicester and, presumably,
Birmingham, were able to restore their power in their respective
county divisions in the years immediately *before* the second Reform Bill
was passed. And the fact that their power was effectively – if only
temporarily – destroyed by the second Reform Act is further
illustration of that occasional ambiguity in the relationship between
change and certain pieces of nineteenth century legislation.

IV

Before 1832, various anti-Tory leaders in the borough of Leicester had
turned to the surrounding county much as the anti-Tory leaders in the
borough of Cambridge had turned to Cambridgeshire. For both
groups of men electoral action in their respective boroughs was
effectively precluded by the nature of the existing borough electorates.
In 1830, in Leicestershire, these urban anti-Tories nominated one of
themselves as candidate for the county – Thomas Paget, the head of a
local nonconformist banking family. He was beaten in 1830. But the
following year the two Tory Members retired. Paget and a Whig
square, Mark Phillips, were returned without a contest.

By the terms of the Act Leicestershire was divided into two constituencies. North Leicestershire was almost totally rural. But South Leicestershire contained various towns, among them the borough of Leicester. In the northern division there were few urban leaders to withdraw from the county area. But in the southern division there were many more. Once the Bill was passed they did withdraw. Paget retired as Member for the county in 1832. Thereafter, he devoted his political energies to borough affairs.[29] Although Phillips was nominated for the southern division in 1832 and returned without a contest he retired in 1835 when two Tories were nominated. Thereafter, until 1867, the southern division had none but Tory or Conservative Members. Nor, until then, were any serious efforts made to return a Whig or Liberal candidate. True, there were two contests in South Leicestershire between the first and second Reform Acts, the first in 1841, the second in 1867. But the contest of 1841 was scarcely a serious contest. It was principally undertaken as a means of punishing the Tories for their refusal to acknowledge their obvious minority status in the borough. As such – and together with the Tories' refusal to acknowledge this status – it represented a clear violation of certain generally recognized norms of political action.

According to these norms a contest should not take place unless those who challenged the existing representative arrangements were confident of victory. As a radical journalist noted, however, in 1839, the Tories had been the first to violate these norms when they precipitated a contest at a by-election in the borough not two years after their defeat at the general election of 1837. And, as he also noted – clearly in further extenuation – South Leicestershire not only contained significant urban areas; the balance of power in the division had never been tested. As he put it,

> We have ever thought that the supineness of the Liberal party in regard to the representation of the Southern Division of this County was inexcusable – comprising, as it does, within its limits, the Market-towns of Leicester, Harborough, Lutterworth, and Hinckley (all polling places), and the great manufacturing villages in the immediate vicinity of these polling places – we have thought (considering the comparatively small expense at which the Liberal constituency could be polled) that our leaders were criminally negligent in not contesting the representation ... We fear that a conventional feeling has mastered and overruled a public duty. However we may value that gentlemanly feeling which would not countenance a contest when the changes are balanced or unfavourable, we think, at any rate, our leaders need fear no hesitation now; even if the prospect was less cheerful than it is, they would be fully justified. The Tories have thrown down the gauntlet

– they have forced a contest upon the town in spite of a majority of 362 at the last election; they have forced a contest upon us without a chance or hope of success – that they never anticipated: and what do they tell us now? – *That, let the chances be what they may, they will force a contest upon us on every occasion.* Be it so, we are content; but if this is to be their system – if these are to be their tactics – we call upon our friends to change their course, to meet them on the same grounds. The election for the county is a week later than the election for the borough. We know too well the spirit, the activity, the untiring zeal of the Liberal canvassers in this town, to doubt for a moment their bringing their whole power to bear upon the Southern Division . . . The expense to us will be trifling – the result, who can divine? . . . The present members sit by sufferance; neither of them have taken the opinion of the electors. With an informidable minority twice ascertained, the Tories still agitate the Borough, and they tell us they will always do so, even if their minority is still weaker. Again we repeat our friends are unpardonable – absolutely inexcusable – if, with a small *supposed* minority *not* ascertained, they do not on the next occasion take the opinion of the electoral body of the Southern Division.

On the eve of the elections of 1841, John Biggs, chairman of the Liberal Registration Association for the southern division – and himself a townsman – noted the grounds on which *his* hopes of a Liberal victory were based: the urban elements in the constituency would overwhelm the rural. Pointing out that most of the men who had voted for Paget in 1830 resided in the southern division he went on to argue that the Tories were seriously disadvantaged by their essentially rural nature. As he put it, 'The greater part of the Electors, who espouse old Tory principles, are furthest from the Polling Places . . . [while] one-fourth of our number [reside] in the town of Leicester alone – within ten minutes walk of the Polling booth.'[31] And, he added, not only was there the borough of Leicester. There were also the towns of Hinckley, Lutterworth, Harborough and Market Bosworth. Since these were all polling places they increased the ease with which an essentially urban electorate could get to the polls. Nor would the Liberals have to poll as many voters as might at first sight be assumed. As he noted, many of the 4,903 entries on the register were multiple entries. And most of the men who were listed more than once were Tories.

Biggs' emphasis upon what might be called the natural or built-in advantages which the Liberals enjoyed suggests that in 1841 the Liberals did little or nothing to develop these advantages. And this was evidently the case. A Reform Society in the borough had devoted some attention to the register for the southern division of the county immediately *after* the election of 1835, when two Tories were returned without a contest. In particular, they objected to the continued registration of some four or five hundred Tories, most of whom resided at some distance from the county. Since it was far easier to sustain an objection against an absentee than it was against a man who was present at the registration court, the members of the Reform Society obviously hoped to improve their own political position in the county be creating insoluble problems of communication and transportation for their opponents. However, the Tories apparently did manage to assemble the necessary men at the registration courts or at least to obtain the information necessary to defend their qualifications. Ostensibly, the Reform Society's efforts had no impact upon the political complexion of the register.[32] Nor, apparently, was anything more effective done before the contest in 1841. The Liberals simply failed to take those steps to prepare their way without which any contest was – at least for the purpose of electing a candidate – a simple exercise in futility.

The poll book confirms the arguments of the radical journalist and of Biggs about the locus of Liberal strength in the division: most of this strength was concentrated in the borough of Leicester. But the question raised, but not answered, by the available evidence remains: would this strength not have been vastly greater had the Liberals really tried to win rather than simply punish the Tories for their own forays into the borough. Even in the borough, where the two Liberal candidates were returned without a contest – clearly the lessons of 1837 and 1839 had been learned – majorities of the county voters polled for the Tories. Outside the borough almost three-quarters of the votes polled for the Tories. Distinguishing the votes cast at the polling booths in the borough – each booth served those voters whose qualifications were located in the parish or cluster of parishes in which the booth was located – from the votes cast at the other polling booths in the division the totals were as indicated in table 20.[33]

Nor did the appearance of the Anti-Corn Law League on the scene mark a significant change of strategy. In 1845 the League paid the expenses of the same man whose earlier expenses had been paid by the Reform Society. In 1845 he brought objections to the continued registration of 1,370 Conservatives. Had these objections been successful the balance of power in the constituency would have been sharply affected – at least temporarily. Ostensibly, these 1,370 men represented more than half of the Tory or Conservative strength. But when the revising barrister held his first court in the division, and when he allowed some of the men to recover costs whose rights to vote had been challenged and who had come some distance to defend their rights, the great majority of the remaining objections were withdrawn.

Table 20

Sources of support for the Conservative and Liberal candidates at the South Leicestershire contest of 1841

Voters who polled at polling booths in:	Numbers of voters	Votes for: Halford (Cons)	Packe (Cons)	% for Halford	Votes for: Gisborne (Lib)	Cheney (Lib)	% for Gisborne
Leicester	1,638	999	992	61.0	639	630	39.0
the 'county'	2,214	1,639	1,630	74.0	574	566	25.9
Totals	3,852	2,638	2,622	68.5	1,213	1,196	31.5

Of the 1,370 objections only some thirty were sustained.[34] Like the contest of 1841 these objections were, for all practical purposes, an exercise in futility. They might vex the Tories. But they could only weaken the Tories if the Tories failed to respond. As such, they are clearly distinguishable from those other efforts to which the editor of the Leicestershire poll book of 1867 referred while recounting the events which had led up to that contest. Some years earlier, he explained, 'A portion of the [Liberal] party [in the constituency], constituting a South Leicestershire Liberal Registration Society ... [had] by its agents paid attention to the Registration, and counteracted the effects of some years of neglect and supineness.'[35] Unfortunately, he did not indicate exactly when this had occurred. But in the autumn of 1858, the two principal Liberal or Radical newspapers in Leicester not only carried their usual reports of the progress of electoral revision in the *borough*. They also carried reports, apparently their first reports, of electoral revision in the *county*. Indeed, one of them even devoted a leading article to the subject, observing that 'A very large addition has been made, by dilligent effort, to the ranks of the Liberals in South Leicestershire, and it is to be hoped that this will not be without fruit in due season.'[36] Their additional comments concerning the registration of nonconformist ministers as 'freeholders' of houses and gardens which they held in respect of their offices suggest a possible dynamic – perhaps the principal dynamic – of the new strategy. Significantly, however, the guiding case concerning the rights of such nonconformist ministers to be registered had been determined several years earlier, by the Court of Common Pleas.[37]

Presumably, the 'dilligent effort ... of the Liberals' accounts for that crucial change in the balance of electoral power in the division which can be seen when the poll book of 1867 is compared with that of 1841.

In 1867 over 40 per cent more voters polled at the polling booths in the borough of Leicester than polled at these booths in 1841. At the other polling booths in the division the increase in the effective electorate was less than 2 per cent. In all probability, had not the radical urban leaders devoted themselves to the registration of their supporters no contest would have occurred in 1867. Indeed, the contest of 1867 would appear to have been the culmination of their efforts. But this much is certain: had those relative increments which were the obvious consequence of their efforts not occurred, the urban candidate would not have won. The 'county' voters preferred Albert Pell, the Conservative, almost exactly as much as the 'borough' voters preferred Thomas Tertius Paget, the son of the former member. But since 1841 the number of 'borough' voters had been so increased that by 1867 they represented more than half of the effective electorate in the division. As table 21 reveals, the increase in the number of 'borough' voters and their increased cohesion were the principal reasons why Paget won.[38]

Table 21

Sources of support for the Conservative and Liberal candidates at the South Leicestershire contest of 1867

Voters who polled at polling booths in:	Numbers of voters		% change	Pell		Paget	
	1841	1867		Votes	%	Votes	%
Leicester	1,638	2,314	+41.2	886	38.8	1,428	61.2
the 'county'	2,214	2,251	+1.2	1,377	60.7	874	39.3
Totals	3,852	4,565	+18.5	2,263	49.6	2,302	50.4

Perhaps more 'borough' voters polled in 1867 than had polled in 1841 because more 'borough' men were qualified. But to explain the full increase in the numbers of 'borough' voters solely in terms of the possible increase in the numbers of qualified men would be to ignore the evidence that from the latter fifties onwards the radical leaders in Leicester were paying more attention to the county register than they had paid before. Furthermore, it would be to ignore the obvious relationship between their increasing attention to the county register and the increasing proportion of the men who were registered to vote in the county in respect of property located in the borough. In 1852 there were 5,118 entries on the electoral register for the division, only slightly more than the 4,903 to which Biggs referred in 1841. In 1857 there were only 5,205 entries. By 1864, the number had grown to 6,238. But the crucial point lies in the fact that most of this increase was among the men who qualified to vote in the county in respect of property located in the borough.

1852 was the first year in which figures were published for the numbers of men registered to vote in county elections in respect of property located in boroughs. Thus, presumably, it was only roughly then that the 'problem' which these men represented began to reappear. Obviously, in many counties or county divisions the 'problem' either did not exist or was effectively controlled. In the kingdom as a whole between 1852 and 1866 the total numbers of entries on the electoral registers for the counties increased by 25.8 per cent, from 396,967 to 499,617. The numbers of entries for men who qualified in respect of property in boroughs increased by 25.1 per cent, from 76,827 to 96,073. But in South Leicestershire the numbers of such entries increased by 75.7 per cent while the total numbers of entries only increased by 21.8 per cent. In 1852 there were 1,318 entries for men who qualified to vote in the county in respect of property in the borough; in 1857 there were 1,580; in 1866 there were 2,316. In South Leicestershire the changes in the numbers of such entries were important not only because they were large but also because, obviously, the registration of such men was one of the principal means by which the local radical leaders tried to rebuild their strength in the county. Meanwhile, since the latter thirties the numbers of tenants-at-will on the register had only increased from 971 to 1,092.[39]

The circumstances surrounding Paget's return raise two important questions: first, why had not he, or someone else representing the same interests, been returned many years earlier and, second, why did his opponents allow him to be returned in 1867? Presumably, the answer to the first lies in the general willingness of the urban leaders to restrict their electoral activities to 'their own' constituency from the time the Bill of 1832 was passed until the latter fifties – a willingness revealed in the premises which the radical journalist articulated in 1839, in the strategy of vexatious objections, and in the general failure to mount contests in the county. Unfortunately, the second cannot be answered without more evidence than is presently available. Possibly, however, the Conservatives had scraped the bottom of their barrel. Possibly, that segment of the population defined by the county franchise provisions of the Act of 1832 as modified by various decisions of the Court of Common Pleas contained few additional men whom they could have registered as a means of retaining their hegemony. If this be so then certain provisions of the second Reform Act, which historians have generally ignored, would have to be recognized as important. Then, too, a dynamics of reform in the sixties which historians have also generally ignored would have to be noted. The growth of urban power in South Leicestershire in the immediate *pre*-reform period was scarcely unique. Nor was the destruction of that power after the passing of the Derby-Disraeli Reform Bill unique.

Of course, on the morrow of their defeat various Conservatives used the opportunity to argue the need for more effective 'organization.' An essential function of local political organization in the mid century is reflected in their claim that there were 'several hundreds of Conservatives entitled to be placed upon the register, and it was by reason of the long apathy of the party that their votes were lost.' Another function of local political organization – and, as time went on an increasingly important function – is reflected in their claim that there were many men in the borough who were already registered 'who would have given their support to Mr. Pell had an organization been in existence . . . to bring them together and cause them to work in earnest unison . . . ,'[40] Whatever the validity of their contention that numerous qualified Conservatives were just waiting to be registered – and their contention is rather at odds with the generally close relationship between registration and political recruitment – it is more than likely that few effective agencies of Conservative recruitment existed in the borough. Both to repair this lack and to provide a medium of joint action for Conservatives in county and borough a new Conservative organization was formed.[41]

This new organization possibly provided the stimulus necessary to beat Paget in 1868. But if this be so a clear distinction must be made between the results of the establishment of this organization and the arguments used to explain why its establishment was necessary. Whether or not the 'borough' and 'county' Conservatives were more united in 1868 than they were in 1867, Paget was beaten not in the 'borough' but in the 'county'. Furthermore, whether or not 'the long apathy of the party' had been ended, it seems probable that the votes which made the difference to the Conservatives in 1868 had simply not been available to them in 1867. In 'borough' as well as 'county' local electoral agreement was somewhat greater in 1868 than it had been in 1867. More important, however, a shift occurred in the relative electoral weights of the urban and rural areas of the county between 1867 and 1868 which more than made up for the earlier shift between 1841 and 1867. Between 1867 and 1868 the numbers of 'borough' voters declined by almost ten per cent. But the numbers of 'county' voters increased by more than seventy per cent. As Table 22 reveals, Paget's defeat both in 1868 and, again, at a by-election in 1870 were principally functions of these relative increments.[42] Thus, to explain them is, in large measure, to explain his defeat.

Of course, had the Conservatives not organized themselves to

Table 22

Sources of support for the Conservative and Liberal candidates at the South Leicestershire contests of 1868 and 1870, and the polls at the contests of 1874 and 1880

Voters who polled at polling booths in:	Numbers of voters			% Change		Poll, 1868			% For		Poll, 1870		% For	
	1867	1868	1870	1867–68	1868–70	Curzon (Cons)	Pell (Cons)	Paget (Lib)	Curzon	Paget	Heygate (Cons)	Paget (Lib)	Heygate	Paget
Leicester	2,314	2,095	2,094	−9.5	0.0	725	704	1,400	34.6	66.8	840	1,254	40.1	59.8
the 'county'	2,251	3,871	3,768	+71.8	−2.6	2,477	2,406	1,446	64.0	37.3	2,452	1,316	65.1	34.9
Totals	4,565	5,966	5,862	+30.7	−1.7	3,202	3,110	2,846	53.6	47.7	3,292	2,570	56.2	43.8

Poll, 1874

Pell (Cons) 3,583
Heygate (Cons) 3,269
Paget (Lib) 2,883

Poll, 1880

Paget (Lib) 3,685
Pell (Cons) 3,453
Heygate (Cons) 3,174

register their own supporters Paget would scarcely have been beaten. But the reports from the revising barrister's courts suggest that the men they principally registered belonged to the various categories of copyholder, leaseholder and occupier who had been enfranchised by the second Reform Act.[43] The relevant provisions of the Act have often been noted. Indeed, the Act has usually been described as if it contained no other important provisions besides those which transferred a few seats from decaying boroughs to growing towns and counties, and which enfranchised the householders in the boroughs and the £12-occupiers, £5-copyholders and leaseholders in the counties. But the shift in the balance of power in South Leicestershire was not only the consequence of the *growth* in the numbers of 'county' voters which the enfranchisement of £12-occupiers, £5-copyholders and leaseholders would explain. It was also the consequence of the *decline* in the numbers of 'borough' voters. The decline was smaller than the growth. Thus, in one sense, the provisions to which the decline should be attributed are less important. But in another sense they are equally important: they provide a further corrective to the tendency to conceive of the second Reform Act as a simple concession to radical demands. Not only did the Act disfranchise many of the smaller borough freeholders in the counties, it also disfranchised many leaseholders and copyholders in the counties whose properties were located in boroughs but who had managed to qualify as county voters by exploiting a technicality in the wording of the first Reform Act, a technicality which the Court of Common Pleas had legalized in 1843.[44]

By and large, the new voters who polled in South Leicestershire in 1868 simply increased the size of the various local electoral blocs. Nor were contemporaries surprised by this. Indeed, while Paget claimed he was the victim of the coercion and intimidation of the new rural voters – and to protect the 'independence' of these men he demanded the secret ballot – his hopes of future victory were entirely based upon the prospect of registering additional numbers of 40s-freeholders in the 'borough'.[45] Unfortunately, the adoption of the secret ballot obscures the answer to the question whether, in fact, it was these men who returned him when he was again returned in 1880. Because the Ballot Act required that the votes cast in a given constituency be counted together it obscured the possible differences of orientation of the men who polled at the different polling booths. Thus, it made it impossible to determine whether a new shift had occurred in the balance of power between 1874 and 1880. But be this as it may, the vice-president of the new Ibstock and Hugglescote Polling District Liberal Association had a ready answer to the question why Paget was returned in 1880: it was the consequence of organization and of the principal activity in which organizations were engaged. Many Liberals, he explained, had been registered in respect of their purchases of land within the county.[46]

Like others of the local political organizations which proliferated in the period after 1868 and, in particular, in the years around 1880, the Ibstock and Hugglescote Polling District Liberal Association had, as its principal objects, the identification and registration of prospective political supporters. Thus, for the vice-president of the Association to claim that Paget's victory was principally a function of the registration of known Liberals was to advertise the ostensible importance of the organization with which he was connected. Once the secret ballot had been adopted the actual importance of registration – and thus the actual importance of the mechanism of registration – cease to be measurable. But whatever the impact of the secret ballot upon the actualities of electoral behaviour the adoption of the secret ballot did not affect the assumptions which these organizations themselves reflected and which were implicit in the mid-century political system – that contests were won less by appealing to bodies of uncommitted men than by bringing to the polls sufficient numbers of men who were committed already and qualified to vote. After 1868, however – and here lies the essential reason why the second Reform Act did not restore the mid-century political system – many urban leaders did not withdraw from the county arena as they had after 1832.

The Liberal leaders in Birmingham had no success comparable with that of Paget in 1867. In modified form, however, the same patterns of behaviour are apparent, among them as among their cousins in Leicester. True, their withdrawal from the county arena was not as complete. Except at by-elections they forced a contest in North Warwickshire on almost every possible occasion. Furthermore, they took various initiatives in registration matters which attracted fairly wide attention.[47] From their standpoint however, these initiatives can scarcely have been satisfactory. In 1831 two reformers had been returned without a contest for the county as a whole. Thereafter, except on one occasion, no Whig or Liberal was ever returned for the northern division. And, according to G. F. Muntz, the Liberal candidate in 1865, the Liberals had only themselves to blame for this. According to him, the potential Liberal voters were there. But nothing had been done to transform them from potential voters into actual voters. As he was pleased to announce, however, in 1865, the Liberal leaders were finally rousing themselves. They were taking active steps to register their own supporters in the county.[48] Where these supporters were – and thus, to some extent, who they were – was clearly indicated in the comments of the Liberal journalist the following autumn at the time of the annual revision of the electoral register: 'If one-half of the persons duly qualified in the parish of Aston alone were to make out claims . . . the county would be secured for ever to two Liberal representatives.' [49] Lying just beyond the parliamentary boundaries of Birmingham, Aston contained, as the boundary commissioners reported, in 1868, 'an urban population in every respect identical in pursuits and interests with that of the Parlimentary Borough.' [50] Clearly, suburban migration had produced a potential political power in the county which had simply not been exploited. Presumably, the attentions of those who might have exploited this power were so firmly fixed upon the town that they failed to see how, because they or others had moved outside the borough boundaries, the opportunity to achieve the political goals which were often associated with the town had been created. Presumably, too, it was only after 1865 that that new political strategy was adopted which was premised upon the recognition of the opportunity. The change is symbolized by the organization of the North Warwickshire Liberal Registration Association. It can be seen both in the sharp increase in the number of claims for registration which were filed on behalf of Liberals, and in the places where the men resided on whose behalf these claims were filed.

In 1863 the Liberal registration agents in the northern division filed 468 claims; in 1864, 411; in 1865, 662; and in 1866, 1,444. Of course, not all of these claims were successful. Furthermore, the Conservative registration agents filed claims of their own which slightly limited the relative gains which otherwise the Liberals would have enjoyed. However, while the numbers of Conservative *objections* increased more or less as the numbers of Liberal claims increased, there was no comparable increase in the number of Conservative *claims*. Indeed, in 1863 the Conservatives filed 333 claims; in 1864, 305; in 1865, 454; but in 1866 only 244. Whether the Conservatives were running out of potential claimants within the population group defined by the franchise provisions of 1832 as modified – and there is no way to answer this question – the major population centres of the county did not have the same importance for them as they had for their opponents. In 1864 the Liberal registration agents presented 234 new claims on behalf of men from the Birmingham, Aston and Edgbaston area; in 1865, 311; and in 1866, 1,263. The respective figures for the Conservatives were .56, 76, and 37. [51] The sharp increase in the number of Liberal claims in 1866 confirms the general tenor of the Liberal journalist's argument the previous year. As such, it prompts the question why this sharp increase had not occurred earlier. But once the urban leaders had adopted this new strategy it seems clear that their rural opponents were in serious trouble.

After the various claims and objections had been heard in 1866, and after the revising barrister had approved the register for the coming year, the North Warwickshire Liberals were jubilant. As a Liberal journalist explained, at the general election in July, 1865, Muntz had been beaten by 466 votes. But since then, and primarily because of the new registrees in the suburb of Aston, the balance of power had been shifted. 'The Liberals', he declared, 'are now a majority of 59!' [52] The victory he anticipated at the next election would have been the consequence of the urban leaders' new effort to exploit their powers beyond the boundaries of 'their own' constituency. Or – to put it differently – it would have been the consequence of their rejection of the sociological premises on which the first Reform Act was based.

For the purposes of the argument it is unfortunate that no vacancy occurred in North Warwickshire when the Liberal leaders might have demonstrated the validity of their claim to a majority of fifty-nine. Unfortunately, no poll books are available for those North Warwickshire contests which did occur. Assuming, however, that the Liberals *did* have a majority of fifty-nine on the register which came into effect in January 1867, then the defeat of the two candidates they nominated in 1868 should be attributed to those provisions of the second Reform Act which were designed to shift the balance of electoral weight in the counties back in favour of the rural areas.

V

Obviously, if the behaviour of these urban leaders may be used to measure their concerns (and how else, in this world which Freud has helped us to understand, *should* their concerns be measured?), during much of the mid-century these men were not really concerned to maximize their powers within the Kingdom as a whole. Instead, they were concerned – or *principally* concerned – to secure their status within the communities in which it was principally enjoyed. As such – because the mid-century political system was a *system,* the various parts supporting the whole – their behaviour helps to explain why, throughout the mid-century, poll books were publishable. Furthermore – because the system was a *system,* changes in one part prompting changes in another – their changes of behaviour help to explain why poll books ultimately became unpublishable.

Obviously, the publishability of poll books was a measure of the generality of the belief that the effective agencies and mechanisms of electoral recruitment were legitimate. Unfortunately, with the evidence presently available these agencies and mechanisms can only be identified in the county constituencies and, in certain cases, within the county constituencies. But clearly, these agencies and mechanisms were not unique to the countryside. In part, this is indicated by the expectation, in borough as well as county, that election managers would be able to forecast the outcome of a prospective contest in the light of their knowledge of the influence or influences which might be brought to bear upon each voter in respect of his 'employer, sect, landlord, customer or creditor'.[53] As the Liberal agent in Marylebone observed, in 1860, many contested elections might be avoided if only a way could be found of using the information which he and other agents possessed.[54] Of course, he warned of the risks any agent would run who agreed too hastily in accepting the information his rivals might offer.[55] Obviously, his warning reveals his distrust of his rivals. It also reveals presumably his understanding of the ways in which, as another Liberal agent explained, 'the normal opinion of the general community of the qualified' in any constituency might be distorted by the activities of the agents themselves.[56] Some years earlier, from the other reach of the political spectrum, similar assumptions were expressed by the witness before the Select Committee on Votes of Electors who criticised the members of the Anti-Corn Law League for trying to create votes in a county for persons who did not reside in the county. As he put it, they were trying to overturn the majority 'which I will call the legitimate majority of the county'.[57] The statements of these men illustrate the tensions between the system as an ideal and the working arrangements which the system encouraged. As such, they suggest an important reason why changes occurred within the system itself.

VI

The very existence of the phrase 'faggot voter' provides a key to the problem. The faggot voter was the man who managed to satisfy the technical qualifications for the franchise but who was not really a member of the category which these qualifications were supposed to describe. The members of the Grey Ministry had tried to describe the categories of men they wished to have vote in the different types of constituency as precisely as possible. But the very need for precision suggests an important reason for the ultimate failure of the effort. No law could be drafted to prevent from qualifying those men who might technically do so. The distinction, while real in the eyes of those who made it, was essentially metaphysical. This was the general problem. Its specific manifestations derived from the fact that the Ministers had, as a rule, used the law of real property to describe the different categories of prospective voter. Thus, as property relationships changed so did the meanings of their descriptions change. The process can be seen from certain changes in the franchise law which were made by the Court of Common Pleas once the Court was given appellate jurisdiction on points of law in registration cases. In particular, there was the problem of the borough copyholders and the borough leaseholders.

In August 1831, when Althorp introduced the amended borough freeholder clause, he also introduced an additional section of this clause dealing with borough copyholders and borough leaseholders. Subsequently, the two sections of this clause were separated into distinct clauses. The restriction against a borough freeholder voting in a county in respect of property which might 'confer on *him* the right of voting for any city or borough, whether *he* shall or shall not have actually acquired the right to vote for such city or borough in respect thereof' was put into clause 24. The restriction against a borough copyholder or leaseholder voting in a county in respect of property which might 'confer on him *or any other person* the right of voting for any city or borough, whether he *or any other person* shall or shall not have actually acquired the right to vote for such city or borough in respect thereof' was put into clause 25.[58] The apparent purpose of this separation is obvious – to emphasize the continued exclusion of borough copyholders and borough leaseholders from the county electorates which had been modified with respect to the borough freeholders. But the purpose was not fully realized. In part the reason obviously lies in the ambiguities of meaning of certain of the words which the legislative draftsman used. But even more it lies in the disappearance of the conditions in the context of which these words had the meaning which, obviously, the legislative draftsman intended.

Graham blamed the draftsman. In 1836 he contended that various men were 'defeating the intentions of the framers of the Act' because, in section 25, the word *occupied* had been used instead of the word *held.*[59] As he explained, quoting from the Act, according to section 25 no person could vote for a county 'in respect of his estate or interest as a copyholder or customary tenant or as such lessee or assignee, . . . in any house, warehouse, countinghouse, shop or other building, or in any land *occupied* together with a house, warehouse, etc. . . . being either separately or together with the land so occupied therewith of such value as would give a right of voting for the city or borough.'[60] The word *occupied,* he contended, had been used in its technical legal sense to signify the tenancy of an estate or interest. But in some places – apparently, in Birmingham in particular – the word was being read in its non-technical sense to signify simple physical possession.[61] Thus, because the word was used to describe the relationship between the individual copyholder or leaseholder of borough property and the property in respect of which *he could not qualify as a county voter* there were cases in which a long term leaseholder was registered to vote in a county in respect of borough property which he *held* but did not *occupy.* To illustrate what was involved Graham described how he might qualify to be registered in Middlesex in respect of his long lease on a house in Grosvenor Place. Attached to the house were both a coach-house and a stable. If he let the one on a long lease for £7 a year, the other for £6 a year, then, since neither rent would be large enough to convey a franchise for the borough of Westminster, and since the aggregate rental he would receive would be more than £10, the amount required for the leasehold franchise, he would be able to qualify as a county voter.[62] To put a stop to such practices he proposed an appropriate amendment to the Registration Bill which the House was then considering. But those whose practices he wished to stop had their defenders in Parliament, and these had effectively redefined 'the intentions of the framers of the Act' to accommodate the practice. Graham insisted that the members of the Grey Ministry had wanted to keep men from voting in counties in respect of copyhold and leasehold property in boroughs.[63] Russell not only confirmed his description of the Ministers' intentions, he even protested his failure to understand how any revising barrister could have allowed such 'fictitious' votes.[64] But the others protested that if Graham's amendment were adopted it would disfranchise 'a thousand good votes in and around Manchester' and a similar number in Birmingham.[65] And they had the votes not only in Manchester and Birmingham but in Parliament as well. Graham's amendment was defeated by 133 to 100.[66] Obviously, the practice reveals the continued interest of certain townsmen in county politics. But in 1836 there were only a few county divisions in which leaseholders comprised significant proportions of the registered voters. Subsequently, significant increments in the numbers of leaseholders on the register only occurred in North and South Lancashire and East Surrey.[67]

But, the problem Graham tried to solve was less the consequence of the fact that the word *occupied* was used instead of the word *held* in section 25 than of the fact that contemporary practice increasingly ruled out the construction Graham obviously wished to put on *estate* or *interest*. When Graham deplored the procedure by which he might acquire a vote for Middlesex he was, in fact, deploring the hypothetical separation of his coachhouse and stable from his house itself. But if there were men who wished to rent such premises, and others who wished to let them, there was no way he could prevent their wishes from affecting the construction. In substance, had it not been one word it would have been another because the problem did not derive from words but from relationships. This is suggested by the reasons given for the decision of the Court of Common Pleas in 1843 in the case of Webb v. the Overseers of Birmingham.

The case was one of the first to be determined by the Court after it had been given appellate jurisdiction on points of law in registration cases. Presumably, when Members of Parliament gave the Court this jurisdiction they scarcely expected the Court to use it to make basic changes in the franchise law. Presumably, when they approved the relevant clause of the Registration Bill of 1843 they merely hoped the decisions of the revising barristers would become more uniform and more in keeping with the intentions of the men who drafted the Reform Act.[68] But the results were somewhat different. If the barristers' decisions became more uniform the uniformity reflected a basic departure from the interest group orientation of the Reform Act.

The circumstances of the case were simple.[69] William Hickman had rented a number of houses in Birmingham for 99 years under a single lease. One of the houses was worth more than £10 a year, the others less. In the aggregate, however, the rents he received for the houses which, individually, were worth less than £10 a year were more than £10 a year. What was in doubt – what the Court was asked to determine – was whether Hickman should have been registered as a county voter even though one of the houses covered in the lease provided a borough vote.

The attorney for the appellant quoted Brougham in 1832, that 'the 25th clause [of the Bill] prevents . . . [a borough leaseholder] from acquiring . . . [a right to vote in a county]. He quoted Graham in 1836. He declared categorically, 'The undisputed intention of the legislature [in 1832] was to keep the county and borough voters distinct.' But the attorney for the Overseers reminded the Court that 'the intentions of the framers of the Reform Act are, to say the least, extra-judicial'. What mattered was the language of the Act even when – or, perhaps, especially when – the language was ambiguous. And what made the language ambiguous was not so much the language itself as the practices which the language served to describe. The question on which the case was determined was whether the word *term* as used in section 20 was used in its technical legal sense, to signify an *estate* or *interest*. or in its popular sense, to signify the *time* a lease had to run.[70] Blackstone was quoted, but to no avail, that 'The word *term* does not merely signify the time specified in the lease, but the estate also and interest that passes by that lease; and therefore the term may expire during the continuance of the *time*; as by surrender, forfeiture and the like.' If *term*, as used in the Act, signified *interest*, and if an *interest* was a single thing, then Hickman would not have been able to qualify for the county franchise because one of the houses included in the lease was the potential source of a borough franchise. As various of the Justices noted, however, properties might be divided. Thus, since an *interest* was a single thing, the word *term*, as used in the Act, must have been used to signify *time*. On this ground they concluded that Hickman's registration as a county voter was justified.

In 1846, in the case of Alexander v. Newman, the Court was less careful to avoid 'extra-judicial' reasoning. As Chief Justice Tindal put it, 'the increasing the numbers of persons enjoying the elective franchise . . . appears to have been the leading object of the legislature in passing the late act "for amending the representaton of the people in England and Wales".' [71] In the light of the problem which the faggot voter signifies his statement not only illustrates a dubious procedure, it also reflects a basic distortion of the Act. It was, however, an important distortion.

The case involved the rights of 35 men in the West Riding of Yorkshire who, as tenants in common, and for the express purpose of obtaining electoral qualifications in the county, had bought some cottages from a neighbouring mill owner which they then leased back to him for an aggregate annual rental of £70. Since this rental was divided equally among them it served to qualify each of them as the owner of real property in the county worth not less than two pounds a year. The revising barrister had approved their claims to be registered as 40s-freeholders. But there was an appeal against his decision on the grounds that it violated the Splitting Act, a measure designed to prevent the creation of faggot votes in the counties. According to the Splitting Act, 'no more than one single voice shall be admitted for one and the same house or tenement'. To this end the Act declared 'That all conveyances of any messuages, lands, tenements, or hereditaments, in any county, city, borough, town corporate, port, or place, in order to multiply voices, or to split and divide the interest in any houses or lands among several persons, to enable them to vote at elections, . . . be void and of none effect. . . .'[72] However, while the intent of the Act is clear, there was no possible way of enforcing it. As Tindal explained, while affirming the barrister's decision, the Splitting Act could scarcely be enforced except in the case of a fraudulent conveyance because, otherwise, it would 'fetter the full and free enjoyment of landed property, and create insecurity in titles to estates.'

The decision affected the very nature of the franchise as the reformers of 1832 had obviously conceived it. Whether or not they had the Splitting Act specifically in mind when they drafted their franchise provisions, these provisions are consistent with that implicit definition of the franchise which the Splitting Act contains: in the first place, that the franchise should be the consequence of the possession or occupation of certain property – not the other way round, the possession or occupation of the property the means of acquiring the franchise; in the second place, that the franchise should be the means by which the head of a household was empowered to vote as the spokesman of the household. As long as real property was principally conceived as family property such – more or less – were the effects of the freehold franchise. But during the course of the nineteenth century real property was effectively redefined as individual property. In effect, the land law was ceasing to re-enforce the essentially dynastic implications of the freehold franchise. Thus, while Tindal's description of the reformers' 'leading object' involved a basic distortion, the distortion may have been required by the logic of the circumstances.

The case of Astbury v. Henderson was scarcely less important.[73] Determined in 1854, it had to do with the question of how the value of a freehold should be decided. According to 8 Henry VI, c. 7, which the Reform Act confirmed, a freehold voter had to have 'free land or tenement to the value of forty shillings by the year, at the least, above all charges.' William Astbury had purchased two lots in East Surrey from a freehold land society on a 99 year building lease. Pending the negotiation of such a lease he claimed to be registered to vote in the division. But the land he had bought was not worth 40s a year except as building land. The revising barrister had noted this fact. He had also observed that he could not consider the prospective or speculative value of the land. In consequence, he had refused to allow Astbury's claim to be registered. As Chief Justice Jarvis noted, however, if the net income of an estate were used to determine whether the owner of the estate were qualified as a 40s-freeholder then a man with an estate worth £10,000 might be disfranchised if the estate were unproductive. On these grounds he determined that the claim was good. But his example served less to describe the case than to accommodate it. The question at issue was not how to appraise the value of an unproductive estate. Rather, it was how to appraise the value of land which was no longer being used for one purpose and not yet being used for another. By determining that Astbury's claim was good the Court was applying an essentially speculative criterion of value. Thereafter, little remained of the implications which the freehold franchise had possessed in 1832. While the reformers of 1832 had clearly recognized the inadequacies of the 40s-freehold franchise as a measure of a settled or permanent interest in the county in which the property was located, it was such an interest which the franchise did symbolize. But once this franchise had been defined as a simple function of investment it no longer even symbolized that interest.

VII

Undoubtedly, the Court's decisions in these and other cases enhanced the powers which the radical urban leaders were able to wield when they returned to the county arena. But in most cases several years elapsed between the relevant cases – many of them were determined in the '40s, most of them by the mid-50s – and the effective return of these men. In substance, the general lack of correspondence between the growth of population and the growth in the numbers of entries on the county registers, and the general time lag between the Court's decisions and the return of the radical urban leaders to the arena of county politics, suggest that until the 60s, or shortly before, most of these men were less concerned to elect Members to Parliament who would vote in particular ways on particular issues than they were to exercise political powers where the exercise of these powers would strengthen or reflect their local status. Of course, local status might require that lip service be paid to some ultimate purpose for which power was sought. And many men in many towns defined this as the curtailment of the powers of the rural leaders. Apparently, however, in many cases at least, all they did was proclaim the goal. The steps which should have been taken to achieve the goal were simply not taken.

Given the existing distribution of parliamentary seats among the different varieties of county and borough, and given the patterns of electoral behaviour which poll books reveal, the goal was not to be achieved unless those who proclaimed it developed bases of power in constituencies other than 'their own'. Because numerous communities of potential radical voters existed in the counties; because the 40s-freehold franchise had been retained in 1832 without any residence qualification; because the initial borough freeholder clause had been amended; and because various decisions of the Court of Common Pleas enabled a far wider spectrum of men to qualify for the county franchise than the reformers of 1832 had intended, the counties were the obvious constituencies in which such bases of power might be developed. Furthermore, because of the actual and symbolic dependence of the rural leaders upon the counties the development of such bases of power not only promised to enhance the general influence of the urban leaders within the State. It also promised to curtail the influence of the rural leaders. Apparently, however, until the latter 50s or early 60s few significant efforts were made to develop such bases of power except in such semi-urban constituencies as the West Riding of Yorkshire. By and large, until then, urban leaders in other counties either restricted their electoral attentions to 'their own' constituencies or, when they did look beyond the boundaries of these constituencies, behaved in ways which reveal their assumption that beyond these boundaries was a territory into which forays might be made but which they could scarcely hope to occupy. This assumption can be seen in the strategic emphasis which the leaders of the Anti-Corn Law League placed upon purging their opponents from the county registers.

In 1845 and 1846 agents of the Anti-Corn Law League challenged the qualifications of almost a third of the men registered in the counties. Ostensibly, they made 143,731 challenges. At the time the registers contained 445,630 entries.[74] Clearly, when they challenged the qualifications of these men they were demonstrating one of the uses to which poll books were put: while they did not object to the registration of every protectionist Tory it was only against protectionist Tories that their objections were brought. Furthermore – and it was one of the principal grounds of complaint of the men who defended the rights of those against whom these objections were brought – by and large, the men who signed the necessary objection forms were not men with any intimate local knowledge. In effect, the objections were mass produced. As such, they offended against the spirit of that political system which the reformers of 1832 had tried to create. Consistent with this spirit was the suggestion that the law be changed so that an objection might only be made by someone who lived in the same district as the man to whom he objected, and thus, had 'the means of becoming acquainted with the nature of the qualification to which he objected.'[75] However, while the indignation which these objections induced may have been prompted by their mass nature it was also their mass nature which limited their effectiveness. In the vast majority of cases objections were dropped as soon as the revising barristers began awarding costs against objections to the registration of men whose substantive qualifications were not really in doubt. In consequence, besides prompting the appointment of the Select Committee on Votes of Electors, in 1846, the indignant complaints to which the Committee listened, and, possibly, the reversal of that earlier decision of the Court of Common Pleas which provided the technical legal grounds on which most of these objections were brought, these objections would appear to have had little effect other than to encourage the protectionists in the affected counties to improve their own organizational efficiency.[76] The social composition of the county electorates was not to be changed until the radical urban leaders began the concerted registration of their own supporters – in effect, until they changed their strategy.

In certain of the semi-urban counties, of course, this strategy was already being implemented before the Select Committee of 1846 was appointed.[77] Indeed, it was because this strategy was being implemented that the members of the Committee were so deeply disturbed by the decision of the Court of Common Pleas in the case of Alexander v. Newman. Fearing that in consequence of this decision the strategy would become universal they even recommended that Parliament override the Court and reiterate the essential intent of the Splitting Act.[78] No one acted on their recommendation. Indeed, they were somewhat silly to imagine that the validity of a conveyance could ever have been made subject to the motives of the parties concerned. But the eventuality which the Committee feared did not occur immediately. In effect, it was not from the law, or from the construction placed upon the law, that the principal danger which they anticipated stemmed. It was from the use that was made of the law, thus from the factors which conditioned its use. The Court's decision in the case of Alexander v. Newman legalized the creation of faggot votes. Their decision in the case of Astbury v. Henderson legalized the freehold land societies as means of altering the social composition of the county electorates. But whatever the impact of these decisions upon the social composition of the *potential* electorates the relevant changes in the *effective* electorates only occurred when the radical urban leaders ceased to restrict their electoral attentions to 'their own' constituencies. It was this element of the problem which Bright ignored when, in 1849, he forecast the imminent collapse of Tory power in the counties. For public consumption, at least, he then argued that it was enough that the freehold land societies existed: in consequence of their existence the county electorates would be doubled or tripled; then, the Tory squires who had provided the core of protectionist strength in Parliament would no longer be returned for the counties.[79] But the individual initiatives on which he dwelt, and on which these societies depended, were not responsible for those changes in the social composition of the county electorates which occurred in various counties in the period immediately before the Derby-Disraeli Reform Bill was passed. Rather, the initiatives were corporate. Thus, in one respect, these changes scarcely mark a break in the mid-century political system: leaders of discrete collectivities were still registering their own supporters. But in another respect they mark a complete break in the system: these leaders were now seriously trying to maximize their political powers within the State. To this end they were now trying to build bases of power in constituencies other than 'their own'. Furthermore, in some cases in 1868 they founded their hopes of success upon the expectation that the nexus which provided them with means of influencing certain voters would prove stronger than the nexus which provided their opponents with means of influencing the same voters.[80] The exploitation of rival nexus was scarcely a new phenomenon. But the concerted exploitation was. The difference was a matter of degree. As indicated, however, by the declining proportions of uncontested elections, the increasing proportions of contests which did not result in changes of representation, and the sharp drop in the numbers of seats which changed hands without a contest, the difference was quite real.[81] The premises of politics were no longer those which the radical journalist in Leicester had implicitly defined when he referred to 'that gentlemanly feeling which would not countenance a contest when the chances are balanced or unfavourable.' In increasing numbers of cases men were no longer granting the legitimacy and invulnerability of the agencies of electoral recruitment on which their rivals' powers were based. However, when they refused to grant the legitimacy and invulnerability of *these* agencies they were not suggesting that agencies of recruitment, as such, were illegitimate. They were only suggesting that the agencies on which their *rivals'* powers were based were illegitimate. Of course, with respect to the ultimate transformation or destruction of the mid-century political system the one refusal was almost as effective as the other. The importance of the point has to do with the question of whether the ultimate transformation or destruction of the system was more intentional than coincidental.

7

The operation of the system

The occurrence of general elections in the mid-nineteenth century was conditioned by several varieties of factor. A general election occurred when a sovereign died. Also, within the limits which the Septennial Act imposed upon the duration of any given Parliament, a general election occurred when a Prime Minister believed that such would allow him to enhance his majorities in the House of Commons or, at least, reduce his minorities. The varieties of factor which conditioned the occurrence of by-elections were far more numerous. But for all practical purposes these may be reduced to one. A by-election occurred in a given constituency when a vacancy occurred in the representation of that constituency. At some general elections, however, a *contest* took place in fewer than half of the constituencies. The point is of more than antequarian interest. It bears upon the essential nature of the mid-century political system because it bears upon the essential nature of the question to which a contested election within the system *was* the answer.

Then, as now, an election determined who would sit in a given Parliament for a given constituency. Thus, then as now, the aggregate results of the elections which occurred at a given general election determined who, for the time being, would fill the offices of State and, indirectly, what policies would be pursued. As a rule, today, it is this function of elections which conditions the terms in which electoral behaviour is discussed. It is generally assumed that the aggregate behaviour of the voters not only *provides* an answer to these questions but *is* an answer to them. Possibly, such an assumption is valid today when a contest occurs in every possible constituency on every possible occasion. But such an assumption could not be valid for a time when

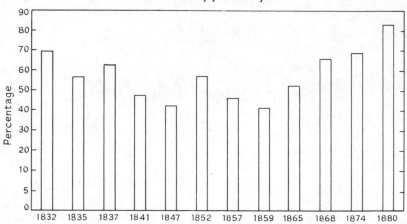

Fig 2

Percentages of United Kingdom constituencies in which contests occurred, 1832-80.

contests were not the rule. Obviously, when contests were not the rule the questions to which a particular contest in a particular constituency *was* the answer were those questions which precipitated the occurrence of *that* contest in *that* constituency.

In the Kingdom as a whole a contest occurred in more constituencies in 1832 than in any subsequent year until 1868. In 1880 the percentage of the constituencies in which a contest occurred was significantly larger again (see figure 2).[1] Obviously, the relatively large numbers of contests in 1832 and 1868 were measures, in part, of the intensities of the political crises in the context of which the first two Reform Bills were passed. But other factors were also involved. This becomes particularly apparent in the light of the evidence for the English county

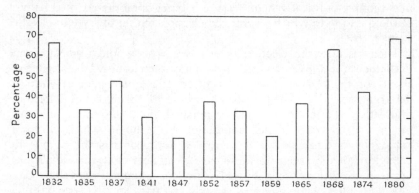

Fig 3

Percentages of English county constituencies in which contests occurred, 1832-80.

constituencies. These provide a limited and somewhat special sample. But the same general trends in the incidence of contests are apparent for the counties as for other categories of constituency with the exception of 1874 (see figure 3).[2] Furthermore, the counties possess a peculiar virtue. Because of the nature of the county franchise it is sometimes possible to see the relationship between the occurrence of a contest in a county constituency and those changes in the levels of local political activity which are themselves revealed in changes in the composition of the local electorate.[3] More generally, the sample *qua* sample facilitates the study of certain other relationships, in particular, those reflected in the changes which occurred in the numbers of seats which changed hands from a member of one 'party' to a member of another without a contest at the polls, and those reflected in the changes in the numbers of contests which occurred without seats changing hands.[4] These changes are important for what they reveal of the changing role of contests within the system, thus for what they suggest of changes within the system itself.

II

For seats changing hands without a contest at the polls the period before 1847 or 1857 – the question of which would be the better date to choose is debatable – is clearly distinguishable from the period after (see figure 4). Between 1835 and 1847, inclusive, 96 English county seats changed hands at general elections from a member of one 'party' to a member of another. Of these, 41 changed hands without a contest at the polls – roughly 43 per cent. At the general elections between 1852 and 1880 – excluding, for 1868, those new county constituencies which the second Reform Act created: for these constituencies no comparisons with prior conditions are possible – 132 English county seats changed hands from a member of one 'party' to a member of another. Of these, only 22 changed hands without a contest – roughly 17 per cent. By-elections tell much the same story. Between December 1832, and August 1847, 13 English county seats changed hands at by-elections from a member of one 'party' to a member of another. Of these, six changed hands without a contest – roughly half. Between August 1847, and April 1880, 20 English county seats changed hands at by-elections from a member of one 'party' to a member of another. Of these, only seven changed hands without a contest – roughly a third.

For contests which did not result in changes of representation three periods suggest themselves (see figure 5). At the general elections of 1835, 1837 and 1841 74 contests occurred in English county constituencies. Seats changed hands in 42 – 57 per cent. At the general elections between 1847 and 1865, inclusive, 101 contests occurred in

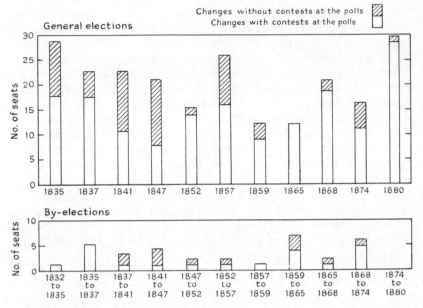

Fig 4

Numbers of English county seats which changed hands from a member of one 'party'
to another at general elections and by-elections between 1835 and 1880 with and
without contests at the polls.

English county constituencies. Seats changed hands in 50 – roughly
half. At the general elections of 1868 1874 and 1880 – again excluding,
for 1868, the new constituencies which the second Reform Act created
– 127 contests occurred in English county constituencies. Seats only
changed hands in 51 – roughly 40 per cent. The significance of these
figures presumably lies in their relationship to the general phenomena
to which the tendency of urban leaders to return to the county arena
should be attributed. This is suggested by the changing orientations of
the different candidates, by their differential success and, even more
clearly, by the changing orientations of the men who claimed seats
which, before the dissolution or vacancy, neither they individually nor
other members of their 'party' had occupied. (see figures 6 and 7).

By and large, the contests of 1835, 1837 and 1841 at which seats did
not change hands were those which Whigs, Liberals or Radicals
precipitated. From the evidence of the polls many of these contests
were obvious violations of the norm which the Radical journalist in
Leicester implicitly described in 1839 when he referred to 'that
gentlemanly feeling which would not countenance a contest when the
chances are balanced or unfavourable'.[5] But the relatively small

number of unsuccessful contests and the relatively large number of seats which changed hands without a contest, suggest that many men were quite willing too grant the invulnerability – if not always the legitimacy – of the principal agencies of electoral recruitment on which their rivals' powers were based.

Between 1832 and 1861, when South Lancashire received a third seat, there were 144 English county seats. In 1832, 120 Whigs or Liberals were candidates for these seats but only 77 Tories or Conservatives. By 1841 this balance had been more than reversed.

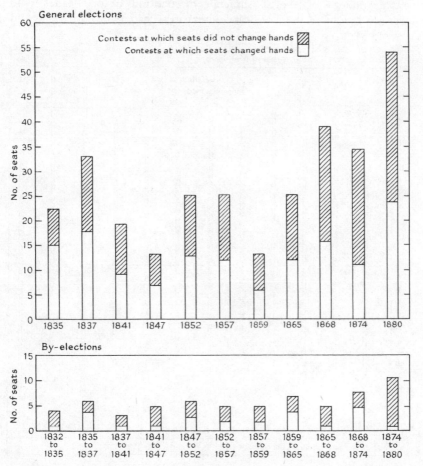

Fig 5

Numbers of contests in English county constituencies at general elections and by-elections between 1832 and 1880 at which seats did and did not change hands from a member of one 'party' to a member of another.

Then, 127 Tories or Conservatives were candidates for these seats but only 42 Whigs or Liberals. The small number of Tory or Conservative candidates in 1832 was principally a measure of the continued disorganization of these men in the various constituencies, and the prevalence of belief in the validity of the grounds for the Tories' opposition to the Bill.[6] But, in the circumstances which the Act itself and continued Radical agitation helped to create these factors were self correctable. In large part, the increased number of Tory or Conservative candidates in 1841 was the consequence of the establishment – or re-establishment – of coalitions of local leaders who were in favour of the Tory or Conservative leaders in Parliament and

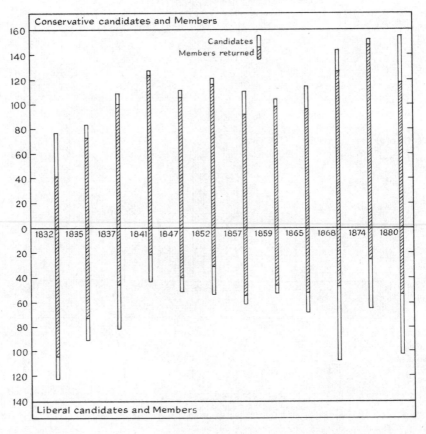

Fig 6

Numbers of 'Conservative' and 'Liberal' candidates at general elections in English county constituencies between 1832 and 1880 and the numbers of such candidates returned. The 'new' and 'old' constituencies are both included for 1868.

whose logic of cohesion was generally phrased in terms of the need to defend the corn laws.

As these local coalitions were established, or re-established, and as their potential electoral strength became apparent, Tory or Conservative candidates claimed more and more county seats. As a

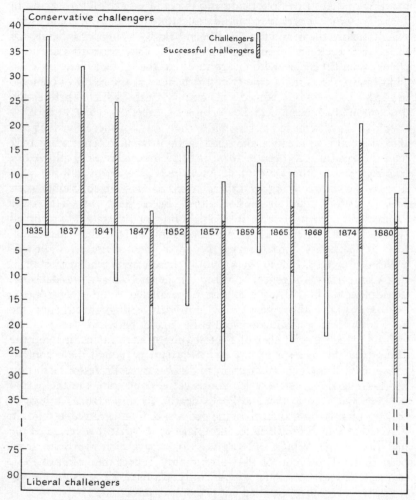

Fig 7

Numbers of 'Conservative' and 'Liberals' who were candidates in English county constituencies at general elections between 1835 and 1880 for seats which, before the dissolution, neither they individually nor other members of their 'parties' had held, and the numbers of such challengers who were successful. Only the 'old' constituencies are included for 1868.

rule, however, they only claimed seats which they had the strength to take. This is suggested by the small number of unsuccessful claims they made. But the frequency with which their claims were contested obviously reflects other factors. In particular, it reflects the reformers' reluctance to acknowledge that they, too, had been carried away by the flow of their own rhetoric during the course of the reform crisis. In 1835, Tory or Conservative candidates claimed 38 English county seats which, before the dissolution, had been held by Whigs or Liberals. Of these, they took 28 – roughly 74 per cent. They took 10 seats in 10 county constituencies without contests at the polls. They took an additional 18 seats in 13 county constituencies as the result of contests. In 1837 they only claimed 32 county seats which, before the dissolution, had been held by Whigs or Liberals. They took 23 – roughly 72 per cent. However, while their rates of success in 1835 and 1837 were almost identical they had to fight far more contests in 1837 than they had had to fight in 1835: in 1837 they were only allowed to take five seats without a contest. Also, in 1837 – and it tells the same story – far more Whig or Liberal candidates claimed county seats which, before the dissolution, had been held by Tories or Conservatives than in 1835. In 1835, Whigs or Liberals only claimed two such seats. Neither claim was successful. In 1837 they claimed 19 seats in 15 county constituencies. None of these claims was allowed without a contest. Indeed, only one of these claims was successful: in East Cumberland the renegade Whig, Sir James Graham, was defeated. Undoubtedly, in 1837, the almost unparalleled number of contests helped to raise the intensity of political feeling throughout the Kingdom. But a distinction must be made between the political feelings which the number of contests might have intensified and the changes in the balance of power in Parliament which these contests occasioned. If the general election of 1837 was, as Professor Gash puts it, 'the crucial contest between conservatives and whigs in the period between the Reform Act and Peel's death', its importance, at least in the counties, lay not so much in the growth of Conservative strength in Parliament which it *allowed* to take place as in what it revealed of the inability of the Whigs and Liberals to *prevent* such a growth from occurring.[7] The events of 1841 presumably, reflect the lesson of 1837. In 1841, Tories or Conservatives only claimed 25 seats in county constituencies which they had not previously possessed. They took 22 – 88 per cent of those they claimed. For 10 seats in 10 county constituencies they had to fight. But they took 13 seats in 11 county constituencies without contests at the polls. Meanwhile, Whig, Liberal or Radical candidates only claimed 11 seats in eight county constituencies. None of their claims was successful. Altogether, at general elections and by-elections between 1832 and 1841 Tory or

Conservative candidates claimed 103 English county seats. They took 79. Altogether, during this period, Whig, Liberal or Radical candidates claimed 37 English county seats. They only took two.

The importance both of the corn law crisis itself and of the resolution of this crisis can be seen in the changes in the situation which the contests between 1832 and 1841 help to illustrate. Initially, in 1846, protectionist associations tried to stem the tide of desertion from the protectionist cause which followed Peel's announcement of his plan to repeal the corn laws.[8] Where they were unable to convince Members who had been elected as protectionists that they should not desert the cause they tried to obtain their resignations and their replacement by sound protectionists. In several cases they succeeded. But in the aftermath of the repeal of the corn law many protectionists simply lost their zest for politics. In many cases their seats were taken by scions of noble, often Tory houses, whose zest for politics was a simple function of their identities. But in some cases, too, their seats were taken by Liberal free traders.

Of course, the very number of English county seats which were held by Tory or Conservative Members in 1847 limited the number of their own prospective claims. But it remains true that in a number of cases in 1847 Tory protectionists simply abandoned their seats to their opponents; also, that in a number of cases in which they did not abandon their seats their continued tenure of them was challenged. Challenge of this sort was not as widespread as it became later, in the late fifties and early sixties, but it was significant. It suggests that the circumstances which had conditioned the observations of the Radical journalist in Leicester in 1839 were changing.

In 1847, Liberal candidates claimed 25 seats in 21 English county constituencies which, before the dissolution, had been held by Tories or Conservatives. They took 16, 10 in nine constituencies without a contest. Meanwhile, Conservatives only claimed two English county seats which they had not previously possessed. They only took one, that without a contest. The revival of protectionist hopes in 1852 brought a partial return to the circumstances of the corn law period. But the return was only partial. Furthermore, it was only temporary. Altogether, in 1852, Conservative candidates claimed 16 English county seats. They took 10, but only one without a contest. Of the 16 seats which protectionists had lost to free traders in 1847 eight were regained in 1852. But four others they failed to regain and the remaining four they made no serious efforts to regain. Meanwhile, in 1852, Liberals also claimed 16 English county seats. They only took three, one without a contest. But in 1857 the numbers of Liberal claims and successes exceeded the numbers of Conservative claims and successes. Liberal candidates claimed 27 English county seats which, before the dissolution, had been held by Conservatives. They took 21, six without contests at the polls. Meanwhile, Conservative candidates only claimed nine English county seats which they had not previously possessed. They only took one and for that they had to fight. In 1859 the former balance was somewhat restored. Conservative candidates claimed 13 English county seats which, previously, they had not possessed. They took eight, two without contests at the polls. Meanwhile, Liberal candidates only claimed five English county seats which, previously, they had not possessed. They took one, that without a contest. But in 1865 Liberal candidates claimed a total of 23 English county seats which, previously, they had not possessed. In each case their claim was contested. They took nine. Conservative candidates, on the other hand, only claimed 11 such seats. In each case, too, their claim was contested. They only took four. In effect, at general elections between 1847 and 1865, inclusive, Liberal candidates claimed 96 English county seats which, before the respective dissolutions, they had not possessed. They took 50, 18 without contests at the polls. Meanwhile, Conservative candidates claimed 51 English county seats which, before the respective dissolutions, they had not possessed. They took 24, only four without a contest. At by-elections, too, there are striking differences between the period before and the period after corn law repeal. At by-elections between 1847 and 1865 Liberal candidates claimed 14 seats, their opponents 10. While Liberals took only five of these seats, their opponents seven, this is very different from the situation which existed before 1847.

It is impossible to determine what would have happened to the Conservative monopoly of English county seats had the Reform Bill of 1866 been passed. But this much is clear: the Bill of 1866 was designed to facilitate the further erosion of those distinctions between borough and county on which the monopoly was largely based. Nor can we determine what would have happened to the Conservative monopoly of English county seats *had not* the Derby-Disraeli Reform Bill been passed. But this much is also clear: the Bill of 1867 was designed to restore the relevant distinctions between borough and county. In effect, it was designed to perpetuate both the Conservative monopoly of these seats and the political system in which this monopoly had come into being. However, since neither the monopoly nor the political system was the product of legislation alone neither could be perpetuated by legislation alone. The end of the mid-century political system is symbolized in the fact that while the Conservative monopoly of English county seats was strengthened in 1868 and further strengthened in 1874 in neither year was it strengthened without opposition. The situation of the thirties no longer existed. Many men, and, in particular, many Radicals, were no longer willing to grant either the legitimacy or the invulnerability of the agencies of electoral recruitment on which their rivals' powers were based.

The fact that new electoral qualifications and, in many cases, new constituency boundaries were defined by the Acts of 1867 and 1868 is presumably largely responsible for the increased number of contested elections in 1868. And, obviously, many Liberals and Radicals believed that the greater the formal changes the more would their powers be enhanced. This is indicated by the fact that proportionately more contests occurred in 1868 in the county constituencies in which the second Reform Act had its largest impact – those which it redivided.

In 1865, in consequence of the division of the West Riding of Yorkshire into two two-member constituencies, there were 147 English county seats; 115 Conservatives were candidates for these seats but only 77 Liberals. After the Derby-Disraeli Reform Bill was passed there were 172 English county seats; 143 Conservatives were candidates for these seats. But the number of Liberal candidates for these seats was 105. In effect, while the number of Conservative candidates increased by 24 per cent over the number in 1865 the number of Liberal candidates increased by 36 per cent. Furthermore, the concentration of Liberal candidates was particularly heavy in the redivided counties. There were 51 Liberal candidates for the 72 seats in these constituencies. Only 54 Liberals were candidates for the 100 seats in the remaining county constituencies.

Presumably, the greater the anticipation of victory the greater the need to find an acceptable excuse for the defeat. If this be so, then the proportions of defeated Liberal candidates, especially in the redivided counties, may be extremely significant. In the counties which were *not* redivided Liberal candidates claimed 22 seats which, before the dissolution, they had not possessed, the Conservatives 11. Each took six. Thus, in these constituencies the balance of power between 'parties' was the same after the elections of 1868 as it had been after the elections of 1865. But in the counties which were redivided a far larger proportion of Conservatives was returned in 1868 than had been returned in 1865. In 1865, 28 Conservatives and 21 Liberals had been returned from these counties. In 1868, 57 Conservatives were returned from them but only 15 Liberals. The rates of success which yielded these results were strikingly different. Among the Conservatives the rate of success was roughly 88 per cent – 65 Conservatives had been candidates for these seats. Among the Liberals the rate of success was roughly 30 per cent – 51 Liberals had been candidates for these seats. Whether more illegitimate influence was exercised at these elections than had been exercised at previous elections it is impossible to say. Quite apart from the problem of evidence there is the far more basic problem of definition. What with the number of disappointed candidates, however, answers were often provided which, by passing both the problem of evidence and the problem of definition, led to but one conclusion – the need for the secret ballot. And what happened to many Liberals in the counties happened to many Conservatives in the boroughs.

In 1874, far more Liberals than Conservatives claimed English county seats which, before the dissolution, they had not possessed: 31 Liberals, 19 Conservatives. As in 1868, however, the rate of success of the Conservative candidates was far higher than the rate of success of the Liberals. Conservative candidates took roughly 84 per cent of the seats they claimed – 16, five without contests at the polls. Meanwhile, Liberal candidates only took some 13 per cent of the seats they claimed – four, none without a contest at the polls. But in 1880 the Liberals' success was far greater than the Conservatives'. Their rate of success scarcely equalled the Conservatives' earlier rates of success but of the 75 seats they claimed in 55 English county constituencies they took 29. Meanwhile, Conservatives only claimed six seats which, before the dissolution, they had not possessed. They only took one.

III

Obviously, a change was occurring in the role which contests performed. Not only were far more contests taking place. Far more contests were taking place without seats changing hands. The explanation presumably lies in several clearly related phenomena.

As long as contests were fairly expensive there were few candidates who were willing to pay the price from their own resources without considerable assurance of success. Nor was it easy, except in times of political excitement, to collect the necessary funds from others. In such times, many candidates were returned 'free of expense'.[10] But at other times this was not the case. Hence the importance of the information in the light of which the requisite assurances were sought. Hence the importance of those organizations through which the relevant information was gathered. And hence the importance of the apparent fact that in the years after 1846 this information tended to lose its relevance.

As long as sufficient proportions of the voters voted as members of clearly definable and publicly identifiable blocs such assurances were generally sought from detailed studies of the groups and networks which these blocs were assumed to reflect. Election managers were expected to be able to 'forecast with tolerable accuracy the result of the election' in the light of their knowledge of each voter's 'employer, sect, landlord, customer or creditor'.[11] But, apparently, in the period *before* the second Reform Bill was passed, the period in which various urban leaders returned to the county arena, election managers ceased to be able to forecast the outcome of a prospective contest in the light of this information with their accustomed accuracy. Was the tendency of urban leaders to return to the county arena more the cause or the consequence of the phenomena to which the declining predictability of electoral behaviour should be attributed? Was the declining predictability of electoral behaviour *more* the consequence of changes in the structure of English society – of the declining cohesion of the traditional agencies of electoral recruitment; or was it *more* the consequence of changes in the electorate – of the increasing proportions of men on the various electoral registers whose behaviour was less affected by the traditional agencies of electoral recruitment? or, again, was it *more* the consequence of the development of organizations through which the relevant information was gathered – of the increasing concentration of effective political power in the hands of men who had a vested interest in maximizing this power or, at least, in creating the presumption of their own relative political strength? The information which these men sought to gather concerning each voter's 'employer, sect, landlord, customer or creditor' possibly became less valuable as a simple consequence of the increasing bureaucratization of the process by which it was gathered; possibly, influence networks were being strained beyond their effectiveness. But this much is clear: the crucial political change in England in the nineteenth century occurred when the information on which the predictability of electoral behaviour was based lost its value. One of the principal symbols of this change lies in the changing role of contests which these various figures suggest.

As long as the information which election managers tried to gather was both relevant and reliable, contests tended to occur not in the context of the question: who will sit in a given Parliament as the representative or representatives of a given constituency? But, rather, in the context of the question – not already fully answered by the information itself – : what is the balance of power within the constituency itself between, or among, the leaders of the various local agencies of electoral recruitment? Of course, the answer to the one question was the answer to the other. Indeed, then as later – and this may help to explain why the relevant change has not been adequately noted – to answer the balance of power question was to answer the parliamentary question. But the reverse was less true: in many cases the uses to which parliamentary majorities were put had only an indirect impact upon the local balances of power. As the poll books for Huntingdonshire, Cambridgeshire and North Northamptonshire reveal, goings-on in Parliament might strengthen or weaken local agencies of electoral recruitment. But these agencies themselves were basic and basically depended upon other varieties of factor. It was presumably, the nature of these factors which conditioned many of the goings-on in Parliament and which also conditioned the terms in which these goings-on were discussed. It was also the importance of these factors which presumably conditioned the reluctance of national leaders to call general elections at times when these would have been in the nature of referenda. As Miss Kemp recently noted, when Peel refused to dissolve Parliament in 1846, following his defeat on the Irish Coercion Bill, he was opposing the principle of parliamentary sovereignty to the principle of electoral or popular sovereignty. He insisted that 'Parliament . . . was sovereign and should decide . . . all . . . questions of policy that arose; [that] the people's function, at general elections, was to choose a House of Commons, not to decide on policy nor to designate a government.' [12] To insist on these points was to insist on protecting the major agencies of electoral recruitment from as many strains as possible. It was the logic of the situation which the author of a highly romanticized description of English rural life recognized when he explained his refusal to discuss county politics.

> Neither I nor my readers, I am sure, would wish to have the uproar and exasperation of a county election introduced into this peaceful volume; enough that when it does come to the county Hall, it comes, often as a hurricane, and frequently shakes it to the foundations, leaving in its track debts and mortgages, shyness between neighbours, and rancour among friends. [13]

National leaders might try to encourage contests in the various constituencies in the hope of increasing their parliamentary followings. The results of these contests might have direct and obvious bearings upon the size of these followings. As the evidence of the county poll books suggests, however, the mid-century political system was only weakly integrated at different levels of action. National questions determined the timing of general elections. However – and, obviously, in some constituencies and on some occasions more than others – the impact of national questions upon the behaviour of the voters was less direct than it was indirect. What conditioned these differences was obviously the relative stability and self-sufficiency of the groups which the different voters comprised. And of course, national leaders made few efforts to appeal to the voters directly until the seventies and eighties by which time the agencies of electoral recruitment on which the mid-century system was based had been significantly weakened. The national leaders' restraint perhaps illustrates their understanding of the social basis of their constitutional principles – their awareness of the fact that they could scarcely hope to condition the behaviour of the voters directly without jeopardizing the traditional structure of the society. But whether they understood the social basis of these principles or — which in practice might come to the same thing — were merely living up to that code of non-interference between a man and his dependents which many of them professed, the system which their behaviour helps to illustrate was fundamentally unstable. The relationships into which national leaders hesitated to intrude were those which election managers studied in detail and not only studied but tried to exploit as means of advancing the interests of the candidates for whom they worked.

Of course, changes in the local balances of power often occurred without the assistance of electoral managers. But, whatever the reason for such a change, until fairly late in the century it was generally one such — and, even more, the question whether a change had in fact taken place — which prompted the occurrence of a contested election. As these questions became more numerous and more difficult to answer in the light of the information which the election managers tried to gather so the contests become more frequent. In effect, the growing incidence of contested elections provides an important measure of change within the system because — and however affected by the growing impetuosity of politicians which, possibly, was an independent variable—it provides a measure of the declining relevance of the information which election managers tried to gather. As the occurrence of uncontested elections suggests, in many constituencies it was obviously assumed that the politically relevant groups did not exist in the context of national or nation-wide relationships but in the context of local, discrete, and largely non-political relationships, those which election managers might hope to understand in the light of their knowledge of each voter's 'employer, sect, landlord, customer or creditor'. In many constituencies, once the balance of power question had been answered this question was clearly not again asked at the polls until something occurred locally which not only cast doubt upon the continuing validity of the answer which the former contest provided but which also cast doubt upon the abilities of men to find an answer except by means of a contest.

In East Norfolk, for example, a contest occurred at a by-election in 1858. Before that no contest had occurred since 1841. But changes had taken place in the representation. Indeed, in 1857, the two Conservative Members for the division, one of whom had sat for the division for 20 years, stepped down. They allowed two Liberals to be returned without a contest. The example is somewhat extreme. But together with the subsequent contest the behaviour of the Conservative Members helps to illustrate the role which contests frequently played as long as the varieties of information which election managers tried to gather were considered relevant.

As the editor of the 1858 poll book explained, the change of representation in 1857 was largely the consequence of the death of the second Baron Wodehouse, a protectionist, and the succession of his grandson, a Liberal. When the succession occurred 'the influence and weight of the noble Lord's property and character' – the formula was standard – were debited 'from the Conservative interest . . . and placed on the side of the Liberal party'.[14] Also, the Liberal leaders in the division began to pay attention to the electoral register. While nine years elapsed between the death of the second Lord Wodehouse and the return of two Liberal Members this was, ostensibly, more a measure of the reluctance of the Liberals to dispossess the Conservative Members of their seats – until 1855, one of these was the new Lord Wodehouse's uncle – than it was of the effective electoral support on which the Conservative Members could depend. But, whatever the reasons for the delay, once the Liberal Lord Wodehouse had joined with the Liberal Earl of Leicester, and once they had agreed to claim one of the two seats for the division, the process was begun which resulted in their temporarily taking both.

Ostensibly, Wodehouse and Leicester merely hoped to induce their opponents to surrender one of the two seats. But their strategy required that they threaten both. As the editor of the subsequent poll book put it, 'It was deemed advisable, . . . in consequence of the long period that had elapsed since a contest, *neither [side] being able to form any direct judgement as to the result* – to endeavour to make an arrangement which would prevent a contest.'[15] But the Conservatives over-reacted. When they looked at the register, and when they discovered that 'many on whose exertions great reliance had been placed . . . declined to give any active support', they simply withdrew.[16] The following year it became apparent that their reaction had been excessive. One of the Liberal Members died. An intemperate Tory precipitated a contest at the ensuing by-election against the recommendations of his more temperate neighbours. He was only beaten by 213 votes out of a total of 5,653 votes cast. In 1859, the 'arrangement' was effected which had previously been sought. One Liberal and one Conservative were returned without a contest. But even though this 'arrangement' was an obvious consequence of the intemperance of the intemperate Tory, he was not the candidate chosen by his Conservative neighbours. In all probability, it was to punish him for his refusal to follow the recommendations of the established Conservative leaders in the constituency that another candidate was chosen.

The effective purpose served by the East Norfolk contest in 1858 helps explain why so many contests occurred in 1832 and 1868: in those years there was often no other way of 'form[ing] any direct judgement as to the result[s]'. A case in point is Cambridgeshire. As a Liberal leader explained, in 1868, he and his colleagues had no wish 'to involve the county unnecessarily in a contest'. But, he went on, they 'believed the Liberal electors were in a *bona fide* majority, and therefore the question ought to be tried'.[17] There had been no contest in the county since 1857, before that since 1835. Before the dissolution there had been two Conservative Members for the county and one Liberal. The contest was precipitated by the candidacy of a second Liberal. As it turned out, the Liberal electors were not in a majority. In a number of other county constituencies, e.g., South Leicestershire, Liberal defeats in 1868 were not accepted as they had been accepted earlier. But in Cambridgeshire Liberal impetuosity was subsequently held in check and, presumably, in large part because after 1872 the Liberal Member, Henry Brand, became Speaker of the House. Thus, if the Liberals again tried to take a second seat, and if they thereby induced their opponents to claim the third, an important seat would be jeopardized. Notwithstanding the urgings of various Liberals, especially urban Liberals, that Liberal candidates be chosen to contest the seats vacated by the death or retirement of Conservative Members,[18] and even that a contest be precipitated at the general elections in 1880,[19] no contest occurred in the county until Brand was elevated to the House of Lords in 1884. Then, of course, it was the Conservatives who precipitated the contest. And they won it.

IV

Presumably, it was fairly common knowledge in East Norfolk which men were the tenants of Lord Wodehouse, which the corn merchants who bought the produce of these men's farms, which the bankers and solicitors who facilitated the relationships of these men with him or his agents, with one another, and with those in the world beyond. Thus, presumably, it was not a very taxing operation to debit 'the influence and weight of the noble Lord's property and character' from the Conservative side of the local political ledger and to credit them to the Liberal side. Nor, in fact, would the mathematical handling of other interests be significantly more complicated. But in many cases the membership of these other interests was rather less clear. And in many cases these interests themselves were less cohesive. It was principally to clarify the membership of these interests and to obtain the information in the light of which their cohesion might be enhanced or weakened that canvassers were used.

As G. Butt explained in his *Suggestions as to the Conduct and Management of a County Contested Election,* first published in 1826, the canvass was the means by which that 'mass of details' was gathered which would allow 'the persons in the management of the contest . . . [to] resolve whether to proceed, or to desist altogether'.[20] Among these details were, first, the exact number of the prospective voters. This was basic. Before electoral registers were available there was no other way of determining how many votes were needed to win. Then, too, these details included the specific grounds of each prospective voter's qualification and, further, whether his qualification could be easily proved. This was scarcely less basic. Without such knowledge the election agent could scarcely defend the rights of friendly voters to vote or challenge the rights of hostile voters. And then, again, these details included which prospective voters were friendly, which were 'hostile', 'doubtful', or 'neutral'.[21] Further, they included, with respect to each 'hostile', 'doubtful', or 'neutral' voter, what influence might be brought to bear upon him to obtain the promise of his support.[22]

As Butt described them, such promises of support were given to candidates as individuals, not as members of parties. Indeed, Butt warned against party attachments or, as such attachments were usually called in the context of an election, 'coalitions' between candidates. His statement was categorical: the 'immediate friends' of each candidate who, with the candidate himself, made all the important decisions, 'should be unconnected, in every way, with the interests of the other candidates'.[23] Whatever the validity of his obvious assumption, that a candidate who coalesced with another would thereby lose more votes than he would gain, the assumption itself was both widespread and enduring. It informed Lord Churston's suggestion, in 1868, that Sir Stafford Northcote and Thomas Walrond, the two Conservative candidates in North Devonshire, might wish to have separate agents 'if they feared to encounter the cry of "coalition" '.[24] By then, the principal grounds for such a fear – the stigma attached to being a 'party man' as long as parties were mainly regarded as agencies for the distribution of patronage – had been significantly weakened.[25] But when it became known that Northcote and Walrond had indeed coalesced, that they had the same agents and canvassers, one Liberal suggested to another that notices be printed 'warning' the voters of their 'coalition'. The suggestion was phrased somewhat cynically. Indeed, it may well have been a joke. 'It only requires to get hold of some terms with which to abuse your opponents', the first Liberal went on, '& "Coalition" is as good as any I know, especially so because but few voters will see the absurdity of it.'[26]

The purposes of the pre-election canvass which Cox and Grady described and recommended some 40 years later were essentially the same. With electoral registers available, however, it was no longer necessary to burden the pre-election canvasser with the tasks of determining the number of the prospective voters, the qualifications of each, or the ease with which his qualification could be proved. Answers to these questions were already at hand. Thus, the pre-election canvasser could focus upon his principal tasks, those of soliciting promises of support, of learning who was neutral, doubtful or hostile, and of providing his election manager with information in the light of which he could perform what Cox and Grady described as his 'real business', that of bringing 'influences ... to bear upon the undetermined [voters], so as to secure them for his own party'. As Cox and Grady put it in their first post-ballot edition, the purpose of the pre-election canvass

> ... was to enable the candidate to ascertain what were his chances of success; which he did by noting the promises secured for himself and those given against him. Thus was obtained also the no less important information what votes remained unpromised, the real business of the manager being to see what influences could be brought to bear upon the undetermined, so as to secure them for his own party. Hitherto no exception has been taken to the act of soliciting the promise of a vote. There was no hesitation about asking or giving it, and, at the close of an active canvass, the residuum of the unpromised was usually so small that on making up the canvass books the manager was enabled to forecast with tolerable accuracy the result of the election. But the vote by ballot has made all these necessary purposes of the canvass altogether worthless. How can a candidate ask an elector to promise a vote which the law has commanded him to keep secret? ... There can now be no anxious casting up of accounts of the canvass at the end of each day; no lists of the unpromised sent to the [local] subcommittees upon whom they are to use their powers of persuasion.[27]

And, they added, thereby revealing their belief that such 'powers of persuasion' were not only legitimate but socially necessary, in the future, 'Elections ... will be carried by wire pullers, who make a profitable business of bringing voters to the polls.'[28]

The contests for which Cox and Grady's handbooks were written — which they tell how to win — were those at which voters were recruited through the basically non-political groups and networks to which they belonged. Butt's handbook had been written for similar contests but in certain important ways things had changed. In part, these changes were the consequence of the increased size of the various electorates, in part, of the increased complexity of the franchise laws. But they were also the obvious consequence of the fact that certain of the questions which, in Butt's time, pre-election canvassers had been used to answer were already answered: electoral registers were at hand, and registers which were annually corrected.

V

Recently, the machinery of registration has been described anew by Mr J. Alun Thomas and Professor H. J. Hanham.[30] Emphasizing the inefficiencies of the men into whose hands formal responsibility for compiling the electoral registers was placed, Mr Thomas and Professor Hanham have also both noted how, in various constituencies, voluntary registration associations came into being which sought to register their own prospective supporters and to prevent the registration of their opponents' prospective supporters. Furthermore, they have emphasized the role of these associations as the local bases of a developing national party system.

Undoubtedly, many overseers were inefficient. Undoubtedly, had local registration associations not come into being the increments which occurred in the various electorates would not have occurred.[31] And again, these local associations did provide the bases of a national party system – especially after the national party leaders had established central registration associations in the sixties as means of encouraging the formation of local associations where such did not exist and of providing essential channels for communication among them.[32] But there are certain aspects of the registration system and certain aspects of these local registration associations which have not been adequately noted. Principally, these have to do with the means by which members of these associations determined which men to propose for registration and which not to propose. In effect, they have to do with the impact of the system upon the principal groups and networks within the society – upon the traditional agencies of electoral recruitment.

Brougham's criticisms of the registration system were immediate but somewhat abstract. Even before the first reformed Parliament had met he was complaining that the registration system was not working as he and his colleagues had hoped. 'The main use of the register', he explained, 'is to have [the voters'] claims decided when men's passions are not aroused ... [But] unless the excitement of a pending contest operate at the moment, voters will not register themselves; ... Moreover, if a contest is going on, the candidates or their partisans are likely to take upon themselves the labour and expense of registering their supporters.'[33] He did not quite put it this way but the thrust of his criticism is contained in the statement that far from guaranteeing that men's claims would be decided 'when men's passions ... [were] not aroused', the registration system simply multiplied the times such passions would be aroused. This was in itself important. But the full measure of its importance lies in the multiplication of times when canvassing was undertaken.

Writing in 1826, Butt emphasized the role of the *pre-election* canvassers in learning the names and numbers of the prospective voters, whether their qualifications could be proved easily, how they intended to vote, and what influences might be brought to bear upon them. In the post-reform period the same information was put to the same uses. But, in consequence of the registration system, some of this information was gathered annually – or even constantly. 'We have *constantly* canvassers all over the City', declared the secretary of the City of London Liberal Registration Association, in 1860, 'approaching everybody; and we know everybody by means of our canvass, for the purpose of registration, and that gives us a great advantage in the election.'[34] Assuming that registration in the City was handled by the book, and that the book was Cox and Grady, the advantage to which he referred would have been, in part, a measure of the value of the very information which the registration canvassers were used to gather, in part, a measure of the value of the experience they acquired in gathering it. Since a given Parliament had no fixed span of life (apart from the legal maximum) it was of the utmost importance to those who were concerned to maximize their political powers – whether in their own constituencies or in Parliament – to have an organized and experienced body of men on hand at all times ready to launch an immediate canvass for the purposes not of registration but of election.[35] Furthermore, if those who were engaged in the registration process did, indeed, gather the information which, according to Cox and Grady, they should gather, then the election manager's job, come election time, would have been that much simpler. As Cox and Grady explained, it was the responsibility of the registration canvassers to learn exactly who on the existing register had died, who had moved away or otherwise lost his qualification, and who had become qualified to be registered, along with 'the nature of their qualification, the objections to it (if any), and their probable politics, with the influences to which they are likely to be subjected'.[36] In earlier editions of their handbook this assertion was hedged in apology. Writing in 1847, before he began his publishing partnership with Grady, Cox observed, 'However we may lament the existence of such influences they are *facts*, having an important bearing upon the result of an election, and which cannot therefore be omitted in the calculations of practical men.'[37] By 1868, however, the apology was dropped. And in their first post-ballot edition they implied that the efforts of election managers to mobilize the relevant influences on which the canvassers reported were far more legitimate than the efforts of others, 'wire pullers' in particular, to bring voters to the polls by other means.

Canvassing was no more a new activity than were the matters on which the canvassers reported. Nor were the purposes of reporting on such matters new. What was new was the enhanced value of the

information which the canvassers gathered, the effective uses to which
it could be put. From this the other novelties derived, in particular, the
registration associations which came into being in many constituencies
as means of gathering this information, and the increased importance of
that enthusiasm which these associations engendered and on which they
depended. In the pre-reform period canvassing was rarely if ever
undertaken except when a contest was in prospect. Also, the men who
conducted these canvasses were not generally organized on a
permanent basis. But with the establishment of electoral registers, and
with the establishment of a process by which these registers could be
corrected annually, such personal and *ad hoc* arrangements could only
survive where the intensity of political life was low. Elsewhere, such
arrangements were rendered obsolete by the possibility which arose
each year of conditioning the local balance of power, and by the
organizational requirements of trying to do so. It was in Dorsetshire
where things political were fairly quiet – there was only one contest in
the county between 1832 and 1885 – that in 1880 the Conservative
committee appointed to investigate the organization of the party in the
different constituencies found that there was absolutely no
Conservative organization – and, presumably, no Liberal organization
either. The local Conservative leaders 'had deliberately come to the
conclusion that it was better to have none, for fear of raising the
activity of the Liberal party'.[38] It was in the City of London where
things political were fairly noisy – contests occurred in the City on
every possible occasion – that canvassing was performed by party
organizations and, ostensibly, not only annually but constantly.

The role of the political bureaucrat was ambiguous. The system
could scarcely have functioned without him. But with him it
functioned in ways which the members of the Grey Ministry scarcely
desired. As far as they were able they had designed the various
franchise qualifications so as to allow certain categories of men to vote
in certain constituencies. Their ideal was that which, implicitly, the
two Liberal agents described in 1860, the one when he referred to 'the
normal opinion of the general community of the qualified' in any
constituency, the other when he observed that many contests might be
avoided if only a way could be found of using the information which
the various election agents possessed.[39] But the 'normal opinion' could
be distorted. And rivals were scarcely to be trusted. In large part, the
existence and nature of the mid-century political system are to be
explained in terms of the fact that the 'normal opinions' of the various
constituencies were frequently re-enforced, not distorted, that no
effective rivals existed. But there was nothing anyone could do to
prevent such distortions or, analogously, to prevent the qualifications
which had been designed to allow certain categories of men to vote in

certain constituencies from becoming challenges to the legal ingenuities of those who were not satisfied by the exploitation of their status where their status was most readily exploitable. In large part, the transformation or destruction of the mid-century political system is to be explained in terms of the refocusing of the relevant ambitions from a local to a national arena. Whatever the total explanation of this phenomenon, a partial explanation obviously lies in the potentialities which the registration system provided of realizing these ambitions. In effect, the transformation or destruction of the system was, in part, the consequence of the fact that the process by which 'the normal opinion of the general community of the qualified' in any constituency could be discovered without a contest was also the first step in the process by which this 'normal opinion' could be changed. It has often been noted that registration was important because an unregistered man could not vote. But the real importance of the registration system derived from its impact upon the traditional agencies of electoral recruitment.

VI

It was presumably, partly because of all this that in many constituencies the more politically conscious or politically ambitious leaders who established registration associations were careful to establish these associations in such ways as would not invade other men's areas of influence. They sought to encourage the others to raise the levels of their political consciousness. But they were often reluctant to insinuate themselves between a man and his dependents or quasi-dependents. Their values were those which the Liberal Marquis of Westminster articulated· in 1841 when he castigated Gladstone for canvassing his tenants without receiving or even asking permission. Of course, in this case the political opposition between Westminster and Gladstone undoubtedly exacerbated the problem. As Westminster wrote in haughty reprimand, 'I did think that interference between a landlord, with whose opinions you are acquainted, and his tenants, was not justifiable according to those laws of delicacy and propriety which I considered binding in such cases.'[40] But even when men were politically allied in Parliament their alliances did not always obviate the need to declare that each would use his separate 'influence' in electoral affairs to help the other.[41] So much the more were men who lived in this world careful lest they presume too much by bureaucratic means. But in some cases in the mid-century, and in many more in the seventies and eighties,[42] their concern to retain their political powers led them to violate the norms of the status hierarchy to which they belonged.

In East Gloucestershire, for example, where a Conservative registration society was established in 1837, the Society had no powers, initially, to interfere with registration activities throughout the constituency.[43] To begin with, all that the members of the Society sought to do was to encourage local activity. Each district in the division was formally autonomous. As a measure of its autonomy, each district was supposed to raise the funds necessary to cover its own registration expenses. Fairly rapidly, however, it became apparent that in certain districts the funds could not be raised. The amounts were not large. In no case did they exceed £50 a year. By 1842, however, in many polling districts, Conservative registration expenses were being paid from a central fund. Significantly, certain of the districts in which this was the case were those in which, at a by-election in 1854, the Liberal candidate received large majorities.

By then the Society had been reorganized. In 1852 a new central committee had been established and given power not only to take steps 'to inspire the careful watching of the Registration of Voters', but also 'to assist the formation of Local Committees in every district'. These, it was noted, should be prepared at all times 'for an immediate Canvass upon the announcement by ... [the central committee] of any Candidate'. To this end the committee opened an office in Gloucester which was staffed by men who were not only supposed 'to assist' the local registration agents but also to take effective direction out of the hands of these agents. 'All necessary arrangements for the conduct of elections' were to be made from the Gloucester office. When the hope that the expenses of this office would be met by a general subscription failed, the burden fell back upon those who had carried it before and who, as members of the new central committee, contributed £50 a year. In effect, in 1852 those men in the county who were concerned to maximize their powers in the constituency – and, presumably, in Parliament – had been led to assume a direct control of the local agencies through which their ambitions might be realized.

In Cambridgeshire the situation was different. Protectionists were active in 1852. They secured the uncontested return of Edward Ball, a nonconformist tenant farmer who had been active on both the local and national scenes in the thirties and forties.[44] But Ball's election expenses were mainly paid by the two principal Conservative peers in the county, the Duke of Rutland and the Earl of Hardwicke.[45] In effect, after 1841 that organization collapsed which had helped to secure the return of a third Conservative Member by providing an election fund of £5,000.[46] In the years before 1868 the entire costs of Conservative registration in the county were paid by Rutland and Hardwicke.[47] Their reasons for paying these costs are understandable. For many years members of their own immediate families held two of the three county seats. But, except in the areas of the county in which their own estates were located, registration activities were apparently minimal. In these areas electoral registration was presumably a function of estate management. Ostensibly, the price which the Conservative gentry paid for this situation was their inability to take the third county seat in 1865 when a crisis occurred within the ranks of the Liberals.[48] Ostensibly, had they been organized, and had their potential supporters been registered, they might have taken the seat. But no contest occurred. Thus, the validity of the contention cannot be measured.

Nor was it easy to organize these men. In January 1868, largely at the instigation of Hardwicke, a meeting was held, Hardwicke in the chair, to form a joint Conservative registration association for the county and borough which would have been affiliated with the new National Union of Conservative and Constitutional Associations, and which would have levied dues from its members to defray the costs of registration.[49] But the rural response was cool. As one of the Conservative leaders in the borough later observed, 'The union between the town and county would be an advantage. But the county was rather apathetic.' And, he added, thus, probably, aggravating the situation, 'Unless the county were more active, the town could not accept them.'[50] In the borough, a fairly effective organization had been in being for many years. But many of the rural leaders were not only reluctant to model their own procedures upon those in the town. They were also extremely jealous of their own prerogatives as 'county' men.[51] The general outlines of the joint association had been approved in January. But a subsequent meeting called to ratify the arrangements – again with Hardwicke in the chair – was attended by only one member of the gentry. In these circumstances the scheme was abandoned.[52]

Presumably the rejection of Hardwicke's scheme by the Conservative gentry was in part a measure of Rutland's influence among them. Hardwicke was identified with the Disraeli wing of the party. Rutland, on the other hand, was identified with the Cranborne wing, those who opposed the second Reform Act.[53] It was common knowledge that if the Liberals did precipitate a contest at the elections to be held in the autumn the seat at stake would be that occupied by Hardwicke's son, Viscount Royston. Hence that combination of plaintiveness and vindictiveness in Royston's statement at the second of the two meetings: 'If the Conservative party in Cambridgeshire are not unanimous enough to keep a registration society going the two members [he and Lord George Manners] would try [to keep their seats], but if they were turned out for party reasons, the responsibility will belong to the county'.[54]

The rejection of Hardwicke's scheme was presumably in part also a measure of the squires' reluctance to be used. As Royston put it earlier, 'The Liberal party might say that … [Rutland and Hardwicke] returned their own representatives for the county.' Nor did he deny the truth of the allegation. But, he insisted, Rutland's and Hardwicke's interests were really those of the constituency itself. 'They were not such bigoted donkeys', he declared, 'as to suppose they could return whom they thought proper; at the same time, they had undoubtedly the right to nominate such persons to represent the county whom they thought would be most acceptable to the constituents.' [55] The association which he and his father tried to organize would probably not have altered the effective concentration of political power in the county. It was perhaps in part because of this that most members of the gentry refused to participate.

Furthermore, the rejection of Hardwicke's scheme was in part the consequence of the fact that on several recent occasions when the Cambridgeshire Hounds had hunted through Wimpole, where Hardwicke's seat was located, there had been such a dearth of foxes as to produce the belief that Hardwicke was opposed to fox hunting. In September, after the Liberals had announced that they would try for the second of the three county seats, and in the context of the argument that an attack upon the Irish Church was really an attack upon the English land system, another Conservative meeting was held, far better attended than the others but unattended by either Hardwicke himself or that member of the gentry who, alone of his ilk, had been present at Hardwicke's second meeting. As the Master of the Cambridgeshire Hounds noted in a letter read at this meeting, the rumour that Hardwicke was 'most inimical to fox-hunting was deterring a certain class of people from supporting Lord Royston in the approaching election'. But these should know, he went on, that 'Lord Hardwicke subscribes one hundred pounds a year to the Cambridgeshire fox hounds, and . . . pays his keepers a sovereign for each fox found in his coverts whenever the hounds go there.' They should also know that there were two litters of cubs at Wimpole. [56] Cheers followed the reading of this letter. Those assembled then agreed to use their influences on behalf of both Royston and Manners. They also agreed to form a Conservative Registration Association — but an Association for the county alone.

This new Association was the means by which the Conservative squires solved their problems of relationship with Rutland and Hardwicke. But it was not the means by which they guaranteed their own concerted action. The Association had a chairman and a vice-chairman. But no decisions could be made except by the committee and the committee, as it was later described, consisted of the chairmen and vice-chairmen of 'independent committees acting in and for the several [polling] districts throughout the County and Isle [of Ely]'. [57] The description was accurate. These committees were nothing if not independent. They were the means by which local men might involve themselves in registration activities in their own polling districts. But the Association had no means of supervising their activities. And, obviously, in some polling districts these were minimal. When reports of registration were published they were sometimes published for only one polling district, not for the county as a whole.[58] Nor could these men act in unison when need arose or resolve their disagreements in the privacy of their own Association. When Hardwicke died, in 1873, and Royston succeeded him, thus creating a vacancy in the county, and, again, in 1874, when Manners died, thus creating another vacancy, the members of these 'independent committees' demonstrated their total lack of institutional or 'party' loyalty by conducting undignified debates in the columns of the local Conservative paper concerning the merits of different candidates and their different supporters.[59] In 1873 the Conservatives were only saved from possible disaster by the Liberals' apparent fears that if they started a candidate of their own when the remaining life of the sitting Parliament was so short they might jeopardize the seat of Henry Brand, Speaker of the House and third Member for the county, who was a Liberal. In 1874 the Conservatives only managed to reduce their candidates to one after the Liberals had begun to talk seriously of running a candidate of their own. The following year, after numerous letters to the editor of the *Cambridge Chronicle* from various of the chairmen and vice-chairmen of the polling district committees the Association was summoned to elect new officers.[60]

It was the same kind of problem – how to get the men whose influence he needed to work in harmony with one another – that Northcote faced in North Devonshire in 1868. But his difficulties did not have to do with the unpopularity of the Conservative candidate, Thomas Walrond. Rather, they had to do with the popularity of the Liberal Member, Sir Thomas Acland. The Conservative enthusiasts in the county who decided to mount a contest against Acland apparently believed that Acland was vulnerable because of the coolness of his own relations, and those of other Liberal squires and peers, with the local nonconformists.[61] But if the coolness of these relations made Acland vulnerable from the one side it was also a source of strength from the other: many Conservatives refused to use their influences against him.

For Northcote himself the contest was both an unwelcome expense – he was not a rich man – and an unwelcome strain upon his friendship with Acland. But Northcote was the hostage of those who, apparently, had been convinced by the Conservative agent in the county that Acland's seat could be taken.[62] As one of Northcote's more party-oriented neighbours explained to him, while the contest might be 'unpleasant', it should be pursued 'as a matter of duty and because

. . . we have a chance which at this moment we ought not to neglect'.[63]
However — and it is this which helps to explain the impatience of many
'party' men with those networks of influence in which they were
enmeshed — this chance was in the power of the others to deny. Some
deplored the contest because of their personal esteem for Acland, others
because of their reluctance to offend the various prominent Liberals
who had estates in the division, others because of their memories of
Acland's father. 'I know [Acland] to be a worthy descendant of a
greatly loved man', wrote one Conservative squire while protesting
against the plans for a contest. 'I *believe* all he does is strictly in harmony
with what he *believes* to be right. He may be mistaken', he added.
'[But] we are all liable to be & I believe him to be an honest man.'[64]
Should the contest really go to the polls, he went on, he would split his
votes between Northcote and Acland. Possibly, similar considerations
prompted Chichester of Hale to deplore a contest. Or it might possibly
have been his reluctance to offend the various other Liberal squires and
peers in the division. In any event, as Northcote's agent explained,
unless Chichester could be induced to support Walrond the votes of his
tenants would be doubly lost for they would be cast for Acland.[65] Nor
was Colonel Fane, Conservative Member for South Hampshire,
enthusiastic at the prospect of a contest. Ostensibly, however, his
reasons were not his own but those he attributed to others. 'I am very
strongly of the opinion', he wrote to Northcote, 'that with the great
influence of Fortescue, Portsmouth, Poltimore, & F. Davie, and others
not to mention the Acland that the success of any such attempt was to
say the least of it doubtful.'[66] The men he mentioned were all Liberals.
Thus, discounting the possibility that Acland would head the poll —
and this was never mentioned — Fane was saying that the influence of
these men would be felt in the numbers of Conservatives they induced
not to vote against Acland — to vote either for Northcote alone or for
Northcote and Acland, in effect, to vote *against* Walrond. But, he went
on, if others insisted on a contest he would agree to use his own
influence 'to forward the views of "the party" '. His choice of words is
significant. They illustrate the fact that there were not one but two
contests going on in the county, the one between Conservatives and
Liberals, the other between those Conservatives who were and those
who were not willing to use their individual influences 'to forward the
views of "the party" '. The former were presumably those who
belonged to the newly organized North Devonshire Conservative
Registration Association.[67] The results of these two contests can be seen
in the final poll.

Northcote (C)	3,967
Acland (L)	3,898
Walrond (C)	3,520

It was presumably Northcote's attitude that his son expressed when, after the contest was over, he observed to his mother that it was too bad it had ever taken place. But, he added, 'we can at least pride ourselves at the thought of how patriotic & unselfish ... [Northcote's] conduct has been in consenting to fight; and how differently and how far more nobly he has behaved than men like the Lincolnshire candidates and others, who without in any way having earned a right to a seat at all have made most shameful compromises in order to avoid a contest.' [68] And while his seat had never been at stake the fact that no subsequent contest occurred in the division suggests that his son was right – that he had, indeed, 'earned' his seat.

VII

The things which the members of registration associations did were not very complex. But they required time, energy and organization. Thus, they encouraged the accumulation of effective political power into the hands of those who were willing both to devote the time and to tolerate the exigencies of organization. As Cox and Grady explained, in 1868, during the summer months those who were involved in registration were fairly busy. [69] But it all started in the late spring and lasted into the autumn. In the late spring the central manager for each party in each constituency was supposed to send the appropriate sections of the constituency register to his agents in each polling district. These sections of the register, they noted, should be marked to show how each voter had voted at the last election or, if he had not voted, what his politics were supposed to be. It was then the duty of the district agent, assisted by his committee, to correct these lists, to make a list of the persons who had become qualified, indicating their qualifications, any objections that might be brought against their qualifications, and, of course, 'their probable politics, with the influences to which they are likely to be subjected', and to return both lists to the central manager by the end of June. Then the central manager was supposed to distribute the forms on which the new claimants might enter their claims. These forms were to be taken to the claimants 'personally' and, once filled out, taken to the overseers 'personally' by 20 July. On 1 August the lists of the claimants were published. The district agents then had 25 days in which to prepare their objections to their opponents' claims. On 1 September the lists of the objections were published. It was then the district agents' responsibility to obtain the information necessary to defend the rights of their own supporters to vote and to arrange for their attendance at the revising barrister's court. These courts were convened in late September or early October.

In many constituencies, by the fifties and sixties, the results of all this activity were published in the local press. But whether published in the press and, as in North Warwickshire, accompanied by the triumphant declaration, 'The Liberals are now a majority of 59!' or communicated privately, the assumptions by which the results were appraised were the same: first, that those who were involved in the registration process knew the political identities of those on whom they reported; and, second, that these identities were fixed. Thus, using the poll book for the last contest as a point of reference, it was possible each year to estimate the new balance of power. In 1846, for example, in North Northamptonshire, the point of reference was 1837. As Earl Fitzwilliam noted, in that year Viscount Maidstone, the weaker of the Tory candidates, defeated Viscount Milton by 397 votes, 1,801 to 1,404. According to Fitzwilliam's calculations, in consequence of deaths and departures Maidstone's majority among the voters who polled in 1837 had been reduced to 255. In consequence of new registrations in the Soke of Peterborough it had been reduced further to 155. There was therefore the question whether, in the context of the possible dissolution of Parliament, those 'little gains' which he had heard had been made in other parts of the division 'amount all together to 155'. It was this question he put to John Gotch, a Liberal banker in Kettering. And, he added, 'What was the temper of the loose voters?'[76] Gotch's reply to these questions was presumably not encouraging. In any event, no contest occurred in the division when Parliament was finally dissolved in 1847.

Such logic of appraisal was basic to the system. Indeed, so basic was it, so standardized the terms in which prospective victory was assumed to be measurable, that printed forms were available both for the reports which many registration agents made annually to their employers and for the reports of the pre-election canvasses. As a rule, 'Summaries of Revision' forms contained spaces in which, for each parish in each polling district, entries could be made of the numbers of Conservatives and Liberals who had died, who had moved away or otherwise lost their qualifications, who had been registered for the first time, and who had been striken from the register. Furthermore – and, presumably, to provide a check upon the efficiency of the registration agents – they also contained spaces where, for each parish, entries could be made of the numbers of Conservatives and Liberals for whom claims had been made but not sustained, and the numbers against whom objections had been made but not sustained. On such 'Summaries of Revision' forms the 'neutral' category was not recognized. The reason is obvious: neutrality made no sense in the context of registration; it only made sense in the context of a particular contest among particular candidates. Thus, the category was included on the forms used for the pre-election canvasses. But 'Summaries of Revision' forms did contain spaces where the same information could be entered about men whose politics were 'Doubtful' as could be entered about 'Conservatives' and 'Liberals'. These categories are significant as indications of the ways the men who used them understood the world in which they lived. But the growing proportions of the 'Doubtful' voters are even more significant as indications of the reasons why the world they claimed to understand was ceasing to exist.

Par excellence, the 'neutral' voter was the non-party man, the man who cast a single vote, or only two votes, in circumstances in which, from a party point of view, it might have been hoped that he would cast two or three. What distinguished him from his Liberal or Conservative neighbours was the lack of correspondence between his concerns and theirs. Presumably, however, both his own concerns and the reasons for them could be discovered. In effect, his own prospective impact could clearly be calculated, and calculated in terms which mid-century election managers were supposed to understand.

But the same was not true of the 'doubtful' voter. He was the man whose prospective behaviour could not be specified. Furthermore, whatever the reasons for this in any given case – whether the 'doubtful' voter was not a member of a definable group or network, or not a member of a group or network which the existing political cadres knew how to reach: and, of course, from their point of view it was six of one and half-a-dozen of the other – the solution to the problem he represented was generally sought not in his 'opinions' but in the networks of influence in which it was assumed he must have been enmeshed. In effect, the 'doubtful' voter was the man whose sociological identity had yet to be discovered. Presumably, in view of the ease with which the necessary identity might be acquired if sufficient money or other inducement were offered, such a definition was not inappropriate. If this be the case then there is a basic distortion of both the mid-century political system and the changes taking place within it, in the suggestion that mid-century politicians could not have known the things they needed to know about the world in which they lived because Dr Gallup had not yet been born.[71]

The usefulness of the procedures which Dr Gallup and others have fashioned to measure the opinions and thus predict the behaviour of present-day voters is undeniable. But those who contend that without Dr Gallup's procedures nineteenth century politicians must have been working in the dark have obviously failed to note that these procedures are the means by which it is hoped that the limitations of the evidence imposed by the secret ballot might be overcome. In effect, when Gladstone explained to the Queen, in 1886, that he had 'no skill in . . . [electoral] matters', he was not describing what was 'typical' of the pre-psephological age.[72] He was in most things *sui generis*. But if others by the mid-eighties were finding that they, too, had 'no skill in such matters' this was only because that world in which the skills they had were useful was ceasing to exist. Within the new world the skills and concepts which Dr Gallup has helped to fashion might be essential. Within the old world, however, there were other skills which were far more useful because they not only provided means of prediction but means of control. These were the skills to which the tardy Liberal canvasser in North Devonshire implicitly referred, in 1868, while expressing the hope that he would be forgiven his tardiness. His report was apparently several days overdue when he wrote to say he had almost finished and added – almost making his tardiness seem intentional, 'I shall probably be able tomorrow to secure through the influence of others some of the doubtful voters.' [73] These were the skills to which the Liberal agent in West Cornwall implicitly referred, also in 1868, when he tried to assure Arthur Pendarves Vivian that he would not let the efforts of certain misguided Liberals jeopardize his return. Apparently, the members of certain of the local Liberal registration committees were trying to register men whose politics were 'doubtful' but who, they believed, could be induced to 'go right'. As the agent explained, however, 'With my knowledge of the views of the different landed proprietors and other influential persons who could bring – should there be an opposition – adverse influences to bear, I am able to correct this over zeal.' [74] These skills remained useful as long as the situation which Cox and Grady described continued: '. . . at the close of an active canvass, the residuum of the unpromised was usually so small that on making up the canvass books the manager was enabled to forecast with tolerable accuracy the result of the election.' But when the numbers of the 'unpromised', or of the irreducibly 'doubtful' – for the two terms were effectively synonymous – passed the critical point the whole set of procedures became useless: those which Butt recommended in 1826; those which Cox and Grady recommended later; and those which were designed, as Cox and Grady put it, 'to enable the candidate to ascertain what were his chances of success'.

Those who worked the system presumably understood it. But there is sparse evidence to illustrate the system as they saw it. While poll books are numerous few canvassing books have been found and few of the notes which election managers wrote or received. These were evidently working papers which, if kept beyond the end of the contest to which they were relevant, were rarely kept beyond one or another subsequent waste paper drive. But where they have been found they reveal the intensity of that concern for the networks of relationship and power which is also revealed in the correspondence of such men as

Northcote. In the aggregate, this evidence explains why poll books were publishable and why in the period immediately following the first Reform Act quite a lot of uncontested elections occurred, quite a lot of seats changed hands without contests at the polls, and rather few contests occurred without seats changing hands. By the same token, it helps to explain why, as time went by, fewer uncontested elections occurred, fewer seats changed hands without contests at the polls, more contests occurred without seats changing hands, and why, ultimately, poll books became unpublishable.

Obviously, when the Liberal canvasser in Cullompton, North Devonshire, reported, in 1868, that Thomas Grant was one of Thomas Walrond's tenants, he was explaining why Grant's prospective votes were being credited to the Conservative candidates.[75] Obviously, when he reported that Richard Burrow was employed by a certain Mr Mortimore, and was thus 'afraid to vote', he was explaining why no prospective votes had been entered for Burrow at all.[76] The relationships which these bits of information reveal are fairly simple. In the town of Honiton things were possibly a bit more complicated. According to one report which the Liberal agent received, the Hon. Colin Lindsay, of Sillwood, Brighton, would be able to overcome certain adverse influences in the town if he could be induced to bring his own influence to bear upon his tenants in the town.[77] According to another report, a certain Sam Pyle was going round the town telling everyone that Walrond was 'a friend of the Squire's'.[78] Possibly, the squire to whom this second report referred was Lindsay. Possibly, he was the man whose influence Lindsay's influence might be expected to counteract. From the available evidence the question cannot be answered. All that is clear is the assumption which the various reports imply, that the men who received the information which the reports contain would know how to use it. Possibly they did. This is suggested by the two reports which the Conservative committee in South West Yorkshire received, in 1868, concerning the parish of Thornhill. A month before polling the committee was told that 45 men from the parish had promised to vote for the Conservative candidates and 20 for the Liberals. Of the 22 remaining, who were described as 'Doubtful', they were told that 'about 5 will be Cons[ervative] but if *Searle* does not interfere more than 5, perhaps $\frac{1}{2}$'.[79] Presumably, whatever the identity of the potent Searle, to report the probable consequence of his prospective 'interference' was to mobilize whatever influences might curtail his 'interference' or counteract it. In any event, three weeks later the committee was told that things had improved in Thornhill. The number of Conservative promises claimed from the parish had risen to 62. The number of Liberal promises recognized from the parish had dropped to 13.[80]

VIII

The recommendations contained in the various electoral handbooks are important because of the assumptions they reveal. But far more important is the evidence of the implementation of these recommendations, that contained in the various surviving canvassing books and, in particular, that contained in three memoranda composed by the Conservative agents in South West Yorkshire, the first in 1868, the second in 1874, the third in 1880, and in certain ancillary figures. These memoranda and figures reconfirm the use that was made of the recommendations. In addition, they reveal the crucial fact that, at least from the point of view of the Conservatives in South West Yorkshire, the proportions of the effectively doubtful voters had so increased *before* 1867 that the procedures recommended by Butt in 1826 and by Cox and Grady later as means of forecasting the result of a prospective contest were ceasing to be relevant.

For the procedures recommended by Butt and Cox and Grady to be relevant the proportions of the doubtful voters would have to be small. Most voters would have to behave as members of definable groups or networks. As long as they did so the ability of an election manager 'to forecast with tolerable accuracy the result of the election' was a simple function of the accuracy of the information which the canvassers were used to gather. These were the conditions which Dudley Baxter and his successors as Conservative agent in South West Yorkshire assumed. In trying to ascertain their candidates' chances of success they depended principally upon two sets of figures, those for the total numbers of registered electors in the constituency and those for the numbers of promises their canvassers reported. They allowed for a certain rate of absenteeism. They also allowed for a certain proportional loss on promises. But in all cases the proportional loss on promises for which they allowed was smaller than the assumed rate of absenteeism. Clearly, they assumed that most of the absentees would be Liberals – that the various nexus to which the Conservativism of the Conservative voters should be attributed would be stronger than those to which the Liberalism of the Liberal voters should be attributed. Then they subtracted the Conservative promises thus reduced from the total registered electorate. In their eyes the remainder represented the maximum number of votes which the Liberal candidates could possibly receive. If the remainder was smaller than the number of promises which their own canvassers reported – this reduced, of course, by the proportional loss on promises – they assumed that victory was assured. Significantly, in performing these calculations they totally ignored both the numbers of prospective voters who had been reported as

'Doubtful' and the numbers who were 'Unaccounted for' at the end of their canvass.

In 1868, in a memorandum drafted while the voters were trooping to the polls, Baxter outlined four sets of possible circumstances. In the first he assumed 22 per cent absenteeism and a 10 per cent loss on promises. In the second he again assumed 22 per cent absenteeism but only five per cent loss on promises. In the third he assumed 25 per cent absenteeism and a five per cent loss on promises. In the fourth he assumed 20 per cent absenteeism and again a five per cent loss on promises. With absenteeism at 22 per cent the effective electorate would have been roughly 15,600. With absenteeism at 25 per cent it would have been roughly 15,000. With absenteeism at 20 per cent it would have been roughly 16,000. Against these figures he applied the 8,700 promises which his canvassers had reported. 'We have 8700 promises,' he wrote.

> Our usual experience has been that we poll within 5% of our promises. At the last election exceptionally we lost 11 $\frac{1}{4}$. If we were now to lose 10% it would leave us polling only 7830 this deducted from the total Riding [assuming twenty-two per cent absentees] would leave for our opponents 7770 giving us a majority of 53. [sic!] These are the most unfavourable circumstances. If on the other hand we poll within 5% as our usual practice has been we shall poll 8265 which would only leave our opponents 7335 & give us a majority of 930.
>
> The most favourable circumstances are that 25% do not poll & that we still poll within 5% of our promises. This would make the total polling only 15,000. Deduct from this our poll 8265 it leaves 6735 for our opponents & gives us a majority of 1520.[81]

Then, assuming 20 per cent absenteeism – this the average between the low of 15 per cent in 1835 and the high of 25 per cent in 1848 – he concluded that in such a circumstance, if no more than five per cent of those who had promised to vote for the Conservative candidates failed to do so, Spencer Stanhope would have a majority of 400 and Starkie would have a majority of 258.

If Baxter's memorandum is any indication, the Conservatives in South West Yorkshire were convinced they would win in 1868. At the polls, Stanhope, their leading candidate, was not badly beaten – by only eight votes. But in comparison with Baxter's expectations his loss was severe (see table 23)[82].

With the assumption of a 10 per cent loss on promises the same formula was used in 1874. Then it worked – at least with respect to the numbers of votes which the Conservative candidates received. As Baxter's successor noted on the morning of polling, there were 22,380 names on the register. If 20 per cent did not poll that would make for

Table 23

*A comparison between the figures in the Conservative canvassers' final reports in
South West Yorkshire, in 1868, and the polls as declared by the sheriff*

	Registered or polled	Stanhope	Starkie	Milton	Beaumont	Doubtful or neutral	Dead	Unaccounted for
Canvassers reports	19,908	8,693	8,435	6,960	6,766	1,452	165	1,890
Poll	15,951	7,935	7,621	8,110	7,943			
Percentage of absentees and agent's errors	20	+8.7	+9.6	−16.5	−17.4			

an effective electorate of 17,904. Half of these were 8,952. If 895 were
added to this – these being the 'ten per cent for those who, having
promised, do not poll' – 9,874 promises would be required 'to insure
success', or, rounding off the figure, '10,000 promises will secure the
seats'. Since Stanhope and Starkie, the same candidates as in 1868, had
10,749 and 10,712 promises, respectively, he had every reason to be
confident. As he noted, a 10 per cent loss on promises would leave
Stanhope with 9,674 votes, a 10 per cent loss on promises would leave
Starkie with 9,641. Nor were his calculations far off. Stanhope received
9,705 votes, 31 more than he anticipated. Starkie received 9,639, two
less than he anticipated.[83] They were both returned. Starkie had a
majority of 1,374 over W. H. Leatham, the stronger Liberal, a majority
of 1,501 over H. F. Beaumont, the weaker Liberal. However, Leatham
and Beaumont perhaps received rather more votes than the agent
expected them to receive. The full figures which the canvassers
reported are not available for 1874 as they are for 1868 and 1880. But in
an undated memorandum headed 'Estimate of Polling', the
Conservative agent grossly underestimated the numbers of votes his
opponents would receive. Leatham received 48 per cent more votes
than he estimated and Beaumont 42 per cent.[84]

The same formula was used again in 1880. But on this occasion it was
a total failure. As the Conservative agent noted, there were now 26,328
names on the register. If 20 per cent did not vote that would make an
effective electorate of roughly 21,128. Half of these, he noted, were
10,564. Adding, 1,050, this being the '10 per cent for those who having
promised do not poll', he concluded that 11,614 promises were
'required to win'. In the light of the fact that Stanhope and Starkie had
12,368 and 12,236 promises, respectively, there was again every reason

to be confident. Assuming a 10 per cent loss on promises the agent observed that Stanhope's 12,368 promises should be worth 11,132 votes, that Starkie's 12,236 promises should be worth 11,012 votes.[85] But these promises – or ostensible promises – notwithstanding, the Conservative candidates were soundly beaten. In part, the agent's errors were caused by absenteeism being at only 18 per cent instead of the 20 per cent he anticipated. Principally, however, they were caused by significantly fewer voters polling for Stanhope and Starkie than the canvassers reported would do so, significantly more voters polling for Fitzwilliam and Leatham, the Liberal candidates, than they reported would do so. The proportional errors were rather greater in 1880 than they had been in 1868 (see table 24).[86] What was, presumably, the

Table 24

A comparison between the figures in the Conservative canvassers' final reports in South West Yorkshire, in 1880, and the polls as declared by the sheriff

	Registered or polled	Stanhope	Starkie	Fitzwilliam	Leatham	Doubtful or neutral	Dead	Unaccounted for
Canvassers' reports	26,328	12,368	12,236	8,558	8,613	1,857	480	1,348
Polled	21,587	10,391	10,020	11,385	11,181			
Percentage of absentees and agent's errors	18	+15.9	+18.9	−33.0	−29.8			

agent's explanation of these errors can be read in his postscript to his memorandum. After the votes had been counted he noted that Stanhope's actual poll of 10,391, was 'exceptionally a loss of 16% instead of 10% on the promises'.[87] His emphasis upon the exceptional nature of these losses suggests his belief that circumstances might soon return to normal. But his description of his calculations as those based on 'the old system' suggests the opposite. Indeed, for him to use such a phrase at a time when many men were questioning the viability of the traditional forms of electoral organization and the traditional mechanisms of electoral appeal suggests that he, too, may have realized that the circumstances on which 'the old system' had been based had gone forever.

IX

After 1868 the growth in the proportions of the doubtful voters was sometimes treated as if it were solely due to the enfranchising provisions of the second Reform Act. In South West Yorkshire, for example, after 1868, the Conservative agents claimed to know the political identities of a far larger proportion of the men who were qualified to vote in respect of what were sometimes called the 'old qualifications' than they did of the men whose qualifications derived from the second Reform Act. This is apparent from their reports of the effects of electoral registration upon the balance of power within the constituency. After the Derby-Disraeli Reform Bill passed the Conservative agents reported the effects of electoral revision under two heads, the one having to do with the effects of revision upon the 'old qualifications' list, the other having to do with the gross balance of power on the 'twelve pound occupier' list. The agents were not themselves responsible for the existence of these separate lists. The two categories of voters were distinguished from one another on the registers. But the agents were responsible for the use they made of this distinction in the annual reports they made to their employers. As the proportions of the admittedly doubtful voters on the 'twelve pound occupier' list suggests, it was no longer possible to estimate the balance of power in the constituency with any degree of assurance.

In 1869, Baxter only really reported on the effects of revision upon the 'old qualifications' list. This was presumably in part a measure of the fact that the effects of revision upon this list were enough, ostensibly, to alter the balance of power which the contest of 1868 had revealed. Applying the same logic that Fitzwilliam had applied earlier in North Northamptonshire, Baxter observed that in 1868 Beaumont, the weaker Liberal candidate, had only beaten Stanhope, the stronger Conservative candidate, by eight votes. According to his report, among those on the 'old qualification' list the Conservatives had a net gain of 231.[xx] He reported no more about the effects of revision upon the 'twelve pound occupier' list than that the Conservatives enjoyed a 'gain of 100' upon it. The roundness of this figure alone makes it somewhat suspect. But the possibility arises that had he provided information in 1869 about the men on this list comparable to that which he and his successors provided about them later he would have had to admit, at least by implication, that he was not as sure as he pretended to be that the Conservatives were now a majority on the register as a whole. This is suggested by the fact that the following year, when his report covered both the political complexion of the men on the 'twelve pound occupier' list and the specific effects of revision upon the 'old qualifications' list, the number of the doubtful

on the 'twelve pound occupier' list was far larger than the majority he
had previously claimed. According to his report in 1869, the doubtful
only constituted some four per cent of the men on the 'old
qualifications' list whose new claims had been sustained before the
revising barrister or whose old claims had been struck off. Between
1870 and 1879 the proportions of such men whom he and his successors
described as doubtful never exceeded five per cent of the totals. Such
would presumably be a rough indication of the total proportions of the
men on this list about whom the agents were willing to admit their
ignorance. But in 1870 almost 20 per cent of the men on the 'twelve
pound occupier' list fell into the doubtful category. In subsequent years
the proportions of the doubtful on this list never fell below 25 per cent.
Clearly, according to these agents, the second Reform Act had
destroyed the grounds on which they might have forecast the outcome
of a contest (see table 25).[89]

Table 25

*Figures included in the reports of the Conservative agents in South West Yorkshire
concerning the results of electoral revision and the political complexion of the £12
occupiers, 1869–79*

'Old Qualifications'

	'New Claims Sustained'			'Old Claims Struck Off'			
Year	'Conservatives'	'Radicals'	'Doubtfuls'	'Conservatives'	'Radicals'	'Doubtfuls'	% of 'Doubtfuls'
1869	843	834	84	595	817	44	4.0
1870	700	568	62	374	564	51	4.8
1873	820	567	10	561	540	64	2.9
1875	629	613	63	487	494	22	3.7
1877	821	618	21	524	538	37	2.3
1878	997	686	32	499	565	11	1.5
1879	1,038	802	32	565	566	22	1.8

'Twelve Pound Occupiers'

Year	'Conservatives'	'Radicals'	'Doubtfuls'	% of 'Doubtfuls'
1870	2,457	2,303	1,126	19.2
1873	2,469	2,130	2,112	31.4
1875	3,496	1,958	1,850	25.4
1878	2,731	1,595	2,577	37.3
1879	3,001	1,817	3,281	40.7

Apparently, the procedure which these agents used in distinguishing between the two lists of voters, those who qualified in respect of pre-1868 qualifications, and those who had been enfranchised by the second Reform Act, was not unique. The same procedure was used by the Reverend Henry Fox Strangeways, in 1882, while submitting his report on the political complexion of the voters in Silverston parish in North Devonshire to the Liberal registration agent of the Cullompton polling district. Furthermore, in North Devonshire as in South West Yorkshire, the procedure reveals the same differential claims of knowledge. As Strangeways explained in the covering letter which accompanied his report, he had corrected both the 'old electors' and the 'new electors' lists by indicating who had died or otherwise left the parish and the 'probable politics' of those remaining. But, he went on, he was not as confident of his conclusions about the 'new electors' list as he was about the other. 'We do not know much [about them],' he explained, 'and only draw our conclusions about their opinions from their associations and from the influence that is likely to be brought to bear upon them.'[90] The formula was, of course, traditional and standard. What was neither traditional nor standard was the admission that the formula might not provide an accurate guide to the 'opinions' of certain voters, the admission that their behaviour might not be predictable in terms of the factors for which the formula implicitly allowed.

But the second Reform Act should not be asked to explain too much – especially when that which the Act is asked to explain is not used to explain the Act itself.[91] Undoubtedly, the enfranchisement of the £12 occupiers aggravated – perhaps *greatly* aggravated – the difficulties which election managers in the counties faced. But in some cases, at least, the procedures by which election managers tried to forecast the outcome of a contest had already begun to lose their relevance before the Derby-Disraeli Reform Bill was passed: an $11\frac{1}{4}$ per cent loss on promises was more than half way between the 5 per cent which had been 'usual' and the 16 and 19 per cents suffered in 1880. Presumably, the explanation lies in part in certain objective changes in the structure of English society which might be attributed to population movement, urbanization and industrialization. Presumably, certain traditional nexus were becoming weaker. Presumably, the tendency for different categories of nexus – e.g., economic, religious and geographic – to re-enforce one another was declining. But presumably the weakening of these nexus was in part the consequence of the working of the system: not only was it the election manager's job to mobilize favourable influences; it was also his job to use the favourable as a means of weakening the unfavourable. Nor should we ignore the fact that local political organization was, apparently, most highly developed where the information which organization was designed to gather was obviously least useful, where its own development would obviously tend to distort the accuracy of this information, and where its own development would obviously tend to weaken the groups or networks whose very existence provided the rationale of organization. The varieties of information which canvassers were used to gather would presumably have been most appropriate in a constituency such as Dorsetshire, less appropriate in a constituency such as the West Riding of Yorkshire, and still less appropriate in a constituency such as the City of London. Ostensibly, however, in 1860, Liberal canvassing was 'constant' in the City of London; ostensibly, in 1868, the Conservative canvassers in South West Yorkshire reached all but 1,890 of the 19,743 registered and living voters; and as late as 1880 there were no political organizations at all in Dorsetshire. The paradox is a further measure of the importance of that corporate and hierarchical model of society which provided the logic of John Stuart Mill's opposition to the secret ballot,[92] which made effective legislation against electoral 'corruption' a practical impossibility,[93] and which made Cox and Grady declare that 'organization' was needed as never before when, following the second Reform Act, many election managers were, as they observed, at a loss to know how the new voters could be 'approached, . . . influenced, . . . [and] won'.[94] The principal functions of the organizations they then went on to describe were not those of appealing to the voters *qua* voters. Rather, they were those of identifying the voters in terms of the groups and networks to which, ostensibly, they belonged. Quite simply, to many men that socio-political world was incomprehensible in which significant proportions of the voters could *not* be recruited through the agencies which organization, as they understood it, was designed to reach and mobilize. In particular, these points are important because they help to describe that partly remembered, partly imagined, world which provided the essential frame of reference of reform legislation in the sixties as in the thirties; because they suggest an additional dynamic of political change which the parliamentary perspective has tended to obscure – that which derived from the simple working of the system; and because they help to explain why the establishment of mass-membership political organizations was so traumatic. Not only did the establishment of such organizations frequently involve the replacement of one body of elite by another. Their establishment occurred in the context of the unresolved question whether, failing traditional modes of electoral appeal based upon traditional varieties of collectivity, other modes could be developed which would forestall anarchy.

What the canvassers reported were the numbers of men who

acknowledged different leaders, the grounds on which they did so, and the grounds on which they might be induced to acknowledge others. To exploit these latter grounds was the road to power. But, of course, a too effective exploitation jeopardized the very system in which such power obtained. The basic instability of the system, that which made 'Finality Jack' Russell's sobriquet something of a joke, derived from the fact which, presumably, every successful election manager thoroughly understood, that all groups and networks were more or less contingent, that all voters were 'doubtful' until proved otherwise. To men who believed that the traditional structure of the society was 'good', that any other structure was 'bad' – or, more to the point, that no other structure was possible – the phenomena which the apparent growth in the numbers of irreducibly 'doubtful' voters reflected was the evidence of a clear and present danger. It was such a danger that Disraeli implicitly referred to when, in 1863, he declared that the government of the kingdom could not be carried on except by the 'united aid and agency' of what were, from certain points of view, non-*political* institutions.[95]

Unfortunately, with the evidence presently available, the growth in the numbers of effectively 'doubtful' voters cannot be chronicled precisely. Thus, the relative importance of the various factors which, in all probability, were responsible for its growth cannot be specified. From the evidence available for South West Yorkshire, however, it appears that the reports of the Conservative canvassers were very much more reliable before 1865 than after, somewhat more reliable in 1868 than in 1865, possibly more reliable in 1874 than in 1868 – but possibly not, and much less reliable in 1880 than they had ever been before. Furthermore – and confirming the thrust of this evidence, it would appear that in 1868, when the greatest detail is available, their reports were least reliable in those polling districts which contained the largest numbers of voters – in effect, in the urban districts – and, among these, least reliable in those in which, subsequently, Liberal majorities were largest (See table 26).[96] Significantly, in almost all cases, the Conservative canvassers *over*-reported promises of support for the Conservative candidates and *under*-reported promises of support for the Liberal candidates.

Such tendencies were nothing new. Nor were they restricted to South West Yorkshire. At the by-election in East Gloucestershire, in 1854, for example, the Conservative canvassers reported that the Conservative candidate would receive 273 *more* votes than he received, that the Liberal candidate would receive 259 *fewer* votes than he received.[97] Nor, again, would this occasion much surprise: they would be attributed to partisan enthusiasm. But the crucial point is this: few if any efforts were made to *compensate* for these tendencies; but various

Table 26

A comparison of the relative reliability of the Conservative canvassers' reports for the different polling districts in South West Yorkshire in 1868, distinguishing those districts in which the Conservative candidates received majorities of the votes cast from those in which the Liberal candidates received majorities of the votes cast, and showing, for each polling district, the numbers of promises which the canvassers reported for Stanhope, the leading Conservative candidate, and for Milton, the leading Liberal candidate, the numbers of votes each received, and the percentage errors of the canvassers

	Stanhope				Milton			
	Promises	Votes	Differences	% Error	Promises	Votes	Differences	% Error
Conservative polling districts								
Doncaster	757	671	+86	11.4	621	632	−11	1.7
Penistone	308	302	+6	1.9	88	100	−12	13.6
Sheffield	1,420	1,235	+185	13.0	922	999	−77	8.3
Thorne	398	362	+36	9.0	166	183	−17	10.2
Wakefield	1,345	1,231	+114	8.4	655	718	−63	9.6
	4,228	3,801	+427	11.2	2,452	2,632	−180	6.9
Liberal polling districts								
Barnsley	690	686	+4	0.6	752	751	+1	0.0
Dewsbury	833	795	+38	4.5	927	1,127	−200	21.5
Dobcross	487	416	+71	14.5	438	419	+19	4.3
Holmfirth	415	386	+29	7.0	483	528	−35	7.2
Huddersfield	1,020	979	+41	4.0	888	1,138	−250	28.2
Scissett	267	207	+60	22.4	297	348	−51	17.1
Rotherham	443	383	+60	13.5	497	854	−357	71.8
Wath	310	282	+28	9.0	226	313	−87	38.4
	4,465	4,134	+331	8.0	4,498	+5,478	−1,010	18.5

suggestions were made for *controlling* them. According to Cox and Grady, it was in part because the information which many canvassers gathered was more optimistic than accurate that many candidates endured 'expense and disappointment' from which, otherwise, they would have been spared.[98] As a means of preventing such errors they suggested that canvassers be required to record their informants' statements both *in extenso* and *verbatim* and, further, that the information which each canvasser gathered be identified with his initials when it was transcribed from his own canvassing book into the book kept by the committee which supervised his efforts 'in order', as they explained, 'that if any question should thereafter arise, the source of the information may be at once referred to'.[99] Obviously, had anyone really tried to apply their suggestions he would have been drowned in the consequent floods of ink and recrimination. But no one who understood the essential nature of the problem would have tried to do so. Cox and Grady's suggestions are further evidence of the premises on which the mid-century political system was based. But the problem itself is evidence of the nature of the factors which were changing or destroying this system. Presumably, principal among these factors were the continuing processes of urbanization and industrialization. Undoubtedly, the accelerating movement of population from the relatively stable communities of the countryside to the relatively unstable communities of the towns – or to the anomie of many urban situations, and the growing impersonality of relationship which obtained in many of the newer and larger economic enterprises, were tending to weaken the various traditional deference communities and deference networks. But there was also an important and somewhat independent institutional component in this process. It was this to which Robert Leader, editor of the *Sheffield Independent,* implicitly referred in 1865, when he observed that unless two Liberal candidates were found in South West Yorkshire who would both go to the polls the local Liberals would become despondent, the Liberal organization would atrophe, and the Liberal registration would 'go to the dogs'.[100]

A contest was an important source of wealth to many of those involved in it, except, of course, the poor candidates and those of their friends who helped them pay the bills. Undoubtedly, for this reason alone many contests occurred. But when election managers and the canvassers on which they depended could do so much to affect the outcome of a contest, their tendency to encourage contests was, presumably, a measure not only of their avarice but of their pride. In such circumstances the failure to encourage a contest was tantamount to an admission of professional incompetence. Then, too, when the failure to mount a contest on one occasion made it difficult to win a contest on another by discouraging those men without whose help a contest could not be won, the occurrence of a contest was clearly in part the price which candidates were forced to pay for the continued support of those whose support they required and whose support could not otherwise be had. In effect, it was necessary to mount a contest to be able to mount a contest. And to mount a contest was not only to exercise – and thus, in certain cases, to strengthen – the ties of influence and deference. In many cases it was to weaken these ties. There are obvious sociological reasons for the editorial statement in the *Cambridge Chronicle,* in 1868, 'Contested elections should be avoided'.[101]

8

Issues and social cohesion

I

The correspondence between constituencies, interest groups and deference communities which came into being after 1832 presumably helped to solve the related problems of confidence, cohesion and social discipline. But if it helped to solve these problems it only did so by confirming the validity of the fears which many anti-reformers and some reformers had expressed during the reform debates to the effect that politics would become dangerously polarized if constituencies were defined in terms of interests. That such had in fact occurred was the thrust of Russell's argument while introducing his Reform Bill of 1854. Indeed, while his analysis of the process was somewhat superficial the process provided the essential rationale of his Bill. As he explained, the Act of 1832 had 'tended to divide the country in a way it was not divided before; in short, into opposite camps according as the districts might be connected with land or trade.' And, he went on, with the events of the previous decade obviously in mind, 'Since the passing of the Act we have seen — what had not occurred before — we have seen county Members too generally exclusive in respect of the interest they cared for, and Members for the great cities too exclusive also for theirs.'[1] Obviously, as Russell saw it, the corn law crisis had been a crisis of confrontation between rival interests; the intensity of the crisis had been a measure of the degree to which these interests were separated from one another into different constituencies. To correct this 'defect' of the Act — as such he described it — he proposed to make the various constituencies, the county constituencies in particular, more heterogeneous: he proposed to introduce elements into their respective electorates which, he observed, would alter the 'special character' of their representatives.[3] In substance, by 1854 Russell had come to believe that the constituency structure which the members of the Grey Ministry had tried to create and which is principally symbolized by their initial borough freeholder clause was not really viable. The corn law crisis had revealed its 'defect'.

Russell's comments throw considerable light upon the nature of the mid-century political system in general and the corn law crisis in particular. From these comments themselves, however, there is still the question of whether he really understood this system, thus whether he really understood the problems with which he was trying to deal. Like most of his contemporaries he seems to have assumed that groups or interests were *a priori* entities. But this they were not. In large measure they were social and ideological constructs, functions of the abilities of the different local elites to legitimize their roles, functions of the willingness of others to acknowledge their rights to perform these roles. Concerned to reduce the intensity of interest-group rivalry in Parliament, he proposed that men be qualified to vote in the different constituencies who were not themselves members of the deference communities on which these constituencies were based. But in the light of the amendments which had been made to the Bill on 19 and 20 August 1831, and in the light of the behaviour of the urban leaders in Birmingham and Leicester, two questions arise: to what extent was the 'defect' a defect of the Act; and, to what extent was it the consequence of the tendency of men to focus their electoral energies within 'their own' constituencies – constituencies they helped to make 'their own' when they focussed their energies without them. The registration of voters was not automatic. Even more to the point, the effective identities of the voters were neither unconditional nor predetermined. As Russel realized, the intensity of the corn law crisis was largely the consequence of the constituency framework which came into being after 1832. What he failed to realize – or at least to mention – was the degree to which this framework was the product not of the Act itself but the efforts of men in the different constituencies who registered certain potential voters and not others and who disseminated certain ideologies among the men they registered. Indeed, in all probability, the intransigence which Russell deplored and which he attributed to the first Reform Act is attributable rather less to the Act itself than to the efforts of men to do what no Act alone could do – legitimize their own social roles within the constituencies in which, principally, these roles were performed.

On two points most protectionists and repealers were agreed, first, that the corn laws not only raised agricultural prices but did so in significant fashion, and, second, that these prices benefited the landed interest. The principal question at issue between them was whether the prices were also a benefit to other interests. By and large, protectionists contended that the prices were a benefit to other interests, in particular, to the manufacturing interest. Their logic was simple: because the members of the landed interest were consumers of urban goods, and because their numbers were large, their prosperity guaranteed the prosperity of the producers of these goods. The repealers' logic was equally simple: because the corn laws raised the costs of domestic industrial production – high food prices required commensurately high wages – and because the corn laws prevented foreign agricultural producers from acquiring the credits in Britain which would enable them to buy more British goods, the corn laws limited the abilities of British industrialists to sell their goods abroad. Hence their conclusion: the sole beneficiaries of the corn laws were the owners of the lands which could not be cultivated at a profit except when prices were high and the owners of the other lands for which the rents were commensurately increased.

Generally, in discussions of the corn laws and corn law repeal these two positions have been played off against one another. The enactment of the Corn Law of 1815 has generally been explained in terms of the simple wish of the spokesmen of the landed interest to perpetuate the high prices of the war period, a wish which their power in Parliament allowed them to realize. Occasionally, the ultimate repeal of the corn laws has been explained in terms of that shift in the locus of power within the State which the first Reform Act ostensibly effected. More reasonably, it has been explained in terms of Peel's decision, that the corn laws would have to go, and the influence he was able to exercise among his parliamentary followers. But the question remains: when and why did he reach this decision? Clearly, he had decided by 1844 that if the corn laws were changed again they should be repealed.[4] Thus, as far as the principle is concerned, the failure of the Irish potato crop in 1845 was irrelevant. At most, the failure of the crop marked the time when the earlier decision was implemented. But even if the decision had been reached in the early forties, what were the grounds for it? In trying to answer this question historians have often made use of Peel's refusal to reply to Cobden's speech on the corn laws on 13 March 1845.[5] At some point while listening to this speech Peel crumpled the notes he was taking, turned to Sidney Herbert, and said, 'You must answer this, for I cannot.'[6] As previously Peel had generally replied to Cobden's speeches on the corn laws the significance of his behaviour seems clear: he had been convinced by the supposedly irrefutable logic of the urban repealers' case. But those who have used Peel's behaviour in 1845 to demonstrate this point have ignored an important fact: in 1845 Cobden was using a new argument, one to which Peel himself had significantly contributed. Before 1845 Cobden had generally argued that the corn laws should be repealed because, while they were a benefit to the landlords, they were an onerous burden to all other groups in the kingdom.[7] But in 1845 he criticised the corn laws because, as he put it, they had come to symbolize the hope that rural prosperity might be restored on the basis of price at a time when these prices themselves were being reduced by increments of production. In effect, before 1845 Cobden's arguments against the corn laws were the standard repealers' arguments. But in 1845 he criticised the corn laws not for raising domestic prices but for deterring domestic agriculturists from investing in agricultural improvements.[8] The points at issue in his new argument were implicit in Peel's 'Account of a Field Thorough-Drained, at Drayton, in Staffordshire', published in 1842.[9]

Both the changes in the logic of Cobden's criticisms of the corn laws and the importance of these changes have presumably been obscured by the constancy of his criticism. But, whatever the cause, the consequence has been unfortunate. As a rule, the relationship between the corn law question and the problems consequent to the developments of agricultural technology has also been obscured. Throughout the corn law period, while importations were marginal and the British population growing rapidly, prices were generally falling. Also, throughout the corn law period and beyond, while many British agriculturists complained of depression others increasingly boasted of their own prosperity. The explanation is obvious: the prices which caused many agriculturists to despair were largely the products of the increasing yields and lower costs which many of their neighbours were managing to achieve. Thus, as means of guaranteeing the prosperity of the countryside, protection against the *foreigner* was losing much of its relevance. Indeed, in the circumstances which derived from 'the second agricultural revolution' those who still complained of depression had but one alternative to bankruptcy: they had to adopt those technological innovations on which their neighbours' prosperity was increasingly based.[10] But there lay the rub. Many of these innovations were still·experimental; many of them could not be applied without considerable capital; furthermore, in many cases the existing laws and customs of rural society made this capital unavailable. And, again, many men feared – and quite rightly – that if the laws and customs of rural society were so altered as to make this capital available the very structure of the society which they were concerned to preserve would be destroyed. This was the structure whose political importance is revealed in the county poll books.

In view of the changes in the logic of Cobden's argument in 1845 we might ask whether, in fact, it was not Peel who 'converted' Cobden rather than Cobden who 'converted' Peel.[11] As Peel reported in his 'Account' of 1842, by draining the field he had managed both to avoid a fallow and to obtain a large crop of turnips. These turnips were important. In particular, they were fed to the sheep whose meat and wool commanded relatively high prices and whose manure was used to increase arable yields. But in the case Peel described these turnips were not obtained without considerable difficulty. The tenant had refused to drain the field himself. The field had only been drained after the tenant had agreed to give it up and Peel had taken it back into his own hands. Perhaps the tenant lacked the necessary capital. Drainage was expensive. Perhaps he lacked the confidence in the wisdom of 'thorough-drainage' which might have prompted him to use the capital he possessed. If so he was not alone. Indeed – and it helps to explain why the problems of rural prosperity were so difficult to solve, why Peel's efforts to solve these problems have been so widely misunderstood – many agriculturists subscribed to the doctrine articulated in 1838 when the English Agricultural Society, later the Royal Agricultural Society of England, was organized, that 'agricultural practice [was] . . . in every point of view a minor department of agriculture.' [12] The Society, of which Peel was a charter member, was organized to encourage such improvements. Its motto was 'Practice with Science'. Clearly, Peel was concerned to reap the benefits of such improvements himself. But he was not unconcerned about the problems which these benefits occasioned for those who failed to reap them. As he observed in his 'Account', he had wished to complete the drainage of the field as rapidly as possible 'for the purpose of encouraging others in my neighbourhood to follow my example'. [13] Clearly, it was the same concern which underlay those various provisions of his 'general scheme' of 1846 – as such he described it – by which he hoped to facilitate the general adoption of technological innovations by those agriculturists whose inabilities to adopt these innovations, or whose refusal to adopt them, were the principal causes of their own continuing economic difficulties. [14] And clearly, too, the reasons why these provisions were contained in his 'general scheme' are the reasons why their existence has been so generally ignored.

Obviously, in the eyes of many repealers and many protectionists the corn laws served either to raise domestic prices or to keep these prices from falling still further. But, the corn laws were obviously not working as these men believed. To note this point is not simply to 'discredit . . . the ability of contemporaries to understand their own affairs'. [15] Even more, it is to ask how, in the light of the existing circumstances their various statements should be understood. In particular, these circumstances are revealed by the fact that while some agriculturists were complaining bitterly of low prices others were not only boasting of their own prosperity but happily proclaiming to the world that they would still be prosperous were prices to fall even further.[16] Presumably, the answer to the question lies in the function, or functions, which their statements performed. Clearly, each agriculturist who focussed upon the foreign threat, and each manufacturer who focussed upon the corn laws, was thereby obscuring the degree to which the problems he faced were really the consequence of his own lack of technological sophistication, and thus could be solved by increasing that sophistication and by effecting those changes of relationship and role which might be required to apply the relevant innovations. He was proposing that legislation be used to solve a problem which legislation could scarcely touch – or, at least, which legislation could scarcely touch through the administrative mechanisms which were then available. Presumably, the efforts of these men to generate the political support which might be needed to secure this legislation helped to intensify the political divisions between borough and county. Presumably, their efforts helped to condition those assumptions concerning the decision-making process in Parliament in the post-reform period which are reflected in the often-repeated proposition that the Anti-Corn Law League was really responsible for the repeal of the corn laws. And presumably, whether or not these efforts served at the time to delay those changes of relationship and role which technological changes required – in effect, whether they delayed these very technological changes – they have helped to obscure the nature of the social problem from which the political problem derived.

In consequence of urbanization, industrialization, deflation, and the adoption of new productive techniques which deflation obviously encouraged, the traditional relationships within British society were being changed. These were the relationships on which the traditional agencies of electoral recruitment were based. Clearly, it was this problem which conditioned many demands for parliamentary reform. Clearly, it was this problem which conditioned the usual formulations of the corn law question. As a rule, in both town and countryside, the corn law question was formulated in such a way as to carry the burden of the argument according to which the growing problems of relationship between employers and employees, between landlords and tenants, were to be attributed, not to these relationships themselves, but to the relationships between the traditional aggregates of urban society on the one hand and the traditional aggregates of rural society on the other. In town and countryside the messages were different but functionally the same: for their own selfish reasons the rural leaders were using their political powers to perpetuate a policy which seriously inhibited urban prosperity; for their own selfish reasons the urban leaders were trying to alter this policy, thus threatening the residual prosperity of the countryside. These messages presumably helped to buttress the traditional agencies of electoral recruitment in town and countryside. By doing so they presumably helped to strengthen that polarization of politics between town and countryside which Russell deplored. However, while the intensity of this polarization made a solution to the corn law question essential, the solution that was sought in 1846 was not sought within the context of the premises which these messages reflect. Rather, it was sought within the context of those technological developments the importance of which has been obscured by these messages themselves.

The essence of the problem is apparent from the very beginning, from the arguments made at the time the Corn Law was passed in 1815. In 1813 the Committee on the Corn Trade recommended that no importations of foreign wheat be allowed until the domestic price reached 103s. per quarter ton. Underlying that recommendation was the concern to encourage domestic agriculturists to increase their investments in the land.[17] These investments were sought as a means of increasing domestic production, thus as a means both of lowering domestic prices and of reducing the general dependence upon those foreign suppliers whose occasional deficiencies of harvest had been responsible, in part, for the high prices of the war period.[18] But, in the context both of these prices themselves, and of the fact that the relationship between investment and productivity in agriculture was not yet well understood even in the countryside itself, the logic of the Committee's argument was obscured by another.[19] This was the argument, often associated with David Ricardo, that the Committee's recommendation was simply evidence of the Committee's wish to perpetuate rural prosperity at the cost of urban depression.[20] In the context of the subsequent urban outcry a Committee on Petitions relating to the Corn Laws was appointed and charged to discover 'the lowest remunerative price' at which wheat could be produced in Britain.[21] Their report reveals a crucial fact: there was nothing in reality which corresponded to the concept of a lowest remunerative price for a given commodity in the Kingdom as a whole. As they noted, remunerative prices varied 'according to the variations of the soil, markets, skill and industry of the occupier, and many other circumstances affecting differently not only different districts but different farms in the same district'.[22] But it was not their job to find out why their job could not be done. From the evidence of various witnesses they also noted that many existing tenancy arrangements were premised upon wheat at 80s. per quarter ton.[23] It was this price upon which the Corn Law of 1815 was based. The subsequent impact of deflation upon price perhaps enlarged the differential efficiencies to which they referred by encouraging the more efficient producers to take further steps in the directions in which they were already moving.

But be that as it may, these differential efficiencies in the countryside, and analogous differential efficiencies in the towns, had important consequences upon the structure of political groups, the content of political discourse, and the policy of the State.

As long as grain prices remained high and large profits could be had by simply ploughing land and planting wheat, differences of skill, capital and technological sophistication made relatively little difference to the prosperity of the individual farmer or to that of his landlord. But when the initial confusion passed which followed the general post-war price collapse all this was changed. What was the cause of those differences of prosperity of different agriculturists which were becoming increasingly difficult to deny? In particular, this question emerged in the context of the grossly uneven way in which agricultural prices declined. In general, these commodities which fell most sharply in price were those which were associated with the heavy clay lands. The price of wheat, the traditional staple of the clays, fell precipitously. But the prices of meat, wool and dairy products held closer to their war-time levels. Among the grains, the prices of the malting barleys held rather better than those of wheat.

In part, these relative price movements were the consequence of shifting demand, especially of the greater importance of meat and dairy products in the British diet and the growing demand for wool. But, they were also the consequence of technological and managerial changes in the countryside, of the expanding popularity of the Norfolk and Northumbrian rotations, of artificial manures, of land drainage – in effect, of the development of the concept of the mixed farm which, as Professor Thompson recently observed, was the 'spearhead' of 'the second agricultural revolution'.[24] To a large extent this 'revolution' was the expression of the wish to increase the fertility of the light lands. However, by means of oil cake and bones, turnips, sheep and cattle – turnips and oil cake to feed the sheep and cattle; sheep, cattle and bones to fertilize the land – certain of the more skilful light land farmers were becoming able to grow wheat where they had never grown it before. Furthermore, what with the normal dependence of the light land farmers upon products other than wheat to pay their rents, these men found themselves able to grow wheat at far lower unit cost than their neighbours who farmed the traditional wheat lands, the heavy clays.

These relative price movements could not be ignored. But temporarily, at least, their implications could be denied – that the light lands, the expensively drained clays, and the more highly skilled and wealthy farmers, were simply driving out the heavy clays, the unimproved lands, and the farmers who still farmed as their fathers and grandfathers had farmed before them.[25] In large measure, the reform crisis was the consequence of the effort to deny these implications. In large measure, it was the expression of the belief that the economic and social problems in town and countryside were principally functions of those governmental policies which could not be changed until the structure of government had been changed. These efforts did not stop after the Bill was passed. Indeed, they increased. In all probability, this was in part a consequence of the increased *need* to deny them, a need which grew as the relevant problems grew. But it was probably also a consequence of the constituency structure which the members of the Grey Ministry had tried to create, a structure based on those various deference communities which the technological changes were threatening.

II

Many men were parliamentary reformers for reasons other than those which the demands for currency reform and malt tax repeal reflected. But, for many months after Parliament met in February 1830, the crucial political questions were those which these men defined. Hence the importance of the date of George IV's death: during the period when these men defined the crucial questions the elections required as a result of his death and his brother's succession were held. At these elections were chosen the men who turned out Wellington's Government. When Grey subsequently announced that the 'first and most anxious object' of his own Government would be 'the relief of distress'[26] he was acknowledging an important political debt.

The debt was never paid. At least, it was never paid in the way the creditors wished. But for several years the question whether their demands for payment might not become irresistible remained open. Throughout 1831 and 1832 Parliament was busy with other matters. But many men hoped – or feared – that once the Bill was passed those fiscal questions would be restored to prominence which, in so many cases, had provided the logic of the demand for parliamentary reform. Indeed, it was such a fear which explains Peel's behaviour following the vote on Thomas Attwood's motion of 21 March 1833, that a committee be appointed 'to inquire into the causes of the general distress existing among the industrious classes'.[27]

Attwood's motion was generally regarded as the beginning of a currency reform campaign. It was defeated by a vote of 192 to 158. But it provided a point of agreement – or at least a point of common action – for an extremely diverse body of M.P.s. Those who voted with him included Daniel O'Connell and his Irish tail, a number of English and Scottish Radicals, a number of English county Members who were generally regarded as Ministerialists, and various Ultra-Tories. It was seconded by William Gillon, a Dissenter, who had previously urged the disestablishment of the Church.[28] That Chandos and Knatchbull should have been willing to vote with him and O'Connell suggests the continuing fluidity of political alliances and the importance of the fiscal or fundholder problem as a factor in them. Noting all this as well as the fact that Chandos, Knatchbull and several others of those who voted with Attwood had *not* been parliamentary reformers Peel concluded that a 'new combination' was coming into being, one based on the currency.[29] It was to help meet the threat of this 'new combination' that he decided to return to active political leadership either by entering into coalition with the Whigs or by trying to form a Government of his own.[30]

Peel's apprehensions were perhaps exaggerated. Whatever the strength of their support in the various constituencies the members of the 'new combination' never constituted a majority of the House. They could always be beaten if the Whips were attentive to their business. Moreover, while they agreed that the fiscal problem was a problem, that it demanded a solution and, as a rule, a solution at the expense of the fundholders, they were not fully agreed about the form the solution should take. Some were inflationists pure and simple. Others were willing to accept tax relief as a compromise. Others, again, while arguing that 'Peel's Act' was the principal source of the kingdom's ills, were opposed to any further tampering with the currency. The removal of certain taxes was all they sought. And these men were split between those whose concerns were principally urban and who focussed their hopes upon the repeal of the house and window taxes – a project which had strong support on both front benches, and those whose concerns were principally rural and who focussed their hopes upon the repeal of the malt tax. Furthermore, there was another split among them quite apart from those which had to do with the Church, Ireland and the corn laws. Or, at least, it was a *potential* split: it did not become fully apparent until 1834. Some of them supported the Poor Law Amendment Bill. Others opposed it. Clearly, by 1834, the former had accepted the argument which the defenders of fiscal orthodoxy were at pains to make, that pauperism and the rising burden of poor rates were *really* the consequence of excessive charity and lax administration. In doing so, they abandoned the alternative explanation which many members of the 'new combination' offered in 1833, and which some continued to offer for many years thereafter, that pauperism and the rising burden of poor rates were really the consequence of lack of money on the part of prospective employers – in other words, a function of deflation. This was the contention of Thomas Attwood and Chandos among others.[31] As this contention reveals, the inquiry they sought would have competed with the one the Poor Law Commissioners were then conducting.

Thomas Attwood's motion did not mention the currency. But Thomas Attwood happily supported the motion of his brother, Matthias, that a committee be appointed 'to inquire into the state of general distress, difficulty and embarrassment which now presses on the various orders of the community; how far the same has been occasioned by the operation of our present monetary system; and to consider the effects produced by that system upon the agriculture, manufacture, and commerce of the United Kingdom'. [32] A few years later the belief that 'Peel's Act' would have been repealed by overwhelming majorities in both Houses if Peers and M.P.s had been able to vote in secret, was attributed to an unnamed Cabinet Minister. [33] But, after three nights of debate on Matthias Attwood's motion, Althorp's amendment was carried by 331 to 139, 'that any alteration of the monetary system of the country, which would have the effect of lowering the standard of value, would be highly inexpedient'. [34] Two nights later Chandos' motion that the agricultural community had a strong claim to fiscal relief in view of the intensity of agricultural depression, was defeated. [35] However, while these and other analogous motions were all defeated there was a solid bloc of men who voted for them. These men never constituted a majority of either House. But they could win when others failed to attend the House, when the question was not the question of the currency pure and simple, and when they were not divided by other rivalries. On the night Chandos' motion was defeated, Sir William Ingilby's motion that the malt tax be reduced by half, was adopted. [36] Later, this vote was rescinded. On the 30th Althorp exploited the rivalry between the urban and rural wings of this 'combination' by moving, as an amendment to Sir John Key's motion to repeal the house and window taxes, that the Government could not afford *both* the reduction of the malt tax and the repeal of the house and window taxes without adopting a property tax which would 'change the whole financial system of the country' and which was therefore 'inexpedient'. [37] More to the point, with a larger House, Ingilby was denied leave to introduce a Bill to implement the vote of the 26th. [38] Then, on 3 May, Althorp proposed the appointment of two committees, the one to investigate 'the state of agriculture, and of the persons employed in it', the other to investigate 'the state of the Trade, Manufactures and Shipping of the United Kingdom'. [39] Earlier, he had declared he would not oppose an inquiry if the question of 'public faith' were not involved. [40] Thus, his proposals of 3 May did not represent a total reversal of his position. But they did represent a change of tactics. Instead of flexing the Government's majorities to defeat the 'new combination' an appeal would be made to their reason. As Althorp put it, the appointment of the two committees 'would have the effect of

showing, that the expectations of the country on the subject of a redress
of grievances in the way desired was impossible.' [41]

The Committee on Manufactures, Commerce and Shipping did no
more than report their evidence. Thus, presumably, they were not very
effective in demonstrating the 'impossibility ... of a redress of
grievances in the way desired'. But the Committee on Agriculture
produced a report which, whatever its actual political impact, reveals
the way the men who sought such an impact hoped to achieve it. They
acknowledged the fact that deflation had been 'proportionately
disadvantageous to many individuals belonging to the productive
classes of the community, and especially to those who had engaged in
speculative adventures of farming or of trade'. [42] But, they went on, the
solution to the problems which these men faced was not to be found in
a further alteration in the standard of value. 'Steadiness of price', they
declared, 'which is conducive to settled habits, and forms the basis of
all fixed engagements, is the primary object never again to be
overlooked.' [43] And, they observed, prices had become steadier since
the adoption of the sliding scale Corn Law of 1828. [44] Furthermore,
rents were coming into line with prices. [45] From their point of view this
served to demonstrate the validity of the general rule in which they
placed their faith: 'Contracts, prices and labour have a strong natural
tendency to adjust themselves to the value of money, once
established.' [46] Nor was their faith disturbed by the obvious fact that in
some cases things had gone beyond the point at which 'natural
adjustments' could greatly help. As they noted, certain of the occupiers
of the heavy clays had so curtailed their investments in their farms as
prices fell that they now found themselves unable to make ends meet:
they were suffering from both declining productivity and declining
prices. And in many cases, the Committee noted, these clays were
'ancient corn land, on which wheat had been grown from time
immemorial'. [47] Furthermore, where poor rates were large the funds
available for such investments as well as for the landlord's rent and the
farmer's profit were seriously depleted. In some such cases, they
observed, land had gone out of cultivation. And even where it had not
gone out of cultivation the mounting poor rate often took its toll. They
cited a parish in the Weald of Sussex where the sum of rent and poor
rate was the same in 1833 as it had been in 1792. 'But these burthens
had changed places: the 8s. an acre, which was rent in 1792, is now
poor-rate; the 4s. per acre, which was the poor-rate then, is now the
rent.' [48] Their comments reveal why, in their eyes, efforts to reduce
poor rates were so important.

Perhaps, the *principal* reason why the 'new combination' disappeared
had to do with the many questions on which its members were
disagreed; perhaps, it had to do with the effects of the Reform Act

which, by destroying the nomination boroughs, destroyed an essential element in the anti-fundholder argument, and which, by helping to create the mid-century constituency system, helped to intensify that urban-rural polarity which the corn law issue reflected; perhaps, it had to do with the fact that since adjustments to the value of money were being made in the context of increasingly rapid technological changes those men who managed to make such adjustments had thereby defined new standards of competition which, like it or not, the others simply had to meet; or perhaps, it had to do with the fact, which numerous division lists reveal, that while the necessary parliamentary majorities could *not* be put together to try to solve the problems of depression by inflating the currency or by reducing the taxes which went to pay interest on the national debt, such majorities *could* be put together to try to solve these problems by trying to do something about poor rates.

Presumably, it was the effort to guarantee such majorities, thus to avoid the alternative solution or solutions, which conditioned the terms in which the poor law question was often discussed. In particular, there was the question when the poor law problem became a *problem*. Clearly, if it only became a problem in 1819 – or, at the earliest, at the end of the wars – then the problem it represented would be largely attributable to the contraction of the currency and could be solved either by reinflating the currency or by reducing taxation. This was the contention of many members of the 'new combination'.[49] But equally as clearly, if the poor law had been a problem from the turn of the century then the problem was attributable not the currency nor to the burden of taxation but to that excessive charity and lax administration with which the allowance system or, as it was often called, the Speenhamland system was commonly associated. This was the contention of the defenders of fiscal orthodoxy, Althorp among them.[50] Then, too, there was the question of what effect the existing poor law had upon the poor. Clearly, if the poor law demoralized the poor and, for whatever reason, aggravated the causes of their poverty, then the amendment of the poor law might be a boon not only to the rate-payers whose rates might thereby be reduced but to the poor themselves. Such was the contention of the defenders of fiscal orthodoxy.[51] But if the existing poor law did not demoralize the poor but succoured them – indeed, if it was an important means of strengthening their confidence in the legitimacy of the existing social hierarchy, then the effort to reduce poor rates might threaten the very structure of society itself. This was the contention of various members of the 'new combination', among them Earl Stanhope and Thomas Attwood.[52] Indeed, in all probability it was in part the need to answer this contention which explains why the poor law commissioners attributed principal responsibility for the existing poor law problems to the allowance system when their own evidence reveals that this system had already been abandoned in most parts of the kingdom.[53] Presumably it was also because the ethic of *noblesse oblige* was so important to the self-image of so many of the gentry, and because this ethic was so grandly symbolized in the rights of J.P.s to order the payment of relief on their own authority, that the Act which removed this right has so often been described as the means of ending the allowance system.[54] Indeed, only recently has it become clear that where the allowance system still obtained in 1834 it continued to obtain for many years to come – in effect, that the local administration of the poor law was not greatly changed in 1834.[55]

But if the arguments of both sets of poor law polemicists were at least somewhat conditioned by their instrumental concerns, the defenders of fiscal orthodoxy had, as a rule, a somewhat clearer view of economic realities. Both groups acknowledged that in town as well as countryside 'Peel's Act' had created serious economic and social problems. But the defenders of fiscal orthodoxy were able to see – as certain of their opponents were not – that some of these problems could not be blamed on the currency or the incidence of certain taxes. It was William Gillon, while seconding Thomas Attwood's motion, who claimed that deflation was responsible for the handloom weavers' distress because it was responsible for the sharp decline in the prices of the goods which the handloom weavers produced.[56] Speaking later the same evening John Fielden argued to much the same effect.[57] As Althorp pointed out, however – and the point he made in this connection was analogous to the point which he and others made about the problems of rural depression – the distress of the handloom weavers could not be attributed to the currency. Rather, 'it was owing to the competition between them and machinery'.[58]

III

It is somewhat ironical, perhaps, that the members of the 'new combination' were principally responsible for eliciting the evidence which destroyed the logic of their own position. But the irony holds the key to an important political question. Seeking parliamentary inquiries in 1833 into the 'causes of general distress' – this as a means of demonstrating the need for some sort of parliamentary action to deal with the causes of distress as they defined them – they had finally obtained the appointment of a Select Committee on Agriculture which recommended parliamentary 'forbearance'.[59] Reluctant to accept defeat, they furthered their organization in the various constituencies with which they were associated. To the Cambridge and Isle of Ely Farmers' Association, which had been organized in the context of the elections of 1832, they added the Northamptonshire Association for the Protection of Agriculture and the various other 'agricultural associations' which, as was noted at the time, had such an important effect upon the county elections of January 1835.[60] The following December, with prices at levels not again reached until the seventies and eighties, some 500 delegates of these associations met in London to form the Central Agricultural Society, to demand a further parliamentary inquiry, and to resolve, by all but unanimous vote, 'that nothing can remove the present overwhelming distress but the adoption of some measure which will either raise the price of produce to the level of the burdens imposed, or bring down the burdens to the level of the present prices.'[61] It was there that Chandos, confirming his right to be known as the 'Farmer's Friend', announced that he would move the appointment of another select committee as soon as Parliament met.

These were the origins of the Select Committee on Agriculture of 1836. As in 1833, however, the Committee scarcely served the purpose its sponsors hoped for. It provided a forum for those who contended that unless Parliament inflated the currency or significantly reduced the taxes which bore upon the landed interest the landed interest would simply vanish. But it also provided a forum for those who argued that there were no real problems in the countryside except on the undrained clays and among the less skilful farmers. These made the case which the chairman of the Committee, Charles Shaw Lefevre, subsequently reiterated, that '. . . the pressure of . . . distress is in a great measure confined' to the occupiers of the cold tenacious soils and to those farmers who rely upon their wheat crop as their major source of profit.'[62]

And, he went on, thus by implication explaining the process from which the political movement derived, '. . . by the introduction of the turnip system of husbandry the poor light lands are made to produce wheat at less cost to the cultivator than the more tenacious soils, and thus the clay lands, which were considered the ancient wheat lands of this country, have to enter into competition with the lighter soils.'[63] Noting that drainage could, in many cases, restore the competitive status of the clays he concluded, in essence, that those who complained of depression were really complaining of their own lack of skill and capital.

In part, of course, the rural problem was a function of price. But even more, it was a function of *remunerative* price and, as Shaw Lefevre noted, there was a wide range of prices at which the same commodities could be sold at a profit by different farmers. The point was the same as that made by the Select Committee on Petitions relating to the Corn Laws some 20 years earlier. But in 1836 it was vastly more important than it had been in 1814. Indeed, if Shaw Lefevre's figures are remotely accurate the difficulties which the less efficient producers faced in the mid-thirties were vastly greater than they had been at the end of the wars. At the end of the wars, he explained, some farmers had been able to sell their wheat at a profit at 80s. per quarter ton. But others had not been able to sell their wheat at a profit at less than 96s. per quarter ton. Clearly, the one represented a serious threat to the other. In 1836, he went on, some farmers were able to sell their wheat at a profit at 40s. per quarter ton. But others could not sell theirs at a profit at less than 56s. per quarter ton.[64] In absolute terms the range was the same in both years. But in relative terms it had doubled. Due in part to deflation, in part to increasing efficiency – while he did not cite these causes they were obviously the operative ones – the more efficient producer had become a far greater threat to his less efficient neighbour. Nor was that the end of the story. In 1844, when wheat was selling at 50s. per quarter ton, and when many farmers were ostensibly failing, Earl Ducie announced that on his model farm in Gloucestershire he could sell wheat at a profit at 28s. per quarter ton.[65]

Speaking in 1830, Peel described the competition between the more and the less efficient producers in terms of the differences in the inherent qualities of the lands they occupied. The 'partial' depression in agriculture, he explained, was the consequence of the fact that the poorer lands which had been brought into cultivation during the wars could not withstand the competition of the better soils of Scotland and Ireland. And, he went on, nothing could be done about the consequent sufferings of the men who owned or farmed these lands.[66] The failure of the efforts of the agricultural members of the 'new combination' to obtain the legislative relief they sought confirms the accuracy of his conclusion: as long as the rural problem was defined in terms of the inherent qualities of different lands the problem was insoluble. Writing in 1836, Shaw Lefevre described the competition between the more and the less efficient producers in terms, principally, of differences in skill and capital. Where depression existed, he explained, it was largely the consequence of the inability of the poorer and, generally, the less innovative farmers, occupying lands which had not been improved, to compete with the richer and, generally, the more skilful farmers, occupying lands which had been improved. Of course, to the farmer who was being squeezed it was six of one and half a dozen of the other whether his problems derived from the quality of his land or from his lack of skill and capital. But when his problems were understood in terms of his lack of skill and capital – and, together with the obvious aggravation of these problems, this was one of the principal consequences of 'the second agricultural revolution' – these problems were no longer insoluble. Of course, many spokesmen of the landed interest continued to argue that the general rural problem would not be solved by raising the levels of efficiency of the less efficient producers. But the problem to which they referred was not the economic problem. It was the social one consequent to those changes of relationship and role which the effort to raise their efficiency inevitably entailed. Thus, in the context of that political system which was in part a product of the first Reform Act, in part a product of the efforts of men to legitimize their own roles in the various constituencies, it became an increasingly important political problem.

IV

Undoubtedly the importance of this problem was in part a measure of the novelty of the procedures to which Shaw Lefevre referred and of the untempered enthusiasm and social background of many of their advocates. Writing in 1840 in the first issue of the *Journal of the Royal Agricultural Society* Philip Pusey, its editor, dated the high farming movement from 1837, the date of publication of John Morton's handbook, *On the Nature and Properties of Soils: their Connexion with the Geological Formation on which they rest; the best Means of permanently increasing their Productiveness, and on the Rent and Profits of Agriculture.*[67]
To some extent, Pusey's statement was an obvious exaggeration. Morton had simply tried to draw the lessons from various of the existing rule of thumb methods. For example, there was the dressing of the Norfolk sands with subsoil chalk and clay. It was in consequence of this practice, he contended, that land 'of the most worthless kind . . . is now converted into good sandy loam, which yields large crops of turnips, barley and wheat'.[68] Also, there were the cutting of drains and the subsoil ploughing of the kind which James Smith, of Deanston, had undertaken in 1823 and on which he had reported in his *Remarks on Thorough Drainage and Deep Ploughing,* published in 1831. As Morton noted, many agriculturists believed that the clays could not be improved. But this, he declared, was not the case. They could be improved by drainage. Furthermore, once drained they could be farmed on the same turnip and sheep system which had proved its worth on the sands. And, he insisted, unless they were drained they were no longer competitive.[69] But the problems which the movement *qua* movement created were no less serious if its beginnings be found in the twenties or even earlier. What was important was the acceleration of the movement, 'he fact that by the middle thirties increasing numbers of farmers were abandoning the more traditional procedures. In the context of this acceleration what was also important was the attitude expressed in the refrain of the song, *The English Farmer,* which was so 'warmly applauded' when sung at the meeting of the Royal

Buckinghamshire Agricultural Association in 1834,
New fangled nonsense an't the thing
To gull the British farmer. [70]

But this attitude was not entirely unreasonable. Various spokesmen of the high farming movement were novices to the field. In consequence, they sometimes showed more enthusiasm than common sense. It was such a one who, attributing an outbreak of cattle disease to 'the poisonous properties of buttercups', declared that the only way to stop the epidemic was to plough up every pasture which contained a buttercup – in effect, every pasture in the kingdom. To this the Duke of Richmond might reply that since buttercups were no novelty they could scarcely be the cause of the new epidemic. [71] But common sense provided no preliminary test of the practicality of the other procedures these men were recommending. It was a Londoner, I. J. Mechi, who bought Tiptree Farm, in Essex for £25 an acre and then proceeded to invest more than £47 pounds an acre in improvements. [72] According to his report, many of his London friends told him he should have invested his money in consols. Instead, he used it to lay drains under all the fields, to cut all his timber trees, to inclose the waste, to build roads, new buildings, a threshing machine, a steam house,in which to prepare food for the cattle, a tank to receive all liquid and solid manure and even to install gutters on all the adjacent buildings so that the manure would not be diluted. When his neighbours asked him how he had learned to spend his money he replied that he had read many books. [73] And now, fresh from the City, he was writing one.

Mechi's arrogance was perhaps more offensive than his affluence, and his affluence than its source. He was tactless. [74] And even for a publicist his behaviour was rather extreme. But he was not alone in believing that the old ways were inefficient and thus contemptible, that new ways, and new capital, would make agriculture prosperous. He was one of the new 'scientific agriculturists' who were described in not altogether complimentary terms, in 1851, as believing,

> ... that it is expedient to make our fields larger and more open to sun and air, by removing hedges and fences; that the shade of trees is injurious to the ripening of grain, and therefore that they should be removed; that 'timber-smothered' land is a reproach to scientific and economical farming; that to keep pace with the advancement of agricultural knowledge, and to meet the activity and competition of the age, the hedge-rows, which have heretofore been considered the beauty of England, must, from considerations of utility, be abandoned; that land must be looked upon as nothing else than a manufactory of agricultural produce; and that farmers who think of anything else than profit, are little better than fools. [75]

These men, it was added, 'are ... those who bring the wisdom of the city countinghouse, or scientific lecture room, to bear upon rural affairs.' And, by doing so, another critic noted, they were undermining the traditional structure of rural society and jeopardizing its values. They were making '. . . stewards of lawyers, who have no real knowledge of farming interests, and can, therefore, have no sympathies with the small farmer or patience with him in the day of his difficulty, and whose only object is to get the greatest rent at the easiest rate.' [76]

What was at stake was extremely important: it was the integrity of the landed estate not only – or not so much – as a source of income to the owner but as a quasi-governmental agency, an arena in which the relationships of the men associated with the estate might be regulated and the status of the man who regulated these relationships re-enforced. It was that to which Disraeli referred, in 1863, when he observed that the formal government of the kingdom could not be carried on except by the 'united aid and agency' of various institutions which, in terms of strictly defined attributes – at least from the point of view of many contemporary political theorists – would scarcely have been defined as governmental. Indeed, his explanation reveals the importance of those overlapping boundaries of function which, in his eyes, many institutions continued to possess: one of the institutions without which the government could not be carried on was 'the hereditary tenure of land'. Obviously, as he saw it, the landed estate performed more than an economic function. He was articulating the essential message which poll books convey when he declared, 'in hours of peril and perplexity, external and domestic, [the landed estate] . . . offers something around which men may rally and save the State.' [77] Twenty years later much the same was said by one of the editors of his speeches. Indeed, notwithstanding the changes in the structure of rural society which were depriving landowners of their status, T. E. Kebbel could still refer to the 'well-ordered hierarchy' of the rural village and observe that the 'authority of the gentry, founded on their property, their jurisdiction, and their hereditary claim to respect, is still active for good.' [78] Nor was it only Tories or Conservatives who expressed such assumptions. Forty years before Disraeli described landed estates as rallying points of effective loyalty, analogous roles were assigned to them, at least by implication, by a man who, in all probability, would have considered it a matter of pride to rehearse his points of substantive disagreement with Disraeli and Kebbel. It reveals the ubiquity of their assumptions concerning the essential structure of English society, the degree to which *some* political theorists did appreciate the political role of non-political institutions, that the landed estate provided the obvious model to which James Mill referred when describing the means by which opinions were formed 'in the great body of society'. As he put it, men naturally adopt the opinions of those 'to whom they fly for advice and assistance in all their numerous difficulties, upon whom they feel an immediate and daily dependence in health and in sickness, in infancy and in old age'.[79]

In the early nineteenth century the English land system was oriented towards the preservation of dynasties and dynastic dependents, not towards the efficient exploitation of the land as such exploitation was being redefined by such men as John Morton. The owners of personal property were allowed to succeed or fail as individuals with a fair amount of freedom as circumstances and their abilities determined. But the main functions of the land law were to protect the owners of real property from themselves and to guarantee that their estates remain inviolate. As the real property commissioners explained, in 1829, by the effects of the land law 'families are preserved'.[80] Because this, from their point of view, was what the land law *should* do their conclusion follows: the land law 'came almost as near to perfection as can be expected of any human institution'.[81]

Obviously, by providing landlords with peculiar privileges English land law helped to postpone the day when an urban patrician class might emerge. Furthermore, as long as politics remained an avocation, and as long as limited liability companies were not yet effectively established as alternative foci for investment, the land law helped to preserve the situation in which landownership remained the primary source of support of the politically active leisure class. As Bagehot explained in the latter fifties, the large proportion of ministerial offices filled by landowners was a simple consequence of the fact that debentures, canal shares and other investments 'not requiring sedulous personal attention, and not liable to be affected by political vicissitudes', had not yet had any appreciable impact upon habits of investment. 'All opulence gravitates towards the land', he declared, '[and] political opulence ... particularly.'[82] But whatever the degree to which these habits of investment were conditioned by the privileges associated with landownership these privileges were becoming increasingly expensive.

As long as capital accumulation progressed relatively slowly the privileges associated with landownership tended to prevent the dissipation of existing units of landed capital while encouraging the purchase of land by would-be *arrivistes*. But, as capital accumulation became increasingly rapid, as the wealth of other social groups came to rival that of the established landed classes, and as the Mortons and Ducies defined new standards of agricultural competition which could only be met by those who were both willing and able to make sizable investments in their estates or farms, the legal privileges associated with landownership became a brake upon the ability of the members of the established landed classes to retain their own prominence. Many landowners were economically immobilized. Furthermore – and thereby was the political problem aggravated and the historical problem obscured – many of them failed to understand the alchemy of circumstance by which a privilege had become a liability.

According to the high farmers, agriculturists would all be prosperous if they adopted the procedures they recommended. But many agriculturists did not understand these procedures. Furthermore, these procedures required larger quantities of working capital than they were in the habit of using – indeed, larger quantities of capital than many of them had available. With prices depressed, one of the primary sources of capital as well as motives for investment which had been so effective during the war years was lacking. Furthermore, in a great many cases the investments which the high farmers recommended not only implied a complete reversal of traditional attitudes towards the land. They were also effectively precluded by the customs of rural society and the laws by which these customs were re-enforced.

The capital which high farming required of the landlord was potentially available from any of three sources: his personal property, the current income of his estate, or a mortgage of the estate. However, with prices depressed many rent rolls declined sharply. Furthermore, what with the widespread continuing scepticism as to the economic value of land improvement, such prices tended to deter many landowners from allowing whatever personal wealth they had to tarnish on the land. Then, again, on settled estates, improvement mortgages were effectively prohibited until the value of land improvement was more clearly and widely recognized. To those who believed that 'new fangled nonsense an't the thing to gull the British farmer', or, with the writer in *Blackwood's Edinburgh Magazine,* in 1850, that 'If high farming could be shown to be productive, high farming would be the rule and not the exception',[83] such mortgages were simply means of weakening the economic basis of the family by burdening the estate to no good purpose. Since the primary function of the land law was to protect the reversioner against the possibility that his estate would be wasted by tenants for life or tenants in tail, strong legal impediments remained against the negotiation of improvement mortgages until – whether rightly or wrongly in the long term – there was general agreement that high farming was worth the cost.[84] The owner in fee might mortgage as he wished. In 1847, however, it was estimated that two-thirds of England land was controlled by testamentary settlement.[85] Before the land law reforms which Peel's 'general scheme' helped to further, and which culminated in the Settled Land Act of 1882, the tenant for life on a settled estate had no powers to negotiate an improvement mortgage unless such powers were expressly granted by the settlement under when he held – and this was rare – or unless he obtained such powers by private Act of Parliament or, after 1833, from the Court of Chancery.[86] Proceedings in Chancery were less expensive than proceedings by private Act. But their expense was one of those impediments to land improvement which it was one of Peel's objects in 1846 to remove.

Nor was it easy to start the flow of capital which high farming required of the agricultural tenant. As Peel noted at the inaugural meeting of the English Agricultural Society, few existing farmers had the necessary capital or the necessary experimental orientation.[87] It was this which prompted Lord Kinnaird to suggest that they be replaced by men from the towns who were endowed with capital and were not afraid to use it, 'knowing', as he put it, 'that thus alone can their land be made productive'.[88] James Caird's cure was not quite as drastic as Kinnaird's. But his diagnosis was similar. And the end result would have been the same. When he emphasized the therapeutic value of high rents – farmers with low rents, he declared, lacked the incentive to be efficient – he, too, was urging a revolution in rural society.[89] Nor did the problem only have to do with the absence of men who fitted Kinnaird's description and the fact that many rents were too low to provide the inducements to efficiency Caird sought. The mobilization of tenant capital was also inhibited by the inherent difficulties of defining the interests of different persons in the same piece of property to their mutual satisfaction. These difficulties derived from the very nature of the English land system. They were particularly prominent on settled estates.

On an estate owned in fee simple an agricultural tenant with a long lease might invest heavily in the operations of his farm in full confidence that unless he failed to pay his rent he would remain in possession long enough to reap the benefits of his investments. If his operations were wise he would be the gainer. On such an estate a tenant-at-will with an adequate tenant-right agreement might make comparable investments in full confidence that unless he failed to pay his rent he would be compensated for the unexhausted value of his improvements in the event of his possession ending. But in the early years of the century a lease on a settled estate only provided the leaseholder with a contingent interest. In law, such a lease might be terminated at the death of the man who granted it.[90] Also, no compensation agreement which was not supported by the neighbourhood or county custom was legally binding upon the successor in inheritance to a settled estate.[91] These customs developed as means of standardizing the compensation agreements – and thus the varieties of investment for which compensation would be provided – on different estates in the same region. Thus, at a time of increasingly rapid technological change they may have inhibited the trial and adoption of new agricultural techniques.[92] But be that as it may, as late as 1847, in large parts of the kingdom, such customs did not exist. In these areas no claim for compensation was legally binding on the successor in inheritance to a settled estate. Such a claim could only be collected from the personal estate of the tenant for life with whom it had been negotiated.[93]

But the more general problems were, perhaps, the more basic. Leases at fixed money rents were scarcely appropriate to the economic circumstances of the post-war period when fluctuations of price were fairly acute. Landowners found that leaseholders tended to bank their profits when prices were high and to plead for abatements when they fell.[94] Also, in circumstances created by changes of agricultural technology, leases ceased to provide an effective mechanism of estate management. Of old, leases had required that the tenant manage his farm 'according to the rules of good husbandry'.[95] From at least the mid-thirties, however, the consensus as to what 'good husbandry' required tended to vanish. Then, too, if the possession of a lease encouraged the leaseholder to spend heavily on his farm during the early years of his tenancy so did it encourage him to exhaust his farm during the latter years lest he leave any of his capital behind in the event of his tenancy was not continuing.[96] It was the assumption that the leaseholder would be prepared to leave his farm at the end of his lease which gave weight to Althorp's arguments against the Chandos clause in 1831.[97] But such assumptions also help to explain why many landowners disliked leases: the farm which the tenant would be willing to leave because it was exhausted was not the farm on which the landowner could obtain a good rent from a new tenant.

Tenancies-at-will were more flexible. But their very flexibility was a serious drawback. In law, any investment which a tenant made in his farm automatically became the property of his landlord. Also, in law, a tenant-at-will could be evicted on six months notice. Thus, without an adequate compensation agreement to override the landlord's legal right of ownership in whatever capital the tenant had invested in his farm, the tenant-at-will who made such investments was simply placing his capital where his landlord might expropriate it by the simple expedient of eviction. In law, all the tenant could claim was the capital represented by the seeds of the standing crops. These crops were his. But nothing more. In effect, while tenancies-at-will might be more appropriate to the fluctuations of price and the increasingly numerous proposals of technological innovation in the post-war period they had a very serious disadvantage from the landlord's point of view: they encouraged the demand for tenant right. Not only did a tenant right agreement violate the purity of the landlord's right of ownership, it was a means of formalizing the traditionally informal relationship between landlord and tenant and of placing the two upon a level of contractual equality. Almost inevitably, the implementation of a tenant right agreement required the appointment of a third party to determine the value of the tenant's unexhausted investments in his farm. As such, a tenant right agreement deprived the landlord of his wonted role as the determinor of the rights of his dependents. For this reason in particular many landlords were immovably opposed to them.[98]

V

Such were the problems. Within the context of the political system which came into being after 1832 they gave rise to two distinct polarizations or conflicts. The one derived from the social dynamics of the various communities in town and countryside, borough and country. It was that to which Russell referred in 1854 when he spoke of the tendencies of the borough and county Members to be 'too generally exclusive in respect of the interest[s] they cared for'; it was that which the usual descriptions of the corn law crisis reflect. The other derived from the differences between the perspectives of these men and the perspectives of those who, for one reason or another, were less strongly conditioned by the various constituency dynamics.

On the one hand were those who contended that rural depression was universal – or, at least, that rural prosperity, where it existed, was not a function of skill, capital and technological sophistication. These tried to bring effective pressures to bear upon Parliament to reform the currency, to repeal the malt tax, and to prevent any further reductions in the levels of protection which, like the Corn Law of 1828, might be designed to enhance the stability of prices in circumstances conditioned by deflation, the increasing volume of domestic production, and the increasing dependence of certain farmers upon products other than wheat to pay their rents. To bring such pressures to bear they organized essentially political agricultural associations in various appropriate constituencies. They · also formed central bodies to co-ordinate the activities of these local bodies and to strengthen their voice. Fairly soon after 1836 the Central Agricultural Society dissolved.[99] But in 1844 many of the men who had been prominent in this Society formed another – although not to agitate for currency reform or malt tax repeal: for all practical purposes those causes had been lost. Rather, they formed the Central Agricultural Protection Association, often called the Anti-League, as a means of organizing resistance to the agitations of the Anti-Corn Law League.[100] But if their substantive concern in the forties was more defensive than it had been in the thirties, their fundamental assumption was the same: prosperity in the countryside could not be a function of productivity but solely a function of price. The point was made at the first anniversary dinner of the Protection Association — the 'Farmer's Friend', now Duke of Buckingham, vice-president — 'The cry on the one side is "Cultivate, cultivate". My answer, in the name of the tenant farmers of England is, "Remunerate, remunerate." ' [101] His declaration was greeted with 'immense cheers'. But if formally, as an Association, they were no longer seeking the panaceas of the thirties, inflation and the reduction of the taxes which bore upon the landed interest, nostalgia was strong. The previous year, Robert Baker, a tenant farmer prominent in the new Association reiterated the earlier arguments. He declared that

> The first object of laws for the regulation of society should be to encourage industry by such enactments as will best secure permanent and profitable employment for those who live by their labour; and unless permanent relief is given by a removal of the taxes or revision of the currency they will be unable to effect this object. [102]

The other principal expression of this constituency dynamic was the Anti-Corn Law League. As Dr McCord has noted, the League was formed in Manchester in 1838 to provide 'an acceptable focus for Radical energies at a time when Radicals were sadly in need of a rallying point'. [103] In the context of the assumption that the corn laws really worked in the ways the Leaguers claimed — not only to raise food prices but to do so in significant fashion, thus to guarantee rural prosperity at the cost of urban depression — these laws 'stood out as the visible legislative symbol of the predominance of the landed interest'. [104] Thus, it was hoped, 'an attack on the Corn Laws would be welcomed by all who resented the privileges and entrenched influence of the aristocracy in national life.' [105] The functional importance of these assumptions, the degree to which they fed the resentments from which they derived, is revealed by the rapid expansion of the League, by the Leaguers' frequent success in weaning men away from goals which were socially divisive to goals which, at least in the towns, were socially unifying, and by the often-repeated proposition that the League was really responsible for the repeal of the corn laws. [106]

But then there were those who, in the context of their commitment to the currency settlement of 1819, not only resisted the demands of the currency reformers and malt tax repealers but tried to facilitate those adjustments to the value of money which the members of the Committee on Agriculture of 1833 had described as 'natural'. These were the men who, as a means of encouraging efforts to increase productivity and reduce costs, met in London in May 1838, under the chairmanship of Earl Spencer, the former Althorp, to form the English Agricultural Society, later the Royal Agricultural Society of England. This Society was insistently non-political. Before the inaugural

meeting efforts were made to assure the presence of Peel and
Wellington, thus to prevent the Society's acquiring a Whig image
because of Spencer's role in its organization.[107] Furthermore, this
meeting adopted the rule that no question might be discussed at any
future meeting 'which shall refer to any matter to be brought forward,
or pending in either of the Houses of Parliament'.[108] The Society also
adopted the motto, 'Practice with Science'. In effect, it was
non-political in both 'party' terms and in terms of the solution to the
rural problem which it symbolized. The solution was not to be sought
by parliamentary action.

   To those who formed the Central Agricultural Society in 1835, and
to most of those who later formed the Central Agricultural Protection
Association, the rule and motto of the English Agricultural Society
were both anathema. It was the secretary of what was by then the
moribund Central Agricultural Society who declared, in 1838, that
'agricultural practice [was] ... in every point of view a minor
department of agriculture.'[109] He was one of the few men associated
with the Central Society to attend the inaugural meeting of the English
Society. He did not speak at this meeting. But his behaviour was
eloquent. He got up and walked out as soon as the motion that a
'non-political agricultural association' was 'delusive in principle', had
been ruled out of order. In his departure he was accompanied, among
others, by the mover of the resolution and by a man who, earlier, had
made 'rude remarks about fat bullocks, dying of apoplexy', which, as
the correspondent of *The Farmers' Magazine* explained in his report,
were 'intended doubtless as a sneer at the noble and excellent
chairman'. Speaking immediately after their departure, Peel observed
that they had opposed the new Society because it was 'advising farmers
to turn experimentalists'. He granted the truth of the charge. But, he
went on,

> ... if it were admitted that the application of science to agriculture
> could improve it, and also admitted that the farmers were too poor
> to carry that improvement into effect themselves, was it not a
> conclusive reason why an assemblage of rich men interested in the
> progress and success of agriculture should combine for the purpose
> of affording to the poor the benefit of the new discoveries?

And, he added, dignifying the contention with the vehemence of his
denial, it was simply not true that scientific farming would set landlord
against tenant. Speaking immediately after Peel that down, Shaw
Lefevre reiterated his essential points. In all probability, those who
walked out would have rejected their premise, that the application of
science to agriculture could improve it, not only because scientific
agriculture was, in their eyes, 'new fangled nonsense', but also because,
Peel's and Shaw Lefevre's statements to the contrary notwithstanding,

the social costs of high farming lay in those changes of relationship and role which threatened the existing structure of rural society. It was this structure which the nominally agricultural but essentially political organizations in the countryside reflected.

These organizations were not 'party' organizations. As a speaker observed to a meeting of the Yorkshire Central Agricultural Association in November 1834, if the Association were 'tinctured with party feeling . . . it would quickly sink into insignificance'. But, he went on, '. . . when he observed the combinations which were forming against the agricultural interest, he thought it important that agriculturists should come forward to protect themselves; and it was that which induced him to become a member.' [110] The following month the same point was made by Chandos' father at a meeting of the Royal Buckinghamshire Agricultural Association. The Association, he declared, was not a 'party' association. But, he went on, it was 'political'. And, he added,

> God forbid it should be otherwise. The time never has been and we hope never would be, in England, when the agriculturists of that country would cease to be, in their assemblies, a political body . . . I say it shall never happen as long as I live, that the agricultural interest shall cease to be a political object. I hold that no Minister, no matter to what party he may belong, or be he who he may, will be supported in this country who does not take into deep consideration the agricultural interests of that country. [111]

Buckingham's statement was a warning to the Tory leaders who had just assumed office. Furthermore, for reasons which the recently acquired royal prefix to the Buckinghamshire Agricultural Association helps to explain, it was not a warning to be taken lightly. A week or so before William IV dismissed Melbourne he identified himself with Chandos and the cause he symbolized by contributing £50 to the Buckinghamshire Agricultural Association. His contribution was acclaimed by those who hoped that Melbourne's dismissal promised that basic change of economic policy which, in so many cases, had provided the logic of the demand for parliamentary reform. [112] The immediate satisfaction of these hopes was disappointed by the events to which Buckingham implicitly referred. After Peel accepted office, and after he offered a post in his Government to Chandos, he refused to accept the terms which Chandos placed upon his joining the Government – that he commit himself to the repeal of the malt tax. But the hopes remained. Indeed, it was to break down Peel's resistance that Disraeli, speaking at this meeting, urged the formation of additional agricultural associations so that petitions for the repeal of the malt tax might be sent to Parliament 'not only . . . [from] every county, but . . . [from] every town in the country'. [113]

But it was Edward Cayley, the Whig, addressing the members of the Yorkshire Central Agricultural Association, who revealed the essential problem when he criticised Spencer for urging farmers to stay out of politics and devote their energies to finding cheap ways to fatten cattle. Such a goal was all very well, Cayley observed. But, he went on, '. . . it was much more desirable, in times like the present, that agriculturists should unite for the purpose of expressing their decided opinions on the policy pursued by the Government, and for endeavouring to rid themselves of the grievances under which they laboured.'[114]

The demands articulated at these meetings and those articulated later at meetings of the Central Agricultural Society and the Central Agricultural Protection Association stemmed from the 'grass roots' and expressed the concern, felt by many, that unless the pressures which were threatening the traditional structure of rural society were relieved this society would crumble. These demands were political in several senses of the term. They reflected the concerns of a definable group. They also reflected the belief of the members of this group – a belief which, in all probability, helped to increase the cohesion of the group itself – that only by means of formal political action could their own roles in society and relationships with one another be perpetuated. However, while the agricultural or county 'interest' was an important political phenomenon, it was not in such terms a party phenomenon. Both the members of the local associations and the delegates to the central societies or associations undoubtedly included more Tories than Whigs. But they included both. Even more importantly, the Tories among them were principally concerned to reverse the policies with which the ministerial leaders of their own party were identified.

Nor were these policies party policies. There were few men of ministerial rank or serious ministerial pretensions in either party who proposed to restore prosperity by inflating the currency. Nor were there many who proposed to do so in the countryside by repealing the malt tax either before or after the significance of the tax was redefined in the light of growing awareness of the relative prosperity of the light land farmers. But the differences between the party leaders and the others was not on substantive points alone. Indeed, the differences on these points reflected differences of general attitude, differences of perspective. On the one hand were those whose vision and understanding were directly related to one or another of the 'interests' on which the Bill was based. On the other hand were those who pretended to a somewhat olympian detachment, who claimed to understand the requirements of the nation as a whole. From their point of view these requirements lay in the interrelatedness of the different sectors of the economy. It was on this point in particular that Althorp criticised Chandos and those who acted with him in 1833. As he put it,

Chandos and his various allies 'appeared to think that there was no relief for the cultivators of the soil, unless taxes which pressed directly upon them were removed'.[115] In this, he declared, they were wrong. He was demonstrating his own ostensible objectivity when he observed that the farmer could only be prosperous if the townsmen who bought his products were prosperous. Thus, he concluded, the repeal of taxes which pressed directly upon the landed interest 'would not relieve them nor the country so much as [the repeal or reduction of] other taxes of a more general nature'.[116]

In agricultural matters Peel scarcely possessed the same reputation as Althorp. But he understood the dynamics of a national policy in similar terms. This is apparent from his agreement with Althorp, in 1834, that landlords and farmers would be served best by steps taken to extend the commerce and manufacturing of the Kingdom as a whole, not by steps taken to assist certain sectors specifically.[117] This is also apparent from his arguments, in 1842, while proposing his new corn law. As he put it, the corn law should be improved, not repealed. Furthermore, it should be improved not as a means of solving the urban problems to which the members of the Anti-Corn Law League had been referring in their own agitations but as a means of enhancing the stability of price. In effect, while describing his new corn law he was reiterating Shaw Lefevre's argument, in 1836, that the advantages of the sliding scale corn law had been somewhat cancelled out by the prices on which the scale was based.[118] The merit of the sliding scale was the merit of price stability. Ostensibly, however, the scale had been set too high. In consequence, it had failed to produce the intended stability. After 1828 importations were legally allowed whatever the going domestic price. But importations were effectively discouraged until the going domestic price had reached such a level as to be significantly affected even by small importations. It was this problem which the Corn Law of 1842 was designed to solve.

Together with the alterations in the corn law which Peel's arguments in 1842 serve to explain these arguments reveal the differences between Peel's concerns and the concerns of the members of the Anti-Corn Law League on the one hand and the members of the Central Agricultural Society and the Central Agricultural Protection Association on the other. However, while these differences are clear today they were scarcely apparent at the time to those who saw things from one or the other of the two principal constituency perspectives. In particular this was the case for many spokesmen of the landed interest. As Sir Richard Vyvyan put it, in passing the new Corn Importation Bill, the Ministers had shown that they only had sympathies for the urban consumer.[119] In effect, he explained the Ministers' behaviour not in terms of the concern which their own arguments and behaviour suggest but in terms of those other concerns which the constituency dynamics would help to explain. But Vyvyan's further argument is somewhat more reasonable – the implementation of this ostensible sympathy had only been possible because the Ministers had 'availed themselves of the influence of the Crown'.[120] As the totality of his argument reveals, the anti-ministerial grievances of 1829 and 1830 were scarcely below the surface of political consciousness. What brought them back to the surface was the realization that however 'delusive' a 'non-political agricultural association' might be 'in principle' in practice it was a force to be conjured with. Matters to be discussed in Parliament might be out of order at meetings of the Royal Agricultural Society. But matters discussed at these meetings had a direct bearing upon matters discussed in Parliament.

Yet, from the point of view of Peel and Spencer and those who acted with them, the rural problem only became a *political* problem because it was made so by those who focussed their electoral energies within the appropriate constituencies. Whatever position they had taken individually concerning the Bill in 1831 and 1832, and whatever position they had taken earlier concerning the desirability or undesirability of parliamentary reform and the reasons why parliamentary reform might be desirable or undesirable, the positions they took in the post-reform period while attacking or defending the landed and urban interests were not only consistent with the essential thrust of the Act. They clearly intensified this thrust. Whether mobilizing support for corn law repeal in the towns or for currency reform and malt tax repeal in the countryside or – after these had lost whatever semblance to practicality they might have possessed – mobilizing opposition to further reductions in the levels of protection, they were clearly strengthening the traditional agencies of electoral recruitment on which they depended.

It was presumably because Peel and Althorp defined the rural problem as a non-political problem that they found it all the easier to understand the redefinition of it which derived from the progress of the 'second agricultural revolution'. Presumably, it was because they defined the problem as non-political that they never bothered to articulate an ideology other than that of trying to survive in circumstances which their own abilities to survive helped to produce. In the years after 1838 a number of technologically oriented local agricultural societies came into being which, patterning themselves on the Royal Agricultural Society, adopted analogous non-political rules. But when the policy implications of high farming became clear in the forties these rules became major impediments to their continued existence.[121] Indeed, from the nature of the case, the effort to organize support for high farming, to transform 'Practice with Science' from motto to rallying cry, was extremely difficult. It was scarcely compatible with the structural exigencies of rural society.

VI

'Look at the facts', Cobden wrote to Peel in the summer of 1846, '... can the country be otherwise ruled ... [than] through the *bona fide* representatives of the middle class? ... The Reform Bill decreed it: the passing of the Corn Bill has realised it.' [122]

Cobden's statements in this letter suggest a clear institutional linkage between the Reform Act and the repeal of the corn laws. Had the Reform Act done no more than abolish the rotten boroughs, distribute the seats thus made available among the previously unrepresented towns and enlarge the electorate; had the corn laws really worked as Cobden generally implied they worked – his argument in 1845 is an exception to his general arguments – and had the corn laws been repealed in 1846 without more ado; then, possibly, the linkage between the Reform Act and corn law repeal might have been that which he suggested. But the Act did contain other provisions; the corn laws did not work in the ways he generally implied; and more was done in 1846 than simply repeal the corn laws. In particular, in 1846, the tenant for life of a settled estate was given the power to borrow money for the improvement of the estate and to make the repayment of the loan a charge upon the estate. But the agricultural tenant was not granted a legal right of ownership in his improvements. The distinction suggests an important aspect of Peel's 'general scheme' which, possibly, has been obscured by statements such as Cobden's about what the 'Reform Bill decreed' and what the 'Corn Bill realised'. The meaning of 'middle class' is dubious at best – except in the light of the concerns of those who use the phrase. But normally such meanings are not found in a 'scheme' designed, insofar as possible, to perpetuate the communities on which a status hierarchy depends. Peel proposed to change the landlord's role *vis-a-vis* those who were not members of his estate. But he did *not* propose to change his role *vis-a-vis* those who were members of his estate – who were his dependents. The 'scheme' reflects the diagnosis of the rural problem as many high farmers saw this problem. It provided means of encouraging the investment of capital in agriculture. But it only did so with respect to the land*owner*. As such, it also reflects the concern of many high farmers to perpetuate the status of the landlord and the integrity of the landed estate. In effect, the 'scheme' reflected the hope that landlords might have their cake and eat it too.

As initially proposed, corn law repeal was not to take effect for three years. But other parts of the 'scheme' were to come into effect immediately. These included a sharp reduction in the duties on grass and clover seeds. As Peel explained to the House on the evening of January 27, since clover seed was produced in only a very few British counties, and since it was required 'where agriculture is most advanced', the reduction in these duties should not be considered a 'removal of protection, but a benefit to agriculture'. [123] Then, maize and buckwheat, which were coming into use as fatteners for cattle, were to be admitted at a nominal duty immediately. Again drawing upon the assumptions symbolized by his charter membership in the English Agricultural Society he reminded his audience, '... there is nothing more important than the fattening of cattle to an improved system of agriculture because no other fertilizer is as good as manure.' [124] The same reasoning lay behind his proposal that the duties on linseed cake and rape cake be reduced at once. [125] He also proposed several ways by which the burden of rates might be reduced, particularly in the countryside. One of these involved reforms of the highway administration. [126] Another, more important, involved reforms of the poor law administration. He proposed to amend the law so that men born in the countryside but employed in a town could not be 'removed' so easily to their parishes of birth when depression hit the towns. [127] The purpose here was to so alter the poor law system that the economic burden of urban unemployment would not be thrown upon the rate-payers in the countryside. But most important of all was the drainage loan. [128]

The drainage loan was not calculated to provide the total capital necessary for land drainage. The amount of the loan was far too small for that. While Peel mentioned no figure in January, the initial sum later set aside under the Public Money Drainage Act, introduced in May and finally passed in August, was a mere £2m. During the previous few years the costs of land drainage had been radically reduced. [129] But even at the reduced costs £2m. would only have drained a small fraction of the land which the high farmers said required it. In effect, the loan was primarily a psychological measure designed to popularize high farming by facilitating the prerequisite land drainage on exactly those estates on which, as the Richmond Committee had reported the previous year, there was a 'natural reluctance of proprietors to expend capital upon the permanent improvement of land.' [130] These were the settled estates.

The proceedings and report of the Richmond Committee illustrate the combination of the two concerns, on the one hand, efficiency, on the other the perpetuation of traditional status. The Committee had been appointed 'to inquire into the expediency of a legislative enactment ... to enable possessors of entailed estates to charge such estates with a sum, to be limited, for the purpose of draining and otherwise improving the same.' Sitting under the chairmanship of the Duke of Richmond, who thus had a foot in both camps, they reiterated the case which the high farmers had been making for years – investments in land improvement were the essential prerequisite to agricultural prosperity. In addition, they noted the fact that in many cases tenants for life of settled estates could not make such investments. However, while recommending that steps be taken to facilitate investment they were adamant in their insistence that the substance of an entailed estate be protected against possible depletion.

The star witness before the Committee – perhaps its guiding light – was Josiah Parkes, a man who combined several significant roles. He was a private drainage contractor, a surveyor for the West of England and South Wales Land Drainage Company, advisor to several of the other witnesses and – thus further revealing the irony of the non-political role of the Royal Agricultural Society – consulting engineer for the Royal Agricultural Society.[131] Parkes' testimony, and that of most of the other witnesses, was focused on two main points: the profits which landowners might enjoy from high farming, and the impossibility of limited owners ever enjoying these profits unless they could mortgage their estates for productive purposes. But there was another question at issue which was raised in the light of Parkes' role as an employee of the West of England and South Wales Land Drainage Company. The Company had been chartered both to lend money for land drainage and to perform drainage work itself. But the Company had found that it could neither raise the money for the one function nor perform the other because of the 'want of power on the part of proprietors of entailed estates to give security on the estates for the money advanced and laid out in draining and other permanent improvements.'[132] Unfortunately for the Company, many of the men who wished to improve their estates held them under settlements which did not allow them to mortgage them for that purpose.

No one appeared before the Committee who was not on Parkes' side of the question. But much of the testimony to which the Committee listened was directed at points they might have raised, e.g., that high farming was particularly foolish when the trends of prices and, on some estates, of rents as well were down, that it was far better to invest in land purchase than land improvement. As Parkes explained, '. . . if rents have a tendency to fall the drainage of an estate which is water-logged may keep them up to what they are now, and even increase them.'[133] Applying Parkes' logic to the problem of the status of the landed classes, the Committee reported, '. . . the operation of draining, properly conducted, not only tends by its immediate effect to increase the produce of the soil and to facilitate its cultivation, but also permanently enhances the value of the inheritance to all future proprietors.'[134] But the Committee did not wish to free the limited owner from all restraint. It was important, they insisted, 'for the security of property, that much caution ... be exercised in the application of any powers which may be given for placing a charge upon the inheritance at the instance of persons having only a limited interest in the estate.'[135] They merely recommended that steps be taken to make it cheaper and easier for limited owners to obtain such powers where they were already available, in Chancery.

Peel tried to solve the same problem. But, rather than simplify procedures in Chancery, he proposed that in all normal cases the matter be taken out of the hands of Chancery. He proposed that unless an objection were filed by someone who had an interest in the estate the tenant for life should be able to obtain the powers necessary to borrow from the funds made available from the Treasury and to make the repayment a prior charge upon the estate by simple bureaucratic procedure. Authority to approve applications for funds and to make the repayment a prior charge upon the estate was to be given to the recently established Enclosure Commissioners. As far as concerned a loan from the public funds recourse to Chancery would only be necessary in the event of an objection.[136]

The essential relationship which Peel conceived between corn law repeal and the drainage loan is apparent from two of his observations. First, he expected that only a few objections would be made to charging an entailed estate with the costs of its own improvement. As he explained, even though repayment of the loan would be the first charge upon the estate – priority was required by the need to obviate any loss to the Treasury – and even without protection, the improvement of the estate would be a guarantee of all other charges.[137] Secondly, while he looked to the loan itself for many improvements, he also anticipated that the spirit of improvement would be strengthened when the effects of these initial improvements were seen.[138] Juxtaposed upon corn law repeal the drainage loan was an obvious attempt to rouse a large portion of the agricultural community from their fears and lethargy. Clearly, Peel was addressing the many men who, either directly or indirectly, still stood out against high farming when he acknowledged the widespread fears of foreign competition and added that with 'the application of capital, skill, and industry' this competition could be beaten.[139] His statement reflected the same confidence in scientific farming which he had expressed at the inaugural meeting of the English Agricultural Society. Lord George Bentinck implicitly acknowledged the same relationship between the corn laws and high farming when he appeared at the last effective meeting of the Central Agricultural Protection Association in May. Beaten politically the previous week when he led the protectionists' last stand in the House of Commons he now acknowledged the economic and ideological corollary of that defeat: he explained that the only salvation for English agriculture lay in the application of capital and science.[140]

Whether the confidence in land improvement was or was not justified in the long term, initially it was far more prevalent in Scotland than in England. The earliest applications for funds under the Drainage Act came largely from Scotland.[141] Only gradually did English landowners acquire the same confidence. By the middle fifties, however, when the funds provided by a second public loan, similar to the first, had been exhausted, a number of private companies were chartered to provide additional funds to meet the then mounting English demand. Like the drainage loan, the Acts chartering these companies contained *ad hoc* reforms of the land law. Furthermore, all but one of them assigned to the Enclosure Commissioners the same two functions of approving the loan and making the repayment a prior charge upon the estate which had been assigned to them under the Drainage Act. Because the rent charges the Commissioners imposed took precedence over all existing charges, even when the need to guarantee the Treasury against loss did not provide the rationale for such an arrangement, the Commissioners' services were often appealed to by owners in fee whose estates were already mortgaged but who wished to obtain additional funds for land improvement. The money on loans the Commissioners approved was available at a far lower rate than it would have been otherwise. That the owners of previous rent charges did not as a rule object to this procedure was a measure of the growing confidence in high farming. One of the Commissioners used the argument which Peel and Parkes had used earlier when, testifying before a subsequent Committee of the House of Lords, he explained that before approving a loan the Commissioners always assured themselves 'that the land [would] be improved to an extent exceeding the amount of the charge created'.[142] Thus, he continued, a landowner could 'get money very much cheaper [by dealing through them than he could otherwise], even assuming he could borrow at all, which of course a tenant for life could not . . .'[143]

As the Commissioner was implicitly explaining, it was the agricultural tenant who paid the immediate costs of land improvement. Improving the land 'to an extent exceeding the amount of the charge created' simply meant raising the rent by an amount exceeding the sum of interest and principal. As the agent of one of the lending companies explained, in most cases the increase in the rental value of an estate was almost double the amount of the rent charge which his company received in respect of the interest and principal on its loan.[144]

Initially, many farmers were obviously willing to shoulder the economic burden. As the same agent explained, 'If one man objected at all to the charge for the improvement, other competitors would appear, and the highest bidder would take the lands and pay the interest for proper improvements.' [145] But as time went on the point was finally reached at which many farmers were no longer willing to pay for these improvements without greater compensation. Nor were they willing to increase their own capital commitments in the exploitation of their farms without a positive guarantee that the ownership of this capital would remain in their hands. In effect, it proved impossible to change the landowner's role *vis-a-vis* those who might be his creditors without also changing his role *vis-a-vis* those who were his dependents.

In retrospect, it is obvious that the drainage loan was a step in each of three complementary processes, two of which culminated in the Settled Land Act of 1882, the third of which culminated in the Agricultural Holdings Act of 1883. By the measure of 1882 the individual tenant for life of a settled estate became an almost totally free agent for purposes of administering his estate while the estate itself was redefined from a unit of land to a unit of value. The tenant for life was empowered on his own authority to sell off portions of the land either to pay for improvements to the remainder or to obtain the capital which he might invest in certain specified securities. Settlement was finally shifted 'from the land to the purchase money.' [146] According to the Agricultural Holdings Act of the following year the agricultural tenant could no longer contract himself out of the right of ownership which he had acquired in 1875 in the unexhausted value of the improvements he might have made to his farm. Thereafter, in most instances, his landlord was legally obligated to compensate him for his improvements at such time as he quitted his farm.

But the men who passed the Drainage Acts or administered them had not tried to create a landless landed gentry or a class of agricultural tenants with legally defined rights in their farms. [147] They were not interested in Joseph Hume's suggestion, in 1847, that, instead of voting additional public funds which landowners might borrow for land improvement, Parliament should allow these landowners to sell off portions of their estates to raise the money necessary for improving the remainders. [148] They were mainly concerned to obviate the need for such sales in Britain, if not in Ireland. Indeed, in the middle fifties the possibility that debts might be incurred which, ultimately, would force the break-up of British estates prompted one of the Enclosure Commissioners to criticize the provisions of one drainage company's charter, according to which a man with a limited interest in an estate could, under certain circumstances, mortgage the estate without the Commissioners' approval, 'and in fact without any control at all.' [149]

While the Commissioner may have been speaking as a jealous bureaucrat the question of his bureaucratic authority was only raised in the context of his concern for the reversioner's interests. As for the creation of a class of agricultural tenants in England with legally defined rights in their farms, many of the men who voted for the drainage loan and for subsequent measures by which the powers of tenants for life of settled estates were enhanced, voted against tenant right legislation from the time such legislation was first proposed until 1883 when, with little left to save of the integrity of the estate, an effective tenant right Bill for England was finally passed. The economic problems were the same in the two cases – how to provide the increasing quantities of capital for which the high farmers were calling. But the social problems were vastly different.

Like Parkes, who appeared before the Richmond Committee in 1845 to argue the merits of allowing tenants for life of settled estates to borrow money for land improvement and to make the repayment of the loan a charge upon the estate, Lord Portman and Philip Pusey, who introduced the first tenant right legislation into Parliament, were intimately associated with the Royal Agricultural Society. But, in a Parliament largely composed of landowners for whom land had not been fully redefined in economic terms, their cause was rather unpopular. It was incontestable that when a farmer invested money in so-called 'permanent improvements' – when he drained, fenced, or erected buildings on his farm – he was contributing to the wealth of his landlord. But to recognize this in law was to alter the relations between landlord and tenant. As proposed in Portman's Bill of 1844, if a tenant wished to make such permanent improvements he should so inform his landlord in writing; if his landlord did not wish to compensate him with a sum representing the 'amount of loss incurred by [him in] quitting the said premises so improved,' this amount to be determined by arbitration in the event of disagreement, he should so inform him in writing within three months of receiving his notice of intention.[150] The subsequent Bills which Pusey introduced were similar. None would have forced a landlord to compensate his tenant beyond a sum he had previously agreed in principle to pay. However, by acknowledging the principle that the tenant should be compensated they proposed what was, in fact, compulsory arbitration. Inevitably, a referee would have had to be appointed to determine the loss which the tenant would incur.

Until the eighties this was too much. It bears directly upon the questions which Cobden implicitly raised – what did the Reform Act 'decree'? and, what did the Corn Importation Act 'realise'? – that tenant right legislation was totally blocked in the forties and often on the grounds that it would not only destroy the 'happy relationship' between landlord and tenant but would also put a stop to land improvement. According tò several M.P.s, no landlord would agree in writing to compensate his tenant if, by doing so, he were to place himself in a position in which his relations with his tenant became a matter which others might judge.[151] As long as the concern for status was as reflected by this argument, and as long as the landed estate was the principal arena in which status was exercised and acknowledged, the most that could be had in the way of tenant right legislation was an Act of 1851 according to which a tenant who had obtained his landlord's consent in writing, and who had put up farm buildings or machinery at his own cost, could remove these at the expiration of his tenancy subject to an option on the landlord's part to buy them at a valuation.[152] Presumably, what made this measure acceptable and the others not, was the fact that the landlord was not thereby coerced. A third party might be required to value the tenant's improvements. But the landlord retained the option whether or not to accept the valuation and to act upon it: he remained the determinor of the rights of his dependents. His need, while doing so, to retain the self-image of fairness and benevolence is suggested by the Duke of Argyle's subsequent criticism of compulsory tenant right: 'Life would be intolerable in any profession, if men were obliged to be looking at everything in a barely legal or barely pecuniary point of view.'[153]

But the informality of relationship on which the traditional status of the landlord was based could scarcely survive the requirement that the agricultural tenant greatly increase his own investments in his farm. Not until the latter seventies did an organization come into being which symbolized the conflict of interest between landlord and tenant. This was the Farmers' Alliance. Ostensibly, the Alliance was responsible for the defeat of various 'landlord' candidates in the English counties in 1880.[154] However, if the structural or sociological implications of high farming were not fully realized until then these had been apparent to many men many years earlier. It was after the vote on one of Pusey's tenant right Bills, in 1847, that a correspondent in the *Mark Lane Express,* the most widely read agricultural weekly, considered the question why the farmers, whom he described as the largest and richest class in the kingdom, were always so badly treated. His conclusions were two: that they had no adequate awareness of their own common interests, and that they were 'dependent for their holdings upon others with whom their own interests are not unfrequently antagonistic'.[155] The importance of the corn law question in the countryside was presumably in part a measure of the strength of the wish, on the part of many tenants as well as many landlords, to perpetuate the circumstances in which such antagonism would be kept in check. It was this which a witness cited, in 1869, while explaining the nature of landlord influence in the countryside to the members of the Select Committee on Parliamentary and Municipal Elections. Tenants, he said, wished to please their landlords because their landlords, and their landlords' agents, could do so much to make life easy for them. There were 'all sorts of petty indulgences', he explained, which it was in the power of the landlord or his agent to give or to withhold, '[money for] small repairs, additional gates, and perhaps a little time to pay his rent'.[156]

VII

Traditionally, the repeal of the corn laws has been used not only to mark a step in the development of a general free trade policy – which, of course, it does – but also to illustrate that growth of urban influence within the State which has often been described as a direct consequence of the first Reform Act. In effect, the story of corn law repeal has often been told as if, in the words which Cobden used in his letter to Peel in the summer of 1846, 'the Corn Bill realised' what 'the Reform Bill decreed'. In part, the corrective to this procedure lies in the various provisions of the Reform Act which historians have tended to ignore. In part, it lies in the differences between the rural problem of the forties as the Ministers and potential Ministers tended to understand it and as most members of the Anti-Corn Law League and most members of the Central Agricultural Protection Association understood it. In part, again, it lies in the apparent paradox which Professor J. B. Conacher recently noted concerning the Peelites, that 'Although progressive in their views on the commercial policy of the newly industrialised Britain, to a curious extent the Peelites represented in their constituencies the old England of the past.' [157] But to criticise Cobden's argument on the grounds that he used a mechanism which did not exist to explain an event which had not occurred is not to dispose of his argument. Rather, it is to raise the question why the argument seemed valid. The answer presumably, lies in the function it performed as an essential corollary to the economic argument or arguments. This function presumably holds the key to an important political question.

As Miss Betty Kemp recently noted, Peel's handling of the various crises of 1845 and 1846 reveals his concern to prevent the substitution of the constitutional principle of electoral or popular sovereignty – that implicit in Cobden's references to what 'the Reform Bill decreed' and what 'the Corn Bill realised' – for the principle of parliamentary sovereignty. In particular, there was his refusal to dissolve Parliament after his defeat on the Irish Coercion Bill in June 1846. By then the Corn Bill had been passed. But the Protectionists had their revenge when they coalesced with various Whigs and Radicals on the Irish question. In these circumstances Peel had two alternatives. He could resign, thus accepting defeat at the hands of these men. Or he could dissolve Parliament, thus, as it were, appealing over their heads to the voters in their constituencies. As Miss Kemp notes, in all probability, had Peel dissolved he would have had his own revenge. However, as she explains, the price of this revenge would have been the violation of his constitutional principles. Such an election would have been a referendum. In his eyes a referendum was a simple perversion. As she puts it, Peel believed that

> Parliament . . . was sovereign and should decide . . . all . . . questions of policy that arose; the peoples' function, at general elections, was to choose a House of Commons, not to decide on policy nor to designate a government . . . His resignation . . . vindicated the right of the Commons to turn out ministers and even, indirectly, the right of the monarch to choose them, and his refusal to fight an election on the personal issue of his retention of office denied both rights to the electorate.[158]

And, she adds, Peel's view of the appropriate functions of voters and M.P.s 'is usually labelled a pre-1832 view'. Her analysis and observation raise the important questions of how and why the one view was replaced by the other. The answers presumably lie in the exigencies of the political system which came into being after 1832.

As suggested by Cobden's letter to Peel — implying, as it does, that the voters were not only choosing M.P.s but determining both how they would behave in Parliament and what policies governments would follow — and as suggested by the analogous statements of the various Protectionists who attributed corn law repeal to the pressures of the Anti-Corn Law League, many of Peel's contemporaries either failed to notice or refused to acknowledge the significance of his own behaviour and the significance of the behaviour of many of his followers.[159] Neither Peel nor his followers were responding directly — and directly is the crucial word — to pressures generated in the various constituencies, pressures which the various constituency perspectives reflected. This is apparent from those provisions of Peel's 'general scheme' which historians have tended to ignore. These reveal the differences between *his* understanding of the economic problems of the forties and the understandings of these problems articulated by the members of the Anti-Corn Law League on the one hand and by the members of the Central Agricultural Protection Association on the other. He and his followers were behaving in terms of a non-constituency perspective, in terms which the various constituency perspectives have tended to obscure. Indeed, the principal impact of constituency pressures in 1846 was not so much to repeal the corn laws as to obscure the concerns which corn law repeal reflected and the mechanisms by which it was effected.

In 1842, when Peel reduced the levels of agricultural protection as a means of enhancing price stability, he created serious problems for the leaders of the Anti-Corn Law League. As Dr McCord notes, these men responded by attributing 'any improvement [in their economic position] to Peel's partial implementation of their theories' – thus, of course, obscuring the point which Peel had been at pains to make: he was *not* implementing *their* theories – and by attributing 'any continuing depression . . . [to] the remaining vestiges of protection and especially . . . [to] the Corn Laws'.[162] In 1846, when Peel proposed not only to give agriculturists three years grace in which to adjust their priorities from price to productivity but also to use the resources of the State to assist them in making this adjustment, he again created problems for the Leaguers. As Dr McCord notes, when the terms of Peel's 'general scheme' were announced 'there were anxious discussions among the Leaguers as to the course to be pursued . . . A number of the more extreme members of the League Council . . . wanted to fight Peel and everyone else unless the League was given full satisfaction.'[161] The question at issue was not repeal itself: that had been promised. It was the Leaguers' ability to claim the trophy which, from their point of view, repeal should have symbolized. In particular, they wanted immediate repeal. In the end the decision was made to 'offer no factious or fanatical opposition to Sir Robert Peel's measure'.[162] But the trophy was claimed in the context of the argument in Cobden's letter: 'the Corn Bill realised' what 'the Reform Bill decreed'. Things had not happened as they implied they had happened. But in helping to create a past they were also helping to mould a future.

Peel's failure to control the understanding of corn law repeal – the fact that the niceties of his constitutional lesson have only recently been noted – should presumably be attributed to that 'defect' of the Reform Act to which Russell referred in 1854, the tendency, as he put it, of the various county and borough Members to be 'too generally exclusive in respect of the interest[s] they cared for'. Russell begged an extremely important question – to what extent this 'defect' was really attributable to the Act. But the importance of this question should not be allowed to obscure the importance of the relationships to which he pointed. Not only do these relationships hold an important key to the nature of the mid-century political system. They also hold an important key to the understanding – or, rather, to the *mis*understanding – of this system as is revealed in Cobden's letter.

And, again, if the usual formulations of the corn law question helped to perpetuate the traditional agencies of electoral recruitment in town and countryside, then, as a further illustration of Lewis Coser's basic proposition concerning the 'Group-binding functions of conflict', we should note that the repeal of the corn laws may have involved a threat to the structure of British society no less real than that involved in the corn law crisis itself.[163] If the belief in the legitimacy of the roles of the various local elites was in part a function of the efforts of these men to identify themselves with the interests their constituencies symbolized and to condition these interests in terms appropriate to their own roles within them, then, presumably, both their status and the structure of the groups in which this status was enjoyed were weakened when the corn laws were repealed. And, furthermore, as a further illustration of Professor Coser's corollary proposition concerning 'The search for enemies', the removal of this issue may hold an important answer to the question why, in the latter fifties and early sixties, many urban leaders returned to the county arena in the context of a new anti-landlord campaign; why election managers found that they were less able to forecast the outcome of a prospective contest with their wonted accuracy in the light of the information they had been in the habit of using; why the Derby-Disraeli Reform Bill was passed; why contested elections became increasingly frequent; why poll books became unpublishable; and why new mass-membership political parties were established.[164]

Part IV

Efforts at repair

9

The second Reform Act

I

Within the context of modern British political culture the assumption
that changes in the distribution of political power can be effected by
legislation is extremely important. Indeed, this assumption not only
provides the formal rationale of much political activity, it provides the
framework in which many such changes have been explained. Clearly,
many of these explanations are valid. But if what is sought is less a
means of confirming certain cultural values – however important – and
more a means of explaining certain changes in the distribution of
political power in the nineteenth century two points should not be
ignored: first, that various changes in the distribution of power were
occasioned more by voluntary political activity than they were by
legislation; and, second, that various pieces of nineteenth century
legislation, while themselves effecting changes in the distribution of
power, were clearly designed to control or counteract other such
changes which were stemming from other sources. Illustrations of the
first point can be seen in the effects of the tendency of the various urban
elites to withdraw from the county arena in the years immediately after
the first Reform Bill was passed and to return to the county arena in the
latter 50s and early 60s. Illustrations of the second can be seen in the
boundary scheme and the borough freeholder clause – even the
amended clause – of the first Reform Act, various provisions of the
second Reform Act which historians have generally ignored, and
certain other provisions of this Act which, although frequently
mentioned, have rarely been probed for anything resembling their full
implication.

As a rule, those who have discussed the second Reform Act have
done so as if the principal – or even the sole – effects of the Act were to

greatly enlarge the borough electorates, to enlarge the county
electorates somewhat less, and to transfer a sizeable number of seats
from the smaller two-Member boroughs to the counties, the largest
existing boroughs, certain of the growing towns which had not
previously been separately represented, and the University of London.
When the Act is thus defined and when the enfranchising provisions of
the Act are given special emphasis – and, generally, these are the
provisions to which special emphasis has been given – its background is
generally sought in the spread of democratic ideals and, as both a
complementary and confirming phenomenon, the ostensibly growing
'fitness' of the so-called 'aristocracy of labour' to share political power
with their 'betters'. The story has often been told how free trade and
abundant gold broadened the ladder up which Britons were climbing
out of the depression of the early 40s; how, as their climb progressed,
many of the higher paid artisans in the newer industries who,
ostensibly, had provided much of the Chartist leadership in the 40s,
abandoned revolutionary goals for reformist goals and associated
bourgeois values; and how, as they adopted these goals and values, those
cross-class alliances were formed which provide the logic of John
Bright's reform proposals and which are institutionally symbolized by
the Reform Union, with its demands for household suffrage and, even
more, by the Reform League, with its demands for manhood suffrage
and the secret ballot. In the context of this story the Act has generally
been described as either the reward which the working classes earned
for their 'good' behaviour or as the concession they won after various
leaders of the Reform League demonstrated their ability to hold reform
demonstrations in Hyde Park in July 1866, and again in May 1867, in
violation of the Home Office orders prohibiting them from doing so.
Nor are these two descriptions so very different from one another.
They are variations on the same basic theme. The Home Office orders
were clearly class measures. As such, they were clearly incompatible
with that ostensible assimilation of *bourgeois* values by the working
classes to which Gladstone implicitly referred, in 1866, when he
explained that the Franchise Bill of the Russell Government had been
largely prompted by the 'moral spectacle of Lancashire during the
cotton famine'.[1] The validity of Gladstone's explanation is confirmed
by the provisions of this Bill and by those of the Redistribution Bill he
subsequently introduced after the Russell Government had conceded to
their critics' demands that they reveal their entire reform scheme before
proceeding with the Franchise Bill. But these Bills were not passed.
The Act of 1867 was a very different measure – and different in certain
important ways which not only explain why the Conservatives
preferred it to the Liberal measures but which suggest a dynamic of
reform which has not been adequately noted.[2]

II

As a rule, historians have focused upon the similarities between the Bill of 1866 and the Act of 1867 and, in the light of these similarities, upon certain differences between the two measures, or sets of measures, which might be explained in terms of the ostensible parliamentary response to radical agitation. In certain respects, of course, the measures were similar. And, in the light of certain assumptions the Act was the more radical. But there were other assumptions in the light of which it was not only less radical but positively anti-radical. Unfortunately, these latter assumptions have not been adequately noted. Nor have those provisions which, in the context of certain phenomena, illustrate the legislative importance of these assumptions. Indeed, as with the first Reform Act, so with the second: historians have tended to focus their attention upon certain provisions while ignoring those other provisions which either conditioned the impact of these provisions or were triggered by them. Furthermore, they have tended to ignore the phenomena to which these other provisions were obviously related. If these other provisions be restored to their legislative context, and if they be seen against the background of the phenomena to which they are obviously related, it becomes clear that the second Reform Act was designed to control or counteract the political impact of the various forces and factors which were tending to alter or destroy the political world which had come into being after 1832.

According to Homersham Cox, that ardent Gladstonian publicist, the Conservative Bill of 1867, in the form in which it was finally passed, was essentially the same as the Liberal Bills of 1866. Ostensibly, the Liberal majority in the House had so altered the Bill as to make it their own. In one of the first histories of the two measures, a work published in 1868, he contended that the only 'exclusively ... Conservative' provisions of the second Reform Act were its title, a clause disfranchising four small boroughs, a clause penalizing the corrupt payment of rates, and a clause indicating who might vote at a contest should one occur before the new registers were completed.[3] Whatever the criteria on which Cox's judgment was based there were, in fact, few significant provisions which the two measures had in common. One of these was the general requirement of a one year's residence in a constituency before a would-be voter could be registered to vote there. Another was the successive occupancy provision: a voter would not lose his qualification if he moved from one qualifying premise to another. And another was the lodger franchise in the boroughs. In its final form the Act allowed – as the Franchise Bill would have allowed –a man to vote in a borough if he occupied lodgings in the borough 'of clear yearly value, if let unfurnished, of

£10'.[4] Indeed, the wording in the one was the same as the wording in the other. However, while these were almost the only provisions they had in common it is questionable exactly how different would have been the impact of certain of the other provisions.

The Franchise Bill would have allowed a man to vote in a borough if he 'occupied premises of any tenure in the borough of clear yearly value of £7'.[5] The Act provided 'household suffrage'. It allowed a man to vote in a borough if he was 'an inhabitant occupier, as owner or tenant, of any dwelling house within the borough'.[6] The phrase, 'household suffrage', had tremendous emotive force. But the question remains whether any significantly larger numbers of men were able to vote in the boroughs in consequence of the enfranchising provisions of the Act than would have been able to vote in the boroughs in consequence of the enfranchising provisions of the Bill. A 'dwelling house' was more restrictive than 'premises'. Furthermore, the Act required that the rates payable on each dwelling house which provided a qualification under the Act be paid at 'an equal amount in the pound to that payable by other ordinary occupiers.'[7] The Bill contained no similar provision. The extra-ordinary occupiers were the so-called compound ratepayers, those whose rates were paid not by themselves directly but by their landlords indirectly. As a rule, these were the men whose rates were the lowest – and this, in part, because many parish authorities were willing to allow reductions of rates where the landlord paid them in a lump sum on behalf of his tenants. Thus, while the Act contained no stipulation concerning the value of the property which the would-be voter had to occupy, or the value of the rates he had to pay,it required that many pay a considerable price for the rights to vote which it offered. These points aside, the principal difference between the borough franchise provisions of the Bill and those of the Act is that between extending the franchise to those men who, for at least a year, had resided in the borough and occupied premises for which they paid 2 shillings 8 pence a week in rent, and extending the franchise to those who, whatever the rent or rates they paid, had resided in the borough and occupied a separate dwelling house in the borough for at least a year. From some points of view there was considerable importance in stipulating the rent or rates the would-be voter would have to pay. As the secretary of the City of London Liberal Registration Association explained, however, in 1860, the £6 occupation franchise in the boroughs which was then being proposed was tantamount to household suffrage because there were few premises available for rent in any borough in the kingdom for less than 2 shillings 6 pence a week.[8]

In a county the Franchise Bill would have given the vote to a man who 'occupied premises of any tenure in the county of clear yearly value of £14'. But it specified that 'where the premises consist partly of a house or other building and partly of land, the building must either be the dwelling house of the occupier, or must itself be of clear yearly value of £6.'[9] Furthermore, while the Bill would not have reduced the existing levels for the copyhold or leasehold franchises it would have removed the distinctions contained in the sections 24 and 25 of the first Reform Act between the rights of a borough freeholder to vote in a county and the rights of a borough copyholder or borough leaseholder to do so. Had the Bill been passed in the form in which it was introduced every £10 copyholder or leaseholder whose property was located in a borough would have been able to qualify to vote in the county in which the borough was located except where he was qualified to vote in the borough in respect of that particular property.[10] In effect, the Bill would have gone a step beyond Webb v. the Overseers of Birmingham in assimilating the rights of copyholders and leaseholders to those of freeholders.[11] Furthermore, the Bill contained an important 'Saving clause' about which there has been an apparent conspiracy of silence. Had the Bill been passed a man who was registered to vote in either borough or county would have remained registered as long as he retained his qualification.[12] The mention of borough voters in this clause was completely gratuitous. No borough voter was remotely threatened with the loss of his vote by any provision of the Bill. But a sizeable number of county voters might have been threatened. The 'Saving clause' would have saved them. In consequence of this clause the generally contingent enlargements of the borough boundaries for which the subsequent Redistribution Bill provided would have had no immediate effect upon the county registers. Those resident borough freeholders would also have been able to retain their county votes whose properties were worth the 40s a year necessary for them to qualify as county voters but less than the £10 a year necessary for them to qualify as borough voters under the provisions of the Act of 1832. In effect, various men would have acquired borough votes as £7 occupiers without sacrificing the county votes they had previously enjoyed as 40s-freeholders in respect of the same properties. The county franchise provisions which the Act contained were fundamentally different.

The Act allowed a man to vote in a county who was 'the occupier, as owner or tenant, of lands or tenements within the county of rateable value of £12'.[13] Obviously, to stipulate 'lands or tenements' was somewhat less restrictive than to stipulate 'premises' – especially when, if the premises consisted of land as well as building, the building had to be either the dwelling house of the occupier or of clear yearly value of £6. Significantly, however, the category of men thereby enfranchised by the Act – those who occupied lands alone, not 'tenements' or 'premises' – scarcely testifies to the importance of that fundamentally urban pressure for reform to which, as a rule, the Act has been attributed, especially if the inclusion of these men be seen in the context of those increments of urban power which occurred in North Warwickshire and South Leicestershire in the latter 50s and early 60s. Nor should it be forgotten that while the £12 figure finally adopted in 1867 was £2 lower than that proposed in the Franchise Bill it was applied to 'rateable value', not to 'clear yearly value'. For a given piece of property the rateable value was generally lower than the clear yearly value. Unfortunately, however, since there was no standard relationship between the two it would be difficult to determine whether the occupation franchise in the counties provided by the Act was more or less generous than that proposed in the Franchise Bill.

But the question of generosity aside, there are certain obvious differences between the county franchise provisions of the two measures. Because of several Liberal amendments the Act reduced the copyhold and leasehold qualifications. It allowed a man to vote in a county if he was a copyholder or leaseholder 'of any lands or tenements ... of clear yearly value of £5'.[14] But it also reiterated sections 24 and 25 of the Act of 1832 – the one excluding a freeholder of borough property from voting in the surrounding county in respect of that property if the property provided *him* with a borough qualification, the other excluding a copyholder or leaseholder of borough property from voting in the surrounding county in respect of that property if the property provided 'him or any other person' with a borough qualification. Furthermore, the Act invoked these sections upon the new borough franchise qualifications.[15] The Act contained a 'Saving clause.' But this clause was no defence against the other. While it stipulated that 'The franchises conferred by this Act shall be in addition to and not in substitution for any existing franchises', it went on to say, ' ... subject to the provisions of this Act, all laws, customs and enactments now in force ... shall remain in force'.[16] The provisions of the Act of 1832 which not only remained in force but were specifically invoked meant that those smaller resident freeholders in the boroughs and leaseholders and copyholders of borough property whose tenants were now enfranchised in the boroughs lost their country votes. The Act did not explicitly reverse the decision of the Court of Common Pleas in the case of Webb v. the Overseers fo Birmingham. But the circumstances to which the decision applied were so greatly changed that the decision lost most of its political significance. *Terms,* meaning estates or tenancies, were still divisible. But there was little purpose in proclaiming their divisibility when most of their parts were useless as electoral qualifications. As Cox and Grady noted, in their edition of 1868,

No freehold dwelling house will now give a vote for the county if in the occupation of the owner. Formerly, all such houses below the value of 10 l. per annum conferred the county franchise . . .

No copyhold or leasehold dwelling house in a borough will now confer a vote for the county . . . nor will a shop or building of less value than 10 l., save in the one case of the leasehold consisting of several houses (not dwelling houses) each of less value than 10 l., for then they would not give a vote for the borough, and therefore, if of the value of 5 l. per annum, they would give a vote for the county.[17]

The importance of the fact that sections 24 and 25 of the Act of 1832 were reiterated in section 59 of the Act of 1867 is apparant from the case of Chorlton v. Johnson, in 1868, when the Court of Common Pleas affirmed the revising barrister's decision, that Henry Bunting should not remain registered for South East Lancashire in respect of his interest as a leaseholder in two dwelling houses in the borough of Manchester for which he had been registered before. As the reporter observed,

By 2 Wm. 4 c. 45, s. 25, it is enacted that no person shall be entitled to vote in the election of knights of the shire in respect of his interest . . . as such lessee as aforesaid . . . in any house . . . of such value as would according to the provisions hereinafter contained confer on him or any other person the right of voting for any city or borough; by 30 & 31 Vict. c. 102, s. 59, the expressions 'as aforesaid' and 'hereinafter contained' are to apply to the provisions of the later Act.

A. was, at the time of the passing of 30 & 31 Vict. c. 102, properly on the list of voters for the county of L., as lessee for a term of sixty years of two dwelling houses, which were situate within the borough of M., the yearly value of neither of them being £10. By that Act, the borough franchise was extended to all inhabitant householders paying rates, and the occupiers of the houses then became entitled to vote for the borough:—

Held, that A. was not entitled to have his name retained on the county list.[18]

There is perhaps not much to choose between the gross redistribution schemes of the two measures. The Redistribution Bill which Gladstone introduced in May 1866, would have transferred 49 seats to the counties, the largest existing boroughs, some previously unrepresented towns, the University of London, and Scotland. These seats would have been taken from 49 of the smallest boroughs. None of these boroughs would have been disfranchised entirely. But most of them would have found themselves sharing their Member or Members with one or more adjacent boroughs whose representative strengths would have been similarly reduced.[19] In its final form the Act transferred 45 seats, 38 from the smaller two-Member boroughs which lost one seat each and 7 from 4 boroughs which were disfranchised for corruption. Most of these seats went to the counties – much as they would have gone to the counties had the earlier Redistribution Bill been passed. Others went to the largest existing boroughs, some previously unrepresented towns, and the University of London.[20] But the counties to which the majority of these seats were assigned were very different constituencies as they were projected in the Act from what they were as projected in the Franchise and Redistribution Bills of 1866. In part these differences were functions of the different franchise provisions. But even more they were functions of the different boundary schemes. Unfortunately, the boundary provisions of the various nineteenth century reform bills have been generally ignored. The provisions of 1866 and 1867 are no exceptions.

III

As Gladstone acknowledged when introducing the Franchise Bill, a 'complete measure' of reform would include more than mere alterations of the franchise. Among other things it would include the redistribution of seats. And along with the redistribution of seats came the question of constituency boundaries. But these other things, he declared, were extremely complex. In consequence, the Government had decided to postpone them until a later session.[21] Whatever his candour in thus explaining it, the Government's decision was widely suspect. As a rule, these suspicions have been explained as products of concern about the survival of one or another particular borough. In effect, they have been explained – as by Dr Smith recently – in the context of redistribution alone and attributed to 'the Whig proprietors and the small borough men'.[22] But there were others, Disraeli among them, who, from what they said in Parliament, were principally concerned lest the boundaries question be handled in the way the 'Saving clause' and the borough copyholder and borough leaseholder provisions suggested it would be handled, not as a means of restoring the distinctions between county and borough which urbanization, population movement and voluntary political activity were tending to weaken, but as a means of weakening these distinctions still further.[23]

Disraeli apparently prepared the motion criticising the Government's procedure which was introduced by Earl Grosvenor on the first night of the second reading of the Franchise Bill.[24] But the discovery of this fact has not affected the tendency to consider the motion, and the behaviour of the large minority of the House who voted for it, solely in the light of the redistribution question, not in the light of Disraeli's expressed concern over the boundaries question, a concern to which Gladstone directly referred in his major speech against the motion.[25] The size of the minority boded ill for the Russell Government. Had party lines held firm the Government would have had a majority of 60 or 70. But on this motion their majority was reduced to 5. 313 Members voted with Grosvenor and Disraeli,

> That this House, while ready to consider, with a view to its settlement, the question of Parliamentary Reform, is of opinion that it is inexpedient to discuss a Bill for the reduction of the Franchise in England and Wales until the House has before it the entire scheme contemplated by the Government for the amendment of the representation of the people.[26]

Grosvenor was a good Whig. While explaining his behaviour in introducing the motion – Disraeli's role was, of course, kept secret – he declared that he had not deserted his party: the Government had done so.[27] Shortly after the vote on his motion the Redistribution Bill was introduced. This revealed both how the Government proposed to redistribute seats from the smallest boroughs to the largest counties and towns and how they proposed to handle the boundaries question. Their redistribution scheme incorporated the principle of grouping. But in other respects it was not unlike that which their opponents later proposed. And too much emphasis should not be placed on the fact that the one scheme incorporated the grouping principle, the other did not. A motion opposing the grouping principle was, indeed, introduced. But it was withdrawn, and largely on Grosvenor's recommendation.[28] On the other hand, there was a world of difference between the boundary scheme which this Bill revealed and that of the later Derby Government.

The boundary scheme which Gladstone described in May 1866, was all that Disraeli feared it would be. In his speech on Grosvenor's motion Disraeli stressed that in his eyes a county franchise should be 'a county franchise . . . a suffrage exercised by those who have a natural relation to the chief property and to the chief industry of the county.'[29] What he sought in a boundary scheme was a means of restoring the powers of the traditional leaders of the landed interest and, more generally, of restoring the integrity of the traditional agencies of electoral recruitment, by restricting the county franchise to those men who possessed the appropriate attributes. His concerns are apparent from his contention that the only defence against the assumption of power by 'demagogues' lay in that correspondence between constituencies and the traditional interest groups in the kingdom which facilitated the return of 'great proprietors' and 'great manufacturers' to Parliament.[30] From Gladstone's point of view, on the other hand – and, presumably, his point of view had been clarified when he was

returned 'unmuzzled' in 1865 from the semi-urban constituency of
South Lancashire – 'to meddle with the boundaries of boroughs for the
sake of affecting questions of town and county representation, and the
balance of interests, would . . . be a gross abuse'.[31] No doubt about it:
Gladstone was a clever advocate. To criticise his opponents for wishing
to do with legislation what he did not need legislation to do for himself
was to obscure the process by which 'questions of town and country
representation, and the balance of interests', were in fact being affected.
He claimed the virtues of non-intervention without noting that such
non-intervention served to strengthen the interests with which he was
increasingly identified.

As he explained, the Russell Government's boundary scheme was
principally designed to assimilate the parliamentary boundaries of the
existing boroughs to their municipal boundaries. Where the municipal
boundaries of a borough extended beyond the parliamentary
boundaries the latter were to be made to coincide with the former.[32]
And this, he contended, should be an on-going process: a Bill would
have been introduced for this purpose.[33] Had these Bills been passed a
principle would have been established: the parliamentary boundaries of
a borough would be extended when, and only when, the area within
which the urban authorities performed their various activities was
enlarged, thus when the area within which the rates were collected
which paid for these activities was enlarged. Whatever the role of the
generally higher urban, rates in inhibiting the extension of the
municipal boundaries, it would scarcely have encouraged the
parliamentary boundaries of a borough to have made their extension
dependent upon the extension of the municipal boundaries. And, in
any event, the political impact of this happening would have been
rather limited.[34] Because the Franchise Bill contained an efficient
Saving clause the extension of the parliamentary boundaries of a
borough would have had no immediate effect upon the number of
urban or suburban votes in the surrounding county. It has been noted
that in relatively few cases were the areas encompassed by the
municipal boundaries of a borough larger than those of the
parliamentary boundaries – in effect few cases where the procedure
described by Gladstone would have worked to extend the
parliamentary boundaries. of the borough.[35] But because the Saving
clause has been ignored, the fact that even where the parliamentary
boundaries of a borough would have been extended this would not
have restored the significance of the county franchise which Disraeli
hoped to restore, has been neglected. There was a community element
in Gladstone's design. But the communities to which it was oriented
were solely the urban communities, not those other communities into
which the urban populations were overflowing. 'A local community,

wherever it is, should be represented', Gladstone declared. But these communities were to be identified principally by those who lived in them, thus were to reflect their concerns. 'We think the best and safest definition of a local community', he went on, 'will be obtained by giving facilities to the inhabitants for fixing its limits from time to time as considerations of their own practical convenience may dictate and require.'[36]   His declaration is consistent with the provisions he described. The only cases in which borough boundaries would have been otherwise determined were those of the boroughs which the Redistribution Bill itself would have created. Tentative boundaries had been assigned to these boroughs. According to the Bill these tentative boundaries would have been examined by men appointed by the Inclosure Commissioners to determine 'whether any enlargement of the boundaries of such boroughs is necessary in order to include within the area thereof the population properly belonging to such boroughs respectively'. Where this was the case the Commissioners were to 'propose such new boundaries (if any) as in their judgment would effect that object'.[37]   Subject to parliamentary confirmation the Commissioners' proposals would have defined the boundaries of *these* boroughs. The criterion and procedure were almost word for word those described in the Conservative Reform Bill of 1859 and the Act of 1867 – saving the point that in the Act the responsibility for determining which populations were 'proper' to which constituency was placed in the hands of specified Boundary Commissioners, not in the hands of the Inclosure Commissioners. But in the Bill of 1859 and in the Act of 1867 the men charged to apply this criterion were charged to apply it to every borough in England and Wales. The difference is crucial.

IV

Had the Bills of 1866 been passed, and had the agencies and mechanisms of electoral recruitment on which the mid-century political system was based retained their efficiency, the powers of the urban interest as it existed in the mid-century would have been considerably enhanced. This would in part have been the consequence of the provisions which these Bills contained. But it would also have been the consequence of the provisions which these Bills did not contain: these Bills would have done nothing to control or counteract the political impact of the on-going processes of urbanization and urban overspill. The Bill of 1859, on the other hand, and the Act of 1867, were designed to restrain the political impact of these processes. Whatever the success of the Act in restraining them – and, obviously its success in this respect could scarcely be measured – one of the principal means by which those who drafted the Act hoped to restrain

them was by enlarging the areas of the boroughs. To enlarge these was
to enlarge the areas within which the new borough franchise
provisions obtained. Thus, it was to enlarge the numbers of borough
voters. As a rule, however, the enlargement of the borough electorates
has been attributed solely to the enfranchising provisions of the Act.[38]
Whatever the reason for this the consequence has been unfortunate. It
has helped to obscure the fundamental differences between the
concerns of the men who drafted the different Bills. Thus it has helped
to obscure the fundamental differences between the 'problems' which
these men hoped to solve. For when we observe that the enlargement
of the borough electorates was in part the consequence of the extension
of the borough boundaries we can scarcely ignore the fact that the
enlargement of borough electorates was in part the consequence of the
effort to restore that separation of interests into different constituencies
which had been such an important goal of the members of the Grey
Ministry. Or, to put it somewhat differently, we can scarcely ignore
the fact that what has generally been described as the pre-eminent
achievement of the second Reform Act was in part the consequence of
the effort to curtail those changes in the distribution of power with
which this achievement is usually associated.

As Disraeli explained in 1859, there were, in fact, two schools of
parliamentary reformers in the kingdom. The one, he declared,
included his colleagues in the Derby Ministry. They hoped to 'adapt
the settlement of 1832 to the England of 1859'. The other included their
political opponents. They hoped 'to realize the opinion of the
numerical majority of the country'.[39] Whatever the degree of
exaggeration on the one side, on the other such descriptions were a
simple parody. Most Conservatives were far too frightened of the
radical associations of reform to appreciate the possibilities of using
reform to protect their own powers within the State. Few Liberals
were in favour of anything remotely approaching manhood suffrage.
But these descriptions are useful none the less. They confirm a point
illustrated by the provisions of the different measures. In the fifties and
sixties a reform of Parliament might have been made in either of two
directions, to control or counteract the changes taking place in the
political system which had come into being after 1832 or to accelerate
these changes. This, of course, was denied by such men as John Bright,
who contended that the Act of 1832 was a means of strengthening
urban power within the State, who contended further that Reform was
a Liberal monopoly, and who criticised the reforms which the
Conservatives proposed.[40] Leaving aside the question of the orientation
of the Act of 1832, their very criticisms contradict their argument. In
effect, while denying the possibility of a Conservative reform they
were implicitly explaining it.

The general boundaries question was perhaps more important in the fifties and sixties than it has been in the thirties. But if this be so then the very factors which made it more important were also reducing its importance: they were destroying the political system in which it was important. Already in the thirties many towns had been growing rapidly, spilling an essentially urban population into the counties. Indeed, the process was a simple extension of that to which Wellington referred, in 1831, when he explained that the close boroughs had become 'the true protectors of the landed interest [because] the increase of manufactures and commerce . . . [had] given great influence to the inhabitants of towns in all county elections'.[41] Whatever the effectiveness of the role which the close boroughs then played – and whatever the importance of this role in conditioning that definition of the landed interest in the light of which their effectiveness might be measured – by the fifties the close boroughs were things of the past. The first Reform Act had done away with them. However great the number of remaining boroughs in which a single dominant influence obtained, urban overspill and the growth in the number of voters in the counties qualified in respect of property in the boroughs were now occurring within a political system in which the powers of the landed interest, the related powers of the Conservative party, and all that the landed interest and the Conservative party had come to symbolize, were largely dependent upon the integrity of the counties as rural constituencies. Hence the different ways in which these phenomena were seen: by some as the source of inevitably dominant power which might be encouraged by judicious legislation or simply allowed to fructify, by others as a serious threat which had to be met before it was too late, and met in ways which the traditional agencies and mechanisms of electoral recruitment served to indicate. Of course, there were others, again, who realized, or came to realize, that neither the hopes nor the fears nor the strategies associated with these hopes and fears were fully justified because the traditional agencies and mechanisms of electoral recruitment were losing their effectiveness. But in the fifties and sixties these men's opinions had little bearing upon the ways in which the problems of politics were discussed.

V

According to Russell, in 1854, reform was needed to correct three principal 'defects' in the mid-century political system which the first Reform Act had either created or left uncorrected. He criticised the Act because of the many remaining boroughs which, he thought, had too few voters to justify the representation they enjoyed. He also criticised it for producing too close a correspondence between constituencies and interest groups and for destroying the relative heterogeneity of the pre-reform borough electorates. But in his eyes the principal 'defect' was obviously the second: the first Reform Act, he declared, had 'tended to divide the country in a way it was not divided before; in short, into opposite camps according as the districts might be connected with land or trade'. Furthermore – and thus was the 'defect' revealed – 'Since the passing of the Act', he explained, 'we have seen – what had not occurred before – we have seen county Members too generally exclusive in respect of the interest they cared for, and Members for the great cities too exclusive also for theirs.'[42] Obviously, when Russell explained the corn law crisis in these terms he was obscuring its essential dynamic. It was not the Act which determined where the various elites would focus their electoral energies or how they would try to rationalize their appeals. But if the polarization of politics between the landed and urban interests is only to be partially attributed to the Reform Act the polarization itself was very real. To correct this as well as the two other principal 'defects' to which Russell referred he proposed, among other things, to enfranchise £6 ratepayers in the boroughs and £10 occupiers in the counties, to transfer a sizeable number of seats from the smallest boroughs to the larger counties and boroughs, and to leave the boundaries of the residual boroughs unchanged – in effect, to do nothing to curtail or counteract the political impact of urbanization and suburban overflow.[43]

The changes which Russell proposed to effect through Parliament would have complemented those which were being effected by other agencies. Indeed when the principal 'defect' of the system was defined as he defined it suburban overflow became an important means of reform. As he noted, if the changes he proposed were made it was 'obvious that the county representation ... [would] have less of a special character than heretofore'.[44] And in the context of the argument which Sir George Cornewall Lewis, his Under-Secretary for Home Affairs from 1848 to 1850, had articulated in 1849 in his *Essay on the Principle of Authority in Matters of Opinion,* such a 'special character' was not only dangerous, as he implied. It was totally unnecessary as a means of perpetuating the roles and status of the appropriate elite. According to Lewis, leadership did not obtain within definable communities; it was not a function of definable nexus. Using a logic similar to that of Bagehot later, but pursuing it a bit further, Lewis proclaimed the ostensibly general rule that while 'persons of sound practical judgment ... may be always expected to be in a minority; .. their opinion is likely to be voluntarily adopted by the majority'.[45] The crucial point is that this voluntary adoption occurred without regard to any possible community of interests however conditioned or advertised.

Needless to say, Russell's reform proposals in 1854, 1860 and 1866 – they were fundamentally the same in all three years – scarcely appealed to those whose power bases were in the counties as the counties had come into being in the years after 1832. Nor did they appeal to those who, unlike Lewis, believed that the welfare of the State – or, to put it differently, their own status and leadership roles – really depended upon the continued existence of those tightly knit communities within which their status was principally recognized and their leadership roles performed. Disraeli's descriptions in 1863 when he addressed the National Conservative Registration Association contained elements of exaggeration or parody similar to those contained in his description, in 1859, of the two schools of parliamentary reformers. But again they are useful. As he explained, giving party names to the attitudes he described, recent legislation had not dealt with questions which revealed the fundamental differences of principle between Liberals and Conservatives. But, he went on, the differences were still there. In the interests of a specious freedom the true Liberal wished to abolish the many traditional institutions which lay between the individual and the State. But the true Conservative wished to preserve these institutions, knowing full well that it was only 'by their united aid and agency that the Government of this country . . . [was] carried on'.[46]

On one point Disraeli in 1859 and Russell in 1854 were agreed: reform was needed as a means of avoiding further confrontations between the landed and urban interests. But the sort of confrontations they hoped to avoid were very different; and so were the means by which they hoped to avoid them; and so, again, were the reasons for their concern.

The confrontations which Russell principally hoped to avoid were those which occurred in Parliament between the spokesmen of the different interests which the first Reform Act had helped to separate. Besides the peace of the kingdom the main questions at stake were those which concerned matters of policy and the ease with which matters of policy might be determined. He hoped to avoid such confrontations and to facilitate the calm determination of policy by reducing the correspondence between constituencies and interest groups.

The confrontations which Disraeli principally hoped to avoid were those which occurred between differently oriented groups within the various county constituencies. He was perhaps less concerned with matters of policy than with matters of status and power. In any event, what mainly concerned him was the integrity of the communities in which this power was exercised and this status enjoyed. For Russell, continuing urbanization was a means of solving the problem which reform was intended to solve. For Disraeli, on the other hand, urbanization was almost synonymous with the problem itself. As he put it, one of the main problems which the members of the Derby Ministry had set themselves to solve was how they could 'restore the county constituency to its natural state'. [47] As he explained, '[In 1832] it was proclaimed with great triumph that when a gentleman stood for a county, his neighbours who dwelt in the county would vote for him.' But now, he went on, because of the growth of suburban populations, and because of the growing practice of 'manufacturing county votes in boroughs', these neighbours were often outvoted. The situation had come into being in which 'some large town in the district . . . pour[s] out its legions by railway, and on the nomination of some club in the metropolis . . . elect[s] the representative for the county.' [48] In part, Disraeli hoped to 'restore the county constituency to its natural state' by constituency boundary adjustments, in part by redistribution, in part by franchise adjustments. The Inclosure Commissioners would have been instructed to 're-arrange [the borough boundaries] according to the altered circumstances of the time'. [49] One seat would also have been taken from each of the fifteen smallest two-Member boroughs and reassigned to various of the more industrial counties and the more rapidly growing towns. These counties would have been redivided as a means of separating their industrial from their non-industrial areas. Receiving borough status, these towns would have been abstracted from their surrounding counties. Furthermore, borough freeholders, borough copyholders and borough leaseholders would have been assigned to vote in the boroughs in which their properties were located; the electorates of both borough and county would have been enlarged by various personal property and other franchises; and the electorates of the counties would have been enlarged by reducing the occupation franchise in the counties from £50 to £10 – in effect, by reducing it to the same level as obtained in the boroughs. This latter proposal provides an important clue to the general socio-political problem as various Conservatives obviously saw it. It was to be hoped that if the occupation franchises in county and borough were made the same the political leaders in the boroughs would be willing to withdraw from the county arena.

The increase in the electorate which the Conservative proposed in 1859 would have been fairly small. But whatever its size, it would not have occurred at random. Indeed, much as the extensions of the franchise which Russell described in 1854 and 1860 and which Gladstone described in 1866 were selective in ways which clearly reflect their understanding of the nature of the mid-century political system and the hopes which this understanding induced, so the extensions of the franchise which the members of the Derby Ministry proposed in 1859 were selective in ways which clearly reflect their understanding of the nature of the mid-century political system and the fears which this understanding induced. The new franchise qualifications which Disraeli described would principally have enlarged the county electorates. As he explained them, however, their major impact would have been felt in the boroughs. They would have served to dissipate that urban suspicion of the nature of political power in the countryside which he atrributed to the 'exclusiveness' of the Chandos clause. Thus, they would have put an end to that 'civil war' between town and countryside pursued by those 'suspicious' townsmen who were both 'manufacturing county votes in boroughs', and exploiting the electoral potentialities of surbuban overflow. Disraeli denied the validity of the argument in which urban suspicion was principally expressed – that the Chandos clause voters were the creatures of their landlords and, as such, had delayed the repeal of the corn laws. There were far too few of them he contended, to have had that power. Indeed, as he pointed out, there were fewer Chandos clause voters than men qualified to vote in the counties in respect of property in boroughs. Furthermore, many landlords were Whigs.[50] But he acknowledged the sociological or psychological importance of the Chandos clause argument. 'There is no doubt', he declared,

> that dissatisfaction, followed by distrust and misrepresentation, did raise in the country an idea that the county representation was an exclusive representation; that it was animated only by one object; that it had a selfish interest always before it, and that it had not that sympathy with the community which we desire in that body to which the privilege of election is entrusted.[51]

When the county franchise was no longer so 'exclusive' the legitimacy of the power base of the leaders of the landed interest would ostensibly no longer be questioned in the towns. Then, the 'civil war' between town and countryside would end. A man would be willing to vote 'for the place where he resides, or for the locality in which he is really and substantially interested'.[52] In effect, by reducing the occupation franchise qualification in the counties the members of the Derby Ministry hoped to deal with what they clearly recognized as the principal problem they faced. Whatever the potential effectiveness of their proposed solution the problem itself was not so much legal as sociological. It was the consequence of the fact that increasing numbers of urban leaders were ceasing to concentrate their electoral energies in what might be called 'their own' constituencies. They were venturing into the counties, complaining the while of the ostensible illegitimacy of their adversaries' powers. As Disraeli explained, only when this 'unnatural state of things' had been ended could they 'bring about that general and constant sympathy between the two portions of the constituent body which ought to exist'.[53] Thus described, the 'sympathy' to which he referred would have been less the consequence of restoring the 'natural state of things' than it would have been the synonym of that restoration.

The Conservatives failed 'to adapt the settlement of 1832 to the England of 1859'. Their Bill was defeated, apparently for two principal reasons: it would have disfranchised borough freeholders in the counties; and it would not have extended the borough franchise in any significant fashion.[54] In 1867, as the Liberals' dilemma reveals, the Conservative measure was far more astutely drafted. Their case was also far more ably argued.

VI

It was obviously a mistake on Disraeli's part, in 1859, to refer to his opponents as those who hoped 'to realize the opinion of the numerical majority of the country'.[55] To refer to them in these terms was to abandon all claim to that amorphous 'popular support' which became an increasingly important concept or commodity as the process he was trying to arrest continued. It was to fail to adjust to the linguistic implications of the process. It was to proceed on the assumption that the process itself was somewhat superficial. But this it was not. That which was weakening the groups and networks on which the 'settlement of 1832' was based, that which prompted the Conservatives' effort to 'adapt the settlement of 1832 to the England of 1859', was also changing the vocabulary of politics and the general vocabulary of social relations. It was enforcing the use of a new language according to which men were members of categories, not members of groups, according to which the electoral recruitment functions of the various institutions without whose 'united aid and agency', as Disraeli put it in 1863, 'the Government . . . [could not be] carried on', were either not performed at all or performed by other agencies. Whatever the degree to which, in fact, men were ceasing to behave as members of groups – whether groups similar to those which the Conservatives wished to buttress, or different ones – the vocabulary of groups was losing its currency. Whatever the reasons for this,[56] Disraeli failed to acknowledge it when he argued his case in 1859.

Disraeli used the new language of politics in 1867 when he criticised his opponents for both the timidity and the selectivity of their franchise proposals. The Liberals, he contended, had sought to enfranchise a 'Praetorian guard' in 1866. The Conservatives were now trying to enfranchise 'the great body of the people'. The Liberals had sought to enfranchise that 'favoured portion of the working classes, who are always treated in this House, and everywhere else publicly in terms of great eulogium'. The Conservatives were now trying to enfranchise 'the larger number [who] would be more national'.[57] Statements such as this have undoubtedly contributed to the belief that the numbers of men who were enfranchised in the boroughs by the enfranchising provisions of the Act greatly exceeded the numbers who would have been enfranchised had the Franchise Bill of 1866 been passed. But the extent of this difference is open to question. Statements such as this have also contributed to the belief that the Act was more the consequence than it was the conditioner of that new 'Tory democracy' which it has occasionally been used to symbolize.[58] Citing Disraeli's name, subsequent 'Tory democrats' spoke of partnerships between distinct *classes* or *categories* of men. They also sometimes spoke of the State as the agency by which social problems might be solved. Whatever the importance of these arguments at the times when they were used, Disraeli's own arguments in the fifties and sixties were scarcely compatible with the existence of a society thus composed or with the efforts of a centralized government to provide for the general welfare through its organs. Rather, his arguments were premised upon the existence of a State with very limited functions, upon the existence of a society in which the crucial relationships were both corporate and hierarchical. They were premised upon that ethic of *noblesse oblige* which could only operate voluntarily and only within the context of strong multi-functional communities. Indeed, the attributes of society and state which subsequent 'Tory democrats' advertised in his name were precisely those whose development he sought to arrest. As he explained, in 1866, while supporting Grosvenor's motion, the ultimate results of a boundaries scheme such as the Saving clause and the borough copyholder and borough leaseholder provisions of the Franchise Bill led him to anticipate would have been to increase the powers of the 'Executive' and to replace the 'great proprietors' and 'great manufacturers' in the House with 'demagogues'.[59] Greater criticism could not have been uttered.

In 1867 Disraeli spoke less — if at all — of the two schools of parliamentary reformers to which he referred in 1859. As various provisions of the Bill suggest, however, his principal concern was the same, to 'restore the county constituency to its natural state'. To whatever the extent this goal might be achieved, the proposal of household suffrage clearly helped towards the passage of the Bill designed to achieve it. What with the Liberals' self-image as the party of reform, and the mounting pressures of radical agitation, the Liberals could not simply oppose the Bill of 1867 as they had the Bill of 1859. They were almost inevitably compelled to urge the removal of those limitations which, initially hedged the proposal of household suffrage. Indeed, their relative concern for these limitations, their relative unconcern for other provisions of the Bill, and the importance of these other provisions to the goal which many Conservatives shared with many Whigs, that of 'restor[ing] the county constituency to its natural state' as part of an effort to restore the mid-century political system, would almost lead one to conclude that these limitations had been placed in the Bill to divert the Liberals' attention from others of its provisions.

Household suffrage was an important phrase. But phrases apart, the important political questions had to do with the ways in which household suffrage – or any other alterations of the franchise whether legislated or not – would affect the nature of the interests within the society and their relative powers within the State. In his speech on the third reading of the Conservative Bill in 1867 Disraeli observed that in 1859 the Derby Ministry 'was unanimous, after utmost deliberation and with the advantage of very large information on the subject, that if we attempted to reduce the borough qualification which then existed we must have recourse to household suffrage'.[60] From several points of view household suffrage was extremely dangerous. From others it was not. And, in any event, from the point of view which Disraeli shared with many others, the existing fissiparous tendencies within society were themselves extremely dangerous – not to mention the various Liberal reform schemes which, again from this point of view, merely threatened to aggravate the dangers resulting from these tendencies.

Robert Lowe was a consumate rationalist and legalist who ignored the changes in the balance of power in the State which were occurring in consequence of non-legislative causes. According to him, the only real danger was that which stemmed from a legislated reduction in the franchise qualifications. And, according to him, such a reduction was dangerous because those who would be thereby enfranchised would act together as a bloc. His argument was a rather crude class argument: because those who had less property were more numerous than those who had more any significant reduction of the franchise requirements would inevitably mean that the existing electorates would be swamped by hordes of new voters who were their economic or class opponents.[61] Northcote's argument, in 1859, was both far less legalistic and far more sophisticated. As he explained in a memorandum on reform,

> In those cases in which . . . [an extension of the franchise] would let in the greatest masses of the *lower* classes of voters, it would do little real harm because generally speaking the members chosen from these places are such as would continue to be chosen by the *lowest* classes. In the counties some danger is probably to be apprehended; but many desirable voters as well as many undesirable ones would be added to the constituencies; and the mischief might be much mitigated. Upon the whole, if the electoral districts remained unchanged, much the same influences would continue to work, and

much the same men would in the long run be returned.[62]

In the light of Lowe's premises the Bill of 1867 was far more radical than the Bill of 1866 because it provided household suffrage. But according to Northcote's premises the Bill of 1867 was not only less radical than the Bill of 1866. It was positively anti-radical. Indeed, to those who believed that the extension of the franchise 'would do little real harm because . . . if electoral districts remained unchanged, much the same influences would continue to work, and much the same men would in the long run be returned', the principal differences between the Conservative Bills of 1859 and 1867 were those which might be expected to increase the Conservatives' chances of passing a Bill designed to restore the general conditions in which a man would be willing to vote 'for the place where he resides, or for the locality in which he is really and substantially interested', or, more particularly, their chances of passing a Bill designed to 'restore the county constituency to its natural state'.

Yet, as revealed by Disraeli's explanation, in 1859, of why the occupation franchise qualification in the counties should be reduced, some men recognized quite clearly that the important questions concerning the nature and distribution of political power in the kingdom were those which legislation could not affect directly. To 'adapt the settlement of 1832 to the England of 1859 [or 1867]' would mean the restoration of conditions in which sufficient proportions of the various elites were satisfied with the powers and status they enjoyed when they restricted their electoral energies to 'their own' constituencies, in which sufficient proportions of the voters were willing to acknowledge themselves as members of the groups or networks of which these men were the leaders. But these conditions could no more be restored — and restored by legislation — than the groups and networks could be restored — and restored by legislation — which these conditions reflected. Whatever the impact of changes in the franchise, in the distribution of seats, and in the boundaries between constituencies, the real changes in the system derived from sources which law could not control. This presumably lay beyond Lowe's comprehension. To those who understood it the Bill of 1867 might have seemed something of a risk. At best, it could not have been a full, much less a permanent, solution to their problems. At worst, it might stimulate exactly those activities they hoped to curtail. But their powers were eroding within the existing system. The results of registration in North Warwickshire in 1866 and, even more clearly, Paget's return for South Leicestershire in 1867 — but this occurred after the Bill had been passed — confirmed Disraeli's argument of 1859. From the point of view of those who drafted the Bill it was obviously far better to try to control the existing fissiparous tendencies within the

society while they had the chance than to let the Liberals aggravate
these tendencies with a Bill of their own – better not only in party
terms but in general societal terms.

VII

The behaviour of the Conservative Ministers in 1867 bears out the
implications of Disraeli's statement in 1866, to the effect that he held no
brief for particular franchise levels.[63] It bears out the implications of
Stanley's suggestion in 1866, once the Redistribution Bill had been
introduced, that the provisions of this Bill be considered before those of
the Franchise Bill because the questions raised in this Bill were both
more complex and more important than those raised in the other.[64] As
a rule, however, the implications of these statements have been
ignored. Generally, when such statements are mentioned at all they are
mentioned not to illustrate Disraeli's or Stanley's priorities or premises
but to buttress the argument that neither man was capable of
understanding the seriousness of the questions with which he was
dealing.[65] By and large, while discussing the Bill of 1867 historians
have tended to focus upon those of its provisions which principally
affected the size of the electorate, especially the borough electorate.
They have tended to ignore those other provisions which, while
indirectly affecting the size of the various electorates, were principally
designed to sort out the various categories of voters, old as well as new,
into different constituencies. Of course, the provisions on which
historians have tended to focus attracted rather more attention at the
time than the others. In the long term they were perhaps the more
important. The agencies of electoral recruitment which provided the
logic of the other provisions were breaking down. Furthermore – and
whether as a separate or related phenomenon – as time went by fewer
men were willing to restrict their electoral energies to 'their own'
constituencies. As a result, the effort to re-segregate the differently
based deference communities was deprived of much of its significance.
But to ignore this effort is both to distort the Bill and to obscure the
concerns of the men who drafted it.

The story has been told many times how, to the amazement of some,
the consternation of others, Disraeli and his colleagues blandly
accepted various of the amendments to their Bill which largely
removed the limitations initially surrounding household suffrage in the
boroughs. And the Ministers' acceptance of these ammendments has
sometimes been used to buttress the argument that they were far less
concerned about the details of the Bill they passed than that the Bill
which was passed should be theirs.[66] The members of the Derby
Government were undoubtedly eager to demonstrate their

governmental competence, their ability to pass a refom bill where Gladstone and the Liberals had failed. But they were not willing to pass just any bill. Indeed, the argument that they were more concerned to have their hands on the wheel than to steer the ship in one direction rather than another – either because they did not really care which way the ship might sail or because they believed there was only one way the ship could sail – is scarcely compatible with the fundamental differences between their Bills and the various Liberal Bills or with their opposition to those amendments to their Bill of 1867 which were designed to weaken its efficiency as a means of restoring the separation of interests into different constituencies. Whatever the possible effectiveness of legislation to this end, two categories of provisions were at stake, those which concerned the rights of borough freeholders, borough copyholders and borough leaseholders to vote in the counties and those which concerned the boundaries of the boroughs. The Conservatives succeeded in their efforts to reduce the numbers of borough voters in the counties. But they failed in their efforts to extend the boundaries of the major boroughs.

VIII

Soon after the Bill was introduced, Hussey Vivian, Liberal Member for Glamorganshire, asked whether the Bill would not deprive the smaller resident borough freeholders of their county votes.[67] Vivian was presumably reassured by Disraeli's reminder that most borough freeholders were non-resident, thus would not acquire borough votes, thus would not be deprived of their county votes.[68] In any event, he made no effort to perpetuate the right to vote in a county of a resident borough freeholder whose freehold was not worth the £10 a year necessary for him to qualify as a borough voter under the Act of 1832. But during the committee stage of the Bill he and Charles Colvile, Liberal Member for South Derbyshire, did their best to provide borough leaseholders and borough copyholders with the same rights of voting in the counties as were enjoyed by borough freeholders.

Their campaign began with Colvile's motion, in May, to reduce the copyhold franchise qualification from £10 to £5. The Government opposed the motion – as Disraeli later put it, because of their wish 'to interfere as little as possible with the old franchises'.[69] But whatever the reasons for it their opposition was unavailing. The motion was carried to 201 to 157.[70] Three days later Disraeli accepted Vivian's motion, that the leasehold franchise qualification be similarly reduced. But the terms of his acceptance drew the sting from both motions. He accepted it 'subject to this – that the £5 qualification was to be enjoyed under similar conditions as the £10 qualification in the Reform Bill of 1832'.[71]

When the exact meaning of this was asked Gathorn Hardy had the
ready answer: 'That the £5 qualification will be enjoyed the same as
the £10 qualification under the 24th and 25th sections of the Reform
Act.'[72] Section 24 defined the rights of borough freeholders to vote in
the counties. Section 25 defined the rights of borough copyholders and
borough leaseholders to vote in the counties. Vivian was hardly pleased
with this arrangement. 'These sections', he declared, 'ought to be
modified'.[73] But subsequent attempts at modification failed.

It was in June that Colvile introduced his motion to repeal that part
of section 25 of the Act of 1832 which forbade borough copyholders
from voting in a county in respect of premises which conferred a
borough franchise 'on any other person'. As Colvile explained, the
repeal was needed because 'a great many copyholders would
[otherwise] be disfranchised by the proposed extension of the borough
boundaries.'[74] From the Ministers' point of view, however, the
question which his motion raised was not the question which he noted.
As Sir Charles Adderley put it, the question was 'whether the property
which gave the vote should be within the place for which the
representative was elected'.[75] Speaking in this context Disraeli
appealed for fairness: 'I should not at all question the propriety of the
representative of a borough resisting any invasion of his rights; but let
the natural feelings of those who represent the rights of counties be also
respected.'[76] And Sir John Rolt indicated what the Government might
do if their opponents used their majority in the House to introduce
what was, in fact, a provision from the Franchise Bill of 1866 into the
Bill of 1867: 'If the Amendment were agreed to, the Bill would have to
be re-cast, and then it would be a question whether the Bill could be
passed this Session.'[77]

Of course, there were several so-called vital points in the Bill which
were abandoned when need arose. But none of these involved the
question of urban penetration of the counties. With respect to Colvile's
motion the need did not arise. The motion was defeated by 171 to
151.[78] Later that evening Vivian's motion to allow borough
leaseholders to vote in the counties in similar circumstances was
defeated by 256 to 230.[79] Thus, it is impossible to determine whether,
had either of these motions been carried, the Government would have
re-cast their Bill or would have accepted their defeat and gone on in
such a way as would confirm the conclusions which have sometimes
been drawn from their acceptance of other amendments. What is clear
is that later a supplementary clause was added to the Bill – it became
section 59 of the Act – according to which the relevant provisions of
the Act were to be read in the light of sections 24 and 25 of the Act of
1832. As some have noted this clause was fairly complex. Indeed, it
perhaps deserves the epithet, 'obscure', which was applied to it at the

time by Homersham Cox and, more recently, by Dr. Smith.[80] But for all its 'obscurity' it served its purpose fairly well. It was the means by which the Conservatives achieved in 1867 one of the principal things they had tried to achieve in 1859; the disfranchisement of most borough copyholders and borough leaseholders in the counties. It was the grounds on which, in November, 1868, in the case of Chorlton v. Johnson, Henry Bunting was deprived of his right to vote in South East Lancashire.[81] The previous June – clearly in anticipation of such a decision – a Liberal leader in Sheffield explained to Lord Halifax that the borough leaseholder section of the Act would greatly aggravate the problems which the Liberals faced in South West Yorkshire. In consequence of this section, he wrote, some 500 Liberal voters in the borough of Sheffield alone would be stricken from the county register.[82]

IX

But when it came to the boundaries question the Ministers were less successful. A few days before the vote on Colvile's and Vivian's amendments Disraeli explained the Government's ostensible reasons for not following the same procedure in dealing with the boundaries question as the Grey Ministers had followed in 1831. Then, he noted, the Ministers had both appointed the Boundary Commissioners and given them their instructions. But some Members had objected. 'We thought . . . that if the House joined with us in appointing these Commissioners it would create a degree of confidence between the House and the Government which was very desirable.'[83] Presumably, what he really sought was not so much the abstract 'confidence' to which he then referred as that moral commitment on the part of the House to accept the Commissioners' handiwork to which he later referred when their handiwork was criticised.[84] Concessions were made in the membership of the Commission to placate such men as John Bright and Denman, who complained that the membership as initially proposed was excessively rural in orientation and thus failed to satisfy the 'reformers'.[85] But the Commissioners' instructions remained intact. They were told to examine the boundaries of every existing borough in England and Wales 'with a view to ascertain whether the boundaries should be *enlarged,* so as to include within the limits of the borough all premises the occupiers of which ought, due regard being had to situation or other local circumstances, to be included therein for Parliamentary purposes.' They also were told to examine the proposed boundaries of the new boroughs 'with power to suggest *such alterations* therein as they may deem expedient'. And, again, they were told to examine the proposed boundaries of the new county divisions 'with a view to ascertain whether, having regard to the natural and legal divisions of each county, and the distribution of the population therein, any, and what, *alterations* should be made'.[86] But whatever the 'confidence' which parliamentary involvement in the appointment and instruction of the Commission produced, this 'confidence' scarcely survived the introduction of the Boundaries Bill based on the Commissioners' report.

Obviously, the approval of the Commissioners' instructions reflected the general consensus that representation in Parliament should be the representation of communities. As Gladstone declared, in 1866, 'A local community, wherever it is, should be represented'.[87] Indeed, the only serious criticism of the Commissioners' instructions were those which might be said to reflect an even fuller expression of the community principle. Complaints were made that in dealing with existing boroughs the Commissioners could only recommend *extensions* of their parliamentary boundaries, not *contractions*.[88] These complaints applied to cases in which the parliamentary boundaries of a borough extended far beyond the boundaries of the town. Unless the Commissioners had the power to contract the parliamentary boundaries of a borough they could not protect the urban voters from being swamped by the rural. In fact, these complaints reflected gross distortions of the circumstances. Boroughs with parliamentary boundaries far beyond the boundaries of the town were scarcely 'urban'. They were boroughs such as those whose parliamentary boundaries had been extended in 1832 in the effort to guarantee adequate constituencies. However, while there was general agreement on the principle that representation in Parliament should be the representation of communities there was widespread disagreement about the application of this principle. This problem marks an important point in the growing tension between interest and principle.

The general agreement that representation in Parliament should be the representation of communities was predicated upon the usually unstated assumption that the communities that were being discussed were legitimate communities, those which legitimate influence helped to define. But there was no agreement on which communities were legitimate and which were illegitimate. Indeed – and there lay the rub – because communities were not *a priori* entities, because they were social and ideological constructs, the very existence of the communities on which the system was based – the very existence of those interest groups whose rivalries are the subject of so much nineteenth century English political history – was largely the product of the belief generally shared by members of each interest group, that the relationships on which the rival interest groups were based were *ille*gitimate. Thus, since the community problem – or, what generally came to the same thing, the constituency boundary problem – only arose where the members of one interest group were invading the precincts of another, and since important questions of political power were generally at stake, there were few cases in which there could be a solution satisfactory to the invaders as well as the invaded.

Looking at the problem from an urban perspective Gladstone described a procedure in 1866 which was attuned to urban institutions and interests. Parliamentary boundaries, he explained, should coincide with municipal boundaries. Furthermore, the municipal boundaries should be those which were needed by the town. 'The best and safest definition of a local community', he declared, 'will be obtained by giving facilities to the inhabitants [of a borough] for fixing its limits from time to time as considerations of their own practical convenience may dictate and require.' [89] Looking at the problem from a rural perspective Disraeli described a procedure in 1867 which was attuned to rural interests. There were no organs of local government in the counties analogous to those in the towns into whose hands could be put the powers to fix the limits of the counties from time to time as considerations of their practical convenience might require. Hence the use of Commissioners. Hence, too, the need to instruct these Commissioners in ways in which, presumably, the very identities of the members of the borough councils would have rendered unnecessary. But different men apparently read these instructions in different ways. If this is understandable it is no less important.

To say that each borough should 'include ... all premises the occupiers of which ought ... to be included therein for Parliamentary purposes was not in itself to specify the criteria of inclusion. But Gladstone, for one, apparently assumed it was. He apparently assumed that the procedures of 1867 would produce results similar to those he had anticipated from the procedures of 1866. As he explained, in 1867, he understood the Commissioners' instructions to mean that they would 'only ... include within the area of such boroughs the populations proper to them'. [90] In fact, of course, there were no 'populations proper' to any constituency. Or − to put it differently − there were no criteria other than political ones by which these populations could be determined. What is important about Gladstone's statement is the evidence it provides of his apparent belief that there were other such criteria.

The following year, when he had the Boundaries Bill before him, he was careful to deny that he was criticising the Bill in 'party' terms, or the Commissioners for recommending boundaries designed to strengthen one 'party' at the expense of the other. The Commissioners, he declared, had not done wrong. But they had had a difficult task. And the House had failed to provide them with adequate guidance as to how they should apply the criteria which the House had defined. [91]

But the source of the problem was not in the failure of the House. Rather, it was the breakdown of the working consensus what constituted a legitimate community.

The Commissioners' instructions were predicated upon the assumption that communities were objectively definable. The Commissioners proceeded on this assumption. They defined their tasks in terms analogous to those which the Commissioners of 1831 had used in defining theirs. They looked to see 'whether there are any considerable number of houses beyond the existing borough boundaries the occupiers of which from community of interests with the Borough or from other local circumstances, may be considered as forming part of the Town population'. [92] They also looked to see whether a borough was increasing rapidly in size and, if so, in which directions. 'A sufficient allowance', they explained, 'should be made for the extension of the Borough in those directions.' [93] But what had served in 1831 no longer served in 1867.

For Birmingham, for example, the Commissioners noted that the town had overflowed the existing parliamentary boundaries, which were also the municipal boundaries. In particular, there was Aston Manor to the north, with some 20,000 inhabitants, and Balsall Heath to the south, with another 10,500. 'Both Aston Manor and Basall Heath', they declared, 'comprise an urban population in every respect identical in pursuits and interest with that of the Parliamentary Borough.' [94] In consequence, they should, both be included. But the borough officers and many inhabitants of the Manor and Heath objected. At most, the extension promised to increase the population of the parliamentary borough by a tenth. But certain objectors contended that this would render the parliamentary constituency 'unmanageable'; that it would limit the choice of candidates to the very rich – no one else would be able to pay the expenses of a contest; that it would 'neutralize' the 'privilege' of the third seat which the borough had just received; that it would project the borough into more than one county; that it might encourage a comparable extension of the municipal boundaries, thus a comparable extension of the area in which the municipal rates were levied; and, finally, that it threatened the investments of the men who had 'invested their earnings in buildings outside the municipality, either to get a county vote or to escape the heavy rate charged on the town'. [95] As the Commissioners noted, none of these objections bore upon the terms of their charge, that they inquire 'whether the occupiers of houses beyond the boundaries of the *borough,* from community of interests and other local circumstances, may be considered as forming part of the *town* population.' [96]

There had been few criticisms of the recommendations of the earlier Boundary Commissioners on these grounds. Back in the thirties, those objective criteria of social identity which were reflected in both sets of instructions had presumably been more widely accepted. The subjective criteria had probably tended to coincide more frequently with the objective. And again, this coincidence was probably strengthened by the fact that many local political leaders had obviously been satisfied with the powers and status they enjoyed when they focused their electoral energies within 'their own' constituencies. Whatever the impact of continued urbanization and population overspill upon the behaviour of local political leaders, many of these men were now trying to maximize their powers in the State in ways which the implementation of the Commissioners' instructions would directly inhibit. Furthermore, they were trying to maximize these powers within the context of the argument that the relationships upon which their opponents' powers were based were somewhat illegitimate. Whatever the degree to which the behaviour and arguments of these men reflected a weakening of the traditional nexus – whatever the degree to which their criticisms of the structure of power within a rival interest group were prompted by efforts to restore waning loyalties within their own interest groups – their behaviour and arguments clearly helped to weaken the traditional nexus still further. As revealed by his explanation, in 1859, of the reasons why the occupation franchise in the counties should be reduced, Disraeli understood something of the nature of the problem: while assuming that political power should be exercised by men of status, and exercised in respect of the roles they performed in their own communities, many men were refusing to grant the legitimacy of these roles or the legitimacy of the communities in which they were performed. There was still general agreement that representation in Parliament should be the representation of communities. Hence the approval of the Commissioners' instructions. But there was no general agreement about the criteria for such communities.

As Gladstone explained, in 1868, the Boundary Commissioners should not have depended upon objective criteria but upon the wishes of those whose interests were at stake – or, at least, upon the wishes of those who had an institutional means of declaring their interests. There should be no enlargement of a borough, he declared, 'unless in cases where the town is willing to be enlarged'. Nor should there be any enlargement except where 'the district [to be included] is willing to be included.'[97] This latter criticism does not reflect any new-found concern for the interests of the countryside. Gladstone was not being objective except from his own perspective. His focus remained urban. He was not concerned for the countrymen who were threatened with the prospect of being engulfed in a borough. Rather, he was concerned for the suburbanites who were threatened with the prospect of losing their county votes. Others spoke of the enlargement of the boroughs as a means of enfranchising more voters.[98] They further contended that Members should be returned for towns, not for parts of towns.[99] This contention is not inconsistent with Gladstone's earlier statement about the representation of communities. But, if given full legislative expression, it threatened to inhibit within the State, the growth of urban power which derived – and, ostensibly, would continue to derive – from urban overspill. And, from the perspective of Gladstone's new followings an inhibition such as this was scarcely desirable. Indeed, a key point in Gladstone's political progress is clearly marked by his emphasis upon the prospective disfranchising impact of the Boundaries Bill. In many cases, he explained, the areas which the Commissioners proposed to include in a borough were inhabited by men of substance who had offices or shops in the borough. Residing within seven miles of the borough these men were able to vote in the borough in respect of their business premises. But since they resided in the counties and either owned their houses or paid adequate rents they were also qualified to vote in the counties. It was these qualifications which concerned him. 'In some cases', he explained, 'it might almost be asserted that the effect of an extension of boundary as proposed will be simple disfranchisement.'[100] Sergeant Gaselee's criticism was conceptually simpler: the Boundaries Bill, he complained, was designed 'to take away voters from the country and place them in the towns, thus eliminating the town voters [from the counties] who were really the Liberal voters.[101]

By the time these criticisms were made it was too late to reopen the entire boundaries question. Whether intentionally or not, the Conservative Ministers had used time to compensate for their lack of numbers in the House. They had waited until the third week of March before introducing the Boundaries Bill according to which the boundaries of eighty-one boroughs were to be extended.[102] What with the pressures of other business – and for this, presumably, they were not ungrateful to Gladstone for taking up so much time with his Irish Church resolutions – the committee stage of the Bill did not begin until May. And the deadline was in early June.[103] By then it would be necessary to start compiling the new registers if elections under the Act were to be held in the autumn of 1868. And before the registers could be compiled the boundaries question had to be settled.

In the context of Gladstone's argument about the impropriety of including men in a borough who did not wish to be included, the Liberal majority in the House forced the appointment of a select committee to reconsider those boundary proposals against which significant local opposition had been voiced.[104] In all, the committee only considered the boundaries of 29 old boroughs. For only 15 of these did they recommend the perpetuation of the existing boundaries.[105] These were the boroughs – Birmingham among them – whose suburbs were growing most rapidly, in effect, those in which, in the light of mid-century assumptions, the boundaries question arose in its most acute form. Paradoxically, however, the very process of suburban exodus, the political impact of which the Conservative Ministers hoped to arrest and their Liberal opponents hoped to maximize, was tending to weaken the validity of the assumptions on which both hopes were based.

X

Writing in 1899, Harold Gorst came close to providing an adequate description of the background of the Act when he explained that, 'principally', Disraeli won the support of the county Members for household suffrage in the boroughs by proposing to extend the boundaries of the boroughs 'so as to embrace the suburban districts, which contained a numerous population which possessed no interests in the county.'[106] Gorst was right in saying that 'in the opinion of the Tory squires ... the admittance of the masses in these urban districts to the county franchise would have resulted ... in the Liberals sweeping the counties at the first election.'[107] He was also right in the reasons he gave for this opinion: the Tory squires 'were convinced that the small householders in the outskirts of the towns would prove 'Radical without exception'.[108] But he ignored the point which explains both the differences between the different Conservative and Liberal Reform Bills and the fact that the usual connotations of 'reform' notwithstanding Conservative Ministers *did* introduce Reform Bills in 1859 and 1867: the danger which Disraeli and the Tory squires both saw was not a future but a present one. It is this which provides the answer to Gorst's complaint that the Bill was misconceived. 'Time has, of course, shown', he declared 'that their fears were groundless, and the winning of Conservative seats in London and in many other towns has been entirely due in several instances to the suburban voters.'[109] This was occurring by 1899. Furthermore, for the twenty-odd years before 1899, Sir John Gorst, Harold's father, had kept insisting – and, generally from his point of view, unsuccessfully insisting – upon the need to reorient the Conservative party in such a way as to capture the support of the new suburban populations.[110] In the sixties however, this suburban Conservatism was still very much a thing of the future. While intimations of it might have been seen in the return of Lord George Hamilton as one of the Members for Middlesex in 1868[111] what time had principally shown by 1867 was the precarious nature of Conservative power in the only constituencies in which it existed to a

significant extent, and the declining efficiency of the traditional
agencies of electoral recruitment. Considered in narrow party terms it
was only the Conservatives who were threatened when the Liberal and
Radical leaders in Birmingham, Leicester, and various other towns
returned to the county arena. But when they challenged the
Conservative hegemony in the counties these men were shaking the
foundations of the mid-century political system. They were
jeopardizing the roles and thus the existence of the traditional agencies
of electoral recruitment. In consequence, they were jeopardizing the
roles and thus the status of the traditional elites.

10

Why poll books became unpublishable

I

The first Reform Act marks a clear divide. After 1832 few if any constituencies remained in which power could be exercised in purely arbitrary fashion. Instead, power was principally the function of social status measured in the constituency in which it was exercised. In creating the mid-century political system, however, the Act's provisions were more permissive than they were prescriptive. The Act determined the configuration and distribution of constituencies, the qualifications which the voters had to have in the different categories of constituency and the mechanisms by which qualified men might be registered. These questions were obviously important. But they were important in the way that limits are important. The Act did not determine which of the qualified men in the different constituencies would be registered or how they would behave if and when they were brought to the polls. Because these were the crucial questions they illustrate the nature of the crucial variables which had far less to do with the distribution of seats, the franchise qualifications in the different constituencies, the boundaries between constituencies, or the mechanisms of registration, than with the patterns of relationship in the context of which particular men in particular constituencies were able to grasp the machinery of power which the law provided. In conditioning the nature of the system and the distribution of power within it law was essentially passive. Social relationships and the various ideologies and issues which legitimized and challenged these relationships were active. Hence the importance of the fact that it was not really alterations in the law which produced those changes in both the system itself and the distribution of power within the system which the men who drafted the second Reform Act hoped to arrest. Law could no more arrest change than it had produced the system and the distribution of power which these changes were affecting. In consequence, the second Reform Act marks no divide comparable to that marked by the first. Indeed, in all probability it merely accelerated the process it was designed to slow down. Yet a divide exists to which the Act is related because a divide exists to which the process is related. It lies at the point at which the traditionally structured deference communities and deference networks ceased to provide the principal agencies and mechanisms of electoral recruitment.

This turning point cannot be located precisely. Nor, indeed, can the process itself be chronicled from the poll books without a far more precise analytical tool than that which the criterion of local electoral agreement provides. This criterion is useful in illustrating the nature of the mid-century political system. But it is far too crude and far too limited in applicability to provide a means of discovering exactly how the electoral blocs which affected the outcome of contests in the sixties differed from those which affected the outcome of contests in the thirties. And, of course, once the Ballot Bill was passed even this criterion becomes useless. Thus analysed the differences between the blocs of the thirties and sixties would appear to have been slight – or even non-existent. In Cambridgeshire and South Leicestershire, for example, the geographically definable blocs revealed by the poll books for 1868 were, if anything, even more solid than those revealed by the poll books for previous contests, those for 1857 and 1835 in Cambridgeshire and for 1867 and 1841 in South Leicestershire.[1] However, this is presumably more a measure of what the criterion shows than of the actual nature of the effective agencies and mechanisms of electoral recruitment. Differences between the electoral blocs of the thirties and sixties would presumably be apparent if these blocs could be seen not as the pool books reveal them but as the election managers tried to see them. This is suggested by the differences in the proportions of English county seats which changed hands without contests at the polls in the thirties and in the sixties and the differences in the proportions of contests which occurred in the English counties without seats changing hands. There is clearly a connection between the fact that not a single English county seat changed hands in 1865 without a contest at the polls, and that in South West Yorkshire, in 1865, the Conservatives' loss on promises was more than twice what their 'usual experience' led them to expect.[2] The evidence is circumstantial. But the fact is no less obvious. There was a breaking down of the political system which the radical journalist in Leicester implicitly described, in 1839, when he referred to that 'gentlemanly feeling which would not countenance a contest when the chances are balanced or unfavourable'.[3] Whatever the numbers of such 'gentlemen' about – and, clearly, their numbers would make an important difference – it was breaking down because the traditionally structured deference communities and deference networks were ceasing to perform their previous roles. In consequence, it was no longer possible to predict the outcome of a prospective contest with that 'tolerable accuracy' to which Cox and Grady referred on the basis of the procedures they described.[4]

Ultimately the general processes of population growth, population movement, urbanization and economic growth were presumably responsible for all this. But something more than the processes themselves is required to explain it. Obviously, the system that was breaking down cannot be explained except in the light of these processes. But the partial autonomy of politics is illustrated by the fact that what served to weaken the local and hierarchical relationships on which the existing interest groups were based also served to re-enforce the cohesion of these groups and the boundaries between them; what encouraged the development of new relationships, new groups and new lines of conflict also provided new weapons in the on-going conflict between the landed and urban interests. Presumably, the key to the paradox – if such it be – lies in the fact that the groups themselves were social and ideological constructs. Clearly, population growth, population movement, urbanization and economic growth affected the circumstances in which the different constructions occurred. As suggested, however, by the general lack of correspondence between the growth of population in the different county constituencies and the growth in the numbers of registered electors in these constituencies, the actual changes in the political system had less to do with these general processes than with the efforts of men to retain, enhance or acquire power within the system.[5] The second Reform Act was designed to perpetuate the system. But the real threats to the system were not of a nature which legislation could control – much less, which legislation could counteract. Indeed, the very effort to restore the mid-century political system, to 'adapt the settlement of 1832 to the England of . . . [1867 and 1868]', may have been that which precipitated the final breakdown of the system.

II

The enlargement in the numbers of qualified men in the different constituencies in 1867 and 1868 – the price paid for the effort to re-segregate the different categories of voter – undoubtedly multiplied the problems which faced the election managers as they tried to identify the prospective voters as members of specific collectivities. And, undoubtedly – the point suggested by differences in knowledge of the 'old' and 'new' voters which was claimed by the registration agents and their informants in both South West Yorkshire and North Devonshire – a smaller proportion of the 'new' voters were members of the collectivities with which the mid-century cadres were familiar.[6] Furthermore, the Act altered the franchise in every constituency and the boundaries of many. This fact provides much of the answer to the question why a contest occurred in a far larger proportion of the constituencies of the Kingdom as a whole in 1868 than in any previous general election since 1832. But it was presumably even more important that the Act was both the product and the stimulus of conflicting hopes. An illustration of the basic source of instability of the mid-century political system is the fact that many of the contests which occurred as means of determining the local balance of power also occurred as means of destroying the relationships in the context of which such a balance of power might be determined.

Cox and Grady's handbook provides a useful key to the mid-century political system because it illustrates the intimate connection between the political system and the social system. As Cox and Grady explained, when a contest occurred it was the election manager's 'real business . . . to see what influences could be brought to bear upon the undetermined [voters], so as to secure them for his own party'.[7] Presumably, as long as the leaders of rival interest groups tended to sort themselves out into the 'appropriate' constituencies, thus indicating their willingness to accept the consequent limitations upon their powers in Parliament and, to the same effect, as long as they tended to observe those 'laws of delicacy and propriety' to which the Marquis of Westminster referred in 1841, those which should have kept Gladstone from interfering 'between a landlord with whose opinions . . . [he was] acquainted, and his tenants', the procedures Cox and Grady went on to describe not only enhanced the 'appropriateness' of the different constituencies but strengthened the related agencies of electoral recruitment.[8] But when the leaders of rival interest groups began seriously trying to maximize their powers in Parliament the procedures Cox and Grady described became the formula for chaos. This was because of the very nature of the agencies and mechanisms of electoral recruitment on which the system was based: as long as the election managers' 'real business' was to mobilize favourable influences, and to do so in part as a means of counteracting the unfavourable, the effort to maximize power in Parliament jeopardized the fundamental groups and networks within the society. Inevitably, it involved the use of one loyalty, the product of one relationship, to tear a voter free from a conflicting loyalty, the product of another relationship.

There was clearly a critical point. This was obviously not reached until after the passing of the second Reform Bill. And until it was reached there was an increasing tendency to assume that the political mobilization of social relationships served to strengthen them. In particular, this is suggested by the grounds on which John Stuart Mill abandoned his earlier advocacy of the secret ballot and by the use others made of his anti-ballot argument. From the early 1850s Mill acknowledged the fact that the discipline exercised by the traditional agencies of social control was becoming weaker. But, he contended, these agencies could be preserved if open voting were retained. His argument contained in his 'Thoughts on Parliamentary Reform', which, according to Professor Hayek, was written in the early 1850s, was repeated word for word in his *Representative Government,* published in 1861. It was cited by many of those who continued to oppose the secret ballot down to the time when the Ballot Bill was passed in 1872. Open voting, he declared, was the means by which 'the voter's personal interest, or class interest, or some mean feeling in his own mind' might be held in check, and held in check by a 'sense of shame or responsibility'.[9]

Mill's argument against the secret ballot implicitly describes the mid-century political system. During the mid-century many voters' 'personal' and 'class' interests – and, presumably, their 'mean feeling[s] – were held in check by their 'sense of shame or responsibility'. Indeed, within the context of Mill's obvious definition of these words such a statement is a simple tautology. But Mill confused the symbol with the cause. It was not open voting which held the various 'personal' and 'class' interests in check. Rather, it was the strength of the various hierarchical relationships which made open voting possible. In effect, Mill begged the fundamental political question, of what constitutes a legitimate group. Of course, there is no answer to this question – or none other than a political answer. But Mill and many of his contemporaries clearly assumed that there was an answer which was not a political answer – that the agencies and mechanisms by which the requisite 'sense of shame or responsibility' was generated were natural, not artificial, given, not constructed. As long as this assumption was effectively unchallenged poll books remained publishable and the traditionally structured deference communities and deference networks continued to provide the principal agencies and mechanisms of electoral recruitment. When the assumption was seriously challenged – and challenged by those who contended that other groups and relationships wee legitimate and these were not – poll books ceased to be publishable. Also, both as symbol and consequence of the challenge, the new mass membership political organizations came into being which provided the basis of the new political system.

III

The adoption of the secret ballot has sometimes been attributed to an ideological *deus ex machina*. It has been described as the application or fulfilment of what might be called the principle of political individualism. But those who have described it thus have generally left vague the answers to the questions exactly how and why, in the years immediately before 1872, the requisite conversions to the principle took place among a majority of M.P.s. Sometimes, the adoption of the secret ballot has been simply attributed to the enlargement of the electorate effected by the second Reform Act and to the further enlargement which many men anticipated in the not too distant future. It was to these that Gladstone referred when he drew the pro-ballot conclusion from Palmerston's argument, that the vote was a 'trust', not a 'right' – which, in fact, was not so very different from Mill's argument, that the voter should be responsible to the community at large as to how he used his vote. As Gladstone explained, when the electorate was increased in size each voter came to hold his 'trust . . . on behalf of his wife and children, all other persons being presumably entitled to act with him on a footing of equality'.[10] From this the logical conclusion might be drawn that because some of those on whose behalf the 'trust' had been held were now themselves partners in holding it, and because others would soon be joining them, it was no longer necessary that the 'trust' be exercised in public. Such an argument illustrates Gladstone's considerable dialectical skill. But as an explanation of the adoption of the secret ballot it scarcely makes up in complexity for what it lacks in relevance. Far more to the point is the Marquis of Hartington's observation that as a result of the elections of 1868 the advocates of the secret ballot had grown from a small band of advanced radicals to include most Liberals and many Conservatives.[11] In part, the merit of his observation lies in the experience on which it was based. He was chairman of the Select Committee on Parliamentary and Municipal Elections appointed in 1869 to investigate the conduct of these elections. But its principal merit lies in the connections it suggests between the passing of the Ballot Bill in 1872, the plethora of contests in 1868, the tactics used at many of these contests, and concern for the impact of these tactics upon the established social nexus and institutions.

One of those whose attitudes towards the secret ballot were changed by the experiences of 1868 was George Latham, a Dissenter, who testified at length before the Hartington Committee about the contest in Mid-Cheshire. His evidence figured prominently in both the Committee's Report and the subsequent debates on the different Ballot Bills. In particular, the points he made derived from the information he had gathered as the Liberal election agent in Mid-Chesire. On the basis of his canvass he had expected the Liberal candidate to be returned with a majority of 180.[12] But he was beaten by almost 600.[13] A member of the Committee implied that this discrepancy was but a measure of the canvassers' extreme partisanship.[14] But Latham had another explanation. After the voting was over he had collated the poll book with the canvassing books. He then discovered 'that nearly 400 men who had pledged to vote for the Liberal side had voted for the Conservative side, and every one of these men was a tenant on a [Conservative] estate'.[15] Before the contest he had been opposed to the secret ballot. He was, as he put it, a 'disciple of Mr. John Stuart Mill'.[16] Ostensibly, the contest convinced him that Mill was wrong. What his evidence principally reveals, however, is not Mill's *error* but the conditional relevance of Mill's argument.

As Latham described the contest it was a confrontation between urban nonconformists and Anglican squires. There had been no contest in the county for 20 years. During this time none but Conservatives had been returned. Ostensibly, however, nine-tenths of the Cheshire farmers were Dissenters.[17] In these circumstances, when the new constituency of Mid-Cheshire was created – a constituency which contained no parliamentary borough but which did contain various sizable towns and various suburbs of Manchester: much was made of these points – Latham and his urban friends decided on a contest.[18] Latham drafted a requisition inviting John Leicester Warren to stand.[19] Warren was the son of the second Baron de Tabley, formerly a Peelite, now a Liberal, who had large estates in the county. Ostensibly, the Dissenting farmers signed this requisition 'almost . . . to a man'.[20] But when it came time to vote, many of them voted not with their nonconformist ministers but with their Conservative landlords. Obviously, what changed Latham's mind about the secret ballot was the relative weakness of the religious nexus when brought up against the fundamentally economic nexus.

Latham acknowledged that most Cheshire farmers had no strong 'political' feelings.[21] But this was the condition he hoped to change. And, clearly, unless this condition were changed – or, to put it differently, unless the farmers' membership of religious communities came to play a more important part in conditioning their votes than their membership of fundamentally economic communities – Latham and his friends would not be able to achieve their political ambitions. At one point in his testimony before the Hartington Committee Latham spoke as if the problem were simple. Had the voters been protected by the secret ballot, he declared, they would have been able to use their own discretion how they would vote 'in the case when the chapel and the landlord were opposed'.[22] In reality, however, the

408   *Efforts at repair*

problem was rather complex. Whether or not he knew this at the time he clearly came to know it. In 1873, the year after the secret ballot was adopted, a vacancy occurred in Mid-Cheshire. On this occasion Latham himself was the Liberal candidate. He was beaten by a far larger margin than Warren in 1868.[23] His explanation for his defeat can presumably be seen in his speech to the newly reconstituted National Reform Union the following year in which he urged the need for land law reform both to provide 'such systems of tenure as will promote the best cultivation of the soil' and to destroy the 'feudal spirit' in the countryside.[24] Indeed, it was this spirit which Latham principally emphasized in his testimony before the Hartington Committee. Few men on the Committee or elsewhere would presumably have argued against the abstract proposition that voters should not be coerced to vote against their better judgment. But when asked what should condition such judgment they were apt to argue with one another.

Throughout his testimony Latham used the term, *coercion*. But what he obviously had in mind was something rather more complex than that which the term is generally used to describe. There were very few cases, he declared, in which a voter had been ordered to vote one way or another under threat of eviction.[25] Instead, voters voted as they did to please those on whom they depended for their economic well-being. Their votes were part of a socio-economic-political bargain. As Latham explained, few Cheshire farmers were rich. They were always wanting 'small repairs, additional gates, and perhaps a little time to pay . . . [their] rent'.[26] Also, few of them had leases.[27] Many farms had been in the same families for generations. At any given moment, however, few farmers had the legal right to continued possession beyond a year. They voted to please their landlords in the hope and expectation that this would not only allow them to remain on their farms but to remain in the best possible circumstances. The conditions he described while trying to explain Warren's defeat in Mid-Cheshire were analogous to those which others described when trying to explain the behaviour of the voters employed in the different mills in Blackburn, or those employed in the different railway works in Carlisle.[28] As a former Liberal mayor of Carlisle put it, most of the men employed at the Carlisle works of the London and North Western Railway Company were members of mechanics' institutes at which mainly Liberal newspapers were read.[29] But, he went on, had those employees of the Company who had the vote in 1868 voted against William Hodgson, the Conservative candidate, it would have been 'like quarrelling with their bread and butter'. Hodgson, he explained, a director of the Company, 'had been the means of getting these works erected, and consequently they were indebted to him for their employment'.[30] Some men regarded behaviour of this sort as evidence of corruption.

Others regarded it as not only legitimate but natural. And others, again, put it somewhere in between. By and large, those who regarded it as evidence of corruption were those whose political ambitions it served to block. By and large, those who regarded it as legitimate and natural were those whose political powers were based upon it. Many of those who put it somewhere in between presumably understood the complexities of the social and political arguments in which the others were engaged.

At stake was the fundamental question of politics in a representative system of government: What varieties of influence or nexus should the results of an election reflect? Some years earlier Samuel Bailey had implicity answered this question in a way which helps to characterize the mid-century political system when he quoted the argument of a hypothetical opponent of the secret ballot:

> We admit . . . that a landlord is not justified in using intimidation to prevent his tenants from voting according to their conscientious convictions; but we hold, that the tenants in general are not under the influence of conscientious motives in voting contrary to the wishes of their landlords: they are, in fact, either bribed to do it, or misled by false representations; and therefore the landlord is fully justified in employing threats or promises as counteractive expedients.[31]

As means of characterizing the system, however, the real importance of these attributed beliefs and admissions lies in the fact that the mechanisms of electoral recruitment which they imply were the same as those which provided the grounds for Bailey's advocacy of the secret ballot. In explaining why the secret ballot was essential this ardent Utilitarian who came to James Mill's aid against Macaulay – who tried to do what Macaulay said could not be done: deduce the science of government from the principles of human nature – referred to the 'unconquerable . . . and beneficial proneness of man, to rely on the judgment and authority of those who are elevated above himself in rank and riches',[33] to

> The propensity of mankind . . . not to make a choice of an individual for a desirable office on account of his bare merits, of his mere aptness of discharge its functions, estimated by their own independent understandings; but . . . to give him their suffrages on account of the opinion entertained of him, and the favour manifested towards him, by those whom they wish to please, and whose judgment they have been accustomed to respect.[34]

In effect, as Bailey described it, the secret ballot would serve not to keep one man from influencing another. Rather, it would serve to strengthen *legitimate* influence. His argument *might* perhaps be used to illustrate a mid-nineteenth century paradox. More to the point, the paradox *should* be used to illustrate the differences between his socio-political assumptions and those in the light of which his argument is, indeed, paradoxical. Bailey assumed that the various opinion leaders would inevitably be drawn from the different elites. He also assumed that these men would exercise their influence in consequence of their combined socio-economic roles. Further, he assumed that their influence would be felt where their roles were acknowledged. It was not he but another who, in explaining the behaviour of the voters employed in the different railway works in Carlisle, in 1868, referred to that *esprit de corps* in the different establishments to go the same way as the leading members'.[35]

Of course, throughout the poll book period various men criticised behaviour of this sort. In the thirties one such was George Grote. Indeed, in 1833 Grote complained that the first Reform Act contained an unwritten clause which divided the voters into two classes, 'the first invested with a will of their own, the second under legal obligation to express only the will of another'.[36] Similar arguments were used subsequently by the Hon. F. H. F. Berkeley, Radical Member for Bristol and by E. A. Leatham, John Bright's brother-in-law.[37] In 1870, generalizing upon Latham's evidence for Mid-Chesire, Leatham referred to that 'prevalent form in influence which . . . results through habit, experience, and tradition from the mutual relations subsisting between landlord and tenant'.[38] From his point of view, such 'mutual relations' did not legitimize the influence which derived from them. Indeed, from his point of view they merely served to perpetuate a power which — according to him — was manifestly corrupt. As he put it, the influence which derived from these relations 'operates as powerfully at an election as though it were backed up by daily acts of oppression'.[39]

Throughout the poll book period many 'acts of oppression' undoubtedly occurred. However, what the publication of poll books principally illustrates is not 'acts of oppression'. Rather, it illustrates those patterns of loyalty which the reformers of 1832 and 1867 had tried to strengthen, which Bailey regarded as 'beneficial', but which were breaking down and which, as Latham's evidence and Leatham's argument suggest, were being challenged with increasing intensity by those whose political ambitions they served to block. By the same token, what the passage of the Ballot Bill illustrates is not Leatham's, or anyone else's ability, to convince a majority of M.P.s that such loyalties were 'illegitimate'. Rather, the passage of the Bill illustrates the only practical means by which those whose political powers depended upon these loyalties could hope to perpetuate them against the challenges of the others. As a matter of principle most Conservatives and, probably, most Liberals continued to oppose the adoption of the secret ballot.

The proper safeguard against bribery and intimidation, declared a writer in the *Edinburgh Review* in 1870, is not the secret ballot but 'the exposure of the intimidator's tyranny'.[40] There was 'no greater mistake', he went on, 'than repressive legislation in matters involving morality'. In such matters the principal solution lay in that 'moral influence' which the secret ballot would effectively destroy.[41] The previous year a leader writer in *The Times* had observed that those who agreed with Leatham 'that a vote was a man's own, to exercise as he pleased', were a small minority of the House.[42] Those who ageed with Mill were the large majority. But whatever the size of this majority, their conviction that voting should be done in public because voting was a public duty was unavailing when the question arose which Mill had begged. In one of its simplest forms, perhaps, the problem can be seen in the advice of the anonymous 'Conservative' in Cambridge, in 1868, that he and his fellows 'adopt the principle of their opponents, and have no dealings whatever with anyone but with sound Conservative Churchmen'.[43] As he explained, Anglicans, by and large, were richer than non-Anglicans. Thus, if Anglicans withdrew their custom from all shopkeepers except those who promised to vote for Conservative candidates, and if they dismissed all employees and evicted all tenants except those who gave the same promise, Conservative candidates would, presumably, be successful not only in Cambridge but in a majority of the constituencies in the kingdom. He presumably believed that the purpose for which this 'influence' would be brought to bear was highly 'moral'. Obviously, without open voting this 'influence' would have been significantly weakened: there would have been no means of telling who had failed to make good his promise, thus who should be appropriately punished. Obviously, others believed that the purpose for which this 'influence' would be used was highly 'immoral'.

It is impossible to determine which side strained its influences the more in 1868, whether corruption was more prevalent then than it had been at earlier general elections, and whether more or less illegitimate influence was exercised then than had been exercised before. Apart from the problem of evidence there is the problem of definition. And the two are closely related. Within the system it was clearly acknowledged that money given to a voter might not be a bribe – that it might be a bit of selectively dispensed charity;[44] that when a landlord seated himself at the hustings where his tenants would come to vote his behaviour was not necessarily evidence of his intent to coerce his tenants – that he might have come merely to greet them.[45] But the willingness to grant such interpretations was itself conditional. And, by and large, those who refused to grant these interpretations – whether justly or not is another question – were those who brought the evidence itself to light. In effect, what marked the passing of the system was the declining willingness to acknowledge the possible legitimacy of the principal agencies and mechanisms of electoral recruitment on which the system was based.

While moving the appointment of what ultimately became the Select Committee on Parliamentary and Municipal Elections Henry Bruce referred to that change of attitude towards the exercise of influence which, ostensibly, had occurred in the fairly recent past. 'Many persons, a few years ago', he declared, 'would have supposed they were only exercising an ordinary right in compelling tenants to vote on their side or in using influence in the strongest way over their workmen.'[46] But this, he went on, was no longer the case. As he described it, the new forebearance was a sign of progress and they should all be proud of it. But the elections of 1868 had raised the question of the adequacy of this progress. It was to answer this question, he explained, that the Committee was needed.

As a rule, the adoption of the secret ballot has been attributed more to the 'progress' of which he boasted than to the inadequacy of this 'progress', more to the ostensibly voluntary separation of the political system from the social system than to the continuing effort – or, possibly, the growing effort – to exploit every possible relationship for every vote it might yield. According to Mill, open voting should be retained as a means of preserving these relationships and the society that was based upon them. As is suggested by the evidence to which the Hartington Committee listened, and by other evidence which was never brought before them, it was to preserve these relationships and thus to preserve this society, that open voting was abandoned.

The Ballot Bill was essentially a tactical measure supported by many M.P.s whose approval did not signify any repudiation of the social values and assumptions which had made open voting possible. Indeed, it was not Leatham's values and assumptions to which W. E. Forster referred when he introduced the Government's first Ballot Bill. It was Bailey's values and assumptions. 'I ask the support of all sides of the house', he declared,

> because I feel sure all are anxious to destroy illegitimate influence, and also, for the reason that the more you destroy that influence the more you will increase the legitimate influence, because any attempt to use illegitimate influence produces needless irritation and prejudices people against persons who may have the power to intimidate them, though they may rarely or never have practised intimidation.[47]

The following year a leader writer in *The Times* observed that 'Large numbers of voters have been encouraged, and are now fixed, in the belief that they will be exposed to unknown evils if they have not the power of screening their votes in darkness.' [48] He believed they were wrong. Previously, he or another had observed 'that notwithstanding all the talk about intimidation, whether by landlords, priests, or trades unions, in most instances the man who is thus influenced, and said to be controlled, really votes the way of his interest and his wishes'.[49] But whatever the reality on which he insisted, by 1872 he recognized the need which the contentions themselves imposed. 'Legislation' he declared, 'must take account of this state of feeling'. On these grounds he advised the Lords to accept the measure which the Commons had passed making it illegal to divulge one's knowledge of the way another man had voted.[50]

IV

If men voted in secret, an anonymous pamphleteer predicted, in 1870,

> ... no representative would thenceforth know who were the supporters upon whom he could surely count, or what might be their political views; nor, in such utter darkness, could any appeal to the public on questions of policy be confidently made by Ministers. Party organization and discipline, an admitted necessity in our representative constitution, must then become impracticable; our rulers could with difficulty ascertain their relative strength in Parliament, and continued instability of Government would be the inevitable result.[51]

Others made similar predictions which, like his, were significantly wrong. In particular, party organization and discipline did not become impracticable. Nor did Government remain or become unstable. But these predictions are no less important for being wrong. Indeed, the very expectations of the secret ballot expressed by these men help to illustrate the importance of those changes in the effective agencies and mechanisms of electoral recruitment which made the secret ballot necessary. In consequence of these changes party organization and discipline both inside Parliament and out became far stricter than they had ever been before. In the context of this organization and discipline Government acquired increased stability. But the party organization was a different sort of organization from that with which these men were familiar, the party discipline was a different sort of discipline, and the stability of Government obtained in respect of vastly extended governmental functions.

Clearly, what vitiated the accuracy of these men's predictions was their failure to recognize that a political system might be based upon other varieties of relationship than those of the mid-century system.

Obviously, the parties which the anonymous pamphleteer had in mind when he referred to the future impracticability of party organization and discipline were parties of the sort which another opponent of the secret ballot implicitly described when he explained that if men voted in secret 'the natural disposition of the tenant to make common cause with his landlord . . . [would be] set aside', there would be no way of discovering 'the balance of parties' in a given constituency without a contest, and candidacies for seats in the House of Commons would be multiplied fourfold.[52] As it happened, candidacies for seats in the House of Commons did become rather more numerous after 1872 than they were before. But this was not only for the reasons he suggested. Indeed, it was mainly for reasons he ignored. In some constituencies before 1872, but in most constituencies after, fundamental changes of political organization occurred. In many cases these organizational changes were accompanied by changes of personnel. In others the same men remained in control of local political affairs. But in almost every constituency changes occurred in the ways in which these affairs were conducted which paralleled changes in both the conduct and content of politics in Parliament. Because of these various changes contested elections became the rule.

As long as sufficient numbers of voters behaved as members of traditionally structured deference communities and deference networks, national parties scarcely existed as agencies of electoral recruitment; national party leaders had little influence except in Parliament, Whitehall, and the constituencies in which their own property interests were located; 'the Executive' lacked the powers which, in 1866, Disraeli warned it would *acquire* if the different categories of constituency ceased to provide for the almost automatic return to Parliament of 'great proprietors' and 'great manufacturers'; by and large, the issues of domestic politics did not have to do with the relationships among the various classes which composed the same deference community or deference network: rather, they had to do with the relationships between the interest groups with which the leaders of these communities and networks were identified.[53] The point is somewhat tautological: generally, as long as sufficient numbers of voters behaved as members of traditionally structured deference communities and deference networks questions of class relationship either did not appear at all on the surface of electoral and parliamentary politics or appeared in such forms as reflected the strength of deferential assumptions: they appeared as moral indictments brought by the spokesmen of one interest group against the spokesmen of a rival group for the latters' ostensible failure to take proper care of their dependents.[54] All this changed when the traditionally structured deference communities and deference networks ceased to provide the effective agencies and mechanisms of electoral recruitment. It was then that mass membership parties came into being and not only sought to recruit the voters directly but to recruit them as partners in the legislative process.

The establishment of these mass membership parties marked the time when local political leadership passed from the hands of men who, by and large, had exercised their leadership roles in consequence of their traditionally based local status. Generally, these roles had not been used to maximize power in Parliament. Rather, they had been used to perpetuate the status on which they were based. In many cases, local power was now being grasped by those who had little or no status to perpetuate. But whether these men still had much status to perpetuate or simply much to gain, they often tried to perpetuate or gain status by promising that they would use the powers of Parliament to solve social problems which, previously, had been handled – when, in fact, they had been handled at all – informally and within the arena of the various traditionally structured deference communities and deference networks. During the mid-century the principal question to which a contested election provided the answer – the question to which many contests *were* the answer – was what were the relative numbers of voters within the constituency in which the contest occurred who could be recruited and organized through the agencies and mechanisms of the differently oriented local deference communities and deference networks. When sufficient proportions of the voters could no longer be recruited and organized through such agencies and mechanisms contested elections acquired a somewhat different function. Whatever the actual agencies and mechanisms, contested elections became the occasions when rival candidates tried to recruit voters by promising, as members of parties, parliamentary action of their behalf. A few years earlier, once the imperatives of the corn law crisis were safely past, many parliamentary candidates happily proclaimed their independence of 'party'; many M.P.s undoubtedly enjoyed the tenure of their seats as a not too arduous diversion during 'the golden age of the private Member'. And the greater their pleasure the more understandable the vehemence of their protests against the new restrictions upon their independence which were associated with the mass-membership parties. But their protests scarcely stemmed the tide of change. Party loyalties and promises of benefits to be had from parliamentary action were coming to provide those mechanisms of electoral recruitment and organization which other loyalties had ceased to provide.

Epilogue: The interpretational problem

I

At the turn of the century Graham Wallas observed, 'The study of politics is just now in a curiously unsatisfactory position.'[1] The reasons for this were simple. He and various others had come to the conclusion that contemporary political phenomena could no longer be handled according to the assumptions of human nature and society which most students of politics were using. The implications of this were also simple. When confidence in the validity of these assumptions waned the question that inevitably arose was whether that political system was really viable whose development was generally attributed to the legislative application of these assumptions.

In the pages of many histories the political reform process had been used to illustrate the ostensible role of formal ideas in effecting political change. Against the background of urbanization and industrialization, and using social unrest both to show the need for political reform and to explain why particular reforms occurred when they occurred, historians had described the development of the English system of representative government in fairly simple terms. Ostensibly, it was a case of those who believed in human rationality and the identity of human interests succeeding in their efforts to enfranchise ever larger numbers of voters, to free these men from all restraint in the expression of their individual political preferences, and to provide an ever closer nexus between these men and the representative they chose. By the turn of the century, however – and it was this which occasioned Wallas' observation – their stories sometimes ended on a rather despairing note. For when the process which they described in these terms was largely complete the results were scarcely such as to encourage confidence in the validity of the relevant assumptions. It was no longer sensible to argue that voters behaved as individual and rational agents, their behaviour conditioned by their objective understanding of the ways in which their individual interests might be furthered. Nor was it sensible to argue that if the final steps in the process were taken – if the electorate were made identical with the total community – this enlarged electorate would choose their representatives and instruct them in ways which would prevent social conflict. Furthermore, while the process had been described, generally, as a means of destroying oligarchical power within the State, new oligarchs had emerged whose powers could be compared with those of the older oligarchs. These were the party leaders and propagandists who appealed not to the rationality of their electoral followers but to their passions and emotions. As for those economic and social problems whose existence in the past had often been attributed to the lack of representative government, these had, if anything, become even more acute than they had been before. In consequence, what with new oligarchs tending to formulate their own electoral appeals in terms of the class issues which these economic and social problems helped to aggravate, the basic question had emerged both for Wallas and for many of his contemporaries whether the English system of government was really viable – or, to put it differently – whether those concepts of human nature and society to which the development of this system was generally attributed had been, in fact, suicidal. The generally accepted historical account was encapsulated in Wallas' statement:

> . . . those who worked to create a democracy of which they had as yet no experience . . . looked on reasoning not as a difficult and uncertain process, but as the necessary and automatic working of man's mind when faced with problems affecting his interest. They assumed, therefore, that the citizens of a democracy would necessarily be guided by reason in the use of their votes, that those politicians would be most successful who made their own conclusions and the grounds for them most clear to others, and that good government would be secured if the voters had sufficient opportunities of listening to free and sincere discussion.[2]

In the context of his general complaint about those who 'exaggerate the intellectuality of mankind' this historical account became the prelude to disaster.[3]

Since Wallas' time the question of the viability of the system has been fairly well laid to rest. The ultimate disaster has not occurred. By and large, survivors of limited disasters have come to accept the realities he deplored, the existence of political blocs, man's tendency to behave emotionally as well as intellectually – or emotionally *instead of* intellectually. This acceptance has not been easy. In some cases it has not progressed very far. The nostalgia there is understandably strong for a world which, whether or not it ever existed, might be described in terms of human rationality and the identity of human interests. But the study of politics is no longer in that 'curious unsatisfactory position' to which Wallas referred. The reasons for this obviously lie partly in the fact that crises notwithstanding the British political system still exists in a form which Wallas might have recognized and partly in the fact that since the end of the second World War in particular the phenomena which occasioned Wallas' concern have become important subjects of study both in Britain and elsewhere. Increasingly, political scientists and sociologists have abandoned those *a priori* assumptions which he criticised – but from which he could not entirely free himself – as to how men *should* behave. Increasingly, they have turned their attentions to the question of how men *do* behave. Their conclusions have confirmed his somewhat agonized contention that men are not rational beings. But they have also shown that his fears that if men were not rational beings representative government could not exist, were unfounded. Which is not to say that they have denied the importance of the *argument* that men are rational beings, or the importance of the *argument* that social conflict will cease if facilities be provided for increased political participation. But they have assigned new roles to these arguments. Wallas' dilemma was essentially a measure of his fear that if men were not really rational, and if human interests were not really identical, that political system which he had learned to regard as the legislative application of the relevant assumptions, would collapse. Apparently, however, what is required for the perpetuation of the system is not so much the *fact* of human rationality, or the *fact* of the identity of human interests, but the confidence which the *belief* in these 'facts' provides. The difference marks the crucial step which neither Wallas nor his contemporaries were able to take.

But certain other questions remain, in particular, why Wallas and so many others have told the story of reform in such a way as not only to illustrate the ostensible role of formal ideas in politics but to illustrate the ostensible role of particular formal ideas. This question scarcely allows of a simple answer. Inevitably, whatever answer is suggested must be somewhat speculative. But various considerations help to focus speculation, especially the evidence which the story has obscured, the evidence which the story has distorted, and the probable role of these obscurations and distortions in creating and – even more, perhaps – in perpetuating the mid-century political system. In particular, the evidence which the story has obscured is that contained in the poll books and in those provisions of the first and second Reform Acts with which the story is scarcely compatible. In particular, the evidence which the story has distorted is that contained in the arguments of the various Benthamites or Utilitarians whom Wallas obviously had in mind when he referred to the men 'who worked to create a democracy of which they had as yet no experience'. In effect, the measures which the story serves to explain were never drafted. Furthermore, the political assumptions which, have frequently been attributed to the Benthamites or Utilitarians as a means of explaining their ostensible responsibility for these measures were not theirs. Obviously, the story has a source other than the phenomena it purports to describe. Presumably, this source lies in the exigencies of the system.

If the evidence which the story obscured be considered it becomes clear that the men who initiated the reform process were not convinced that their fellow subjects could be trusted to make individual evaluations of issues, or that social peace was to be had if adequate constitutional channels were provided for their ostensible rationality. Rather, the men who initiated the reform process were concerned to perpetuate both the integrity of the traditional groups in English society and the status of the leaders of these groups. The importance of these groups in their eyes was an obvious measure of the strength of their belief that men would only act wisely when they acted as members of such groups, and that social peace was a function of the discipline which the leaders of such groups exercised within them or which the members of such groups exercised over one another – in either case a discipline which was weakened when the cohesion of the groups was weakened. When the relevant legislative provisions are seen, and seen in the context of the poll book evidence, then the basic problem for which these provisions were the ostensible solution becomes clear: the nexus by which these groups were held together were weakening.

It is presumably this which explains the relationship between the actualities of the reform process and the traditional story of reform. For the men who drafted the relevant legislation of the thirties and sixties these traditional groups provided the essential frame of reference. By means of franchise adjustments within constituencies, boundary adjustments between constituencies, the abolition of constituencies, and the creation of constituencies, the reformers tried to adapt the constituency structure of the Kingdom so that it would correspond to the traditional group structure: in so far as possible, no constituency which did not provide for the representation of such a group and no constituency in which the leaders of rival varieties of group would compete with one another. Within the structure thus created, and in the context of appropriate issues – those which the leaders of these groups helped to define – significant proportions of the voters behaved as members of these groups. However, it was apparently the weakening of the nexus which these groups reflected which conditioned the terms in which their behaviour was often described. Frequently, men who behaved as members of clearly defined groups were said to be behaving as rational individuals. And the political reform process which reflected the effort to perpetuate the traditional varieties of group – and thus the status of the traditional elites – was said to reflect the belief that men were rational individuals capable of judging their own interests. Such arguments presumably, helped to perpetuate the groups in terms of which many men continued to behave. But these groups were not perpetuated as what they were. They were perpetuated as what they were not, as products of the ostensible rationality of their members.

The paradox has significant epistemological implications. The traditional story distorts the development it purports to describe. But in all probability the development could not have occurred without the distortion. It was the sort of thing which Sorel called a myth.

By now, the myth has presumably long since served its purpose. But its effects can still be seen in both the descriptions of the first and second Reform Acts which are scarcely compatible with the provisions these measures contained and in the tendency to ignore certain crucial structural or sociological assumptions in the political arguments of various of the Benthamites or Utilitarians. Of course, few historians today would attribute as much responsibility for the political reform process to the Benthamites as Wallas did. But assertions similar to his about 'those who . . . looked on reasoning not as a difficult and certain process' can still be found in a number of recent studies of the Benthamites, in particular of James Mill. Demythification not only requires that the reform process itself be clarified, it also requires the clarification of the assumptions of those men to whom responsibility for this process and, in particular, responsibility for the first Reform Act has often been attributed.

II

Wallas cited Thomas Macaulay's 'celebrated attack' on James Mill's *Essay on Government.*[4] But Wallas obviously overlooked one of the major points Macaulay tried to make, that Mill's effort in the *Essay* to deduce a science of government from certain principles of human nature was rather unconvincing because, in the course of his argument, he had used two sets of principles which were inconsistent with one another.[5] In the subsequent journalistic debate this point was generally ignored. As Mill claimed in his own rejoinder, Macaulay had criticised him not for his logic but for his attempt to be logical.[6] Joining the controversy a few years later, Bailey reiterated Mill's argument.[7] In effect, both men ignored Macaulay's essential points, first, that different men had different natures – and the same men more than one[8] – and, second, that because Mill had granted this implicitly at several places in his argument his argument was vitiated by a basic inconsistency.[9] He had used one set of principles of human nature – what might be called his 'classical' principles – while discussing the needs from which government arose and while criticising monarchy and aristocracy. While recommending and discussing representative government, however, he used another. For the former purpose men were rational individuals driven by limitless greed for wealth and power. For the latter, their greed for wealth and power was effectively submerged beneath their corporate awareness of their common human interests and – even more significantly – beneath the willingness of certain definable groups of men to recognize as their spokesmen particular men who were above them in rank and station and with whom they had contacts of an intimate and enduring nature.

As Mill explained while recapitulating those sections of his argument which bore upon the origin of government and the reasons why monarchy and aristocracy were bad forms of government,

> The positions which we have already established with regard to human nature, and which we assume as foundations, are these: that the actions of men are governed by their wills, and their wills by their desires; that their desires are directed to pleasure and relief of pain as *ends,* and to wealth and power as the principal means; that to the desire of these means there is no limit; . . .[10]

This is sufficiently rational and individualistic to suit anyone's fancy. But some of the fancies thus suited have evidently failed to note that this argument was not used to show how voters would vote. It was used to show why governments were necessary and why monarchy and aristocracy were bad forms of government.

According to Mill, it was human intelligence driven by human cupidity which lay behind the need for government. 'Since every man who has not all the objects of his desire has inducement to take them from any other man who is weaker than himself' – here his classical definition of human nature – government had been instituted. However – and here he introduced a social or corporate element which is scarcely compatible with his classical definition of human nature – government was instituted when 'a number of men combine[d] and delegate[d] to a small number the power necessary for protecting them all'.[11] According to Mill, monarchy and aristocracy were bad forms of government because neither contained any formal institutional means of restraining that selfishness which was logically related to the definition of man as a rational individual driven by limitless greed for wealth and power. But Mill returned to his modified definition of human nature when he concluded that the only good form of government was one in which 'the community in a body ... [could] be present to afford protection to each of its members.' [12] And this other definition of human nature also underlay his argument that while 'The people as a body ... [could] not perform the business of government for themselves' they could choose representatives who, while not ruling themselves, could 'operate as a check' upon those who did. [13]

As Macaulay suggested, there was something inconsistent in all this. If Mill's classical definition of human nature was really accurate then how could he assume that even with frequent elections representatives could be chosen who would not comprise a functional aristocracy just as predatory as that which they were elected to check? [14] But an even greater problem of logical consistency arose in connection with Mill's subsequent argument, that a portion of the total community might have interests identical with those of the total community itself. While discussing the process by which representatives should be chosen Mill relied upon the frequency of elections to prevent these representatives from using their power 'like any other men ... not for the advantage of the community, but for their own advantage'. [15] While discussing the necessary composition of the electorate, however, he was willing to grant that such formal institutional guarantees might not be needed. Adequate guarantees might be found in certain social nexus.

It has often been noted that Mill was willing to condone the continued disfranchisement of 'children' and women; also, that he may have been willing to condone the continued disfranchisement of sizable proportions of the general adult male population. As a rule, however, the grounds on which he was willing to do so have not been noted. These provide the crucial key to his argument. According to Mill it was not necessary to enfranchise 'children' – and he was willing to include as 'children' all persons below the age of 40 – because their 'interests ... [were] involved in those of their parents'. [16] Nor was it necessary to enfranchise women, 'the interests of almost all of whom is involved in that of their fathers or in that of their husbands'. [17] And the same assumptions concerning the importance of certain definable social nexus and the importance of the role of these nexus in allowing the identification of persons who had certain common interests, also allowed him to argue, other things being equal, that it would make no effective difference whether the electorate was composed of the total adult male population or merely of those men who had some property and who he assumed would comprise 'the great majority of the people'. [18] By and large, however, as applied to *this* question the role of these assumptions has been ignored. As a rule, it has been overlooked that according to Mill, 'all those men who have attentively considered the formation of opinions in the great body of society, or, indeed, the principles of human nature in general', would accept the following proposition:

> . . . that the opinions of that class of the people who are below the middle rank are formed, and their minds are directed by that intelligent, that virtuous rank *who come the most immediately in contact with them, who are in the constant habit of intimate communication with them, to whom they fly for advice and assistance in all their numerous difficulties, upon whom they feel an immediate and daily dependence in health and in sickness, in infancy and in old age; to whom their children look up as models for their imitation, whose opinions they hear daily repeated and account it their honor to adopt.* [19]

These comments occur during Mill's discussion of the nature and role of the 'middle rank' of society. They serve to describe the means by which he believed the influence of the 'middle rank' was felt throughout society. Of course, considerable attention has been devoted to Mill's emphasis upon the role of the 'middle rank'. But the *means* by which the influence of the 'middle rank' was felt – and, presumably, would continue to be felt – has been effectively ignored. According to Mill, the 'middle rank . . . [was that which] gives to science, to art, and to legislation itself their most distinguished ornaments, and is the chief source of all that has exalted and refined human nature'. [20] He made a clear distinction between the 'middle rank' and the aristocracy. 'Under the present state of education and the diffusion of knowledge', he declared,

> the class which is universally described as both the most wise and the most virtuous part of the community, the middle rank, are wholly included in that part of the community which is *not* the aristocratical. [21]

But the mechanisms were both local and hierarchical – that is to say, the mechanisms were essentially 'aristocratical' – by which the influence of the 'middle rank' was supposedly felt throughout the society.

In some cases, what with the obviously synonymous meanings which 'rank' and 'class' had for Mill, what with the general tendency to conceive of English politics in the nineteenth century in terms of generalized classes, and what with the almost equally general tendency to conceive of the Benthamites as spokesmen of the 'middle class', Mill's *Essay* has been read as an argument for a narrowly restricted franchise, or, as it was recently put, as an argument why 'the wealthy minority should rule the entire society'. [22] And considering the limited educational provisions in England at the time this reading is not inconsistent with Mill's classical definition of human nature. It is this which undoubtedly explains Professor Shields' effort to rub away the meaning of those passages in the *Essay* which, as he notes, 'appear to

justify the exercise of political power by the "lower orders" '.[23] But
the effort is only required because Mill's sociological premises have
been ignored. Shields has clearly sought in Mill's argument a total
meaning which would be consistent with Mill's classical definition of
human nature. As he put it, what Mill had in mind was

> ... that only persons capable of rational action should possess
> political power. The suffrage should be granted to those individuals
> able to judge rationally their self interest ... Only adult males, age
> forty, with a substantial amount of property qualify: age and wealth
> are evidence of suitable 'rationality'. Anyway, members of the
> working class, poor and illiterate, do not really understand what is
> to their best interests. They should be guided by their betters, the
> reputable members of the middle class, who have clearly
> demonstrated their competence for rational pursuit of self interest.[24]

But an argument such as this not only denies Mill's explicit advocacy of
universal suffrage,[25] it misses the entire point of the grounds on which
he rationalized the continued exclusion of women and 'children' – that
their interests were *identical* with those of their husbands and fathers. As
to the grounds for the possible exclusion of the 'lower orders', Shields
has reversed Mill's argument, implying that their dependence upon the
'middle rank' is a reason not for including them but for leaving them
outside the pale of the constitution.

Professor Hamburger noted this latter point when arguing that Mill
was trying to make a case for universal suffrage, not for restricting the
franchise to the middle class.[26] He also noted that when Mill referred to
the 'middle rank' he was not referring to the 'middle class' as an
economic group – to an industrial or commercial middle class – but to
a group whose 'intellectual eminence' he admired.[27] But the
recognition of these points notwithstanding, Hamburger asserts that
'Mill's consideration of the suffrage was shaped by his belief that men
would choose their representatives according to their individual wishes
and interests'.[28] This statement is scarcely compatible with Mill's
emphasis upon the nature of the relationship between the members of
the 'middle rank' and those who, he explained, 'are in the constant
habit of intimate communication with them'.

Nowhere does Hamburger mention this aspect of Mill's argument.
Indeed, while he quotes Mill's contention, that 'the opinions of that
class of the people who are below the middle rank are formed, and
their minds are directed by that intelligent, that virtuous rank', he ends
his quotation at that point.[29] In effect, he ignores the crucial assumption
revealed in the following statement, that the influence of the 'middle
rank' was expressed through certain quite specific nexus. He may be
quite right in saying that Mill intended his general statement about the
influence of the 'middle rank' to be 'a factual description of the way

working class opinions were formed in the England of his time'.[30] But he ignored the nexus upon which, according to Mill, this influence essentially depended.

Historians and political scientists have evidently sometimes assumed that James Mill could not have meant what he said. The reader who had only Elie Halevy's *Growth of Philosophic Radicalism* to guide him would find that at one point in the *Essay on Government* Mill had written,

> ... for if the whole mass of the people who have some property would make a good choice, it will hardly be pretended that, added to them, the comparatively small number of those who have none ... would be able to make the choice a bad one.[31]

In effect, the Mill whom Halevy quoted argued his case against a property qualification for the franchise on the grounds that rich and poor would probably behave very much alike and, even if this were not so, that the poor were not very numerous. But according to Mill, if the rich and poor behaved alike it was because the rich would influence the poor. Halevy's ellipsis stands in place of a crucial assertion which is scarcely compatible with the general description of Mill's argument which he provided. As Mill himself had put it,

> ... for if the whole mass of the people who have some property would make a good choice, it will hardly be pretended that, added to them, the comparatively small number of those who have none, *and whose minds are naturally and almost necessarily governed by the minds of those who have,* would be able to make the choice a bad one.[32]

But according to Mill the poor would not be powerless. As he explained elsewhere, once they had the protection of the secret ballot – and the secret ballot was crucial to his scheme – their individual response to the influences of the individual rich would serve to distinguish between the 'legitimate' influences of some and the 'illegitimate' influences of others. For Mill the logic of the secret ballot did not derive from the premise of rationality. Rather, it derived from the incontestable fact of influence. As he explained in his 'Thoughts on Moderate Reform in the House of Commons', property might have either of two varieties of influence or power, the one good, the other bad. 'It is possible', he declared,

> for a man who is possessed of this power [derived from property], to exercise it in such a manner as to become the object of affection and reverence, not only to all those who come within the sphere of his virtues, but, by sympathy with them, of all those to whom the knowledge of this character is diffused. The opinion, the wishes of such a man become a motive to his fellow creatures.[33]

And, in his *History of British India* he distinguished between those circumstances in which the secret ballot might be 'advantageous', and those in which it might be 'hurtful'. The grounds for this distinction were pragmatic: whether internal or external influences − '[those] which have their origin primarily in [the voter] himself . . . [or] in other men' − would be more effective in prompting the voter to vote 'in the right direction' or 'in the opposite direction'. 'In all cases', he explained,

> in which the independent interests of the voter . . . would dictate the good and useful vote; but in which cases . . . he is liable to be acted upon . . . by men whose interests would dictate a base and mischievous vote, the ballot is a great and invaluable security . . . There is, however, another set of cases in which those interests of the voter, which have their origin primarily in himself, and not in other men, draw in the hurtful direction . . . If allowed, in this set of cases, to vote in secret, he will be sure to vote as the sinister interest impels. If forced to vote in public, he will be subject to all the restraint which the eye of the community, fixed upon his virtue or knavery, is calculated to produce; and in such cases, the ballot is only an encouragement to evil.[34]

Of course, Mill argued that the ballot was a 'great and invaluable security . . . [in] the important instance of the votes of people for representatives in the legislative assembly of a nation'.[35] But he also acknowledged that 'a majority out of any number of voters . . . [might] be acted upon by the will of other men, whose interests are opposite to those of the nation.'[36] At the time he wrote it was this possibility which underlay his argument for the secret ballot. By the early fifties, however, it was this possibility which underlay his son's opposition to it.[37]

As these various statements reveal, James Mill's plea for the secret ballot was not premised upon the assumption that if voters could vote in secret they would all vote as individuals. Rather, it was premised upon the assumption that if voters could vote in secret many of them would vote in response to the influences which emanated from the 'virtues' of men of property. His plea for the ballot, like his criticism of the aristocracy, was not predicated upon any inherent dislike of social gradations, or of that influence which, in England in the early nineteenth century, derived from these gradations.[38] Rather, his plea was predicated upon his dislike of the particular ways in which influence was often exercised. The changes he hoped to see in English society and politics were not changes of *structure* but changes of *mode*. By means of the ballot he sought to moralize the effective influences within the society. If electoral influence were to depend upon 'virtue' then, obviously, only the virtuous men would be influential. But while the non-virtuous men would lose their influence, the scope of the influence of the virtuous men would be delimited by the radii of the areas through which the knowledge of their characters was diffused. And, with such a scope, the channels through which their influences would be felt would not be formal and institutional – except to the degree to which an estate or mill or factory might be considered a formal institution. Rather, they would be informal and personal. According to Mill, a choice should be made among rival opinions in terms of the social factors which might induce specific groups of men to adopt the opinions of those to whom they '[flew] for advice and assistance in all their numerous difficulties', or in terms of the cohesion of clearly defined communities, those whose 'eyes' might restrain the 'knavery' of their errant members. Of course, except where such communities existed in some relation to the influences which affected them – except where they corresponded with 'the sphere of . . . [the] virtues' of a man of property – they remained undefined. But his failure to define them more fully should not be allowed to obscure their importance in the logic of his argument. For Mill, the price of political power should be social benevolence. Or, looked at from the other side, the effective choice among political alternatives should be made in terms of the moral standing of the men with whom they were associated. And, because standing could only be judged by members of small face-to-face communities, his handling of the problem of the 'formation of opinions in the great body of society' is not inconsistent with his handling of the franchise and of the secret ballot. On the other hand, as Macaulay noted, the premises underlying his handling of the franchise were enough to upset the entire logic of his effort to show that monarchy and aristocracy were, *by nature,* bad forms of government.

Generally, Macaulay's criticisms of Mill have been read as Mill obviously wished to have them read, not as criticisms of his logic but of his effort to be logical and to be logical in a particular way – to deduce the science of government from the principles of human nature. It was against this charge that he defended himself. And, as a rule, historians and political scientists have assumed that his defence was appropriate to the charge. Thus, they have generally ignored Macaulay's reference to that 'delicious *bonne bouche* of wisdom', as he called it, the passage in the *Essay on Government* in which Mill explained how 'the opinions of that class of the people who are below the middle rank are formed, and their minds are directed'. After quoting this passage at length, not stopping with the simple assertion of the role of the 'middle rank', but including Mill's explanation of how the role was performed, Macaulay went on to declare that if Mill's arguments in this passage were valid then 'his whole system falls to the ground'.[39] And it fell to the ground because of the logical inconsistencies it contained. Mill had used one set of principles of human nature to show why monarchy and aristocracy were bad forms of government. He had used another set to show how representative government would work. But if the principles of human nature which he had used to show how representative government would work were applied to monarchy and aristocracy then his argument that monarchy and aristocracy were, *by nature,* bad forms of government collapsed. By the same token, if the principles of human nature which he had used to show why monarchy and aristocracy were bad forms of government were applied to representative government then his argument that representative government was, *by nature,* a good form of government collapsed.

III

As James Mill's argument reveals, when John Stuart Mill found much that was congenial in Coleridge's concern for 'the conditions of the permanent existence of the social union', he had not gone so very far from home.[40] The son's complaint against the father, that 'he refused to let his praise or blame be influenced by the motive of the agent' is understandable in generational terms.[41] But it scarcely provides an adequate key to the father's various theoretical positions. A far more useful key lies in the son's observation that the Benthamites – and, presumably, his father among them – were critical of 'the *selfish* interests of aristocracies, or priests, or lawyers, or some other species of *imposter*'.[42] However, perhaps because the imposter is, by definition, hard to distinguish from those he seeks to emulate, the son's implicit distinction has been largely ignored. It was the *imposter* in the role, and his selfish motives, which incited the principal animosity of the Benthamites. But the role itself they scarcely criticised. Nor did they criticise the hierarchical structure which allowed the role to be played. In effect, in criticising their society the Benthamites did not criticise its *values.* Rather, they used these values as a frame of reference. It was the younger Mill, at that time even less far from home, who declared, in 1831, that England was in 'a *transitional* condition', one in which there were 'no persons to whom the mass of the uninstructed habitually defer, and in whom they trust for finding the right, and for pointing it out'.[43] But he looked forward to the return of what he described as 'the *natural* state of society . . . that . . . in which the opinions and feelings of the people are, with their voluntary acquiescence, formed *for* them . . . .[44]

The process by which John Stuart Mill hoped 'the *natural* state of society' would be restored was not a legislative process. It was a social process the course of which could be measured by the emergence and, even more, by the recognition of a new elite. 'Society may be said to be in its *natural* state', he declared, when worldly power, and moral influence, are habitually and undisputedly exercised by the fittest persons whom the existing state of society affords. Or, to be more explicit; when on the one hand, the temporal, or, as the French would say, the material [sic!] interests of the community, are managed by those of its members who possess the greatest capacity for such management; and on the other hand, those whose opinions the people follow, whose feelings they imbibe, and who practically and by common consent, perform, no matter under what original title, the office of thinking for the people, are persons better qualified than any others whom the civilization of the age and the country affords, to think and judge rightly and usefully.[45]

The goal of the Grey Ministers is clear. In particular, it is revealed by the boundary and franchise provisions of their Bill, those by which they hoped to restore the foundations of the status of the various existing elites. But their hopes of restoring these foundations in any permanent fashion were inevitably doomed to disappointment. It may still have been possible in the early thirties to divide the kingdom into appropriate constituencies. It may still have been possible in the latter sixties to try to restore the structure which the earlier reformers had tried to create. But it was scarcely possible either in the early thirties or in the latter sixties to perpetuate the integrity of these constituencies against the effects of accelerating technological change, increasing population movement, and growing intellectual ferment. Even less was it possible to perpetuate their integrity when it also depended upon the willingness of rival politicians to restrict their electoral efforts to those constituencies which had been designed with them in mind, and upon the willingness of others to acknowledge the legitimacy of those social groups upon which this constituency structure was based.

The goals of James Mill and John Stuart Mill were equally clear – if clarity belongs to metaphysics – to concentrate power in the hands of the proper members of 'the middle rank' or in the hands of those who were really 'the fittest persons'. But as the son acknowledged, in a '*transitional* condition' there was some difficulty in reaching any general agreement as to exactly who 'the fittest persons' might be. Indeed, the difficulty served to define the 'condition'.[46] Nor did the father do much better. On the one hand he declared, 'the middle rank are wholly included in that part of the community which is *not* the aristocratical'. This might perhaps be called a step towards precision. On the other hand, he provided a functional definition so open ended as to cast considerable doubt upon the inexorability of what has been called his 'truly inexorable ... logic'.[47] 'The middle rank', he explained, were those to whom members of the class below them '[flew] for advice and assistance in all their numerous difficulties'. In effect, while '[giving] to science, to art, and to legislation itself their most distinguished ornaments, and . . . [while being] the chief source of all that has exalted and refined human nature', the members of 'the middle rank' were those whom men in the class below them chose. But the point of all this is not to show that the son and the father both failed to provide useful answers to the question of who 'the fittest persons' might be, or how the real members of 'the middle rank' should be distinguished from the others, or how to deal with those men who, perhaps for perverse reasons of their own, refused 'to fly for advice and assistance' to those to whom they should have flown, or refused to accept the opinions of those who really were 'the fittest persons'. Neither the father nor the son should be unduly criticised for failing to provide answers to these questions because they are unanswerable. Rather, the point is this: these were the questions which both the father and the son tried to answer.

Historians and political scientists have frequently described the political reform process not only as the means by which, ultimately, universal suffrage became established but also as the means by which, ultimately, all restraints upon the expression of individual political preferences were removed with the exception of those which the voter chose to impose upon himself, those which are implicit in any choice because any choice precludes an alternative. Historians and political scientists have also frequently attributed responsibility for this process and thus for the ultimate removal of these restraints, to the Benthamites or Utilitarians. Clearly, universal suffrage has come into being in consequence of changes in the law. Indeed, that scarcely needs saying. But to endow the reform process with the function of removing all restraint from the expression of individual political preferences is to fail to take account of those provisions of the first and second Reform Acts by which the members of the Grey Ministry and, subsequently, the members of the Derby-Disraeli Ministry, obviously tried to increase the strength of the traditional social nexus by defining and redefining the various constituencies in terms of the traditional groups and communities. To claim, as some historians and political scientists have claimed, that men such as James Mill provided the theoretical grounds for the removal of such restraints is to fail to take account of what might be called the anti-liberalism of their arguments. But details aside, such descriptions of the political reform process, requiring the identification of those hypothetical men who, as Wallas put it, 'worked to create a democracy of which they had as yet no experience', involves a basic confusion about the relationship between legislation and changes in the distribution of political power.

The Grey Ministers tried to create a political structure within which the legitimate influences of the established leaders of English society might be perpetuated. James Mill and John Stuart Mill expressed similar structural assumptions with – as is obvious – a different social focus. However, while the concept of legitimate influence was as basic to the arguments of the Mills as it was to the reform scheme of the Grey Ministers the concept of legitimate influence was losing its essential validity. The Grey Ministers might try to restore the integrity of the traditional groups and communities of English society. But they could scarcely arrest those various processes to which, in large measure, the problems should be attributed with which they sought to deal. Towns continued to be established where none had been before; cities continued to overflow their boundaries. And even when these things did not occur ambitious politicians kept trying to elbow their way into places where they did not 'belong'. Furthermore, while doing so these men often argued that the powers of those against whom they contended were illegitimate, and that their own followers followed them not because of any influence they exercised over them but rather because of their intelligence. In these circumstances the distinction between legitimate and illegitimate influence was obscured, the groups or communities to which the concept of legitimate influence was related were obscured, and the mechanisms through which the so-called legitimate influences were channelled were obscured. In place of the distinction between legitimate and illegitimate influence another emerged, that between free individuals and individuals who were not free. According to this distinction all influence was illegitimate. It was this which George Grote implied when he complained, in 1833, about that unwritten clause in the first Reform Act as a result of which the voters were divided into two classes, 'the first invested with a will of their own, the second under legal obligation to express only the will of another'.[48] According to Grote, the men with wills of their own were not 'the fittest persons' to whom John Stuart Mill had referred. They were mere landlords or employers. And because of this he demanded the secret ballot.

The logic of Grote's demand for the secret ballot was basically different from the logic of James Mill's demand. James Mill recognized the existence of groups and the function of groups in the formation of opinions. But Grote implied that electoral choices should be made by individuals 'invested with a will of their own'. Of course, he did not say how such individuals might be created. Or rather – to put it somewhat differently – he implied that such was the nature of man. His argument was used to criticise the Act. But his argument may well have helped to provide the context of Wallas' later assertion, that the men responsible for the Act, 'those who worked to create a democracy of which they had as yet no experience . . . looked on reasoning not as a difficult and uncertain process, but as the necessary and automatic working of man's mind when faced with problems affecting his interest'.

In polemical terms Grote's formulation is understandable. Indeed, representative systems of government can perhaps only exist if it is assumed that Grote's formulation is accurate. A distinction must be made, however – and many historians and political scientists who have dealt with nineteenth century English politics have been reluctant to make this distinction – between the psychological and sociological myths which representative government requires and the psychological and sociological realities which these myths render endurable. In one respect Grote was right: most of the men who exercised electoral influence in the early and mid-nineteenth century were the voters' landlords or employers. But he grossly distorted the problems of nineteenth century electoral behaviour when he implied that influence could have no effect upon opinion. In many cases – indeed, probably, in most cases – the orientation of influence tended to accord with the personal preferences of the voters, as these preferences were themselves conditioned both by influence itself and by the organizations and mass media which supplemented the strength of influence. Historians, however, who have generally assumed that Grote's formulation is the right one, have not only obscured the question to which Grote's formulation provided the answer – how could traditionally based influences be rendered viable? – they have also obscured the novelty of the problems which emerged as those hierarchical groups and communities lost that cohesion to which Mill *père* and Mill *fils* both implicitly referred, and as new groups and communities came into being. In effect, many nineteenth century Englishmen, reformer and anti-reformer alike, were totally unprepared to deal with a society in which, increasingly, influence was exercised not *across* class lines but within them.

IV

The characteristic sociological assumptions of the early and mid-nineteenth century reflect indealizations of the pre-industrial world. The norms were those in which economic classes possessed no organizational importance or in which ostensibly such classes did not exist. And, in the early part of the century, by and large, those men who believed that classes should not possess organizational important – that employers and employees, landlords and tenants and labourers, should form coherent groups – sought to legitimize the various ranks or hierarchies of status in terms of the functions performed by different ranks of men within their own local groups or communities. By the early part of the century, however, the various relationships which did, to some extent, characterize the pre-industrial world, those which these assumptions reflected, were already being replaced by other varieties of relationship. And many of the local functions which, in the pre-industrial world, served to legitimize the status of the various elites had already been transferred to the State. However, while social divisions along class lines were becoming increasingly important such divisions were often – perhaps even generally – regarded not as the characteristic attributes of a new social order but as symptoms of 'transition' or as symptoms of disorder. As Francis William Newman put it, in 1852, this was 'the great disease of modern Europe, *that the cohesions of society are in horizontal layers alone*'.[49]

Writing in the twenties and thirties, James Mill had still been able to legitimize the traditional social hierarchy in terms of the functions which the various elites performed – or, at least, which the *virtuous* elites performed – within their own local communities. And, for him, the secret ballot would strengthen these virtuous elites. However, as the century wore on and more and more of these local functions were transferred to the State, it became progressively more difficult to legitimize the traditional hierarchy in terms of these local functions. As Newman put it, in 1852, what with the growing number of State activities, and what with the growing efficiency of State administration, the 'upper classes' were ceasing to perform their self-legitimizing roles. ' . . . When the work of governing is done well for them, [they] no longer trouble themselves about it, and, finding no necessity to care for the public, care only for their own pleasures or their own tastes . . .'.[50] In these circumstances the status of the various elites could no longer be legitimized – or rationalized – in terms of their local functions. Nor could those communities of deferential men which figure so prominently in the logic of James Mill's arguments on the franchise be handled in the way he handled them, as groups whose own cohesion was largely related to the influences to which they responded.

Mid-century electoral behaviour was group behaviour of a sort which confirms the enduring relevance of James Mill's description. But in much the same way that the terms of Mill's description were forgotten so were the realities of this behaviour ignored – at least in public discussion. When the basic nexus of traditional society were being brought into question many men came to argue that English society was – or should be – composed of rational individuals, not of groups or communities. And they also argued that the reform process was the means of emancipating such rational individuals. Of course, the cultural values which their arguments reflect were at hand. But these did not underlie the reform process anymore than they underlay James Mill's arguments on the franchise. Rather, they helped to obscure the essential assumptions on which Mill's arguments were based, certain essential provisions of the first two Reform Acts, and the essential nature of the problems which these provisions were designed to solve. By means of these values the traditional groups or communities of English society were legitimized. And by means of these values the status of those men was legitimized who were either members of the traditional elites or members of those new elites which John Stuart Mill, among others, hoped would replace the traditional ones. But these groups or communities were not legitimized as social entities. They were legitimized, rather, as products of the ostensible rationality of their members. Nor was status legitimized in terms of functions performed within the group or community. Rather, it was legitimized as being the automatic right of these men who possessed the necessary qualities of intelligence and wealth. And, as Walter Bagehot put it, only a fairly intelligent man could be expected to recognize the greater intelligence of those who were elevated above him in rank and station.

V

The notion that deference was an important factor in nineteenth century English politics is particularly associated with Bagehot. However, while the notion has often been cited it has seldom been used in analyses of nineteenth century English politics. The reasons for this presumably lie in the fact that in Bagehot's hands deference was not an analytical concept. It was principally a means of legitimizing the structure of English society as, apparently, he understood it. In gross terms, Bagehot's framework of political analysis has proved useful. In one way or another, many historians and political scientists have availed themselves of the distinction he made between the 'dignified' parts of the constitution, those from which the Government derived its powers, and the 'efficient' parts, those through which these powers were exercised. Rarely, however, have they used the concept of deference, defined as he defined it, to explain how the 'dignified' parts of the constitution functioned. Their procedure is understandable both logically and evidentially. According to Bagehot, elective systems of Government were only possible where the mass of the people were intelligent, educated, and fairly well off, as in America, or deferential, as in England.[51] Having made this distinction, however, he quickly destroyed it. Not only did he fail to deal with the crucial empirical question of why *certain* Englishmen habitually deferred to *certain* others, he scarcely recognized the question as a question. He attributed the deferential nature of the mid-century English electorate in part to their corporate susceptibility to the '*theatrical show* of society', in part to their *moderate* intelligence, their *moderate* education, and their *moderate* affluence.

The results of deference were there for him to see, revealed in the continued social, economic and political pre-eminence of the aristocracy, the gentry, and the urban magnates. And, apparently, Bagehot assumed that the cause must be of the same nature as the result. 'In fact', he explained,

> the mass of the English people ... defer to what we may call the *theatrical show* of society. A certain state passes before them; a certain pomp of great men; a certain spectacle of beautiful women; a wonderful display of wealth and enjoyment is displayed, and they are coerced by it. Their imagination is bowed down; they feel they are not equal to the life which is revealed to them. Courts and aristocracies have the great quality which rules the multitude, though philosophers can see nothing in it – visibly. Courtiers can do what others cannot. A common man may as well try to rival the actors on the stage in their acting, as the aristocracy in *their* acting. The higher world, as it looks from without, is a stage on which the actors walk their parts much better than the spectators can.[52]

Certainly, the *'theatrical show'* must have had its effects. 'The mass of the English people' could not have felt equal to the life of the aristocracy. But this is scarcely relevant. Of course they accepted the differences of wealth, rank and status which Bagehot described. This is not at issue. The issue is, why did they accept them? Possibly, Bagehot realized the folly of his formulation. Writing *after* 1867 he urged the members of the aristocracy and plutocracy to act at once to prevent political questions from arising which would bind the poor together as a class in opposition to the rich.[53] But in dealing with the mid-century he begged the essential questions of class or group relations. His *'theatrical show'* argument provides no means of explaining anything other than a cheering crowd on a summer day. His *moderate* intelligence, *moderate* education, and *moderate* affluence argument perhaps explains even less.

The argument is to be found in the Introduction to the 2nd edition of *The English Constitution,* published in 1872. It is related to his analysis of English society into three distinct categories of men. The first of these categories was composed of the small minority who, because of their property and common sense, were competent to rule. The second was composed of a larger minority many of whom had been enfranchised in 1832. The members of this category, he declared, were not themselves competent to rule.

> They were just competent to make a selection between two sets of superior ideas; or rather – for the conceptions of such people are more personal than abstract – between two opposing parties, each professing a creed of such ideas. But they could do no more. Their own notions, if they had been cross-examined upon them, would have been found always most confused and often most foolish. They

were competent to decide on issues selected by the higher classes,
but they were incompetent to do more.[54]
The third category was composed of the majority of the population,
many of whom were enfranchised in 1867. According to Bagehot,
these needed even more guidance than the members of the second
category. Hence the problem as he saw it after 1867: 'Will they defer
in the same way [as the members of the second category] to wealth and
rank, and to the higher qualities of which these are the rough symbols
and the common accompaniments'?[55]

The conceptual model of society which such a question helps to
illustrate is one which Bagehot shared with many of his
contemporaries. It was, of course, the model of a 'class' society – if
classes be defined in simple hierarchical terms. But the classes which
composed this society did not exist in any political or dynamic sense.
Nor did the society possess definable networks, loyalties, or lines of
cohesion. James Mill's conceptual model was totally different.
Whatever the usefulness of his concept of 'the middle rank', when he
described the means by which the influence of 'the middle rank' was
felt throughout English society he was describing something at least
potentially·real. According to him, when the lower orders deferred to
the higher their behaviour was a measure of the latters' benevolence
exercised within quite specific communities and networks. For him, the
concept of deference made a certain amount of sociological sense. It
was a function of the face-to-face community, an attribute of the
Gemeinschaft. As used by Bagehot, on the other hand, the concept of
deference made very little sense. Nor did it make any greater sense as
used by Sir George Cornewall Lewis.

Lewis' work is scarcely as well known as Bagehot's. Indirectly,
however, its importance may be as great. Indeed it was possibly Lewis
who helped to obscure elements in his predecessors' arguments by
distorting their essential logic. In his *Essay on the Influence of Authority in
Matters of Opinion,* first published in 1849, Lewis quoted extensively
from Samuel Bailey's *The Rationale of Political Representation,* a work of
Benthamite popularization. But Lewis significantly distorted the logic
of Bailey's argument. And, writing later, Bagehot saw Bailey through
Lewis' eyes.

In particular, Lewis quoted a passage from Bailey in which he
referred to the 'unconquerable . . . and beneficial proneness in man, to
rely on the judgment and authority of those who are elevated above
himself in rank and riches'.[56] In the logic of Bailey's argument this
statement served to define the general political consequences of a local
and hierarchical society. It served to buttress his argument that the
secret ballot would not reduce the legitimate influence of intelligence
and property within the State but would increase it by reducing the

strength of illegitimate influence. James Mill had said as much – with similar limiting conditions. Lewis, however, ignored these limiting conditions. Just as recent historians and political scientists have tended to ignore James Mill's implicit specification of the means by which, ostensibly, the influence of 'the middle rank' was felt throughout the society, so Lewis ignored the fact that when Bailey referred to the 'unconquerable . . . and beneficial proneness of man, to rely on the judgment and authority of those who are elevated above himself in rank and riches', he was only making a conditional statement. The conditions were those he went on to define when he referred to

> The propensity of mankind . . . not to make a choice of an individual for a desirable office on account of his bare merits, of his mere aptness of discharge its functions, estimated by their own independent understandings; but . . . to give him their suffrages *on account of the opinion entertained of him, and the favour manifested towards him, by those whom they wish to please, and whose judgment they have been accustomed to respect.*[57]

Just as recent historians and political scientists have tended to cut their quotations from Mill at the point before he explained the mechanisms of influence of 'the middle rank', so Lewis cut his quotation from Bailey at the point before he referred to the wish to please and the custom to respect. It scarcely exaggerates the case to say that according to Lewis elevated status provided its own validation without regard to the relationships between those who enjoyed this status and those who recognized their claims to enjoy it. According to Lewis, 'persons of sound practical judgment . . . may be always expected to be in a minority; but their opinion is likely to be voluntarily adopted by the majority'.[58]

Reading Bailey through Lewis's eyes, Bagehot obviously assumed that they were saying the same thing. And because he agreed in part with what he *thought* they were saying – because he agreed in part with Lewis' formulation of deference – his efforts to distinguish his own beliefs from theirs are all the more revealing of the change in the concept of deference which occurred during the middle years of the century. According to Bagehot, Lewis and Bailey had both provided 'appropriate description[s] of the popular association of superiority of judgment with superiority in station'.[59] But, he went on, they had drawn an inappropriate inference from their descriptions because they failed to recognize what he believed to be the case, that only moderately intelligent men would be deferential.

Bagehot's comments might perhaps be appropriate to Lewis' concept of deference. But they are scarcely appropriate to Bailey's concept of deference. Ignoring the basic point of disagreement between Lewis and Bailey, Bagehot declared that the two men had been right in saying 'that as the higher orders are felt by the lower to be more capable of governing, they will be chosen by the lower if the latter *are left free to choose*.'[60] What is important in his argument is the implicit definition of 'freedom'. 'If the acquisition of power is left to the unconscious working of the natural influences of society', he explained,

> the rich and cultivated will certainly acquire it; they obtain it insensibly, gradually, and without the poorer orders knowing that they are obtaining it. But the result is different when, by the operation of a purely democratic constitution, the selection of rulers is submitted to the direct vote of the populace. The lower orders are then told that they are *perfectly able to judge;* demagogues assert it to them without ceasing: the constitution itself is appealed to as an incontrovertible witness to the fact; as it has placed the supreme power in the hands of the lower and more numerous classes, it would be contravening it to suppose that the real superiority was in the higher and fewer . . . In consequence, history teaches that under a democratic government those who speak the feelings of the majority themselves have a greater chance of being chosen to rule, than any of the higher orders, who, under another form of government, would be admitted to be the better judges. The natural effect of such a government is to mislead the poor.[61]

In effect, according to Bagehot, 'freedom to choose' should only be given to those who were 'able to judge'. Professor Shields' gloss on James Mill, '[that] only persons capable of rational action should possess political power', distorts the thrust of Mill's argument. Had it been applied to Bagehot, however, it would have been appropriate. And the reasons are clear. According to Mill's social model, 'right voting' did not have to be an individual act, or even a rational act. It could be a social act, an act conditioned either by the 'affection and reverence' which the voter felt for a specific superior, or by 'the eye of the community fixed on his virtue or knavery'. Mill made no distinction between social and political relationships because, according to him, it was only within the context of certain social relationships that political relationships possessed the legitimacy he believed to be essential. And the same is true of Bailey. Hence their advocacy of the secret ballot. Within the logic of their arguments the ballot would increase the effective strength of legitimate influence, that which derived from the 'virtues' of the various elites. It would do so because it would allow the virtuous men of property to be distinguished from the others. For Bagehot, on the other hand, who conceived of society not in terms of groups and networks but in terms of categories of men, voters were required who would themselves be 'competent to make a selection between two sets of superior ideas'. Bagehot did not impose very high intellectual requirements. Formally, however, the

requirements were intellectual. For Mill and Bailey the secret ballot
provided the prospective guarantee that only those men would possess
political power who should possess it. For Bagehot, on the other hand,
who opposed the ballot, the question whether those who possessed
political power should possess it was not to be raised. In effect, he
disposed of the question whether the right men possessed political
power by means of the somewhat circular argument – this must be the
case because those men believed it to be the case who thereby
demonstrated their intelligence.

VI

The essential problem was the same in Bagehot's time as it had been in
Mill's – how to guarantee the legitimate exercise of political power.
But there had been a change in the terms in which the problem was
discussed. While dealing with what was still in large measure a locally
and traditionally structured society James Mill assumed that this
localism and traditionalism could provide the essential means by which
the legitimacy of power could be determined – by which power could
be assigned and kept in the hands in which it belonged. But the
cohesions on which his argument depended continued to break down.
Their legitimacy was increasingly called into question. In these
circumstances, Bagehot and many of Bagehot's contemporaries applied
those principles of human nature to the functioning of representative
government which Mill had primarily used to show why monarchy
and aristocracy were bad forms of government. Like Bagehot, many of
these men continued to refer to the 'deferential nature' of the English
electorate. Like Bagehot, again, they tended to deal with the deference
question not as a *structural question* – why do certain men recognize
certain leaders and, in recognizing these leaders, constitute a group?
Rather, they dealt with the deference question as a *non-structural question*
– what are the qualities which enable men to recognize what might be
described as the true attributes of leadership?

   Writing in the twenties James Mill had cited the paternal behaviour
of the various elites in their various local communities to explain why
the minds of those men who had no property were governed by the
minds of those who had. And, according to Mill, the same social
relations would continue to obtain in the future between the same two
categories of men. In effect, he dealt with the problems of opinion and
electoral behaviour in terms of those patterns of influence and
deference which the traditional nexus provided. Writing in the fifties
and sixties, on the other hand, when many of the traditional nexus
were becoming weaker and when new nexus were coming into being,
many men tended to imply that the problems of opinion and electoral
behaviour were – or, at least, should be – discrete problems unrelated

440 *Epilogue*

to any questions of social structure or social nexus. And, while doing so, they produced an appropriate theory of society, an appropriate theory of politics, and an appropriate criterion of political morality. According to them, politics was – or, at least, should be – a matter of applied intelligence; according to them, the traditional groups within the society were not really groups but aggregates of individuals; and, according to them – and the point is crucial – the new groups which were emerging in the context of industrialization were either products of the demagogues or functions of the discreditable feelings of their members which open voting would help to keep in check.

Since the mid-nineteenth century or, more specifically, since the time Graham Wallas was writing, a crucial change has occurred in the terms of political discussion. One important fact has to some extent been assimilated: society itself did not break down when those relationships which had provided the essential units of cohesion of pre-industrial society lost the organizational importance. To some extent the structural exigencies of society have been acknowledged – and acknowledged in more than the limited sense in which John Stuart Mill acknowledged them when he referred to 'the *natural* state of society'. In consequence, various collectivities are frequently regarded as legitimate bodies. If they have discrete political goals of their own these goals are often treated as adjuncts to the identity of the collectivities themselves. In effect, in the world today the politician is – at least within limits – the recognized advocate of the voters who choose him. The premise is often granted in terms of which his actual behaviour is regarded as legitimate. Deplorable, perhaps, by those who oppose him. But legitimate nonetheless. Thus, when he rewards his electoral followers by voting for legislation conceived on their behalf he is not doing anything which violates present-day social assumptions, or the related assumptions as to how a political system really functions.

But in the mid-nineteenth century the premise was somewhat different, that politics was – or, at least, that politics ought to be – a matter of applied intelligence, not a matter of group action. And, within the context of this premise, no legitimate political rewards could exist except those which derived from the simple satisfaction of each man's individual integrity. It was this premise which informed the arguments of many mid-century men when they came to deal with the problem of political corruption. According to them, political activity should not provide any tangible rewards for those engaged in it. Rather, it should be undertaken from purely altruistic motives. And this norm defined the terms in which they discussed the problem of how to deal with the various infractions of the norm. The problem was not that the norm was placed 'too high'. Rather, that the norm was the product of a myth.

The reform process reflected the effort to maximize 'legitimate' political behaviour. As such, it has generally been described as a single process definable in terms of the progressive realization of a single idea, or – in these years when Hegel is somewhat out of fashion – in terms of the progressive achievement of a single criterion of legitimacy. Within the context of this argument no changes occurred in the *meaning* of legitimate political behaviour. The only changes which occurred were changes in the *legitimacy* of the behaviour itself. But such an argument not only obscures the differences among the various measures of reform, it also obscures the difficulties which many men faced when trying to apply the altruistic norm. These were the difficulties on which William Greg focused in an article which won John Stuart Mill's hearty approbation.

' . . . A seat in the legislature is an object of personal ambition', Greg declared,

> it is so honourably and justifiably . . . Long may it be so regarded . . . Very well: on this object . . . [the candidate] sets his heart; . . . *he is naturally grateful to all who aid him in his purpose;* . . . they have furthered his objects: he naturally wishes to further theirs. [But] the law forbids him to do this, or to promise to do this: it commands him to confine his gratitude to 'words and becks and wreathed smiles'; it says to him, 'you shall show no hospitality to those who are toiling and sweating in your cause: if you give them a breakfast you shall be unseated; if you are detected in paying their expenses, or compensating them for the day's wages they have lost, or the mischievous enmity they have incurred in your service, you shall be fined and punished.' – Well! the verdict of public opinion will not ratify this language of the law: is it wholly unreasonable in this refusal?[62]

And from this his conclusion followed:

> . . . the law cannot distinguish between . . . that *understood* gratitude for electoral support at which purity itself can scarcely frown, and that open purchase of reluctant votes which the most law profligacy would not dream of defending.[63]

To the modern reader the points included in Greg's argument are rather less striking than those omitted from it. Greg's examples of what candidates might do in rewarding or recompensing their supporters – and of what the law forbade them to do – seem almost ludicrous when compared with what Members of Parliament were doing and, with increasing intensity, what they have continued to do. To pay for their supporters' breakfasts, or to pay them the day's wages they had lost by voting, are so inconsequential when compared with the enactment of legislation in their interest which, in this world of limited abundance, must be legislation in someone else's *dis*interest. Greg ignored this aspect of politics just as he ignored the social realities related to it: that groups existed, and existed in respect of the common goals or interests which their members recognized. Conceiving of politics in rational terms, he conceived of political corruption either as that which interfered with the expression of human rationality as he defined it, or as that which derived from the unfortunate participation in politics of men who lacked the requisite integrity, who regarded their votes as 'a private property to be sold – not a public trust to be exercised'. [64]

It was on these grounds – that more and more men regarded their votes as means of benefiting themselves either individually or corporately – that the younger Mill came to oppose the secret ballot. After quoting that passage in his father's *History of British India* in which his father had explained that 'There are occasions on which the use of the ballot is advantageous; [and] ... occasions on which is hurtful', John Stuart Mill went on to declare: [65]

> Thirty years ago, it was still true that in the election of members of Parliament, the main evil to be guarded against was that which the ballot would exclude – coercion by landlords, employers and customers. At present, I conceive, a much greater source of evil is the selfishness, or the selfish partialities of the voter himself. A 'base and mischievous vote' is now, I am convinced, much oftener given from the voter's personal interest, or class interest, or some mean feeling in his own mind, than from any fear of consequences at the hands of others: and to these evil influences the ballot would enable him to yield himself up, free from all shame or responsibility ... [And, he went on,] The growth of bribery, so loudly complained of, and the spread of the contagion to places formerly free from it, are evidence that the local influences are no longer paramount; that the electors now vote to please themselves, and not other people. [66]

However, while John Stuart Mill referred to 'local influences' in favourable terms – clearly, according to him, they might serve to counteract both the mounting 'contagion' of bribery and the not unrelated phenomenon of voting to please oneself alone – he scarcely analyzed these influences or the ways in which they might work. In effect, he ignored the relationships between those groups or communities through which a countervailing 'shame or responsibility' might be channelled and the traditional structure of society which this 'shame or responsibility' might serve to protect. The same was true of Greg. Both men described as *'moral'* that which served to protect a given pattern of relationships. As Greg put it,

> ... when plain and simple bribery has been cured or reduced within the scantiest limits, we should have to be on our guard against the increase of a different, and a subtler, and perhaps in effect a more noxious species of corruption. If corrupt and low-minded voters still

retain the franchise, they will still seek to sell their votes, though they will have to look for payment in a different coin. If candidates are not more stern and lofty in their integrity than heretofore, they will be exposed to temptations of another sort, even more difficult to resist, more easy to palliate to their consciences. If they may not any longer open their purses to gratify the inferior class of electors, they will be expected to warp their principles to suit them. They will be urged to purchase votes as before – and to purchase them at a far higher and more fatal price. They will be pressed, and often, we fear, induced, to lower their political creed, to modify and impair their genuine opinions, to 'file their mind' (as Shakespeare hath it), to profess views they do not hold, to give pledges they cannot redeem, in order to obtain the suffrages of men to whom the suffrage ought never to have been vouchsafed.[67]

The third Earl Grey's statement was conceptually identical:

To give money bribes to electors is not worse, or rather not nearly so bad, as to court their favour by flattering their passions and prejudices, and by encouraging them knowingly, in mischievous political errors. More real guilt is incurred because greater injury is done to the Nation, by having recourse to the arts of the demagogue, than by the illicit use of money for the purpose of carrying an election, and at the present moment the former abuse seems to be more common than the latter.[68]

Within the context of these assumptions the ideal parliamentary candidate was the man who merely wished to serve the State. And the ideal voter was the man who voted without thought of reward of any kind, either personal or corporate – except, of course, that of having done the right thing – and without regard to any permanent nexus which might exist either between him and the candidate or candidates for whom he voted, or between him and others who might support the same candidate or candidates. On this level the point that politics in general and electoral behaviour in particular were matters of group action was totally ignored. On another level it was clearly acknowledged – poll books continued to be published; M.P.s debated the question whether leaseholders of borough property should be allowed to vote in the counties in which the boroughs were located. But the two levels only impinged in the context of the question whether altruistic voters might be recompensed for their their votes even when, legally, such recompense was frowned upon.

According to Professor Gash, 'the real stumbling block [in the elimination of corrupt practices lay in the fact that] the electors even more perhaps than the elected were prepared to connive at the evasion of the anti-bribery law.' And this, as he put it, was because 'the exchange of money or other favours was firmly rooted in the electoral system.' [69] Whatever the relative moralities of nineteenth and twentieth century Englishmen, 'the exchange of money or other favours' has scarcely been rooted out of the electoral system. Indeed, it might be said that such exchanges are inherent in any electoral system. If tangible political rewards did not exist, political activity would be inconceivable – or conceivable only in that never-never land which Greg, Grey and the younger Mill tried to describe. As a rule, however, such exchanges occur today in only one of the two general forms in which they occurred a century and more ago. Rarely, today, do candidates bribe voters individually. But the practice which, according to Greg, Grey and the younger Mill, was far more deplorable, that by which candidates promise rewards to whole groups or classes of voters to gain their support is now general. Of course, today, such appeals are seldom regarded as corrupt. But that is the point exactly.

In the context of the declining organizational importance of traditional hierarchical communities, and the growing organizational importance of other nexus, it is significant that according to John Stuart Mill and many of his contemporaries those men who acted in terms of their group interests were not behaving legitimately. And it is also significant that many of these men tended to argue that when voters behaved as members of hierarchical communities or networks they were not really behaving as such but as rational individuals. In effect, in their public discussions – and, presumably, in their private discussion as well – these men tended to ignore the mechanisms which served to counteract the structural consequences of economic and social change.

Yet the mechanisms were basic. And, at least implicitly, their role was sometimes acknowledged. Indeed, as John Stuart Mill's reference to 'local influences' reveals, he, like his father before him, looked to the group or community as the guarantor of political legitimacy. But in the hands of the son – and the same is true of many of the son's contemporaries – these groups or communities were somewhat anomalous. In the logic of their arguments they often performed an essential function. But the question of how this function was performed was significantly avoided. And, presumably, it was avoided because, in the circumstances which obtained from the mid-century on, the son and his contemporaries could not distinguish – as the father had distinguished before them – between legitimate and illegitimate influence. According to James Mill the distinction was clear. Legitimate influence was that which obtained where wealth was used benevolently. It was a consequence of the 'affection and reverence' of members of a community for their benefactor. The other was a simple perversion. It obtained where wealth was used not to confer benefits but to 'control the will'. [70] Of course, some men continued to recognise this distinction – and, for example, to refer to the 'legitimate influence which a popular and respected landlord must always exercise in his neighbourhood'.[71] But these men's assumptions were generally buried beneath others. When the structure of society was changing, when, possibly, 'the upper classes . . . [found] the work of governing . . . done well for them . . . and, finding no necessity to care for the public, care[d] only for their own pleasures or their own tastes', the distinction to which they referred was obscured.[72] Influence became synonymous with corruption and the obvious communities and networks within the kingdom were either ignored or were understood in terms of the ostensible rationality and individualism – virtuous individualism – of their members, not as social entities whose cohesion was largely a function of the personal influences within them.

Of course, there is still the possibility that the tendency to substitute the concept of the individual – and often the concept of the *rational* individual – for the concept of the group was simply a measure of the weakening of those nexus on which James Mill and Samuel Bailey based their arguments. What with the widespread notion that politics was – or should be – a matter of applied intelligence, however, and what with the relationship which Bagehot and many of his contemporaries made between individualism and cosmopolitan deference, it seems probable that the actual weakening of these nexus affected their arguments rather less than the difficulties involved in trying to understand an increasing non-traditional society in terms of traditional frames of reference. At a time when the traditional structure of society was changing – when the traditional nexus of society were being brought into question – many men sought to defend this structure and these nexus with ideological weapons which the structure and nexus themselves provided. Their frame of reference was reflected in the assumption which the younger Mill articulated in 1831, the assumption of the *'natural* state of society', that in which 'the opinions and feelings of the people are, with their voluntary acquiescence, formed *for* them.' Presumably, it was the strength of this assumption which informed the arguments which largely obscured the assumption itself. Nor should it be argued simply that their formulations were 'class' formulations. While the class implication of their arguments are clear enough, their own complaints of the weakening of hierarchical status were matched by others' complaints that those welfare functions which had served to legitimize status were ceasing to be performed. In effect, it was not only the traditional elites and the new elites who complained of the new structure of society. They might protest that they were being abandoned by those who should follow them. But at other levels of the status hierarchy men also complained that they were being abandoned by those who should succour them.

VII

As poll books reveal, deference was a crucial factor in nineteenth century English politics. But deference was not the cosmopolitan phenomenon which Bagehot and many of his contemporaries described. Deference was not the consequence of generalized relationships among the members of different classes. Rather, it was the consequences of specific relationships among the members of specific groups and networks. In sociological terms Bagehot's arguments and the arguments of various of his contemporaries make very little sense. And the patterns of electoral behaviour which poll books reveal are not those which their arguments would lead one to expect. But while their formulations are scarcely descriptive of the world in which they lived their formulations are useful nonetheless. Not only do they help to explain how the actual behavioural patterns of the society were obscured and thus how significant aspects of the structure of the society were also obscured. Their formulations also perhaps help to explain why these patterns and structure both endured. Presumably, the effects of the arguments which Bagehot and many of his contemporaries used – that the men enfranchised in 1832 had, as a rule, approved of the social structure of the kingdom because of their *wisdom* – were not inconsiderable.

Arguments such as these carried their own interpretational corollaries. As Bagehot put it, 'the first Reform Act had been a means of transfer[ring] predominant influence in the state from certain special classes to the general aggregate of fairly intelligent men.' [73] And Gladstone agreed. But Gladstone went further than Bagehot. Indeed, Gladstone transformed the ostensible consequence into the cause. Defining the first Reform Act in class terms – as the means by which the middle class had been enfranchised – Gladstone claimed that the middle class had been enfranchised in 1832

> . . . because they were loyal to our institutions, sober and thoughtful in disposition, having access to political information, reasonably capable of forming a judgment on political affairs, [and] well disposed to defer to those who might be more capable still. [74]

Arguments such as these are perhaps politically essential. As a rule, however, historians have dealt with such arguments not as parts of a necessary mythology, a mythology required by the exigencies of both the changing structure of society and the political system which had been changed to deal with these changes. Rather, they have dealt with such arguments as if they were both descriptive and explanatory – descriptive of the political system, and explanatory of the way this system cane into being. In consequence, they have not only granted the premise that the first Reform Act was primarily a class measure. They have also granted its corollaries, implicit in Gladstone's observation, that once the middle class had been brought out on the political stage those other classes which were waiting in the wings could not long remain unenfranchised. The essential correctives to this interpretation lie in the poll books and in those provisions of the first two Reform Acts whose importance can be seen once those patterns of behaviour which the pool books reveal are seen.

Wallas had presumably not considered the evidence of group behaviour revealed by the poll books. He had presumably not considered those particular provisions of the first Reform Act whose importance becomes apparent in the light of the poll book evidence. But in any event, he obviously read James Mill through the haze which the subsequent myth produced. In these circumstances his statement is understandable: 'The study of politics is just now in a curiously unsatisfactory position.'

Notes to the text

Prologue: The evidential problem

1. Edward W. Cox and Standish Grove Grady, *The New Law and Practice of Registration and Elections,* 10th ed. (London, 1868), xcviii.
2. Cox and Grady, *The New Law,* 11th ed. (London, 1872), p lxxix.
3. See, in particular, chapter 7.
4. The importance of this point is discussed below.
5. J. R. Vincent, *Pollbooks: How Victorians Voted* (Cambridge, 1967), pp. 61-3.
6. T. J. Nossiter, 'Aspects of electoral behaviour in English constituencies, 1832-1868', in Erik Allardt and Stein Rokkan (eds.), *Mass Politics: Studies in Political Sociology* (New York, 1970), pp. 160-89.
7. Vincent, *Poll books,* p. 27.
8. Vyvyan Papers, 22 February 1825 et seq., 22M/80/36/44/10-15, Cornwall Record Office.
9. Ryland to Cartwright, 27 July [1837], Cartwright Papers, Box 30, Northamptonshire Record Office.
10. These conclusions derive from a study of *South Nottinghamshire Election, The Poll Book* (Newark, 1846).
11. Sessional Papers, 1868-69, VIII, q. 12,540.
12. The statement was reported in the *Cambridge Chroniclee,* 22 May 1852.
13. Unfortunately, when statistics were published on the geographical distribution of the various religious groups, in 1852, they were published on the basis of 'registration districts', not of parishes. Because many registration districts were fairly large the differences which, in many cases, probably obtained among the several parishes within each district are obscured. For Cambridgeshire no districts are shown in which absolutely no one attended a nonconformist service on 31 March 1851. But in all probability many individual parishes were not so heterogeneous. As it is, the range of variation among the different registration districts is great enough to suggest that the range of variation among individual parishes was far more so. The proportions of

Dissenters varied between 40 per cent and 78.7 per cent. Significantly, the former proportion obtained in the south of the county, in the district of Linton, where most of the parishes had been enclosed for many years and where landownership was largely concentrated in the hands of Anglican squires. The latter proportion obtained in the fenland district of North Witchford where a number of parishes were still unenclosed (Parliamentary Papers, 1852-53, LXXXIX, 341-2). While the situation in Wales was somewhat more extreme than the situation in England – religious lines cut sharper social demarcation – it was apparently not until after the contest of 1859 that certain Anglican landlords in Merioneth established religious qualifications for their tenantry. See I. G. Jones, 'Merioneth politics in mid-nineteenth century', *Journal of the Merioneth Historical and Record Society*, V (1968), esp. 306-11.

14. David Spring, *The English Landed Estate in the Nineteenth Century: Its Administration* (Baltimore, 1963).
15. 3 *Hansard*, LXVII (24 March 1843), 1423.
16. Cox and Grady, *The New Law*, 10th ed. p. xcviii.
17. This point is illustrated and discussed in chapters 1-3.
18. Concerning recent American elections the distinction was made by Talcott Parsons, 'Voting and the equilibrium of the American Political System', in Eugene Burdick and J. A. Brodbeck (eds.), *American Voting Behavior* (Glencoe, 1959), esp. pp. 92-96.
19. Such a definition is implicit in Lewis Coser, *The Functions of Social Conflict* (London, 1964).
20. These points are discussed in the Epilogue.
21. Cox and Grady, *The New Law*, 11th ed. p. lxxx.
22. This point is discussed in chapter 8.
23. 10 May 1872.

Part I

Introduction

1. See the division list, 3 *Hansard*, I (15 November 1830), 549 ff.
2. See the division list, 3 *Hansard*, IV (6 July 1831), 907-16.
3. See the division list, 3 *Hansard*, LIX (27 August 1841), 450-5.
4. E.g., Charles Seymour, *Electoral Reform in England and Wales* (New Haven, Conn., 1915), p. 81.
5. E.g., Norman Gash, *Politics in the Age of Peel* (London, 1953), p. 320.
6. The Chandos amendment was one which the members of the Grey Ministry strenuously opposed but which they were forced to accept in August 1831. As it was ultimately embodied in the Bill it extended the right to vote in county elections to men who were tenants-at-will of lands or tenements for which they paid an annual rent of not less than £50. The significance of the amendment is discussed below.
7. These various questions are discussed below.
8. As reported in Henry Stooks Smith, *The Parliament of England from 1715 to 1847*, ed., F. W. S. Craig (Chichester, 1973), contests occurred in 1826 in Bedfordshire, Cambridgeshire, Devonshire – where the polls only

remained open one day – Huntingdonshire, Northumberland, Oxfordshire, Somersetshire, Surrey, Sussex and Westmoreland; contests occurred in 1830 in Cambridgeshire, Devonshire, Durham, Essex, Huntingdonshire, Leicestershire, Oxfordshire, Suffolk, Surrey and Yorkshire – where the polls only remained open two days; and contests occurred in 1831 in Bedfordshire, Buckinghamshire, Cambridgeshire – a by-election – Cornwall, Cumberland, Dorset – at both the general election and at a by-election – Essex, Northamptonshire, Oxfordshire, Shropshire and Worcestershire.

Chapter 1

1. The terms Tory and Whig, are extremely useful. Nonetheless it must be remembered that electoral coalitions were fluid and factional and that there is considerable evidence in the poll books to indicate that 'parties' were not themselves agencies of electoral recruitment.
2. J. B. Rooper, of Abbotts Ripton, reported to Lord Milton that before Fellowes retired he had come to an agreement with Strathaven. See Rooper to Milton, 3 July 1830, Fitzwilliam Papers, Northamptonshire Record Office.
3. *The Times,* 27 July 1830.
4. J. B. Ulph to Lord Milton, 19 May 1830, Fitzwilliam Papers, N.R.O.
5. George G. Day to Lord Milton, 23 June 1830, Fitzwilliam Papers, N.R.O.
6. Precision was not the *forte* of those who counted votes in the nineteenth century or compiled poll books. Thus, there are often differences between the total polls as announced by the sheriff or other returning officer and the total polls as reported in a poll book. There are also differences between different poll books for the same contest. In such cases it is impossible to say who was right. But poll books were not published as proofs of the statistical accuracy of the announced polls. Rather, they were published as records of how the different voters had voted. The following tables are consonant with that purpose and have been compiled from *A Copy of the Poll for Two Knights of the Shire for the County of Huntingdon* (Huntingdon, [1826]), *The Poll for Two Knights of the Shire for the County of Huntingdon* (Cambridge, [1831]), and *Copy of the Poll Taken at the General Election for the county of Huntingdon* (Huntingdon, [1837]). Unfortunately, only a portion of *A Copy of the Poll, . . . in 1830* (London, [1830]), has been found.
7. *The Times,* 10 May 1831.
8. William Page and Granville Proby, 'Parliamentary History', *Victoria History of the County of Huntingdon* (London, 1932), II, 54.
9. The Carysfort interest had abandoned its exclusively Whig orientation in 1830. See below.
10. Rooper to Milton, 25 April 1831, Fitzwilliam Papers, N.R.O.
11. Quoted by Page and Proby, 'Parliamentary History', p. 55.
12. *Ibid.*
13. An outvoter was a man who lived outside the constituency in which he

was qualified to vote – in particular, a freeholder who lived outside the county, or counties, in which his freehold, or freeholds, were located. Since there were no residence requirements for the freeholder, there were often a lot of franchise outvoters.

14. See note 6 page 450.

15. Table 3 shows, for each parish in the county, the polls of the voters in 1826 and 1831 who were resident in the county and, for 1837, the polls of the resident voters together with those of the outvoters who voted in respect of property located in the parish. As a means of simplifying the table, the parishes have been grouped together in which majorities of the voters voted more or less the same way at these contests.

  Strictly speaking, the figures for the contests of 1826 and 1831 are not comparable with those for the contest of 1837. To have made them strictly comparable it would have been necessary either to identify the outvoters of 1826 and 1831 in terms of the parishes in which their properties were located and to add their votes to those cast by the voters resident in these parishes, or to subtract the votes of the outvoters of 1837 from the various parish totals in that year. The problem arises because the table was compiled principally from the tables which the different poll books contain. Thus, the table reflects the different ways in which the poll books were organized. In the poll books of 1826, 1830 and 1831 the voters who resided in the same parish were listed together. In the poll book of 1837 the voters whose qualifications were located in the same parish were listed together – this an obvious consequence of the first Reform Act which required the compiling of electoral registers which were themselves organized on the basis of the parish of residence. Had there been any significant differences between the patterns of behaviour of the resident voters and those of the outvoters whose properties were located in the different parishes then the effort to distinguish the two categories of voter would have been essential as a means of posing the question why these differences existed. A sampling of the evidence in numerous county poll books, among them those for Huntingdonshire, Cambridgeshire, and Northamptonshire, suggests that the same factors generally affected the behaviour of the outvoters whose qualifications were located within a given parish as affected the behaviour of the voters resident in the parish.

16. In consequence of 2 William IV, c. 45, s. 24, a freeholder of property in a borough lost his right to vote in a county election in respect of that property if the property provided him with a right to vote in the borough. This provision is discussed below.

17. Principally, information on Huntingdonshire landownership has been taken from *Post Office Directory of . . . Hunts* (London, [1847-8]).

18. See J. B. Rooper to Milton, 3 July 1830, Fitzwilliam Papers, N.R.O.

19. The poll book, once owned by James Duberly, is in the collection of the Guildhall Library, London.

20. Duberly to Milton, 5 July 1830, Fitzwilliam Papers, N.R.O.

21. Bedford's motives in voting with Wellington were perhaps implicit in his son, the Marquis of Tavistock's description of the political spectrum

within his family and his own position. In a letter to Milton, he said that
there was his father on the one side, his brother, Lord John Russell, on
the other, and himself in the middle, lacking his father's positive
confidence in Wellington's Government, but seeing more good in it
than his brother saw. Explaining his own position he cited the mischief
which strong Government had done: they had made wars, suspended
liberties, laid on taxes, 'ruined all, corrupted all.' But Wellington's
Government was, as he saw it, 'too weak for evil, & yet strong enough
to carry through any good measure that may be forced [?] upon them.'
(8 July 1830, Fitzwilliam Papers, N.R.O.). Peel perhaps suggested a
complementary motive when he observed, in connection with Bedford's
vote on this occasion, that Bedford should be given the first vacant
garter. See Francis Bamford and the Duke of Wellington (eds.), *The
Journals of Mrs Arbuthnot* (Louds, London, 1950). II, pp. 367-8.

22. See below.
23. Tycho Wing to Milton, 19 July 1830, Fitzwilliam Papers, N.R.O.
24. John Proby, second Earl of Carysfort, sat as Whig Member for
    Buckingham, 1805-6, and for Huntingdonshire, 1806-7, and 1814-18. By
    1828, when he succeeded to the title, he was insane. Writing to Milton
    on 5 July 1830, and reporting that the Carysfort steward had instructed
    the tenants to delay before promising their votes to any candidate, J. M.
    Symonds asked Milton to discover how the dowager Countess and the
    Carysfort trustees intended to exercise their influence. These latter, he
    declared, were Lord Holland, T. Grenville and C. Wynne. As Austin
    Mitchell notes in *The Whigs in Opposition, 1815-1830* (Oxford, 1967), p.
    219, Holland was among the Whigs who, in the immediate pre-reform
    period, were 'prepared to praise [the Tory] ministers for their internal
    policies . . . '
25. But in Oxfordshire 320 of the 1,316 votes cast for Lord Norreys, the
    anti-Bill candidate in 1831, were cast for him by voters who also voted
    for one or the other of the two pro-Bill candidates. See *The Copy of the
    Poll of the Freeholders for Knights of the Shire for the County of Oxford*
    (Oxford, 1831).
26. *Cambridge Independent Press,* 11 August 1838.
27. *Cambridge Chronicle,* 5 August 1837.
28. W. Pears to Milton, 18 July 1830, Fitzwilliam Papers, N.R.O.
29. George G. Day, in *Cambridge Independent Press,* 11 August 1838.

Chapter 2
1. Information on Cambridgeshire landownership has been taken,
   principally, from Robert Gardiner, *History, Gazetteer and Directory of
   Cambridgeshire* (Peterborough, 1851), supplemented by E. P. Kelly, (ed.)
   The Post Office Directory of Cambridgeshire (London, 1846).
2. T. H. B. Oldfield, *The Representative History of Great Britain and Ireland* (6
   vols., London, 1816), III, p. 118.
3. D. Cook, 'Parliamentary History since 1660,' *Victoria County History of
   Cambridge and the Isle of Ely* (London, 1948) II, 417.

4. *The Times*, 3 October 1818.   5. *Ibid.* 12 June 1826.   6. *Ibid.*, 15 June 1826.   7. *Ibid.*, 16 June 1818.

8. The electoral figures in tables 5-11 have been compiled from *A Copy of the Poll for Knights of the Shire for Cambridgeshire, . . .* (London, 1722), *The Poll for the Election of Two Representatives in Parliament for the County of Cambridgeshire . . .* (Cambridge, 1780), *A State of Polls for the Two Elections of Representatives in Parliament for the County of Cambridgeshire . . .* (London, 1802), *The Poll for Election of Two Representatives in Parliament for the County of Cambridge* (Cambridge, 1826), *The Poll for Two Knights of the Shire for the County of Cambridge* (Cambridge, 1830), *The Poll of an Election of a Representative in Parliament for the County of Cambridgeshire* (Cambridge, 1831), *The Poll of the Election of Three Knights of the Shire for the County of Cambridgeshire*, and *The Poll of the Election of Three Knights of the Shire for the County of* Cambridgeshire (Cambridge, 1835). The population figures in table 5 are from the census reports

9. 3 *Hansard*, CLXXX (12 June 1865), 25.

10. Asa Briggs, 'The background of the parliamentary reform movement in three English cities,' *Cambridge Historical Review*, X, 3 (1952), 295.

11. *The Times*, 27 June 1826. This was presumably, the Wells of Huntingdon with whom Cobbett stayed during his visit to Huntingdon in 1830. See *Political Register*, 17 April 1830.

12. *The Times*, 23 June 1826.

13. *Ibid.*, 14 August 1830.

14. *The Poll of the Election of a Representative for the County of Cambridgeshire* (Cambridge, 1831), p. 56.

15. *Ibid.*, 27 October 1831.

16. See the division list, 3 *Hansard*, VIII (7 October 1831), 339.

17. This question is discussed below and is illustrated in table 8.

18. See Bourn in group 18 of table 7.

19. See Stapleford in group 18 of table 7. Leed's opposition to the Bill possibly also explains Osborne's resignation from the seat he could not fill conscientiously except by opposing his father's wishes.

20. *The Times*, 13 August 1830.

21. *Ibid.*, 14 August 1830.

22. *Ibid.*

23. See 3 *Hansard*, VI (18 August 1831), 286.

24. See the list of this committee, *Cambridge Independent Press*, 8 October 1831.

25. *Cambridge Chronicle*, 21 March 1857.

26. Doddington was one of the very few parishes in the county where majorities of the voters followed the same progression between 1826 and 1835 as that of majorities of the Thorney voters. See below.

27. See *The New Cambridge Guide* (Cambridge, 1826), p. 99.

28. *Cambridge Chronicle*, 31 December 1832. Evidently, he did so, in the parish of Whittlesey. And, later, in 1868, it was reported that his nephew, the Rt. Hon. Hugh Childers, not only canvassed the tenants on his estate the day of the elections of 1868, but 'took his place at the hustings to see that all the tenants, as far as could be ascertained, should

record their votes for the Liberal candidates.' *Ibid.*, 5 December 1868.

29. *Ibid.*, 21 December 1832.
30. Such was reported *ibid.*, 14 September 1832.
31. *Ibid.*, 17 August and 14 September 1832.
32. *Cambridge Independent Press*, 16 February 1833.
33. *Ibid.*
34. The statement was contained in a letter to the editor, *Cambridge Advertiser*, 14 August 1839.
35. These are discussed in chapter 6.
36. See, in particular, Ebenezer Foster's statements at the dinner celebrating Townley's return, *Cambridge Independent Press*, 24 January 1835.
37. See *Cambridge Chronicle*, 15 March 1833 and 30 January 1841, and *Cambridge Independent Press*, 15 March 1835, 14 March 1836 and 28 April 1838.
38. *Cambridge Chronicle*, 21 December 1832.
39. Twiss' activities in connection with the Association were noted, *ibid.*, 30 November 1832. His political role was noted, *ibid.*, 2 August 1833.
40. See the report of the dinner, *ibid.*, 2 August 1833.
41. These conclusions derive from an analysis of the voting behaviour of the men who attended the various meetings of the Association which were reported in the local press from 15 March 1833 to 30 January 1841.
42. See the comments of Mr. Cotton, reported in *Cambridge Chronicle*, 8 May 1852.
43. See Henry Grylls, jun., to Arthur Pendarves Vivian, 25 and 26 May 1881, and Vivian to Grylls, 26 May 1881 (copy), Vivian Papers, DDPV.I.8., Cornwall Record Office.
44. See the reports of the meetings of the Association, *Cambridge Chronicle*, 15 March 1833, 11 January 1840 and 23 January 1841, and *Cambridge Independent Press*, 7 March 1835 and 2 February 1839.
45. This statement from an unidentified 'Conservative journal' was quoted in *The Farmer's Magazine*, II, 3 (March 1835), 158-9, original emphasis. One of the associations mentioned was the Northamptonshire Agricultural Protection Association, for which see below.
46. *Ibid.*
47. See the report of this meeting, *Cambridge Chronicle*, 12 December 1834.
48. *Ibid.*, 16 January 1835.
49. *Cambridge Independent Press*, 7 March 1835.
50. *Cambridge Chronicle*, 15 March 1833.
51. *Cambridge Independent Press*, 14 March 1835.
52. *Cambridge Chronicle*, 5 August 1837. The tax is discussed below.
53. *Ibid.*, 12 December 1834.
54. Such was reported in a letter to the editor, *Cambridge Advertiser*, 14 August 1839.
55. See the report of the meeting of the Association, *Cambridge Chronicle*, 11 January 1840.
56. See the report of the year's activities, *ibid.*, 30 January 1841.
57. *Ibid.*, 15 May 1841.
58. *Cambridge Advertiser*, 11 August 1847.

59. St. Quintin's statement at a Conservative meeting was reported in *Cambridge Chronicle*, 22 July 1865.
60. *The Times*, 27 October 1831.
61. *Cambridge Independent Press*, 26 June 1841.
62. The poll books for 1826 and 1831 were organized on the basis of the parish of residence. Those for 1830, 1832 and 1835 were organized on the basis of the parish of qualification. These differences are reflected in tables 6 and 7. Table 7 shows, for each parish in the county, the polls of the resident voters in 1826 and 1831 and, for 1830, 1832 and 1835, the polls of the resident voters combined with the polls of the outvoters whose properties were located in the parish. Thus, as for the Huntingdonshire poll books arranged in table 3, the figures for the various years are not strictly comparable. But sampling suggests that in most cases the same factors affected the behaviour of the outvoters as affected the behaviour of the resident voters. In consequence, in its present form, and without significant distortion, table 7 illustrates the differences of sequential behaviour of the majorities of voters in the different parishes. In addition, it helps to reveal the varieties of factor to which the differences of result of the different contests should be attributed. Subsequent contests for which poll books exist occurred in 1857 and 1868. To consider these contests would unduly complicate the present analysis.
63. *Cambridge Independent Press*, 26 June 1841.
64. *Cambridge Chronicle*, 19 June 1841.
65. *Ibid.*, 5 August 1837 and *Cambridge Advertiser*, 7 July 1841.
66. *The Times*, 14 August 1830.
67. *Cambridge Chronicle*, 12 December 1834.
68. *Ibid.*, 16 January 1835.
69. Such parishes were Arrington, Eversden Great, Eversden Little, Steeple Morden, West Wickham, Whaddon and Wimpole.
70. Letter to the editor, *Cambridge Advertiser*, 14 August 1839.
71. In 1873 there were more than 40 persons resident in Soham who owned land from which the gross estimated rental was less than £10 a year. Return of Owners of Land, 1873, Sessional Papers, 1874, LXXI, Part 1, Cambridge.
73. Letter to the editor, *Cambridge Advertiser*, 14 August 1839.
73. *Ibid.*, 11 August 1847.
74. In 1844 Elizabeth Peyton was married to Francis John Russell, the younger brother of Lord John Russell.
75. For reasons discussed below this number must remain unknowable.
76. *Cambridge Independent Press*, 16 February 1833.

Chapter 3

1. William Hanbury to Viscount Milton, 22 April 1831, and Bouverie to Milton, 25 April 1831, Fitzwilliam Papers, Northamptonshire Record Office.
2. C. Hill to Milton, 25 April 1831, Fitzwilliam Papers, N.R.O.
3. Charles Arbuthnot to Mrs. Arbuthnot, 13 February 1831. A. Aspinall

(ed.), *The Correspondence of Charles Arbuthnot* (London, 1941), p. 135.

4. H. B. Harrison to Cartwright, 25 August 1830, Cartwright Papers, Box 12, N.R.O.

5. Charles Arbuthnot to Mrs. Arbuthnot, 13 February 1831, in Aspinall, *The Correspondence of Charles Arbuthnot*, p. 135.

6. *The Times,* 16 April 1831.

7. See below.

8. 'A Plain Catechism,' Scrap Book, Cartwright Papers, N.R.O.

9. See *The Times,* 16 November 1835, and Maunsell's statement at the anniversary dinner of the North Northamptonshire Conservative Association, *ibid.,* 12 December 1835.

10. The following tables have been compiled from *A Copy of the Poll of the Freeholders as taken at the Election of Knights of the Shire for the County of Northamptonshire, 1831* . . . (Northampton, 1832), *Copy of the Poll, for Two Knights, for the Northern Division of the County of Northampton* . . . *1832* . . . (Kettering, 1833), *A Copy of the Poll, taken at the General Election for the Northern Division of the County of Northampton; . . . 1835* . . . (Northampton, 1836), and *A Copy of the Poll for one Knight of the Shire, for the Northern Division of the County of Northampton* (Northampton, 1858). The poll book of 1835 was mistitled. There was no contest in the division at the general election in January, 1835. But there was a contest at the by-election the following December. It was this contest which the poll book reflected. Unfortunately, efforts to locate the poll book for the contest of 1837 have been unavailing.

11. *Morning Chronicle* (London), 16, 20, 21 and 23 May 1831 contain fairly extensive reports on the Northamptonshire contest.

12. Information on Northamptonshire landownership has been taken from William Whelan and Co., *History, Gazetteer and Directory of Northamptonshire* (London, 1949).

13. Unfortunately, the question — or questions — cannot be answered: no contest occurred in South Northamptonshire until 1841. Presumably, by then, whatever differential increments might have occurred in the numbers of voters from the different categories of parishes between 1831 and 1832, the effects of these increments would have been overlaid by the effects of other occurrences. In 1841, the anti-Tory candidate was badly beaten. Cartwright received 2,436 votes, Knightley, 2,324, and the Earl of Euston only 925. But the degree to which Euston's defeat is attributable to the changes in the balance of political power which might have been the consequence of an equalization of the ratio of voters to population cannot be measured.

14. 'Men contributing to Cartwright's and Knightley's expenses — 1831,' Cartwright Papers, Box 12, N.R.O.

15. The nominations in 1835 were reported in *The Times,* 16 December 1835. The nominations in 1832 were reported, *ibid.,* 18 December 1832. The anniversary dinner was reported, *ibid.,* 12 December 1835.

16. Ostensibly, Lilford threatened to evict any tenant who voted for Maunsell in 1835. See *ibid.,* 3 December 1835.

17. While canvassing the voters in Raunds, Hanbury made extensive use of a

letter in which Langham ostensibly promised him the votes of his tenants. See *ibid.*, 8 December 1835.

18. 3 *Hansard*, IV (21 June 1831), 107.
19. *The Times*, 17 January 1835.
20. *Ibid.*, 17 December 1835.
21. See below.
22. *The Times*, 12 December 1835.
23. See the agreement, dated 27 October 1831, Knightley Papers, K. CLVIII, 1391-1404, N.R.O.
24. J. S. Bentor to Cartwright, 16 June 1833, Cartwright Papers, Box 12, N.R.O.
25. *Ibid.*
26. *The Farmer's Magazine*, II, 3 (March 1835), 158-9.
27. Rooper to Milton, 3 July 1830, Fitzwilliam Papers, N.R.O.
28. Trollope to Milton, 24 April 1831, Fitzwilliam Papers, N.R.O.
29. See the report of the meeting, *The Times*, 26 January 1835.
30. See his letter to the editor, *The Farmer's Magazine*, II, 3 (March 1835), 186-7.
31. See the leader, *ibid.*, 158-9.
32. *The Times*, 17 January 1835.

Part II

Chapter 4

1. 3 *Hansard*, VII (4 October 1831), 1193-4.
2. *Ibid.*, 1195.
3. *Ibid.*, 1198.
4. 3 *Hansard*, II (1 March 1831), 1076.
5. Aspinall, *The Correspondence of Charles Arbuthnot*, p. 135.
6. See chapter 2, pp. 00-00.
7. E.g., The Rev. G. R. Gleig, from Kent, The Duke of Wellington, (ed.), *Despatches, Correspondence, and Memoranda of Field Marshal Arthur Duke of Wellington* (8 vols., London, 1878), VII, esp. pp. 467-8.
8. These questions are discussed in chapter 5.
9. The 'county borough' problem is discussed in more detail below.
10. E.g., [David Robinson], 'The Reform of the House of Commons', *Blackwood's Edinburgh Magazine*, XXCII (April 1830), 648 ff., Various of these plaints are considered in chapter 5.
11. 27 July 1830.
12. Arthur Stanley Turberville and Frank Beckwith, 'Leeds and Parliamentary Reform, 1820-1832', *Thoresby Society Publications*, XLI (1946), 17.
13. 3 *Hansard*, VI (17 August 1831), 167.
14. W. W. Bean, *The Parliamentary Representation of the Six Northern Counties of England* (Hull, 1890), p. 659.
15. W. G. Rimmer, *Marshall's of Leeds, Flax Spinners, 1788-1886* (Cambridge, 1960), p. 112.
16. 3 *Hansard*, III (28 March 1831), 1063. Brougham's statement is obviously

one of those which Professor George Woodbridge failed to notice before
he administered the would-be *coup de grace* to that portion of my general
argument which concerns the growth of urban influences in the counties
before 1832 by declaring: 'Never [during the debates on the Bill] was it
claimed that the inhabitants of the large centers of population already
controlled the county elections', *The Reform Bill of 1832* (New York,
1970), p. 88. John Cannon's effort to show that this part of my argument
'is without foundation' by calculating the proportions of the voters at
various county contests between 1802 and 1831 who polled from towns
from which more than 100 voters polled, would have been more
effective had he been able to show that there were no changes in the
proportions of urban voters, and that these men did not comprise
electoral blocs whose importance increased in the immediate pre-reform
period. See *Parliamentary Reform 1640-1832* (Cambridge, 1973),
Appendix 5. However, he only did his calculations for only one contest
in each county and, in Appendix 5, provides no evidence to how these
'urban' voters did vote. At one point in his text he does note the
interesting fact – but this while *criticising* my argument – that at a
by-election in Warwickshire in 1820 367 of the 399 voters who polled
for property in Birmingham voted for one of the candidates, only 32 for
the other. *Ibid.*, pp. 248-9.

17. 3 *Hansard*, XII (24 May 1832), 22.
18. 3 *Hansard*, VI (17 August 1831), 167. For the period before 1832 there is
     no way of telling how many men were *qualified to vote* in any county. All
     that can be told is *how many voters polled* at any given contest.
19. *John Bull* (London), 8 May 1831.
20. 3 *Hansard*, VI (17 August 1831), 190.
21. See chapter 3.
22. See chapter 2.
23. Such is revealed by *The Copy of the Poll of the Freeholders for Knights of the
     Shire for the County of Oxford* . . . (Oxford, 1831).
24. 3 *Hansard*, III (28 March 1831), 1063.
25. Cannon, *Parliamentary Reform*, p. 247, footnote 1.
26. In all, there were three Bills. The first was introduced on 1 March, the
     second on 24 June, the third on 12 December 1831.
27. One of the clearest analyses of the redistribution provisions of the first
     Bill was that which Russell made while introducing it, 3 *Hansard*, II (1
     March 1831), 1072 ff.
28. Evidently, such is Cannon's understanding of the emphasis. See Cannon,
     Parliamentary Reform, p. 246.
29. In my discussion of the Bills themselves I shall for simplicity ignore the
     fact that the franchise provisions which the Bills contained did not define
     rights to vote but rights to be registered to vote. The reasons why the
     point is important – because the electorates themselves were not given
     entities but functions of the political activities of the men who used them
     to support their own political ambitions – will, presumably, have
     become apparent from Part I. They are discussed in greater detail below
     as they were manifest in the post-reform period.

30. 'A Bill to amend the Representation of the People in England and Wales', clause 18, Sessional Papers, 1831, III, 13-14. There were minor changes of wording in the clause between this first published version of the second Bill and the second published version of the first Bill. But there were major changes of wording between the first and second published versions of the first Bill. See Sessional Papers, 1830-31, II, 199 and 223.

31. According to Peel, there were 5 'boroughs' in which the freeholders voted in the 'borough', Bristol, Haverfordwest, Litchfield, Norwich and Nottingham; 4 in which they voted in the surrounding county, Canterbury, Poole, Southampton, and part of York; and 10 in which they had no rights to vote in either the county or the 'borough', Carmarthen, Chester, Coventry, Exeter, Gloucester, Kingston-on-Hull, Lincoln, London, Newcastle-on-Tyne, and Worcester (3 *Hansard*, VI (17 August 1831), 173). Edward Porritt disagreed. According to him, there were 6 in which the freeholders voted in the 'borough' – Peel's list plus Carmarthen; 4 in which they voted in the surrounding county – the same 4 as were specified by Peel; and 9 in which they had no rights to vote in either the county or the 'borough' – Peel's list less Carmarthen (*The Unreformed House of Commons* (Cambridge, 1903), I, p. 18). However, while Porritt's numbers are accurate his lists contain two apparent errors. Ultimately, the relevant provision was amended so that where a freeholder had voted in the 'borough' in the pre-reform period he would continue to vote in the 'borough'. Assuming that those who amended the provision knew what rules obtained in the different 'boroughs' in the pre-reform period, then the 6 'boroughs' in which freeholders voted in the 'borough' in the pre-reform period were Bristol, Exeter, Haverfordwest, Litchfield, Norwich and Nottingham; assuming that Peel and Porritt were right where they agreed, then the 4 'boroughs' in which freeholders had voted in the surrounding county were Canterbury, Poole, Southampton and part of York; thus, the 9 'boroughs' in which freeholders had no rights to vote in either the 'borough' or the surrounding county were Carmarthen, Chester, Coventry, Gloucester, Kingston-on-Hull, Lincoln, London, Newcastle-on-Tyne and Worcester. Since freeholders in only part of York voted in the surrounding county John Cannon is not 'wrong' when he lists 'parts of York' among the towns in which freeholders did not have the right to vote in the surrounding county (Cannon, *Parliamentary Reform*, p. 249, footnote 1). On the other hand, because the point bears upon his argument, although in minor fashion, he should have included the other part of York among the towns in which freeholders did have the right to vote in the surrounding county. The omission of Exeter from his list of 'boroughs' in which the freeholders continued to vote in the 'borough' in the post-reform period (*ibid.*, footnote 3) is an error.

32. 3 *Hansard*, VI (20 August 1831), 354.

33. The relationship between these two clauses somewhat dulls the thrust of John Cannon's effort to show, in the light of clause 15 alone, that the

members of the Grey Ministry were not really concerned to isolate the counties from the towns, and thus, by extension, that there was no real urban penetration of the counties which might have prompted such a concern. As Cannon notes – and on this point he is quite right – the urban penetration of the counties in the pre-reform period was somewhat limited by the existence of the 'county boroughs' in which the freeholders had no rights to vote in the surrounding counties. He is also right in saying that the Ministers' handling of the 'boroughs' in which the freeholders had not voted in the 'borough' in the pre-reform period 'can be regarded as a further test of . . . [their] intentions'. Hence the importance of the partial inaccuracy of his statement: 'the first and second Bills proposed that these towns should henceforth vote in the counties', Cannon, *Parliamentary Reform,* p. 249. Apparently, the point escaped him that while clause 15 of the second Bill would have made every 'county borough', for purposes of election, part of the county proper in which it was located, clause 18 of this Bill would have deprived every borough freeholder of his county vote – including, of course, the freeholders in the 'county borough' except where the freehold property was worth between 40s. and £10 a year. In criticising my argument he declares: 'Had . . . [the Ministers] been determined, at all costs, to separate town and country, they would presumably have continued the exclusion of these sixteen towns [*Sic!* The figure is reached by including York among the 'county boroughs' in which freeholders did not vote in the surrounding county in the pre-reform period. See footnote 31 above], and quoted precedent to defend their action', *ibid.* Whatever the significance of the phrase, 'at all costs', the first and second Bills, as introduced, would have excluded most of the freeholders in the 'county boroughs' from voting in the counties proper. Also, it was 'precedent' which determined the 'boroughs' in which the freeholders continued to vote in the 'borough' in the post-reform period. See 3 *Hansard,* IX (12 December 1831), 169.

34. 3 *Hansard,* V (4 August 1831), 752.
35. The amendment was made by dropping the phrase, 'or any other person', from the formula, 'he or any other person'. According to 2 William IV, c. 45, s. 24, ' . . . no Person shall be entitled to vote in the Election of a Knight or Knights of the Shire to serve in any future Parliament in respect of his Estate or Interest as a Freeholder in any House, Warehouse, Counting-house, Shop, or other Building occupied by himself, or in any Land occupied by himself together with any House, Warehouse, Counting-house, Shop or other Building, such House, Warehouse, Counting-house, Shop or other Building being, either separately, or jointly with the Land so occupied therewith, of such Value as would, according to the Provisions herein-after contained, confer on him the Right of voting for any City or Borough, whether he shall or shall not have actually acquired the Right to vote for such City or Borough in respect thereof'. Omitting certain technicalities, 'the Provisions herein-after contained' were those according to which a man might qualify to vote in a borough if he occupied premises in the

borough worth at least £10 a year, and if he either resided in the borough or within a 7 mile radius of it. (s. 27).

36. Russell described the change while introducing the third Bill. See 3 *Hansard*, IX (12 December 1831), 169.

37. The faggot voters and these concerns are discussed below.

38. 3 *Hansard*, IX (27 January 1832), 983-4.

39. The thought is mentioned by John Milton-Smith, 'Earl Grey's Cabinet and the Objects of Parliamentary Reform', *The Historical Journal*, XV (1972), 70.

40. Henry Earl Grey, (ed.), *The Reform Act, 1832: The Correspondence of the late Earl Grey with his Majesty King William IV and with Sir Herbert Taylor* . . . (2 vols., London, 1867), I, p. 467, emphasis added.

41. Brook, *The Great Reform Act*, p. 369, footnote 82.

42. *Electoral Reform in England and Wales* (New Haven, 1915), p. 13-15.

43. Cannon, *Parliamentary Reform*, p. 247.

44. Brock, *The Great Reform Act*, p. 226.

45. B. M. Add. Mss., 51,867, ff. 79-80. I am grateful to Dr E. P. Hennock for bringing this statement to my attention.

46. 3 *Hansard*, VI (26 August 1831), 689, J. J. Barrow, (ed.), *The Mirror of Parliament* contains substantially the same report. 1831, II, 1,694.

47. Dr Hennock's contention that Althorp was wrong on 26 August is discussed below.

48. Grey, *The Reform Act, 1832*, I, p. 106.

49. 3 *Hansard*, VI (17 August 1831), 163.

50. *Ibid.*, III (28 March 1831), 1010, 998.

52. *Ibid.*, XIII (24 May 1832), 21, and III (28 March 1831), 998.

54. *Ibid.*, XIII (24 May 1832), 22.

55. Peel to Henry Hobhouse, July 1831, B. M. Add. Mss., 40, 402, ff. 98-101.

56. 3 *Hansard*, V (4 August 1831), 752.

57. *Ibid.*, (12 August 1831), 1317.

58. *Ibid.*, VI (17 August 1831), 182.

59. 'The sociological premises of the first Reform Act: a critical note', *Victorian Studies*, XIV (1971), 325-6. Since electoral registers did not exist until the Act created them the statement that the amendment of the borough freeholder clause resulted in 'the admission of borough freeholders to the county register' can be confusing. The unwary reader might miss the point, which I have already explained, that while the amendment of the clause allowed more borough freeholders to vote in the counties than would have been qualified to do so had the clause not been amended the numbers who remained qualified were still fewer than the numbers who had been qualified in the pre-reform period. Perhaps Dr Hennock was himself confused on this point? This is suggested by his differing descriptions of the effects of the amendment. On the one hand, while paraphrasing Althorp's announcement of the 17th, he explains – and the explanation is correct – that in consequence of the amendment no borough freeholder 'was deprive[d] . . . of his vote in the county unless he was entitled on the strength of that property to a borough vote instead' (p. 325). On the other hand, he declares that the amendment

'*increase[d]* the number of urban freeholders on the county register' (*ibid.*, emphasis added), that in consequence of the amendment '*aditional voters were . . . admitted* to the county register' (*ibid.*, emphasis added), and, while considering the question from a somewhat different angle, that 'it was the opinion of His Majesty's ministers that freeholders in boroughs should not be allowed to come in [sic!] and *overpower* the constituency of the counties' (p. 326, original emphasis). He is, of course, quite right in saying that the Ministers did not intend that the counties be 'overpowered' from the towns. But he distorts Althorp's argument when he uses the latter's statement to this effect on 20 August to suggest that the Ministers intended an 'admixture' of urban and rural voters in the counties, but one in which the urban elements would not 'overpower' the rural. When Althorp declared the Ministers' concern that the counties 'not be overpowered by the inhabitants of the towns' he was not referring to the situation which the amended clause would produce. Rather, he was referring to the situation which had existed in the pre-reform period, the situation which the clause – even the amended clause – would, he hoped, correct (3 *Hansard*, VI (20 August 1831), 339).

60. 3 *Hansard*, VI (26 August 1831), 687-8.
61. *Ibid.*, 689.
62. 1831, II, 1,694.
63. 3 *Hansard*, VI (17 August 1831), 193.
64. *Ibid.*, 165.
65. *Ibid.*, 167.
66. *Ibid.*
67. *Ibid.*, 165.
68. *Ibid.*, 163.
69. *Ibid.*
70. *Ibid.*, 183-4.
71. *Ibid.*, 183-6.
72. *Ibid.*, 186.
73. While *Hansard* only contains a list of the majority on Davies' motion, and no list at all on Chandos' motion, *The Times* for 18 August 1831 contains a list of 12 usual ministerialists who voted with Davies and, for 19 August, a list of the usual ministerialists who participated in the Chandos clause division, showing how each had voted. All but one of the men who voted with Davies voted with Chandos. Evidently, that one did not take part in the Chandos clause division.
74. Brock, *The Great Reform Act*, p. 228.
75. 3 *Hansard*, VI (26 August 1831), 689.
76. 3 *Hansard*, II (3 March 1831), 1329.
77. These are discussed in chapters 5 and 9.
78. Cannon, *Parliamentary Reform*, p. 247.
79, E.g., Lord Milton, 3 *Hansard*, VI (17 August 1831), 200.
80. *Ibid.*, 200-1.
81. The so-called Chandos amendment was first proposed by Colonel Sibthorp, Member for Lincoln, as an amendment to the first Bill. See Sessional Papers, 1830-31, II, 257. During the committee stage of the

second Bill Sibthorp proposed the amendment again. But his knowledge of parliamentary procedure failed him. At the time he moved his amendment the committee had not yet reached that line in the clause in which he proposed to insert it. Thus, his motion was ruled out of order. Also, he had committed himself. Speaking later the same evening Chandos proposed to insert an almost identical amendment at an earlier line in the clause than that at which Sibthorp had declared he wished to insert his. The consideration and adoption of the Chandos amendment precluded the consideration of Sibthorp's. Thus is fame lost and anger aroused. See 3 *Hansard*, VI (18 August 1831), 270-83.

82. 3 *Hansard*, VI (18 August 1831), 272. In 1837, when there were 5,760 entries on the register for Buckinghamshire only 47 of these were for men who were registered as leaseholders. Sessional Papers, 1838, XLIV, 553. The reasons why the number should be referred to as the number of entries on the register, not as the number of registered electors, is discussed in Chapter VI.

83. 3 *Hansard*, VI (18 August 1831), 281-2.

84. *Ibid.*

85. *Ibid.*, 272, and Althorp's analysis of Chandos' arguments, *ibid.*, 280-3.

86. *Ibid.*, 284.

87. *Ibid.*, 280.

88. See 'Orator' Hunt's comments, *ibid.*, 277-8.

89. This was John Arthur Roebuck's subsequent explanation of the Radical's behaviour. *History of the Whig Ministry of 1830* ... (2 vols., London, 1852), II, p. 198.

90. *3 Hansard*, VI (17 August 1831), 202.

91. *Ibid.*, 287.

92. 3 *Hansard*, V (11 August 1831), 1227.

93. *Ibid.*, (12 August 1831), 1319.

94. 3 *Hansard*, VI (18 August 1831), 287.

95. *Ibid.*, (19 August 1831), 298.

96. *Ibid.*, (20 August 1831), 338.

97. These phenomena are discussed below.

98. 3 *Hansard*, CLII (28 February 1859), 990.

99. These points are discussed below.

100. 3 *Hansard*, VI (20 August 1831), 339.

101. *Ibid.*, 345.

102. *Ibid.*, 349.

103. 3 *Hansard*, IV (14 July 1831), 1284, emphasis added.

104. As Russell did, 3 *Hansard*, V (27 July 1831), 422.

105. The point was Croker's, *ibid.*, IV (15 July 1831), 1343.

106. See the description of these modifications, 3 *Hansard*, VI (1 September 1831), 984 ff.

107. 'Instructions transmitted by direction of Lord Melbourne', 24 October 1831, Sessional Papers, 1831-32, XXXVI, 17.

108. See Russell's analysis of the ways in which the new criteria differed from the old, 3 *Hansard*, IX (12 December 1831), 159 ff.

109. *Ibid.*, 163.

110. *Ibid.*, 159.
111. Lord Melbourne to Lieutenant T. Drummond, R.E., 8 August 1831, Sessional Papers, 1831-32, **XXXVI**, 11.
112. 'Instructions transmitted by direction of Lord Melbourne', 24 November 1831, *ibid.*, 20.
113. 'Instructions, etc . . . addressed to the Gentlemen engaged in collecting Information respecting the Boundaries of the Cities and Boroughs of England and Wales', 23 August 1831, *ibid.*, 12.
114. 'Report from Edward J. Littleton, Esq., Captain F. Beaufort, R.N. and Lieut. T. Drummond, R.E., to the Right Honourable Viscount Melbourne, on proposed Boundaries of the Boroughs of England and Wales', 10 February 1832, *ibid.*, 6.
115. Melbourne to Drummond, 8 August 1831, *ibid.*, 11.
116. 'Instructions, etc . . . addressed to the Gentlemen engaged in collecting Information respecting the Boundaries of the Cities and Boroughs of England and Wales', 23 August 1831, *ibid.*, 13.
117. Reports from Commissioners on Proposed Division of Counties and Boundaries of Boroughs, Sessional Papers, 1831-32, **XL**, 19.
118. *Ibid.*
119. *Ibid.*
120. Reports from Commissioners on Proposed Division of Counties and Boundaries of Boroughs, Sessional Papers, 1831-32, **XXXIX**, 37.
121. Report from Edward J. Littleton, Esq., M.P., Captain F. Beaufort, R.N. and Lieut. T. Drummond, R.E., to the Right Honourable Viscount Melbourne, on Proposed Boundaries of the Boroughs of England and Wales, Sessional Papers, 1831-32, **XXXVI**, 5.
122. *Ibid.*
123. General Remarks on the Proposed Division of the . . . Counties; . . . /s/ J. G. Shaw Lefevre, Sessional Papers, 1831-32, **XXXVIII**, 22.
124. Reports from Commissioners on Proposed Division of Counties and Boundaries of Boroughs, Sessional Papers, 1831-32, **XXXIX**, 33.
125. *Ibid.*
126. *Ibid.*, 85. Such comments provide the answer to Dr. Hennock's recent suggestion, that the Government's instructions to the borough boundary commissioners to, in certain cases, project the boundaries of a borough beyond the boundaries of the existing town, reveal their concern not to isolate the counties from the towns but rather to guarantee the satisfaction of expanding borough populations. As he put it, 'everyone knew [that the] borough qualifications were more generous than those for the county, and when the opposite was the case (as with the 40 shilling freeholders who were not £10 householders) they did not preclude the exercise of a county vote. Had the commissioners not been instructed to make a liberal allowance for the foreseeable growth of towns, in next to no time a class of unenfranchised ten pound householders would have clamoured for the franchise which their neighbours possessed a few streets away. Such an obvious anomaly would have made a frequent re-drawing of constituency boundaries necessary, involving an administrative burden, a parliamentary squabble,

and the frequent disturbance of local political alignments.' Hennock, 'The Sociological Premises of the First Reform Act', p. 326-7. Notwithstanding the somewhat anachronistic aspect of the argument – that men made the decisions they made because of their concern to simplify the solution of administrative problems which they scarcely yet recognized as such – it might possibly be cogent if the instructions issued to the borough boundary commissioners were considered in isolation from other relevant evidence. But, in the light of the comments which accompanied the reports on the boundaries of the counties, its cogency becomes somewhat limited. The same concern was expressed for the boundaries between the divisions of a county as for the boundaries between county and borough, that they serve to separate interests. And, of course, on the two sides of the boundary between the division of a county the same franchise obtained.

127. *The Times,* 12 July 1831, original emphasis.
128. 3 *Hansard,* V (11 August 1831), 1227.
129. *Ibid.*
130. *Ibid.,* 1228.
131. *Ibid.*
132. 3 *Hansard,* XIII (22 June 1832), 962-4.
133. E.g., the Cambridgeshire by-election of May 1802, which reportedly cost the Duke of Rutland and the rival Earl of Hardwick over £40,000, a figure approaching £14 per voter. D. Cook, 'Parliamentary History since 1660', *Victoria County History of Cambridge and Ely* (London, 1948), II, 417.
134. G. Butt, *Suggestions as to the Conduct and Management of a County Contested Election* (London, 1826), p. lv.
135. *Ibid.,* p. 57-9.
136. The outcome of the Northamptonshire contest of 1831 was determined by the assessor's decision on the question whether some 500 Northampton freemen should be regarded as 40 shilling freeholders because of their rights in respect of some common lands in the borough. The question is discussed in chapter 3. At the Essex contest of 1830 approximately 900 would-be voters whose properties were not assessed to the land tax were challenged. *The Poll for Two Knights of the Shire . . . for the County of Essex* (Chelmsford, 1830), iii-iv. Unfortunately, the editor of the poll book, who provided this information in his Introduction, failed to indicate how many of these men convinced the assessor that their rights to vote were good and were thus included among the 5,318 listed in the poll book. The Dorsetshire by-election of October 1831, was finally decided by an election committee of the House of Commons, when it received proof that the properties of 150-odd voters from the village of Mortcombe Lake were exempt from the land tax. When the polls closed W. F. S. Ponsonby, the reform candidate, trailed Lord Ashley, the anti-reform candidate, by 1,811 votes to 1,847. He petitioned against Ashley's return on the grounds that many of the men whose votes for Ashley had been counted, including the vast majority of those who polled from Mortcombe Lake, should not have

been allowed to vote because they were not assessed to the land tax. The proof of exemption from the land tax resulted in Ashley being seated. From 8 to 19 March 1832 *The Times* carried extensive reports of the committee hearings.

137. As the *Morning Chronicle* observed on 26 July 1830, 'Reform will take place to a considerable extent in England, not because the voters are less mercenary, ... but because they are not worth purchasing . . . We now see profligate voters holding out their hands every where to profligate Members; but as the latter are no longer full-handed their profligacy is no longer profitable.'

138. 3 *Hansard,* VI (2 September 1831), 1048.
139. *Ibid.,* 1050.
140. *Ibid.,* 1049.
141. *Ibid.,* 1051.
142. Clause 36 of the third Bill. The most readily available copy of this draft of the Bill is that published as an appendix to 3 *Hansard,* IX.
143. 3 *Hansard,* X (11 February 1832), 228.
144. *Ibid.,* (20 February 1832), 543.
145. *Ibid.,* (11 February 1832), 242.
146. Such beliefs are reported in abundance by Joseph Hamburger, *James Mill and the Art of Revolution* (New Haven, 1963).
147. Cannon, *Parliamentary Reform,* p. 263.
148. Such, apparently, is Dr. Hennock's understanding of my earlier efforts to describe these questions. See 'The Sociological Premises of the First Reform Act', p. 321.
149. Norman Gash, *Politics in the Age of Peel* (London, 1953), p. 16.
150. *Ibid.*
151. 3 *Hansard,* II (3 March 1831), emphasis added.
152. Gash, *Politics in the Age of Peel,* p. 9.
153. This point is discussed below.
154. 'Internal Policy', *Quarterly Review,* XXXII (January, 1830), 271. The author of this piece was either John Fullarton or John Miller. See Walter E. Houghton (ed.), *The Wellesley Index of Victorian Periodicals,* (Toronto, 1966).
155. Gash, *Politics in the Age of Peel,* p. 9.
156. Milton-Smith, 'Earl Grey's Cabinet,' p. 58.
157. *Ibid.*
158. Cannon, *Parliamentary Reform,* p. 250.
159. *Ibid.*
160. 3 *Hansard,* XXXIX (20 November 1837), 44-7.
161. *Ibid.,* (21 November 1837), 107-8.
162. E. L. Woodward, *The Age of Reform, 1815-1870* (Oxford, 1949), p. 77.

Chapter 5
1. 3 *Hansard,* VII (4 October 1831), 1188.
2. 3 *Hansard,* II (3 March 1831), 1337.
3. *Hansard,* N. S., XXIV (14 May 1830), 731 ff.

4. W. R. Brock, *Lord Liverpool and Liberal Toryism* (Cambridge, 1941), p. 78-9.

5. [Lord John Russell] *Essays and Sketches of Life and Character, by a Gentleman who has left his lodgings* (London, 1820), p. 146.

6. *Ibid.*

7. *Ibid.*, p. 148.

8. Brock, *Lord Liverpool*, p. 96.

9. [Sir James Mackintosh], 'Parliamentary Reform,' *Edinburgh Review*, XIV, 28 (July 1809), 285-6.

10. *Ibid.*, p. 278.

11. *Ibid.*

12. *Ibid.*, p. 283.

13. *Ibid.*, p. 286-7.

14. *Ibid.*, p. 278.

15. *Ibid.*, p. 288.

16. *Ibid.*, p. 287-8.

17. *Ibid.*

18. *Ibid.*, p. 290.

19. *Ibid.*

20. *Ibid.*, original emphasis.

21. *Ibid.*

22. *Hansard*, N. S. XV (27 April 1826), 661.

23. The malt tax question is discussed below.

24. Sir James Graham, *Corn and Currency*, new ed. (London, 1826) pp. 79-81.

25. *Ibid.*, p. 14-5.

26. *Ibid.*, p. 11. The logic (obscured by such an argument) of the corn law of 1815 as conceived by various of its sponsors was that high prices would encourage investments, that investments would increase production as well as efficiency, and that these together would result in lower prices for the consumer and equivalent or greater prosperity for the producer. These points are discussed in chapter 8.

27. *Ibid.*, p. 12.

28. *Ibid.*, p. 44.

29. David Ricardo, *On Protection to Agriculture*, 4th ed. (London, 1822), reprinted in E. C. K. Gonner, (ed.), *Economic Essays* (London, 1923), p. 275-6.

30. These points are discussed at greater length in chapter 8.

31. Graham, *Corn and Currency*, p. 49-50.

32. *Ibid.*, 6.

33. Russell, *Essays and Sketches*, p. 147.

34. *Hansard*, N. S. XXIV (14 May 1830), 734.

35. *Morning Herald* (London), 20 May 1830.

36. *Hansard*, N. S., XXI (2 June 1829), 1677.

37. *Ibid.*

38. 3 *Hansard*, I (2 November 1830), 65.

39. *Hansard*, N. S., XXI (2 June 1829), 1677.

40. C. M. Wakefield, *Life of Thomas Attwood* (London, 1885), p. 137.

41. *Hansard*, N. S. XXI (2 June 1829), 1685.

42. *Ibid.*
43. Elie Halevy, *A History of the English People, 1815-1830,* translated by E. I. Watkin (London, 1926), pp. 281-2.
44. A. Aspinall, (ed.), *Three Early Nineteenth Century Diaries* (London, 1952), p. xxvii.
45. 'On Parliamentary Reform and the French Revolution', *Blackwood's Edinburgh Magazine,* **XXX** (October 1831), 613.
46. Cannon, *Parliamentary Reform,* p. 244.
47. Brock, *Lord Liverpool,* p. 226.
48. See below.
49. *Morning Journal* (London), 12 September 1829.
50. *Morning Herald* (London), 27 December 1829.
51. *Standard* (London), 24 December 1829. Charges of libel were also brought against the *Standard* but were not pursued.
52. *Examiner* (London), 3 January 1830. Tenterden had signed a requisition calling for a testimonial dinner for the Protestant stalwart, Sir Edward Knatchbull, at Maidstone. See *The Times,* 14 November 1829.
53. *The Times* (London), 24 and 26 December 1829.
54. *Morning Chronicle* (London), 30 December 1829.
55. [David Robinson] 'The Reform of the House of Commons', *Blackwood's Edinburgh Magazine,* **XXVII** (April 1830), 643.
56. *Morning Herald,* 16 July 1829.
57. *Ibid.,* 12 October 1829.
58. *Hansard,* N. S., **XXIII** (16 March 1830), 395.
59. *Hansard,* N. S., **XXII** (18 February 1830), 678-98.
60. *Ibid.*
61. *Standard,* 19 February 1830.
62. *Ibid.,* 20 February 1830.
63. Robinson, 'The Reform of the House of Commons', p. 647.
64. *Ibid.,* p. 648.
65. *Ibid.,* p. 651.
66. *Examiner,* 26 June 1829.
67. *Ibid.,* 7 June 1829.
68. Reported in *The Times,* 14 November 1829.
69. *Ibid.* The possible electoral effects in Northamptonshire of Winchelsea's flirtation with reform are discussed in chapter 3.
70. Reported in *The Times,* 14 November 1829.
71. *Hansard,* N. S., **XXII** (4 February 1830), 3 and 69 ff.
72. *Ibid.,* (4 February 1830), 9.
73. *Hansard,* N. S., **XXIII** (16 March 1830), 429.
74. *Hansard,* N. S., **XXII** (4 February 1830), 38.
75. *Ibid.,* (4 February 1830), 71.
76. *Ibid.,* 38.
77. *Hansard,* N. S., **XXIII** (19 March 1830), 667, and *ibid.,* (23 March 1830), 817.
78. *Ibid.*
79. These questions are discussed in chapter 8.
80. *The Times,* 1 December 1829.

81. *Ibid.*
82. *Ibid.*, 12 December 1829.
84. *Morning Herald,* 14 December 1829. This controversy was carried on against the background of the Government's efforts to avail themselves of the current low rates of interest to convert £150,000,000 of four per cent stock to three and a half per cent. While recognizing the Government's obligation to reduce the interest on the national debt – and thus the need for taxes to pay this interest – if money rates fell naturally *The Times* (15 December 1829 and 7 January 1830) was not sure these rates were not being manipulated. Such doubts were consistent with the protests made by a committee of fundholders, to the effect that the Government was simply trying to economize at their expense. Observing that the Government could do nothing without their consent – that they could demand repayment of the capital which, they believed, the Government could never raise – they tried to organize themselves to reject the plan. See 'To the proprietors of 4 per cents', *ibid.*, 17 December 1829. Ultimately, the conversion took place.
85. *Morning Herald,* 14 December 1829, original emphasis.
86. *Ibid.*, 15 January 1830.
87. *Standard,* 28 December 1829.
88. *Ibid.*, 29 December 1829.
89. See, for example, the arguments of Colonel E. F. Bromhead at the Lincolnshire county meeting, reported in *Political Register,* 23 January 1830, and those of the Marquis of Chandos while introducing his motion to repeal the malt tax, 3 *Hansard,* XXVI (10 March 1835), 739.
90. On this question see in particular, *Essay on the Repeal of the Malt Tax* (London, 1846). This *Essay* was published under the auspices of the Total Repeal Malt Tax Association.
91. E.g., the letter to the editor from Henry Blackman, *The Farmers' Magazine,* II (April 1835), 280-81.
92. 3 *Hansard,* XXVI (10 March 1835), 756-63.
93. E.g., the statements of Sir Montague Cholmeley at the Lincolnshire county meeting, reported in *Political Register,* 23 January 1830.
94. On the preliminaries of these meetings see *Morning Herald,* 7 October and 5 and 7 December 1829. At the public meeting in London from which the call went out for other meetings throughout the kingdom it was reported that meetings had already been held in Berkshire, Kent, Suffolk and Sussex. (*Ibid.*, 16 December, *The Times,* 16 December, and *Examiner,* 20 December 1829.) Subsequently, meetings were held in, among other places, Essex (*Morning Herald,* 21 December 1829), Sussex again (*Ibid.*, 14 January 1830), Norfolk (*Ibid.*, 18 January and *Political Register,* 24 and 30 January 1830), Lincolnshire (*Political Register,* 23 January 1830), Cambridgeshire (*The Times,* 23 January 1830), Cheshire and Cumberland (*Examiner,* 31 January 1830), Hampshire (*Morning Herald,* 3 February 1830), and Kent and Hampshire again (*Political Register,* 20 March 1830).
95. *Morning Herald,* 16 December 1829.
96. *Ibid.*

97. *Aris's Birmingham Gazette,* 1 February 1830.
98. Arbuthnot to Peel, 16 February 1830, B. M. Add. Mss., 40, 340, f. 218.
99. 8 February 1830.
100. 6 February 1830.
101. *Hansard,* N. S., XXIV (29 April 1830), 215.
102. See especially *Morning Chronicle,* 3 February 1830, and *The Times,* 10 February 1830.
103. 15 January 1830.
104. 21 September 1830.
105. 22 September 1830.
106. 3 *Hansard,* I (2 November 1830), 53.
107. [William Johnstone] 'The Present Crisis', *Blackwood's Edinburgh Magazine,* XXXVIII (October, 1830), 693-4.
108. [Thomas de Quincey] 'French Revolution', *ibid.,* (September 1830), 556.
109. [Thomas de Quincey] 'France and England', *ibid.,* (October 1830), 717.
110. See the excerpts published in the ministerial *Morning Post* (London), 30 October 1830.
111. B. M. Add. Mss., 40, 340, f. 236-7.
112. See the comments of the *Examiner,* 26 September 1830, on the sudden hostility of the *Morning Chronicle* and the *Edinburgh Review* towards Wellington. As the *Examiner* put it, there was 'but one sentence of real meaning' in the *Edinburgh Review* to explain their change of attitude towards Wellington: 'Why is Lord Grey excluded from the Administration?'
113. Bamford and Wellington, (eds.) *The Journal of Mrs Arbuthnot,* II, p. 395.
114. *Ibid.,* p. 396.
115. From Milan, 15 May 1831, Louis J. Jennings, (ed.), *The Croker Papers . . .* (London, 1884), II, p. 126.
116. *Hansard,* N. S., XXIV (29 April 1830), 215.
117. 14 July 1830.
118. 3 *Hansard,* I (22 November 1830), 608.
119. 23 November 1830.
120. *Ibid.*
121. Marquis of Londonderry to the Duke of Buckingham, 5 January 1831, Duke of Buckingham and Chandos, *Memoirs of the Courts and Cabinets of William IV and Victoria* (2 vols., London, 1861), I, p. 189.
122. 27 January 1831.
123. 31 January 1831.
124. 2 February 1831.
125. 8 February 1831.
126. 12 February 1831.
127. 18 February 1831.
128. *Ibid.*
129. 28 February 1831.
130. 2 March 1831.
131. As the *Examiner* had put it the previous 7 November, 'Panic is now the respectable principle of Parliamentary support, and in every riot and street brawl a reason is seen for rallying to the Duke of Wellington's

Government.'
132. 21 August 1830.
133. E.g., *The Times,* 17 November 1830 and the *Standard,* 23 November 1830.
134. *The Times,* 12 February 1831.
135. *3 Hansard,* II (1 March 1831), 1096.
136. *Ibid.,* (2 March 1831), 1171.
137. *Ibid.,* (1 March 1831), 1091.
138. *Ibid.,* 1115. E.g., Horace Twiss, *ibid.,* 1132, and Lord Francis Leveson-Gower, *ibid.,* 1149.
139. *3 Hansard,* VII (4 October 1831), 1200.
140. Croker to Lord Fitzgerald, 28 August 1832, Jennings L. J. (ed.), *The Croker Papers,* 2nd ed. (3 vols, London, 1885), II, p. 185.
141. *Ibid.*
142. *3 Hansard,* XVI (21 March 1833), 918 ff. These points are discussed at greater length in chapter 8.
143. Croker to Lord Hertford, 25 March 1833, Jennings, *The Croker Papers,* II, p. 205.
144. William Thurnall, Chairman of the Cambridge and Ely Farmers' Association, reported in the *Independent Press,* 14 May 1836.
145. E.g., Brock *The Great Reform Act,* p. 142: 'The ideas of the ministers on Reform cannot be compressed into a single, internally consistent theory.'
146. *3 Hansard,* II (3 March 1831), 1329, emphasis added.
147. Cannon, *Parliamentary Reform,* p. 262.
148. *Ibid.*
149. *Ibid.*
150. *Ibid.*
151. *Ibid.*
152. *Ibid.*
153. The judgment was declared in the author's 'Concession or cure: the sociological premises of the first Reform Act', *Historical Journal,* IX (1966), 44-5.
154. *3 Hansard,* II (1 March 1831), 1086-7.
155. *Ibid.*
156. *3 Hansard,* III (8 March 1831), 225.
157. *Ibid.*
158. T. H. B. Oldfield, *History of the Boroughs* (3 vols., London, 1792), II, p. 213.
159. The process is discussed in chapter 11.
161. Viz. Brock, *The Great Reform Act,* p. 28 and p. 142
162. Wellington to G. R. Gleig, 4 July 1831, The Duke of Wellington, (ed.) *Despatches, Correspondence, and Memoranda of Field Marshal Arthur Duke of Wellington, K. G.,* (London 1878), VII, p. 466.
163. Croker to Peel, 11 November 1831, Jennings, *The Croker Papers* II, p. 136-7.
164. *3 Hansard,* II (2 March 1831), 1171.
165. *Ibid.,* XI (23 March 1832), 756-7.
166. *Ibid.,* V (2 August 1831), 614.

167. *Ibid.*, CXXX (13 February 1854), 495.
168. *Ibid.*, 498.
169. This question is discussed below.
170. Cannon, *Parliamentary Reform,* p. 262.
171. *Ibid.*
172. 3 *Hansard,* IX (27 January 1832), 983-4.
173. *Ibid.*, VI (20 August 1831), 339.
174. *Ibid.*, 345.
175. E.g., Brock, *The Great Reform Act,* p. 17.
176. Cannon, *Parliamentary Reform,* p. 246, footnote 2.
177. Quoted by Joseph Hamburger, *James Mill and the Art of Revolution* (New Haven, 1963), p. 36.
178. Quoted *ibid.*, p. 35.
179. 3 *Hansard,* III (28 March 1831), 1062-3.
180. *Ibid.*
181. James Mill, *An Essay on Government,* ed. Currin V. Shields, (New York, 1955), p. 90.
182. Brock, *The Great Reform Act,* p. 142.
183. Joseph Hamburger, 'James Mill on Universal Suffrage and the Middle Classes', *The Journal of Politics,* XXIV (1962), 172.

Chapter 6

1. A. V. Dicey, *Introduction to the Study of the Law of the Constitution,* 8th ed. (London, 1926), esp. pp. 411 ff.: 'The Connection between the Law of the Constitution and the Convention of the Constitution'; E. A. Freeman, *The Growth of the English Constitution from the Earliest Times* (London, 1872), esp. chapter 3.
2. It is instructive to consider the grounds on which John Cannon has tried to show that 'the increase in the electorate effected by the act was nearer to 80% than the 50% usually quoted' (*Parliamentary Reform,* p. 259). For the pre-reform period, when most of the borough electorates were fairly small, the essential problem which Cannon faces is how to determine the number of eligible men in the counties. His proposed solution is simple: 'For the county computation [in the pre-reform period]', he declares, 'I have taken as the basis the highest poll recorded between 1800 and 1831. For the 9 counties where there were no contests in this period, or only token ones, I have assumed the increase in the electorate to be proportionate to the overall increase' (p. 290). He notes the fact that 'a calculation on this basis will leave a number of freeholders unaccounted for'. But, he goes on, 'the number is unlikely to be great, since most of the polls continued ten or fifteen days' (*ibid.*) In effect, his *terminus a quo* is fashioned in the light of the assumption that the factors which conditioned electoral participation were *not political,* that if the voters were given sufficient *opportunity* to vote they would vote. But if the situation described above for Cambridgeshire be any guide, calculations based upon such an assumption might be grossly in error – and grossly in error in ways that are undefinable and thus uncorrectable. In 1826 the

poll was open in Cambridgeshire for seven days. But according to the poll book figures only 2,252 voters polled. Thus, had there been no subsequent contests in Cambridgeshire the county would have added only 2,252 men to Cannon's ostensible total of eligible voters in the pre-reform period. Presumably, his computation reflects the fact that 3,717 voters are listed in the Cambridgeshire poll book for 1830. But even assuming that this was the total of eligible voters – and how often does electoral participation approach 100 per cent? – the differences between this number and the number listed in the 1826 poll book suggest an important element of possible error to which his general procedure might lead. In effect, if he wishes to estimate 'the increase in the electorate effected by the act' he must start by answering a question which simply cannot be answered: what were the degrees of absenteeism in the various counties in which one or more contests occurred between 1800 and 1831?

John Cannon's *terminus ad quem* is fashioned in the light of the analogously non-political assumption that if men were given sufficient opportunity to register themselves they would do so. 'The electorate in 1833', he declares, 'is known from registration and was 652,777' (p. 259, footnote 3). Whatever the meaning of the term, 'electorate' in this statement – while referring to a *registered electorate* he is comparing this electorate to a *participating electorate* which, he assumes, was equivalent to the *number of eligible men* in the pre-reform period – he is begging the question of agency and, even more important, perhaps, ignoring the fact that the question of what the figure 652,777 really signifies simply cannot be answered. Presumably one of the components of this figure are the 344,564 entries on the county registers in 1833. But in the light of the subsequent increase in the numbers of men registered in the counties – in 1834 there were 366,222; in 1836 there were some 440,000 (as noted below, there were several gaps in the Returns of the numbers of electors entitled to vote in 1836; the round number is an estimate produced by filling these gaps with figures available for these constituencies in other years) – the figure for 1833 should scarcely be used to measure the *number of eligible men* in 1833. Nor should it be used to measure the number of men who might have voted at a contest. The reasons for this are discussed below.

3. See the cases for Dorsetshire and Essex noted in chapter 4, note 136.
4. Sessional Papers 1837-38, XLIV, 554. The same points had been made for South Notts. in 1833: 'In this division there are instances of the same person being several times inserted in respect of property in different places' (*Ibid.*, 1833, XXVII, 85), and for East Worcestershire, in 1836, where the number of entries on the register was reported 'without deducting those who are registered more than once, which would occasion great trouble' (*Ibid.*, 1836, XLIII, 380).
5. Such a case was noted by T. Rogers, a registration agent for Bedfordshire, in his testimony before the Select Committee on Registration of County Voters, Sessional Papers, 1864, X, q. 1032.
6. Such a case was noted by John Biggs, chairman of the South

Leicestershire Liberal Registration Association. See *Leicestershire Mercury,* 5 June 1841.

7. As a witness explained to the Select Committee on Votes of Electors, there were over 1,200 different ways a man might qualify for the county franchise. Sessional Papers, 1846, VIII, q. 3306. Obviously, Edward Porritt's assertion, based on Hume's statement (3 *Hansard,* XCIX (20 June 1848,) 893.), that after 1832 'there were no fewer than eighty-five avenues through which the Parliamentary franchise could be reached [in the counties]', is unnecessarily modest. See Porritt, *The Unreformed House of Commons,* I, p. 23.

8. The roles of these men are described in particularly useful fashion in Report of the Select Committee on Registration of County Voters, Sessional Papers, 1864, X, q. 15.

9. 3 *Hansard,* XXXIII (20 May 1836), 1134 and 1136.

10. Such was Russell's argument. See *ibid.,* 1137. Comparable assumptions informed the logic of the argument of Sir John Campbell, the Attorney General, against the establishment of special registrars of voters. He saw no other means of appointing such registrars except to place their appointment in the hands of the Government of the day. But, he argued, if this were done the registrars' impartiality would inevitably be suspect. See *ibid.,* XXXII (18 April 1836), 1176.

11. These unintended consequences of the Act are discussed below.

12. This provision, 30 & 31 Vict. c. 102., s. 59., is discussed in chapter 9.

13. Sessional Papers, 1870, VI, 195.

14. The Return of the Number of Electors in every County and Division of a County in Great Britain, according to the Registers of Electors of 1850 ... [to] 1856 ... Sessional Papers, 1857 (2nd Session), XXXIV, 83 ff., contains a note to the effect that since there were an 'estimated' 2,513 persons registered for more than one qualification in the West Riding of Yorkshire in 1856 there were probably no more than 35,000 potential voters in the division. According to this 'estimate' roughly 6 per cent of the entries were duplicates. But the roundness of the number of ostensibly actual voters who remained after the 'estimated' number of duplicate entries had been subtracted suggests that the 'estimate' was merely a guess. The register contained 37,513 entries. Ostensibly, in 1860, almost a quarter of the entries on the Bristol register were duplicates. But Bristol was a special case. Not only did it contain significant numbers of freemen voters; it was one of the six boroughs with county status in which freeholders continued to vote in the 'borough' after 1832. It was claimed, in 1860, that 1,600 men were registered in Bristol both as freemen and as occupiers, and that an additional 1,482 men were registered both as freeholders and as occupiers. Thus, of the 12,837 entries on the register, some 3,082, or 24 per cent, were duplicates. (Report from the Select Committee appointed to inquire what would be the probable increase of the number of electors in the counties and boroughs of England and Wales from a reduction of the franchise, ... Sessional Papers, 1860, XII, qs. 1204-7.) In all probability, the situation in Liverpool was rather more usual. There, in

1868, it was claimed that only some 3.5 per cent of the entries on the register were duplicate entries, only 1,408 out of 39,645. (Report from the Select Committee on Registration of Voters, Sessional Papers, 1868-69, VII, qs. 271-4.)

15. Report from the Select Committee on Election Expenses, Sessional Papers, 1834, IX, 263 ff.

16. Individually, the returns of 1836 and 1837 contained a number of gaps. However, when the returns for both years are used the only remaining gap is for the northern parts of Cambridgeshire, the Isle of Ely. Had the figures for the Isle been included they would have raised the total from approximately 437,000 to 440,000. The returns for these years were published together in Sessional Papers, 1837-38, XLIV, 553 ff.

17. *Ibid.*, 1847, XLVI 335 ff.

18. *Ibid.*, 1865, XLIV, 549 ff.

19. Walter Bagehot, *Essay on Parliamentary Reform* (London, 1859), p. 9.

20. These are discussed in the Epilogue.

21. Report from the Select Committee of the House of Lords appointed to inquire what would be the probable increase of the number of electors in the counties and boroughs of England and Wales from a reduction of the franchise, . . . Sessional Papers, 1860, XII, q. 2110.

22. E.g., in South Northamptonshire, where Captain George Ashby informed the Conservative registration agent on 8 July 1870 that he had 'a new tenant to vote but I doubt whether he will be allowed to go on this year as I did not get his rateable value increased till I think it was January . . .' Noting that he had another 'who only came in on Ladyday', he went on to express his regret that Lord Clifden had a lot more on the other side. Daventry Papers, N. R. O.

23. Table 19 has been compiled from Returns published in Sessional Papers, 1833, XXVII, 21 ff.; 1834, IX, 602 ff.; 1857 (2), XXXIV, 83 ff.; and 1865, XLIV, 549 ff., which show the ostensible numbers of registered electors in 1832, 1833, 1835, 1857 and 1864 — the 1833 return containing no information for Cambridgeshire, Herefordshire or Huntingdonshire: for these counties the figures are for 1833 and come from the 1834 return; from the Return published in *ibid.*, 1866, LVII, 569 ff., which shows the population of the counties or county divisions exclusive of represented cities and boroughs for 1831 and 1861; and from that published in *ibid.*, 1866, LVII, 573 ff., which shows the populations of the boroughs in each county or county division in 1831 and 1861.

24. Sessional Papers, 1837-38, XLIV, 553 ff.

25. E.g., in Mid-Cheshire. See George William Latham's comments, Report from the Select Committee on Parliamentary and Municipal Elections, Sessional Papers, 1868-9, VIII, q. 6469.

26. These shifts in Cambridgeshire and North Northamptonshire are discussed in chapters 2 and 3. In Oxfordshire similar shifts occurred. There, the total effective electorate was increased by roughly 40 per cent, from a pre-reform maximum of 2,934 in 1831, to 4,120, in 1837. However, in the 21 towns and villages from which over half the voters polled in 1831 the average increase was less than 2 per cent. Among the

other 300 odd villages in the county the average increase was over 80 per cent. These conclusions derive from analyses of *The Copy of the Poll of the Freeholders for Knights of the Shire for the County of Oxford* ... (Oxford, 1831), and *The Copy of the Poll of the Freeholders for Knights of the Shire for the County of Oxford* ... (Oxford, 1837). On the continuing activities of urban leaders in the politics of the West Riding of Yorkshire see F. M. L. Thompson, 'Whigs and Liberals in the West Riding, 1830-60', *English Historical Review,* LXXXXIV (1959), 214-39. Since no contests occurred in Yorkshire in the immediate pre-reform period there is no evidence which might be brought to bear on the question whether changes occurred in the relative electoral weights of the different varieties of community in Yorkshire at the time the Act was passed. As Professor Thompson notes, however, it was reported in 1848 that 13,612 of the 32,948 registered electors in the West Riding resided in manufacturing areas, 8,575 in agricultural areas, and 8,761 in so-called 'mixed' areas. And, as he points out, these three categories scarcely do justice to the urban nature of the constituency since the 'mixed' areas included such places as Leeds, Wakefield, Barnsley and Rotherham.

27. H. Stiles to Sir Michael Edward Hicks Beach, 5 October 1863, St. Aldwyn Papers, Misc. PP/17.

28. The South Leicestershire by-election of 1867 and the development of the ostensible Liberal majority on the North Warwickshire register are discussed below.

29. These are described by A. Temple Patterson, *Radical Leicester* (Leicester, 1954), *passim.*

30. *Leicestershire Mercury,* 30 March 1839, original emphasis.

31. *Ibid.,* 5 June 1841.

32. Report from the Select Committee on Votes of Electors, Sessional Papers, 1846, VIII, qs. 2308 and 2381.

33. Table 20 has been compiled from *The Poll for the Election of Two Knights of the Shire to serve in Parliament for the Southern Division of the County of Leicester* (Leicester, 1841).

34. Report from the Select Committee on Votes of Electors, Sessional Papers, 1846, VIII, qs. 2312-20.

35. *The Poll taken at the Election of a Knight of the Shire, November 28th 1867,* ... (Leicester, n.d.), p. 130.

36. *Leicester Chronicle,* 23 October 1858. See also *ibid.,* 4 and 25 September and 16 October 1858, and *Leicestershire Mercury,* 25 September 1858.

37. Burton v. Brooks, determined in 1851. Alfred J. P. Lutwyche, *Reports of Cases argued and determined in the Court of Common Pleas on Appeal from Decisions of the Revising Barristers* (2 vols., London, 1847-54), II 197.

38. Table 21 has been compiled from the 1841 and 1867 poll books noted above.

39. These various figures are to be found in Sessional Papers 1837-38, XLIV, 553 ff.; *ibid.,* 1852, XLII, 303 ff.; *ibid.,* 1857-58, XLVI, 571 ff.; *ibid.,* 1865, XLIV 549 ff; and *ibid.,* 1866, XVII, 15ff.

40. *Leicester Journal,* 6 December 1867.

41. *Ibid.*

42. Table 22 has been compiled from the 1867 poll book noted above, *The Poll for the Election of two Knights of the Shire for the Southern Division of the County of Leicester* (Leicester, 1869), *The Poll taken at the Election of a Knight of the Shire* (Leicester, 1870), and J. Vincent and M. Stenton, (eds.), *McCalmont's Parliamentary Poll Book British Election Results 1832-1918,* 8th ed. (Brighton, 1971).
43. See *Leicester Journal,* 25 September and 2, 9 and 16 October 1868, and *Leicester Chronicle,* 26 September and 3, 10 and 17 October 1868, for cursory reports of proceedings at the revising barrister's court.
44. These points are discussed below.
45. See his Address following his defeat, *Leicester Chronicle,* 28 November 1868.
46. See his speech, reported *ibid.,* 3 July 1880.
47. These involved the exploitation of section 25 of the first Reform Act. See below.
48. See his speech, reported in *Birmingham Journal,* 8 July 1865.
49. *Ibid.,* 21 October 1865.
50. Sessional Papers, 1867-8, **XX**, 29.
51. *Birmingham Journal,* 29 October 1864, 21 October 1865 and 11 October 1866.
52. *Ibid.,* 11 October 1866.
53. Cox and Grady, *The New Law* 10th ed., p. xcviii.
54. Report from the Select Committee of the House of Lords appointed to inquire what would be the probable increase of the number of electors in the counties and boroughs of England and Wales from a reduction of the franchise, . . . Sessional Papers, 1860, **XII**, qs. 3179-81.
55. *Ibid.*
56. *Ibid.,* qs. 2110-6.
57. Testimony of William Wyndham Burrell, Sessional Papers, 1846, **VIII**, q. 5491.
58. Emphasis added.
59. 3 *Hansard,* **XXXIV** (21 June 1836), 701-2.
60. *Ibid.*
61. In explaining the problem to Peel, Graham referred to the practice as the 'Birmingham mode of manufacturing county votes out of building leases in towns'. Graham to Peel, 11 May 1836, BM, Add. Mss., 40,318, f. 37.
62. 3 *Hansard,* **XXXIV** (21 June 1836), 701-2.
63. *Ibid.*
64. *Ibid.,* 702-3 and 705.
65. *Ibid.,* 703. Their figures were perhaps accurate with respect to Manchester. With respect to Birmingham, however, they were grossly exaggerated. In 1836, 2,251 of the 17,576 entries on the electoral register for South Lancashire were for men registered as leaseholders. But in North Warwickshire the number of entries for men registered as leaseholders was only 407 out of a total of 6,632. See Sessional Papers, 1837-38, **XLIV**, 553 ff.
66. 3 *Hansard,* **XXXIV** (27 June 1836), 971.
67. This is apparent from a comparison of the figures in Sessional Papers,

1837-38, XLIV, 553 ff.; 1844, XXXVIII, 427 ff.; 1854, LIII, 211 ff. and 1865, XLIV, 549 ff.

68. 6 Victoria c. 17., s. 42.

69. The case is reported in Lutwyche, *Reports of Cases argued,* I, p. 26-7, and E. W. Cox and H. T. Atkinson, *Registration Appeals, determined by the Court of Common Pleas, under the 6 Vict. c. 18. argued during the Michaelmas term, 1843* [London, 1844], pp. 6-8. The following description is taken from these reports.

70. According to section 20, '. . . every male person . . . who shall be entitled, either as lessee or assignee, to any lands or tenements, . . . for the unexpired residue, whatever it may be, of any term originally created for a period of not less than 60 years . . . of the clear yearly value of not less than £10 . . . or for the unexpired residue, whatever it may be, of any term originally created for a period of not less than 20 years . . . of the clear yearly value of not less than £50 . . . shall be entitled to vote in the election of a knight or knights of the shire . . .

71. Reported in Lutwyche, *Reports of Cases argued,* I, p. 413.

72. 7 & 8 William III, c. 25, s. 7.

73. Reported in D. D. Keane and James Grant, *Reports of Cases argued and determined in the Court of Common Pleas, on appeal from the decisions of the revising barristers* . . . (London, 1863), p. 9.

74. 3 *Hansard,* CV (5 June 1849), 1193.

75. Report from the Select Committee on Votes of Electors, Sessional Papers, 1846, VIII, q. 219.

76. Most of the objections brought by agents of the Anti-Corn Law League were based on the decision of the Court of Common Pleas in 1843 in the case of Bartlett v. Gibbs. This decision concerned section 40 of the Registration Act of 1843. According to this section, if an error occurred in any entry which an electoral register contained, or if the entry did not include all the items of information which were legally required, and if the error or omission were not corrected to the revising barrister's satisfaction, the entry was to be expunged. In Bartlett v. Gibbs it was held that where street numbers existed the legal requirement of adequate description of property was not satisfied unless such numbers were included in the register; also, that the revising barrister had no power to amend an entry except where no objection had been brought – in effect, that where an objection had been brought the objection could not be dealt with simply by correcting the entry or by supplying the missing information. In such a case the right to vote had to be proved. Most of the objections initiated by League agents concerned the omission of street numbers. In a large number of cases, however, Tory registration agents either secured the presence in the registration courts of the men against whom the objections had been brought, or obtained the information necessary to defend their contested rights. As a rule, the revising barristers allowed those men who had appeared in court and who had successfully defended their qualifications to recover costs. Usually, too, further objections were dropped as soon as the revising barrister had allowed costs. Thus further costs were avoided. By this means, however,

where the objections had been based on errors or omissions of information these errors or omissions could be amended without more ado.

According to various League spokesmen the campaign as a whole was an immense success. Ostensibly, 96½ per cent of their objections were sustained in North Warwickshire, 98 per cent in North Staffordshire, 92 per cent in Buckinghamshire, etc ... However, in arriving at these figures these spokesmen obviously ignored those objections which had been dropped. Of the 710 objections served in one polling district in North Warwickshire, in 1845, only 11 or 12 were sustained. The remainder were dropped after the revising barrister had begun awarding costs. Of the 1,370 objections served in South Leicestershire, in 1845, only 30 were sustained. Roughly a thousand were served in Buckinghamshire, in 1845, but only 15 were sustained. (See Report from the Select Committee on Votes of Electors, qs. 4, 2323 and 1650.) As Dr Norman McCord notes, the expenses of this campaign were considerable. So, too, the expenses of the somewhat different campaign designed not to purge the various county registers of their opponents but to provide free traders with freehold qualifications. 'Undoubtedly', he observes, 'the manipulation of the electoral roles in these ways was a formidable engine of agitation; it is impossible to say how far it might have been decisive, for the final crisis supervened before these activities had reached their peak.' (See *The Anti-Corn Law League* (London, 1958), p. 154.) But something can be said: in Lucknett v. Knowles, in 1846, the Court of Common Pleas reversed that portion of their decision in the case of Bartlett v. Gibbs which concerned the revising barristers' powers. They decided that the revising barristers *did* have the power to amend an entry even where an objection had been brought. (On the legal grounds of the League objections see Lutwyche *Reports of Cases argued*, I, pp. 74-91 and pp. 452-3, and Report from the Select Committee on Votes of Electors, qs. 4 and 59-61. On the abandonment of further objections as soon as costs were awarded, see *ibid.*, qs. 4, 2321-2, and 2655-6. On the 'success' or 'failure' of the campaign as a whole, see *ibid.*, qs. 2310 and 2650, and the exchange between John Bright and Charles Newdegate, 3 *Hansard*, LXXXXII [5 May 1847], 398-402.)

77. According to one of the Conservative registration agents in the West Riding, over £90,000 had passed through the hands of the Anti-Corn Law League for the purchase of qualifications in the West Riding of Yorkshire, South Lancashire and North Cheshire. See Report from the Select Committee on Votes of Electors, q. 4813.
78. Sessional Papers 1846, VIII, 179.
79. 3 *Hansard*, CV (5 June 1849), 1197.
80. See below, on the Mid-Cheshire contest.
81. These phenomena are discussed below.

Chapter 7
1. The information on which figure 2 is based has been taken from William O. Aydelotte, 'A data archive for modern British political history', in

Val R. Lorwin and Jacob M. Price (eds.), *The Dimensions of the Past: materials, problems and opportunities for quantitative work in history* (New Haven, 1972), pp. 333-59.

2. The information on which figs 3-7 are principally based has been taken from J. Vincent and M. Stenton (eds.), *McCalmont's Parliamentary Poll Book.*

3. E.g., in South Leicestershire in 1867. See chapter 6.

4. In *McCalmont's Parliamentary Poll Book* candidates and Members were identified by their political orientations or affiliations. These provide the basis of the identification in figures 4-7. The usual categories of identification, T[ory], C[onservative], W[hig] and L[iberal] raise few procedural questions as long as the figures are recognized as heuristic rather than descriptive – in effect, as long as the question whether coherent political groups which would warrant the use of such terms really existed, is kept in abeyance. It is to be hoped that the importance of the questions raised by the comparisons which the figures allow will more than compensate for possible confusion on this point. But procedural questions do arise for candidates and Members who were not identified as T, C, W or L. The principal alternative identifications used by F. H. McCalmont were P[rotectionist] 'and L[iberal]-C[onservative]. As a rule, Ps and L-Cs have been assimilated to Ts and Cs. This rule has been broken, however, when it seemed necessary to do so in the light of a subsequent identification provided by McCalmont or some other source – e.g., in the case of Sidney Herbert, Member for South Wiltshire from 1832 until 1861, who is first identified as C, then as LC, and then as L. The LC designation was used by McCalmont between 1847 and 1855. At the risk of entering into controversy with Professor J. B. Conacher and Professors W. D. Jones and A. Erickson, who have studied the Peelites and tried to specify the dates when different Peelites joined the Whigs and Radicals to form the new Liberal party, (*The Peelites and the Party System, 1846-52* (Newton Abbot, Devon, 1972), *The Aberdeen Coalition 1852-1855: a study of mid-nineteenth century party politics* (Cambridge, 1968), and *The Peelites 1846-1857* (Columbus, Ohio, 1972) Herbert *et al.* have been identified as Liberals from 1847. While the legitimacy of this procedure is obviously open to question, any other procedure would tend to greatly increase the complexity of the figures without significantly adding to their usefulness.

5. See chapter 6.

6. The disorganization of the Conservatives in Cornwall has been discussed by W. Brian Elvins, 'The Reform Movement and County Politics in Cornwall 1808-52', unpublished MA thesis, University of Birmingham, 1959, esp. chapter 8.

7. Gash, *Politics in the Age of Peel,* p. 239.

8. See the notices of meetings of agricultural protection societies in *John Bull,* 3 January 1846, and the observation, *ibid.,* 10 January, that because the Ministers had not expected agriculturists to react with so much vigour there was talk of a possible ministerial defeat and dissolution.

9. However many M.P.s ultimately voted against Peel because of these

pressures, very few resigned. Lord Ashley and Charles Sturt, two of the three Members for Dorsetshire, did so. Initially, they intended to seek re-election. But they refused to fight against John Floyer and Henry Ker Seymer who had been chosen as candidates at a combined meeting of agricultural protection societies in the county chaired by Floyer. See the report of the meeting, *The Times,* 10 February 1846. In East Gloucestershire the Hon F. Charteris retired in consequence of a requisition drawn up by the Gloucestershire Protection Society. See *ibid.,* 7 and 16 February 1846. In South Nottinghamshire the protectionists exploited the opportunity provided by the appointment of Lord Lincoln to a new office in the Government Peel formed in December 1845. Earlier, Lincoln had been asked to resign by the members of the Nottinghamshire Agricultural Protection Society. *Ibid.,* 9 February 1846. He had refused to resign. But his appointment to a new office required his re-election and, at the by-election, he was badly beaten by the protectionist candidate, T. B. T. Hildyard. This contest is mentioned above.

10. E.g., in Cambridgeshire, in 1831. See *The Times,* 27 October 1831.
11. Cox and Grady, *The New Law,* 10th ed., p. xcviii.
12. Betty Kemp, 'Reflections on the repeal of the corn laws', *Victorian Studies,* V (1962), 201.
13. William Howitt, *The Rural Life of England* (London, 1840), p. 77-8.
14. *The Poll for a Knight of the Shire for the Eastern Division of the County of Norfolk* (Norwich, 1858), p. ix.
15. *Ibid.,* p. xiv, emphasis added,
16. *Ibid.,* p. xiv-xvi.
17. C. W. Townley, reported in *The Times,* 23 November 1868.
18. See, in particular, the letters to the editor of the *Cambridge Independent Press* in September and October, 1874, following the death of Lord George Manners, and the letters to the editor, *ibid.,* in January, 1879, following the death of the Hon. Eliot C. Yorke.
19. See *ibid.,* 20 March 1880.
20. G. Butt, *Suggestions* p. 62.
21. The 'neutral' category reflected the statistical fact that in a multi-member constituency where each voter could cast as many votes as there were seats to be filled the voter who did not cast all his votes was taking a 'neutral' position with respect to the candidates for whom he did not vote. The importance of such 'neutral' behaviour in Huntingdonshire, in 1831, and in North Northamptonshire, in 1832, is discussed in chapters 1 and 3.
22. Butt, *Suggestions,* p. 64 and lvii.
23. *Ibid.,* p. 68.
24. Lord Churston to Sir Stafford Northcote, 7 January 1868, BM, Add. Mss., 50037, f. 68.
25. This was the role which Sir Charles Trevelyan attributed to parties when, in writing to Gladstone on 28 November 1853 concerning the proposed civil service reforms, he observed, 'The Government Patronage is habitually employed in influencing, or according to a

stricter morality, corrupting Representatives and Electors at the expense both of their independence and of the public interests'. Quoted by Edward Hughes, 'Sir Charles Trevelyan and Civil Service Reform, 1853-5', *English Historical Review,* LXIV (1949), 68.

26. William Partridge to A. W. Leigh, 3 October 1868, Burrows Papers, Devonshire Record Office, DRO 74B/MV54.
27. Cox and Grady, *The New Law,* 11th ed., pp. lxxix-lxxx.
28. *Ibid.,* p. lxxxi.
30. J. Alun Thomas, 'The system of registration and the development of party organisation, 1832-1870', *History,* **XXXV** (1950), 81-98. H. J. Hanham, *Elections and Party Management* (London, 1959), Appendix II, C: 'A note on registration in England', pp. 399-403 and *passim.*
31. But the statement 'that but for party action in the constituencies the three Reform Acts of the nineteenth century would have remained paper enactments only' reflects a grossly distorted view of the contents of the various Reform Acts. Thomas, 'The system of registration', p. 81. These measures contained many other provisions besides those which altered the franchise qualifications.
32. The central registration associations are discussed by Hanham, *Elections and Party Management* pp. 347 ff. The importance of the outvoter as a factor whose existence prompted the development of these central associations is suggested by the various printed forms – unfortunately blank – among the Daventry Papers in the Northamptonshire Record Office which were supposed to be used by Conservative agents in London in reporting the politics of outvoters residing in London to the appropriate registration agents, and by other printed forms – also, unfortunately, blank – on which the Conservative registration agent in one constituency might request information from his counterpart in another concerning the politics of a particular individual and the possible grounds on which an objection might be brought against his qualification. The establishment of central registration associations and the printing of such forms presumably simplified the process revealed in the letter of 15 August 1873 from William Burnett, one of the Conservative registration agents in South West Lancashire, to John Jeffrey, the Conservative registration agent in South Northamptonshire, requesting information concerning the politics of George Turner, of Kilsby, Northamptonshire, who had recently submitted a claim to be registered for property located in South West Lancashire. Daventry Papers, Northamptonshire Record Office.
33. 'The reformed parliament – the ballot', *Edinburgh Review,* LVI (January 1833), 544. The attribution to Brougham is from the *Wellesley Index to Victorian Periodicals.*
34. Report from the Select Committee of the House of Lords appointed to inquire what would be the probable increase of the number of electors in the counties and boroughs of England and Wales from a reduction of the franchise, . . . Sessional Papers, 1860, XII, q. 793, emphasis added.
35. The importance of preparation was frequently noted, e.g., in the undated manuscript history of the East Gloucestershire [Conservative]

Registration Society from its inception in 1837 until 1855, St. Aldwyn Papers, Misc/PP/11/1.

36. Cox and Grady, *The New Law,* 10th ed., p. xcviii.
37. Edward W. Cox, *The Law and Practice of Registration and Elections* 5th ed. (London, 1847), p. 144.
38. Edward Stanhope to Salisbury, 12 May 1880, Salisbury Papers.
39. Report from the Select Committee of the House of Lords appointed to inquire what would be the probable increase of the number of electors in the counties and boroughs of England and Wales from a reduction of the franchise, . . . Sessional Papers, 1860, XII, qs. 2114-6 and 3181.
40. John Morley, *The Life of William Ewart Gladstone* 3 vols., London 1903), I, p. 239.
41. See, for example, the undated letter from the Duke of Rutland to the Earl of Hardwicke thanking Hardwicke for 'kindly promising to support [Lord] George [Manners],' Adeane Papers, Misc. 17, and the letter of 27 March 1857 from Rutland to Hardwicke, marked 'Confidential', thanking Hardwicke for promising to 'support [Edward] Ball as well as . . . George', Adeane Papers. The significance of Hardwicke's promise perhaps derived from the fact that a few years later his eldest daughter was married to the Whig squire, Henry John Adeane, the fourth candidate at the contest of 1857, a man who enjoyed wide support against Ball, the non-conformist tenant farmer who had been returned as a protectionist in 1852.
42. See below.
43. The following description is taken from the undated manuscript history of the East Gloucestershire [Conservative] Registration Society, St. Aldwyn Papers, Misc/PP/11/1.
44. Ball's activities are mentioned in chapter 2.
45. Reported by John Fairlie, Rutland's agent, at the meeting of Ball's supporters, the *Cambridge Chronicle,* 22 May 1852.
46. See chapter 2.
47. Reported by Viscount Royston at the meeting of the Cambridge Conservative Club, the *Cambridge Independent Press,* 25 January 1868.
48. See the discussion of the problem in the report of the Conservative luncheon, the *Cambridge Chronicle,* 22 July 1865.
49. The meeting was reported in both the Conservative *Cambridge Chronicle* and the Liberal *Cambridge Independent Press,* 4 January 1868. In the latter was discussed at considerable length the question whether Hardwicke had not violated his non-political status as lord lieutenant of the county by participating. 18 January 1868.
50. *Cambridge Independent Press,* 25 January 1868.
51. The problem emerged in acute form in September 1874, following the death of Lord George Manners. Many of the rural Conservatives objected to the prospective candidacy of Francis Sharp Powell, who had sat for the borough of Cambridge from 1863 until 1868. Complaining that Powell was a 'town man', and 'blushing for the county that they could not find a county gentleman' to replace Manners, they ultimately secured Powell's withdrawal and the uncontested return of Hunter

Rodwell, of Ampton Hall, Suffolk. The controversy was extensively reported in the *Cambridge Chronicle* between 26 September and 17 October 1874.

52. *Cambridge Independent Press,* 21 March 1868.

53. Such was the interpretation of the *Cambridge Independent Press,* 21 March 1868.

54. *Ibid.*

55. *Ibid.*, 25 January 1868. This right was specifically acknowledged by the editor of the North Lincolnshire poll book for 1852. There was nothing unconstitutional, he contended, when 'a nobleman or gentleman representing a powerful party, and possessing the confidence of that party . . . [selects] a particular candidate . . . [In doing so, he] exercises only the legitimate sway of property and character combined'. But, he went on, the 'constitutional power to nominate' was perverted into an unconstitutional power to dominate' when the necessary confidence lapsed. *North Lincolnshire Poll Book* (Boston, 1852), p. xii.

56. The meeting was reported in both the *Cambridge Chronicle* and the *Cambridge Independent Press,* 12 September 1868.

57. *Cambridge Chronicle,* 17 October 1874.

58. E.g., *ibid.*, 8 October 1870.

59. *Ibid.*, 11 October, 18 October and 15 November 1873 and 26 September to 7 November 1874.

60. *Ibid.*, 24 April 1875.

61. Directly or indirectly, these relations are revealed in Thomas Acland to Earl Fortescue, 24 and 26 March 1865, Fortescue to Earl Russell (draft), 25 April 1866, and Edward Drewe to Fortescue, 30 April and 12 May 1866, Fortescue Papers, and the letter from Edwin S. Coleridge, 26 August 1868, and the letter from Robert J. Crosse to A. W. Leigh, 31 August 1868, Burrow Papers, DRO, 74B/MV54.

62. According to Northcote's son the contest had been 'forced by the electioneering agents'. W. S. Northcote to Lady Northcote, his mother, 20 November 1868, BM, Add. Mss., 50,031, ff. 27-30.

63. Lord Clinton to Northcote, 28 August 1868, BM, Add. Mss., 50,037, ff. 115-6.

64. Letter to Northcote, 29 August 1868, BM, Add. Mss., 50,037, f. 123.

65. Thomas Bembridge to Northcote, 29 August 1868, BM. Add. Mss., 50,037, ff. 121-2.

66. H. H. Fane to Northcote, 25 August 1868, BM, Add. Mss., 50,037, ff. 111-2.

67. Whether or not a Conservative Registration Association had existed in the county before 1868, a new association was organized in January. The meeting at which it was formed was reported to Northcote by Lord Churston on 7 January 1868, BM, Add. Mss.

68. W. S. Northcote to Lady Northcote, 20 November 1868, BM, Add. Mss., 50,031, ff. 27-30.

69. Cox and Grady, *The New Law,* 10th ed. pp. lxxiv ff.

70. Fitzwilliam to Gotch, 24 April 1846, Gotch Papers, Northamptonshire Record Office, G. K. 654.

71. The suggestion is made by J. P. D. Dunbabin, 'Parliamentary elections in Great Britain, 1868-1900: a psephological note', *English Historical Review*, LXXXI (1966), 82-3.
72. Typicality is claimed *ibid.*
73. Cox & Son to A. W. Leigh, 2 October 1868, Burrow Papers, Devonshire Record Office, 74B/MV54.
74. Downing to Arthur Pendarves Vivian, 10 July 1868, Vivian Papers, Cornwall Record Office D.D.P.V., Box 1, bundle 1. Downing who was Vivian's agent in Redruth, later observed that he had 'at last' managed to convice the members of the committee that they should only propose the registration of the 'right people'. Downing to Vivian, 15 July 1868. Earlier, he had explained that the 'large properties' were being 'worked by stewards' 6 July 1868. But evidently, at least in some cases, these stewards were assisted by committees. This was the case in the parishes in which the Earl of Falmouth's estates were located. Downing to Vivian, 17 July, 1868.
75. 'Liberal Canvassing Book, Cullompton', Burrow Papers, 74B/MV3.
76. *Ibid.*
77. Letter from Edwin S. Coleridge, 26 August 1868, Burrow Papers, 74B/MV54.
78. Robert J. Crosse to A. W. Leigh, 5 September 1868, Burrow Papers, 74B/MV54.
79. 'Minutes of the Conservative Committee, 22 October 1868', Nostell Papers, D3.8.1., original emphasis.
80. 'Minutes of the Conservative Committee, 12 November 1868', *ibid.*
81. 'Mr Baxter's Calculations, 21 November [1868]', 7,830 less 7,770 is, of course, not 53 but 60. Obviously, the Liberals in South West Yorkshire were making their calculations in terms of the same assumptions. As Robert J. Bentley, a prominent Liberal from Rotherham, observed to Sir Charles Wood within a week of the polling in 1865, if the same proportion of the registered voters polled in 1865 as had polled in 1859, 14,614 would vote. Thus, since Viscount Milton had only 7,180 promises and H. F. Beaumont only 7,017, he was somewhat apprehensive. And, he added, the figures he reported included the promises of many of the outvoters. But not of all. Indeed, it was there his hope resided: there remained some 1,100 outvoters about whom no reports had been received at the Liberal headquarters. If 320 of these could be secured for Milton, he observed, and 483 for Beaumont, he would 'feel safe'. Presumably, he was only allowing for a much smaller proportionate loss on promises than the Conservatives allowed for. But whether or not this was so, the dependence upon the outvoters, he noted, would greatly increase the expense of the contest. It was this which brought him to his principal question, how could the money be raised? Bentley to Wood, 13 July 1865, Hinckleton Papers, A4/42.
82. Table 23 has been compiled from the figures contained in 'Fourth canvass, 20 November 1868', and those contained in 'Final poll as declared by sheriff, 26 November 1868', Nostell Papers, D3.8.1.
83. 'Calculations, morning of the polling, 10 February 1874', *ibid.*

Notes to chapter 8

84. 'Estimate of Polling', *ibid.*
85. 'Calculations on the old system, 9 April 1880', *ibid.*
86. Table 24 has been compiled from the figures contained in 'Final canvass, 8 April 1880', *ibid.*, and those contained in the official poll.
87. 'Calculations on the old system, 9 April 1880', *ibid.*
88. 'Revision, 1869', *ibid.*
89. Table 25 has been compiled from the various reports of the revision of electoral registers which Baxter and his successors as Conservative agent submitted to their employers, Nostell Papers, D3.8.1. The figures for 1871 and 1872 were somewhat less complete than those for the other years and have therefore been omitted. No reports have been found for 1874 and 1875. The report for 1877 did not cover the political complexion of the 12 occupiers. After 1873 the term, 'Radical', was replaced by the term, 'Liberal'.
90. Covering letter from Strangeways, 6 July 1882, Burrow Papers, 74B/MV48.
91. This question is discussed in chapter 9.
92. His opposition is discussed in chapter 11.
93. This question is discussed in chapter 11.
94. Cox and Grady, 10th ed., *The New Law* p. lxxxviii.
95. Reported in *The Times,* 29 June 1863.
96. Table 26 has been compiled from figures contained in 'Fourth canvass, 20 November 1868', and those contained in 'Final poll as declared by sheriff, 26 November 1868', Nostell Papers, D3.8.1.
97. According to the Conservative canvassers' final reports, Sir Michael H. Hicks Beach, the Conservative candidate and father of the later Earl St. Aldwyn, had 3,636 promises and Edward Holland, the Liberal candidate, 2,095. At the polls Hicks Beach received 3,363 votes and Holland 2,344. The report of the canvass was pasted into Hicks Beach's copy of *A Correct List of the Poll at the Election of a Knight of the Shire for the Eastern Division of the County of Gloucester,* . . . (Gloucester, n.d.), St. Aldwyn Papers, Misc. PP/10/5a.
98. Cox and Grady, 10th ed., *The New Law* p. xcvii.
99. *Ibid.*, p. xcviii.
100. R. Leader to Sir Charles Wood, 28 June 1865, Hinckleton Papers, A4/42.
101. 5 September 1868.

Chapter 8
1. 3 *Hansard,* CXXX (13 February 1854), 498.
3. *Ibid.*, 495, 504.
4. Norman Gash, *Sir Robert Peel* (London, 1972), II, p. 429.
5. E.g., by Anthony Wood, *Nineteenth Century Britain, 1815-1914* (London, 1960), p. 142; D. G. Barnes, *A History of the English Corn Laws from 1660-1846,* reprinted (London, 1960), p. 266; and John Morley, *The Life of Richard Cobden,* 14th ed., (London, 1920), p. 318.
6. Morley, *The Life of Richard Cobden,* p. 318.
7. E.g., 3 *Hansard,* LXXIV (15 May 1844), 386 ff.
8. See, especially, 3 *Hansard,* LXXVIII (13 March 1845), 796.
9. *The Journal of the Royal Agricultural Society of England,* III (1842), 18-21.

10. F. M. L. Thompson, 'The Second Agricultural Revolution, 1815-1880', *The Economic History Review*, 2nd Ser., XXI (1968), 62-77.
11. The word is used by Barnes, *A History of the English Corn Laws*, p. 269.
12. *Bell's Weekly Messenger*, 26 February 1838.
13. *Journal of the Royal Agricultural Society*, III p. 19.
14. 3 *Hansard*, LXXXIII (27 January 1846), 276.
15. These are the grounds on which Mrs. Fairlie criticises those who contend that the corn laws did not have the effects which *certain* contemporaries attributed to them. S. Fairlie, 'The Nineteenth-Century Corn Law Reconsidered', *The Economic History Review*, 2nd Ser., XVIII (1965), 562.
16. See the discussion in *The Farmer's Magazine*, 2nd Ser., X (August 1844), 133 ff., of Earl Ducie's claim that he could sell wheat at a profit from his model farm in Gloucestershire were the price to drop to 28 shillings per quarter ton.
17. As Sir Henry Parnell put it while presenting the Committee's Report, the Committee's 'whole object . . . [was] to prove the evils which belong to . . . [the corn law] system as it now exists, and to obtain such an alteration in the law as shall draw forth our own means into operation of growing more corn, by increasing the capital that is now vested in agriculture.' *Hansard*, XXVI (15 June 1813), 645.
18. This was the essential point of his argument: that if domestic producers were given a monopoly of the domestic market they would so increase their investments as to raise their production, '. . . at the same time with diminishing expences in producing it, and at reduced prices to the consumer. For if the agricultural capital is considerably increased, its effects on the quantity produced, and the expence of production, and also in lowering prices, will be the same as when employed in manufactures. Every one knows how it operates in increasing the quantity of manufactures; and that those who employ it in manufactures can afford to sell them at very reduced prices, in consequence of the reduced expences at which with its help they can make them. In the same way the farmer by being able to render his land more productive in proportion as he improves it, and at a small expence according as he makes use of good implements, will be able to sell his corn at reduced prices; and in this manner the increase of agricultural capital will secure us a sufficiency of food independent of foreign supply, and at the same time at a reduced price to the consumer.' *Ibid.*
19. The logic of Parnell's argument was frequently denied in the countryside, e.g., by the witness before the Lords' Committee appointed to enquire into the State of the Growth, Commerce and Consumption of Grain, and all Laws relating thereto, who contended, in 1814, that, unless wheat prices rose from the 70-80s. range which they obtained, his own prior investments would become worthless. Communicated by the Lords, Parliamentary Papers, 1814-15, V, 1102 ff. See also the somewhat equivocal review of Sir Humphry Davy's *Elements of Agricultural Chemistry* in *Quarterly Review*, XI (July 1814), 318-31.
20. According to Ricardo, while investments in industry were inherently capable of reducing the unit costs of production, investments in

agriculture would inevitably raise these unit costs. See 'Influence of a low price of corn on the profits of stock' in E. C. K. Gonner, (ed.) *Economic Essays* (London, 1923), esp. pp. 274-5. In 1847, the logic of Parnell's argument was acknowledged by a writer in *Westminster Review* who noted that Ricardo had been 'hardly correct' in assuming that each successive dose of capital applied to the land returned a smaller yield. ('Improvement of Landed Property', XCIV (October 1847), 3.) But if Ricardo was 'hardly correct' the landlords were hardly innocent: the article was a general indictment of landlords in the name of the national interest for their failure to invest adequate quantities of capital in the land.

21. *Hansard*, XXVII (6 June 1814), 1084 ff.
22. Report from the Select Committee on Petitions relating to the Corn Laws of this Kingdom, Parliamentary Papers, 1813-14, III, 198.
23. *Ibid.*
24. Thompson, 'The Second Agricultural Revolution', p. 63.
25. Such a denial is contained in E. S. Cayley, *A Letter to H. Handley, Esq., M. P.,* ... (London, 1836), p. 8, from which the essential phrasing is taken.
26. 3 *Hansard*, I (22 November 1830), 608.
27. 3 *Hansard*, XVI (21 March 1833), 918 ff.
28. 3 *Hansard*, XV (5 February 1833), 208.
29. Jennings, *The Croker Papers*, II, p. 205.
30. *Ibid.*
31. For Attwood's views on this question see 3 *Hansard*, XVI (21 March 1833), esp. 922; for Chandos' views, see *ibid.*, XXIV (7 July 1834), esp. 1256.
32. See 3 *Hansard*, XVII (22 April 1833), 384-463; (23 April 1833), 469-537; and (24 April 1833), 540-91.
33. This was reported by Earl Stanhope to the inaugural meeting of the Central Agricultural Society, *The Farmer's Magazine*, IV (January 1836), 10. Speaking later at this meeting, Edward Ball observed: 'This afforded matter for deep consideration, and it was necessary that it should be well and maturely pondered ... [The farmers] had not been importunate – they had not been turbulent – they had not wielded the bludgeon or hurled the brick-bat, but had entreated so gently, in voice so faint and meek, in whispers so low and soft, that the ministers of the day had always found it more convenient to listen to the louder and more threatening petitioners, and to pass by the prayers of the meek and gentle unheeded and uncared for. It was time that the farmers of England should adopt a bolder and more determined tone' (14). Ball's activities in Cambridgeshire in this period are noticed in chapter 2.
34. 3 *Hansard*, XVII (24 April 1833), 582.
35. *Ibid.*, (26 April 1833), 678-89.
36. *Ibid.*, 689-718.
37. *Ibid.*, (30 April 1833), 776.
38. *Ibid.*, 833.
39. *Ibid.*, (3 May 1833), 958-9.

40. 3 *Hansard,* XVII (22 April 1833), 416.

41. 3 *Hansard,* XVII (3 May 1833), 958.

42. Report from the Select Committee on Agriculture, Parliamentary Paers, 1833, V, x.

43. *Ibid.,* xi.

44. *Ibid.*

45. *Ibid.*

46. *Ibid.,* xiii.

47. *Ibid.,* iv.

48. *Ibid.*

49. E.g., Thomas Attwood, for whom see 3 *Hansard,* XXIII (26 May 1834), 1337-8; Chandos, for whom see *ibid.,* XXIV (7 July 1834), 1256-8; and E. S. Cayley, for whom see *ibid.,* XXVIII (1 June 1835), 244 ff.

50. 3 *Hansard,* XXII (17 April 1834), 878.

51. *Ibid.,* 877.

52. Stanhope and various of the other currency reformers did not participate in the debates on the Poor Law Amendment Bill itself. But Stanhope was eloquent in his defence of the labourer's 'right to require employment to be found for him, and that he be sufficiently paid for that employment' at a meeting of the Central Agricultural Society, *The Farmer's Magazine,* V (July, 1836), 3-6. According to the report of this meeting, the last effective meeting of the Society, Stanhope was cheered at numerous points in his speech. But many in his audience objected strenuously to the criticisms he directed at the New Poor Law. At the end of the meeting he and several others resigned from the Society. The disagreements over the poor law question were obviously partly responsible for the subsequent collapse of the Society. Speaking later in the House of Lords Stanhope observed that if labourers were deprived of the 'property' they enjoyed 'by right' of the Elizabethan poor law they would scarcely continue to respect the property which others enjoyed by other rights. See 3 *Hansard,* XXXVIII (27 June 1837), 1635 ff. Thomas Attwood's criticisms of the poor law amendment scheme were reported in 3 *Hansard,* XXIII (26 May 1834), 1337-8.

53. This paradox is discussed by Mark Blaug, 'The Myth of the Old Poor Law and the Making of the New', *The Journal of Economic History,* XXIII (1963), 151-84, and 'The Poor Law Report Re-examined', *ibid.,* XXIV (1964), 229-45.

54. E.g., by Lord Ernle, *English Farming Past and Present,* 6th ed. (London, 1961), p. 331.

55. E.g., E. C. Midwinter, *Social Administration in Lancashire, 1830-60* (Manchester, 1969), esp. pp. 60-1; Anthony Brundage, 'The landed interest and the new poor law: a reappraisal of the revolution in government', *The English Historical Review,* LXXXVII (1972), 27-48.

56. 3 *Hansard,* XVI (21 March 1833), 938-9.

57. *Ibid.,* 953-5.

58. *Ibid.,* 941.

59. Report from the Select Committee on Agriculture, Parliamentary Papers, 1833, V, xiii.

60. *The Farmer's Magazine,* II (March 1835), 158-9.
61. *Ibid.,* IV (January 1836), 8-16.
62. Charles Shaw Lefevre, *Remarks on the Present State of Agriculture* (London, 1836), p. 6.
63. *Ibid.,* p. 11.
64. *Ibid.,* p. 24.
65. See the discussion of the questions whether and, if so, how wheat could be produced at a profit at 28s per quarter ton in *The Farmer's Magazine,* 2nd Ser., X (August 1844), 113 ff. Among those who refused to believe the accuracy of Ducie's announcement were those who contended that turnips were not worth the problems involved in their production. Among those who may have believed him were those who pointed to the fact that at a time when few farmers had more than five pounds per acre of working capital Ducie's farmer had £15 per acre.
66. *Hansard,* N. S., XXIII (19 March 1830), 667; and *ibid.,* (23 March 1830), 817.
67. 'Some Introductory Remarks on the Present State of Agriculture as a Science in England', *Journal of the Royal Agricultural Society,* I (1840), 4-5.
68. John Morton, *On the Nature and Property of, Soils:* . . . 2nd ed. (London, 1840), p. 85.
69. *Ibid.*
70. See the report of the meeting, *The Farmer's Magazine,* II (January 1835), 59-63.
71. The meeting of the Royal Agricultural Society at which the discussion occurred was reported in *The Times,* 11 June 1840. Later; Spencer noted at a meeting of the Royal Agricultural Society that, while the Society had hoped to help farmers during this epidemic by circulating a paper on the causes of the disease 'authorities' had not been able to agree as to the nature of these causes. Thus, no paper was circulated. *John Bull,* 24 July 1841.
72. I. J. Mechi, *Letters on Agricultural Improvement* (London, 1844), pp. 1-2.
73. *Ibid.*
74. In 1855, while addressing the Witham Agricultural Society, Mechi observed that he doubted whether many in his audience were 'convinced that drainage, irrigation, steam power, and other things which involved a large amount of capital were really essential to farming profitably'. He was there to convince them. See *The Times,* 15 October 1855.
75. William Johnstone, *England as it is* . . . (London, 1851), I, pp. 4-5.
76. William Howitt, *The Rural Life of England* (London, 1840), p. 101.
77. Speech at the anniversary dinner of the National Conservative Registration Association, reported in the *Standard* (London), 27 June 1863. According to Sir Edward Clarke, he and Henry Cecil Raikes were 'greatly influenced' by this speech in which Disraeli 'laid down in striking language and with keen political instinct the main principles of his political faith'. Ostensibly, this speech had much to do with Raikes' decision 'to attempt the work of gathering into a single organisation the various Conservative and Constitutional Associations which were scattered over the country'. Ultimately, Raikes' efforts and the efforts of

others resulted in the establishment of the National Union of Conservative and Constitutional Associations. As Clarke notes, this speech has been 'strangely overlooked by the statesman's biographers, and still more strangely omitted from the reprints of his speeches'. Sir Edward Clarke, *The Story of My Life* (London, 1918), p. 96.

78. T. E. Kebbel, 'The county system', *Fortnightly Review*, N. S., XXXIII (1883), 423-4.
79. Mill, *An Essay on Government* p. 90.
80. First Report of H. M. Commissioners appointed to inquire into the laws of England respecting Real Property, Parliamentary Papers, 1829, X, 7.
81. *Ibid.*, 6.
82. Walter Bagehot, *Essay on Parliamentary Reform* (London, n.d.), p. 8.
83. 'British agriculture and foreign competition', *Blackwood's Edinburgh Magazine,* LXVII (January 1850), 96-7.
84. See F. M. L. Thompson, *English Landed Society in the Nineteenth Century* (London, 1963), esp. chapters 9 and 10.
85. Report from the Select Committee on Agricultural Customs, Parliamentary Papers, 1847-8, VII, q. 56.
86. Arthur Underhill, 'Changes in the English Law of Real Property during the Nineteenth Century', *Select Essays in Anglo-American Legal History* (Boston, Massachusetts, 1909), III, 673 ff.
87. See the report of the meeting, *The Farmer's Magazine,* VIII (June 1838), 440-5.
88. Lord Kinnaird, *Profitable investment of capital, or eleven years practical experience in farming: a letter from Lord Kinnaird to his tenantry* 2nd ed. (Edinburgh, 1849), pp. 5-6.
89. James Caird, *English Agriculture in 1850-51* (London, 1852), p. 477.
90. William Woodfall, *The Law of Landlord and Tenant* 7th ed. (London 1829), pp. 57 ff.
91. The point was made in testimony before the Select Committee on Agricultural Customs, Parliamentary Papers, 1847-8, VII, q. 145.
92. See *Law Times,* 27 September 1845.
93. The point was made in testimony before the Select Committee on Agricultural Customs, qs. 704-15.
94. See the discussion of this question at the Harleston Farmers' Club, reported in *The Farmer's Magazine,* 2nd Ser., V (January 1842), 1-5. A slightly different point was made by Peel at a meeting of the Lichfield Agricultural Association in 1843. He hoped that 'confidence between landlord and tenant' would provide a basis for agricultural improvement in the Lichfield area similar to that which leases often provided in Scotland. While he had no leases on his own estates he observed that if any of his tenants wanted leases they might have them. But, he went on, he doubted that any of his tenants would apply for them. See the report of the meeting, *ibid.*, 2nd Ser., VIII (November 1843), 335-9. The problem to which he implicitly referred was that to which the anonymous writer of a letter to the editor of the *Bedfordshire Reporter* referred when he suggested that any significant tenant investments would have to wait until the Chandos clause had been repealed. The

letter was reprinted *ibid.*, 2nd Ser., VII (March 1843), 188-9.
95. *The Times*, 23 December 1842.
96. The point was made in the discussion at the Harleston Farmers' Club, *The Farmer's Magazine*, 2nd Ser., V (January 1842), 1-5.
97. 3 *Hansard*, VI (18 August 1831), 281-2.
98. See the debates on the question, 3 *Hansard*, LXXIV (26 April 1844), 280 ff.; XC (22 February 1847), 383 ff.; XCI (26 March 1847), 541 ff.; XCII (12 May 1847), 719 ff.; and CX (1 May 1850), 1061 ff.
99. In part, the dissolution occurred over the poor law question. See the report of the last effective meeting of the Central Agricultural Society, *The Farmer's Magazine*, V (July 1836), 3-6.
100. The list of officers of the Central Agricultural Protection Association can be found in E. S. Cayley, *Reasons for the Formation of the Agricultural Society* (London, 1844).
101. See the report of this dinner, *The Farmer's Magazine*, 2nd Ser., XI (January 1845), 23-56.
102. Reported in *The Farmer's Magazine*, 2nd Ser.,XI (January 1845), 23-5.
103. Norman McCord, *The Anti-Corn Law League 1838-1846* (London, 1958), p. 16.
104. *Ibid.*, p. 21.
105. *Ibid.*, p. 22.
106. As Donald Read notes, 'After 1842, . . . we find popular feeling slowly coming over to support of the middle-class League. This development helped to close the social gulf in local society. The coming together of middle and working classes in support of repeal of the corn laws smoothed away much of that atmosphere of social tension which the Chartists had exploited for so long, and encouraged in its stead an atmosphere of social union between masters and men'. Donald Read, 'Chartism in Manchester' in Asa Briggs, (ed.), *Chartist Studies* (London, 1959), p. 58.
107. Charles Arbuthnot to Peel, 2 April 1838, B.M., Add. Mss., 40,341, f. 5. Wellington had already joined. It was his request which Arbuthnot conveyed.
108. See the report of the meeting, *The Farmer's Magazine*. VIII (June 1838), 440-5.
109. *Bell's Weekly Messenger*, 26 February 1838.
110. See the report of the meeting, *The Farmer's Magazine*, II (January 1835), 3 ff.
111. *Ibid.*, 59.
112. See Cayley's statement at the meeting of the Yorkshire Central Agricultural Association, *ibid.*, 3.
113. *Ibid.*, 63.
114. *Ibid.*, 3.
115. 3 *Hansard*, XVII (26 April 1833), 680.
116. *Ibid.*
117. *Ibid,*, XXI (21 February 1834), 690.
118. *Ibid.*, LX (9 February 1842, 204 ff., esp. 226, and Shaw Lefevre, *Remarks on the Present State of Agriculture*, p. 23.

119. *A Letter from Sir Richard Vyvyan, Bart., M.P., to his Constituents* (London, 1842), p. 17. ·

120. *Ibid.*, p. 5.

121. See the discussion of the question whether the non-political rule of the Braintree and Bocking Farmers' Club should be altered, *The Farmers' Magazine*, 2nd Ser., V (April 1842), 247-55; the editorial recommendation that those farmers' clubs and agricultural societies which were not inhibited by such rules make their voices heard to protest the Corn Law of 1842, *ibid.*, 308; Robert Baker's observation, in 1843, that by adopting non-political rules for their various clubs and societies farmers had weakened their abilities to respond to the agitations of the Anti-Corn Law League, *ibid.*, 2nd Ser., IX (January 1844), 26-8, and his recommendation that the members of the newly formed London Farmers' Club 'unite to oppose the Anti-Corn Law League', *ibid.*, 39-40. The problem was particularly acute for the Central Agricultural Protection Association. While this Association had been established 'to maintain protection' its initial rules forbade its involvement in 'party politics' and its 'interference in parliamentary elections'. See *ibid.*, 2nd Ser., IX (March 1844), 277. In 1846 delegates resolved to expunge the rule forbidding the Association from interfering in elections in an obvious effort to bring countervailing pressures to bear upon many M.P.s who were abandoning their protectionist positions out of loyalty to Peel. See *John Bull*, 17 January 1846. Later, in an obvious effort to show that local agricultural protection societies had not only been violating their own non-political rules but had been trying to swamp the 'legitimate majority' in various counties in ways analogous to those charged against the Anti-Corn Law League, much was made of the fact that a solicitor in Coventry who had been active in registration affairs in Warwickshire as an agent of the Loyal and Constitutional Association in the county was also a member of the Warwickshire Association for the Protection of Agriculture (see the Report from the Select Committee on Votes of Electors, 1846, VIII, qs. 303, 418 ff. and 5491), and that the Sussex Agricultural Protection Society, of which the Duke of Richmond was president – he was also president of the Central Agricultural Protection Association – had been behaving unconstitutionally when the Society placed an advertisement in a local paper 'inviting persons wishing to procure [electoral] qualifications' to apply to a certain solicitor in Brighton. Q. 5415. In answer, it was said that neither the solicitor in Coventry nor the one in Brighton had been paid by the local protectionist societies, qs. 420-1 and 5424, and that the advertisement had not been authorized by the Sussex Agricultural Protection Society. Q. 5470.

122. Quoted by John Morley, *Richard Cobden*, p. 395.

123. 3 *Hansard*, LXXXIII (27 January 1846), 255.

124. *Ibid.*

125. *Ibid.*, 256.

126. *Ibid.*, 264-6.

127. *Ibid.*, 266-8.

128. *Ibid.*, 268-70.
129. In an article published in 1840, 'Some introductory remarks on the present state of agriculture as a science in England', *Journal of the Royal Agricultural Society,* I (1840), 3, Philip Pusey gave figures as high as eight or 10 pounds an acre. In 1845, several witnesses before the Select Committee of the House of Lords appointed to inquire into the expediency of a legislative enactment being introduced to enable possessors of entailed estates to charge such estates with a sum, to be limited, for the purpose of draining and otherwise improving the same, Parliamentary Papers, 1845, XXI, reported successful drainage at a quarter of the earlier cost. See qs. 57 and 1415.
130. *Ibid.*, 113.
131. See his testimony, *ibid.*, qs. 56 ff.
132. Qs. 423-4.
133. Q. 148.
134. *Ibid.*, 111.
135. *Ibid.*, 114.
136. 3 Hansard, LXXXIII (27 January 1846), 269-70. Recently, both Professor David Spring and Mr O. R. McGregor have called attention to Peel's drainage loan. But neither has recognized the true nature of the loan or the relationship between the loan and the repeal of the Corn Laws. In part, this may be because neither seems to realize that the loan was outlined in the speech in which Peel described his plans for repeal. In part, it may be because neither seems to be aware of the intensity of opposition to high farming. Professor Spring's assertion that 'The Public Money Drainage Act first came before the House of Commons at the end of May, 1846 . . . is somewhat misleading, especially since he follows it by saying that 'the immediate background of the Act remains obscure', and since he fails to note that the main provisions of the loan had already been sketched in January. See Spring, *The English Landed Estate* p. 149. In his discussion of the Enclosure Commissioners Professor Spring has redeemed the loan from the obscurity into which it had been allowed to fall by previous historians who focused their attention solely on the corn laws. But he has followed them in refusing to recognize any essential relationship between the two measures. 'The improvement party', he explains, 'of which Peel was a notable member, had for some years been moving towards a scheme such as that embodied in the [Public Money Drainage] Act.' Repeal merely provided a 'welcome opportunity for the improvement party to fashion legislation on a subject which had deeply interested them for some time'. *Ibid.*, p. 150. The problems of chronology and of opposition to high farming are also apparent in Mr McGregor's description of the loan as 'a *quid pro quo* for the landed interest after the repeal of the Corn Laws'. See his Introduction, Part II: after 1815', p.cxiii, in Ernle, *English Farming*. Possibly, in one respect, he comes closer to the truth of the matter because he recognizes the close relationship between the loan and corn law repeal. But he distorts the nature of this relationship. Evidently, he neglected to consider the *political* impact of the various changes in agricultural technology which

he discusses, the degree to which these changes had produced that situation in which protection was no longer the effective guarantee of rural prosperity which *certain* agriculturists continued to assume it was. In the light of these changes the drainage loan could scarcely be described as 'a *quid pro quo*'.

137. 3 *Hansard*, LXXXIII (27 January 1846), 269-70.
138. *Ibid.*
139. *Ibid.*, 268.
140. *Bell's Weekly Messenger*, 25 May 1846.
141. A Return of the number of applications ... under the Act of the last session, c. 101, in England, Ireland, and Scotland, ... and the total sums applied for in each country ... 1847, XXXIV, 301, indicates that through the end of January, 1847, there had been 168 applications from Scotland amounting to approximately £800,000, and 48 applications from England, amounting to approximately £200,000.
142. Henry Charles Mules, before the Select Committee of the House of Lords appointed to consider whether it would not be desirable that the powers now vested in the companies for the improvement of land should be made subject to general regulation, Sessional Papers, 1854-5, VII, q. 31.
143. Q. 58.
144. Q. 322.
145. Q. 347.
146. Arthur Underhill, 'Property', *Law Quarterly Review*, LI (1935), 225.
147. The editor of the 8th edition of Sir Bernard Burke, *History of the Landed Gentry of Great Britain and Ireland* (London, 1894), explained that some families who had made use of the Settled Land Act had been cast into oblivion and had 'severed their connection with their ancestral homes'. By 1921, however, the sins of which these men were guilty had come to define a new norm. As the editor of the thirteenth edition explained, '... the history of a family is retained after its head has ceased to be a landowner.'
148. 3 *Hansard*, XC (23 February 1847), 405.
149. Parliamentary Papers, 1854-5, VII, q. 4.
150. A Bill intituled An Act to amend the Law relating to Landlord and Tenant, clauses II and III, Parliamentary Papers, 1844, IV, 509-10.
151. 3 *Hansard*, LXXIV (26 April 1844), 280; XC (22 February 1847), 382-5; XCI (26 March 1847), 541-3; XCII (12 May 1847), 719-21; and CX (1 May 1850), 1061-6.
152. 14 & 15 Victoria, c. XXV.
153. 'The Agricultural Holdings Act of 1875', *Contemporary Review*, XXVII (1876), 498.
154. W. E. Bear, 'The revolt of the counties', *Fortnightly Review*, N.S., XXVII (1880), 720-25.
155. *Mark Lane Express*, 10 May 1847.
156. Testimony of George W. Latham before the Select Committee on Parliamentary and Municipal Elections, Parliamentary Papers, 1868-9, VIII, q. 6419.

157. J. B. Conacher, *The Peelites,* pp. 67-8.
158. Kemp, 'Reflections on the repeal of the corn laws', pp. 201, 203.
159. See the discussion at the meeting of the Central Agricultural Protection Association, *John Bull,* 17 January 1846.
160. McCord, *The Anti-Corn Law League,* p. 118.
161. *Ibid.,* p. 200.
162. *Ibid.,* p. 202.
163. Lewis A. Coser, *The Functions of Social Conflict* paperback, (London, 1964), pp. 33 ff.
164. *Ibid.,* pp. 104 ff.

Chapter 9

1. 3 *Hansard,* CLXXXIII (27 April 1866), 148. One of the clearest statements of the theme is to be found in F. E. Gillespie, *Labor and Politics in England 1850-1867* (Durham, North Carolina, 1927). Its two principal variations have been developed recently by Royden Harrison, *Before the Socialists: studies in labour and politics 1861-1881* (London, 1965), pp. 78-137: 'The 10th April of Spencer Walpole: the problem of revolution in relation to reform, 1865-1867', first published in the *Inter-National Review of Social History,* VII (1963), and F. B. Smith, *The Making of the Second Reform Bill* (London, 1966).
2. On various substantive points the following argument is not inconsistent with that contained in Maurice Cowling, *1867, Disraeli, Gladstone and Revolution, the Passing of the second Reform Bill* (Cambridge, 1967). It principally differs from Mr Cowling's in emphasizing the importance of certain extra-parliamentary processes which lie beyond the scope of his analysis.
3. Homersham Cox, *A History of the Reform Bills of 1866 and 1867* (London, 1868), p. 281, footnote.
4. 30 & 31 Vict. c. 102., s. 4.; 'A Bill to extend the right of voting at elections of Members of Parliament in England and Wales', clause 7, Parliamentary Papers, 1866, V, 87 ff.
5. Clause 5.
6. Section 3.
7. *Ibid.*
8. Report from the Select Committee of the House of Lords appointed to inquire what would be the probable increase of the number of electors in the counties and boroughs of England and Wales from a reduction of the franchise . . . Transmitted to the Commons, Parliamentary Papers, 1860, XII, q. 658.
9. Clause 4.
10. Clause 15: 'Sections 24 and 25 of the Act of the 2nd year of William IV, c. 45, shall be repealed, and in place thereof be it enacted. No person shall be entitled to be registered as a voter for a county Member or Members in respect of any premises situate in a borough, if he would be entitled to be registered in respect of such premises as a voter for a Member or Members of Parliament to serve for such Borough.'
11. See above.

12. Clause 20: 'Nothing herein contained shall affect the right which any person may have acquired of voting at the election of a Member or Members to serve in Parliament for a County or Borough in pursuance of any Register of Voters in force at the Time of the passing of this Act, so long as such voter retains the Qualification in respect of which he is registered at the time of the passing of this Act.'
13. Section 5.
14. *Ibid.*
15. Section 59: 'This act, so far as is consistent with the tenor thereof, shall be construed as one with the enactments for the time being in force relating to the representation of the people and with the registration acts; and in construing the provisions of the 24th and 25th sections of the act of the 2nd year of king William IV, c. 45., the expressions 'the provisions hereinafter contained' and 'as aforesaid' shall be deemed to refer to the provisions of this act conferring rights to vote as well as to the provisions of the said act.'
16. Section 56.
17. Cox and Grady, *The New Law,* 10th ed., pp. xix–xx.
18. Law Reports, Common Pleas, IV, 32 Vict., 426.
19. 3 *Hansard* CLXXXIII (7 May 1866), 493–7.
20. 30 & 31 Vict. c. 102., ss. 17–25.
21. 3 *Hansard,* CLXXXII (12 March 1866), 26–7.
22. Smith, *The Second Reform Bill,* p. 84.
23. 3 *Hansard,* CLXXXIII (27 April 1866), esp. 83 and 86.
24. Smith, *The Second Reform Bill,* p. 84.
25. 3 *Hansard,* CLXXXIII (27 April 1866), 134.
26. 3 *Hansard,* CLXXXII (12 April 1866), 1156.
27. *Ibid.,* 1154.
28. 3 *Hansard,* CLXXXIII (4 June 1866), 1810 ff.
29. *Ibid.,* (27 April 1866), 86.
30. *Ibid.,* 93.
31. 3 *Hansard,* CLXXXII (12 March 1866), 24.
32. 3 *Hansard,* CLXXXIII (7 May 1866), 501.
33. *Ibid.*
34. One of the reasons for protest against the recommendation by the Boundary Commissioners appointed in 1867 that the parliamentary boundaries of Birmingham be extended was the fear that the municipal boundaries would also be extended and consequently the area in which municipal burdens were imposed increased. 'Petition from the Manor of Aston, the Board of Repair of Highways, the Board of Inspectors of Lighting, and the Executive Committee of an Association in the Manor to oppose Annexation.' Parliamentary Papers, 1867-8, LVI, 195.
35. Smith, *The Second Reform Bill,* p. 96.
36. 3 *Hansard,* CLXXXIII (7 May 1866), 502.
37. 'A Bill for the redistribution of Seats', clause 28, Parliamentary Papers, 1866, V, 33 ff.
38. E.g., Smith, *The Second Reform Bill,* p. 236-7.
39. 3 *Hansard,* CLII (28 February 1859), 973.

40. *Ibid.*, 1022 ff.
41. 3 *Hansard*, VII (4 October 1831), 1193-4.
42. 3 *Hansard*, CXXX (13 February 1854), 498.
43. Clause 9 of the Bill of 1854 provided for the settlement of the boundaries of the new boroughs which would have been created but said nothing about the boundaries of the existing boroughs. Parliamentary Papers, 1854, V, 375 ff.
44. 3 *Hansard*, CXXX (13 February 1854), 504.
45. Sir George Cornewell Lewis, *An Essay on the Principle of Authority in Matters of Opinion*, 2nd ed. (London, 1875), p. 147.
46. *Standard*, 27 June 1863.
47. 3 *Hansard*, CLII (28 February 1859), 991.
48. *Ibid.*, 990.
49. *Ibid.*, 992.
50. *Ibid.*, 989-90.
51. *Ibid.*
52. *Ibid.*
53. *Ibid.*, 991.
54. 3 *Hansard*, CLIII (21 March 1859), 405.
55. 3 *Hansard*, CLII (28 February 1859), 973.
56. These are discussed in chapter 11.
57. 3 *Hansard*, CLXXXVIII (15 July 1867), 1603-4.
58. E.g., by Gertrude Himmelfarb, 'The politics of democracy: the English Reform Act of 1867', *The Journal of British Studies*, VI (1966), 97-138.
59. 3 *Hansard*, CLXXXIII (27 April 1866), 93.
60. 3 *Hansard*, CLXXXVIII (15 July 1867), 1602.
61. See in particular 3 *Hansard*, CLXXVIII (3 May 1865), 1423 ff.; CLXXXII (13 March 1866), 141 ff.; and *ibid.*, (26 April 1866), 2077 ff.
62. Memorandum on reform, 5 February 1859, BM., Add. Mss., 50043, f. 101., emphasis added.
63. 3 *Hansard*, CLXXXIII (27 April 1866), 86.
64. *Ibid.* (7 June 1866), 2057 H.
65. E.g., by Homersham Cox, *A History of the Reform Bills*, p. 63.
66. E.g., by Smith, *The Second Reform Bill*, esp. p. 229.
67. 3 *Hansard*, CLXXXVI (21 March 1867), 283.
68. *Ibid.*
69. 3 *Hansard*, CLXXXVII (23 May 1867), 997.
70. *Ibid.* (20 May 1867), 850.
71. *Ibid.* (23 May 1867), 997.
72. *Ibid.*, 998.
73. *Ibid.*
74. 3 *Hansard*, CLXXXVIII (24 June 1867), 457-8.
75. *Ibid.*, 461.
76. *Ibid.*, 467.
77. *Ibid.*, 465.
78. *Ibid.*, 471.
79. See the division list, *ibid.*, 476-9.
80. Homersham Cox, *A History of the Reform Bills*, p. 213, and Smith, *The*

Second Reform Bill, p. 206.
81. Law Reports, Common Pleas, IV, 32 Vict., 426.
82. T. Dunn to Lord Halifax, 10 June 1868, Hinckleton Papers, A4/46.
83. 3 *Hansard,* CLXXXVIII (21 June 1867), 270.
84. 3 *Hansard,* CXCII (14 May 1868), 255.
85. 3 *Hansard,* CLXXXVIII (21 June 1867), 274 and 276-7.
86. *Ibid.,* (25 June 1867) 528, emphases added.
87. 3 *Hansard,* CLXXXIII (7 May 1866), 502.
88. Especially by John Bright and Darby Griffith, 3 *Hansard,* CLXXXVIII (21 June 1867), 274, and *ibid.* (25 June 1867), 522-4.
89. 3 *Hansard,* CLXXXIII (7 May 1866), 502.
90. 3 *Hansard,* CLXXXVIII (25 June 1867), 532.
91. 3 *Hansard,* CXCII (14 May 1868), 248.
92. Report of the Boundary Commissioners for England and Wales, Sessional Papers, 1867-88, XX, ix.
93. *Ibid.*
94. *Ibid.,* 29.
95. Copy of all Petitions, Letters, Papers, and Memorials laid before the Select Committee on the Boundaries of Boroughs, together with the Reports of the Assistant Commissioners, Sessional Papers, 1867-68, LVI, 193 ff.
96. *Ibid.,* 193.
97. 3 *Hansard,* CXCII (14 May 1868), 250.
98. E.g., Russell Gurney, who had been a member of the Commission, *ibid.,* 272.
99. *Ibid.* (11 June 1868), 1418.
100. *Ibid.* (14 May 1868), 250.
101. 3 *Hansard,* CXCI (20 April 1868), 1014.
102. *Ibid.* (24 March 1868), 196.
103. See Gathorn Hardy's comments when Hibbert asked when the Bill would be brought on, *ibid.* (5 May 1868), 1786.
104. 3 *Hansard,* CXCII (14 May 1868), 248 ff.
105. Report from the Select Committee on Boundaries of Boroughs, Sessional Papers, 1867-68, VIII, vi.
106. Harold E. Gorst, *The Earl of Beaconsfield* (London, 1900), p. 96.
107. *Ibid.*
108. *Ibid.*
109. *Ibid.*
110. *Ibid.*
111. Lord George Hamilton, *Parliamentary Reminiscences and Reflections, 1868-1885* (London, 1917), pp. 12-15.

Chapter 10

1. *The Poll taken at the Election of Three Knights of the Shire for the County of Cambridgeshire and the Isle of Ely* (Cambridge, 1869), *passim,* and *The Poll for the Election of two Knights of the Shire for the Southern Division of the County of Leicester* (Leicester, 1869), *passim.*
2. The points are discussed in chapter 6.

3. *Leicestershire Mercury,* 30 March 1839.
4. These are discussed in chapter 6.
5. This is discussed in chapter 6.
6. The point is discussed in chapter 8.
7. Cox and Grady, *The New Law,* 11th ed., pp. lxxix-lxxx.
8. Morley, *Gladstone,* I, p. 239.
9. John Stuart Mill, *Considerations on Representative Government* (London, 1861), pp. 195-7; 'Thoughts on Parliamentary Reform', *Essays on Politics and Culture by John Stuart Mill,* ed. Gertrude Himmelfarb, (New York, 1963), pp. 325-7. Concerning the date when the pamphlet was written, see F. A. Hayek, *John Stuart Mill and Harriet Taylor* (Chicago, 1951), pp. 188 and 307.
10. 3 *Hansard,* CCIII (27 July 1870), 1031.
11. *Ibid.,* CC (16 March 1870), 32.
12. Report of the Select Committee on Parliamentary and Municipal Elections, Sessional Papers, 1868-9, VIII, q. 6447.
13. As subsequently reported the votes were as follows:

The Hon. Wilbraham Egerton (Cons)	3071
G. C. Legh (Cons)	3057
The Hon. J. B. L. Warren (Lib)	2482

14. Report of the Select Committee on Parliamentary and Municipal Elections, q. 6450.
15. *Ibid.,* q. 6418.
16. *Ibid.,* q. 6462.
17. *Ibid.,* q. 6414.
18. *Ibid.*
19. *Ibid.,* q. 6494.
20. *Ibid.,* q. 6416.
21. *Ibid.,* q. 6451.
22. *Ibid.,* q. 6538.
23. As subsequently reported the votes were as follows:

Colonel Egerton Leigh (Cons)	3508
G. W. Latham (Lib)	2118

24. *National Reform Union, Conference Report* (Manchester, 1875), pp. 32-3.
25. Report of the Select Committee on Parliamentary and Municipal Elections, q. 6419.
26. Qs. 6419, 6427 and 6438.
27. Q. 6428.
28. Qs. 10718-10731; Shorthand Writers' Notes of the Judgments delivered by the Judges selected in pursuance of 'The Parliamentary Elections Act, 1868,' for the Trial of Election Petitions, Sessional Papers, 1868-9, XLVIII, 11-25: Blackburn Election.
29. Report of the Select Committee on Parliamentary and Municipal Elections, q. 9365.
30. Q. 9371.
31. Samuel Bailey, *The Rationale of Political Representation* ... (London, 1835), p. 265.

33. *Ibid.*, p. 15 and pp. 269-70.
34. *Ibid.*, p. 271.
35. Report of the Select Committee on Parliamentary and Municipal Elections, q. 12540.
36. 3 *Hansard,* XVII (25 April 1833), 610.
37. *Ibid.*, C (8 August 1848), 1225 ff.; CLXXI (16 June 1863), 984 ff.; CLXXX (16 June 1865), 421 ff.
38. *Ibid.*, CC (16 March 1870), 13.
39. *Ibid.*
40. 'Ballot not Secret Voting', *Edinburgh Review,* CXXI (April 1870), 564.
41. *Ibid.*, p. 566.
42. *The Times,* 17 March 1869.
43. *Cambridge Chronicle,* 19 September 1868.
44. The point is discussed in chapter 11.
45. The Conservative *Cambridge Chronicle* reported that on the day of the elections of 1868 Hugh Childers 'took his place at the hustings to see that all the tenants [on his Whittlesey estate], as far as could be ascertained, should record their votes for the Liberal candidates.' 5 December 1868. Their charge was clearly a response to the claims of Richard Young, one of the Liberal candidates, that he had been beaten by 'the screw'. He had ostensibly gone into the contest with 4,159 promises of support. *Cambridge Independent Press,* 28 November 1868. If this were the case then 869 voters deserted him at the polls. Charges and countercharges, reflecting contrary interpretations of the same events, filled the local papers for weeks after the contest.
46. 3 *Hansard,* CLXXXXIV (4 March 1869), 652.
47. *Ibid.*, CCIV (20 February 1871), 546.
48. 10 May 1872.
49. 2 August 1869.
50. 10 May 1872.
51. H. C. M. P., *The Ballot, Three Letters* (London, 1870), p. 6.
52. 'The Ballot Bill', *Blackwood's Edinburgh Magazine,* CX (August 1871), 264.
53. 3 *Hansard,* CLXXXIII (27 April 1866), 92-3.
54. In a revealing aside Harriet Martineau observed that many farmers and labourers had deserted their landlords over the corn law question because they found 'that their interests were not identical with those of the receivers of rent, *though it was true that they ought to be.*' *The History of England during the Thirty Years' Peace: 1816-1846* (12 vols., London, 1850), II, p. 611, my emphasis.

Epilogue: The interpretational problem

1. Graham Wallas, *Human Nature in Politics,* 3rd ed. (New York, 1921), p. 25.
2. *Ibid.*, pp. 187-8.
3. *Ibid.*, p. 45.
4. *Ibid.*, p. 46.
5. [Thomas Macaulay] 'Utilitarian Logic and Politics', *Edinburgh Review,*

XCVII (March 1829), esp. 184.

6. [James Mill] ' "Greatest Happiness" Principle', *Westminster Review,* XI (July 1829), 254; 'The pith of the charge against the author of the Essays is, that he has written 'an elaborate treatise on government', and 'deduced the whole science from the assumption, of certain propensities of human nature'. Now in the name of Sir Richard Birnie and all saints, from what else *should* it be deduced?' Original emphasis.

7. Samuel Bailey, *The Rationale of Political Representation* . . ., p. 15.

8. As Macaulay put it, 'If all men preferred the moderate approbation of their neighbours, to any degree of wealth, or grandeur, or sensual pleasure, government would be unnecessary. If all men desired wealth so intensely as to be willing to brave the hatred of their fellow creatures for sixpence, Mr Mill's argument against monarchies and aristocracies would be true to the full extent. But the fact is, that all men have some desires which impel them to injure their neighbours, and some desires which impel them to benefit their neighbours'. 'Utilitarian Logic and Politics', p. 168.

9. *Ibid.,* p. 176, 178 and 184.

10. Mill, *An Essay on Government,* ed. Shields, pp. 62-3, original emphasis.

11. *Ibid.,* p. 49-50.

12. *Ibid.,* p. 51.

13. *Ibid.,* pp. 66-7.

14. Macaulay, 'Utilitarian Logic and Politics', p. 176.

15. Mill, 'Greatest Happiness Principle', p. 69.

16. *Ibid.,* p. 73.

17. *Ibid.,* pp. 73-4.

18. *Ibid.,* p. 75.

19. *Ibid.,* p. 90, emphasis added.

20. *Ibid.*

21. *Ibid.,* p. 89, emphasis added.

22. Mill, *An Essay on Government,* ed. Shields. Editor's 'Introduction' p. 38.

23. *Ibid.*

24. *Ibid.*

25. E.g. Mill, ' "Greatest Happiness" Principle', p. 264.

26. Joseph Hamburger, 'James Mill on Universal Suffrage and the Middle Class', *The Journal of Politics,* XXIV (1962), 173.

27. *Ibid.,* p. 179, note 29.

28. *Ibid.,* p. 172.

29. *Ibid.,* pp. 167-8.

30. *Ibid.,* p. 178.

31. Elie Halevy, *The Growth of Philosophic Radicalism,* tr. Mary Morris (Boston, Massachusetts, 1955), p. 423.

32. *Ibid.,* pp. 75-6, emphasis added.

33. [James Mill] 'Thoughts on Moderate Reform in the House of Commons', *Westminster Review,* XIII (July 1830), 7.

34. James Mill, *The History of British India,* 2nd ed. (London, 1820), III, pp. 451-2.

35. *Ibid.*

36. *Ibid.*
37. See below.
38. 'Think what a society must be, in which all that is respectable in intellect and correct in conduct is the object of display . . . Where such is the style . . . in the leading class – a class not separated from, but intimately mixed with, the rest of the community, the imitation of it is inevitable.' [James Mill] 'Aristocracy', *London Review,* II (January 1836), 290-91.
39. Macaulay, 'Utilitarian Logic and Politics, 184. The passage to which Macaulay referred is that quoted on pp. 423 above.
40. 'Coleridge', *Essays on Politics and Culture,* ed. Gertrude Himmelfarb, p. 142.
41. John Stuart Mill, *Autobiography* (London, 1873), p. 49.
42. 'Coleridge', p. 122, emphases added.
43. 'The Spirit of the Age', *Essays on Politics and Culture,* ed. Gertrude Himmelfarb, p. 36, original emphasis.
44. *Ibid.*, original emphasis.
45. *Ibid.*, p. 17, original emphasis.
46. *Ibid.*, p. 44.
47. This claim is made on his behalf by Wendell Robert Carr, 'James Mill's Politics Reconsidered: Parliamentary Reform and the Triumph of Truth', *The Historical Journal,* XIV (1971), 580.
48. 3 *Hansard,* XVII (25 April 1833), 610.
49. [Francis William Newman] 'The Tendencies of England', *Westminster Review,* LVIII (July 1852), 67, original emphasis.
50. *Ibid.*, p. 68.
51. Bagehot, *The English Constitution,* pp. 262-3.
52. *Ibid.,* pp. 266-7.
53. Introduction to Walter Bagehot, *The English Constitution,* 2nd ed. pp. xxi-xxii.
54. *Ibid.*, pp. xii-xiii.
55. *Ibid.*, pp. xiv.
56. Sir George Cornewall Lewis, *An Essay on the Influence of Authority in Matters of Opinion,* 2nd ed. (London, 1875), p. 157. The passage comes from Bailey, *The Rationale of Political Representation,* pp. 269-71.
57. Bailey, *The Rationale of Political Representation,* p. 271, emphasis added.
58. Lewis, *An Essay on the Influence of Authority,* p. 147.
59. Walter Bagehot, *Parliamentary Reform: an essay* (London, [1859]), p. 19.
60. *Ibid.*, emphasis added.
61. *Ibid.*, pp. 19-20, emphasis added.
62. [William Greg] 'Parliamentary Purification', *Edinburgh Review,* XCVIII (October 1853) 574, original emphasis. The article was attributed to Greg by Mill, who, in a letter to his wife of 9 January 1854, also remarked that Greg must have seen a letter of their own on the same subject, '. . . for he has adopted nearly every idea in the letter almost in the very words'. Hayek, *John Stuart Mill,* p. 187.
63. *Ibid.*, p. 576.
64. *Ibid.*, p. 577.
65. The passage is quoted on p. 426 above.

66. 'Thoughts on Parliamentary Reform', *Essays on Politics and Culture*, ed. Gertrude Himmelfarb, pp. 325-7; Mill, *Considerations on Representative Government*, pp. 195-7.

67. Greg, 'Parliamentary Purification', p. 586.

68. Earl Grey, *Parliamentary Government Considered with Reference to a Reform of Parliament* (London, 1858), p. 120.

69. Gash, *Politics in the Age of Peel,* p. 122.

70. James Mill, 'Thoughts on Moderate Reform in the House of Commons', pp. 7-8.

71. Hartington's Draft Report of the Select Committee on Parliamentary and Municipal Elections, Sessional Papers, 1868-69, VIII, xvii. The phrase appeared in the final Report of the Committee, Sessional Papers, 1870, vi, 135.

72. Newman, 'The Tendencies of England', p. 68.

73. Bagehot, *Parliamentary Reform,* p. 4.

74. W. E. Gladstone, 'The county franchise and Mr. Lowe thereon', *Nineteenth Century,* II (November 1877), 541.

Works Cited

Manuscript Collections

Adeane Papers, Babraham, Cambridgeshire
Burrows Papers, Devonshire Record Office
Cartwright Papers, Northamptonshire Record Office
Daventry Papers, Northamptonshire Record Office
Fitzwilliam Papers, Northamptonshire Record Office
Fortescue Papers, Castle Hill, Devonshire
Gotch Papers, Northamptonshire Record Office
Hickleton Papers, Garrowsby, Yorkshire
Holland Papers, British Library
Iddesleigh Papers, British Library
Knightley Papers, Northamptonshire Record Office
Nostell Papers, Nostell Priory, Yorkshire
Peel Papers, British Library
St. Aldwyn Papers, Williamstrip Park, Gloucestershire
Salisbury Papers, Christ Church, Oxford
Vivian Papers, Cornwall Record Office
Vyvyan Papers, Cornwall Record Office

Sessional (or Parliamentary) Papers

1813-14, III. Report from the Select Committee on Petitions relating to the Corn Laws of this Kingdom.

1814-15, V. Report from the Lords' Committee appointed to enquire into the State of the Growth, Commerce and Consumption of Grain, and all Laws relating thereto, . . .

1829, X. First Report of H. M. Commissioners appointed to enquire into the Laws of England respecting Real Property.

1830-31, II. A Bill to amend the Representation of the People in England and Wales.

1831, III. A Bill to amend the Representation of the People in England and Wales.

1831-32, XXXVI. Report from Edward J. Littleton, Esq., Captain F. Beaufort, R.N., and Lieut. T. Drummond, R. E., to the Right Honourable Viscount Melbourne, on proposed Boundaries of the Boroughs of England and Wales, 10 February 1832.

Lord Melbourne to Lieutenant R. Drummond, R. E., 8 August 1831.

Instructions, etc. ... addressed to Gentlemen engaged in collecting Information respecting the Boundaries of the Cities and Boroughs of England and Wales, 23 August 1831.

Instructions transmitted by direction of Lord Melbourne, 24 October 1831

Instructions transmitted by direction of Lord Melbourne, 24 November 1831.

1831-32, XXXVIII. General Remarks on the Proposed Division of the ... Counties.

, XL. Reports from Commissioners on Proposed Division of Counties and Boundaries of Boroughs.

1833, V. Report from the Select Committee on Agriculture.

XXVII, 21 ff. Number of Electors Inrolled in Each County, City, etc. ... under 2 & 3 William IV, c. 45.

1834, IX, 263 ff. Report from the Select Committee on Election Expenses.

1836, XLIII, 373 ff. Number qualified to vote at the last General Election; also Gross Number who actually voted. . .

1837-38, XLIV, 553 ff. Return from every County, City and Borough of the Number of Electors registered in each, for 1836 and 1837, classifying them under their respective qualifications . . .

1844, XXXVIII, 427 ff. Abstract return of the Number of Electors on the Register for each County, City, etc. in England, Wales and Scotland in the years 1839-40 and 1842-43, distinguishing their different Qualifications . . .

1845, XII, 111 ff. Report from the Select Committee of the House of Lords appointed to inquire into the expediency of a legislative enactment being introduced to enable possessors of entailed estates to charge such estates with a sum, to be limited, for the purpose of draining and otherwise improving the same.

1846, VIII, 175 ff. Report from the Select Committee on Votes of Electors.

1847, XXXIV, 301 ff. Return of the number of applications that have been made for advances of Public Money under the Act of the last session, c. 101, in England, Ireland, and Scotland, respective, the total sum applied for in each country, and the amounts sanctioned by the Government.

XLVI, 335 ff. Return of the Number of Electors on the Register.

1847-48, VII. Report from the Select Committee on Agricultural Customs.

1852, XLII, 303 ff. Abstract of return of the Number of County Electors in each County or Division of a County in England and Wales registered for Property situated within the Limits of any Borough; distinguishing the Total Number registered in each Constituency, and the Number of County Electors registered for Property in each Borough.

1852-53, LXXXIX. Religious Worship (England and Wales)

1854, V, 375 ff. Bill further to amend the laws relating to the Representation of People in England and Wales.

LIII, 211 ff. Return of the Number of Electors in each County and Parliamentary Division of a County in England and Wales, registered at the last Registration of 1853-54, distinguishing the Number under each Qualification.

1854-55, VII, 245 ff. Report from the Select Committee of the House of Lords appointed to consider whether it would not be desirable that the powers now vested in the companies for the improvement of land should be made subject to general regulation.

1857 (2nd Session), XXXIV, 83 ff. Return of the Number of Electors in every County and Division of a County in Great Britain, according to the register of electors for 1850, 1851, 1852, 1853, 1854, 1855 and 1856, and as they appear in the Register of Electors for 1856 and 1857, . . .

1857-58, XLVI, 571 ff. Number of Registered Electors in England and Wales, who are entitled (by the Provisions of the Act 2 William IV, c. 45) to vote at Elections for Knights of the Shire, in respect of Freehold or other Property situate within the precincts of any City or Borough that returns a Member or Members to Parliament; . . .

1859, II, 649 ff. A Bill to amend the Laws relating to the Representation of the People in England and Wales, . . .

1860, V, 597 ff. Bill further to amend the Laws relating to the Representation of the People in England and Wales.

, XII. Report from the Select Committee of the House of Lords appointed to inquire what would be the probable increase of the number of electors in the counties and boroughs of England and Wales from a reduction of the franchise, . . .

1864, X, 403 ff. Report of the Select Committee on Registration of County Voters.

1865, XLIV, 549 ff. Return, in a Tabular Form, for the Year 1864, of the Number of Electors on the Register of each County in England and Wales, exhibiting the several Qualifications, . . .

1866, V, 33 ff. A Bill for the Redistribution of Seats. 87 ff. A Bill to extend the right of voting at elections of Members of Parliament in England and Wales.

LVII, 15 ff. Return in respect of each county or electoral division of a county in England and Wales, of the number of persons on the register having a qualification, whose qualifying property is situate within the limits of a Parliamentary city or borough; . . .

569 ff. Return showing Population of Counties and Parliamentary Divisions, of Parliamentary Cities and Boroughs in the United Kingdom in 1821, 1831, and 1861; Number of Members under Reform Act; Increase and Decrease of Population since 1831; Number of Electors in 1832 and 1862; . . .

1867-68, XX. Report of the Boundary Commissioners of England and Wales.

LVI, 183 ff. Copy of all Petitions, Letters, Papers, and Memorials laid before the Select Committee on Boundaries of Boroughs, together with the Reports of the Assistant Commissioners.

1868-69, VII, 301 ff. Report from the Select Committee on Registration of Voters.

VIII. Report from the Select Committee on Parliamentary and Municipal Elections.

1868-69, XLVIII. Shorthand Writers' Notes of the Judgements delivered by the Judges selected in pursuance of 'The Parliamentary Elections Act, 1868', for the Trial of Election Petitions.

1870, VI, 191 ff. Report from the Select Committee on Registration of Voters in Counties (England and Wales); . . .

Parliamentary Debates

Hansard's Parliamentary Debates
The Mirror of Parliament, J. H. Barrow, (ed.), London.

Directories

The New Cambridge Guide (Cambridge 1826).
Gardiner, Robert, *History, Gazetteer and Directory of Cambridgeshire* (Peterborough 1851).
Kelly, E. P. (ed.), *The Post Office Directory of Cambridgeshire* (London, 1846).
Post Office Directory of . . . Hunts (London [1847-48]).
Whelan, William, and Co., *History, Gazetteer and Directory of Northamptonshire* (London, 1849).

Newspapers

Published in Birmingham
Aris's Birmingham Gazette
Birmingham Journal

Published in Cambridge
Cambridge Advertiser
Cambridge Chronicle
Cambridge Independent Press

Published in Leicester
Leicester Chronicle
Leicestershire Mercury

Published in London
Bell's Weekly Messenger
John Bull
Examiner
The Farmer's Magazine
Law Reports, Common Pleas
Law Times
Mark Lane Express
Morning Chronicle
Morning Herald
Morning Journal
Morning Post
Political Register
Standard
The Times

Pollbooks

Cambridgeshire
A Copy of the Poll for Knights of the Shire for Cambridgeshire . . . (London, 1722).
The Poll for the Election of Two Representatives in Parliament for the County of Cambridgeshire . . . (Cambridge, 1780).

A State of Polls for the Two Elections of Representatives in Parliament for the County of Cambridgeshire . . . (London, 1802).

The Poll for Election of Two Representatives in Parliament for the County of Cambridge (Cambridge, 1826).

The Poll for Two Knights of the Shire for the County of Cambridge (Cambridge, 1830).

The Poll of an Election of a Representative in Parliament for the County of Cambridgeshire (Cambridge, 1831).

The Poll of the Election of Three Knights of the Shire for the County of Cambridgeshire (London, 1833).

The Poll of the Election of Three Knights of the Shire for the County of Cambridgeshire (Cambridge, 1835).

The Poll taken at the Election of Three Knights of the Shire for the County of Cambridgeshire and the Isle of Ely (Cambridge, 1869).

Essex

The Poll for Two Knights of the Shire . . . for the County of Essex (Chelmsford, 1830).

Gloucestershire

A Correct List of the Poll at the Election of a Knight of the Shire for the Eastern Division of the County of Gloucester . . . (Gloucester, [1854]).

Huntingdonshire

A Copy of the Poll for Two Knights of the Shire for the County of Huntingdon (Huntingdon, [1826]).

A Copy of the Poll, taken at the General Election for the County of Huntingdon (London [1830]).

The Poll for Two Knights of the Shire for the County of Huntingdon (Cambridge, [1831]).

Copy of the Poll taken at the General Election for the County of Huntingdon (Huntingdon, [1837]).

Leicestershire

The Poll for the Election of Two Knights of the Shire to serve in Parliament for the Southern Division of the County of Leicester (Leicester, 1841).

The Poll taken at the Election of a Knight of the Shire, November 28, 1867 . . . (Leicester, n.d.).

The Poll for the Election of two Knights of the Shire for the Southern Division of the County of Leicester (Leicester, 1869).

The Poll taken at the Election of a Knight of the Shire (Leicester, 1870).

Lincolnshire

North Lincolnshire Poll Book (Bolston, 1852).

Norfolk

The Poll for a Knight of the Shire for the Eastern Division of the County of Norfolk (Norwich, 1858).

Northamptonshire
  A Copy of the Poll of the Freeholders as taken at the Election of Knights of the Shire
    for the County of Northamptonshire, 1831 . . . (Northampton, 1832).
  Copy of the Poll, for Two Knights, for the Northern Division of the County of
    Northampton . . . 1832 . . . (Kettering, 1833).
  A Copy of the Poll, taken at the General Election for the Northern Division of the
    County of Northampton; . . . 1835 . . . (Northampton, 1836).
  A Copy of the Poll for one Knight of the Shire, for the Northern Division of the
    County of Northampton (Northampton, 1858).

Nottinghamshire
  South Nottinghamshire Election, The Poll Book (Newark, 1846).

  Oxfordshire
  The Copy of the Poll of the Freeholders for Knights of the Shire for the County of
    Oxford . . . (Oxford, 1831).
  The Copy of the Poll of the Freeholders for Knights of the Shire for the County of
    Oxford . . . (Oxford, 1837).

Other Materials

[Alison, Archibald] 'On Parliamentary Reform and the French Revolution',
    Blackwood's Edinburgh Magazine, XXX (October 1831), 600-15.
Anon., *Essay on the Repeal of the Malt Tax* (London, 1846).
Anon., 'Improvement of Landed Property', *Westminster Review*, XLVIII
    (October 1847), 1-23.
Anon., 'Review of Sir Humphry Davy, *Elements of Agricultural Chemistry*',
    Quarterly Review, XI (July 1814), 318-31.
Argyle, Duke of, 'The Agricultural Holdings Act of 1875', *Contemporary
    Review*, XXVII (1876), 497-521.
Aspinall, A., (ed.), *Three Early Nineteenth Century Diaries*, (London, 1952).
    (ed.), *The Correspondence of Charles Arbuthnot* (London, 1941).
Atkinson, H. T., *Registration Appeals determined by the Court of Common Pleas,
    under the 6 Vict. c. 18 argued during the Michaelmas Term, 1843*, [London,
    1844].
Aydelotte, William O., 'A data archive for modern British political history',
    in Val R. Lorwin and Jacob M. Price, (eds.), *The Dimensions of the Past:
    materials, problems and opportunities for quantitative work in history*, (New
    Haven, 1972).
[Aytoun, E. E.] 'British agriculture and foreign competition', *Blackwood's
    Edinburgh Magazine*, LXVII (January 1850), 222-248.
Bagehot, Walter, *The English Constitution*, new ed., (London, 1872). *Essay on
    Parliamentary Reform* (London, 1859).
Bailey, Samuel, *The Rationale of Political Representation* . . . (London, 1835).
Bamford Francis and Wellington, Duke of, (eds.), *The Journals of Mrs.
    [Harriet] Arbuthnot*, (2 vols., London 1950).
Barnes, D. G., *A History of the English Corn Laws from 1660 to 1846*, reprinted
    (London, 1960).

Bean, W. W., *The Parliamentary Representation of the Six Northern Counties of England,* (Hall, 1890).

Bear, W. E., 'The revolt of the counties', *Fortnightly Review,* N.S., **XXVII** (1880), 720-5.

Blaug, M., 'The myth of the Old Poor Law and the Making of the New', *The Journal of Economic History,* **XXIII** (1963), 151-84.
'The Poor Law Report Re-examined', *The Journal of Economic History,* **XXIV** (1964), 229-45.

Briggs, Asa, 'The background of the parliamentary reform movement in three English cities', *Cambridge Historical Journal,* **X** (1952), 293-317.

Brock, Michael, *The Great Reform Act* (London, 1973).

Brock, W. G., *Lord Liverpool and Liberal Toryism* (Cambridgeshire, 1941).

Brougham, Henry, 'The reformed parliament – the ballot', *Edinburgh Review,* **LVI** (January 1833), 543-64.

Brundage, Anthony, 'The landed interest and the new poor law: a reappraisal of the revolution in government', *The English Historical Review,* **LXXXVII** (1972), 27-48.

Buckingham and Chandos, Duke of, *Memoirs of the Courts and Cabinets of William IV and Victoria* (2 Vols., London, 1861).

Burke, Sir Bernard, *History of the Landed Gentry of Great Britain and Ireland,* 8th ed. (London, 1894).
History of the Landed Gentry of Great Britain and Ireland, 13th ed. (London, 1921).

Butt, G., *Suggestions as to the Conduct and Management of a County Contested Election* (London, 1826).

C., H., M.P., *The Ballot, Three Letters* (London, 1870).

Caird, James, *English Agriculture in 1850-51* (London, 1852).

Cannon, John, *Parliamentary Reform, 1640-1832* (Cambridge, 1973).

Carr, Wendell Robert, 'James Mill's Politics Reconsidered: Parliamentary Reform and the Triumph of Truth', *The Historical Journal,* **XIV** (1971), 553-80.

Cayley, E. S., *A Letter to H. Handley, Esq., M.P. . . .* (London, 1836).
Reasons for the Formation of the Agricultural Society (London, 1844).

Clarke, Sir Edward, *The Story of My Life* (London, 1918).

Conacher, J. B., *The Aberdeen Coalition 1852-1855: a study of mid-nineteenth century party politics.* (Cambridge, 1968).
The Peelites and the Party System, 1846-52 (Newton Abbot, 1972).

Cook, D., 'Parliamentary History since 1660', *Victoria County History of Cambridge and the Isle of Ely* (London, 1948).

Coser, Lewis A., *The Functions of Social Conflict* (London, 1964).

Cox, Edward W., *The Law and Practice of Registration and Elections,* 5th ed. (London, 1847).

Cox, Edward W. and Grady, Standish Grove, *The New Law and Practice of Registration and Elections,* 10th ed. (London, 1868); 11th ed. (London, 1872).

Cox, Homersham, *A History of the Reform Bills of 1866 and 1867* (London, ·1868).

Dicey, A. W. *Introduction to the Study of the Law of the Constitution,* 8th ed.

(London, 1926).

Elvins, W. Brian, 'The Reform Movement and County Politics in Cornwall, 1809-52', Unpublished M. A. thesis, University of Birmingham, 1959.

Fairlie, S., 'The Nineteenth Century Corn Law Reconsidered', *The Economic History Review*, 2nd ser., XVIII (1965), 562-75.

Freeman, E. A., *The Growth of the English Constitution from the Earliest Times* (London, 1872).

[Fullarton, John, or Miller, John] 'Internal Policy', *Quarterly Review*, XXXXII (January 1830), 228-77. (See Walter E. Houghton (ed.), *The Wellesley Index of Victorian Periodicals*, Toronto, 1966).

Gash, Norman, *Politics in the Age of Peel* (London, 1953).

Gillespie, F. E., *Labor and Politics in England, 1850-1867* (Durham, North Carolina, 1927).

Gladstone, W. E., 'The county franchise and Mr. Lowe thereon', *Nineteenth Century*, II (November 1877), 537-60.

[Gleig, G. R.] 'The Ballot Bill', *Blackwood's Edinburgh Magazine*, CX (August 1871), 257-70.

Gorst, Harold E., *The Earl of Beaconsfield* (London, 1900).

Graham, Sir James, *Corn and Currency*, new ed. (London, 1826).

[Greg, W. R.] 'Parliamentary Purification', *Edinburgh Review*, XCVIII (October 1853), 566-624.

Grey, Earl, *Parliamentary Government Considered with Reference to the Reform of Parliament* (London, 1859).

(ed.), *The Reform Act, 1832: The Correspondence of the late Earl Grey with his Majesty King William IV and with Sir Herbert Taylor* (2 vols., London, 1867).

Halevy, Elie, *The Growth of Philosophic Radicalism*, tr. by Mary Morris (Boston, Massachusetts, 1955).

A History of the English People in the Nineteenth Century, vol. II: *The Liberal Awakening*, tr. by E. I. Watkin, 2nd ed. (London, 1949).

Hamburger, Joseph, *James Mill and the Art of Revolution* (New Haven, 1963).

'James Mill on Universal Suffrage and the Middle Classes', *The Journal of Politics*, XXIV (1962), 167-90.

Hamilton, Lord George, *Parliamentary Reminiscences and Reflections, 1868-1885* (London, 1917).

Hanham, H. J., *Elections and Party Management* (London, 1959).

Harrison, Royden, 'The 10th April of Spencer Walpole: the problem of revolution in relation to reform, 1865-1867', in *Before the Socialists: studies in labour and politics, 1861-1881* (London, 1965).

Hayek, F. A., *John Stuart Mill and Harriet Taylor* (Chicago, 1951).

Hennock, E. P., 'The sociological premises of the first Reform Act: a critical note', *Victorian Studies*, XIV (1971), 321-7.

Himmelfarb, Gertrude, 'The politics of democracy: the English Reform Act of 1867', *The Journal of British Studies*, VI (1966), 97-138.

Howitt, William, *The Rural Life of England* (London, 1840).

Hughes, Edward, 'Sir Charles Trevelyan and Civil Service Reform, 1853-5', *The English Historical Review*, LXIV (1949), 53-88, 203-234.

Jones, I. G., 'Merioneth Politics in Mid Nineteenth Century', *Journal of* the Merioneth Historical and Record Society, V (1968), 273-334.

Jones, W. D. and Erickson, A., *The Peelites, 1846-1837* (Columbus, Ohio, 1792).

Johnstone, William, *England as it is,* . . . (London, 1851).

[Johnstone, William] 'The Present Crisis', *Blackwood's Edinburgh Magazine,* XXXVIII (October   ).

Jennings, L. J. (ed.), *The Croker Papers,* 2nd ed. (2 vols., London 1885).

Keane, D. D. and Grant, James, *Reports of Cases argued and determined in the Court of Common Pleas, on Appeal from the Decisions of the Revising Barristers* . . . (London, 1863).

Kebbel, T. E., 'The county system', *Fortnightly Review,* N.S., XXXIII (1883), 417-36.

Kemp, Betty, 'Reflections on the repeal of the corn laws', *Victorian Studies,* V (1962), 189-204.

Kinnaird, Lord, *Profitable investment of capital, or eleven years practical experience in farming: a letter from Lord Kinnaird to his tenantry,* 2nd ed. (Edinburgh, 1849).

Lefevre, Charles Shaw, *Remarks on the Present State of Agriculture* (London, 1836).

Lewis, Sir George Cornewall, *An Essay on the Influence of Authority in Matters of Opinion,* 2nd ed. (London, 1875).

Lutwyche, Alfred J. P., *Reports of Cases argued and determined in the Court of Common Pleas on Appeal from Decisions of the Revising Barristers* (2 vols., London, 1847-54).

McCalmont's Parliamentary Poll Book, British Election Results 1832-1918 ed. J. Vincent and M. Stenton, 8th ed. (Brighton, 1971).

McCord, Norman, *The Anti-Corn Law League 1838-1846* (London, 1958).

McGregor, O. R., 'Introduction, Part II: after 1815', Lord Ernle, *English Farming Past and Present,* 6th ed., (London, 1961).

[Macaulay, T. B.] 'Utilitarian Logic and Politics', *Edinburgh Review,* XCVII (March 1829), 159-89.

Mackintosh, Sir James] 'Parliamentary Reform', *Edinburgh Review,* XIV (July 1809), 277-306.

[Maitland, Edward] 'Ballot not secret voting', *Edinburgh Review,* CXXI (April 1870), 540-66.

Martineau, Harriet, *The History of England during the Thirty Years' Peace: 1816-1846* (2 vols., London 1850).

Mechi, I. J., *Letters on Agricultural Improvement* (London, 1844).

Midwinter, E. C., *Social Administration in Lancashire, 1830-60* (Manchester, 1969).

[Mill, James] 'Aristocracy', *London Review,* II (January 1836), 283-306.

Mill, James, *An Essay on Government,* ed. Currin V. Shields (New York, 1955).

[Mill, James] 'Greatest Happiness Principle', *Westminster Review,* XI (July 1829), 254-68.

Mill, James, *The History of British India,* 2nd ed. (6 vols., London, 1820).

[Mill, James] 'Thoughts on Moderate Reform in the House of Commons', *Westminster Review,* XIII (July 1830).

Mill, John Stuart, *Autobiography,* (London, 1873).

'Coleridge', *Essays on Politics and Culture by John Stuart Mill,* ed. Gertrude Himmelfarb (Garden City, New York, 1963), 132-86.

'The Spirit of the Age', *Ibid.,* 3-50.

'Thoughts on Parliamentary Reform', *Ibid.,*

Considerations on Representative Government (London, 1861).

[Miller, John or Fullarton, John] 'Internal Policy', *Quarterly Review,* **XXXXII** (January 1830), 228-77.

Milton-Smith, John 'Earl Grey's Cabinet and the Objects of Parliamentary Reform', *The Historical Journal,* XV (1972), 55-74.

Mitchell, Austin, *The Whigs in Opposition, 1815-1830* (Oxford 1967).

Moore, D. C., 'Concession or cure: the sociological premises of the first Reform Act', *The Historical Journal,* IX (1966), 39-59.

'The other face of reform', *Victorian Studies,* V (1961), 7-34.

Morley, John, *The Life of Richard Cobden* (London, 1920).

The Life of William Ewart Gladstone (3 vols., London, 1903).

Morton, John, *On the Nature and Property of Soils;* . . . 2nd ed. (London, 1840).

National Reform Union, *Conference Report* (Manchester, 1875).

[Newman, Francis William] 'The Tendencies of England', *Westminster Review,* LVIII (July 1852), 110-28.

Nossiter, T. J., 'Aspects of electoral behavior in English constituencies, 1832-1868', in Erik Allardt and Stein Rokkan (eds.), *Mass Politics: Studies in Political Sociology,* (New York, 1970).

Oldfield, T. H. B., *History of the Boroughs* (3 vols., London, 1792).

The Representative History of Great Britain and Ireland (6 vols., London, 1816).

Page, William, and Proby, Granville, 'Parliamentary History', *Victoria History of the County of Huntingdon* (London, 1932) II, 22-61.

Parsons, Talcott, 'Voting and the equilibrium of the American Political System' in Eugene Burdick and J. A. Brodbeck, (eds.), *American Voting Behavior* (Glencoe 1959), pp. 80-120.

Patterson, A. Temple, *Radical Leicester* (Leicester, 1954).

Peel, Sir Robert, 'Account of a Field Thorough-Drained, at Drayton, in Staffordshire', *The Journal of the Royal Agricultural Society,* III (1842),

Porritt, Edward, *The Unreformed House of Commons,* 2 vols., (Cambridge, 1903).

Pusey, Philip, 'Some Introductory Remarks on the Present State of Agriculture as a Science in England', *The Journal of the Royal Agricultural Society,* I (1840),

[de Quincey, Thomas] 'France and England', *Blackwood's Edinburgh Magazine,* XXVIII (October, 1830), 699-718.

'French Revolution', *Blackwood's Edinburgh Magazine,* XXVIII (September 1830), 542-58.

Read, Donald, 'Chartism in Manchester', in Asa Briggs, (ed.), *Chartist Studies* (London, 1959), 29-64.

Ricardo, David, *Influence of a low price of corn on the 4th ed.* (London 1822), *profits of stock,* E. C. K. Gonner (ed.) reprinted in *Economic Essays,* (London, 1923).

On Protection to Agriculture, 4th ed. (London, 1822), reprinted. E. C. K.

Gonner, (ed.), *Economic Essays*, (London, 1923).

Rimmer, W. G., *Marshall's of Leeds, Flax Spinners, 1788-1886* (Cambridge, 1960).

Roebuck, John Arthur, *History of the Whig Ministry of 1830* (2 vols., London, 1852).

[Robinson, David] 'The Reform of the House of Commons', *Blackwood's Edinburgh Magazine*, XXVII (April 1830), 640-58.

[Russell, Lord John] *Essays and Sketches of Life and Character by a Gentleman who has left his lodgings* (London, 1820).

Seymour, Charles, *Electoral Reform in England and Wales* (New Haven, 1915).

Shields, Currin V., 'Editor's Introduction', to James Mill, *An Essay on Government* (New York, 1955).

Smith, F. B., *The Making of the Second Reform Bill* (London, 1966).

Smith, Henry Stooks, *The Parliaments of England from 1715 to 1847*, ed. F. W. S. Craig, (Chichester, 1973).

Spring, David, *The English Landed Estate in the Nineteenth Century: Its Administration* (Baltimore, 1963).

Thomas, J. Alun, 'The system of registration and the development of party organization', *History*, XXV (1940), 81-98.

Thompson, F. M. L., *English Landed Society in the Nineteenth Century* (London, 1963).

'The Second Agricultural Revolution', *The Economic History Review*, 2nd ser., XXI (1968), 62-77.

'Whigs and Liberals in the West Riding, 1830-1860', *The English Historical Review*, LXXXXIV (1959), 214-39.

Turberville, Arthur Stanley, and Beckwith, Frank, 'Leeds and Parliamentary Reform, 1820-1832', *Thoresby Society Publications*, XLI (1946), 1-88.

Underhill, Arthur, 'Changes in the English Law of Real Property during the Nineteenth Century', *Select Essays in Anglo-American Legal History* (3 vols., Boston, Massachusetts, 1909).

'Property', *Law Quarterly Review*, LI (1935),

Vincent, J. R., *Pollbooks: How Victorians Voted* (Cambridge, 1967).

Vyvyan, Sir Richard, *A Letter from Sir Richard Vyvyan, Bart., M.P., to his Constituents* (London, 1842).

Wakefield, C. M., *Life of Thomas Attwood* (London, 1885).

Wallas, Graham, *Human Nature in Politics*, 3rd ed. (New York, 1921).

Wellington, Duke of (ed.), *Wellington, Arthur Duke of, Despatches, Correspondence, and Memoranda of Field Marshal*, (8 vols., London, 1867-1880).

Wood, Anthony, *Nineteenth Century Britain, 1815-1914* (London, 1960).

Woodbridge, George, *The Reform Bill of 1832* (New York, 1970).

Woodfall, William, *The Law of Landlord and Tenant*, 7th ed., (London, 1829).

Woodward, E. L., *The Age of Reform, 1815-1870* (Oxford, 1949).

Index

Aboyne, Earls of, 42

Absenteeism, 314-15, 317

Acland, Sir Thomas, 307-8

Adderley, Sir Charles, 392

Adeane, Henry John, and borough freeholders clause, 167, 169; in Cambridgeshire elections, 41, 46, 49-53, 61-2, 64, 80, 83-8 *passim*, 90, 102

Agricultural-aristocratic 'party', 51, 57

Agricultural associations, 56, 131, 339, 348, 351-4

Agricultural Holdings Act 1883, 360

Agricultural revolution, second, 332, 340, 354

Agriculture, agricultural practices; barley growing, 213-14; depression in, 214-15, 325, 338-40, 348; Government policies for, 351-5; investment in 345-6, 355-62; and legislation, 330; report on, 336; technological development in 200, 211-12, 328-9, 331-2, 339-47, 350, 355-60

Alliances, *see* Coalitions

Allix, John Peter, 54, 57-8, 64, 83

Alexander v Newman, 274-5, 278-9

Althorp, Lord, later 3rd Earl Spencer, 110; and agriculture, 349-50, 352-4; and borough freeholders clause, 145, 152, 154-8, 160-4 *passim*, 169-70, 177, 239, 272; on boundaries question, 178-9; and Chandos amendment, 166-8 *passim*, 347; and currency reform, 335,

338; on electoral registers, 182-3; in Northamptonshire elections, 103-5, 108, 113, 128, 130-2 *passim*; as reformer, 187; and transfer taxes, 221

Anglicans, 9-10, 48

Anti-Corn Law league, 261, 271, 277, 330, 349, 353, 363-5,

Anti-League, *see* Central Agricultural Protection Association

Anti-reformers, 148-9, 153, 185, 188; Associations of 236; and borough freeholders clause, 236; coalition of 148, 157-9; and influence, 234-5, 236-9; and introduction of Reform Bill, 224-8

Arbuthnot, Charles, 139, 215, 218

Arbuthnot, Mrs, 219

Argyle, Duke of, 362

Aristocracy, and close boroughs, 218; criticism of, 421, 426-8 *passim*, 439; and deference, 435; influence of 162, 167, 180-1, 196, 233, 349; and middle class, 223; *also see* Landed interest; Landowners

Aspinall, A., 203

Astbury v Henderson, 276, 279

Attwood, Matthias, 335

Attwood, Thomas, 202, 210-11, 215, 226-7, 333-5, 337

Bagehot, Walter, 12-13, 250, 344, 382, 434-9, 445-6

Other History Titles

Michael J. CULLEN
**The Statistical Movement in Early Victorian Britain: The
Foundations of Empirical Social Research**

The early Victorians, in an age of serious social tension and the threat of tumultuous
unrest, found it imperative to know the reasons behind multiplying challenges to their
society. Faced with 'the condition of England' question, they sought for its causes. At
the root of that search was the cluster of values known as the ideology of
'improvement'. This book is the first deep analysis of the ideas, institutions and men
which coalesced into the characteristically Victorian statistical movement to probe,
measure, quantify and reform, − 'to prevent misfortune and vice, sickness and
improvidence'.

Dr. Cullen, through close analysis of the empirical enquiries carried out by
government agencies, statistical societies and private men, explores the motives of
change. Trained in both history and mathematics, he grounds his work in voluminous
sources. It fills a substantial gap and is based on work originally carried out at the
University of Edinburgh which won Dr. Cullen the Jeremiah Dalziel Prize in History
for outstanding work.

The book is set in two chief contexts: the statistical movement is seen as an
outgrowth of a long period of development in the use of quantification to study social
problems (here surveyed) and it is seen as a response to the social and political needs of
the time when information and analysis was crucial to government. Dr. Cullen's book
forges a valuable intellectual link in the chain that unites the earliest forms of social
enquiry with Henry Mayhew, Charles Booth, Seebohm Rowntree and the modern
statistical sciences of society.

'This is an interesting and scholarly book on a greatly neglected subject.'
Professor Asa Briggs.

Tom J. NOSSITER
**Influence, Opinion and Political Idioms in Reformed England:
Case Studies from the North-East, 1832–1874**

How did the Victorian political system of popular democracy actually work? What
was its precise nature in town and country in a variety of situations? What was the
impact − and in what proportions − of 'influence', the purse, and the exercise of the
individual political conscience? Aside from the legislative framework, what was the
local reality and what were the underlying conceptions of politics which guided actions?
This study seeks to answer these important questions.

Dr. Nossiter makes rich use of poll-book, which recorded votes until 1872 − and shows that the interaction between magnate influence, corrupt practices and opinion was a complex one. Nevertheless, he finds patterns in voting behaviour able to be expressed in terms both of social structure of individual constituencies, and the conceptions men held about the nature of politics. Industrialisation and urbanisation played their part, but Dr. Nossiter argues that the key factor was the distribution of social and economic power. Dr. Nossiter's hypothesis is that influence, corruption and opinion were expressions of basic differences in man's conceptualisation of the nature of society, which themselves gave rise to typical forms of political organisation.

Influence, Opinion and Political Idioms in Reformed England should have a wide appeal to historians and political scientists, the more so as it is written in a lively as well as a scholarly way.

Michael BARKER
Gladstone and Radicalism; The Reconstruction of Liberal Policy in Britain 1885-1894

New study of the final decade of Gladstone's political life, the most controversial and yet neglected episode in the long and distinguished career of the man who was four times Prime Minister.

Those years are rife with paradoxes: why should it have been Gladstone rather than Joseph Chamberlain who absorbed radical doctrines, stood in the van of many Labour and trade union issues, and extinguished the control of the landed whig aristocracy?

Dr. Barker, University of Wales Fellow in History, examines these paradoxes, and investigates the sources both of Liberal intellectual vitality and of political weakness. He undertakes the first comprehensive survey of the composite nature of the party, which drastically influenced policy formation and its political fortunes after Gladstone's death.

The author also offers the first widespread survey of Liberal pressure groups, stressing the manner in which the composite nature of the party drastically influenced the formation of policy. Semi-autonomous units in Wales and London posed peculiar difficulties for the party leaders: the conflicting aims of talented Radical idealists and Fabian Socialists, and the disruptive role of the Labouchere faction, produced an embarrassing degree of discord.

Barker maintains that these divisions were as much a source of intellectual vitality as the political weakness, and substantiates this proposition by undertaking a full examination of the ambiguous role allotted to the National Liberal Federation. This is a work whose quality and originality is immediately impressive. There is material here of high importance for the understanding of Gladstone and of late-Victorian politics.

FONTANA ECONOMIC HISTORY OF EUROPE
Editor: Carlo M. Cipolla

Carlo M. CIPOLLA, (ed.)
The Emergence of Industrial Societies – Part 1
'Fontana Economic History of Europe.'

This volume, which complements *The Industrial Revolution,* is especially concerned with the impact and development of industrialisation on individual European countries. It is divided, for the user's convenience, into two Parts, published as separate volumes. In both parts great stress has been laid on the need to consider the subject in a way that goes much beyond the usual limited discussion where the place of Britain crowds out the other countries. Thus *Germany, France, The Low Countries and The Habsburg Empire and Italy* are fully dealt with in this volume (forming Part 1). In Part 2 Russia, Spain, Switzerland and the Nordic Countries are fully covered

Contents: France 1700-1914; CLAUDE FOHLEN; Germany 1700-1914, KNUT BORCHARDT; Great Britain, PHYLLIS DEANE; The Habsburg Monarchy 1750-1914, N. T. GROSS; Italy 1830-1914, LUCIANO CAFAGNA; The Low Countries 1700-1914, JAN DHONDT and MARINETTE BRUWIER; Maps; Notes on Authors.

Carlo M. CIPOLLA, (ed.)
The Industrial Revolution, 1700-1914
'Fontana Economic History of Europe.'

Between 1780 and 1850 in less than three generations, a far-reaching revolution, without precedent in the history of Mankind, changed the face of England. Here ten substantial studies examine the roots and consequences of the Industrial Revolution throughout Europe. No revolution has been as dramatically revolutionary as the Industrial Revolution; few subjects are so much studied today. *This book stands alone for the breadth and depth of its coverage.*

Contents: The Industrial Revolution, C. M. CIPOLLA; Population in Europe 1700-1914, ANDRE ARMENGAUD; Patterns of Demand 1750-1914, WALTER MINCHINTON; Technological Progress and the Industrial Revolution 1700-1914, SAMUEL LILLEY; Banking and Industrialisation in Europe 1730-1914, BERTRAND GILLE; The State and the Industrial Revolution 1700-1914. BARRY SUPPLE; The Service Revolution; The Growth of Services in Modern Economy 1700-1914, R. M. HARTWELL; The Industrial Bourgeoisie and the Rise of the Working Class 1700-1914, J-F. BERGIER; Agriculture and the Industrial Revolution 1700-1914, PAUL BAIROCH; The Emergence of Economics as a Science 1750-1870, DONALD WINCH; Industrial Archaeology, M. J. T. LEWIS; Notes on Authors; Index of Persons; Index of Places; General Index.

Carlo M. CIPOLLA, (ed.)
The Emergence of Industrial Societies – Part 2
'Fontana Economic History of Europe.'

This is the second volume complementing the volume on *The Industrial Revolution, 1700-1914* and in dealing with the impact of industrialisation on individual countries it covers Russia, Spain, Switzerland and the Nordic Countries.

Contents: The Nordic Countries 1850-1914, LENNART JORBERG; Russia and the Soviet Union, GREGORY GROSSMAN; Spain 1830-1914, JORDI NADAL; Switzerland 1700-1914, B. M. BIUCCHI; The Emergence of an International Economy 1700-1914. WILLIAM WOODRUFF, Statistical Appendix, B. R. MITCHELL.

Carlo M. CIPOLLA, (ed.)
The Middle Ages
'Fontana Economic History of Europe.'

Eight substantial chapters present what modern Economic historians know of the period A.D. 500 to 1500.

Contents: The Origins, CARLO CIPOLLA; Population in Europe 500-1500, J. C. RUSSELL; The Town as an Agent of Civilisation 1200-1500, JACQUES LE GOFF; Patterns and Structure of Demand, RICHARD ROEHL; The Expansion of Technology 500-1500, LYNN WHITE JR.; Medieval Industry, SYLVIA THRUPP; Trade and Finance in the Middle Ages, 900-1500, JACQUES BERNARD; Government Economic Policies and Public Finance, 1000-1500, EDWARD MILLER, Maps showing main trade routes of the Mediterranean. Notes on Authors, Index of Persons, Index of Places. General Index.

Alan and Veronica PALMER
Quotations in History. A Dictionary of Historical Quotations, c. A.D. 800 to the Present

An entirely new reference book, prepared by the author of the *Penguin Dictionary of Modern History,* together with Veronica Palmer.

With some one thousand six hundred entries – with a subject-index and appropriate cross-references – it fills a surprising gap in reference and in historical literature.

Quotations in History presents the great moments of history captured in a single pithy phrase, and brings together the great figures of history in their own words

The book ranges over 1,200 years, from the crowning of Charlemagne and his 'Holy Roman' Empire in the West (in A. D. 800) to Neil Armstrong's first foot-fall on the Moon, and even more recent events through to the end of 1975

Its accuracy and authority are undoubted. Alan Palmer is both an established historian and compiler of reference works with more than a dozen successful books to his credit. Veronica Palmer, an expert on the classical and medieval periods, has previously assisted her husband on the preparation and writing of earlier books.

The book includes not only the famous phrases (which everyone knows, but can never quite place exactly and date precisely) but longer passages that capture the essence of an historical figure's character or the spirit of a particular historical event.

Particular care has been given to establishing the date of quotations wherever possible. With some of the better-known remarks the authors have chosen to present rather more of their context than is customary. At the same time phrases of dubious authenticity have been noted, and the authors have tried to discover the original versions upon which the legendary remarks have been built up (Did George Washington *really say* . . . ?)

J. R. VINCENT
The Formation of the British Liberal Party, 1857-1868
2nd revised edition, with new introduction

'It will probably turn out in the long run that Mr. Vincent has reshaped British political history of the mid-nineteenth century.' A. J. P. Taylor.

This brilliant, influential and irreplaceable work is a set-book wherever British political history is taught. For this second edition Professor Vincent has written a substantial new introduction titled 'Afterthoughts'.

The book describes how, at root level, the Parliamentary Whig Party developed into a national Liberal movement. The action takes place in the 1860s; the leading parts are played by a cluster of great men – Gladstone, Bright, Palmerston, Russell and Mill – who, as well as coming to represent great forces in the nation, were capable of working to consolidate the existing system of aristocratic parties.

For the voter, Liberalism often involved a sense of individual self-determination, novel both in that it operated in previously dependent sections of society, and that the purpose to which this new freedom was put was more acceptance of the political system than rebellion against it. For the political system Liberalism meant that an important section of the landowners changed their role to meet urban conditions by ruling not as the holders of power in rural society, but as the impartial managers of conflict between all other groups.

In the years 1857-68 the conquest of public opinion by the Liberal Party moved at a gallop in the constituencies. The agencies at work here were, in a minor degree, patronage and organisation, but much more occurred through channels that were part of the everyday life of millions; the cheap press, militant Dissent, organised labour, the Reform agitation, the working class club and society movement, and the explosive ardour flashing between great names and great crowds.

A. B. Cooke and J. R. Vincent

The Governing Passion: Cabinet Government and Party Politics in Britain, 1885-1886

The Governing Passion is not a conventional history book. Its structure. evidence and arguments seek to break new ground.

It departs from the dominant tradition in the writing of British political history by which a general interpretation of complicated events is argued from carefully selected evidence.

Instead, in this book the results of deep research are presented in two ways. A long interpretative survey attempts to explain the meaning of events in the crisis and upheaval of Gladstone's Home Rule government, which shifted the entire basis of late-Victorian politics. There then follows an extensive body of evidence, in the form of a day-by-day chronicle, of the exceptionally difficult political situation between January 1885 and July 1886.

This evidence and its interpretation has a wide relevance to the analysis of high politics, at least from 1867 and into this century.

Above all else, *The Governing Passion* seeks to focus on the relationship between party politics and cabinet government. It provides the first full account of the processes by which three late-Victorian cabinets reached their decisions. It illustrates contrasting methods of government and offers explanations for the motives and meanings of these cabinets.

Cooke and Vincent argue that in 1885-86 cabinet (and shadow cabinet) policy cannot be understood as a response to pressure from below. Foreign policy excepted, cabinet ministers derived their energy from the need to maintain (and sometimes to find) the correct party structure which provided berths for themselves. Thus, the debate over Ireland assumed the proportions that it did, not only because there was an acute administrative problem, but because the outcome was expected to decide the shape of the party structure – and, therefore, the future careers of all leading politicians – for the next decade.

There has been no comprehensive survey of any aspect of politics in 1885-86 since J. L. Hammond's *Gladstone and the Irish Nation* was published in 1938. *The Governing Passion* is not intended to supersede Hammond, which gave special attention to Liberal Irish Policy. Yet by using some 70 collections of private papers, most of which were unavailable when Hammond wrote, it substantially supplements his account and is as much concerned with the Tories as with their opponents.

Perhaps the most startling single discovery which emerges from this new material is that Lord Randolph Churchill, frequently pilloried as a mere compulsive intriguer, took a more sustained and intelligent interest in Ireland than any other British politician of that time – including Gladstone, who, in the authors' view, never came near to losing his heart (or his head) to Ireland. There is also close study of the only other politician who might have solved the Irish question in 1885-86: the greatly underestimated Lord Hartington.

This is a major book. It is based upon the most detailed and precise research into one of the greatest disruptions of the British party system. For general readers and students, the first part supplies a general interpretation not dominated by detail. For specialists, the second part will supply the data from which they can draw their own conclusions.